CORPORATIONS

Holger Spamann
Professor of Law, Harvard Law School

Guhan Subramanian
Joseph H. Flom Professor of Law and Business, Harvard Law School
H. Douglas Weaver Professor of Business Law, Harvard Business School

Spring 2018

This collection of materials is adapted from Spamann's Corporations materials as initially created and available on H2O, an online learning and content platform.

Acknowledgements

We thank the authors and copyright holders for granting permission to include the following works in this casebook:

Anand, Geeta, Jerry Markon, and Chris Adams, *ImClone's Ex-CEO Arrested, Charged with Insider Trading*, Wall Street Journal, June 13, 2002. Copyright 2002 by Dow Jones & Company, Inc. Reprinted with permission of Dow Jones & Company, Inc. through the Copyright Clearance Center.

Flom, Joseph H., *Mergers & Acquisitions: The Decade in Review*, University of Miami Law Review, 2000. Copyright 2000 by University of Miami Law Review. Reprinted with permission of University of Miami Law Review.

Friedman, Milton, *The Social Responsibility of Business Is to Increase Its Profits*, New York Times Magazine, Sept. 13, 1970. ©1970 by The New York Times. All rights reserved.

Isaacson, Walter, *Steve Jobs*, Simon & Schuster, Inc., 2011. Copyright 2011 by Walter Isaacson. Reprinted with permission of the author.

Jenkins, Holman W., Jr., *Minority Shareholders Wise Up in 2016*, Wall Street Journal, Dec. 26, 2016. Copyright 2016 by Dow Jones & Company, Inc. Reprinted with permission of Dow Jones & Company, Inc. through the Copyright Clearance Center.

McDonald, Duff, *Harvard Business School and The Propagation of Immoral Profit Strategies*, text (adaptation as appeared in *Newsweek*, Apr. 6, 2017) from *The Golden Passport*. Copyright 2017 by Duff McDonald. Reprinted with permission of HarperCollins Publishers.

Nudelman, Mike, Chart of Alphabet in *One Chart That Explains Alphabet, Google's Parent Company* by Rob Price and Mike Nudelman, Business Insider, Jul. 23, 2016. Copyright 2016 by Business Insider. Chart reprinted with permission of the graphics editor.

Parloff, Roger, *The Gray Art of Not Quite Insider Trading*, Fortune, Aug. 15, 2013. © 2013 Time Inc. All rights reserved. Reprinted from Fortune and published with permission of Time Inc. Reproduction in any manner in any language in whole or in part without written permission is prohibited.

We also thank Dami Seung of the Harvard Law School for her tireless efforts on this casebook. We are grateful for all her help. – HS & GS

Contents

Chapter 1 – An Introduction to Corporate Law

The corporation is the greatest invention of humankind. You are no doubt skeptical of this claim. Surely it must be the wheel? Or the light bulb? Or the airplane? Or the iPhone (6 not 7)? But the corporation has been the engine through which these transforming technologies have created massive societal value. Without the corporation, Thomas Edison could not have created General Electric; the Wright Brothers could not have created what is now known today as the Curtiss-Wright Corporation; and Steve Jobs, of course, could not have created Apple (at least, not the Apple we know today).

The corporate form unites crucial features that work together. The corporation can sue and be sued, have rights, and owe duties, in its own name (**legal personhood**). Shareholders, the "residual claimants" on the corporation's cash flows, elect a board of directors, but, for the rest, control of the corporation is centralized in the hands of that board (**centralized management**). Shares are fungible and **freely transferrable**, a feature that is only possible because shareholders are not liable for debts of the corporation (**limited liability**) and the corporation is not liable for debts of its shareholders (**entity shielding**). (Together, limited liability and entity shielding are also known as **asset partitioning**.) Nor can shareholders take their money out except by decision of the board (**capital lock-in**). All of these characteristics of the corporate form improve upon prior forms of business organization. Taken together, they make the corporation the ultimate wealth creation machine (to paraphrase the slogan of BMW—another corporation).

In the beginning, there is always an idea, usually for a better product or service. If it makes it all the way to a corporate law opinion or a corporate law case study, it was probably a very good idea. The players in our various cases tend to be smart, sophisticated, ambitious, and wealthy—as one prominent Delaware judge put it, the fights in corporate law are typically between "the haves and the haves." In the U.S., one can have a very comfortable lifestyle working for a salary, but to amass "generational wealth" usually requires creating something great, and having an equity interest in it. It also means that you have (usually) improved the lives of others along the way: e.g., customers, suppliers, employees, and local communities. Steve Jobs, Mark Zuckerberg, and Oprah Winfrey (who, after all, is more of a business woman than an entertainer) have probably done more good for the world than Mother Teresa.

Of course, with such concentration of wealth and power comes important challenges. Management might shirk their duties. The board might run off with the shareholders' money. Controlling shareholders (i.e., shareholders who hold more than 50% of the voting power, and sometimes less) might act opportunistically against minority shareholders. The board might act in ways that benefit shareholders but hurt creditors, thereby reducing the overall value of the corporation. Here is where corporate law comes in. It provides the rules to manage the complex relationships between the board, management, employees, shareholders, creditors, and other constituencies.

What is a Corporation?

Formally speaking, a corporation is nothing but an **abstraction** to which we assign rights and duties. It exists independently of humans in the sense that it has indefinite life, and its assets and obligations are legally separate from those of any humans involved in its founding or administration.

The corporate abstraction is an extraordinarily useful and widely used device for organizing relationships between various people and different assets. Most importantly, a group of people can pool their assets by transferring them to a corporation that will act as a single contracting interface with third parties (and with the owners among themselves, for that matter). Or a single person can set up multiple corporations to hold different assets and to enter into contracts relating to those assets. You can and should, therefore, also think of the corporation as a **contracting technology**. It facilitates contracting by partitioning and pooling assets.

The corporate form facilitates the division of labor. Consider the famous pin factory example from Chapter 1, Book 1 of Adam Smith's *Wealth of Nations* (1776):

> To take an example, therefore, from a very trifling manufacture; but one in which the division of labour has been very often taken notice of, the trade of the pin-maker; a workman not educated to this business (which the division of labour has rendered a distinct trade), nor acquainted with the use of the machinery employed in it (to the invention of which the same division of labour has probably given occasion), could scarce, perhaps, with his utmost industry, make one pin in a day, and certainly could not make twenty. But in the way in which this business is now carried on, not only the whole work is a peculiar trade, but it is divided into a number of branches, of which the greater part are likewise peculiar trades. One man draws out the wire, another straights it, a third cuts it, a fourth points it, a fifth grinds it at the top for receiving, the head; to make the head requires two or three distinct operations; to put it on is a peculiar business, to whiten the pins is another; it is even a trade by itself to put them into the paper; and the important business of making a pin is, in this manner, divided into about eighteen distinct operations, which, in some manufactories, are all performed by distinct hands, though in others the same man will sometimes perform two or three of them. I have seen a small manufactory of this kind where ten men only were employed, and where some of them consequently performed two or three distinct operations. But though they were very poor, and therefore but indifferently accommodated with the necessary machinery, they could, when they exerted themselves, make among them about twelve pounds of pins in a day. There are in a pound upwards of four thousand pins of a middling size. Those ten persons, therefore, could make among them upwards of forty-eight thousand pins in a day. Each person, therefore, making a tenth part of forty-eight thousand pins, might be considered as making four thousand eight hundred pins in a day. But if they had all

wrought separately and independently, and without any of them having been educated to this peculiar business, they certainly could not each of them have made twenty, perhaps not one pin in a day. . . .

Discussion Questions:

1. What, if anything, prevents the workers in Adam Smith's pin factory from achieving the same efficiencies by just contracting with each other? (I.e., why do they need to be 'housed' within the same business entity to be able to achieve the efficiencies that Smith describes?)

2. More generally, what does corporate law provide that cannot be provided entirely through contract law? Put another way, if the corporation is nothing more than a contracting technology, then why do we need corporate law as a distinct body of law?

Precursors of the corporate form can be found at least as early as in ancient Rome. Until the 19th century, however, the full package—legal personhood, centralized management, transferable shares, asset partitioning, and capital lock-in—was either not available at all or only with strings attached. In particular, in the United States before the nineteenth century, creating a corporation required a "special act", typically done only for charitable or political (not business) purposes. In the 19th century, however, the U.S.—and the world generally—quickly deregulated to permit private corporations, for business purposes, without governmental approval. New York provided the first broadly available incorporation statute in 1811, and Connecticut followed in 1837 (not coincidentally, just as the Industrial Revolution was beginning in the U.S.).

In 1888, New Jersey took the further step of allowing corporations to own the stock of other corporations, which facilitated holding company structures. Companies headquartered in surrounding states quickly migrated to New Jersey to take advantage of this rule. In 1910, however, Woodrow Wilson was elected governor of New Jersey on a platform that was more skeptical toward private enterprise. In his 1912 annual message, Governor Wilson stated: "The corporation laws of the State notoriously stand in need of alteration. They are manifestly inconsistent with the policy of the Federal Government and with the interests of the people. . . ." In 1913 New Jersey accordingly changed course, no longer permitting holding company structures under its corporate law.

Meanwhile, "little Delaware," which had in 1899 amended its corporate code to mirror that of New Jersey, filled the void and began attracting out of state businesses with lower fees and tax rates than what had been available in New Jersey. Companies quickly migrated to Delaware, and Delaware never looked back. By 1965, 35% of companies listed on the New York Stock Exchange (NYSE) were incorporated in Delaware; and today, more than 2/3 of all publicly traded corporations are incorporated in Delaware.

Today, a curious fact that startles many casual observers is that ten judges (five on the Delaware Chancery Court and five on the Delaware Supreme Court) make the corporate law that governs more than two-thirds of the public shareholder wealth of the country. Even the Delaware corporate code is not drafted by elected officials: the Council of Corporation Law, a group of 25 well-respected attorneys (mostly from prominent Wilmington, Delaware law firms) plus the Deputy Secretary of State proposes all amendments to the Delaware corporate code.[1] The Council writes the Delaware General Corporate Law (DGCL), and, by extension, the corporate law of the country. As a practical matter, approval by the Council is a necessary and sufficient condition for approval by the Delaware legislature. Throughout the course we will focus primarily on the corporate law of Delaware for the same reason that Willie Sutton robbed banks ("because that's where the money is.") We will also discuss the pros and cons of this unusual arrangement in the production of corporate law.

The basic **default governance** of a corporation is simple: (common) shareholders elect the board (DGCL 211(b)), which formally manages the corporation (DGCL 141(b)), mostly by appointing the chief executive officer and other top management, who in turn act on behalf of the corporation in day-to-day matters. As to consuming the profits, the board may decide to distribute available funds to shareholders—or not (DGCL 170(a)). By default, each share confers one vote and the right to equal distributions per share (DGCL 212(a))—the more shares you own, the more votes you have and the more of any distribution you get.

Technically, the corporation is not the only abstraction available for asset pooling and partitioning. There are variants such as the limited liability company (LLC) that have all or most of the features discussed here, and are subject to very similar rules. From the perspective of this introductory course, the differences are minor, and hence not covered.

What the Corporation is Not

The corporation is **not a person** like a human being. To be sure, we sometimes refer to corporations as "legal persons." But you should realize that this is just legalistic shorthand to emphasize the fact that a corporation can be the object and subject of legal claims. It does not mean that a corporation is a person in the sense that it has the same rights and obligations as human beings. Or have you ever heard of a corporation being drafted into military service? Or invoking a human right not to be tortured? (Though in 2012, Presidential candidate Mitt Romney, a Harvard JD/MBA graduate, famously seemed to muddy the waters a bit on whether a corporation is in fact a person. See https://www.youtube.com/watch?v=E2h8ujX6T0A).

The corporation is also **not the same as a business**. A corporation may "own" a business, but they are not the same thing. A business is a collection of assets and a set of real world activities. A corporation is an abstract legal reference point to which we assign those assets. (Another formal note: In most jurisdictions, one technically cannot own a "business." Rather, one owns the assets that form the business, which include not only chattel and real property but also contracts, intellectual property, etc.)

---

[1] For the curious, the current list of Council Members is available at: http://www.dsba.org/sections-committees/sections-of-the-bar/corporation-law/.

Example 1: Mike's Pizza

To make this more concrete, think of your local pizza store. Perhaps it is called "Mike's Pizza," and Mike indeed runs the place. You might think that Mike is the "owner" of the store. In all likelihood, however, the formal "owner" of the pizza place—or rather the contracting party on the relevant contracts—is actually a corporation. The corporation might be called "Mike's Pizza Place Inc.," or "XYZ Corp." for that matter. XYZ Corp. might be (a) the lessee under any lease contract for the store building or other leased items, (b) the employer of any employees, (c) the owner of any real estate or chattel such as the pizza oven or the store sign, and (d) the contracting party with the payment system operator (so your payment for the pizza might show up under "XYZ Corp." on your credit card statement).

Of course, Mike might be XYZ Corp.'s sole shareholder, director, and chief executive officer (CEO). As shareholder, Mike would elect the board (here a single director), which in turn appoints the CEO. As CEO and director, Mike would then have plenary power to administer the business. And as shareholder, he might receive any profits as dividend. For many practical purposes, it is thus irrelevant if Mike owns the store outright or through a corporation. So what's the point of incorporating?

One benefit of incorporating can be convenience in contracting in certain transactions. If Mike ever wanted to sell the pizza place after incorporating, he would just sell the corporation—a single asset (or to be more precise, all his shares in the corporation, still just one collection of a uniform asset). By contrast, as a single owner, he would have to transfer all the assets individually.

Another convenience is that incorporating changes the default rule from unlimited liability to **limited liability**. The default rule for corporations is that shareholders, directors, and corporate officers are not liable for corporate debts (but they do stand to lose any assets they invested in the corporation as shareholders: hence the expression "limited liability" rather than "no liability"). By contrast, the default rule for single owners is the same as that for any other individual debt: full liability except for protection under the bankruptcy code. It is extremely important that you realize these are only default rules. Contracts can and often do transform limited liability into unlimited liability and vice versa. For example, a no-recourse mortgage contractually limits the borrower's liability to the value of the underlying real estate. Most importantly for present purposes, controlling shareholders such as Mike often contractually guarantee particular corporate debts such as bank loans (i.e., they contractually promise to pay the corporate debt if the corporation does not). In contractual relationships, the legal concept of "limited liability" is thus neither necessary nor sufficient to provide actual limited liability for shareholders; it merely facilitates it. The situation is different (and controversial) for most tort liability, as most tort creditors never consented, even implicitly, to the limited liability arrangement.

Another benefit is **entity shielding**. Entity shielding refers to a liability barrier in the opposite direction: Mike's personal creditors cannot demand payment or seize any assets from XYZ Corp. The personal creditors can only seize Mike's shares in XYZ Corp. Entity shielding is extremely useful because it allows those interacting with XYZ Corp. to focus their attention on the pizza store's assets and financial prospects, and not worry about Mike's other businesses. Imagine for example that Mike also runs a construction business in a different city. Without entity shielding, creditors from the construction business might seize assets of the pizza store, and vice versa. As a consequence, the two businesses' financial health could not be assessed independently of each other. By contrast, with entity shielding, a bank making a loan to develop the pizza store need only assess the financial prospects of the pizza store, i.e., XYZ Corp. And if the construction business does fail, XYZ Corp. can nevertheless continue business as usual. Entity shielding is more than a mere convenience in that it cannot be accomplished by contracting in the technical sense of the term (i.e., as opposed to the broader set of voluntary arrangements discussed below, which include corporate charters). That being said, the law also provides entity shielding to other entities such as partnerships.

One can neatly summarize limited liability and entity shielding with the simple legal construction of the corporation as a separate "legal person." "Naturally," one might say, separate persons are not liable for each other's debts. Importantly, however, the legal construction is only a convenient summary of policy choices that must be grounded elsewhere. For there is nothing natural about declaring the corporation a separate legal person in the first place (nor, for that matter, would there be anything natural about the opposite arrangement, in particular holding investors liable for all debts of the business). It is a convenient fiction, and the law does not adhere to it strictly. We will encounter exceptions in corporate law (notably "piercing the veil"), and there are many more in tax, antitrust, etc.

Example 2: Apple Inc.

We have just argued that the corporation can be useful for small, single-owner-manager businesses such as Mike's Pizza. But the corporation's full advantages only come into play in larger businesses with multiple shareholder-investors, many or most of whom have no direct involvement in management. Almost all large firms are organized as corporations. And the majority of economic activity is bundled in large firms.

Think of Apple Inc. When its legendary co-founder and CEO Steve Jobs died, from a legal perspective all that happened was that the board of Apple Inc. had to appoint a new CEO. By contrast, if Steve Jobs had been the single owner of Apple, the entire business would have been part of his estate, presumably with deleterious consequences. Similarly, if the board of Apple Inc. decides to replace the CEO, it does so by simple resolution—it does not need to expropriate the old CEO.

Even more important than independence from its managers, Apple is independent from its shareholders, and the shareholders are excluded from management. Think of Apple Inc.'s millions of shareholders. Imagine the mayhem if any one of them could demand participation in Apple's management, or liquidation and distribution of Apple's assets. Or if the creditors of any one shareholder could demand payment from Apple, even just for a limited amount, and seize Apple's assets to the extent the payment is not forthcoming. And of course it would be impossible for Apple to enter into a contract or file a suit if this required the signatures of all its shareholders, just as no plaintiff could sue "Apple" if it required naming every single shareholder as a defendant. In other words, Apple Inc. as we know it could not exist without the convenience of a single fictitious "legal person," restricting shareholder involvement in management, and entity shielding.

Many think that Apple Inc. and other large corporations also could not exist without limited liability. The argument is that shareholder liability would deter wealthy investors (who are the ones most likely to be sued), would make the corporation's credit-worthiness dependent on its fluctuating shareholder base, and would interfere with diversification (the strategy to invest in many different assets so as to not put all eggs into one basket). There is reason to doubt this common wisdom, however. Limited liability distorts shareholders' incentives because they (fully) benefit from the upside but do not (fully) bear the downside of risky investments. And the problems of unlimited shareholder liability may be minor if liability is proportional to the number of shares held. Empirically, California provided for proportional shareholder liability until 1931, and American Express was organized with unlimited shareholder liability until 1965. It appears that shareholders largely viewed the shift to limited liability with indifference both in California and in American Express.

Back to indefinite life, and the inability of individual shareholders to demand liquidation. If an Apple shareholder wants to cash out, he or she can simply sell the shares. The default rule is that **shares are freely transferable**. This default rule complements indefinite life. It reconciles the corporation's need for continuity with individual shareholders' need for liquidity, i.e., the ability to convert their investment to cash. In smaller corporations, particularly family firms, however, the charter or shareholder agreements sometimes restrict transferability of shares. And even if sale is not restricted, there is often no market for a small corporation's shares at a price that fully reflects the corporation's value. In these cases, liquidity can be a major source of disagreement between shareholders.

In general, multi-member organizations also have governance problems that Mike's Pizza does not have. (We write "organizations" because the problems are not specific to corporations.) When the only shareholder (Mike) is also the only director, the only manager, and the only employee, there are no conflicts to resolve. But when there are millions of shareholders or more generally investors, a multi-member board, dozens of managers, and thousands of employees, conflicts abound. Millions are not necessary for conflicts to arise, however. The conflicts can be even more acrimonious when there are only two shareholders. Mitigating these conflicts is the main preoccupation of corporate law and of this course.

Holding Companies and Subsidiaries

Large businesses are usually not one but many corporations. Usually, a so-called "holding company" sits at the top of a pyramid of several layers of fully-owned subsidiary corporations. That is, the holding company owns 100% of the shares of several direct subsidiaries. These direct subsidiaries in turn own 100% of the shares of some other, indirect subsidiaries. And so on. This is a further illustration of the point that a corporation and a business are not the same thing. The average Fortune 500 company has approximately 150 wholly-owned subsidiaries. One such example is Alphabet, Inc., which was formed in 2015 as the holding company for all of Google's activities. *Business Insider* depicted Alphabet's corporate structure as follows:

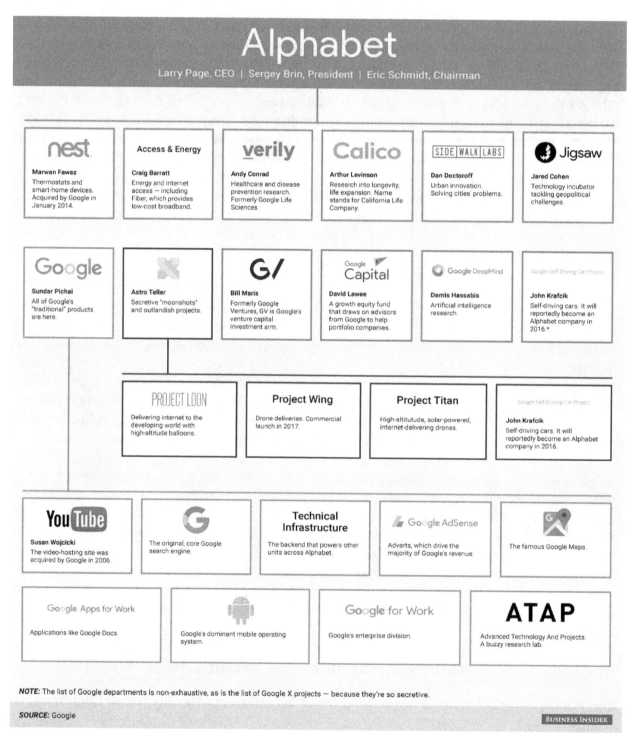

Some advantages of the subsidiary structure are similar to the advantages of incorporating Mike's Pizza. Others include tax considerations and regulatory requirements. For example, Apple Inc. has become infamous for its use of Irish subsidiaries to "manage" its corporate tax liability.

In this course, we usually focus on the top level holding company because that is where the governance problems arise.

Partnerships and Other Entity Types

You may wonder what would happen if a multi-person firm did *not* incorporate. The answer is that "the association of two or more persons to carry on as co-owners a business for profit forms a partnership, whether or not the persons intend to form a partnership." See Section 202 of the Uniform Partnership Act of 1997.

This is a very dangerous default rule. Absent agreement to the contrary, (1) all partners have unlimited liability for partnership debt, (2) all partners have equal rights to participate in management, (3) any partner may be able to demand dissolution at any time, and (4) partnership interests are not transferable. It is a recipe for disaster.

See again Apple, one last time (for now):

Excerpt from Walter Isaacson in *Steve Jobs* (2011)

Now that they had decided to start a business, they needed a name. Jobs had gone for another visit to the All One Farm, where he had been pruning the Gravenstein apple trees, and Wozniak picked him up at the airport. On the ride down to Los Altos, they bandied around options. They considered some typical tech words, such as Matrix, and some neologisms, such as Executek, and some straightforward boring names like Personal Computers Inc. The deadline for deciding was the next day, when Jobs wanted to start filing the papers. Finally Jobs proposed Apple Computer. "I was on one of my fruitarian diets," he explained. "I had just come back from the apple farm. It sounded fun, spirited, and not intimidating. Apple took the edge off the word 'computer.' Plus, it would get us ahead of Atari in the phone book." He told Wozniak that if a better name did not hit them by the next afternoon, they would just stick with Apple. And they did.

Apple. It was a smart choice. The word instantly signaled friendliness and simplicity. It managed to be both slightly off-beat and as normal as a slice of pie. There was a whiff of counterculture, back-to-nature earthiness to it, yet nothing could be more American. And the two words together—Apple Computer—provided an amusing disjuncture. "It doesn't quite make sense," said Mike Markkula, who soon thereafter became the first chairman of the new company. "So it forces your brain to dwell on it. Apple and computers, that doesn't go together! So it helped us grow brand awareness."

Wozniak was not yet ready to commit full-time. He was an HP company man at heart, or so he thought, and he wanted to keep his day job there. Jobs realized he needed an ally to help corral Wozniak and adjudicate if there was a disagreement. So he enlisted his friend Ron Wayne, the middle-aged engineer at Atari who had once started a slot machine company.

Wayne knew that it would not be easy to make Wozniak quit HP, nor was it necessary right away. Instead the key was to convince him that his computer designs would be owned by the Apple partnership. "Woz had a parental attitude toward the circuits he developed, and he wanted to be able to use them in other applications or let HP use them," Wayne said. "Jobs and I realized that these circuits would be the core of Apple. We spent two hours in a roundtable discussion at my apartment, and I was able to get Woz to accept this." His argument was that a great engineer would be remembered only if he teamed with a great marketer, and this required him to commit his designs to the partnership. Jobs was so impressed and grateful that he offered Wayne a 10% stake in the new partnership, turning him into a tie-breaker if Jobs and Wozniak disagreed over an issue.

"They were very different, but they made a powerful team," said Wayne. Jobs at times seemed to be driven by demons, while Woz seemed a naïf who was toyed with by angels. Jobs had a bravado that helped him get things done, occasionally by manipulating people. He could be charismatic, even mesmerizing, but also cold and brutal. Wozniak, in contrast, was shy and socially awkward, which made him seem childishly sweet. "Woz is very bright in some areas, but he's almost like a savant, since he was so stunted when it came to dealing with people he didn't know," said Jobs. "We were a good pair." It helped that Jobs was awed by Wozniak's engineering wizardry, and Wozniak was awed by Jobs's business drive. "I never wanted to deal with people and step on toes, but Steve could call up people he didn't know and make them do things," Wozniak recalled. "He could be rough on people he didn't think were smart, but he never treated me rudely, even in later years when maybe I couldn't answer a question as well as he wanted."

Even after Wozniak became convinced that his new computer design should become the property of the Apple partnership, he felt that he had to offer it first to HP, since he was working there. "I believed it was my duty to tell HP about what I had designed while working for them. "That was the right thing and the ethical thing." So he demonstrated it to his managers in the spring of 1976. The senior executive at the meeting was impressed, and seemed torn, but he finally said it was not something that HP could develop. It was a hobbyist product, at least for now, and didn't fit into the company's high-quality market segments. "I was disappointed," Wozniak recalled, "but now I was free to enter into the Apple partnership."

On April 1, 1976, Jobs and Wozniak went to Wayne's apartment in Mountain View to draw up the partnership agreement. Wayne said he had some experience "writing in legalese," so he composed the three page document himself. His "legalese" got the better of him. Paragraph 1 began with various flourishes: "Be it noted herewith . . . Be it further noted herewith . . . Now the refore [sic], in consideration of the respective assignments of interests . . ." But the division of shares and profits was clear—45%-45%-10%—and it was stipulated that any expenditures of more than $100 would require agreement of at least two of the partners. Also, the responsibilities were spelled out. "Wozniak shall assume both general and major responsibility for the conduct of Electrical Engineering: Jobs shall assume general responsibility for Electrical Engineering and Marketing, and Wayne shall assume major responsibility for Mechanical Engineering and Documentation." Jobs signed in lowercase script, Wozniak in careful cursive, and Wayne in an illegible squiggle.

Wayne then got cold feet. As Jobs started planning to borrow and spend more money, he recalled the failure of his own company. He didn't want to go through that again. Jobs and Wozniak had no personal assets, but Wayne (who worried about a global financial Armageddon) kept gold coins hidden in his mattress. Because they had structured Apple as a simple partnership rather than a corporation, the partners would be personally liable for the debts, and Wayne was afraid potential creditors would go after him. So he returned to the Santa Clara County office just eleven days later with a "statement of withdrawal" and an amendment to the partnership agreement. "By virtue of a re-assessment of understandings by and between all parties," it began, "Wayne shall hereinafter cease to function in the status of 'Partner.' " It noted that in payment for his 10% of the company, he received $800, and shortly afterward $1,500 more.

Had he stayed on and kept his 10% stake, at the end of 2012 it would have been worth approximately $54 billion. Instead he was then living alone in a small home in Pahrump, Nevada, where he played the penny slot machines and lived off his social security check. He later claimed he had no regrets. "I made the best decision for me at the time. Both of them were real whirlwinds, and I knew my stomach and it wasn't ready for such a ride."

Discussion Questions:

1. What should Steve, Steve, and Wayne have done to mitigate Wayne's concern that "potential creditors would go after him"? (Does it concern you that Wayne—an attorney—did not think of this himself?)

2. Why do you think Steve & Steve didn't have the same concern as Wayne?

3. In view of your answers to (1) and (2), why do you think the *Economist* stated nearly a century ago that:

> The economic historian of the future may assign to the nameless inventor of the principle of limited liability, as applied to trading corporations, a place of honour with Watt and Stephenson, and other pioneers of the Industrial Revolution. The genius of these men produced the means by which man's command of natural resources has multiplied many times over; the limited liability company the means by which huge aggregations of capital required to give effect to their discoveries were collected, organized, and efficiently administered.[2]

---

[2] As quoted in Paul Halpern, Michael Trebilcock & Stuart Turnbull, *An Economic Analysis of Limited Liability in Corporate Law*, 30 U. TORONTO L. REV. 117 (1980).

You might now wonder how businesses could even operate before incorporation became generally available in the 19th century. There are three answers: First, some were lucky enough to procure a special corporate charter from the king or legislature. Second, some businesses may indeed not have commenced or grown beyond a certain point because the corporate form was not available.

Third, and most importantly, the partnership rules described above are merely the default rules. They can and usually are heavily tailored in the partnership agreement, provided that the partners are aware that they are forming a partnership. For example, the partnership agreements of contemporary law firm partnerships reserve management to a committee, and provide for a regulated cash-out without dissolution if a partner wants to exit the partnership. The one thing that the partnership agreement cannot exclude in a traditional partnership is unlimited liability. To limit liability in a practical way, the law firm must choose a different entity type, such as a Limited Liability Partnership (LLP). But these limited-liability variations on the partnership form were not available until the past decade or so.

Discussion Questions:

Take a look at the websites of three to four of your favorite corporate law firms.

1. Which of these have adopted LLP status? Can you find any that do not seem to have adopted any kind of limited liability status? (And what makes you think they have not?)

2. What features of a law firm practice would make LLP status more likely? And in view of your answer, why do you think certain firms have not adopted LLP status?

Contractual Freedom

Almost everything in corporate law can be modified by contract, at least if we understand contract in a broader sense to include charters and bylaws. For example, the charter can create separate classes of stock with different voting and distribution rights (DGCL 151(a), 212(a)). Even if a rule is mandatory on its face, like unlimited liability for partners in general partnerships, one can usually circumvent it by choosing an economically equivalent but legally different transaction or entity type, such as the limited liability partnership (LLP).

To see different examples of this "make your own" approach to the corporate form, take a look at the Articles of Incorporation (a.k.a. "the charter") for Alphabet, Inc. (the company formerly known as Google, as we have already seen) and for Kona Grill, Inc. (a restaurant chain with 30+ locations around the U.S.; see www.konagrill.com). Both companies are incorporated in Delaware, yet their foundational documents establish different rights and responsibilities in these two companies.

Discussion Questions:

1. How do Alphabet and Kona Grill differ in how shareholders vote? What business reasons might explain this difference?

2. How do Alphabet and Kona Grill differ in how the board of directors is elected? What consequences do you think this would have for how the corporation is governed? (Consider an analogy to how the U.S. House of Representatives is elected versus the U.S. Senate.)

3. Can shareholders remove directors, and if so, do they need cause? See DGCL 141(k)(1).

4. Can shareholders act by written consent? Can they call a special meeting? Compare the charters of both companies against the default provisions for acting by written consent (DGCL 228(a)) and calling a special meeting (DGCL 211(d)).

5. Who can amend the bylaws? See DGCL 109(a) and DGCL 102(b)(4). In contrast, how does amending the charter work? See DGCL 242(b)(1). What is the voting threshold for shareholders to amend the bylaws at Kona Grill? Why would the Kona Grill incorporators want a supermajority vote for amending the bylaws? And is this supermajority vote permissible under DGCL 109(a)? (What if the threshold were 99%?)

6. Take a look at Alphabet Article VII, Section 1, and Kona Grill Article V Section 6. See also DGCL 102(b)(7). Why do you think Delaware corporate law permits such a provision in the charter? Do you think such a provision would improve corporate governance? If no, why do you think Alphabet and Kona Grill both have such a provision?

7. Take a look at Kona Grill Article V Section 8(a). Does Alphabet, Inc. have a similar provision? Based solely on this provision, which company would you want to invest in as a shareholder? Is it a good idea as a policy matter (before you answer, see below).

8. What happens at Alphabet if a Founder (defined as Larry Page or Sergey Brin) sells his stock? See Article IV, Section 2(f) et seq. Extra credit: What happens when one of them dies?

The Really Big Picture (and some basic corporate finance)

Note: This section matters as much for terminology as for substance. If you have no background in business and finance, you should read it extremely carefully and look up any terms that you do not understand after reading twice.

17

As already mentioned above, the corporation is the vehicle of choice for pooling the resources of many investors. Before studying this vehicle in detail, it is worth zooming out for a moment to appreciate why these details matter—a lot!

The basic corporate investment relationship

The corporation is at the center of an elaborate system that matches cash-rich investors to cash-poor firms, and thereby enables life as we know it. On one side are **savers** who invest. For the time being, you can think of such savers as yourself when you start saving for retirement, usually through a tax-deferred plan like a 401(k). Savers invest first and foremost to **transfer value through time**, from today to the future: you put money into your 401(k) today and get it out when you retire in 40 years or so. On the other side are **firms** (or, in the beginning, a simple entrepreneur). Firms also wish to transfer value through time, but in the opposite direction, i.e., from the future to today: the firm expects to generate lots of cash in the future and offers to share it in return for financing today, without which it would not be able to generate the future cash in the first place ("Have idea, need money!").

To be sure, individual savers and entrepreneurs could decide to go it alone and put only their own money into a small-scale self-financed business. But in most industries, the investment required for efficient production far exceeds the wealth of individuals and thus requires **pooling resources**. For example, Apple has in excess of $300 billion in assets, financed by countless investors. Even if an individual could afford to finance an entire firm, it is generally preferable to spread the individual's wealth over many firms so as not to put all eggs into one basket, i.e., to reduce risk through **diversification**.

The importance of large-scale matching of savers and firms cannot be overstated. Without it, life as we know it would be impossible. There would be no personal computers, no smart phones, no cars (electric or not), and no electric skateboards. Nor should we take this matching for granted. In the U.S. and some other developed economies, the system matches savers and firms without much friction (cost): many firms can finance themselves on a grand scale at reasonable rates, and a great number of savers can expect returns not much below the rates paid by the firms. Elsewhere in the world, the spread between what savers get and what firms must pay is large, firms often find it hard to impossible to obtain funding at all, and saving is a treacherous affair. Given the enormous temptations for the recipients of financing not to pay it back, it is easy to see why the system might not work ("Tens of trillions of dollars entrusted to money-driven, focused people by naïve and absent-minded savers – what could go wrong?"). The astonishing thing is that it works so well in some parts of the world – and corporate law has a large part in that.

Investors, intermediaries, and the lifecycle of firms

In fact, the system achieves nothing short of a miracle once you consider that the typical retirement plan saver invests the money for decades and never looks closely at what firms do with the money or even which firms have the money (more on this below). Firms, on the other hand, come and go and mutate all the time, as new ideas are born and old ones adapt or disappear. Throughout this lifecycle of firms, investors have to make important decisions or risk wasting their money on bad firms or being taken to the cleaners by the firms' managers or other investors. Fortunately, most of these decisions are made by professional investment managers—intermediaries—to whom the ultimate investors like us have entrusted their savings, relying on a well-functioning legal system and other institutions to ensure that we will eventually get our money back, and more.

A thumbnail sketch of a firm's lifecycle might be: In the beginning, an entrepreneur solicits financing from so-called **venture capital funds (VCs)** that specialize in early-stage financing. 90% of early stage companies fail. The VCs make their money off of the 10% that do not and reach the next stage: a "trade sale" to another company, or an **initial public offering (IPO)** of the corporation's stock to investors at large by means of registration with the S.E.C. and listing on a stock exchange. Depending on how the business develops, the corporation might later offer more stock to the public in a so-called **secondary equity offering (SEO)**, be acquired by another company, acquire other companies, or go bankrupt – or all of the above in various permutations.[3] Along the way, the corporation holds numerous shareholder votes and investor calls, engages in all sorts of financing transactions, and, last but decidedly not least, runs its business. This happens at tens of thousands of firms. Meanwhile, all that the ultimate investors are doing is to put their money into a bank account, annuity contract, retirement plan, etc., wait a couple decades, and leave the rest to financial intermediaries.

Such intermediaries include **banks and insurance companies**. Banks use funds received as deposits or savings to make loans. Insurance companies offer annuity products by taking savers' premia and investing them in firms; they also invest premia received from other insurance clients. Prudential regulation generally prohibits banks and insurance companies from investing in stocks, however, and thus they will feature less prominently in this course.

Retail investors' main way to invest in stocks and bonds (= tradeable debt) is through **mutual funds**. As the name suggests, mutual funds pool individual investor' funds and invest them in a pre-specified type of assets (e.g., S&P 500 stocks); each individual investor owns a share of the fund. By size, mutual funds are the big dog among intermediaries, especially in stocks: as of 2017, U.S. mutual funds had almost 20 trillion U.S. dollars under management. However, mutual funds are not the most active participants in corporate governance, nor are they present in all types of firms. This is largely because, in the name of investor protection, the Investment Company Act and the Investment Advisers Act, respectively, impose considerable restrictions on mutual funds and their management companies (like Fidelity or Vanguard). In particular, mutual funds must offer daily

---

[3] Note in this regard that bankruptcy usually means restructuring or sale rather than liquidation, and firms not only buy but also sell a/k/a "spin off" subsidiaries and other parts of their business. For example, United Airlines was founded as Boeing Air Transport by William Boeing in 1927, merged with his Boeing Airplane Company in 1929, and spun out as United Airlines in 1934; it filed for bankruptcy in 2002, emerged from bankruptcy in 2006, and merged with Continental Airlines in 2013.

redemption at the fund's then-current net asset value (NAV), which makes it difficult to impossible for mutual funds to invest in illiquid assets, i.e., assets that do not trade in thick markets and hence cannot be sold quickly except at a major discount. Mutual funds therefore mostly invest in public securities, i.e., securities that are registered with the S.E.C. and, usually, admitted to trading on a trading venue such as a stock exchange. Moreover, mutual funds' diversification requirement and prohibition of performance fees makes it relatively unattractive for mutual fund managers to expend resources on effecting change at individual firms in the fund's portfolio.

Private funds—funds open only to select investors—are not subject to these restrictions and are thus present in all asset classes. They provide high-powered incentives to their managers for active management, and thus generate a disproportionate amount of trading and engagement. One small but important group of private funds are the aforementioned VCs. A larger group of private funds called **private equity (PE)** buys mature companies (usually using plenty of additional debt financing), holds and reshapes them for a couple years, and then resells them. Both VCs and private equity funds have investment horizons of at least several years up to a decade and require their own investors to commit their capital for similar periods. All other private funds go by the catch-all name **hedge funds**. Their investment strategies and horizons differ greatly. Of particular importance for this course, so-called **activist** hedge funds seek to profit from changing the way a public company conducts its business, having taken a sizeable equity stake in the company that will increase in value if the company improves. **Merger arbitrage** hedge funds specialize in buying the equity of corporations that have announced to merge.

Investors in private funds include institutional investors such as public and private pension funds (e.g., CalPERS), endowments (e.g., Harvard's), and sovereign wealth funds (e.g., Saudi Arabia's). (The teams managing institutional investors are themselves intermediaries for the ultimate beneficiaries, such as employees and retirees.) Other investors in private funds are wealthy individuals, particularly ultra wealthy individuals who often have their own wealth management teams ("family offices"). In this connection, it is worth pointing out that the "savers" that invest their money in firms are not the average Joe: in the U.S., the top 1% own one third of all equity in public firms, and the top 10% own four fifths (these numbers include indirect ownership through pension funds etc.).

Capital structure and corporate governance

As hinted above, there are two broad categories of financial claims that investors acquire in firms, in return for their investment: debt and equity. **Debt** is an IOU—a fixed claim. It includes loans from banks and others, as well as publicly traded debt securities called *bonds*. These payment claims can be enforced in court: creditors can sue for payment, and seize the corporation's assets if payment is not forthcoming. **Equity** (a/k/a shares, stock), on the other hand, provides no right to payment but usually provides voting rights to elect the corporation's board, which *may* determine to pay money to equity holders as a dividend or to buy back their stock.

If the corporation cannot pay its creditors—i.e., if it is *insolvent*—, unpaid creditors or the corporation itself may petition the bankruptcy court to open a **bankruptcy** procedure. Bankruptcy does not mean that the business of the corporation is liquidated. Rather, bankruptcy is a collective proceeding to settle various investors' claims, while preserving the business's going concern value, if any (potentially simply by selling the business, and then dividing the sale price between existing claimants). The most important tool of bankruptcy law is its *automatic stay* of individual proceedings, which prevents inefficient liquidation by individual creditors racing to grab the corporation's assets and explains the expression "filing for bankruptcy *protection*." In bankruptcy, claimants are supposed to be paid in order of their seniority (see below). In particular, equity holders are supposed to get paid only after all creditors have been paid in full. Hence equity holders are often referred to as the corporation's *residual claimants*.

Debt and equity come in various flavors, including hybrids. This is especially true for debt. Not only do debt claims come in different maturities and with different ancillary rights, such as creditor undertakings to do or not to do something (**covenants**). Importantly, debt claims also differ in their **seniority**. Some creditors—so-called juniors—may contractually agree to subordination to certain other creditors—so-called seniors—in bankruptcy, i.e., to receive payment only after the latter have been paid in full. (Bankruptcy law itself also contains some seniority rules for special groups of creditors.) The debtor may grant a **security interest** in particular assets (e.g., a mortgage) to so-called secured creditors, which enables the secured creditors to obtain satisfaction of their claim from the sale of the asset prior to any other creditors, provided certain formalities, usually including a filing, have been complied with. (Security interests are also called collateral.) The debt contract may provide that the debt is **convertible** into equity at the election of the creditor and/or the corporation. The debt may also be issued together with **options**—known as **warrants** when issued by the corporation—, i.e., rights to purchase stock of the corporation at a pre-specified price (cf. DGCL 157).

Equity tends to be less varied, and most corporations only have one class of common stock. Of late, however, many prominent tech corporations such as Google, Facebook, or Snap have gone public with two or more different classes of stock ("**dual class**") to preserve the founders' control: one high-voting class reserved to the founders, and one low- or even non-voting class for outside investors. Many corporations also issue so-called **preferred stock**, which tends to have no voting rights but a dividend preference, i.e., the right to receive some specified minimum amount of dividends before any dividends can be paid to common stockholders (cf. DGCL 151(c)/(d)). Anything goes under Delaware corporate law: DGCL 151(a)). Voting and other rights may even be extended to creditors (DGCL 221).

A very important point is that the so-called capital structure formed by the combination of different claims on the corporation is just that: a structure to raise capital and ultimately to divide the returns, if any. There is nothing essential or even permanent about any of the claims or the investors who hold them. The same investors often hold different parts of the capital structure, such as debt and equity, simultaneously or at different points in time. Investors may trade in an out of the corporations' claims at any time (at least if they are traded in a liquid market). The corporation frequently extinguishes some claims by paying

21

or buying them back and creates others by selling them in return for new investment. For example, the corporation may borrow money to buy back stock ("leveraged recapitalization"), issue stock to pay off debt, repay one loan by taking on another ("refinancing"), or offer to exchange one type of stock for another. (However, sensibly enough, shares owned by the corporation itself—"treasury shares"—do not have voting rights etc., see DGCL 160(c).)

Does capital structure matter? It obviously matters for the pricing of individual claims, as investors only pay for what they get. But what the corporation gives to holders of one claim it cannot give to another, and in light of the previous paragraph, the value of individual claims is hardly of deep interest (except, of course, to those buying or holding those claims!). The real question is whether the total value of all claims that the corporation can sell, and hence the total amount of financing it can raise, depends on the way the claims are delineated by contract, charter, and law? Specifically, does it matter which part of the dollars taken in by the firm (cash flows) go to which investors under which circumstances (**cash flow rights**), and what rights do those investors have to influence the decisions taken by the firm (**control rights**)?

Modigliani and Miller's famous benchmark result in corporate finance is that *if* the firm's cash flows were fixed and some other conditions held, it would not matter what sort of financial claims the firm issued – the total value of the claims would always be the same. As Miller once explained this proposition, it does not matter how you slice a pizza – it will always be the same amount of pizza. A corporation, however, is not a pizza: its cash flows depend crucially on how it is managed, which in turn depends on how it is governed, i.e., who has which control rights and how they exercise them. Cash flow rights provide incentives to exercise control rights in a certain manner. These incentives can be more or less aligned with increasing the value of the pie (or size of the pizza, if you will). The division and bundling of cash flow and control rights thus matters a great deal.

Corporate and bankruptcy law have some role in the division and bundling of rights, but most of it is done by contract writ large, including the corporate charter. This is inevitable because businesses differ and hence need different governance terms adjusted to the business. In particular, businesses differ in the amount of debt they can service. Debt offers important advantages. First, it is tax advantaged: interest is tax deductible, while dividends are not. Second, debt is less information-sensitive: creditors only need to assess the corporation's ability to repay the loan rather than the corporation's full potential. Last but not least, creditors' return expectations are backed up by a hard legal claim and its threat of judicial enforcement and bankruptcy, whereas shareholders are at the mercy of the board. This last feature, however, also makes debt inflexible: it will lead to costly litigation, bankruptcy, or even liquidation whenever the actual cash flows fall short of projected cash flows, or at least give creditors the ability to extract concessions in renegotiating the debt. That is why only stable businesses with predictable cash flows tend to use a lot of debt, while more volatile businesses, particularly startups, rely mostly or exclusively on equity financing. Most of this course will be concerned with the ways in which corporate law seeks to ensure that shareholders will get a return even though they lack a hard claim to repayment.

A final note on capital structure and corporate governance is that every possible arrangement is a compromise, and perfection is impossible. Ex ante, every participant in the business would agree that the goal is to maximize the size of the total pie (or pizza, if you prefer) because that will enable everyone to get a bigger slice (the division can be adjusted by side payments). Once the business gets under way, however, whoever has control over a decision will be tempted to use that control to get a bigger slice, even if doing so reduces the size of the total pie. For example, managers may favor growing the business beyond the efficient size if they enjoy the greater power and prestige that comes from running a bigger firm. Creditors may favor inefficient liquidation if continuation, while profitable in expectation, is also risky, such that creditors stand to lose but not much to gain from continuation (remember that creditors' claims are fixed!). Inversely, shareholders may favor inefficient continuation if continuation, while unprofitable in expectation, presents at least the possibility of a positive outcome whereas the liquidation proceeds would go fully or mostly to creditors. The point is that as soon as people pool resources, conflicts of interest are unavoidable. The goal is to mitigate such conflicts; they cannot be eliminated.

Valuation

Reassuring note: This subsection is conceptually denser and more algebraic than anything else in this course. You may find it challenging on first reading.

Above, I said tongue-in-cheek that the value of individual claims does not matter in the big scheme of things. Of course, to individual investors, the value of their claim is all that matters. And because of that, understanding how different actions affect the value of individual claims is crucial to understand the incentives of those holding those claims.

To value a claim, one usually starts with the claim's **expected future cash flows**. Expected cash flows are the probability-weighted average of the cash flows that the investor will receive in all the conceivable scenarios. For example, if the investment will return either $2 million or nothing with equal probability, the expected cash flows are 50% × $2 million + 50% × 0 = $1 million. In the real world, estimating expected cash flows requires understanding the business and the capital structure, particularly—for debt—the seniority structure and security interests. Usually, such estimates are fraught with very considerable uncertainty, especially for equity (cf. discussion of information-sensitivity above).

The next step is to **discount** the future cash flows **to present value** for the time value of money and a risk premium, to name only the most important ones. The **time value of money** arises from the simple fact that in the world we live in, all investors have the alternative to put their money into other investments that are expected to pay back the same amount of money *plus a positive return* in the future. In particular, investors have the alternative to invest in U.S. government bonds that will pay back the same amount of money plus interest with certainty. Thus, to persuade investors to give their money to the corporation, the corporation has to offer more than the interest paid by the government.

How much more? That depends on the risk of the corporation's claim. Risk in this context does not mean the probability of non-payment per se: that is already accounted for in the calculation of *expected* future cash flows. Rather, risk here means the variance or volatility of the expected cash flows. For example, for their retirement, most people would rather have $1 million for sure rather than a 50/50 chance of $2 million or nothing (note that the expected cash flows are the same, namely 50% × $2 million + 50% × 0 = 100% × $1 million). That said, investors can diversify away most risk by investing small amounts in many different assets rather than everything in one asset. By and large, investors thus receive a **risk premium** only for **systematic risk**, i.e., risk that is undiversifiable because it is likely to hit all assets at the same time, such as a global recession. (Of course, individual investors would prefer to receive premia for all sorts of things, but in a competitive financial market, investors compete away most other premia – ultimately, the **expected return** on an investment is set by the supply and demand for capital.)

Let us consider an extremely stylized example. Imagine we knew for certain that a firm will be in operation for only one year, after which it will liquidate all its assets and distribute them to its investors. Imagine further that we magically know that there are only three possible outcomes, all equally likely: after liquidation but before distribution, the firm will hold (1) $0, (2) $100, or (3) $200. What is this firm worth? Start with the expected future cash flows: $\frac{1}{3} \times \$0 + \frac{1}{3} \times \$100 + \frac{1}{3} \times \$200 = \$100$. To discount those future cash flows to present value, we need to know the time value of money and the firm-specific risk premium. As mentioned above, the time value of money is what you could earn on a government bond of the same duration.[4] Let's assume the government currently offers 1% on a one year bond. What is the right risk premium? It depends on the firm! The more the success of the firm is correlated with the health of the economy, the higher the risk premium. How high? It depends on what financial markets demand—or equivalently, what investors can get elsewhere—, which in practice we would estimate by looking at similar firms. Imagine we found the right premium to be 10%. In that case, our firm would be worth $\$100/(1+1\%+10\%)=\$90.09$.[5]

Having valued the firm as a whole, let us value individual claims on it. Imagine the firm is organized as a corporation and only has two claimants: a creditor owed $100, and a shareholder.

Let us start with the creditor and observe that the creditor's claim is not necessarily worth $100—the corporation has promised $100, but whether it will pay that much is an entirely different question, and how to value those payments yet another.[6] Concretely, the

---

[4] Well, actually, the government bond also pays you a compensation for expected inflation. But we'll assume our business's outcomes are measured in nominal terms, so including an inflation premium is appropriate.

[5] At the limit, if the success of the firm were purely idiosyncratic—e.g., it depends on whether or not a patent will be upheld in court—, then the appropriate risk premium would be zero, and our firm would be worth $\$100/(1+1\%+0\%)=\$99.01$.

[6] Nor did the creditor necessarily invest $100 – that is merely the **face value** of the claim, i.e., the promised amount. In fact, given the time value of money, the investor presumably invested less

corporation will not be able to pay anything to the creditor in case 1 where it ends up holding $0 (perhaps the shareholder would be able to pay, but, because of limited liability, the shareholder will not need to pay and presumably won't). In the other two cases 2 and 3, the corporation will be able to pay $100 but will not pay more than that (in case 3, it *could* pay more but it won't because the creditor only has a fixed claim $100). Thus, the expected cash flows to the creditor are ⅓×$0+⅓×$100+⅓×$100=$66.67. As to the appropriate discount rate, observe that the creditor's claim is less volatile than the firm as a whole: in two out of three states, the creditor gets the same amount of money. The appropriate risk premium will thus be lower than for the firm as a whole (which was 10%); assume it is 7%. The time value of money is still 1%. Thus, the creditor's claim is worth $66.67/(1+1%+7%)=$61.73.

Meanwhile, the shareholder as residual claimant gets whatever is left over after paying the creditor, which is nothing in cases 1 and 2 and $100 in case 3, for an expected cash flow of ⅓×$0+⅓×$0+⅓×$100=$33.33 (alternatively, we could have found this number by subtracting the creditor's expected cash flows from those of the corporation as a whole). The shareholder's claim is riskier than the firm as a whole because the shareholder will only be paid in the best possible case; let us assume the appropriate risk premium is 16.5%. Then, the shareholder's claim is worth $33.33/(1+1%+16.5%)=$28.37.[7]

For obvious reasons, the valuation approach exposited above is called **discounted cash-flow analysis (DCF)**. An alternative to DCF is to use **comparables**: one calculates some valuation ratio (or "multiple") for comparable claims, and then assumes that the same ratio will hold for the claim under examination. For example, to value the shares of company A (say, Pepsi), one might look at comparable company B (say, Coca-Cola), calculate the ratio of company B's stock price to B's current earnings per share (EPS; roughly, firm profits divided by number of shares outstanding), and then calculate company A's share value as A's EPS times B's share value divided by B's EPS. (Thus, if Coca-Cola's share is worth $150, Coca-Cola's EPS is $10 per share, and Pepsi's EPS is $8 per share, then Pepsi's share is worth $8 × $150/$10 = $120, as valued by EPS multiple.) The advantage of the comparables approach to valuation is that it avoids the difficult task of estimating company A's expected cash flows. The disadvantage is that one must not only assume that company B is already correctly valued, but also that both companies will develop in parallel from

---

than $100!

[7] In this example, the value of the creditor's claim and the value of the shareholder's claim add up to the value of the firm as a whole. This might appear unsurprising because the two claims are the only claims on the firm, and value cannot evaporate or appear from out of nowhere. Notice, however, that the algebraic equivalence depended on the risk premia: it would not hold with different risk premia (e.g., a lower risk premium for equity). Modigliani and Miller, mentioned above, are famous for showing that, under certain conditions, risk premia must be such that the equivalence does hold. As also mentioned above, however, Modigliani-Miller is merely a benchmark result. In reality, risk premia may not obey the equivalence exactly. More importantly, Modigliani-Miller applies to fixed cash flows; if capital structure influences cash flows, then all bets are off. In the example above, an important omission was taxes: the mix of debt and equity generally influences tax burdens, and it would not even make sense to value "the firm" without taking into account its financing and associated expected taxes.

their current starting point. The latter assumption is never exactly true and even the approximation may be very bad. In practice, most valuations triangulate from a combination of DCF and multiple comparable firms.

Finally, knowing a claim's present value, or PV, is not enough to make an investment decision. At the risk of stating the obvious, the price of the claim also matters. The investment is appealing only if the **net present value (NPV)**, i.e., PV minus price, is positive.

What is the Goal of the Corporation?

Milton Friedman, *The Social Responsibility of Business is to Increase its Profits*
The *New York Times Magazine* **(Sept. 13, 1970)**

When I hear businessmen speak eloquently about the "social responsibilities of business in a free-enterprise system," I am reminded of the wonderful line about the Frenchman who discovered at the age of 70 that he had been speaking prose all his life. The businessmen believe that they are defending free enterprise when they declaim that business is not concerned "merely" with profit but also with promoting desirable "social" ends; that business has a "social conscience" and takes seriously its responsibilities for providing employment, eliminating discrimination, avoiding pollution and whatever else may be the catchwords of the contemporary crop of reformers. In fact they are—or would be if they or anyone else took them seriously—preaching pure and unadulterated socialism. Businessmen who talk this way are unwitting puppets of the intellectual forces that have been undermining the basis of a free society these past decades.

The discussions of the "social responsibilities of business" are notable for their analytical looseness and lack of rigor. What does it mean to say that "business" has responsibilities? Only people can have responsibilities. A corporation is an artificial person and in this sense may have artificial responsibilities, but "business" as a whole cannot be said to have responsibilities, even in this vague sense. The first step toward clarity in examining the doctrine of the social responsibility of business is to ask precisely what it implies for whom.

Presumably, the individuals who are to be responsible are businessmen, which means individual proprietors or corporate executives. Most of the discussion of social responsibility is directed at corporations, so in what follows I shall mostly neglect the individual proprietors and speak of corporate executives.

In a free-enterprise, private-property system, a corporate executive is an employee of the owners of the business. He has direct responsibility to his employers. That responsibility is to conduct the business in accordance with their desires, which generally will be to make as much money as possible while conforming to the basic rules of the society, both those embodied in law and those embodied in ethical custom. Of course, in some cases his employers may have a different objective. A group of persons might establish a corporation for an eleemosynary purpose—for example, a hospital or a school. The manager of such a corporation will not have money profit as his objective but the rendering of certain services.

In either case, the key point is that, in his capacity as a corporate executive, the manager is the agent of the individuals who own the corporation or establish the eleemosynary institution, and his primary responsibility is to them.

Needless to say, this does not mean that it is easy to judge how well he is performing his task. But at least the criterion of performance is straightforward, and the persons among whom a voluntary contractual arrangement exists are clearly defined.

Of course, the corporate executive is also a person in his own right. As a person, he may have many other responsibilities that he recognizes or assumes voluntarily—to his family, his conscience, his feelings of charity, his church, his clubs, his city, his country. He may feel impelled by these responsibilities to devote part of his income to causes he regards as worthy, to refuse to work for particular corporations, even to leave his job, for example, to join his country's armed forces. If we wish, we may refer to some of these responsibilities as "social responsibilities." But in these respects he is acting as a principal, not an agent; he is spending his own money or time or energy, not the money of his employers or the time or energy he has contracted to devote to their purposes. If these are "social responsibilities," they are the social responsibilities of individuals, not of business.

What does it mean to say that the corporate executive has a "social responsibility" in his capacity as businessman? If this statement is not pure rhetoric, it must mean that he is to act in some way that is not in the interest of his employers. For example, that he is to refrain from increasing the price of the product in order to contribute to the social objective of preventing inflation, even though a price in crease [sic] would be in the best interests of the corporation. Or that he is to make expenditures on reducing pollution beyond the amount that is in the best interests of the corporation or that is required by law in order to contribute to the social objective of improving the environment. Or that, at the expense of corporate profits, he is to hire "hardcore" unemployed instead of better qualified available workmen to contribute to the social objective of reducing poverty.

In each of these cases, the corporate executive would be spending someone else's money for a general social interest. Insofar as his actions in accord with his "social responsibility" reduce returns to stockholders, he is spending their money. Insofar as his actions raise the price to customers, he is spending the customers' money. Insofar as his actions lower the wages of some employees, he is spending their money.

The stockholders or the customers or the employees could separately spend their own money on the particular action if they wished to do so. The executive is exercising a distinct "social responsibility," rather than serving as an agent of the stockholders or the customers or the employees, only if he spends the money in a different way than they would have spent it. But if he does this, he is in effect imposing taxes, on the one hand, and deciding how the tax proceeds shall be spent, on the other.

This process raises political questions on two levels: principle and consequences. On the level of political principle, the imposition of taxes and the expenditure of tax proceeds are governmental functions. We have established elaborate constitutional, parliamentary and judicial provisions to control these functions, to assure that taxes are imposed so far as possible in accordance with the preferences and desires of the public—after all, "taxation without representation" was one of the battle cries of the American Revolution. We have a system of checks and balances to separate the legislative function of imposing taxes and enacting expenditures from the executive function of collecting taxes and administering expenditure programs and from the judicial function of mediating disputes and interpreting the law.

Here the businessman—self-selected or appointed directly or indirectly by stockholders— is to be simultaneously legislator, executive and, jurist. He is to decide whom to tax by how much and for what purpose, and he is to spend the proceeds—all this guided only by general exhortations from on high to restrain inflation, improve the environment, fight poverty and so on and on.

The whole justification for permitting the corporate executive to be selected by the stockholders is that the executive is an agent serving the interests of his principal. This justification disappears when the corporate executive imposes taxes and spends the proceeds for "social" purposes. He becomes in effect a public employee, a civil servant, even though he remains in name an employee of a private enterprise. On grounds of political principle, it is intolerable that such civil servants—insofar as their actions in the name of social responsibility are real and not just window-dressing—should be selected as they are now. If they are to be civil servants, then they must be elected through a political process. If they are to impose taxes and make expenditures to foster "social" objectives, then political machinery must be set up to make the assessment of taxes and to determine through a political process the objectives to be served.

This is the basic reason why the doctrine of "social responsibility" involves the acceptance of the socialist view that political mechanisms, not market mechanisms, are the appropriate way to determine the allocation of scarce resources to alternative uses.

On the grounds of consequences, can the corporate executive in fact discharge his alleged "social responsibilities?" On the other hand, suppose he could get away with spending the stockholders' or customers' or employees' money. How is he to know how to spend it? He is told that he must contribute to fighting inflation. How is he to know what action of his will contribute to that end? He is presumably an expert in running his company—in producing a product or selling it or financing it. But nothing about his selection makes him an expert on inflation. Will his holding down the price of his product reduce inflationary pressure? Or, by leaving more spending power in the hands of his customers, simply divert it elsewhere? Or, by forcing him to produce less because of the lower price, will it simply contribute to shortages? Even if he could answer these questions, how much cost is he justified in imposing on his stockholders, customers and employees for this social purpose? What is his appropriate share and what is the appropriate share of others?

And, whether he wants to or not, can he get away with spending his stockholders', customers' or employees' money? Will not the stockholders fire him? (Either the present ones or those who take over when his actions in the name of social responsibility have reduced the corporation's profits and the price of its stock.) His customers and his employees can desert him for other producers and employers less scrupulous in exercising their social responsibilities. . . .

Many a reader who has followed the argument this far may be tempted to remonstrate that it is all well and good to speak of Government's having the responsibility to impose taxes and determine expenditures for such "social" purposes as controlling pollution or training the hard-core unemployed, but that the problems are too urgent to wait on the slow course of political processes, that the exercise of social responsibility by businessmen is a quicker and surer way to solve pressing current problems.

Aside from the question of fact—I share Adam Smith's skepticism about the benefits that can be expected from "those who affected to trade for the public good"—this argument must be rejected on grounds of principle. What it amounts to is an assertion that those who favor the taxes and expenditures in question have failed to persuade a majority of their fellow citizens to be of like mind and that they are seeking to attain by undemocratic procedures what they cannot attain by democratic procedures. In a free society, it is hard for "evil" people to do "evil," especially since one man's good is another's evil.

I have, for simplicity, concentrated on the special case of the corporate executive, except only for the brief digression on trade unions. But precisely the same argument applies to the newer phenomenon of calling upon stockholders to require corporations to exercise social responsibility (the recent G.M crusade for example). In most of these cases, what is in effect involved is some stockholders trying to get other stockholders (or customers or employees) to contribute against their will to "social" causes favored by the activists. Insofar as they succeed, they are again imposing taxes and spending the proceeds. . . .

[T]he doctrine of "social responsibility" taken seriously would extend the scope of the political mechanism to every human activity. It does not differ in philosophy from the most explicitly collectivist doctrine. It differs only by professing to believe that collectivist ends can be attained without collectivist means. That is why, in my book *Capitalism and Freedom*, I have called it a "fundamentally subversive doctrine" in a free society, and have said that in such a society, "there is one and only one social responsibility of business—to use its resources and engage in activities designed to increase its profits so long as it stays within the rules of the game, which is to say, engages in open and free competition without deception or fraud."

Duff McDonald, *Harvard Business School and the Propagation of Immoral Profit Strategies*
Text (adaptation as appeared in *Newsweek*, Apr. 6, 2017) from *The Golden Passport* (2017)

In 1970, Nobel Prize–winning economist Milton Friedman published an essay in *The New York Times Magazine* titled "The Social Responsibility of Business Is to Increase Its Profits."

Flouting the midcentury view (and that of the most influential faculty at the Harvard Business School) that the best type of CEO was one with an enlightened social conscience, Friedman claimed that such executives were "highly subversive to the capitalist system." His tone was snide. . . .

Friedman was suggesting the release of those people from their obligations—contractual or otherwise—to anyone but the shareholder. They'd let their good nature get in the way of getting the job done, he was arguing, and it was time to throw off such naïve notions for the good of the country—nay, for capitalism itself.

It was a remarkable intellectual sleight of hand. Executives who act in ways most of us would consider moral—with an eye to the environment or some other social goal—are, Friedman said, acting immorally. When Joel Bakan interviewed Friedman for his 2005 book, *The Corporation: The Pathological Pursuit of Profit and Power*, the economist repeated the point he'd made nearly 40 years before, but with a twist. In Friedman's view, "hypocrisy is virtuous when it serves the bottom line," Bakan observed, "[whereas] moral virtue is immoral when it does not."

Even in 2005, Bakan was able to find a professor at HBS who was willing to channel Friedman's "brand of cynicism [that is] old-fashioned, mean-spirited, and out of touch with reality." According to then–HBS professor Debora Spar, corporations "are not institutions set up to be moral entities.... They are institutions which really only have one mission, and that is to increase shareholder value."

Just a small sample of people who've actually "set up" corporations would seem to suggest that such a blanket statement is entirely without merit. Yvon Chouinard, the CEO of Patagonia, certainly had a larger mission in mind. John Mackey, co-founder of Whole Foods, wouldn't agree with that premise. It also seems likely that the founders of Harvard, itself a corporation, wouldn't have either.

What's truly unfortunate is that if one considers the work of midcentury thinkers at HBS, the faculty stood almost alone in insisting that character had a part to play in management. Until it decided to hire the man who thought managers had no character at all. . . .

The main way it did so was by endorsing the innocuously named "principal-agent theory" popularized by Friedman. While much of the faculty of HBS was still trying to figure out how to help American management resurrect its reputation and its fortunes as the 1980s began, Michael Jensen, then a professor at the University of Rochester's business school steeped in the University of Chicago's free market tradition, was making sure the good name of managers stayed buried. Along with William Meckling, the dean of Rochester's business school (and a graduate student of Friedman's), Jensen wrote a 1976 paper that would change everything. In "Theory of the Firm: Managerial Behavior, Agency Costs and Ownership Structure," he laid the groundwork for the most radical change in the hierarchy of power in corporate America since the robber barons gave way to professional managers.

Arguing that managers had become too entrenched and lacked discipline and accountability, Jensen and Meckling posited that investors were more trustworthy than managers as custodians of the American corporation. Managers weren't going to voluntarily reform, they said, so the system had to be adjusted so that they would be forced to do so. No longer would they be their own judge, or be judged by a jury they had picked, that is, their board. The market was henceforth to be judge, jury and executioner....

In a 1994 paper Jensen wrote with Meckling, "The Nature of Man," he cited the story of George Bernard Shaw asking an actress if she would sleep with him for a million dollars. When she agreed, he changed his offer to $10, to which she responded with outrage, asking him what kind of woman he thought she was. His reply: "We've already established that. Now we're just haggling about the price." The authors then concluded that we're all whores. "Like it or not, individuals are willing to sacrifice a little of almost anything we care to name, even reputation or morality, for a sufficiently large quantity of other desired things."

The solution they offered was premised on this cynical view of man and, having started from the assumption that we are all whores, they naturally ended up with prescriptions for making us well-behaved whores. "Unlike theories in the physical sciences," wrote Sumantra Ghoshal, a professor at the London Business School, in his 2005 paper, "Bad Management Theories Are Destroying Good Management Practice," "theories in the social sciences tend to be self-fulfilling.... This is precisely what has happened over the last several decades, converting our collective pessimism about managers into realized pathologies in management behaviors."

In other words, if everybody assumes you're a whore, you might as well grab as much money as possible while you're still in demand. "[By] propagating ideologically inspired amoral theories, business schools have actively freed their students from any sense of moral responsibility," concluded Ghoshal. Managers were not to be trusted; shareholders were. It was one of the most remarkable about-faces in the history of education. And by hiring Jensen, HBS threw its lot in with the cynics.

Graduates of HBS had always been drawn to finance, but in the 1980s they began heading to Wall Street and private equity firms in droves. Whereas in 1965 only 11 percent of HBS MBAs entered the fields of consulting or investment banking, by 1985 the two fields took in 41 percent of the school's graduating class. And many of them would play a significant role in downsizing—that is to say, gutting—the traditional manufacturing and product firms that previous HBS graduates had helped build.

The shift is indicative of the MBA's nose for power. Before the 1970s, companies' increasing cash piles had lessened their dependence on banks. But as those cash piles evaporated, the pendulum had swung back in finance's favor. In a capitalist economy, power equals money, and between 1983 and 1992, the proportion of professional managers in the nation's top 1 percent of household wealth holders showed a marked decline, while that of people working in finance spiked. And so that's where the MBAs went. "For most of the 20th century, social organization in the United States orbited around the large corporation like moons around a planet," wrote University of Michigan business administration professor

Gerald Davis in "Corporate Power in the 21st Century." But by the time Jensen was through, "any lingering doubt about the purpose of the corporation, or its commitment to various stakeholders, had been resolved. The corporation existed to create shareholder value; other commitments were means to that end."

"Business educators legitimized the notion that good management might mean dissolving the firm to improve shareholder return," wrote management historian J.C. Spender in BizEd magazine in 2016, "without concern for the social costs to employees who lost their jobs or to communities that lost employers."

Ah, yes: all that nonsense about the social responsibility of business. It turned out that was all just posturing. Recent studies by the Aspen Institute show that when students enter business school, they believe that the purpose of a corporation is to produce goods and services for the benefit of society. When they graduate, they believe that it is to maximize shareholder value....

Way back in 1951, the chairman of Standard Oil of New Jersey—the company founded by the ultimate robber baron, John D. Rockefeller—said: "The job of management is to maintain an equitable and working balance among the claims of the various directly affected interest groups...stockholder, employees, customers, and the public at large." During the Jensen era, many people forgot about that.

But then we all sort of remembered it again. Even shareholder-friendly Jack Welch, the longtime CEO of General Electric, eventually came around. In March 2009, he told the *Financial Times*, "On the face of it, shareholder value is the dumbest idea in the world. Shareholder value is a result, not a strategy.... Your main constituencies are your employees, your customers and your products. Managers and investors should not set share price increases as their overarching goal.... Short-term profits should be allied with an increase in the long-term value of a company."

Maybe, just maybe, we're not all whores....

Walmart Press Release: *More Than One Million Walmart Associates to Receive Pay Increase in 2016* (Jan., 20, 2016)

2016 action lifts average hourly full-time rate to $13.38; New paid time off plan gives full- and part-time associates greater control

BENTONVILLE, Ark., Jan. 20, 2016 – More than 1.2 million Walmart U.S. and Sam's Club associates will receive a pay increase under the second phase of the company's two-year, $2.7 billion investment in workers. The pay raise, which takes effect Feb. 20, will be one of the largest single-day, private-sector pay increases ever. As an industry leader for competitive pay and benefits, Walmart is also implementing new short-term disability and simplified paid time off (PTO) programs. The combined changes will expand support for associates dealing with extended health issues and provide associates greater control over their paid time away from work.

"We are committed to investing in our associates and to continuing to simplify our business. When we do so, there is no limit to what our associates can accomplish," said Judith McKenna, chief operating officer for Walmart U.S. "Our customers and associates are noticing a difference. We're seeing strong increases in both customer experience and associate engagement scores. Five straight quarters of positive comps in our U.S. business is just one example of how helping our associates grow and succeed helps the company do the same."

Discussion Questions:

1. To the extent that the two conflict, do you believe that the goal of the corporation should be "to produce goods and services for the benefit of society" or "to maximize shareholder value?"

2. Assume that the Walmart pay increase described above goes beyond what is required in the various labor markets that Walmart operates in, i.e., Walmart could attract qualified employees at a lower wage rate. Further assume that Walmart receives little to no public-relations benefit, employee morale benefit, employee productivity benefit, etc. (and therefore no benefit in terms of revenues) from the wage increase. If you were a member of the Walmart board of directors, would you vote for the pay increase?

3. If you answered yes to the first question, would you vote for $15 per hour, as some commentators have said Walmart can also afford? (See, e.g., http://www.cnbc.com/2016/06/03/walmart-can-afford-15-minimum-wage-commentary.html). In answering please make the same assumptions as above.

eBay, Inc. v. Newmark et al.
16 A.3d 1 (2010)

CHANDLER, Chancellor

[...]

I. FACTS

Since the time the parties completed their post-trial briefing, I have examined carefully the briefs, exhibits, deposition testimony and trial transcript. I have also reflected at length on my observations of witness testimony during trial, including my impressions regarding the credibility and demeanor of each witness. The following are my findings of the relevant facts in this dispute, based on evidence introduced at trial and my post-trial review.

A. Oil and Water

In 1995, two individuals in northern California began to develop modest ideas that would take hold in cyberspace and grow to become household names. Craig Newmark, founder of craigslist, started an email list for San Francisco events that in time has morphed into the most-used classifieds site in the United States. Pierre Omidyar, founder of eBay, Inc., started an online auction system that has grown to become one of the largest auction and shopping websites in the United States. As they grew, both companies expanded overseas and established a presence in international markets.

Now, even though both companies enjoy household-name status, craigslist and eBay are, to put it mildly, different animals. Indeed, the two companies are a study in contrasts, with different business strategies, different cultures, and different perspectives on what it means to run a successful business. It is curious these two companies ever formed a business relationship. Each, however, felt it had something to offer to and gain from the other. Thus, despite all differences, eBay and craigslist formed a relationship.

The dissimilarities between these two companies drive this dispute, so I will spend a moment discussing them. I will begin with craigslist. Though a for-profit concern, craigslist largely operates its business as a community service. Nearly all classified advertisements are placed on craigslist free of charge. Moreover, craigslist does not sell advertising space on its website to third parties. Nor does craigslist advertise or otherwise market its services. craigslist's revenue stream consists solely of fees for online job postings in certain cities and apartment listings in New York City.

Despite ubiquitous name recognition, craigslist operates as a small business. It is headquartered in an old Victorian house in a residential San Francisco neighborhood. It employs approximately thirty-four employees. It is privately held and has never been owned by more than three stockholders at a time. It is not subject to the reporting requirements of federal securities laws, and its financial statements are not in the public domain. It keeps its internal business data, such as detailed site metrics, confidential.

Almost since its inception, the craigslist website has maintained the same consistent look and simple functionality. Classified categories the site offers are broad (for example, antiques, personal ads, music gigs, and legal services), but craigslist has largely kept its focus on the classifieds business. It has not forayed into ventures beyond its core competency in classifieds. craigslist's management team—consisting principally of defendants Jim [Buckmaster], CEO and President of craigslist, and Craig [Newmark], Chairman and Secretary of the craigslist board—is committed to this community-service approach to doing business. They believe this approach is the heart of craigslist's business. For most of its history, craigslist has not focused on "monetizing" its site. The relatively small amount of monetization craigslist has pursued (for select job postings and apartment listings) does not approach what many craigslist competitors would consider an optimal or even minimally acceptable level. Nevertheless, craigslist's unique business strategy continues to be successful, even if it does run counter to the strategies used by the titans of online commerce. Thus far, no competing site has been able to dislodge craigslist from its perch atop the pile of most-used online classifieds sites in the United States, craigslist's lead position is made more enigmatic by the fact that it maintains its dominant market position with small-scale physical and human capital. Perhaps the most mysterious thing about craigslist's continued success is the fact that craigslist does not expend any great effort seeking to maximize its profits or to monitor its competition or its market share.

Now to eBay. Initially a venture with humble beginnings, eBay has grown to be a global enterprise. eBay is a for-profit concern that operates its business with an eye to maximizing revenues, profits, and market share. Sellers who use eBay's site pay eBay a commission on each sale. These commissions formed the initial revenue stream for eBay, and they continue to be an important source of revenue today. Over the years eBay has tapped other revenue sources, expanding its product and service offerings both internally and through acquisitions of online companies such as PayPal, Skype, Half.com, and Rent.com. eBay advertises its services and actively seeks to drive web traffic to its sites. It has a large management team and a formal management structure. It employs over 16,000 people at multiple locations around the world. It actively monitors its competitive market position. Its shares trade on the NASDAQ. It maintains a constant focus on monetization, turning online products and services into revenue streams. In terms of business objectives, eBay is vastly different from craigslist; eBay focuses on generating income from each of the products and services it offers rather than from only a small subset of services. It might be said that "eBay" is a moniker for monetization, and that "craigslist" is anything but.

[...]

II. ANALYSIS

Jim and Craig owe fiduciary duties to eBay because they are directors and controlling stockholders of craigslist, and eBay is a minority stockholder of craigslist. All directors of Delaware corporations are fiduciaries of the corporations' stockholders. Similarly, controlling stockholders are fiduciaries of their corporations' minority stockholders. Even though neither Jim nor Craig individually owns a majority of craigslist's shares, the law treats them as craigslist's controlling stockholders because they form a control group, bound together by the Jim-Craig Voting Agreement, with the power to elect the majority of the craigslist board.

eBay's complaint asserts that Jim and Craig breached the fiduciary duties they owed to eBay by implementing the 2008 Board Actions. [In which Jim and Craig took defensive actions—most importantly, installing a "Rights Plan" a/k/a "poison pill" (the mechanics of which we will discuss later in the course)—to block eBay from gaining control of craigslist in the future][...]

Jim and Craig contend that they identified a threat to craigslist and its corporate policies that will materialize after they both die and their craigslist shares are distributed to their heirs. At that point, they say, "eBay's acquisition of control [via the anticipated acquisition of Jim or Craig's shares from some combination of their heirs] would fundamentally alter craigslist's values, culture and business model, including departing from [craigslist's] public-service mission in favor of increased monetization of craigslist." To prevent this unwanted potential future reality, Jim and Craig have adopted the Rights Plan *now* so that their vision of craigslist's culture can bind *future* fiduciaries and stockholders from beyond the grave.

[...]

Ultimately, defendants failed to prove that craigslist possesses a palpable, distinctive, and advantageous culture that sufficiently promotes stockholder value to support the indefinite implementation of a poison pill. Jim and Craig did not make any serious attempt to prove that the craigslist culture, which rejects any attempt to further monetize its services, translates into increased profitability for stockholders. I am sure that part of the reason craigslist is so popular is because it offers a free service that is also extremely useful. It may be that offering free classifieds is an essential component of a successful online classifieds venture. After all, by offering free classifieds, craigslist is able to attract such a large community of users that real estate brokers in New York City gladly pay fees to list apartment rentals in order to access the vast community of craigslist users. Likewise, employers in select cities happily pay fees to advertise job openings to craigslist users. Neither of these fee-generating activities would have been possible if craigslist did not provide brokers and employers access to a sufficiently large market of consumers, and brokers and employers may not have reached that market without craigslist's free classifieds.

Giving away services to attract business is a sales tactic, however, not a corporate culture. Jim, Craig, and the defense witnesses advisedly described craigslist's business using the language of "culture" because that was what carried the day in *Time.* To the extent business measures like loss-leading products, money-back coupons, or putting products on sale are cultural artifacts, they reflect the American capitalist culture, not something unique to craigslist. Having heard the evidence and judged witness credibility at trial, I find that there is nothing about craigslist's corporate culture that *Time* or *Unocal* protects. The existence of a distinctive craigslist "culture" was not proven at trial. It is a fiction, invoked almost talismanically for purposes of this trial in order to find deference under *Time's* dicta.

The defendants also failed to prove at trial that when adopting the Rights Plan, they concluded in good faith that there was a sufficient connection between the craigslist "culture" (however amorphous and intangible it might be) and the promotion of stockholder value. No evidence at trial suggested that Jim or Craig conducted any informed evaluation of alternative business strategies or tactics when adopting the Rights Plan. Jim and Craig simply disliked the possibility that the Grim Reaper someday will catch up with them and that a company like eBay might, in the future, purchase a controlling interest in craigslist. They considered this possible future state unpalatable, not because of how it affects the value of the entity for its stockholders, but rather because of their own personal preferences. Jim and Craig therefore failed to prove at trial that they acted in the good faith pursuit of a proper *corporate* purpose when they deployed the Rights Plan. Based on all of the evidence, I find instead that Jim and Craig resented eBay's decision to compete with craigslist and adopted the Rights Plan as a punitive response. They then cloaked this decision in the language of culture and *post mortem* corporate benefit. Although Jim and Craig (and the psychological culture they embrace) were the only known beneficiaries of the Rights Plan, such a motive is no substitute for their fiduciary duty to craigslist stockholders.

Jim and Craig did prove that they personally believe craigslist should not be about the business of stockholder wealth maximization, now or in the future. As an abstract matter, there is nothing inappropriate about an organization seeking to aid local, national, and global communities by providing a website for online classifieds that is largely devoid of monetized elements. Indeed, I personally appreciate and admire Jim's and Craig's desire to be of service to communities. The corporate form in which craigslist operates, however, is not an appropriate vehicle for purely philanthropic ends, at least not when there are other stockholders interested in realizing a return on their investment. Jim and Craig opted to form craigslist, Inc. as a *for-profit Delaware corporation* and voluntarily accepted millions of dollars from eBay as part of a transaction whereby eBay became a stockholder. Having chosen a for-profit corporate form, the craigslist directors are bound by the fiduciary duties and standards that accompany that form. Those standards include acting to promote the value of the corporation for the benefit of its stockholders. The "Inc." after the company name has to mean at least that. Thus, I cannot accept as valid for the purposes of implementing the Rights Plan a corporate policy that specifically, clearly, and admittedly seeks *not* to maximize the economic value of a for-profit Delaware corporation for the benefit of its stockholders—no matter whether those stockholders are individuals of modest means or a corporate titan of online commerce. If Jim and Craig were the only stockholders affected by their decisions, then there would be no one to object. eBay, however, holds a significant stake in craigslist, and Jim and Craig's actions affect others besides themselves.

[...]

. . . I find that defendants failed to prove, as a factual matter, the existence of a distinctly protectable craigslist culture and further failed to prove, both factually and legally, that they actually decided to deploy the Rights Plan because of a craigslist culture. I find, instead, that Jim and Craig acted to punish eBay for competing with craigslist. Directors of a for-profit Delaware corporation cannot deploy a rights plan to defend a business strategy that openly eschews stockholder wealth maximization—at least not consistently with the directors' fiduciary duties under Delaware law.

[...] To the extent I assume for purposes of analysis that a craigslist culture was something that Jim and Craig reasonably could seek to protect, the Rights Plan nonetheless does not fall within the range of reasonable responses. In evaluating the range of reasonableness, it is important to note that Jim and Craig actually do not seek to protect the craigslist "culture" today. They are perfectly able to ensure the continuation of craigslist's "culture" so long as they remain majority stockholders. What they instead want is to preserve craigslist's "culture" over some indefinite period that starts at the (happily) unknowable moment when their natural lives come to a close. The attenuated nature of that goal further undercuts the degree to which "culture" can provide a basis for heavy-handed defensive action.

[...]

Because defendants failed to prove that they acted to protect or defend a legitimate corporate interest and because they failed to prove that the rights plan was a reasonable response to a perceived threat to corporate policy or effectiveness, I rescind the Rights Plan in its entirety.

[...]

E. Attorneys' Fees

eBay asks the Court to order Jim and Craig to reimburse craigslist for all of the legal fees incurred in this action and for the legal fees relating to the 2008 Board Actions. eBay also asks the Court to award eBay the legal fees it has incurred in this action. I decline to order any shifting of fees.

eBay is not entitled to fees under § 9.8 of the Shareholders' Agreement because eBay did not bring a claim for breach of the Shareholders' Agreement or for breach of the implied covenant of good faith and fair dealing inherent in the Shareholders' Agreement. More importantly, however, the equities in this case do not mandate a shifting of attorneys' fees. Under Delaware law, parties are ordinarily responsible for paying their own attorneys' fees. Equity may make an exception and shift fees to a party that has acted in bad faith in connection with the prosecution or defense of the litigation. Fees may also be shifted to a losing party whose pre-litigation conduct was undertaken in bad faith and "was so egregious as to justify an award of attorneys' fees as an element of damages." The Court typically will not find a litigant acted in bad faith for purposes of shifting attorneys' fees unless the litigant's conduct rose to the level of "glaring egregiousness." "[M]erely being adjudicated a wrongdoer under our corporate law is not enough to justify fee shifting."

Neither Jim nor Craig engaged in behavior that could be characterized as bad faith for purposes of fee shifting. Their conduct during litigation was typical of litigants before this Court; they vigorously defended their legal position without making frivolous arguments. Moreover, the 2008 Board Actions cannot be described as "glaring[ly] egregious" pre-litigation conduct. As should be evident by this point in the narrative, this is a unique case with distinct facts and difficult legal issues. I find, as a matter of fact, after evaluating the credibility and demeanor of Jim and Craig, that both men subjectively believed the 2008 Board Actions, despite their uniqueness, were legally permissible under Delaware law. Their judgment was wrong, in my view, with respect to the Rights Plan and the ROFR/Dilutive Issuance. But that does not mean that Jim and Craig implemented the Rights Plan and the ROFR/Dilutive Issuance in bad faith. Neither Jim nor Craig acted with the sort of vexatious, wanton, or frivolous conduct consistent with bad faith. Rather, they deliberated with counsel over a period of six months regarding the 2008 Board Actions, considered the possibility of a legal challenge to the Actions, and decided to move forward after concluding, albeit incorrectly, that the Actions were consistent with law.

[...]

Discussion Questions:

1. What action did eBay challenge in this lawsuit, and what remedy did it obtain? In particular, did Chancellor Chandler order Jim and Craig to monetize craigslist? (Hint: take a look at the site today.)

2. What should be the goal of the corporation? In the eBay case, do you agree with the Court that Jim and Craig, as controlling shareholders of craigslist, cannot run craigslist as a non-profit if they want to?

3. Notice that eBay never formally alleged that Jim and Craig breached their contractual agreements to eBay (see Part E, second paragraph, first sentence). If this is correct, then how could Jim and Craig possibly breach their fiduciary duty? Put differently, why should fiduciary duty require more than just compliance with the contractual documents? (And an optional follow-on question, for a gold star: given your explanation for why a "fiduciary duty overlay" exists in corporate law, what kind of actors—e.g., top managers, low-level managers, directors, major shareholders, etc.—should fiduciary duty apply to?)

4. craigslist is a Delaware corporation. Approximately 30 other states (but not Delaware) have so-called "constituency statutes." Pennsylvania's constituency statute is typical (PCBL § 1715(a)):

    > **General Rule.** -- In discharging the duties of their respective positions, the board of directors, committees of the board and individual directors of a business corporation may, in considering the best interests of the corporation, consider to the extent they deem appropriate:
    >
    > (1) The effects of any action upon any or all groups affected by such action, including shareholders, employees, suppliers, customers and creditors of the corporation, and upon communities in which offices or other establishments of the corporation are located.
    >
    > (2) The short-term and long-term interests of the corporation, including benefits that may accrue to the corporation from its long-term plans and the possibility that these interests may be best served by the continued independence of the corporation.
    >
    > (3) The resources, intent and conduct (past, stated and potential) of any person seeking to acquire control of the corporation.

(4)   All other pertinent factors.

Would the case have come out differently in Pennsylvania?

5.   The past few years have seen the rapid rise of a new idea: the benefit corporation. As provided for by state law, benefit corporations declare a public mission in their articles of incorporation—a social or environmental objective, for example. The company is required to take this mission into account in its decision-making, and to report annually on how it is carrying out its mission, measured by a third-party standard. While benefit corporations do not have a special tax status, they do provide management and directors with legal cover to make decisions based on public motives, as well as profit motives. Delaware's B-Corp statute reads, in relevant part:

§ 362. Public benefit corporation defined; contents of certificate of incorporation.

(a) A "public benefit corporation" is a for-profit corporation organized under and subject to the requirements of this chapter that is intended to produce a public benefit or public benefits and to operate in a responsible and sustainable manner. To that end, a public benefit corporation shall be managed in a manner that balances the stockholders' pecuniary interests, the best interests of those materially affected by the corporation's conduct, and the public benefit or public benefits identified in its certificate of incorporation. In the certificate of incorporation, a public benefit corporation shall:

(1) Identify within its statement of business or purpose pursuant to § 102(a)(3) of this title 1 or more specific public benefits to be promoted by the corporation; and

(2) State within its heading that it is a public benefit corporation.

(b) "Public benefit" means a positive effect (or reduction of negative effects) on 1 or more categories of persons, entities, communities or interests (other than stockholders in their capacities as stockholders) including, but not limited to, effects of an artistic, charitable, cultural, economic, educational, environmental, literary, medical, religious, scientific or technological nature. "Public benefit provisions" means the provisions of a certificate of incorporation contemplated by this subchapter...

§ 365. Duties of directors.

(a) The board of directors shall manage or direct the business and affairs of the public benefit corporation in a manner that balances the pecuniary interests of the stockholders, the best interests of those materially affected by the corporation's conduct, and the specific public benefit or public benefits identified in its certificate of incorporation.

(b) A director of a public benefit corporation shall not, by virtue of the public benefit provisions or § 362(a) of this title, have any duty to any person on account of any interest of such person in the public benefit or public benefits identified in the certificate of incorporation or on account of any interest materially affected by the corporation's conduct and, with respect to a decision implicating the balance requirement in subsection (a) of this section, will be deemed to satisfy such director's fiduciary duties to stockholders and the corporation if such director's decision is both informed and disinterested and not such that no person of ordinary, sound judgment would approve....

§ 366. Periodic statements and third-party certification.

(a) A public benefit corporation shall include in every notice of a meeting of stockholders a statement to the effect that it is a public benefit corporation formed pursuant to this subchapter.

(b) A public benefit corporation shall no less than biennially provide its stockholders with a statement as to the corporation's promotion of the public benefit or public benefits identified in the certificate of incorporation and of the best interests of those materially affected by the corporation's conduct. The statement shall include:

(1) The objectives the board of directors has established to promote such public benefit or public benefits and interests;

(2) The standards the board of directors has adopted to measure the corporation's progress in promoting such public benefit or public benefits and interests;

(3) Objective factual information based on those standards regarding the corporation's success in meeting the objectives for promoting such public benefit or public benefits and interests; and

(4) An assessment of the corporation's success in meeting the objectives and promoting such public benefit or public benefits and interests.

(c) The certificate of incorporation or bylaws of a public benefit corporation may require that the corporation:

(1) Provide the statement described in subsection (b) of this section more frequently than biennially;

(2) Make the statement described in subsection (b) of this section available to the public; and/or

(3) Use a third-party standard in connection with and/or attain a periodic third-party certification addressing the corporation's promotion of the public benefit or public benefits identified in the certificate of incorporation and/or the best interests of those materially affected by the corporation's conduct.

The B-Corp form was not available when Jim and Craig incorporated craigslist. But if it were, do you think Jim and Craig would have used this form? If so, why did they not simply craft their own "B-Corp" by means of an appropriate charter provision? Would the case have come out differently if they had?

Chapter 2 – Shareholder Voting

Shareholders vote to elect the board and to approve fundamental changes, such as charter amendments (DGCL 242(b)) or mergers (cf. DGCL 252(c)). Other matters *may* be submitted to a shareholder vote as well.

"Shareholder Democracy"

Shareholder voting is often labeled "shareholder democracy." It differs considerably, however, from political elections in contemporary democracies such as the U.S.

First, the default rule in corporations is one vote per share ("one share one vote"), rather than one vote per shareholder (DGCL 212(a)).

Second, voting rights are determined on the "record date," 10-60 days *before* the actual vote (DGCL 213). At least in practice, one keeps one's voting rights even if one sells the shares in between. (Any problem with this?)

Third, incumbents enjoy a large advantage. They control the voting process, and the corporation pays for their solicitation of votes.

Fourth, rational apathy is more pronounced in shareholder voting than in (national) political elections. In large corporations with dispersed ownership, an individual small shareholder has practically no influence on the outcome. It is thus rational for the shareholder not to spend time and resources learning about the issues at stake ("rational apathy"). So-called institutional investors such as pension funds or mutual funds might have more influence but their decision-makers lack the incentive to use it: The decision-makers are the funds' managers, but the benefits of higher share value accrue primarily to the funds' beneficiaries. (You might think that a fund manager benefits indirectly by attracting more new customers if the fund generates a higher return for existing customers. This is true for some idiosyncratic funds. But many funds, particularly index fund, invest in the same assets as their competitors and are evaluated relative to one another. The only way such funds can distinguish themselves from their competitors is through lower cost. For these funds, spending resources on voting *hurts* their competitive position relative to passive competitors even if the voting does lead to higher asset values.)

Fifth, shareholders do not run the corporation—the board does. That is, the corporate form is a representative democracy, not a direct democracy. Even if 99% of shareholders instruct the board "Do X," the board does not have to do X if they believe, in good faith, that doing so is not in the best interests of the corporation.

Voting Rules and Frequency

Unless otherwise provided in the charter or the statute, a majority of the shares entitled to vote constitutes a quorum (DGCL 216(i)), and the affirmative vote of a majority of the shares present is required to pass a resolution (DGCL 216(ii)).

The default for director elections is different (plurality voting, DGCL 216(iii)), but most large corporations have instituted some form of majority voting rule for director elections as well. This matters mostly when shareholders express their dissatisfaction through a "withhold campaign" against a particular director. Under the default plurality voting rule, the director could be elected with a single vote (if running unopposed, as is the norm). Under a majority vote rule, each director must get more votes cast in favor than withheld. The net effect of a majority voting rule is that every director X is running against "not X" (in the form of withhold votes). A majority voting rule makes even ostensibly uncontested elections, in effect, contested elections; or, put differently, it gives withhold votes substantive rather than just symbolic bite.

A more radical but rare deviation from the default rule is cumulative voting. Under a cumulative voting regime, each shareholder gets votes equal to the number of shares owned times the number of seats to be filled. They can then distribute their votes across candidates, or cast all their votes for a single candidate. As a practical matter, a cumulative voting regime increases the likelihood of minority representation on the board.

The corporation must hold a stockholder meeting at least once a year, DGCL 211(b). By default, all board seats are up for election every year. Under DGCL 141(d), however, the charter or a qualified bylaw can provide that as few as one third of the seats are contestable each year, i.e., that directors hold staggered terms of up to three years. This so-called "staggered board" (equivalently, "classified board") probably seems like technical minutiae to you now. But it turns out to be an extremely important provision because it may critically delay anybody's attempt to take control of the board. (We will first see this in *Blasius*, below.) An important complementing rule is that unlike standard boards, staggered boards are subject to removal only for cause (DGCL 141(k)(1); *cf.* DGCL 141(k)(2) for the case of cumulative voting).

In addition to an annual shareholder meeting (ASM), companies can allow shareholders to act by written consent and/or act at a special meeting. DGCL § 211(d) allows the board to call a special meeting, though shareholders can be given the right to call a special meeting in the charter or bylaws. DGCL § 228(a) provides that any action that may be taken at a meeting of shareholders may also be taken through written consent of the shareholders, though this power can be taken away through the charter.

Discussion Questions:

1. HLS Corp. has 300 shares outstanding; Reinier owns 199 shares and Lucian owns 101 shares. HLS Corp. has a three-person board elected to annual terms. Reinier and Lucian do not see eye-to-eye, and prefer different candidates for the board. Under a

"straight" voting system, Reinier would win each seat 199 to 101. What would happen under a cumulative voting system?

2. Village, Inc., is a corporation engaged in the business of providing online fashion advice and consulting services to law students and young lawyers.[8] The firm had its initial public offering (IPO) two years ago, and after a meteoric rise, the stock has fallen steadily since then. GianCarlo Morrison, who is Village's CEO, owns 25 percent of its single class of stock. The balance of the stock is widely held. Morrison's block has allowed him to control the outcome of board elections. The bylaws specify that the number of directors shall be fixed at nine and divided into three equal classes, each of whose term shall expire in successive years. The word on the street, however, is that the nosedive of the stock has sparked the interest of others in gaining control. Under these circumstances, the board recommends and the shareholders approve an amendment of the Village charter to provide that the power to amend the bylaws shall be vested exclusively in the directors and to provide for cumulative voting.

    Six months later a well-known takeover artist, Cesar Manning, purchases 51 percent of the outstanding Village, Inc. stock from numerous holders and consults you to devise some method of immediately assuming and exercising actual control over company policy. What advice would you give him under Delaware law?

    Assess Mr. Manning's ability to use the following possible actions to advance his plan: (1) amending the certificate of incorporation, (2) amending the bylaws; (3) increasing the size of the board, (4) removing one or more directors, and (5) dissolving the company and distributing its assets. Please consider DGCL §§ 109(a), 141(d), 141(k), 223(a), 242(b)(1), 275.

3. It is late at night and you are just about to send your memo to Cesar Manning. Just then your new associate from Harvard Law School runs in and says, "Wait! The bylaws that stagger the board weren't put in at the IPO and weren't approved by the Village, Inc. shareholders!" Your associate seems to get excited about very minor things. Nevertheless, revise your memo as needed, and send.

Proxies

In principle, shareholders still vote at a physical "meeting." But in large corporations, few shareholders attend such meetings in person, and those who do may not be the most important ones. Instead, shareholders vote by mail—sort of. U.S. corporations do not mail shareholders a proper ballot. Instead, the board solicits "proxies" on behalf of, and paid by, the corporation. Shareholders "vote" by granting or withholding proxies, and by choosing between any options that the proxy card may provide.

---

[8] This problem is adapted from Allen, Kraakman & Subramanian, *Commentaries and Cases on the Law of Business Organizations* (4th ed. 2012) at 158.

A proxy is a power of attorney to vote a shareholder's shares (see DGCL 212(b)). The board solicits proxies on behalf of the corporation to ensure a quorum, to prevent a "coup" by a minority stockholder, and because the stock-exchange rules require it (see, e.g., NYSE Listed Company Manual 402.04). The board decides which proposals and nominees to include on the corporation's proxy card, with the exception of SEC proxy rule 14a-8, which allows shareholders to submit certain proposals for the corporation's proxy card (see below).

This explains why it is so important who or what gets onto the corporation's proxy card. If it's not on the corporation's card, it won't receive any votes at the meeting, even if properly moved during the meeting. As far as the board is concerned, that's not a problem. They'll put onto the corporation's card whatever resolution and candidate they support. By contrast, challengers must rely on the law to get their proposals onto the corporation's card, otherwise boards happily reject the challengers' proposals. The "Proxy Access" section below deals with this issue directly.

The Federal Proxy Rules

Proxy solicitations are heavily regulated by the SEC's proxy rules (Regulation 14A promulgated under section 14 of the Securities Exchange Act). As a result, the rules of corporate voting in the U.S. are a complicated interaction of federal proxy rules, state law, and a corporation's bylaws and charter.

The federal proxy rules are tedious. One of us provides a guide at simplifiedcodes.com. For a first course on corporations, you only need to know the following:

1. Before any proxy solicitation commences, a proxy statement must be filed with the SEC (Rule 14a-6(b)). In contested matters, a preliminary proxy statement must be filed 10 days before any solicitation commences (Rule 14a-6(a)).

2. The content and form of the proxy materials are heavily regulated (rules 14a-3, -4, and -5, and Schedule 14A). Virtually everything you see in an actual proxy statement is prescribed by the rules.

3. "Proxy" and "solicitation" are defined extremely broadly (Rule 14a-1(f) and (l)(1)). Accordingly, the sweep of the proxy rules is very wide. In the past, the proxy rules impeded even conversations among shareholders about their votes. Certain exceptions to the definitions (particularly Rule 14a-1(l)(2)(iv)) or requirements (particularly Rules 14a-2(a)(6) and 14a-2(b)(1)-(3)) are therefore extremely important—you should read them.

4. Rule 14a-8 is the only federal rule requiring corporations to include shareholder proposals in the corporation's proxy materials. Under the rule, corporations must include in their proxy certain precatory resolutions and bylaw amendments sponsored by shareholders. By contrast, the rule does not cover director nominations or anything else that would affect "the upcoming election of directors"

(*see* official note 8 to paragraph (i) of the rule). You should read the rule—unlike the rest of the proxy rules, it's written in plain English.

5. There is a special anti-fraud provision (Rule 14a-9).

Dual Class Stock

We have already seen dual class stock in the Alphabet, Inc. Articles of Incorporation. The general point is that some companies depart from the standard model of a single class of stock to having two or more classes of stock. Typically, as in the Alphabet case, one class of stock is low-voting, and one class of stock is high-voting. Often, these classes of stock have identical cash flow rights. So if the founders control the high-voting stock, they can control the annual meeting of shareholders, and therefore control the board, even if they own a small share of the cash flow rights.

Facebook, for example, has had two classes of shares: Class A shares, which have one vote per share; and Class B shares, which have ten votes per share. Through his ownership or control of 0.17% of the Class A shares and 85.3% of the Class B shares, Mark Zuckerberg controls 57% of the Facebook votes, even though he only owns approximately 28% of Facebook's cash flow rights. In fact, many Internet companies have dual-class structures—in addition to Facebook and Alphabet, LinkedIn, Zynga, Yelp, Zillow, Kayak, and Groupon all have a dual-class structure (among others).

In the old days, the NYSE required one-share, one-vote—i.e., dual-class structures were prohibited. In the mid-1980s, companies started to demand dual class structures as a takeover defense, and the NASDAQ allowed it, so the NYSE began to allow it as well. However, in the late-1980s, the SEC became alarmed at the proliferation of dual-class companies and passed Rule 19c-4, which prohibited dual-class recapitalizations (basically, offering shareholders the ability to trade in their low-vote stock for no-vote stock + a small dividend), but the SEC allowed dual-class structures at the initial public offering (IPO). But in 1990, the Business Roundtable (a consortium of large public companies) got Rule 19c-4 struck down in the D.C. Circuit on the grounds that the SEC lacked statutory power. But at this point no one cared—hostile takeovers were down, and other defensive measures (e.g., the poison pill) were just as good as a dual-class structure. Finally, in 1995, the NYSE, the American Stock Exchange, and NASDAQ adopted a uniform voluntary rule that basically re-adopts the old Rule 19c-4—prohibiting dual-class recapitalizations but allowing dual class structures at the IPO. Alphabet (then Google, of course), Facebook, Snap, and all the other tech companies went public with a dual-class structure under this new arrangement.

Discussion Questions:

1. We haven't studied hostile takeovers yet, but how do you think dual-class structures serve as a (very potent) takeover defense?

2. Why was the SEC so concerned about dual-class recapitalizations? (Sometimes called "midstream" recapitalizations, because they happen after the company's stock has already started trading on a national exchange.)

3. Why are dual-class IPOs less objectionable than dual-class recapitalizations?

4. Taking a step back, why would anyone invest in Facebook, Google, Snap, Zynga, or any of these other dual-class companies, if they are entirely at the mercy of the controlling shareholder?

5. What would you predict about the long-term stock performance of dual-class companies vs. non-dual-class companies? (Does your prediction depend on what industry the company is in?) Before answering, consider the Facebook post below.

Mark Zuckerberg (Sept. 5, 2016)

Happy 10th birthday, News Feed!

This invention is one of my favorite stories from Facebook's history. Sometimes people talk about the "idea" behind Facebook, as if it was a single concept that came out fully formed. But Facebook, like everything, is made of many ideas and inventions.

At the beginning of Facebook, there was no News Feed. For more than two years, Facebook was just a collection of profiles. You could visit a friend's page to look up some basic details about them, but there was no way to see updates from all your friends or be sure they saw yours.

With News Feed, all of a sudden you could share with all your friends at once. And you could see what was happening with all your friends in one place. News Feed was the first real social feed. It was such a fundamental idea that now, 10 years later, every major social app has its own equivalent of News Feed.

Not everyone liked the idea immediately. . . . About 1 million people joined a protest group threatening to quit if we didn't change Facebook back. I remember there were actual protesters in the streets outside our office demanding we change.

But one of the things I'm most proud of about Facebook is that we believe things can always be better, and we're willing to make big bets if we think it will help our community over the long term. News Feed has been one of the big bets we've made in the past 10 years that has shaped our community and the whole internet the most.

Technically, News Feed is one of the most advanced systems we've built. For more than 1 billion people every day, it considers everything your friends are posting and all of the media content you might be interested in, it considers how much you might care about

---

updates from each person or interest, and then it tries to show you what you'll find most important. Nothing like it has ever been built before.

So thank you to the members of our team—past and present—who have built and improved News Feed over the years. And thanks to our community for growing with us. Everyone's News Feed is unique because each of you is unique, and we'll keep working to make Facebook a better place for all the moments you share.

Shareholder Proxy Access

In everyday corporate governance, the board nominates the slate of candidates for the next election of directors. In this process it would be highly unusual for directors to nominate more than the number of candidates. As a result, the vast majority (99%+) of corporate elections are uncontested—i.e., X candidates for X seats on the board. In the traditional model of corporate governance, then, the only way that a director candidate will not be elected to the board is if there is a full-blown proxy contest, in which an insurgent runs a competing slate of directors. This is an expensive and time-consuming affair, and for this reason unlikely to happen unless undertaken in conjunction with a hostile takeover bid. Putting aside proxy contests, the saying (never verified, but likely to be true) is that a person is more likely to be struck by lightning than voted off a corporate board.

All of this changed with "proxy access." In August 2010, the SEC adopted Rule 14a-11, which gave shareholders (or a shareholder group) that owned 3% of the voting power continuously for a 3-year period the right to nominate directors for up to 25% of the company's board seats at each election. In contrast to a traditional shareholder candidate, these candidates would appear on the company's own proxy statement—thereby avoiding the massive costs involved with circulating a separate proxy to solicit shareholder votes.

Suddenly, the prospect emerged of (say) 11 candidates for 10 seats on the board. With a flip of a switch, corporate elections would suddenly become meaningful. The Business Roundtable pronounced that "[f]ew issues have generated more disagreement or stronger passions" than proxy access. A Wachtell, Lipton memo to clients stated that "[p]roxy access is expected to significantly impact the dynamics of shareholder engagement, and, in some cases, the composition of boards." *Corporate Board Member* magazine told its members that "few things make boards more nervous" than proxy access.

The Business Roundtable and the U.S. Chamber of Commerce challenged Rule 14a-11, arguing that the rule was "arbitrary and capricious" and did not "promote efficiency, competition, and capital formation." Surprising many commentators, the D.C. Circuit Court of Appeals agreed, finding that the Rule violated the Administrative Procedure Act because the SEC had failed "adequately to consider the Rule's effect upon efficiency, competition, and capital formation." In March 2012, the SEC announced that it would abandon its effort for a blanket proxy access rule, and instead would permit a company-by-company approach through Rule 14a-8 shareholder proposals.

One might think that this was the end of proxy access. And so it was, until some high-profile companies (e.g., Hewlett-Packard, General Electric), under pressure from shareholder groups, began providing proxy access. By 2016, the scales had tipped: more than 40% of the S&P 500 companies had adopted proxy access, up from about 1% in 2014. The typical rule is similar to the original Rule 14a-11: giving shareholders owning three percent of a company for three or more years the right to list their director candidates, representing up to 25 percent of the board, on the company's own proxy statement.

While nearly half of S&P 500 companies provide proxy access, to date *only one* proxy access candidate has actually been run (at National Fuel Gas Company) and even this candidate was unsuccessful. Critics of proxy access point to this experience as evidence that boards are doing their job (i.e., nominating the right people to serve on the board), and that proxy access is therefore unnecessary. Proponents of proxy access argue that the prospect of a proxy access candidate serves as a useful prod to directors, even if actual proxy access candidates are few and far between.

Blasius Industries, Inc. v. Atlas Corp.
564 A.2d 651 (Del. Ch. 1988)

[...]

ALLEN, Chancellor.

[...]

[These facts] present the question whether a board acts consistently with its fiduciary duty when it acts, in good faith and with appropriate care, for the primary purpose of preventing or impeding an unaffiliated majority of shareholders from expanding the board and electing a new majority. For the reasons that follow, I conclude that, even though defendants here acted on their view of the corporation's interest and not selfishly, their December 31 action constituted an offense to the relationship between corporate directors and shareholders that has traditionally been protected in courts of equity. As a consequence, I conclude that the board action taken on December 31 was invalid and must be voided. [...]

I. *Blasius Acquires a 9% Stake in Atlas.*

Blasius is a new stockholder of Atlas. It began to accumulate Atlas shares for the first time in July, 1987. On October 29, it filed a Schedule 13D with the Securities Exchange Commission disclosing that, with affiliates, it then owed 9.1% of Atlas' common stock. It stated in that filing that it intended to encourage management of Atlas to consider a restructuring of the Company or other transaction to enhance shareholder values. It also disclosed that Blasius was exploring the feasibility of obtaining control of Atlas, including instituting a tender offer or seeking "appropriate" representation on the Atlas board of directors.

Blasius has recently come under the control of two individuals, Michael Lubin and Warren Delano, who after experience in the commercial banking industry, had, for a short time, run a venture capital operation for a small investment banking firm. Now on their own, they apparently came to control Blasius with the assistance of Drexel Burnham's well noted junk bond mechanism. Since then, they have made several attempts to effect leveraged buyouts, but without success.

In May, 1987, with Drexel Burnham serving as underwriter, Lubin and Delano caused Blasius to raise $60 million through the sale of junk bonds. A portion of these funds were used to acquire a 9% position in Atlas. According to its public filings with the SEC, Blasius' debt service obligations arising out of the sale of the junk bonds are such that it is unable to service those obligations from its income from operations.

The prospect of Messrs. Lubin and Delano involving themselves in Atlas' affairs, was not a development welcomed by Atlas' management. Atlas had a new CEO, defendant Weaver, who had, over the course of the past year or so, overseen a business restructuring of a sort. Atlas had sold three of its five divisions. It had just announced (September 1, 1987) that it would close its once important domestic uranium operation. The goal was to focus the Company on its gold mining business. By October, 1987, the structural changes to do this had been largely accomplished. Mr. Weaver was perhaps thinking that the restructuring that had occurred should be given a chance to produce benefit before another restructuring (such as Blasius had alluded to in its Schedule 13D filing) was attempted, when he wrote in his diary on October 30, 1987:

> 13D by Delano & Lubin came in today. Had long conversation w/MAH & Mark Golden [of Goldman, Sachs] on issue. All agree we must dilute these people down by the acquisition of another Co. w/stock, or merger or something else.

The Blasius Proposal of A Leverage Recapitalization Or Sale.

Immediately after filing its 13D on October 29, Blasius' representatives sought a meeting with the Atlas management. Atlas dragged its feet. A meeting was arranged for December 2, 1987 following the regular meeting of the Atlas board. Attending that meeting were Messrs. Lubin and Delano for Blasius, and, for Atlas, Messrs. Weaver, Devaney (Atlas' CFO), Masinter (legal counsel and director) and Czajkowski (a representative of Atlas' investment banker, Goldman Sachs).

At that meeting, Messrs. Lubin and Delano suggested that Atlas engage in a leveraged restructuring and distribute cash to shareholders. In such a transaction, which is by this date a commonplace form of transaction, a corporation typically raises cash by sale of assets and significant borrowings and makes a large one time cash distribution to shareholders. The shareholders are typically left with cash and an equity interest in a smaller, more highly leveraged enterprise. Lubin and Delano gave the outline of a leveraged recapitalization for Atlas as they saw it.

Immediately following the meeting, the Atlas representatives expressed among themselves an initial reaction that the proposal was infeasible. On December 7, Mr. Lubin sent a letter detailing the proposal. In general, it proposed the following: (1) an initial special cash dividend to Atlas' stockholders in an aggregate amount equal to (a) $35 million, (b) the aggregate proceeds to Atlas from the exercise of option warrants and stock options, and (c) the proceeds from the sale or disposal of all of Atlas' operations that are not related to its continuing minerals operations; and (2) a special non-cash dividend to Atlas' stockholders of an aggregate $125 million principal amount of 7% Secured Subordinated Gold-Indexed Debentures. The funds necessary to pay the initial cash dividend were to principally come from (i) a "gold loan" in the amount of $35,625,000, repayable over a three to five year period and secured by 75,000 ounces of gold at a price of $475 per ounce, (ii) the proceeds from the sale of the discontinued Brockton Sole and Plastics and Ready-Mix Concrete businesses, and (iii) a then expected January, 1988 sale of uranium to the Public Service Electric & Gas Company.

Atlas Asks Its Investment Banker to Study the Proposal.

This written proposal was distributed to the Atlas board on December 9 and Goldman Sachs was directed to review and analyze it.

The proposal met with a cool reception from management. On December 9, Mr. Weaver issued a press release expressing surprise that Blasius would suggest using debt to accomplish what he characterized as a substantial liquidation of Atlas at a time when Atlas' future prospects were promising. He noted that the Blasius proposal recommended that Atlas incur a high debt burden in order to pay a substantial one time dividend consisting of $35 million in cash and $125 million in subordinated debentures. Mr. Weaver also questioned the wisdom of incurring an enormous debt burden amidst the uncertainty in the financial markets that existed in the aftermath of the October crash.

Blasius attempted on December 14 and December 22 to arrange a further meeting with the Atlas management without success. During this period, Atlas provided Goldman Sachs with projections for the Company. Lubin was told that a further meeting would await completion of Goldman's analysis. A meeting after the first of the year was proposed.

The Delivery of Blasius' Consent Statement.

On December 30, 1987, Blasius caused Cede & Co. (the registered owner of its Atlas stock) to deliver to Atlas a signed written consent (1) adopting a precatory resolution recommending that the board develop and implement a restructuring proposal, (2) amending the Atlas bylaws to, among other things, expand the size of the board from seven to fifteen members-the maximum number under Atlas' charter, and (3) electing eight named persons to fill the new directorships. [...]

The reaction was immediate. Mr. Weaver conferred with Mr. Masinter, the Company's outside counsel and a director, who viewed the consent as an attempt to take control of the

Company. They decided to call an emergency meeting of the board, even though a regularly scheduled meeting was to occur only one week hence, on January 6, 1988. The point of the emergency meeting was to act on their conclusion (or to seek to have the board act on their conclusion) "that we should add at least one and probably two directors to the board ..." A quorum of directors, however, could not be arranged for a telephone meeting that day. A telephone meeting was held the next day. At that meeting, the board voted to amend the bylaws to increase the size of the board from seven to nine and appointed John M. Devaney and Harry J. Winters, Jr. to fill those newly created positions. Atlas' Certificate of Incorporation creates staggered terms for directors; the terms to which Messrs. Devaney and Winters were appointed would expire in 1988 and 1990, respectively.

The Motivation of the Incumbent Board In Expanding the Board and Appointing New Members.

In increasing the size of Atlas' board by two and filling the newly created positions, the members of the board realized that they were thereby precluding the holders of a majority of the Company's shares from placing a majority of new directors on the board through Blasius' consent solicitation, should they want to do so. Indeed the evidence establishes that that was the principal motivation in so acting.

The conclusion that, in creating two new board positions on December 31 and electing Messrs. Devaney and Winters to fill those positions the board was principally motivated to prevent or delay the shareholders from possibly placing a majority of new members on the board, is critical to my analysis of the central issue posed by the first filed of the two pending cases. If the board in fact was not so motivated, but rather had taken action completely independently of the consent solicitation, which merely had an incidental impact upon the possible effectuation of any action authorized by the shareholders, it is very unlikely that such action would be subject to judicial nullification. ... The board, as a general matter, is under no fiduciary obligation to suspend its active management of the firm while the consent solicitation process goes forward.

There is testimony in the record to support the proposition that, in acting on December 31, the board was principally motivated simply to implement a plan to expand the Atlas board that preexisted the September, 1987 emergence of Blasius as an active shareholder. I have no doubt that the addition of Mr. Winters, an expert in mining economics, and Mr. Devaney, a financial expert employed by the Company, strengthened the Atlas board and, should anyone ever have reason to review the wisdom of those choices, they would be found to be sensible and prudent. I cannot conclude, however, that the strengthening of the board by the addition of these men was the principal motive for the December 31 action. As I view this factual determination as critical, I will pause to dilate briefly upon the evidence that leads me to this conclusion.

The evidence indicates that CEO Weaver was acquainted with Mr. Winters prior to the time he assumed the presidency of Atlas. When, in the fall of 1986, Mr. Weaver learned of his selection as Atlas' future CEO, he informally approached Mr. Winters about serving on the board of the Company. Winters indicated a willingness to do so and sent to Mr. Weaver a copy of his *curriculum vitae.* Weaver, however, took no action with respect to this matter until he had some informal discussion with other board members on December 2, 1987, the date on which Mr. Lubin orally presented Blasius' restructuring proposal to management. At that time, he mentioned the possibility to other board members.

Then, on December 7, Mr. Weaver called Mr. Winters on the telephone and asked him if he would serve on the board and Mr. Winters again agreed.

On December 24, 1987, Mr. Weaver wrote to other board members, sending them Mr. Winters *curriculum vitae* and notifying them that Mr. Winters would be proposed for board membership at the forthcoming January 6 meeting. It was also suggested that a dinner meeting be scheduled for January 5, in order to give board members who did not know Mr. Winters an opportunity to meet him prior to acting on that suggestion. The addition of Mr. Devaney to the board was not mentioned in that memo, nor, so far as the record discloses, was it discussed at the December 2 board meeting.

[...]

In this setting, I conclude that, while the addition of these qualified men would, under other circumstances, be clearly appropriate as an independent step, such a step was in fact taken in order to impede or preclude a majority of the shareholders from effectively adopting the course proposed by Blasius. Indeed, while defendants never forsake the factual argument that that action was simply a continuation of business as usual, they, in effect, admit from time to time this overriding purpose. [...]

The January 6 Rejection of the Blasius Proposal.

On January 6, the board convened for its scheduled meeting. At that time, it heard a full report from its financial advisor concerning the feasibility of the Blasius restructuring proposal. The Goldman Sachs presentation included a summary of five year cumulative cash flows measured against a base case and the Blasius proposal, an analysis of Atlas' debt repayment capacity under the Blasius proposal, and pro forma income and cash flow statements for a base case and the Blasius proposal, assuming prices of $375, $475 and $575 per ounce of gold.

After completing that presentation, Goldman Sachs concluded with its view that if Atlas implemented the Blasius restructuring proposal (i) a severe drain on operating cash flow would result, (ii) Atlas would be unable to service its long-term debt and could end up in bankruptcy, (iii) the common stock of Atlas would have little or no value, and (iv) since Atlas would be unable to generate sufficient cash to service its debt, the debentures contemplated to be issued in the proposed restructuring could have a value of only 20% to 30% of their face amount. Goldman Sachs also said that it knew of no financial restructuring that had been undertaken by a company where the company had no chance of repaying its debt, which, in its judgment, would be Atlas' situation if it implemented the Blasius restructuring proposal. Finally, Goldman Sachs noted that if Atlas made a meaningful commercial discovery of gold after implementation of the Blasius restructuring proposal, Atlas would not have the resources to develop the discovery.

The board then voted to reject the Blasius proposal. Blasius was informed of that action. The next day, Blasius caused a second, modified consent to be delivered to Atlas. A contest then ensued between the Company and Blasius for the votes of Atlas' shareholders. The facts relating to that contest, and a determination of its outcome, form the subject of the second filed lawsuit to be now decided. That matter, however, will be deferred for the moment as the facts set forth above are sufficient to frame and decide the principal remaining issue raised by the first filed action: whether the December 31 board action, in increasing the board by two and appointing members to fill those new positions, constituted, in the circumstances, an inequitable interference with the exercise of shareholder rights.

II.

Plaintiff attacks the December 31 board action as a selfishly motivated effort to protect the incumbent board from a perceived threat to its control of Atlas. Their conduct is said to constitute a violation of the principle, applied in such cases as Schnell v. Chris Craft Industries, Del. Supr., 285 A.2d 437 (1971), that directors hold legal powers subjected to a supervening duty to exercise such powers in good faith pursuit of what they reasonably believe to be in the corporation's interest. The December 31 action is also said to have been taken in a grossly negligent manner, since it was designed to preclude the recapitalization from being pursued, and the board had no basis at that time to make a prudent determination about the wisdom of that proposal, nor was there any emergency that required it to act in any respect regarding that proposal before putting itself in a position to do so advisedly.

Defendants, of course, contest every aspect of plaintiffs' claims. They claim the formidable protections of the business judgment rule. [...]

They say that, in creating two new board positions and filling them on December 31, they acted without a conflicting interest (since the Blasius proposal did not, in any event, challenge *their* places on the board), they acted with due care (since they well knew the persons they put on the board and did not thereby preclude later consideration of the recapitalization), and they acted in good faith (since they were motivated, they say, to protect the shareholders from the threat of having an impractical, indeed a dangerous, recapitalization program foisted upon them). Accordingly, defendants assert there is no basis to conclude that their December 31 action constituted any violation of the duty of the fidelity that a director owes by reason of his office to the corporation and its shareholders.

[...]

III.

One of the principal thrusts of plaintiffs' argument is that, in acting to appoint two additional persons of their own selection, including an officer of the Company, to the board, defendants were motivated not by any view that Atlas' interest (or those of its shareholders) required that action, but rather they were motivated improperly, by selfish concern to maintain their collective control over the Company. That is, plaintiffs say that the evidence shows there was no policy dispute or issue that really motivated this action, but that asserted policy differences were pretexts for entrenchment for selfish reasons. If this were found to be factually true, one would not need to inquire further. The action taken would constitute a breach of duty. [...]

In support of this view, plaintiffs point to the early diary entry of Mr. Weaver, to the lack of any consideration at all of the Blasius recapitalization proposal at the December 31 meeting, the lack of any substantial basis for the outside directors to have had any considered view on the subject by that time—not having had any view from Goldman Sachs nor seen the financial data that it regarded as necessary to evaluate the proposal—and upon what it urges is the grievously flawed, slanted analysis that Goldman Sachs finally did present.

While I am satisfied that the evidence is powerful, indeed compelling, that the board was chiefly motivated on December 31 to forestall or preclude the possibility that a majority of shareholders might place on the Atlas board eight new members sympathetic to the Blasius proposal, it is less clear with respect to the more subtle motivational question: whether the existing members of the board did so because they held a good faith belief that such shareholder action would be self-injurious and shareholders needed to be protected from their own judgment.

On balance, I cannot conclude that the board was acting out of a self-interested motive in any important respect on December 31. I conclude rather that the board saw the "threat" of the Blasius recapitalization proposal as posing vital policy differences between itself and Blasius. It acted, I conclude, in a good faith effort to protect its incumbency, not selfishly, but in order to thwart implementation of the recapitalization that it feared, reasonably, would cause great injury to the Company.

The real question the case presents, to my mind, is whether, in these circumstances, the board, even if it *is* acting with subjective good faith (which will typically, if not always, be a contestable or debatable judicial conclusion), may validly act for the principal purpose of preventing the shareholders from electing a majority of new directors. The question thus posed is not one of intentional wrong (or even negligence), but one of authority *as between the fiduciary and the beneficiary* (not simply legal authority, *i.e.,* as between the fiduciary and the world at large).

IV.

It is established in our law that a board may take certain steps-such as the purchase by the corporation of its own stock-that have the effect of defeating a threatened change in corporate control, when those steps are taken advisedly, in good faith pursuit of a corporate interest, and are reasonable in relation to a threat to legitimate corporate interests posed by the proposed change in control. [...] Does this rule-that the reasonable exercise of good faith and due care generally validates, in equity, the exercise of legal authority even if the act has an entrenchment effect-apply to action designed for the primary purpose of interfering with the effectiveness of a stockholder vote? Our authorities, as well as sound principles, suggest that the central importance of the franchise to the scheme of corporate governance, requires that, in this setting, that rule not be applied and that closer scrutiny be accorded to such transaction.

1. *Why the deferential business judgment rule does not apply to board acts taken for the primary purpose of interfering with a stockholder's vote, even if taken advisedly and in good faith.*

A. *The question of legitimacy.*

The shareholder franchise is the ideological underpinning upon which the legitimacy of directorial power rests. Generally, shareholders have only two protections against perceived inadequate business performance. They may sell their stock (which, if done in sufficient numbers, may so affect security prices as to create an incentive for altered managerial performance), or they may vote to replace incumbent board members.

It has, for a long time, been conventional to dismiss the stockholder vote as a vestige or ritual of little practical importance. It may be that we are now witnessing the emergence of new institutional voices and arrangements that will make the stockholder vote a less predictable affair than it has been. Be that as it may, however, whether the vote is seen functionally as an unimportant formalism, or as an important tool of discipline, it is clear that it is critical to the theory that legitimates the exercise of power by some (directors and officers) over vast aggregations of property that they do not own. Thus, when viewed from a broad, institutional perspective, it can be seen that matters involving the integrity of the shareholder voting process involve consideration not present in any other context in which directors exercise delegated power.

B. *Questions of this type raise issues of the allocation of authority as between the board and the shareholders.*

The distinctive nature of the shareholder franchise context also appears when the matter is viewed from a less generalized, doctrinal point of view. From this point of view, as well, it appears that the ordinary considerations to which the business judgment rule originally responded are simply not present in the shareholder voting context.[2] That is, a decision by

---

[2] Delaware courts have long exercised a most sensitive and protective regard for the free and effective exercise of voting rights. This concern suffuses our law, manifesting itself in various settings. For example, the perceived importance of the franchise explains the cases that hold that a director's fiduciary duty requires disclosure to shareholders asked to authorize a transaction of all material information in the corporation's possession, even if the transaction is not a self-dealing one. A similar concern, for credible corporate democracy, underlies those cases that strike down board action that sets or moves an annual meeting date upon a finding that such action was

the board to act for the primary purpose of preventing the effectiveness of a shareholder vote inevitably involves the question who, as between the principal and the agent, has authority with respect to a matter of internal corporate governance. That, of course, is true in a very specific way in this case which deals with the question who should constitute the board of directors of the corporation, but it will be true in every instance in which an incumbent board seeks to thwart a shareholder majority. A board's decision to act to prevent the shareholders from creating a majority of new board positions and filling them does not involve the exercise of *the corporation's power* over its property, or with respect to *its* rights or obligations; rather, it involves allocation, between shareholders as a class and the board, of effective power with respect to governance of the corporation. . . . Action designed principally to interfere with the effectiveness of a vote inevitably involves a conflict between the board and a shareholder majority. Judicial review of such action involves a determination of the legal and equitable obligations of an agent towards his principal. This is not, in my opinion, a question that a court may leave to the agent finally to decide so long as he does so honestly and competently; that is, it may not be left to the agent's business judgment.

[...]

In two recent cases dealing with shareholder votes, this court struck down board acts done for the primary purpose of impeding the exercise of stockholder voting power. In doing so, a *per se* rule was not applied. Rather, it was said that, in such a case, the board bears the heavy burden of demonstrating a compelling justification for such action. [citations omitted]

[...]

I therefore conclude that, even finding the action taken was taken in good faith, it constituted an unintended violation of the duty of loyalty that the board owed to the shareholders. I note parenthetically that the concept of an unintended breach of the duty of loyalty is unusual but not novel. [...] That action will, therefore, be set aside by order of this court.

[...]

Discussion Questions:

1. Why was Atlas' board-packing maneuver so effective in thwarting Blasius? More specifically, why couldn't Atlas just propose a shareholder resolution to get rid of the two new directors that have just been added? (Hint: What kind of board does

---

intended to thwart a shareholder group from effectively mounting an election campaign. The cases invalidating stock issued for the primary purpose of diluting the voting power of a control block also reflect the law's concern that a credible form of corporate democracy be maintained. Similarly, a concern for corporate democracy is reflected (1) in our statutory requirement of annual meetings (8 Del.C. § 211), and in the cases that aggressively and summarily enforce that right.

Atlas have?) And why can't Blasius just change the number of directors? *Cf.* DGCL 223(a)(1).

2. Did the Atlas board do anything that violated the charter or bylaws of the company? If not, what did they do wrong?

3. What is the rule articulated by Chancellor Allen in *Blasius*? Is invocation of this rule outcome-determinative? (Can you conceive of situations where *Blasius* is triggered but the defendants still win?)

4. Liquid Audio (LA) was one of the early entrants in the Internet-music industry, but it quickly ran into trouble because competitors were giving away similar services for free. (How's that for a business problem?) By 2001 the company had $86 million of cash but a $52 million market capitalization. MM Companies announced a plan to (1) challenge the two incumbent LA directors who were up for re-election at the next annual meeting; and (2) propose a bylaws amendment expanding the board from five to nine members. Before the annual meeting, LA added two directors, increasing the board size from five to seven. At the annual meeting, shareholders elected the two MM candidates to replace the LA incumbents, but rejected the MM proposal to add four more board seats. MM brought suit challenging LA's board expansion, alleging (among other things) *Blasius* violations. If you were representing Atlas, could you distinguish *Blasius*? If you were the judge, would you distinguish *Blasius*?

5. Consider the following account from George Cloutier, Harvard Business School sectionmate of Circon Chairman and CEO Richard Auhll, in connection with a hostile takeover bid from U.S. Surgical, a competitor in the industry:

> Richard was looking around for a new director because he had to replace some people on the board. It looked like a couple directors would be leaving and I think he was getting the feeling that they were getting squirrelly on him because the [hostile] offer [from U.S. Surgical] had been lowered and he wasn't meeting his business plan. So he was getting into a place where he needed someone to buck him up, and he probably perceived me as that, and I perceived me as that. I knew that by coming onto the board, I was stepping into automatic lawsuits. Richard had to have someone willing to step in and not care, and that was me. 'Hey Richard, we'll take these guys and slap them around and get them straightened out here.' That was my position: we fight until the last minute, last day, last hour, and something will happen. At that point I was probably more aggressive because for me it was riding into an unknown

59

battle. It was just an emotional friendship move—charge in to defeat the Hun.[9]

Would *Blasius* apply to Cloutier's addition? And if so, would the addition be invalidated under *Blasius*?

---

[9] From Brian Hall, Christopher Rose & Guhan Subramanian, Circon (A), HBS Case 9-801-403.

Chapter 3 – Conflicted Behavior: The Duty of Loyalty

We have already seen in a few cases—e.g., *eBay*, *Blasius*—that the fluid concept of fiduciary duty is the centerpiece of corporate law. (While a student at Harvard Law School in the 1980s, U.S. Supreme Court Justice Elena Kagan received her only A+ in Corporations.[10] When one of us pointed this out to her on a summer stroll through Harvard Yard, she commented: "Yeah… it all boils down to fiduciary duty, doesn't it?") There are two core duties: the duty of loyalty and the duty of care. We discuss each in turn.

Directors and officers (D&Os) of the corporation owe a *duty of loyalty* to the corporation. In a nutshell, this means that D&Os must act in the corporation's best interest and may not act in their own self-interest. The concept is simple, but the application (at least in the cases we will examine) is rarely straightforward. The following cases explore the contours of this bedrock principle of corporate law. We begin with one of the most venerable cases in all of corporate law (though it actually involves a joint venture, not a corporation), Justice Cardozo's opinion in *Meinhard v. Salmon*.

Meinhard v. Salmon
164 N.E. 545 (N.Y. 1928)

CARDOZO, C.J.:

On April 10, 1902, Louisa M. Gerry leased to the defendant Walter J. Salmon the premises known as the Hotel Bristol at the northwest corner of Forty-Second street and Fifth Avenue in the city of New York. The lease was for a term of 20 years, commencing May 1, 1902, and ending April 30, 1922. The lessee undertook to change the hotel building for use as shops and offices at a cost of $200,000. Alterations and additions were to be accretions to the land.

Salmon, while in course of treaty with the lessor as to the execution of the lease, was in course of treaty with Meinhard, the plaintiff, for the necessary funds. The result was a joint venture with terms embodied in a writing. Meinhard was to pay to Salmon half of the moneys requisite to reconstruct, alter, manage, and operate the property. Salmon was to pay to Meinhard 40 percent of the net profits for the first five years of the lease and 50 percent for the years thereafter. If there were losses, each party was to bear them equally. Salmon, however, was to have sole power to "manage, lease, underlet and operate" the building. There were to be certain preemptive rights for each in the contingency of death.

The two were coadventurers, subject to fiduciary duties akin to those of partners. *King v. Barnes*, 109 N.Y. 267, 16 N.E. 332. As to this we are all agreed. The heavier weight of duty

---

[10] For reasons that are not obvious, this fact is in the public record. See http://online.wsj.com/public/resources/documents/kagangrades0514.pdf.

rested, however, upon Salmon. He was a coadventurer with Meinhard, but he was manager as well. During the early years of the enterprise, the building, reconstructed, was operated at a loss. If the relation had then ended, Meinhard as well as Salmon would have carried a heavy burden. Later the profits became large with the result that for each of the investors there came a rich return. For each the venture had its phases of fair weather and of foul. The two were in it jointly, for better or for worse.

When the lease was near its end, Elbridge T. Gerry had become the owner of the reversion. He owned much other property in the neighborhood, one lot adjoining the Bristol building on Fifth avenue and four lots on Forty-Second street. He had a plan to lease the entire tract for a long term to some one who would destroy the buildings then existing and put up another in their place. In the latter part of 1921, he submitted such a project to several capitalists and dealers. He was unable to carry it through with any of them. Then, in January, 1922, with less than four months of the lease to run, he approached the defendant Salmon. The result was a new lease to the Midpoint Realty Company, which is owned and controlled by Salmon, a lease covering the whole tract, and involving a huge outlay. The term is to be 20 years, but successive covenants for renewal will extend it to a maximum of 80 years at the will of either party. The existing buildings may remain unchanged for seven years. They are then to be torn down, and a new building to cost $3,000,000 is to be placed upon the site. The rental, which under the Bristol lease was only $55,000, is to be from $350,000 to $475,000 for the properties so combined. Salmon personally guaranteed the performance by the lessee of the covenants of the new lease until such time as the new building had been completed and fully paid for.

The lease between Gerry and the Midpoint Realty Company was signed and delivered on January 25, 1922. Salmon had not told Meinhard anything about it. Whatever his motive may have been, he had kept the negotiations to himself. Meinhard was not informed even of the bare existence of a project. The first that he knew of it was in February, when the lease was an accomplished fact. He then made demand on the defendants that the lease be held in trust as an asset of the venture, making offer upon the trial to share the personal obligations incidental to the guaranty. The demand was followed by refusal, and later by this suit. A referee gave judgment for the plaintiff, limiting the plaintiff's interest in the lease, however, to 25 percent. The limitation was on the theory that the plaintiff's equity was to be restricted to one-half of so much of the value of the lease as was contributed or represented by the occupation of the Bristol site. Upon cross-appeals to the Appellate Division, the judgment was modified so as to enlarge the equitable interest to one-half of the whole lease. With this enlargement of plaintiff's interest, there went, of course, a corresponding enlargement of his attendant obligations. The case is now here on an appeal by the defendants. . . .

Joint venturers, like copartners, owe to one another, while the enterprise continues, the duty of the finest loyalty. Many forms of conduct permissible in a workaday world for those acting at arm's length, are forbidden to those bound by fiduciary ties. A trustee is held to something stricter than the morals of the market place. Not honesty alone, but the punctilio of an honor the most sensitive, is then the standard of behavior. As to this there has developed a tradition that is unbending and inveterate. Uncompromising rigidity has been the attitude of courts of equity when petitioned to undermine the rule of undivided loyalty by the "disintegrating erosion" of particular exceptions. . . . Only thus has the level of conduct for fiduciaries been kept at a level higher than that trodden by the crowd. It will not consciously be lowered by any judgment of this court.

The owner of the reversion, Mr. Gerry, had vainly striven to find a tenant who would favor his ambitious scheme of demolition and construction. Baffled in the search, he turned to the defendant Salmon in possession of the Bristol, the keystone of the project. He figured to himself beyond a doubt that the man in possession would prove a likely customer. To the eye of an observer, Salmon held the lease as owner in his own right, for himself and no one else. In fact he held it as a fiduciary, for himself and another, sharers in a common venture. If this fact had been proclaimed, if the lease by its terms had run in favor of a partnership, Mr. Gerry, we may fairly assume, would have laid before the partners, and not merely before one of them, his plan of reconstruction. The pre-emptive privilege, or, better, the preemptive opportunity, that was thus an incident of the enterprise, Salmon appropriated to himself in secrecy and silence. He might have warned Meinhard that the plan had been submitted, and that either would be free to compete for the award. If he had done this, we do not need to say whether he would have been under a duty, if successful in the competition, to hold the lease so acquired for the benefit of a venture then about to end, and thus prolong by indirection its responsibilities and duties. The trouble about his conduct is that he excluded his coadventurer from any chance to compete, from any chance to enjoy the opportunity for benefit that had come to him alone by virtue of his agency. This chance, if nothing more, he was under a duty to concede. The price of its denial is an extension of the trust at the option and for the benefit of the one whom he excluded.

No answer is it to say that the chance would have been of little value even if seasonably offered. Such a calculus of probabilities is beyond the science of the chancery. Salmon, the real estate operator, might have been preferred to Meinhard, the woolen merchant. On the other hand, Meinhard might have offered better terms, or reinforced his offer by alliance with the wealth of others. Perhaps he might even have persuaded the lessor to renew the Bristol lease alone, postponing for a time, in return for higher rentals, the improvement of adjoining lots. We know that even under the lease as made the time for the enlargement of the building was delayed for seven years. All these opportunities were cut away from him through another's intervention. . . .

Little profit will come from a dissection of the precedents. None precisely similar is cited in the briefs of counsel. What is similar in many, or so it seems to us, is the animating principle. Authority is, of course, abundant that one partner may not appropriate to his own use a renewal of a lease, though its term is to begin at the expiration of the partnership. *Mitchell v. Read,* 61 N.Y. 123, 19 Am. Rep. 252; Id., 84 N.Y. 556. The lease at hand with its many changes is not strictly a renewal. Even so, the standard of loyalty for those in trust relations is without the fixed divisions of a graduated scale. There is indeed a dictum in one of our decisions that a partner, though he may not renew a lease, may purchase the reversion if he acts openly and fairly. *Anderson v. Lemon,* 8 N.Y. 236. It is a dictum, and no more, for on the ground that he had acted slyly he was charged as a trustee. The holding is thus in favor of the conclusion that a purchase as well as a lease will succumb to the infection of secrecy and silence. Against the dictum in that case, moreover, may be set the opinion of Dwight, C., in *Mitchell v. Read*, where there is a dictum to the contrary. (61 N.Y. 123, at page 143) . . . .

We have no thought to hold that Salmon was guilty of a conscious purpose to defraud. Very likely he assumed in all good faith that with the approaching end of the venture he might ignore his coadventurer and take the extension for himself. He had given to the enterprise time and labor as well as money. He had made it a success. Meinhard, who had given money, but neither time nor labor, had already been richly paid. There might seem to be something grasping in his insistence upon more. Such recriminations are not unusual when coadventurers fall out. They are not without their force if conduct is to be judged by the common standards of competitors. That is not to say that they have pertinency here. Salmon had put himself in a position in which thought of self was to be renounced, however hard the abnegation. He was much more than a coadventurer. He was a managing coadventurer. *Clegg v. Edmondson*, 8 D. M. & G. 787, 807. For him and for those like him the rule of undivided loyalty is relentless and supreme. . . .

A question remains as to the form and extent of the equitable interest to be allotted to the plaintiff. The trust as declared has been held to attach to the lease which was in the name of the defendant corporation. We think it ought to attach at the option of the defendant Salmon to the shares of stock which were owned by him or were under his control. The difference may be important if the lessee shall wish to execute an assignment of the lease, as it ought to be free to do with the consent of the lessor. On the other hand, an equal division of the shares might lead to other hardships. It might take away from Salmon the power of control and management which under the plan of the joint venture he was to have from first to last. The number of shares to be allotted to the plaintiff should, therefore, be reduced to such an extent as may be necessary to preserve to the defendant Salmon the expected measure of dominion. To that end an extra share should be added to his half . . . .

ANDREWS, J. (dissenting) . . . .

. . . It may be stated generally that a partner may not for his own benefit secretly take a renewal of a firm lease to himself. . . . [But] [w]here the trustee, or the partner or the tenant in common, takes no new lease but buys the reversion in good faith a somewhat different question arises. Here is no direct appropriation of the expectancy of renewal. Here is no offshoot of the original lease. . . . There was no general partnership, merely a joint venture for a limited object, to end at a fixed time. The new lease, covering additional property, containing many new and unusual terms and conditions, with a possible duration of 80 years, was more nearly the purchase of the reversion than the ordinary renewal with which the authorities are concerned. . . .

In many respects, besides the increase in the land demised, the new lease differs from the old. Instead of an annual rent of $55,000 it is now from $350,000 to $475,000. Instead of a fixed term of twenty years it may now be, at the lessee's option, eighty. Instead of alterations in an existing structure costing about $200,000 a new building is contemplated costing $3,000,000. Of this sum $1,500,000 is to be advanced by the lessor to the lessee, 'but not to its successors or assigns,' and is to be repaid in installments. Again no assignment or sale of the lease may be made without the consent of the lessor...

I assume that where parties engage in a joint enterprise each owes to the other the duty of the utmost good faith in all that relates to their common venture. Within its scope they stand in a fiduciary relationship. I assume *prima facie* that even as between joint adventurers one may not secretly obtain a renewal of the lease of property actually used in the joint adventure where the possibility of renewal is expressly or impliedly involved in the enterprise. I assume also that Mr. Meinhard had an equitable interest in the Bristol Hotel lease. Further, that an expectancy of renewal inhered in that lease. Two questions then arise. Under his contract did he share in that expectancy? And if so, did that expectancy mature into a graft of the original lease? To both questions my answer is 'No.'

The one complaint made is that Mr. Salmon obtained the new lease without informing Mr. Meinhard of his intention. Nothing else. There is no claim of actual fraud. No claim of misrepresentation to any one. Here was no movable property to be acquired by a new tenant at a sacrifice to its owners. No good will, largely dependent on location, built up by the joint efforts of two men. Here was a refusal of the landlord to renew the Bristol lease on any terms; a proposal made by him, not sought by Mr. Salmon, and a choice by him and by the original lessor of the person with whom they wished to deal shown by the covenants against assignment or under-letting, and by their ignorance of the arrangement with Mr. Meinhard. . . . No fraud, no deceit, no calculated secrecy is found. Simply that the arrangement was made without the knowledge of Mr. Meinhard. I think this not enough.

Discussion Questions:

1. What exactly is the duty that Salmon owes Meinhard, and how far does this obligation run? For example, do you think Salmon would have to share with Meinhard an opportunity to start a laundromat around the corner? Another hotel, but in Cleveland? What rule would you propose to determine what opportunities belonged to the joint venture, and what opportunities Salmon could take for himself?

2. In effect, Justice Cardozo is supplying a term to an incomplete contract. In this task, law & economics scholars urge the court to provide the term that the parties would have wanted, had they thought about the issue. What term do you think Meinhard and Salmon would have wanted?

State ex rel. Hayes Oyster Co. v. KeyPoint Oyster Co.
391 P.2d 979 (Wash. 1964)

DENNEY, J.:

Verne Hayes was CEO, director, and 23 percent shareholder of Coast Oyster Co., a public company that owned several large oyster beds. Verne's employment contract barred him from taking part in any business that would compete with Coast except for his activities in

Hayes Oyster Co., a family corporation in which he owned 25 percent of the shares and his brother, Sam, owned 75 percent. In the spring of 1960, when Coast was badly in need of cash to satisfy creditors, Hayes suggested that Coast sell its Allyn and Poulsbo oyster beds. Hayes then discussed with Engman, a Coast employee, how Hayes Oyster might help Engman finance the purchase.

On August 11, 1960, Coast's board approved Hayes's plan to sell the Allyn and Poulsbo beds to Keypoint Oyster Co., a corporation to be formed by Engman, for $250,000, payable $25,000 per year, with 5 percent interest, thus improving Coast's cash position and relieving it of the expenses of harvesting the oysters in those beds. On September 1, 1960, Hayes and Engman agreed that Keypoint's shares would be owned half by Engman and half by Hayes Oyster. At a Coast shareholders' meeting on October 21, 1960, the shareholders approved the sale to Keypoint—Hayes voting his Coast shares and others for which he held proxies (in total constituting a majority) in favor. At none of these times did any person connected with Coast (other than Hayes and Engman) know of Hayes's or Hayes Oyster's interest in Keypoint.

In 1961 and 1962, Hayes sold his Coast shares and executed a settlement agreement with respect to his Coast employment contract. Shortly thereafter, Coast's new managers brought suit against Verne and Sam Hayes for their Keypoint shares and all profits obtained by Hayes as a result of the transaction. The trial court absolved Hayes of any breach of duty to Coast.

Coast does not seek a rescission of the contract with Keypoint, nor does it question the adequacy of the consideration which Keypoint agreed to pay for the purchase of Allyn and Poulsbo, nor does Coast claim that it suffered any loss in the transaction. It does assert that Hayes, Coast's president, manager and director, acquired a secret profit and personal advantage to himself in the acquisition of the Keypoint stock by Hayes or Hayes Oyster in the side deal with Engman; and that such was in violation of his duty to Coast, and that, therefore, Hayes or Hayes Oyster should disgorge such secret profit to Coast.

Certain basic concepts have long been recognized by courts throughout the land on the status of corporate officers and directors. They occupy a fiduciary relation to a private corporation and the shareholders thereof akin to that of a trustee, and owe undivided loyalty, and a standard of behavior above that of the workaday world. . . .

Directors and other officers of a private corporation cannot directly or indirectly acquire a profit for themselves or acquire any other personal advantage in dealings with others on behalf of the corporation. . . .

Respondent [Hayes] is correct in his contention that this court has abolished the mechanical rule whereby any transaction involving corporate property in which a director has an interest is voidable at the option of the corporation. Such a contract cannot be voided if the director or officer can show that the transaction was fair to the corporation. However, nondisclosure by an interested director or officer is, in itself, unfair. This

66

wholesome rule can be applied automatically without any of the unsatisfactory results which flowed from a rigid bar against any self-dealing. . . .

The trial court found that any negotiations between Hayes and Engman up to . . . September 1, 1960, resulted in no binding agreement that Hayes would have any personal interest for himself or as a stockholder in Hayes Oyster in the sale of Allyn and Poulsbo. The undisputed evidence, however, shows that Hayes knew he might have some interest in the sale. It would have been appropriate for Hayes to have disclosed his possible interest at the informal meeting in Long Beach on August 4, 1960, and particularly at the meeting of Coast's board of directors on August 11, 1960. It is not necessary, however, for us to decide this case on a consideration of Hayes' obligation to Coast under the circumstances obtaining at that time.

Subsequent to the agreement with Engman, Hayes attended the meeting of Coast stockholders on October 21, 1960, recommended the sale, and voted a majority of the stock, including his own, in favor of the sale to Keypoint. On the same day, . . . he signed the contract which, among other things, required Keypoint to pay 10 monthly payments amounting to $25,000 per year, to pay interest on [a] deferred balance at 5 percent, to make payments on an option agreement which Coast had with one Smith, to plant sufficient seed to produce 45,000 gallons of oysters per year, inform Coast of plantings, furnish annual reports to Coast, operate the oysterlands in good workmanlike manner, keep improvements in repair, pay taxes, refrain directly or indirectly from engaging in growing, processing or marketing dehydrated oysters or oyster stew, give Coast first refusal on purchase of Keypoint oysters of 10,000 gallons per year or one- fourth of Keypoint's production. Title was reserved in Coast until payment in full of the purchase price of $250,000. . . .

At this juncture, Hayes was required to divulge his interest in Keypoint. His obligation to do so [arose] from the possibility, even probability, that some controversy might arise between Coast and Keypoint relative to the numerous provisions of the executory contract. Coast shareholders and directors had the right to know of Hayes' interest in Keypoint in order to intelligently determine the advisability of retaining Hayes as president and manager under the circumstances, and to determine whether or not it was wise to enter into the contract at all, in view of Hayes' conduct. In all fairness, they were entitled to know that their president and director might be placed in a position where he must choose between the interest of Coast and Keypoint in conducting Coast's business with Keypoint.

Furthermore, after receipt of the Keypoint stock, Hayes instructed the treasurer of Coast to make a payment on the Smith lease-option agreement which Keypoint was required to pay under the provisions of the contract. This action by Hayes grew out of a promise which Hayes made to Engman during their negotiations before the sale to reduce the sale price because of mortality of oysters on Allyn and Poulsbo. There was a clear conflict of interest.

The cases relied upon by respondent are not opposed to the rule condemning secrecy when an officer or director of a corporation may profit in the sale of corporate assets. In *Leppaluoto v. Eggleston,* 57 Wash. 2d 393, 357 P.2d 725, Eggleston secretly chartered his own equipment to a corporation in which he had one-half interest, for $25,000, without the knowledge of the owner of the remaining stock. We held that Eggleston was not required to return the $25,000 to the corporation because there was no proof that the charter arrangement was unfair or unreasonable and no proof that Eggleston made any profit on the transaction and that, absent proof of loss to the corporation or profit to Eggleston, no recovery could be had. In the case before us, profit to Hayes or Hayes Oyster in acquiring 50 percent of Keypoint stock is clear and undisputed. . . .

It is true that Hayes hypothecated his stock in Coast to one of Coast's creditors in early August, 1960. Undoubtedly, this aided Coast in placating its creditors at that time and showed absence of an intent to defraud Coast. It is not necessary, however, that an officer or director of a corporation have an intent to defraud or that any injury result to the corporation for an officer or director to violate his fiduciary obligation in secretly acquiring an interest in corporate property. . . .

Actual injury is not the principle upon which the law proceeds in condemning such contracts. Fidelity in the agent is what is aimed at, and as a means of securing it, the law will not permit the agent to place himself in a situation in which he may be tempted by his own private interest to disregard that of his principal. . . .

Respondent asserts that action by Coast shareholders was not necessary to bind Coast to the sale because it had already been approved by Coast's board of directors. Assuming this to be true, Hayes' fiduciary status with Coast did not change. He could not place himself in an adverse position to Coast by acquiring an interest in the executory contract before the terms of said contract had been performed by Keypoint. Coast had the option to affirm the contract or seek rescission. It chose the former and can successfully invoke the principle that whatever a director or officer acquires by virtue of his fiduciary relation, except in open dealings with the company, belongs not to such director or officer, but to the company. . . .

This rule appears to have universal application. . . . The trial court's finding that Hayes acted on behalf of Hayes Oyster in all of his negotiations with Engman subsequent to July, 1960, does not alter the situation. Sam Hayes knew that Verne Hayes was president and manager of Coast and owed complete devotion to the interests of Coast at the time Verne Hayes first approached him on the subject of sharing with Engman in the purchase of Allyn and Poulsbo. Sam Hayes knew and agreed that any interest of Verne Hayes or Hayes Oyster in Keypoint was to be kept secret and revealed to no one, including Coast. Sam Hayes authorized Verne Hayes to proceed with the deal on behalf of Hayes Oyster on this basis. Verne Hayes became the agent of Hayes Oyster in negotiating with Engman.

. . . Every sound consideration of equity affects Hayes Oyster as well as Verne Hayes. Neither can profit by the dereliction of Verne Hayes. . . .

The decree and judgment of the trial court. . . is reversed with direction to order Keypoint Oyster Company to issue a new certificate for 250 shares of its stock to Coast Oyster

Company and cancel the certificates heretofore standing in the name of or assigned to Hayes Oyster Company....

Discussion Questions:

1. Is there any allegation that the sale of the two oyster beds from Coast Oyster to Keypoint was unfair to Coast? If not, then what did Verne Hayes do wrong?

2. Calculate Verne Hayes' ownership interest in Coast Oyster and in Keypoint. Based on these calculations, would Verne prefer a higher price or a lower price in the sale of the two oyster beds?

3. Note the remedy: the Court cancels the shares of Keypoint held by Hayes Oyster, and orders Keypoint to issue 250 new shares to Coast Oyster. Does this over- or under-compensate Coast? What policy reasons might you give for this result?

Cookies Food Products v. Lakes Warehouse
430 N.W.2D 447 (Iowa 1988)

NEUMAN, JUSTICE.

This is a shareholders' derivative suit brought by the minority shareholders of a closely held Iowa corporation specializing in barbecue sauce, Cookies Food Products, Inc. (Cookies). The target of the lawsuit is the majority shareholder, Duane "Speed" Herrig and two of his family-owned corporations, Lakes Warehouse Distributing, Inc. (Lakes) and Speed's Automotive Co., Inc. (Speed's). Plaintiffs alleged that Herrig, by acquiring control of Cookies and executing self-dealing contracts, breached his fiduciary duty to the company and fraudulently misappropriated and converted corporate funds. Plaintiffs sought actual and punitive damages. Trial to the court resulted in a verdict for the defendants, the district court finding that Herrig's actions benefited, rather than harmed, Cookies. We affirm....

L. D. Cook of Storm Lake, Iowa, founded Cookies in 1975 to produce and distribute his original barbeque sauce. Searching for a plant site in a community that would provide financial backing, Cook met with business leaders in seventeen Iowa communities, outlining his plans to build a growth-oriented company. He selected Wall Lake, Iowa, persuading thirty-five members of that community, including Herrig and the plaintiffs, to purchase Cookies stock. All of the investors hoped Cookies would improve the local job market and tax base. The record reveals that it has done just that.

Early sales of the product, however, were dismal. After the first year's operation, Cookies was in dire financial straits. At that time, Herrig was one of thirty-five shareholders and held only two hundred shares. He was also the owner of an auto parts business, Speed's Automotive, and Lakes Warehouse Distributing, Inc., a company that distributed auto parts from Speed's. Cookies' board of directors approached Herrig with the idea of distributing the company's products. It authorized Herrig to purchase Cookies' sauce for twenty percent

69

under wholesale price, which he could then resell at full wholesale price. Under this arrangement, Herrig began to market and distribute the sauce to his auto parts customers and to grocery outlets from Lakes' trucks as they traversed the regular delivery route for Speed's Automotive.

In May 1977, Cookies formalized this arrangement by executing an exclusive distribution agreement with Lakes. Pursuant to this agreement, Cookies was responsible only for preparing the product; Lakes, for its part, assumed all costs of warehousing, marketing, sales, delivery, promotion, and advertising. Cookies retained the right to fix the sales price of its products and agreed to pay Lakes thirty percent of its gross sales for these services.

Cookies' sales have soared under the exclusive distributorship contract with Lakes. Gross sales in 1976, the year prior to the agreement, totaled only $20,000, less than half of Cookies' expenses that year. In 1977, however, sales jumped five-fold, then doubled in 1978, and have continued to show phenomenal growth every year thereafter. By 1985, when this suit was commenced, annual sales reached $2,400,000.

As sales increased, Cookies' board of directors amended and extended the original distributorship agreement. In 1979, the board amended the original agreement to give Lakes an additional two percent of gross sales to cover freight costs for the ever expanding market for Cookies' sauce. In 1980, the board extended the amended agreement through 1984 to allow Herrig to make long-term advertising commitments. Recognizing the role that Herrig's personal strengths played in the success of the joint endeavor, the board also amended the agreement that year to allow Cookies to cancel the agreement with Lakes if Herrig died or disposed of the corporation's stock.

In 1981, L. D. Cook, the majority shareholder up to this time, decided to sell his interest in Cookies. He first offered the directors an opportunity to buy his stock, but the board declined to purchase any of his 8100 shares. Herrig then offered Cook and all other shareholders $10 per share for their stock, which was twice the original price. Because of the overwhelming response to these offers, Herrig had purchased enough Cookies stock by January 1982 to become the majority shareholder. His investment of $140,000 represented fifty-three percent of the [outstanding shares]. . . .

Shortly after Herrig acquired majority control he replaced four of the five members of the Cookies' board with members he selected. . . . Subsequent changes made in the corporation under Herrig's leadership formed the basis for this lawsuit.

First, under Herrig's leadership, Cookies' board has extended the term of the exclusive distributorship agreement with Lakes and expanded the scope of services for which it compensates Herrig and his companies. In April 1982, when a sales increase of twenty-five percent over the previous year required Cookies to seek additional short-term storage for the peak summer season, the board accepted Herrig's proposal to compensate Lakes at the "going rate" for use of its nearby storage facilities. . . .

Second, Herrig moved from his role as director and distributor to take on an additional role in product development. This created a dispute over a royalty Herrig began to receive. . . . Herrig developed a recipe [for taco sauce] because he recognized that taco sauce, while requiring many of the same ingredients needed in barbeque sauce, is less expensive to produce. . . . In August 1982, Cookies' board approved a royalty fee to be paid to Herrig for this taco sauce recipe. This royalty plan was similar to royalties the board paid to L. D. Cook for the barbeque sauce recipe. That plan gives Cook three percent of the gross sales of barbeque sauce; Herrig receives a flat rate per case. Although Herrig's rate is equivalent to a sales percentage slightly higher than what Cook receives, it yields greater profit to Cookies because this new product line is cheaper to produce.

Third, since 1982 Cookies' board has twice approved additional compensation for Herrig. In January 1983, the board authorized payment of a $1000 per month "consultant fee" in lieu of salary, because accelerated sales required Herrig to spend extra time managing the company. Averaging eighty-hour work weeks, Herrig devoted approximately fifteen percent of his time to Cookies and eighty percent to Lakes business. In August, 1983, the board authorized another increase in Herrig's compensation. Further, at the suggestion of a Cookies director who also served as an accountant for Cookies, Lakes, and Speed's, the Cookies board amended the exclusive distributorship agreement to allow Lakes an additional two percent of gross sales as a promotion allowance to expand the market for Cookies products outside of Iowa. As a direct result of this action, by 1986 Cookies regularly shipped products to several states throughout the country.

As we have previously noted, however, Cookies' growth and success has not pleased all its shareholders. The discontent is motivated by two factors that have effectively precluded shareholders from sharing in Cookies' financial success: the fact that Cookies is a closely held corporation, and the fact that it has not paid dividends. Because Cookies' stock is not publicly traded, shareholders have no ready access to buyers for their stock at current values that reflect the company's success. Without dividends, the shareholders have no ready method of realizing a return on their investment in the company. This is not to say that Cookies has improperly refused to pay dividends. The evidence reveals that Cookies would have violated the terms of its loan with the Small Business Administration had it declared dividends before repaying that debt. That SBA loan was not repaid until the month before the plaintiffs filed this action.

Unsatisfied with the status quo, a group of minority shareholders commenced this equitable action in 1985. Based on the facts we have detailed, the plaintiffs claimed that the sums paid Herrig and his companies have grossly exceeded the value of the services rendered, thereby substantially reducing corporate profits and shareholder equity. Through the exclusive distributorship agreements, taco sauce royalty, warehousing fees, and consultant fee, plaintiffs claimed that Herrig breached his fiduciary duties to the corporation and its shareholders because he allegedly negotiated for these arrangements without fully disclosing the benefit he would gain. The plaintiffs sought recovery for lost profits, an accounting to determine the full extent of the damage, attorneys fees, punitive damages, appointment of a receiver to manage the company properly, removal of Herrig from control, and sale of the company in order to generate an appropriate return on their investment.

Having heard the evidence presented on these claims at trial, the district court filed a lengthy ruling that reflected careful attention to the testimony of the twenty-two witnesses and myriad of exhibits admitted. The court concluded that Herrig had breached no duties owed to Cookies or to its minority shareholders. . . .

II. FIDUCIARY DUTIES

Herrig, as an officer and director of Cookies, owes a fiduciary duty to the company and its shareholders. . . . Herrig concedes that Iowa law imposed the same fiduciary responsibilities based on his status as majority stockholder. . . . Conversely, before acquiring majority control in February 1982, Herrig owed no fiduciary duty to Cookies or plaintiffs. . . . Therefore, Herrig's conduct is subject to scrutiny only from the time he began to exercise control of Cookies. . . .

[T]he legislature enacted section 496A.34, . . . that establishes three sets of circumstances under which a director may engage in self-dealing without clearly violating the duty of loyalty:

> No contract or other transaction between a corporation and one or more of its directors or any other corporation, firm, association or entity in which one or more of its directors are directors or officers or are financially interested, shall be either void or voidable because of such relationship or interest . . . if any of the following occur:
>
> 1. The fact of such relationship or interest is disclosed or known to the board of directors or committee which authorizes, approves, or ratifies the contract or transaction . . . without counting the votes . . . of such interested director.
>
> 2. The fact of such relationship or interest is disclosed or known to the shareholders entitled to vote [on the transaction] and they authorize . . . such contract or transaction by vote or written consent.
>
> 3. The contract or transaction is fair and reasonable to the corporation.

Some commentators have supported the view that satisfaction of any *one* of the foregoing statutory alternatives in and of itself, would prove that a director has fully met the duty of loyalty. . . . We are obliged, however, to interpret statutes in conformity with the common law wherever statutory language does not directly negate it. . . . Because the common law and section 496A.34 require directors to show "good faith, honesty, and fairness" in self-dealing, we are persuaded that satisfaction of any one of these three alternatives under the statute would merely preclude us from rendering the transaction void or voidable *outright* solely on the basis "of such [director's] relationship or interest.". . . We thus require directors who engage in self-dealing to establish the additional element that they have acted in good faith, honesty, and fairness. . . .

. . . The crux of appellants' claim is that the [trial] court should have focused on the fair market value of Herrig's services to Cookies rather than on the success Cookies achieved as a result of Herrig's actions.

We agree with appellants' contention that corporate profitability should not be the sole criteria by which to test the fairness and reasonableness of Herrig's fees. . . .

Given an instance of alleged director enrichment at corporate expense. . . the burden to establish fairness resting on the director requires not only a showing of "fair price" but also a showing of the fairness of the bargain to the interests of the corporation. . . . Applying such reasoning to the record before us, however, we cannot agree with appellants' assertion that Herrig's services were either unfairly priced or inconsistent with Cookies corporate interest.

There can be no serious dispute that the four agreements in issue—for exclusive distributorship, taco sauce royalty, warehousing, and consulting fees—have all benefited Cookies, as demonstrated by its financial success. Even if we assume Cookies could have procured similar services from other vendors at lower costs, we are not convinced that Herrig's fees were therefore unreasonable or exorbitant. Like the district court, we are not persuaded by appellants' expert testimony that Cookies' sales and profits would have been the same under agreements with other vendors. As Cookies' board noted prior to Herrig's takeover, he was the driving force in the corporation's success. Even plaintiffs' expert acknowledged that Herrig has done the work of at least five people—production supervisor, advertising specialist, warehouseman, broker, and salesman. While eschewing the lack of internal control, for accounting purposes, that such centralized authority may produce, the expert conceded that Herrig may in fact be underpaid for all he has accomplished. We believe the board properly considered this source of Cookies' success when it entered these transactions, as did the district court when it reviewed them. . . .

[T]he record before us aptly demonstrates that all members of Cookies' board were well aware of Herrig's dual ownership in Lakes and Speed's. We are unaware of any authority supporting plaintiffs' contention that Herrig was obligated to disclose to Cookies' board or shareholders the extent of his profits resulting from these distribution and warehousing agreements; nevertheless, the exclusive distribution agreement with Lakes authorized the board to ascertain that information had it so desired. Appellants cannot reasonably claim that Herrig owed Cookies a duty to render such services at no profit to himself or his companies. Having found that the compensation he received from these agreements was fair and reasonable, we are convinced that Herrig furnished sufficient pertinent information to Cookies' board to enable it to make prudent decisions concerning the contracts. . . .

AFFIRMED.

SCHULTZ, J. (dissenting)....

Much of Herrig's evidence concerned the tremendous success of the company. I believe that the trial court and the majority opinion have been so enthralled by the success of the company that they have failed to examine whether these matters of self-dealing were fair to the stockholders. While much credit is due to Herrig for the success of the company, this does not mean that these transactions were fair to the company.

I believe that Herrig failed on his burden of proof by what he did not show. He did not produce evidence of the local going rate for distribution contracts or storage fees outside of a very limited amount of self-serving testimony. He simply did not show the fair market value of his services or expense for freight, advertising and storage cost. He did not show that his taco sauce royalty was fair. This was his burden. He cannot succeed on it by merely showing the success of the company.

The shareholders, on the other hand, . . . have put forth convincing testimony that Herrig has been grossly overcompensated for his services based on their fair market value. . . .

Discussion Questions:

1. The opinion provides the relevant language of the Iowa "safe harbor" statute for self-dealing transactions. Delaware's equivalent is provided at DGCL 144(a). Based purely on the statutory language, which approach provides greater insulation for self-dealing transactions? Which approach (do you think) requires a court to engage in a fairness inquiry more often?

2. At the time of the case Cookies is a thriving company—so why are minority shareholders in Cookies "discontent" and "unsatisfied"?

3. Which prong of the Iowa safe harbor statute did Cookies and Herrig attempt to satisfy? Why does the Cookies court nevertheless engage in a fairness inquiry?

4. Notice that the majority and the dissent agree that the Court should engage in a fairness inquiry, but they disagree on how it should be applied. Which approach do you prefer?

5. Consider a common scenario: a board member has an interest in a separate business, and that business contracts with the corporation. There is full disclosure to the board, and the disinterested directors approve the transaction. Should this process "cleanse" the taint of unfairness, such that a reviewing court should only apply deferential business judgment review? Or should the court engage in entire fairness review? If it depends, what factors would it depend on?

Pappas et al. v. Tzolis

N.Y. Slip Op. 06455, App. Div. 1ST Dept. (Sept. 15, 2011)

MAZZARELLI, J.P.

Plaintiffs and defendant Steve Tzolis formed defendant Vrahos LLC for the specific purpose of entering into a long-term lease on a building in Manhattan. Vrahos was created as a Delaware limited liability company, although the operating agreement expressly provided that the agreement was governed by New York law. The lease, which commenced in January 2006, required the payment of a security deposit of $1,192,500 and personal guarantees from Tzolis and plaintiff Steve Pappas. The operating agreement specified that Tzolis would advance the security deposit. It further provided that, as consideration for his furnishing of the security deposit, Tzolis would have the right to enter into a sublease of the property with Vrahos. This was conditioned on his paying additional monies to Vrahos above the rental payments that Vrahos was required to pay directly to the landlord.

[Paragraph 11 of] [t]he operating agreement also contained the following relevant provision:

> "Any Member may engage in business ventures and investments of any nature whatsoever, whether or not in competition with the LLC, without obligation of any kind to the LLC or to the other Members."

Tzolis exercised his right to sublease the building. However, he failed to make the additional payments to Vrahos that were required by the operating agreement. In September 2006, a few months after the subtenancy began, Tzolis suggested to plaintiffs that they assign their interests in Vrahos to him. He claimed that he did not want to make the additional rent payments and would rather take over the prime lease. Plaintiffs agreed, and negotiated buyouts of $1,000,000 for Pappas and $500,000 for plaintiff Constantine Ifantopoulos. The assignment agreements between plaintiffs and Tzolis provided that the assignment would become effective on the later of the date on which the landlord released Pappas from his personal guarantee and the date on which Pappas received the assignment fee. If either of those events had not taken place by February 5, 2007, the assignment would be rendered null and void. At the same time as they executed their assignment agreement, plaintiffs and Tzolis signed a handwritten "certificate," which provided, in pertinent part, that "each of the undersigned Sellers, in connection with their respective assignments to Steve Tzolis of their membership interests in Vrahos LLC, has performed their own due diligence in connection with such assignments. Each of the undersigned Sellers has engaged its own legal counsel, and is not relying on any representation by Steve Tzolis or any of his agents or representatives, except as set forth in the assignments & other documents delivered to the undersigned Sellers today. Further, each of the undersigned Sellers agrees that Steve Tzolis has no fiduciary duty to the undersigned Sellers in connection with such assignments."

The assignments to Tzolis became effective shortly after February 20, 2007, the date on which Pappas was released from his personal guarantee. Six months later, Vrahos, now wholly owned by Tzolis, assigned its lease to nonparty Charlton Soho LLC for $17.5 million. Pappas claims that he later discovered that, unbeknownst to plaintiffs at the time, Tzolis had begun negotiating the assignment of the lease to nonparty Extell Development Company, Charlton's owner, months before plaintiffs assigned their interests in Vrahos to Tzolis.

The complaint asserts [first] ... that Tzolis, ... in failing to disclose to [plaintiffs] ... that he and Extell were negotiating a lucrative sale of Vrahos's leasehold interest, and then engineering the buyout of their interests, ... breached a fiduciary duty that he owed to plaintiffs. The second claim is for misappropriation of a business opportunity of Vrahos....

Tzolis ... [a]rgued that he ... had no duty to disclose his negotiations with Extell. He further asserted that Delaware law governed Vrahos's internal affairs, and that it permitted the elimination of fiduciary duties among members, which he contended was achieved by paragraph 11 of the operating agreement... He further argued that because plaintiffs executed the certificate and willingly entered into the assignment agreement, none of the causes of action stated a claim against him.

The motion court ... found that under both Delaware law and New York law, plaintiffs had no cause of action. The court found that paragraph 11 of the operating agreement "eliminates the fiduciary relationship that would, otherwise, be owed by the members to each other and to the LLC."

***

[In contract, we decide that] Tzolis had the burden of "clearly" establishing that paragraph 11 of the operating agreement eliminated the particular fiduciary duty that plaintiffs contend he breached.

Paragraph 11 of the operating agreement may have permitted Tzolis to pursue a business opportunity unrelated to Vrahos, for his exclusive benefit, without having to disclose it to plaintiffs or otherwise present it first to Vrahos. However, we find that the provision does not "clearly" permit Tzolis to engage in behavior such as that alleged here, which was to surreptitiously engineer the lucrative sale of *the sole asset owned by Vrahos,* without informing his fellow owners of that entity.

Even under Delaware law, which permits parties to a limited liability company agreement such as this one to eliminate traditional fiduciary duties (Del Code Ann tit 6 § 18–1101[c]), Tzolis has not established that the parties eliminated all fiduciary duties that they owed to each other. That is because, under Delaware law, "unless the LLC agreement in a manager-managed LLC *explicitly* ... restricts or eliminates traditional fiduciary duties, managers owe those duties to ... [the LLC's] members" (*Kelly v. Blum*, 2010 WL 629850, ... [Del Ch 2010] [emphasis added]).

We turn now to the effect of the certificate . . . in which [plaintiffs] acknowledged that the assignments of their interests in Vrahos were not based on any representations by Tzolis and that Tzolis owed them no fiduciary duties whatsoever. This Court addressed that very issue *in Blue Chip Emerald v. Allied Partners* (299 A.D.2d 278 [2002]), [where] . . . the parties were joint venturers who formed an entity for the sole purpose of owning a commercial building. The plaintiffs sold their interests in the entity to the defendants based on a valuation of the building that was a small fraction of the price that the defendants received when they sold the building two weeks later. This Court [stated in *Blue Chip*]:

> "The key fact [is that the] defendants, as coventurers and, in particular, as managing coventurers, were fiduciaries of [the entity] in matters relating to the Venture until the moment the buy-out transaction closed, and therefore owe[d] [the entity] a duty of undivided and undiluted loyalty. Consistent with this stringent standard of conduct, which the courts have enforced with [u]ncompromising rigidity, it is well established that, when a fiduciary, in furtherance of its individual interests, deals with the beneficiary of the duty in a matter relating to the fiduciary relationship, the fiduciary is strictly obligated to make full disclosure of all material facts. Stated otherwise, the fiduciary is obligated in negotiating such a transaction to disclose any information that could reasonably bear on [the beneficiary's] consideration of [the fiduciary's] offer."

[This court held that] the defendants in *Blue Chip* had an obligation, in negotiating the buyout agreement, to divulge to the plaintiffs "material facts concerning their efforts to sell or lease the Venture's Property, such as, for example, the prices prospective purchasers were offering to pay" (id. at 280, 750 N.Y.S.2d 291). This obligation attached even though the plaintiffs were commercially sophisticated.

[We] are compelled to act with the same uncompromising rigidity here as in *Blue Chip.* Thus, notwithstanding the certificate in which plaintiffs acknowledged performing their own due diligence and stated that "Tzolis has no fiduciary duty to the undersigned Sellers in connection with such assignments," we find that Tzolis had an overriding duty to disclose his dealings with Extell to plaintiffs before they assigned their interests in Vrahos to him . . . [A]s this Court stated in *Blue Chip,* "[A] fiduciary cannot by contract relieve itself of the fiduciary obligation of full disclosure by withholding the very information the beneficiary needs in order to make a reasoned judgment whether to agree to the proposed contract."

[T]he dissent cites *Centro* (17 N.Y.3d 269 [2011]), as support for its position that the certificate effectively released Tzolis from the claims now at issue. However, the plaintiffs [in *Centro*] alleged that the defendants . . . induced them to sell their interest in a telecommunications company by misrepresenting the value of the enterprise. The [New York] Court of Appeals, in affirming the dismissal of the plaintiffs' fraud claim, noted that the "plaintiffs knew that defendant . . . had not supplied them with the financial information necessary to properly value [their interest], and that they were entitled to that information . . . In short, this is an instance where plaintiffs have been so lax in protecting themselves that they cannot fairly ask for the law's protection." . . . In contrast, defendants here have made no showing that plaintiffs had any reason to suspect Tzolis of deceit.

Moreover, *Centro* involved an exceedingly broad release that extinguished defendants' liability "in all manner of actions . . . whatsoever . . . whether past, present or future . . . resulting from the ownership of membership interests in [the entity] or having taken or failed to take any action in any capacity on behalf of [the entity] or in connection with the business of [the entity]" (*id.* at *3). No such document was signed by plaintiffs here.

[T]he motion court erred in dismissing plaintiffs' claims for breach of fiduciary duty and fraud.

FREEDMAN, J. (dissenting).

I would affirm the dismissal of the complaint in its entirety, because contractual disclaimers by plaintiffs preclude the causes of action that the majority has reinstated.

In January 2006, plaintiffs . . . and defendant Steve Tzolis formed a Delaware limited liability company, Vrahos LLC, as a vehicle for entering into a 49–year lease of a commercial building in Manhattan, and operating and developing the property. Pursuant to Vrahos's operating agreement, also executed in January 2006, Pappas, Ifantopoulos, and Tzolis were named as the company's sole members and managers, with Pappas and Tzolis each holding a 40% interest and making a $50 thousand capital contribution and Ifantopoulos holding a 20% interest and making a $25 thousand contribution.

Tzolis assumed Vrahos's control and management, and, with plaintiffs' consent, Vrahos subleased the Manhattan property to Tzolis in June 2006 for $20 thousand per month. In late 2006, Tzolis approached Pappas and Ifantopoulos about buying out their interests in Vrahos . . . [His] given reason for the buyout was that "he [did] not want to pay rent" and that "he owns his own buildings." But by this time, plaintiffs allege, Tzolis knew of but did not disclose a profitable opportunity for Vrahos to assign its lease interest to nonparty Charlton Soho LLC, a real estate developer.

[The plaintiffs agreed to] assign their interests in Vrahos to Tzolis, in exchange for which Tzolis would pay [plaintiff] Pappas $1 million and [plaintiff] Ifantopoulos $500,000, or 20 times what they had invested one year earlier. At the closing, the [plaintiffs] and Tzolis executed a certificate stating that each of the plaintiffs "has performed [his] own due diligence in connection with [his] assignment]," and that each of them "has engaged its own legal counsel, and is not relying on any representation by Steve Tzolis or any of his agents or representatives." . . . The certificate further stated that "Steve Tzolis has no fiduciary duty to [Pappas and Ifantopoulos] in connection with [the] assignments."

About [seven] months later, . . . Tzolis, now Vrahos's sole member, assigned the Vrahos lease to Charlton Soho for $17.5 million, thus realizing a very large profit on his investment in the LLC. Plaintiffs' central allegation against Tzolis is that he cheated [them] out of a share of the profit from the Charlton Soho deal by buying out their interests in Vrahos without disclosing to them that a potential deal was in the offing.

***

[This Court should dismiss the allegation] that Tzolis breached his fiduciary duty to them by buying their LLC interests without telling them about what they contend were ongoing negotiations with Charlton Soho . . . [The plaintiffs explicitly agreed in the closing certificate] that Tzolis had no fiduciary duty to them in connection with the assignment, stated that they were not relying on Tzolis' external representations, and represented that they had protected their interests by performing due diligence and engaging separate counsel. Although Tzolis had a fiduciary relationship with Pappas and Ifantopoulos before the closing, the certificate specifically . . . released Tzolis from any liability arising from his fiduciary duty.

Moreover, [the LLC operating agreement stated] . . . that "[a]ny [m]ember may engage in business ventures and investments *of any nature whatsoever,* whether or not in competition with the LLC, *without obligation of any kind* . . . to the other [m]embers" (emphasis supplied). Under Delaware law, which, . . . governs the breach of fiduciary duty claim, an LLC member's fiduciary duty to another member "may be expanded or restricted or eliminated by provisions in the limited liability company agreement" (Del Code Ann tit 18 § 1101[c]). While the operating agreement . . . alone did not eliminate all of Tzolis's fiduciary duties to [the plaintiffs], it afforded Tzolis latitude to pursue his individual business interests for his own gain regardless of his co-members' interests.

The [New York] Court of Appeals recently held that "[a] sophisticated principal is able to release its fiduciary from claims—at least where . . . the fiduciary relationship is no longer one of unquestioning trust—so long as the principal understands that the fiduciary is acting in its own interest and the release is knowingly entered into" [citing *Centro*]. In *Centro* . . . the plaintiffs, who were minority shareholders in a closely held corporation, claimed that the defendant majority shareholder . . . fraudulently induced them both to sell their shares (by misrepresenting their value) and to execute a broad release from claims, [and that] [t]he defendant [as the plaintiffs' fiduciary] was required to "disclose any information that could reasonably bear on plaintiffs' consideration of [its purchase] offer" . . . Despite [the defendant's] fiduciary obligation, the Court of Appeals held that the plaintiffs' claims [of a]breach of fiduciary duty . . . [was] barred by the release they granted defendants as a condition of the sale.

In this case, . . . plaintiffs [had] fair notice that plaintiffs were engaging in an arm's-length business transaction with Tzolis.

The majority's reliance on *Blue Chip* . . . is misplaced. In *Centro* . . . the Court of Appeals made clear that one party could release another from claims arising from a fiduciary duty that existed before the release, and called our holding in *Blue Chip* . . . into question by stating that "[t]o the extent that Appellate Division decisions . . . suggest otherwise, they misapprehend our case law" (2011 Slip Op 04720, *6).

Discussion Questions:

1. Shouldn't Pappas and Ifantopoulos know that "something is up" when Tzolis offers to pay them 20 times what they had invested one year earlier, but asks them to sign a very broad release? As a policy matter, why should we give these parties (who are financially sophisticated) the protection of fiduciary duty?

2. This case is our only case from the context of a limited liability company (LLC). In general, the differences between LLCs and corporations are beyond the scope of our course, but one important difference worth noting is that the parties to a LLC agreement can eliminate fiduciary duties among the parties. Del Code Ann tit 6 § 18-1101[c]. In contrast, in the corporate form, only certain kinds of fiduciary duties can be waived—see, e.g., DGCL 102(b)(7), discussed in the next chapter, and DGCL 122(17), discussed below. As a policy matter, should the Delaware courts permit a complete waiver of fiduciary duties among parties to an LLC agreement? Or should there still remain some g-string of a fiduciary duty overlay?[11] Put differently, if the parties to an LLC agreement are sophisticated and want to create a shark tank among themselves, why not let them do so?

Corporate Opportunity Doctrine

Corporate opportunity doctrine is one specific application of the duty of loyalty. If a director or officer owes a duty to the corporation, then this must mean that the director or officer cannot take an opportunity for himself that belongs to the corporation. The difficult questions arise, however, over (1) determining when an opportunity belongs to the corporation; and (2) if the opportunity does belong to the corporation, what constitutes adequate rejection of the opportunity by the corporation such that the director/officer can nevertheless take it.

Unfortunately the case law on these questions is not completely clear. There are three primary approaches. The classic articulation of the Delaware doctrine of corporate opportunity comes from *Guth v. Loft*, Inc., 5 A.2d 503 (Del. 1939) which articulates a four-factor test:

A corporate officer or director may not take a business opportunity for his own if:

(1)   the corporation is financially able to exploit the opportunity;

(2)   the opportunity is within the corporation's line of business;

(3)   the corporation has an interest or expectancy in the opportunity; and

---

[11] Thanks to Professor Reinier Kraakman for this colorful analogy.

(4)   by taking the opportunity for his own, the corporate fiduciary will thereby be placed in a position inimical to his duties to the corporation.

The Court in *Guth* also derived a corollary which states that a director or officer *may* take a corporate opportunity if:

(1)   the opportunity is presented to the director or officer in his individual and not his corporate capacity;

(2)   the opportunity is not essential to the corporation;

(3)   the corporation holds no interest or expectancy in the opportunity; and

(4)   the director or officer has not wrongfully employed the resources of the corporation in pursuing or exploiting the opportunity. *Guth,* 5 A.2d at 509.

Discussion Questions:

1. Imagine you are the in-house lawyer for a real estate developer, Rosalind Franklin Broes. Broes is doing business through RFB Condominiums Inc. ("RFBC"), a Delaware corporation. Broes is RFBC's sole shareholder and president. You are technically an employee of RFBC. RFBC develops and administers condo complexes in the Midwestern United States, mainly in Michigan.

   Broes now wants your opinion on the following issue. One of RFBC's bankers, John Cash of Big Bank, has asked Broes to join the board of another real estate developer, CIS Inc., also a Delaware corporation. CIS is an erstwhile competitor of RFBC. It has been in chapter 11 for the last two years, however, and lost or sold most of its properties and contracts during that time. When it emerges from bankruptcy next month, it will only have interests in Texas. Cash sits on CIS' creditor committee on behalf of Big Bank, a major creditor of CIS. Cash would like to get Broes's experience onto CIS' board.

   Broes is concerned that service on CIS' board will expose her to conflicts of interest. She has shared these concerns with Cash. In Cash's view, the concerns are unfounded. After all, he, Cash, also has access to much confidential information from both CIS and RFBC in his role as their banker. Besides, he argues, CIS and RFBC will no longer be operating in the same areas. Lastly, even if CIS wanted to expand back into the Midwest, Cash points out that CIS would find it very difficult to do so under the restrictive post-bankruptcy loan covenants that prohibit most acquisitions or additional financing.

Can she or can she not serve on CIS' board without getting into trouble? What would you advise Broes to do?

2. DGCL 122(17) permits waiver of corporate opportunities for officers or directors. For example, Dreamworks SKG waived corporate opportunity restrictions for its three founders, Steven Spielberg, Jeff Katzenberg, and David Geffen:

> None of the Founding Stockholders [Spielberg, Katzenberg, and Geffen] shall have any duty to refrain from engaging directly or indirectly in the same or similar business activities or lines of business as the Corporation and that might be in direct or indirect competition with the Corporation.

> In the event that any Founding Stockholder acquires knowledge of a potential transaction or matter that may be a corporate opportunity for any Founding Stockholder . . . none of the Founding Stockholders shall have any duty to communicate or offer such corporate opportunity to the Corporation. . . .

> [A]nd any Founding Stockholder shall be entitled to pursue or acquire such corporate opportunity for itself or to direct such corporate opportunity to another person and the Corporation shall have no right in or to such corporate opportunity."

Why would Spielberg, Katzenberg, and Geffen put such a provision in their charter? Maybe more importantly, why would prospective investors buy shares in such a company?

Chapter 4 – Unconflicted Behavior: The Duty of Care

The duty of care is a bedrock principle of corporate law. Delaware does not provide a single articulation of the duty of care, but the American Law Institute (ALI) Principles of Corporate Governance § 4.01(a) provides a reasonable formulation:

> A director or officer has a duty to the corporation to perform the director's or officer's functions: in good faith; in a manner that he or she reasonably believes to be in the best interests of the corporation; and with the care that an ordinarily prudent person would reasonably be expected to exercise in a like position and under similar circumstances.

The business judgment rule then provides an overlay on the duty of care. Again, the ALI Principles of Corporate Governance (§ 4.01(c)) provide a working definition:

> A director or officer who makes a business judgment in good faith fulfills the duty under this section if the director or officer: (1) is not interested in the subject of the business judgment; (2) is informed with respect to the subject of the business judgment to the extent that the director or officer reasonably believes is appropriate under the circumstances; and (3) rationally believes that the business judgment is in the best interests of the corporation.

In effect, the business judgment rule converts a substantive inquiry (did the director or officer act with due care?) into a procedural inquiry (did the director or officer engage in a reasonable process?).

In general, the duty of care is a very deferential standard of review. Unlike the duty of loyalty, which triggers rigorous "entire fairness" review, the duty of care does not attempt to second-guess the decisions of directors or officers as long as the process they used was reasonable. If the business judgment rule applies, then that determination is (virtually) outcome determinative: the defendants win. If the business judgment rule does not apply, plaintiffs must show that the defendant directors or officers were "grossly negligent" in order to demonstrate a duty of care violation. *Aronson v. Lewis*, 473 A.2d 805 (Del. 1984).

In applying this general approach in *Smith v. Van Gorkom*, the Delaware Supreme Court sent shockwaves through corporate America.

Smith v. Van Gorkom
488 A.2d 858 (Del. 1985)

HORSEY, Justice (for the majority):

This appeal from the Court of Chancery involves a class action brought by shareholders of the defendant Trans Union Corporation ("Trans Union" or "the Company"), originally seeking rescission of a cash-out merger of Trans Union into the defendant New T Company ("New T"), a wholly-owned subsidiary of the defendant, Marmon Group, Inc. ("Marmon"). Alternate relief in the form of damages is sought against the defendant members of the Board of Directors of Trans Union, New T, and Jay A. Pritzker and Robert A. Pritzker, owners of Marmon.

Following trial, the former Chancellor granted judgment for the defendant directors by unreported letter opinion dated July 6, 1982. Judgment was based on two findings: (1) that the Board of Directors had acted in an informed manner so as to be entitled to protection of the business judgment rule in approving the cash-out merger; and (2) that the shareholder vote approving the merger should not be set aside because the stockholders had been "fairly informed" by the Board of Directors before voting thereon. The plaintiffs appeal.

Speaking for the majority of the Court, we conclude that both rulings of the Court of Chancery are clearly erroneous. Therefore, we reverse and direct that judgment be entered in favor of the plaintiffs and against the defendant directors for the fair value of the plaintiffs' stockholdings in Trans Union, in accordance with *Weinberger v. UOP, Inc.*, Del.Supr., 457 A.2d 701 (1983).

We hold: (1) that the Board's decision, reached September 20, 1980, to approve the proposed cash-out merger was not the product of an informed business judgment; (2) that the Board's subsequent efforts to amend the Merger Agreement and take other curative action were ineffectual, both legally and factually; and (3) that the Board did not deal with complete candor with the stockholders by failing to disclose all material facts, which they knew or should have known, before securing the stockholders' approval of the merger.

I.

The nature of this case requires a detailed factual statement. The following facts are essentially uncontradicted:

A.

Trans Union was a publicly-traded, diversified holding company, the principal earnings of which were generated by its railcar leasing business. During the period here involved, the Company had a cash flow of hundreds of millions of dollars annually. However, the Company had difficulty in generating sufficient taxable income to offset increasingly large investment tax credits (ITCs). Accelerated depreciation deductions had decreased available taxable income against which to offset accumulating ITCs. The Company took these deductions, despite their effect on usable ITCs, because the rental price in the railcar leasing market had already impounded the purported tax savings.[12]

---

[12] In other words, Trans Union's "problem" was that it could not make full use of the available massive tax breaks. These tax breaks would reduce the corporate income tax. But Trans Union benefitted from so many tax breaks that it was already not paying corporate income tax. The

In the late 1970's, together with other capital-intensive firms, Trans Union lobbied in Congress to have ITCs refundable in cash to firms which could not fully utilize the credit. During the summer of 1980, defendant Jerome W. Van Gorkom, Trans Union's Chairman and Chief Executive Officer, testified and lobbied in Congress for refundability of ITCs and against further accelerated depreciation. By the end of August, Van Gorkom was convinced that Congress would neither accept the refundability concept nor curtail further accelerated depreciation.

Beginning in the late 1960's, and continuing through the 1970's, Trans Union pursued a program of acquiring small companies in order to increase available taxable income. In July 1980, Trans Union Management prepared the annual revision of the Company's Five Year Forecast. This report was presented to the Board of Directors at its July, 1980 meeting. The report projected an annual income growth of about 20%. The report also concluded that Trans Union would have about $195 million in spare cash between 1980 and 1985, "with the surplus growing rapidly from 1982 onward." The report referred to the ITC situation as a "nagging problem" and, given that problem, the leasing company "would still appear to be constrained to a tax breakeven." The report then listed four alternative uses of the projected 1982-1985 equity surplus: (1) stock repurchase; (2) dividend increases; (3) a major acquisition program; and (4) combinations of the above. The sale of Trans Union was not among the alternatives. The report emphasized that, despite the overall surplus, the operation of the Company would consume all available equity for the next several years, and concluded: "As a result, we have sufficient time to fully develop our course of action."

B.

On August 27, 1980, Van Gorkom met with Senior Management of Trans Union. Van Gorkom reported on his lobbying efforts in Washington and his desire to find a solution to the tax credit problem more permanent than a continued program of acquisitions. Various alternatives were suggested and discussed preliminarily, including the sale of Trans Union to a company with a large amount of taxable income.[13]

Donald Romans, Chief Financial Officer of Trans Union, stated that his department had done a "very brief bit of work on the possibility of a leveraged buy-out."[14]

---

remaining tax breaks were thus "wasted," unless Trans Union could persuade Congress to pay out those breaks in cash (i.e., to allow income taxes to be negative in this case -- from the Treasury to firms) or find other taxable income to use the tax breaks on. – Eds.

[13] The buyer could then merge with Trans Union and, under applicable IRS rules and certain conditions, apply the tax credits of the former Trans Union to the combined taxable income of the merged entities. – Eds.

[14] A leveraged buyout (LBO) is a purchase financed largely with debt. The debt is usually secured by the purchased corporation's assets. LBOs became frequent and spectacularly large in the 1980s. For the LBO to succeed post-acquisition, the target corporation must produce high and steady cash flows to service the high levels of debt incurred. Otherwise, the target will end up in bankruptcy. We will discuss these issues in much greater detail when we discuss Unocal later in the course. – Eds.

This work had been prompted by a media article which Romans had seen regarding a leveraged buy-out by management. The work consisted of a "preliminary study" of the cash which could be generated by the Company if it participated in a leveraged buyout. As Romans stated, this analysis "was very first and rough cut at seeing whether a cash flow would support what might be considered a high price for this type of transaction."

On September 5, at another Senior Management meeting which Van Gorkom attended, Romans again brought up the idea of a leveraged buy-out as a "possible strategic alternative" to the Company's acquisition program. Romans and Bruce S. Chelberg, President and Chief Operating Officer of Trans Union, had been working on the matter in preparation for the meeting. According to Romans: They did not "come up" with a price for the Company. They merely "ran the numbers" at $50 a share and at $60 a share with the "rough form" of their cash figures at the time. Their "figures indicated that $50 would be very easy to do but $60 would be very difficult to do under those figures." This work did not purport to establish a fair price for either the Company or 100% of the stock. It was intended to determine the cash flow needed to service the debt that would "probably" be incurred in a leveraged buyout, based on "rough calculations" without "any benefit of experts to identify what the limits were to that, and so forth." These computations were not considered extensive and no conclusion was reached.

At this meeting, Van Gorkom stated that he would be willing to take $55 per share for his own 75,000 shares. He vetoed the suggestion of a leveraged buy-out by Management, however, as involving a potential conflict of interest for Management. Van Gorkom, a certified public accountant and lawyer, had been an officer of Trans Union for 24 years, its Chief Executive Officer for more than 17 years, and Chairman of its Board for 2 years. It is noteworthy in this connection that he was then approaching 65 years of age and mandatory retirement.

For several days following the September 5 meeting, Van Gorkom pondered the idea of a sale. He had participated in many acquisitions as a manager and director of Trans Union and as a director of other companies. He was familiar with acquisition procedures, valuation methods, and negotiations; and he privately considered the pros and cons of whether Trans Union should seek a privately or publicly-held purchaser.

Van Gorkom decided to meet with Jay A. Pritzker, a well-known corporate takeover specialist and a social acquaintance. However, rather than approaching Pritzker simply to determine his interest in acquiring Trans Union, Van Gorkom assembled a proposed per share price for sale of the Company and a financing structure by which to accomplish the sale. Van Gorkom did so without consulting either his Board or any members of Senior Management except one: Carl Peterson, Trans Union's Controller. Telling Peterson that he wanted no other person on his staff to know what he was doing, but without telling him why, Van Gorkom directed Peterson to calculate the feasibility of a leveraged buy-out at an assumed price per share of $55. Apart from the Company's historic stock market price, and

Van Gorkom's long association with Trans Union, the record is devoid of any competent evidence that $55 represented the per share intrinsic value of the Company.

Having thus chosen the $55 figure, based solely on the availability of a leveraged buy-out, Van Gorkom multiplied the price per share by the number of shares outstanding to reach a total value of the Company of $690 million. Van Gorkom told Peterson to use this $690 million figure and to assume a $200 million equity contribution by the buyer. Based on these assumptions, Van Gorkom directed Peterson to determine whether the debt portion of the purchase price could be paid off in five years or less if financed by Trans Union's cash flow as projected in the Five Year Forecast, and by the sale of certain weaker divisions identified in a study done for Trans Union by the Boston Consulting Group ("BCG study"). Peterson reported that, of the purchase price, approximately $50-80 million would remain outstanding after five years. Van Gorkom was disappointed, but decided to meet with Pritzker nevertheless.

Van Gorkom arranged a meeting with Pritzker at the latter's home on Saturday, September 13, 1980. Van Gorkom prefaced his presentation by stating to Pritzker: "Now as far as you are concerned, I can, I think, show how you can pay a substantial premium over the present stock price and pay off most of the loan in the first five years. * * * If you could pay $55 for this Company, here is a way in which I think it can be financed."

Van Gorkom then reviewed with Pritzker his calculations based upon his proposed price of $55 per share. Although Pritzker mentioned $50 as a more attractive figure, no other price was mentioned. However, Van Gorkom stated that to be sure that $55 was the best price obtainable, Trans Union should be free to accept any better offer. Pritzker demurred, stating that his organization would serve as a "stalking horse" for an "auction contest" only if Trans Union would permit Pritzker to buy 1,750,000 shares of Trans Union stock at market price which Pritzker could then sell to any higher bidder. After further discussion on this point, Pritzker told Van Gorkom that he would give him a more definite reaction soon.

On Monday, September 15, Pritzker advised Van Gorkom that he was interested in the $55 cash-out merger proposal and requested more information on Trans Union. Van Gorkom agreed to meet privately with Pritzker, accompanied by Peterson, Chelberg, and Michael Carpenter, Trans Union's consultant from the Boston Consulting Group. The meetings took place on September 16 and 17. Van Gorkom was "astounded that events were moving with such amazing rapidity."

On Thursday, September 18, Van Gorkom met again with Pritzker. At that time, Van Gorkom knew that Pritzker intended to make a cash-out merger offer at Van Gorkom's proposed $55 per share. Pritzker instructed his attorney, a merger and acquisition specialist, to begin drafting merger documents. There was no further discussion of the $55 price. However, the number of shares of Trans Union's treasury stock to be offered to Pritzker was negotiated down to one million shares; the price was set at $38-75 cents above the per share price at the close of the market on September 19. At this point, Pritzker insisted that the Trans Union Board act on his merger proposal within the next three days, stating to Van Gorkom: "We have to have a decision by no later than Sunday [evening, September 21] before the opening of the English stock exchange on Monday morning." Pritzker's lawyer was then instructed to draft the merger documents, to be reviewed by Van Gorkom's lawyer, "sometimes with discussion and sometimes not, in the haste to get it finished."

On Friday, September 19, Van Gorkom, Chelberg, and Pritzker consulted with Trans Union's lead bank regarding the financing of Pritzker's purchase of Trans Union. The bank indicated that it could form a syndicate of banks that would finance the transaction. On the same day, Van Gorkom retained James Brennan, Esquire, to advise Trans Union on the legal aspects of the merger. Van Gorkom did not consult with William Browder, a Vice-President and director of Trans Union and former head of its legal department, or with William Moore, then the head of Trans Union's legal staff.

On Friday, September 19, Van Gorkom called a special meeting of the Trans Union Board for noon the following day. He also called a meeting of the Company's Senior Management to convene at 11:00 a.m., prior to the meeting of the Board. No one, except Chelberg and Peterson, was told the purpose of the meetings. Van Gorkom did not invite Trans Union's investment banker, Salomon Brothers or its Chicago-based partner, to attend.

Of those present at the Senior Management meeting on September 20, only Chelberg and Peterson had prior knowledge of Pritzker's offer. Van Gorkom disclosed the offer and described its terms, but he furnished no copies of the proposed Merger Agreement. Romans announced that his department had done a second study which showed that, for a leveraged buy-out, the price range for Trans Union stock was between $55 and $65 per share. Van Gorkom neither saw the study nor asked Romans to make it available for the Board meeting.

Senior Management's reaction to the Pritzker proposal was completely negative. No member of Management, except Chelberg and Peterson, supported the proposal. Romans objected to the price as being too low; he was critical of the timing and suggested that consideration should be given to the adverse tax consequences of an all-cash deal for low-basis shareholders; and he took the position that the agreement to sell Pritzker one million newly-issued shares at market price would inhibit other offers, as would the prohibitions against soliciting bids and furnishing inside information to other bidders. Romans argued that the Pritzker proposal was a "lock up" and amounted to "an agreed merger as opposed to an offer." Nevertheless, Van Gorkom proceeded to the Board meeting as scheduled without further delay.

Ten directors served on the Trans Union Board, five inside (defendants Bonser, O'Boyle, Browder, Chelberg, and Van Gorkom) and five outside (defendants Wallis, Johnson, Lanterman, Morgan and Reneker). All directors were present at the meeting, except O'Boyle who was ill. Of the outside directors, four were corporate chief executive officers and one was the former Dean of the University of Chicago Business School. None was an investment banker or trained financial analyst. All members of the Board were well informed about the Company and its operations as a going concern. They were familiar with the current financial condition of the Company, as well as operating and earnings projections reported in the recent Five Year Forecast. The Board generally received regular and detailed reports and was kept abreast of the accumulated investment tax credit and accelerated depreciation problem.

Van Gorkom began the Special Meeting of the Board with a twenty-minute oral presentation. Copies of the proposed Merger Agreement were delivered too late for study before or during the meeting. He reviewed the Company's ITC and depreciation problems and the efforts theretofore made to solve them. He discussed his initial meeting with Pritzker and his motivation in arranging that meeting. Van Gorkom did not disclose to the Board, however, the methodology by which he alone had arrived at the $55 figure, or the fact that he first proposed the $55 price in his negotiations with Pritzker.

Van Gorkom outlined the terms of the Pritzker offer as follows: Pritzker would pay $55 in cash for all outstanding shares of Trans Union stock upon completion of which Trans Union would be merged into New T Company, a subsidiary wholly-owned by Pritzker and formed to implement the merger; for a period of 90 days, Trans Union could receive, but could not actively solicit, competing offers; the offer had to be acted on by the next evening, Sunday, September 21; Trans Union could only furnish to competing bidders published information, and not proprietary information; the offer was subject to Pritzker obtaining the necessary financing by October 10, 1980; if the financing contingency were met or waived by Pritzker, Trans Union was required to sell to Pritzker one million newly-issued shares of Trans Union at $38 per share.

Van Gorkom took the position that putting Trans Union "up for auction" through a 90-day market test would validate a decision by the Board that $55 was a fair price. He told the Board that the "free market will have an opportunity to judge whether $55 is a fair price." Van Gorkom framed the decision before the Board not as whether $55 per share was the highest price that could be obtained, but as whether the $55 price was a fair price that the stockholders should be given the opportunity to accept or reject.

Attorney Brennan advised the members of the Board that they might be sued if they failed to accept the offer and that a fairness opinion was not required as a matter of law.

Romans attended the meeting as chief financial officer of the Company. He told the Board that he had not been involved in the negotiations with Pritzker and knew nothing about the merger proposal until the morning of the meeting; that his studies did not indicate either a fair price for the stock or a valuation of the Company; that he did not see his role as directly addressing the fairness issue; and that he and his people "were trying to search for ways to justify a price in connection with such a [leveraged buy-out] transaction, rather than to say what the shares are worth." Romans testified:

> I told the Board that the study ran the numbers at 50 and 60, and then the subsequent study at 55 and 65, and that was not the same thing as saying that I have a valuation of the company at X dollars. But it was a way—a first step towards reaching that conclusion.

Romans told the Board that, in his opinion, $55 was "in the range of a fair price," but "at the beginning of the range."

Chelberg, Trans Union's President, supported Van Gorkom's presentation and representations. He testified that he "participated to make sure that the Board members collectively were clear on the details of the agreement or offer from Pritzker;" that he "participated in the discussion with Mr. Brennan, inquiring of him about the necessity for valuation opinions in spite of the way in which this particular offer was couched;" and that he was otherwise actively involved in supporting the positions being taken by Van Gorkom before the Board about "the necessity to act immediately on this offer," and about "the adequacy of the $55 and the question of how that would be tested."

The Board meeting of September 20 lasted about two hours. Based solely upon Van Gorkom's oral presentation, Chelberg's supporting representations, Romans' oral statement, Brennan's legal advice, and their knowledge of the market history of the Company's stock, the directors approved the proposed Merger Agreement. However, the Board later claimed to have attached two conditions to its acceptance: (1) that Trans Union reserved the right to accept any better offer that was made during the market test period; and (2) that Trans Union could share its proprietary information with any other potential bidders. While the Board now claims to have reserved the right to accept any better offer received after the announcement of the Pritzker agreement (even though the minutes of the meeting do not reflect this), it is undisputed that the Board did not reserve the right to actively solicit alternate offers.

The Merger Agreement was executed by Van Gorkom during the evening of September 20 at a formal social event that he hosted for the opening of the Chicago Lyric Opera. Neither he nor any other director read the agreement prior to its signing and delivery to Pritzker.

* * *

On Monday, September 22, the Company issued a press release announcing that Trans Union had entered into a "definitive" Merger Agreement with an affiliate of the Marmon Group, Inc., a Pritzker holding company. Within 10 days of the public announcement, dissent among Senior Management over the merger had become widespread. Faced with threatened resignations of key officers, Van Gorkom met with Pritzker who agreed to several modifications of the Agreement. Pritzker was willing to do so provided that Van Gorkom could persuade the dissidents to remain on the Company payroll for at least six months after consummation of the merger.

Van Gorkom reconvened the Board on October 8 and secured the directors' approval of the proposed amendments—sight unseen. The Board also authorized the employment of Salomon Brothers, its investment banker, to solicit other offers for Trans Union during the proposed "market test" period.

The next day, October 9, Trans Union issued a press release announcing: (1) that Pritzker had obtained "the financing commitments necessary to consummate" the merger with Trans Union; (2) that Pritzker had acquired one million shares of Trans Union common stock at $38 per share; (3) that Trans Union was now permitted to actively seek other offers and had retained Salomon Brothers for that purpose; and (4) that if a more favorable offer were not received before February 1, 1981, Trans Union's shareholders would thereafter meet to vote on the Pritzker proposal.

It was not until the following day, October 10, that the actual amendments to the Merger Agreement were prepared by Pritzker and delivered to Van Gorkom for execution. As will be seen, the amendments were considerably at variance with Van Gorkom's representations of the amendments to the Board on October 8; and the amendments placed serious constraints on Trans Union's ability to negotiate a better deal and withdraw from the Pritzker agreement. Nevertheless, Van Gorkom proceeded to execute what became the October 10 amendments to the Merger Agreement without conferring further with the Board members and apparently without comprehending the actual implications of the amendments.

* * *

Salomon Brothers' efforts over a three-month period from October 21 to January 21 produced only one serious suitor for Trans Union—General Electric Credit Corporation ("GE Credit"), a subsidiary of the General Electric Company. However, GE Credit was unwilling to make an offer for Trans Union unless Trans Union first rescinded its Merger Agreement with Pritzker. When Pritzker refused, GE Credit terminated further discussions with Trans Union in early January.

In the meantime, in early December, the investment firm of Kohlberg, Kravis, Roberts & Co. ("KKR"), the only other concern to make a firm offer for Trans Union, withdrew its offer under circumstances hereinafter detailed.

On December 19, this litigation was commenced and, within four weeks, the plaintiffs had deposed eight of the ten directors of Trans Union, including Van Gorkom, Chelberg and Romans, its Chief Financial Officer. On January 21, Management's Proxy Statement for the February 10 shareholder meeting was mailed to Trans Union's stockholders. On January 26, Trans Union's Board met and, after a lengthy meeting, voted to proceed with the Pritzker merger. The Board also approved for mailing, "on or about January 27," a Supplement to its Proxy Statement. The Supplement purportedly set forth all information relevant to the Pritzker Merger Agreement, which had not been divulged in the first Proxy Statement.

* * *

On February 10, the stockholders of Trans Union approved the Pritzker merger proposal. Of the outstanding shares, 69.9% were voted in favor of the merger; 7.25% were voted against the merger; and 22.85% were not voted.

II.

We turn to the issue of the application of the business judgment rule to the September 20 meeting of the Board.

[...]

Under Delaware law, the business judgment rule is the offspring of the fundamental principle, codified in 8 *Del.C.* § 141(a), that the business and affairs of a Delaware corporation are managed by or under its board of directors. *Pogostin v. Rice,* Del.Supr., 480 A.2d 619, 624 (1984); *Aronson v. Lewis,* Del.Supr., 473 A.2d 805, 811 (1984); *Zapata Corp. v. Maldonado,* Del.Supr., 430 A.2d 779, 782 (1981). In carrying out their managerial roles, directors are charged with an unyielding fiduciary duty to the corporation and its shareholders. *Loft, Inc. v. Guth,* Del.Ch., 2 A.2d 225 (1938), *aff'd,* Del.Supr., 5 A.2d 503 (1939). The business judgment rule exists to protect and promote the full and free exercise of the managerial power granted to Delaware directors. *Zapata Corp. v. Maldonado, supra* at 782. The rule itself "is a presumption that in making a business decision, the directors of a corporation acted on an informed basis, in good faith and in the honest belief that the action taken was in the best interests of the company." *Aronson, supra* at 812. Thus, the party attacking a board decision as uninformed must rebut the presumption that its business judgment was an informed one. *Id.*

The determination of whether a business judgment is an informed one turns on whether the directors have informed themselves "prior to making a business decision, of all material information reasonably available to them." *Id.*

Under the business judgment rule there is no protection for directors who have made "an unintelligent or unadvised judgment." *Mitchell v. Highland-Western Glass,* Del.Ch., 167 A. 831, 833 (1933). A director's duty to inform himself in preparation for a decision derives from the fiduciary capacity in which he serves the corporation and its stockholders. [...] Since a director is vested with the responsibility for the management of the affairs of the corporation, he must execute that duty with the recognition that he acts on behalf of others. Such obligation does not tolerate faithlessness or self-dealing. But fulfillment of the fiduciary function requires more than the mere absence of bad faith or fraud.

Representation of the financial interests of others imposes on a director an affirmative duty to protect those interests and to proceed with a critical eye in assessing information of the type and under the circumstances present here. [...]

Thus, a director's duty to exercise an informed business judgment is in the nature of a duty of care, as distinguished from a duty of loyalty. Here, there were no allegations of fraud, bad faith, or self-dealing, or proof thereof. Hence, it is presumed that the directors reached their business judgment in good faith, *Allaun v. Consolidated Oil Co.,* Del. Ch., 147 A. 257 (1929), and considerations of motive are irrelevant to the issue before us.

The standard of care applicable to a director's duty of care has also been recently restated by this Court. In *Aronson, supra,* we stated:

> While the Delaware cases use a variety of terms to describe the applicable standard of care, our analysis satisfies us that under the business judgment rule director liability is predicated upon concepts of gross negligence. (Footnote omitted)

473 A.2d at 812.

We again confirm that view. We think the concept of gross negligence is also the proper standard for determining whether a business judgment reached by a board of directors was an informed one.

In the specific context of a proposed merger of domestic corporations, a director has a duty under 8 *Del.C.* 251(b), along with his fellow directors, to act in an informed and deliberate manner in determining whether to approve an agreement of merger before submitting the proposal to the stockholders. Certainly in the merger context, a director may not abdicate that duty by leaving to the shareholders alone the decision to approve or disapprove the agreement. *See Beard v. Elster,* Del.Supr., 160 A.2d 731, 737 (1960). Only an agreement of merger satisfying the requirements of 8 *Del.C.* § 251(b) may be submitted to the shareholders under § 251(c). *See generally Aronson v. Lewis, supra* at 811-13; *see also Pogostin v. Rice, supra.*

It is against those standards that the conduct of the directors of Trans Union must be tested, as a matter of law and as a matter of fact, regarding their exercise of an informed business judgment in voting to approve the Pritzker merger proposal.

III.

[...]

[T]he question of whether the directors reached an informed business judgment in agreeing to sell the Company, pursuant to the terms of the September 20 Agreement presents, in reality, two questions: (A) whether the directors reached an informed business judgment on September 20, 1980; and (B) if they did not, whether the directors' actions taken subsequent to September 20 were adequate to cure any infirmity in their action taken on September 20. We first consider the directors' September 20 action in terms of their reaching an informed business judgment.

-A-

On the record before us, we must conclude that the Board of Directors did not reach an informed business judgment on September 20, 1980 in voting to "sell" the Company for $55 per share pursuant to the Pritzker cash-out merger proposal. Our reasons, in summary, are as follows:

The directors (1) did not adequately inform themselves as to Van Gorkom's role in forcing the "sale" of the Company and in establishing the per share purchase price; (2) were uninformed as to the intrinsic value of the Company; and (3) given these circumstances, at a minimum, were grossly negligent in approving the "sale" of the Company upon two hours' consideration, without prior notice, and without the exigency of a crisis or emergency.

As has been noted, the Board based its September 20 decision to approve the cash-out merger primarily on Van Gorkom's representations. None of the directors, other than Van Gorkom and Chelberg, had any prior knowledge that the purpose of the meeting was to propose a cash-out merger of Trans Union. No members of Senior Management were present, other than Chelberg, Romans and Peterson; and the latter two had only learned of the proposed sale an hour earlier. Both general counsel Moore and former general counsel Browder attended the meeting, but were equally uninformed as to the purpose of the meeting and the documents to be acted upon.

Without any documents before them concerning the proposed transaction, the members of the Board were required to rely entirely upon Van Gorkom's 20-minute oral presentation of the proposal. No written summary of the terms of the merger was presented; the directors were given no documentation to support the adequacy of $55 price per share for sale of the Company; and the Board had before it nothing more than Van Gorkom's statement of his understanding of the substance of an agreement which he admittedly had never read, nor which any member of the Board had ever seen.

Under 8 *Del.C.* § 141(e), "directors are fully protected in relying in good faith on reports made by officers." [...] The term "report" has been liberally construed to include reports of informal personal investigations by corporate officers, *Cheff v. Mathes*, Del.Supr., 199 A.2d 548, 556 (1964). However, there is no evidence that any "report," as defined under § 141(e), concerning the Pritzker proposal, was presented to the Board on September 20.[16] Van Gorkom's oral presentation of his understanding of the terms of the proposed Merger Agreement, which he had not seen, and Romans' brief oral statement of his preliminary study regarding the feasibility of a leveraged buy-out of Trans Union do not qualify as § 141(e) "reports" for these reasons: The former lacked substance because Van Gorkom was basically uninformed as to the essential provisions of the very document about which he was talking. Romans' statement was irrelevant to the issues before the Board since it did not purport to be a valuation study. At a minimum for a report to enjoy the status conferred by § 141(e), it must be pertinent to the subject matter upon which a board is called to act, and otherwise be entitled to good faith, not blind, reliance. Considering all of the surrounding circumstances—hastily calling the meeting without prior notice of its subject

---

[16] In support of the defendants' argument that their judgment as to the adequacy of $55 per share was an informed one, the directors rely on the BCG study and the Five Year Forecast. However, no one even referred to either of these studies at the September 20 meeting; and it is conceded that these materials do not represent valuation studies. Hence, these documents do not constitute evidence as to whether the directors reached an informed judgment on September 20 that $55 per share was a fair value for sale of the Company.

matter, the proposed sale of the Company without any prior consideration of the issue or necessity therefor, the urgent time constraints imposed by Pritzker, and the total absence of any documentation whatsoever—the directors were duty bound to make reasonable inquiry of Van Gorkom and Romans, and if they had done so, the inadequacy of that upon which they now claim to have relied would have been apparent.

The defendants rely on the following factors to sustain the Trial Court's finding that the Board's decision was an informed one: (1) the magnitude of the premium or spread between the $55 Pritzker offering price and Trans Union's current market price of $38 per share; (2) the amendment of the Agreement as submitted on September 20 to permit the Board to accept any better offer during the "market test" period; (3) the collective experience and expertise of the Board's "inside" and "outside" directors; and (4) their reliance on Brennan's legal advice that the directors might be sued if they rejected the Pritzker proposal. We discuss each of these grounds *seriatim:*

(1)

A substantial premium may provide one reason to recommend a merger, but in the absence of other sound valuation information, the fact of a premium alone does not provide an adequate basis upon which to assess the fairness of an offering price. Here, the judgment reached as to the adequacy of the premium was based on a comparison between the historically depressed Trans Union market price and the amount of the Pritzker offer. Using market price as a basis for concluding that the premium adequately reflected the true value of the Company was a clearly faulty, indeed fallacious, premise, as the defendants' own evidence demonstrates.

The record is clear that before September 20, Van Gorkom and other members of Trans Union's Board knew that the market had consistently undervalued the worth of Trans Union's stock, despite steady increases in the Company's operating income in the seven years preceding the merger. The Board related this occurrence in large part to Trans Union's inability to use its ITCs as previously noted. Van Gorkom testified that he did not believe the market price accurately reflected Trans Union's true worth; and several of the directors testified that, as a general rule, most chief executives think that the market undervalues their companies' stock. Yet, on September 20, Trans Union's Board apparently believed that the market stock price accurately reflected the value of the Company for the purpose of determining the adequacy of the premium for its sale.

In the Proxy Statement, however, the directors reversed their position. There, they stated that, although the earnings prospects for Trans Union were "excellent," they found no basis for believing that this would be reflected in future stock prices. With regard to past trading, the Board stated that the prices at which the Company's common stock had traded in recent years did not reflect the "inherent" value of the Company. But having referred to the "inherent" value of Trans Union, the directors ascribed no number to it. Moreover, nowhere did they disclose that they had no basis on which to fix "inherent" worth beyond an impressionistic reaction to the premium over market and an unsubstantiated belief that the value of the assets was "significantly greater" than book value. By their own admission

95

they could not rely on the stock price as an accurate measure of value. Yet, also by their own admission, the Board members assumed that Trans Union's market price was adequate to serve as a basis upon which to assess the adequacy of the premium for purposes of the September 20 meeting.

The parties do not dispute that a publicly-traded stock price is solely a measure of the value of a minority position and, thus, market price represents only the value of a single share. Nevertheless, on September 20, the Board assessed the adequacy of the premium over market, offered by Pritzker, solely by comparing it with Trans Union's current and historical stock price. (*See supra* note 5 at 866.)

Indeed, as of September 20, the Board had no other information on which to base a determination of the intrinsic value of Trans Union as a going concern. As of September 20, the Board had made no evaluation of the Company designed to value the entire enterprise, nor had the Board ever previously considered selling the Company or consenting to a buy-out merger. Thus, the adequacy of a premium is indeterminate unless it is assessed in terms of other competent and sound valuation information that reflects the value of the particular business.

Despite the foregoing facts and circumstances, there was no call by the Board, either on September 20 or thereafter, for any valuation study or documentation of the $55 price per share as a measure of the fair value of the Company in a cash-out context. It is undisputed that the major asset of Trans Union was its cash flow. Yet, at no time did the Board call for a valuation study taking into account that highly significant element of the Company's assets.

We do not imply that an outside valuation study is essential to support an informed business judgment; nor do we state that fairness opinions by independent investment bankers are required as a matter of law. Often insiders familiar with the business of a going concern are in a better position than are outsiders to gather relevant information; and under appropriate circumstances, such directors may be fully protected in relying in good faith upon the valuation reports of their management. *See 8 Del.C.* § 141(e). *See also Cheff v. Mathes, supra.*

Here, the record establishes that the Board did not request its Chief Financial Officer, Romans, to make any valuation study or review of the proposal to determine the adequacy of $55 per share for sale of the Company. On the record before us: The Board rested on Romans' elicited response that the $55 figure was within a "fair price range" within the context of a leveraged buy-out. No director sought any further information from Romans. No director asked him why he put $55 at the bottom of his range. No director asked Romans for any details as to his study, the reason why it had been undertaken or its depth. No director asked to see the study; and no director asked Romans whether Trans Union's finance department could do a fairness study within the remaining 36-hour[18] period available under the Pritzker offer.

---

[18] Romans' department study was not made available to the Board until circulation of Trans Union's Supplementary Proxy Statement and the Board's meeting of January 26, 1981, on the eve of the

Had the Board, or any member, made an inquiry of Romans, he presumably would have responded as he testified: that his calculations were rough and preliminary; and, that the study was not designed to determine the fair value of the Company, but rather to assess the feasibility of a leveraged buy-out financed by the Company's projected cash flow, making certain assumptions as to the purchaser's borrowing needs. Romans would have presumably also informed the Board of his view, and the widespread view of Senior Management, that the timing of the offer was wrong and the offer inadequate.

The record also establishes that the Board accepted without scrutiny Van Gorkom's representation as to the fairness of the $55 price per share for sale of the Company—a subject that the Board had never previously considered. The Board thereby failed to discover that Van Gorkom had suggested the $55 price to Pritzker and, most crucially, that Van Gorkom had arrived at the $55 figure based on calculations designed solely to determine the feasibility of a leveraged buy-out.[19] No questions were raised either as to the tax implications of a cash-out merger or how the price for the one million share option granted Pritzker was calculated.

We do not say that the Board of Directors was not entitled to give some credence to Van Gorkom's representation that $55 was an adequate or fair price. Under § 141(e), the directors were entitled to rely upon their chairman's opinion of value and adequacy, provided that such opinion was reached on a sound basis. Here, the issue is whether the directors informed themselves as to all information that was reasonably available to them. Had they done so, they would have learned of the source and derivation of the $55 price and could not reasonably have relied thereupon in good faith.

None of the directors, Management or outside, were investment bankers or financial analysts. Yet the Board did not consider recessing the meeting until a later hour that day (or requesting an extension of Pritzker's Sunday evening deadline) to give it time to elicit more information as to the sufficiency of the offer, either from inside Management (in particular Romans) or from Trans Union's own investment banker, Salomon Brothers, whose Chicago specialist in merger and acquisitions was known to the Board and familiar with Trans Union's affairs.

---

shareholder meeting; and, as has been noted, the study has never been produced for inclusion in the record in this case.

[19] As of September 20 the directors did not know: that Van Gorkom had arrived at the $55 figure alone, and subjectively, as the figure to be used by Controller Peterson in creating a feasible structure for a leveraged buy-out by a prospective purchaser; that Van Gorkom had not sought advice, information or assistance from either inside or outside Trans Union directors as to the value of the Company as an entity or the fair price per share for 100% of its stock; that Van Gorkom had not consulted with the Company's investment bankers or other financial analysts; that Van Gorkom had not consulted with or confided in any officer or director of the Company except Chelberg; and that Van Gorkom had deliberately chosen to ignore the advice and opinion of the members of his Senior Management group regarding the adequacy of the $55 price.

Thus, the record compels the conclusion that on September 20 the Board lacked valuation information adequate to reach an informed business judgment as to the fairness of $55 per share for sale of the Company.

(2)

This brings us to the post-September 20 "market test" upon which the defendants ultimately rely to confirm the reasonableness of their September 20 decision to accept the Pritzker proposal. In this connection, the directors present a two-part argument: (a) that by making a "market test" of Pritzker's $55 per share offer a condition of their September 20 decision to accept his offer, they cannot be found to have acted impulsively or in an uninformed manner on September 20; and (b) that the adequacy of the $17 premium for sale of the Company was conclusively established over the following 90 to 120 days by the most reliable evidence available—the marketplace. Thus, the defendants impliedly contend that the "market test" eliminated the need for the Board to perform any other form of fairness test either on September 20, or thereafter.

Again, the facts of record do not support the defendants' argument. There is no evidence: (a) that the Merger Agreement was effectively amended to give the Board freedom to put Trans Union up for auction sale to the highest bidder; or (b) that a public auction was in fact permitted to occur. The minutes of the Board meeting make no reference to any of this. Indeed, the record compels the conclusion that the directors had no rational basis for expecting that a market test was attainable, given the terms of the Agreement as executed during the evening of September 20. We rely upon the following facts which are essentially uncontradicted:

The Merger Agreement, specifically identified as that originally presented to the Board on September 20, has never been produced by the defendants, notwithstanding the plaintiffs' several demands for production before as well as during trial. No acceptable explanation of this failure to produce documents has been given to either the Trial Court or this Court. Significantly, neither the defendants nor their counsel have made the affirmative representation that this critical document has been produced. Thus, the Court is deprived of the best evidence on which to judge the merits of the defendants' position as to the care and attention which they gave to the terms of the Agreement on September 20.

Van Gorkom states that the Agreement as submitted incorporated the ingredients for a market test by authorizing Trans Union to receive competing offers over the next 90-day period. However, he concedes that the Agreement barred Trans Union from actively soliciting such offers and from furnishing to interested parties any information about the Company other than that already in the public domain. Whether the original Agreement of September 20 went so far as to authorize Trans Union to receive competitive proposals is arguable. The defendants' unexplained failure to produce and identify the original Merger Agreement permits the logical inference that the instrument would not support their assertions in this regard. *Wilmington Trust Co. v. General Motors Corp.,* Del.Supr., 51 A.2d 584, 593 (1947); II *Wigmore on Evidence* § 291 (3d ed. 1940). It is a well established principle that the production of weak evidence when strong is, or should have been, available can lead only to the conclusion that the strong would have been adverse. *Interstate Circuit v. United States,* 306 U.S. 208, 226, 59 S.Ct. 467, 474, 83 L.Ed. 610 (1939); *Deberry v. State,* Del.Supr., 457 A.2d 744, 754 (1983). Van Gorkom, conceding that he never read the Agreement, stated that he was relying upon his understanding that, under corporate law, directors always have an inherent right, as well as a fiduciary duty, to accept a better offer notwithstanding an existing contractual commitment by the Board. (See the discussion *infra,* part III B(3) at p. 55.)

The defendant directors assert that they "insisted" upon including two amendments to the Agreement, thereby permitting a market test: (1) to give Trans Union the right to accept a better offer; and (2) to reserve to Trans Union the right to distribute proprietary information on the Company to alternative bidders. Yet, the defendants concede that they did not seek to amend the Agreement to permit Trans Union to solicit competing offers.

Several of Trans Union's outside directors resolutely maintained that the Agreement as submitted was approved on the understanding that, "if we got a better deal, we had a right to take it." Director Johnson so testified; but he then added, "And if they didn't put that in the agreement, then the management did not carry out the conclusion of the Board. And I just don't know whether they did or not." The only clause in the Agreement as finally executed to which the defendants can point as "keeping the door open" is the following underlined statement found in subparagraph (a) of section 2.03 of the Merger Agreement as executed:

> The Board of Directors shall recommend to the stockholders of Trans Union that they approve and adopt the Merger Agreement (`the stockholders' approval') and to use its best efforts to obtain the requisite votes therefor. *GL acknowledges that Trans Union directors may have a competing fiduciary obligation to the shareholders under certain circumstances.*

Clearly, this language on its face cannot be construed as incorporating either of the two "conditions" described above: either the right to accept a better offer or the right to distribute proprietary information to third parties. The logical witness for the defendants to call to confirm their construction of this clause of the Agreement would have been Trans Union's outside attorney, James Brennan. The defendants' failure, without explanation, to call this witness again permits the logical inference that his testimony would not have been helpful to them. The further fact that the directors adjourned, rather than recessed, the meeting without incorporating in the Agreement these important "conditions" further weakens the defendants' position. As has been noted, nothing in the Board's Minutes supports these claims. No reference to either of the so-called "conditions" or of Trans Union's reserved right to test the market appears in any notes of the Board meeting or in the Board Resolution accepting the Pritzker offer or in the Minutes of the meeting itself. That evening, in the midst of a formal party which he hosted for the opening of the Chicago Lyric Opera, Van Gorkom executed the Merger Agreement without he or any other member of the Board having read the instruments.

The defendants attempt to downplay the significance of the prohibition against Trans Union's actively soliciting competing offers by arguing that the directors "understood that the entire financial community would know that Trans Union was for sale upon the announcement of the Pritzker offer, and anyone desiring to make a better offer was free to do so." Yet, the press release issued on September 22, with the authorization of the Board, stated that Trans Union had entered into "definitive agreements" with the Pritzkers; and the press release did not even disclose Trans Union's limited right to receive and accept higher offers. Accompanying this press release was a further public announcement that Pritzker had been granted an option to purchase at any time one million shares of Trans Union's capital stock at 75 cents above the then-current price per share.

Thus, notwithstanding what several of the outside directors later claimed to have "thought" occurred at the meeting, the record compels the conclusion that Trans Union's Board had no rational basis to conclude on September 20 or in the days immediately following, that the Board's acceptance of Pritzker's offer was conditioned on (1) a "market test" of the offer; and (2) the Board's right to withdraw from the Pritzker Agreement and accept any higher offer received before the shareholder meeting.

(3)

The directors' unfounded reliance on both the premium and the market test as the basis for accepting the Pritzker proposal undermines the defendants' remaining contention that the Board's collective experience and sophistication was a sufficient basis for finding that it reached its September 20 decision with informed, reasonable deliberation.[21] [...]

(4)

Part of the defense is based on a claim that the directors relied on legal advice rendered at the September 20 meeting by James Brennan, Esquire, who was present at Van Gorkom's request. [...]

Several defendants testified that Brennan advised them that Delaware law did not require a fairness opinion or an outside valuation of the Company before the Board could act on the Pritzker proposal. If given, the advice was correct. However, that did not end the matter. Unless the directors had before them adequate information regarding the intrinsic value of

---

[21] Trans Union's five "inside" directors had backgrounds in law and accounting, 116 years of collective employment by the Company and 68 years of combined experience on its Board. Trans Union's five "outside" directors included four chief executives of major corporations and an economist who was a former dean of a major school of business and chancellor of a university. The "outside" directors had 78 years of combined experience as chief executive officers of major corporations and 50 years of cumulative experience as directors of Trans Union. Thus, defendants argue that the Board was eminently qualified to reach an informed judgment on the proposed "sale" of Trans Union notwithstanding their lack of any advance notice of the proposal, the shortness of their deliberation, and their determination not to consult with their investment banker or to obtain a fairness opinion.

the Company, upon which a proper exercise of business judgment could be made, mere advice of this type is meaningless; and, given this record of the defendants' failures, it constitutes no defense here.

[...]

A second claim is that counsel advised the Board it would be subject to lawsuits if it rejected the $55 per share offer. It is, of course, a fact of corporate life that today when faced with difficult or sensitive issues, directors often are subject to suit, irrespective of the decisions they make. However, counsel's mere acknowledgement of this circumstance cannot be rationally translated into a justification for a board permitting itself to be stampeded into a patently unadvised act. While suit might result from the rejection of a merger or tender offer, Delaware law makes clear that a board acting within the ambit of the business judgment rule faces no ultimate liability. *Pogostin v. Rice, supra.* Thus, we cannot conclude that the mere threat of litigation, acknowledged by counsel, constitutes either legal advice or any valid basis upon which to pursue an uninformed course.

[...]

-B-

We now examine the Board's post-September 20 conduct for the purpose of determining first, whether it was informed and not grossly negligent; and second, if informed, whether it was sufficient to legally rectify and cure the Board's derelictions of September 20.

(1)

First, as to the Board meeting of October 8 [...]

the primary purpose of the October 8 Board meeting was to amend the Merger Agreement, in a manner agreeable to Pritzker, to permit Trans Union to conduct a "market test."[24] Van Gorkom understood that the proposed amendments were intended to give the Company an unfettered "right to openly solicit offers down through January 31." Van Gorkom presumably so represented the amendments to Trans Union's Board members on October 8. In a brief session, the directors approved Van Gorkom's oral presentation of the substance of the proposed amendments, the terms of which were not reduced to writing

---

[24] As previously noted, the Board mistakenly thought that it had amended the September 20 draft agreement to include a market test. A secondary purpose of the October 8 meeting was to obtain the Board's approval for Trans Union to employ its investment advisor, Salomon Brothers, for the limited purpose of assisting Management in the solicitation of other offers. Neither Management nor the Board then or thereafter requested Salomon Brothers to submit its opinion as to the fairness of Pritzker's $55 cash-out merger proposal or to value Trans Union as an entity. There is no evidence of record that the October 8 meeting had any other purpose; and we also note that the Minutes of the October 8 Board meeting, including any notice of the meeting, are not part of the voluminous records of this case.

until October 10. But rather than waiting to review the amendments, the Board again approved them sight unseen and adjourned, giving Van Gorkom authority to execute the papers when he received them.[25]

[...]

The October 10 amendments to the Merger Agreement did authorize Trans Union to solicit competing offers, but the amendments had more far-reaching effects. The most significant change was in the definition of the third-party "offer" available to Trans Union as a possible basis for withdrawal from its Merger Agreement with Pritzker. Under the October 10 amendments, a better *offer* was no longer sufficient to permit Trans Union's withdrawal. Trans Union was now permitted to terminate the Pritzker Agreement and abandon the merger only if, prior to February 10, 1981, Trans Union had either consummated a merger (or sale of assets) with a third party or had entered into a "definitive" merger agreement more favorable than Pritzker's and for a greater consideration—subject only to stockholder approval. Further, the "extension" of the market test period to February 10, 1981 was circumscribed by other amendments which required Trans Union to file its preliminary proxy statement on the Pritzker merger proposal by December 5, 1980 and use its best efforts to mail the statement to its shareholders by January 5, 1981. Thus, the market test period was effectively reduced, not extended. (*See infra* note 29 at 886.)

In our view, the record compels the conclusion that the directors' conduct on October 8 exhibited the same deficiencies as did their conduct on September 20. The Board permitted its Merger Agreement with Pritzker to be amended in a manner it had neither authorized nor intended. [...]

We conclude that the Board acted in a grossly negligent manner on October 8 [...]

(2)

Next, as to the "curative" effects of the Board's post-September 20 conduct, we review in more detail the reaction of Van Gorkom to the KKR proposal and the results of the Board-sponsored "market test."

The KKR proposal was the first and only offer received subsequent to the Pritzker Merger Agreement. The offer resulted primarily from the efforts of Romans and other senior officers to propose an alternative to Pritzker's acquisition of Trans Union. In late September, Romans' group contacted KKR about the possibility of a leveraged buy-out by all members of Management, except Van Gorkom. By early October, Henry R. Kravis of KKR

---

[25] We do not suggest that a board must read *in haec verba* every contract or legal document which it approves, but if it is to successfully absolve itself from charges of the type made here, there must be some credible contemporary evidence demonstrating that the directors knew what they were doing, and ensured that their purported action was given effect. That is the consistent failure which cast this Board upon its unredeemable course.

gave Romans written notice of KKR's "interest in making an offer to purchase 100%" of Trans Union's common stock.

Thereafter, and until early December, Romans' group worked with KKR to develop a proposal. It did so with Van Gorkom's knowledge and apparently grudging consent. On December 2, Kravis and Romans hand-delivered to Van Gorkom a formal letter-offer to purchase all of Trans Union's assets and to assume all of its liabilities for an aggregate cash consideration equivalent to $60 per share. The offer was contingent upon completing equity and bank financing of $650 million, which Kravis represented as 80% complete. The KKR letter made reference to discussions with major banks regarding the loan portion of the buy-out cost and stated that KKR was "confident that commitments for the bank financing * * * can be obtained within two or three weeks." The purchasing group was to include certain named key members of Trans Union's Senior Management, excluding Van Gorkom, and a major Canadian company. Kravis stated that they were willing to enter into a "definitive agreement" under terms and conditions "substantially the same" as those contained in Trans Union's agreement with Pritzker. The offer was addressed to Trans Union's Board of Directors and a meeting with the Board, scheduled for that afternoon, was requested.

Van Gorkom's reaction to the KKR proposal was completely negative; he did not view the offer as being firm because of its financing condition. It was pointed out, to no avail, that Pritzker's offer had not only been similarly conditioned, but accepted on an expedited basis. Van Gorkom refused Kravis' request that Trans Union issue a press release announcing KKR's offer, on the ground that it might "chill" any other offer. Romans and Kravis left with the understanding that their proposal would be presented to Trans Union's Board that afternoon.

Within a matter of hours and shortly before the scheduled Board meeting, Kravis withdrew his letter-offer. He gave as his reason a sudden decision by the Chief Officer of Trans Union's rail car leasing operation to withdraw from the KKR purchasing group. Van Gorkom had spoken to that officer about his participation in the KKR proposal immediately after his meeting with Romans and Kravis. However, Van Gorkom denied any responsibility for the officer's change of mind.

At the Board meeting later that afternoon, Van Gorkom did not inform the directors of the KKR proposal because he considered it "dead." Van Gorkom did not contact KKR again until January 20, when faced with the realities of this lawsuit, he then attempted to reopen negotiations. KKR declined due to the imminence of the February 10 stockholder meeting.

GE Credit Corporation's interest in Trans Union did not develop until November; and it made no written proposal until mid-January. Even then, its proposal was not in the form of an offer. Had there been time to do so, GE Credit was prepared to offer between $2 and $5 per share above the $55 per share price which Pritzker offered. But GE Credit needed an additional 60 to 90 days; and it was unwilling to make a formal offer without a concession from Pritzker extending the February 10 "deadline" for Trans Union's stockholder meeting. As previously stated, Pritzker refused to grant such extension; and on January 21, GE Credit

103

terminated further negotiations with Trans Union. Its stated reasons, among others, were its "unwillingness to become involved in a bidding contest with Pritzker in the absence of the willingness of [the Pritzker interests] to terminate the proposed $55 cash merger."

* * *

In the absence of any explicit finding by the Trial Court as to the reasonableness of Trans Union's directors' reliance on a market test and its feasibility, we may make our own findings based on the record. Our review of the record compels a finding that confirmation of the appropriateness of the Pritzker offer by an unfettered or free market test was virtually meaningless in the face of the terms and time limitations of Trans Union's Merger Agreement with Pritzker as amended October 10, 1980.

(3)

Finally, we turn to the Board's meeting of January 26, 1981. The defendant directors rely upon the action there taken to refute the contention that they did not reach an informed business judgment in approving the Pritzker merger. [...]

* * *

Upon the basis of the foregoing, we hold that the defendants' post-September conduct did not cure the deficiencies of their September 20 conduct; and that, accordingly, the Trial Court erred in according to the defendants the benefits of the business judgment rule.

[...]

VI.

To summarize: we hold that the directors of Trans Union breached their fiduciary duty to their stockholders (1) by their failure to inform themselves of all information reasonably available to them and relevant to their decision to recommend the Pritzker merger; and (2) by their failure to disclose all material information such as a reasonable stockholder would consider important in deciding whether to approve the Pritzker offer.

We hold, therefore, that the Trial Court committed reversible error in applying the business judgment rule in favor of the director defendants in this case.

On remand, the Court of Chancery shall conduct an evidentiary hearing to determine the fair value of the shares represented by the plaintiffs' class, based on the intrinsic value of Trans Union on September 20, 1980. Such valuation shall be made in accordance with *Weinberger v. UOP, Inc., supra* at 712-715. Thereafter, an award of damages may be entered to the extent that the fair value of Trans Union exceeds $55 per share.

* * *

REVERSED and REMANDED for proceedings consistent herewith.

McNEILLY, Justice, dissenting:

The majority opinion reads like an advocate's closing address to a hostile jury. And I say that not lightly. Throughout the opinion great emphasis is directed only to the negative, with nothing more than lip service granted the positive aspects of this case. In my opinion Chancellor Marvel (retired) should have been affirmed. [...]

The majority has spoken and has effectively said that Trans Union's Directors have been the victims of a "fast shuffle" by Van Gorkom and Pritzker. That is the beginning of the majority's comedy of errors. The first and most important error made is the majority's assessment of the directors' knowledge of the affairs of Trans Union and their combined ability to act in this situation under the protection of the business judgment rule.

Trans Union's Board of Directors consisted of ten men, five of whom were "inside" directors and five of whom were "outside" directors. The "inside" directors were Van Gorkom, Chelberg, Bonser, William B. Browder, Senior Vice-President-Law, and Thomas P. O'Boyle, Senior Vice-President-Administration. At the time the merger was proposed the inside five directors had collectively been employed by the Company for 116 years and had 68 years of combined experience as directors. The "outside" directors were A.W. Wallis, William B. Johnson, Joseph B. Lanterman, Graham J. Morgan and Robert W. Reneker. With the exception of Wallis, these were all chief executive officers of Chicago based corporations that were at least as large as Trans Union. The five "outside" directors had 78 years of combined experience as chief executive officers, and 53 years cumulative service as Trans Union directors.

The inside directors wear their badge of expertise in the corporate affairs of Trans Union on their sleeves. But what about the outsiders? Dr. Wallis is or was an economist and math statistician, a professor of economics at Yale University, dean of the graduate school of business at the University of Chicago, and Chancellor of the University of Rochester. Dr. Wallis had been on the Board of Trans Union since 1962. He also was on the Board of Bausch & Lomb, Kodak, Metropolitan Life Insurance Company, Standard Oil and others.

William B. Johnson is a University of Pennsylvania law graduate, President of Railway Express until 1966, Chairman and Chief Executive of I.C. Industries Holding Company, and member of Trans Union's Board since 1968.

Joseph Lanterman, a Certified Public Accountant, is or was President and Chief Executive of American Steel, on the Board of International Harvester, Peoples Energy, Illinois Bell Telephone, Harris Bank and Trust Company, Kemper Insurance Company and a director of Trans Union for four years.

Graham Morgan is a chemist, was Chairman and Chief Executive Officer of U.S. Gypsum, and in the 17 and 18 years prior to the Trans Union transaction had been involved in 31 or 32 corporate takeovers.

Robert Reneker attended University of Chicago and Harvard Business Schools. He was President and Chief Executive of Swift and Company, director of Trans Union since 1971, and member of the Boards of seven other corporations including U.S. Gypsum and the Chicago Tribune.

Directors of this caliber are not ordinarily taken in by a "fast shuffle". [...] These men knew Trans Union like the back of their hands and were more than well qualified to make on the spot informed business judgments concerning the affairs of Trans Union including a 100% sale of the corporation. Lest we forget, the corporate world of then and now operates on what is so aptly referred to as "the fast track". These men were at the time an integral part of that world, all professional business men, not intellectual figureheads.

[...]

I have no quarrel with the majority's analysis of the business judgment rule. It is the application of that rule to these facts which is wrong. An overview of the entire record, rather than the limited view of bits and pieces which the majority has exploded like popcorn, convinces me that the directors made an informed business judgment which was buttressed by their test of the market.

[...]

CHRISTIE, Justice, dissenting:

I respectfully dissent.

Considering the standard and scope of our review under *Levitt v. Bouvier,* Del. Supr., 287 A.2d 671, 673 (1972), I believe that the record taken as a whole supports a conclusion that the actions of the defendants are protected by the business judgment rule. *Aronson v. Lewis,* Del.Supr., 473 A.2d 805, 812 (1984); *Pogostin v. Rice,* Del.Supr., 480 A.2d 619, 627 (1984). I also am satisfied that the record supports a conclusion that the defendants acted with the complete candor required by *Lynch v. Vickers Energy Corp.,* Del.Supr., 383 A.2d 278 (1978). Under the circumstances I would affirm the judgment of the Court of Chancery.

[...]

Note:

Van Gorkom is often cited as the one instance in Corporate America where director defendants had to pay out-of-pocket for breach of the duty of care. However, this is a misconception. The settlement in the Van Gorkom case worked out to $23 million, $10 million of which was covered by insurance. Jay Pritzker picked up the remaining $13 million, in part because some of the Trans Union directors could not pay their share, and in part because Pritzker believed that the Trans Union board had done nothing wrong.

Discussion Questions:

1. According to the majority opinion, what did the directors do wrong? In other words, what should the directors have done differently? Why did the business judgment rule not apply? What are the dissenters' counter-arguments?

2. *Van Gorkom* was remanded for a determination of the value of the Trans Union shares at the time of the board's decision, and for an award of damages to the extent that the fair value exceeded $55 per share. The case was settled prior to this determination for an additional $1.87 per share. So putting it all together, the stock was trading at $35, the company was sold for $55, and "fair value" according to the settlement was $56.87. Does this settlement influence your judgment on what the defendant directors did wrong?

3. How do you think directors in other companies directed to this decision—what, if anything, did they most likely do differently after *Van Gorkom*?

Van Gorkom caused a firestorm. Liability insurance rates for directors skyrocketed. The Delaware legislature intervened by enacting DGCL 102(b)(7), which allows exculpatory charter provisions to eliminate damages for breaches of the duty of care. Such charter provisions are now standard. Even without them, however, it is unlikely that a Delaware court would impose liability on these facts today. The courts seem to have retrenched—not in their doctrine but in how they apply it. *Cf. Disney* below. You should, therefore, read the case not as an exemplary application of the duty of care, but as a policy experiment: why is the corporate world so opposed to monetary damages on these facts?

After *Smith v. Van Gorkom, Disney* is the closest Delaware courts have come to imposing monetary liability on disinterested directors. The litigation was heavily colored by Disney's 102(b)(7) waiver, which Disney and most other large corporations had adopted after *Van Gorkom*. The Delaware Supreme Court, however, chose first to make an affirmative finding that the defendants met even the default standard of due care. As you read that part of the opinion (chiefly IV.A.1), ask yourself why the court reached the opposite result from *Van Gorkom*. The *Disney* court also addresses "good faith," which is a necessary condition for liability protection under DGCL 102(b)(7) (as well as for indemnification under DGCL 145(a) and (b)).

In re The Walt Disney Company Derivative Litigation
906 A.2d 27 (Del. 2006)

JACOBS, Justice.

In August 1995, Michael Ovitz ("Ovitz") and The Walt Disney Company ("Disney" or the "Company") entered into an employment agreement under which Ovitz would serve as President of Disney for five years. In December 1996, only fourteen months after he commenced employment, Ovitz was terminated without cause, resulting in a severance payout to Ovitz valued at approximately $130 million.

In January 1997, several Disney shareholders brought derivative actions in the Court of Chancery, on behalf of Disney, against Ovitz and the directors of Disney who served at the time of the events complained of (the "Disney defendants"). The plaintiffs claimed that the $130 million severance payout was the product of fiduciary duty and contractual breaches by Ovitz, and breaches of fiduciary duty by the Disney defendants, and a waste of assets. After the disposition of several pretrial motions and an appeal to this Court, the case was tried before the Chancellor over 37 days between October 20, 2004 and January 19, 2005. In August 2005, the Chancellor handed down a well-crafted 174 page Opinion and Order, determining that "the director defendants did not breach their fiduciary duties or commit waste." The Court entered judgment in favor of all defendants on all claims alleged in the amended complaint.

The plaintiffs have appealed from that judgment, claiming that the Court of Chancery committed multitudinous errors. We conclude, for the reasons that follow, that the Chancellor's factual findings and legal rulings were correct and not erroneous in any respect. Accordingly, the judgment entered by the Court of Chancery will be affirmed.

I. THE FACTS

We next summarize the facts as found by the Court of Chancery that are material to the issues presented on this appeal. The critical events flow from what turned out to be an unfortunate hiring decision at Disney, a company that for over half a century has been one of America's leading film and entertainment enterprises.

In 1994 Disney lost in a tragic helicopter crash its President and Chief Operating Officer, Frank Wells, who together with Michael Eisner, Disney's Chairman and Chief Executive Officer, had enjoyed remarkable success at the Company's helm. Eisner temporarily assumed Disney's presidency, but only three months later, heart disease required Eisner to undergo quadruple bypass surgery. Those two events persuaded Eisner and Disney's board of directors that the time had come to identify a successor to Eisner.

Eisner's prime candidate for the position was Michael Ovitz, who was the leading partner and one of the founders of Creative Artists Agency ("CAA"), the premier talent agency whose business model had reshaped the entire industry. By 1995, CAA had 550 employees and a roster of about 1400 of Hollywood's top actors, directors, writers, and musicians. That roster generated about $150 million in annual revenues and an annual income of over $20 million for Ovitz, who was regarded as one of the most powerful figures in Hollywood.

Eisner and Ovitz had enjoyed a social and professional relationship that spanned nearly 25 years. Although in the past the two men had casually discussed possibly working together, in 1995, when Ovitz began negotiations to leave CAA and join Music Corporation of America ("MCA"), Eisner became seriously interested in recruiting Ovitz to join Disney. Eisner shared that desire with Disney's board members on an individual basis.

A. Negotiation Of The Ovitz Employment Agreement

Eisner and Irwin Russell, who was a Disney director and chairman of the compensation committee, first approached Ovitz about joining Disney. Their initial negotiations were unproductive, however, because at that time MCA had made Ovitz an offer that Disney could not match. The MCA-Ovitz negotiations eventually fell apart, and Ovitz returned to CAA in mid-1995. Business continued as usual, until Ovitz discovered that Ron Meyer, his close friend and the number two executive at CAA, was leaving CAA to join MCA. That news devastated Ovitz, who concluded that to remain with the company he and Meyer had built together was no longer palatable. At that point Ovitz became receptive to the idea of joining Disney. Eisner learned of these developments and re-commenced negotiations with Ovitz in earnest. By mid-July 1995, those negotiations were in full swing.

Both Russell and Eisner negotiated with Ovitz, over separate issues and concerns. From his talks with Eisner, Ovitz gathered that Disney needed his skills and experience to remedy Disney's current weaknesses, which Ovitz identified as poor talent relationships and stagnant foreign growth. Seeking assurances from Eisner that Ovitz's vision for Disney was shared, at some point during the negotiations Ovitz came to believe that he and Eisner would run Disney, and would work together in a relation akin to that of junior and senior partner. Unfortunately, Ovitz's belief was mistaken, as Eisner had a radically different view of what their respective roles at Disney should be.

Russell assumed the lead in negotiating the financial terms of the Ovitz employment contract. In the course of negotiations, Russell learned from Ovitz's attorney, Bob Goldman, that Ovitz owned 55% of CAA and earned approximately $20 to $25 million a year from that company. From the beginning Ovitz made it clear that he would not give up his 55% interest in CAA without "downside protection." Considerable negotiation then ensued over downside protection issues. During the summer of 1995, the parties agreed to a draft version of Ovitz's employment agreement (the "OEA") modeled after Eisner's and the late Mr. Wells' employment contracts. As described by the Chancellor, the draft agreement included the following terms:

> Under the proposed OEA, Ovitz would receive a five-year contract with two tranches of options. The first tranche consisted of three million options vesting in equal parts in the third, fourth, and fifth years, and if the value of those options at the end of the five years had not appreciated to $50 million, Disney would make up the difference. The second tranche consisted of two million options that would vest immediately if Disney and Ovitz opted to renew the contract.

> The proposed OEA sought to protect both parties in the event that Ovitz's employment ended prematurely, and provided that absent defined causes, neither party could terminate the agreement without penalty. If Ovitz, for example, walked away, for any reason other than those permitted under the OEA, he would forfeit any benefits remaining under the OEA and could be

109

enjoined from working for a competitor. Likewise, if Disney fired Ovitz for any reason other than gross negligence or malfeasance, Ovitz would be entitled to a non-fault payment (Non-Fault Termination or "NFT"), which consisted of his remaining salary, $7.5 million a year for unaccrued bonuses, the immediate vesting of his first tranche of options and a $10 million cash out payment for the second tranche of options.

As the basic terms of the OEA were crystallizing, Russell prepared and gave Ovitz and Eisner a "case study" to explain those terms. In that study, Russell also expressed his concern that the negotiated terms represented an extraordinary level of executive compensation. Russell acknowledged, however, that Ovitz was an "exceptional corporate executive" and "highly successful and unique entrepreneur" who merited "downside protection and upside opportunity." Both would be required to enable Ovitz to adjust to the reduced cash compensation he would receive from a public company, in contrast to the greater cash distributions and other perquisites more typically available from a privately held business. But, Russell did caution that Ovitz's salary would be at the top level for any corporate officer and significantly above that of the Disney CEO. Moreover, the stock options granted under the OEA would exceed the standards applied within Disney and corporate America and would "raise very strong criticism." Russell shared this original case study only with Eisner and Ovitz. He also recommended another, additional study of this issue.

To assist in evaluating the financial terms of the OEA, Russell recruited Graef Crystal, an executive compensation consultant, and Raymond Watson, a member of Disney's compensation committee and a past Disney board chairman who had helped structure Wells' and Eisner's compensation packages. Before the three met, Crystal prepared a comprehensive executive compensation database to accept various inputs and to conduct Black-Scholes analyses to output a range of values for the options. Watson also prepared similar computations on spreadsheets, but without using the Black-Scholes method.

On August 10, Russell, Watson and Crystal met. They discussed and generated a set of values using different and various inputs and assumptions, accounting for different numbers of options, vesting periods, and potential proceeds of option exercises at various times and prices. After discussing their conclusions, they agreed that Crystal would memorialize his findings and fax them to Russell. Two days later, Crystal faxed to Russell a memorandum concluding that the OEA would provide Ovitz with approximately $23.6 million per year for the first five years, or $23.9 million a year over seven years if Ovitz exercised a two year renewal option. Those sums, Crystal opined, would approximate Ovitz's current annual compensation at CAA.

During a telephone conference that same evening, Russell, Watson and Crystal discussed Crystal's memorandum and its assumptions. Their discussion generated additional questions that prompted Russell to ask Crystal to revise his memorandum to resolve certain ambiguities in the current draft of the employment agreement. But, rather than address the points Russell highlighted, Crystal faxed to Russell a new letter that expressed Crystal's concern about the OEA's $50 million option appreciation guarantee. Crystal's concern, based on his understanding of the current draft of the OEA, was that Ovitz could hold the first tranche of options, wait out the five-year term, collect the $50 million guarantee, and then exercise the in-the-money options and receive an additional windfall. Crystal was philosophically opposed to a pay package that would give Ovitz the best of both worlds—low risk and high return.

Addressing Crystal's concerns, Russell made clear that the guarantee would not function as Crystal believed it might. Crystal then revised his original letter, adjusting the value of the OEA (assuming a two year renewal) to $24.1 million per year. Up to that point, only three Disney directors—Eisner, Russell and Watson—knew the status of the negotiations with Ovitz and the terms of the draft OEA.

While Russell, Watson and Crystal were finalizing their analysis of the OEA, Eisner and Ovitz reached a separate agreement. Eisner told Ovitz that: (1) the number of options would be reduced from a single grant of five million to two separate grants, the first being three million options for the first five years and the second consisting of two million more options if the contract was renewed; and (2) Ovitz would join Disney only as President, not as a co-CEO with Eisner. After deliberating, Ovitz accepted those terms, and that evening Ovitz, Eisner, Sid Bass and their families celebrated Ovitz's decision to join Disney.

Unfortunately, the celebratory mood was premature. The next day, August 13, Eisner met with Ovitz, Russell, Sanford Litvack (an Executive Vice President and Disney's General Counsel), and Stephen Bollenbach (Disney's Chief Financial Officer) to discuss the decision to hire Ovitz. Litvack and Bollenbach were unhappy with that decision, and voiced concerns that Ovitz would disrupt the cohesion that existed between Eisner, Litvack and Bollenbach. Litvack and Bollenbach were emphatic that they would not report to Ovitz, but would continue to report to Eisner. Despite Ovitz's concern about his "shrinking authority" as Disney's future President, Eisner was able to provide sufficient reassurance so that ultimately Ovitz acceded to Litvack's and Bollenbach's terms.

On August 14, Eisner and Ovitz signed a letter agreement (the "OLA"), which outlined the basic terms of Ovitz's employment, and stated that the agreement (which would ultimately be embodied in a formal contract) was subject to approval by Disney's compensation committee and board of directors. Russell called Sidney Poitier, a Disney director and compensation committee member, to inform Poitier of the OLA and its terms. Poitier believed that hiring Ovitz was a good idea because of Ovitz's reputation and experience. Watson called Ignacio Lozano, another Disney director and compensation committee member, who felt that Ovitz would successfully adapt from a private company environment to Disney's public company culture. Eisner also contacted each of the other board members by phone to inform them of the impending new hire, and to explain his friendship with Ovitz and Ovitz's qualifications.

That same day, a press release made the news of Ovitz's hiring public. The reaction was extremely positive: Disney was applauded for the decision, and Disney's stock price rose 4.4 % in a single day, thereby increasing Disney's market capitalization by over $1 billion.

Once the OLA was signed, Joseph Santaniello, a Vice President and counsel in Disney's legal department, began to embody in a draft OEA the terms that Russell and Goldman had agreed upon and had been memorialized in the OLA. In the process, Santaniello concluded that the $50 million guarantee created negative tax implications for Disney, because it might not be deductible. Concluding that the guarantee should be eliminated, Russell initiated discussions on how to compensate Ovitz for this change. What resulted were several amendments to the OEA to replace the back-end guarantee. The (to-be-eliminated) $50 million guarantee would be replaced by: (i) a reduction in the option strike price from 115% to 100% of the Company's stock price on the day of the grant for the two million options that would become exercisable in the sixth and seventh year of Ovitz's employment; (ii) a $10 million severance payment if the Company did not renew Ovitz's contract; and (iii) an alteration of the renewal option to provide for a five-year extension, a $1.25 million annual salary, the same bonus structure as the first five years of the contract, and a grant of three million additional options. To assess the potential consequences of the proposed changes, Watson worked with Russell and Crystal, who applied the Black-Scholes method to evaluate the extended exercisability features of the options. Watson also generated his own separate analysis.

On September 26, 1995, the Disney compensation committee (which consisted of Messrs. Russell, Watson, Poitier and Lozano) met for one hour to consider, among other agenda items, the proposed terms of the OEA. A term sheet was distributed at the meeting, although a draft of the OEA was not. The topics discussed were historical comparables, such as Eisner's and Wells' option grants, and also the factors that Russell, Watson and Crystal had considered in setting the size of the option grants and the termination provisions of the contract. Watson testified that he provided the compensation committee with the spreadsheet analysis that he had performed in August, and discussed his findings with the committee. Crystal did not attend the meeting, although he was available by telephone to respond to questions if needed, but no one from the committee called. After Russell's and Watson's presentations, Litvack also responded to substantive questions. At trial Poitier and Lozano testified that they believed they had received sufficient information from Russell's and Watson's presentations to exercise their judgment in the best interests of the Company. The committee voted unanimously to approve the OEA terms, subject to "reasonable further negotiations within the framework of the terms and conditions" described in the OEA.

Immediately after the compensation committee meeting, the Disney board met in executive session. The board was told about the reporting structure to which Ovitz had agreed, but the initial negative reaction of Litvack and Bollenbach to the hiring was not recounted. Eisner led the discussion relating to Ovitz, and Watson then explained his analysis, and both Watson and Russell responded to questions from the board. After further deliberation, the board voted unanimously to elect Ovitz as President.

At its September 26, 1995 meeting, the compensation committee determined that it would delay the formal grant of Ovitz's stock options until further issues between Ovitz and the Company were resolved. That was done, and the committee met again, on October 16, 1995, to discuss stock option-related issues. The committee approved amendments to the

Walt Disney Company 1990 Stock Incentive Plan (the "1990 Plan"), and also approved a new plan, known as the Walt Disney 1995 Stock Incentive Plan (the "1995 Plan"). Both plans were subject to further approval by the full board of directors and the shareholders. Both the amendment to the 1990 Plan and the Stock Option Agreement provided that in the event of a non-fault termination ("NFT"), Ovitz's options would be exercisable until the later of September 30, 2002 or twenty-four months after termination, but in no event later than October 16, 2005. After approving those Plans, the committee unanimously approved the terms of the OEA and the award of Ovitz's options under the 1990 Plan.

B. Ovitz's Performance As President of Disney

Ovitz's tenure as President of the Walt Disney Company officially began on October 1, 1995, the date that the OEA was executed. When Ovitz took office, the initial reaction was optimistic, and Ovitz did make some positive contributions while serving as President of the Company. By the fall of 1996, however, it had become clear that Ovitz was "a poor fit with his fellow executives." By then the Disney directors were discussing that the disconnect between Ovitz and the Company was likely irreparable and that Ovitz would have to be terminated.

The Court of Chancery identified three competing theories as to why Ovitz did not succeed:

> First, plaintiffs argue that Ovitz failed to follow Eisner's directives, especially in regard to acquisitions, and that generally, Ovitz did very little. Second, Ovitz contends Eisner's micromanaging prevented Ovitz from having the authority necessary to make the changes that Ovitz thought were appropriate. In addition, Ovitz believes he was not given enough time for his efforts to bear fruit. Third, the remaining defendants simply posit that Ovitz failed to transition from a private to a public company, from the "sell side to the buy side," and otherwise did not adapt to the Company culture or fit in with other executives. In the end, however, it makes no difference why Ovitz was not as successful as his reputation would have led many to expect, so long as he was not grossly negligent or malfeasant.

Although the plaintiffs attempted to show that Ovitz acted improperly (*i.e.*, with gross negligence or malfeasance) while in office, the Chancellor found that the trial record did not support those accusations. Rejecting the plaintiffs' first factual claim that Ovitz was insubordinate, the Court found that although many of Ovitz's efforts failed to produce results, that was because his efforts often reflected a philosophy opposite to "that held by Eisner, Iger, and Roth." That difference did not mean, however, "that Ovitz intentionally failed to follow Eisner's directives or that [Ovitz] was insubordinate."

The Chancellor also rejected the appellants' second claim—that Ovitz was a habitual liar. The Court found no evidence that Ovitz ever told a material falsehood or made any false or misleading disclosures during his tenure at Disney. Lastly, the Chancellor found that the record did not support, and often contradicted, the appellants' third claim—that Ovitz had violated the Company's policies relating to expenses and to reporting gifts he received while President of Disney.

Nonetheless, Ovitz's relationship with the Disney executives did continue to deteriorate through September 1996. In mid-September, Litvack, with Eisner's approval, told Ovitz that he was not working out at Disney and that he should start looking for a graceful exit from Disney and a new job. Litvack reported this conversation to Eisner, who sent Litvack back to Ovitz to make it clear that Eisner no longer wanted Ovitz at Disney and that Ovitz should seriously consider other opportunities, including one then developing at Sony. Ovitz responded by telling Litvack that he was not leaving and that if Eisner wanted him to leave Disney, Eisner could tell him that to his face.

On September 30, 1996, the Disney board met. During an executive session of that meeting, and in small group discussions where Ovitz was not present, Eisner told the other board members of the continuing problems with Ovitz's performance. On October 1, Eisner wrote a letter to Russell and Watson detailing Eisner's mounting difficulties with Ovitz, including Eisner's lack of trust of Ovitz and Ovitz's failures to adapt to Disney's culture and to alleviate Eisner's workload. Eisner's goal in writing this letter was to prevent Ovitz from succeeding him at Disney. Because of that purpose, the Chancellor found that the letter contained "a good deal of hyperbole to help Eisner 'unsell' Ovitz as his successor." Neither that letter nor its contents were shared with other members of the board.

Those interchanges set the stage for Ovitz's eventual termination as Disney's President.

C. Ovitz's Termination At Disney

After the discussions between Litvack and Ovitz, Eisner and Ovitz met several times. During those meetings they discussed Ovitz's future, including Ovitz's employment prospects at Sony. Eisner believed that because Ovitz had a good, longstanding relationship with many Sony senior executives, Sony would be willing to take Ovitz in "trade" from Disney. Eisner favored such a trade, which would not only remove Ovitz from Disney, but also would relieve Disney of any obligation to pay Ovitz under the OEA. Thereafter, in October 1996, Ovitz, with Eisner's permission, entered into negotiations with Sony. Those negotiations did not prove fruitful, however. On November 1, Ovitz wrote a letter to Eisner notifying him that the Sony negotiations had ended, and that Ovitz had decided to recommit himself to Disney with a greater dedication of his own energies and an increased appreciation of the Disney organization.

In response to this unwelcome news, Eisner wrote (but never sent) a letter to Ovitz on November 11, in which Eisner attempted to make it clear that Ovitz was no longer welcome at Disney. Instead of sending that letter, Eisner met with Ovitz personally on November 13, and discussed much of what the letter contained. Eisner left that meeting believing that "Ovitz just would not listen to what he was trying to tell him and instead, Ovitz insisted that he would stay at Disney, going so far as to state that he would chain himself to his desk."

During this period Eisner was also working with Litvack to explore whether they could terminate Ovitz under the OEA for cause. If so, Disney would not owe Ovitz the NFT payment. From the very beginning, Litvack advised Eisner that he did not believe there was cause to terminate Ovitz under the OEA. Litvack's advice never changed.

At the end of November 1996, Eisner again asked Litvack if Disney had cause to fire Ovitz and thereby avoid the costly NFT payment. Litvack proceeded to examine that issue more carefully. He studied the OEA, refreshed himself on the meaning of "gross negligence" and "malfeasance," and reviewed all the facts concerning Ovitz's performance of which he was aware. Litvack also consulted Val Cohen, co-head of Disney's litigation department and Joseph Santaniello, in Disney's legal department. Cohen and Santaniello both concurred in Litvack's conclusion that no basis existed to terminate Ovitz for cause. Litvack did not personally conduct any legal research or request an outside opinion on the issue, because he believed that it "was not a close question, and in fact, Litvack described it as 'a no brainer.'" Eisner testified that after Litvack notified Eisner that he did not believe cause existed, Eisner "checked with almost anybody that [he] could find that had a legal degree, and there was just no light in that possibility. It was a total dead end from day one." Although the Chancellor was critical of Litvack and Eisner for lacking sufficient documentation to support his conclusion and the work they did to arrive at that conclusion, the Court found that Eisner and Litvack "did in fact make a concerted effort to determine if Ovitz could be terminated for cause, and that despite these efforts, they were unable to manufacture the desired result."

Litvack also believed that it would be inappropriate, unethical and a bad idea to attempt to coerce Ovitz (by threatening a for-cause termination) into negotiating for a smaller NFT package than the OEA provided. The reason was that when pressed by Ovitz's attorneys, Disney would have to admit that in fact there was no cause, which could subject Disney to a wrongful termination lawsuit. Litvack believed that attempting to avoid legitimate contractual obligations would harm Disney's reputation as an honest business partner and would affect its future business dealings.

The Disney board next met on November 25. By then the board knew Ovitz was going to be fired, yet the only action recorded in the minutes concerning Ovitz was his renomination to a new three-year term on the board. Although that action was somewhat bizarre given the circumstances, Stanley Gold, a Disney director, testified that because Ovitz was present at that meeting, it would have been a "public hanging" not to renominate him. An executive session took place after the board meeting, from which Ovitz was excluded. At that session, Eisner informed the directors who were present that he intended to fire Ovitz by year's end, and that he had asked Gary Wilson, a board member and friend of Ovitz, to speak with Ovitz while Wilson and Ovitz were together on vacation during the upcoming Thanksgiving holiday.

Shortly after the November 25 board meeting and executive session, the Ovitz and Wilson families left on their yacht for a Thanksgiving trip to the British Virgin Islands. Ovitz hoped that if he could manage to survive at Disney until Christmas, he could fix everything with Disney and make his problems go away. Wilson quickly dispelled that illusion, informing

Ovitz that Eisner wanted Ovitz out of the Company. At that point Ovitz first began to realize how serious his situation at Disney had become. Reporting back his conversation with Ovitz, Wilson told Eisner that Ovitz was a "loyal friend and devastating enemy," and he advised Eisner to "be reasonable and magnanimous, both financially and publicly, so Ovitz could save face."

After returning from the Thanksgiving trip, Ovitz met with Eisner on December 3, to discuss his termination. Ovitz asked for several concessions, all of which Eisner ultimately rejected. Eisner told Ovitz that all he would receive was what he had contracted for in the OEA.

On December 10, the Executive Performance Plan Committee met to consider annual bonuses for Disney's most highly compensated executive officers. At that meeting, Russell informed those in attendance that Ovitz was going to be terminated, but without cause.

On December 11, Eisner met with Ovitz to agree on the wording of a press release to announce the termination, and to inform Ovitz that he would not receive any of the additional items that he requested. By that time it had already been decided that Ovitz would be terminated without cause and that he would receive his contractual NFT payment, but nothing more. Eisner and Ovitz agreed that neither Ovitz nor Disney would disparage each other in the press, and that the separation was to be undertaken with dignity and respect for both sides. After his December 11 meeting with Eisner, Ovitz never returned to Disney.

Ovitz's termination was memorialized in a letter, dated December 12, 1996, that Litvack signed on Eisner's instruction. The board was not shown the letter, nor did it meet to approve its terms. A press release announcing Ovitz's termination was issued that same day. Before the press release was issued, Eisner attempted to contact each of the board members by telephone to notify them that Ovitz had been officially terminated. None of the board members at that time, or at any other time, objected to Ovitz's termination, and most, if not all, of them thought it was the appropriate step for Eisner to take. Although the board did not meet to vote on the termination, the Chancellor found that most, if not all, of the Disney directors trusted Eisner's and Litvack's conclusion that there was no cause to terminate Ovitz, and that Ovitz should be terminated without cause even though that involved making the costly NFT payment.

A December 27, 1996 letter from Litvack to Ovitz, which Ovitz signed, memorialized the termination, accelerated Ovitz's departure date from January 31, 1997 to December 31, 1996, and informed Ovitz that he would receive roughly $38 million in cash and that the first tranche of three million options would vest immediately. By the terms of that letter agreement, Ovitz's tenure as an executive and a director of Disney officially ended on December 27, 1996. Shortly thereafter, Disney paid Ovitz what was owed under the OEA for an NFT, minus a holdback of $1 million pending final settlement of Ovitz's accounts. One month after Disney paid Ovitz, the plaintiffs filed this action.

II. SUMMARY OF APPELLANTS' CLAIMS OF ERROR

As noted earlier, the Court of Chancery rejected all of the plaintiff-appellants' claims on the merits and entered judgment in favor of the defendant-appellees on all counts. On appeal, the appellants claim that the adverse judgment rests upon multiple erroneous rulings and should be reversed, because the 1995 decision to approve the OEA and the 1996 decision to terminate Ovitz on a non-fault basis, resulted from various breaches of fiduciary duty by Ovitz and the Disney directors.

The appellants' claims of error are most easily analyzed in two separate groupings: (1) the claims against the Disney defendants and (2) the claims against Ovitz. The first category encompasses the claims that the Disney defendants breached their fiduciary duties to act with due care and in good faith by (1) approving the OEA, and specifically, its NFT provisions; and (2) approving the NFT severance payment to Ovitz upon his termination—a payment that is also claimed to constitute corporate waste. It is notable that the appellants do *not* contend that the Disney defendants are directly liable as a consequence of those fiduciary duty breaches. Rather, appellants' core argument is indirect, *i.e.,* that those breaches of fiduciary duty deprive the Disney defendants of the protection of business judgment review, and require them to shoulder the burden of establishing that their acts were entirely fair to Disney. That burden, the appellants contend, the Disney defendants failed to carry. The appellants claim that by ruling that the Disney defendants did not breach their fiduciary duty to act with due care or in good faith, the Court of Chancery committed reversible error in numerous respects. Alternatively, the appellants claim that even if the business judgment presumptions apply, the Disney defendants are nonetheless liable, because the NFT payout constituted corporate waste and the Court of Chancery erred in concluding otherwise.

Falling into the second category are the claims being advanced against Ovitz. Appellants claim that Ovitz breached his fiduciary duties of care and loyalty to Disney by (i) negotiating for and accepting the NFT severance provisions of the OEA, and (ii) negotiating a full NFT payout in connection with his termination. The appellants' position is that by concluding that Ovitz breached no fiduciary duty owed to Disney, the Court of Chancery reversibly erred in several respects.

In this Opinion we address these two groups of claims in reverse order. In Part III, we analyze the claims relating to Ovitz. In Part IV, we address the claims asserted against the Disney defendants.

III. THE CLAIMS AGAINST OVITZ

The appellants argue that the Chancellor erroneously rejected their claims against Ovitz on two distinct grounds. We analyze them separately.

A. Claims Based Upon Ovitz's Conduct Before Assuming Office At Disney

First, appellants contend that the Court of Chancery erred by dismissing their claim, as a summary judgment matter, that Ovitz had breached his fiduciary duties to Disney by negotiating and entering into the OEA. On summary judgment the Chancellor determined that Ovitz had breached no fiduciary duty to Disney, because Ovitz did not become a fiduciary until he formally assumed office on October 1, 1995, by which time the essential terms of the NFT provision had been negotiated. Therefore, the Court of Chancery held, Ovitz's pre-October 1 conduct was not constrained by any fiduciary duty standard.

That ruling was erroneous, appellants argue, because even though Ovitz did not formally assume the title of President until October 1, 1995, he became a *de facto* fiduciary before then. [...]

the *de facto* officer argument lacks merit, both legally and factually. A *de facto* officer is one who actually assumes possession of an office under the claim and color of an election or appointment and who is actually discharging the duties of that office, but for some legal reason lacks *de jure* legal title to that office. Here, Ovitz did not assume, or purport to assume, the duties of the Disney presidency before October 1, 1995. [...]

B. Claims Based Upon Ovitz's Conduct During His Termination As President

The appellants' second claim is that the Court of Chancery erroneously concluded that Ovitz breached no fiduciary duty, including his duty of loyalty, by receiving the NFT payment upon his termination as President of Disney. The Chancellor found:

> Ovitz did not breach his fiduciary duty of loyalty by receiving the NFT payment because he played no part in the decisions: (1) to be terminated and (2) that the termination would not be for cause under the OEA. Ovitz did possess fiduciary duties as a director and officer while these decisions were made, but by not improperly interjecting himself into the corporation's decisionmaking process nor manipulating that process, he did not breach the fiduciary duties he possessed in that unique circumstance. Furthermore, Ovitz did not "engage" in a transaction with the corporation—rather, the corporation imposed an unwanted transaction upon him.

> Once Ovitz was terminated without cause (as a result of decisions made entirely without input or influence from Ovitz), he was contractually entitled, without any negotiation or action on his part, to receive the benefits provided by the OEA for a termination without cause, benefits for which he negotiated at arm's length *before* becoming a fiduciary.

[...]

The Court made no error in arriving at that determination and we uphold it.

IV. THE CLAIMS AGAINST THE DISNEY DEFENDANTS

We next turn to the claims of error that relate to the Disney defendants. Those claims are subdivisible into two groups: (A) claims arising out of the approval of the OEA and of Ovitz's election as President; and (B) claims arising out of the NFT severance payment to Ovitz upon his termination. We address separately those two categories and the issues that they generate.

A. Claims Arising From The Approval Of The OEA And Ovitz's Election As President

As earlier noted, the appellants' core argument in the trial court was that the Disney defendants' approval of the OEA and election of Ovitz as President were not entitled to business judgment rule protection, because those actions were either grossly negligent or not performed in good faith. The Court of Chancery rejected these arguments, and held that the appellants had failed to prove that the Disney defendants had breached any fiduciary duty.

For clarity of presentation we address the claimed errors relating to the fiduciary duty of care rulings separately from those that relate to the directors' fiduciary duty to act in good faith.

1. The Due Care Determinations

The plaintiff-appellants advance five contentions to support their claim that the Chancellor reversibly erred by concluding that the plaintiffs had failed to establish a violation of the Disney defendants' duty of care. The appellants claim that the Chancellor erred by: (1) [...] (2) ruling that the old board was not required to approve the OEA; (3) [...] (4) concluding that the compensation committee members did not breach their duty of care in approving the NFT provisions of the OEA; and (5) holding that the remaining members of the old board (*i.e.,* the directors who were not members of the compensation committee) had not breached their duty of care in electing Ovitz as Disney's President.

To the extent that these claims attack legal rulings of the Court of Chancery we review them *de novo.* To the extent they attack the Court's factual findings, those findings will be upheld where they are based on the Chancellor's assessment of live testimony. The issue these claims present is whether the Court of Chancery legally (and reversibly) erred in one or more of the foregoing respects. We conclude that the Chancellor committed no error.

(a)

[...]

(b) RULING THAT THE FULL DISNEY BOARD WAS NOT REQUIRED TO CONSIDER AND APPROVE THE OEA

The appellants next challenge the Court of Chancery's determination that the full Disney board was not required to consider and approve the OEA, because the Company's governing instruments allocated that decision to the compensation committee. This challenge also cannot survive scrutiny.

As the Chancellor found, under the Company's governing documents the board of directors was responsible for selecting the corporation's officers, but under the compensation committee charter, the committee was responsible for establishing and approving the salaries, together with benefits and stock options, of the Company's CEO and President. The compensation committee also had the charter-imposed duty to "approve employment contracts, or contracts at will" for "all corporate officers who are members of the Board of Directors regardless of salary." That is exactly what occurred here. The full board ultimately selected Ovitz as President, and the compensation committee considered and ultimately approved the OEA, which embodied the terms of Ovitz's employment, including his compensation.

The Delaware General Corporation Law (DGCL) expressly empowers a board of directors to appoint committees and to delegate to them a broad range of responsibilities, which may include setting executive compensation. Nothing in the DGCL mandates that the entire board must make those decisions. At Disney, the responsibility to consider and approve executive compensation was allocated to the compensation committee, as distinguished from the full board. The Chancellor's ruling—that executive compensation was to be fixed by the compensation committee—is legally correct.

[...]

(c)

[...]

(d) HOLDING THAT THE COMPENSATION COMMITTEE MEMBERS DID NOT FAIL TO EXERCISE DUE CARE IN APPROVING THE OEA

The appellants next challenge the Chancellor's determination that although the compensation committee's decision-making process fell far short of corporate governance "best practices," the committee members breached no duty of care in considering and approving the NFT terms of the OEA. That conclusion is reversible error, the appellants claim, because the record establishes that the compensation committee members did not properly inform themselves of the material facts and, hence, were grossly negligent in approving the NFT provisions of the OEA.

The appellants advance five reasons why a reversal is compelled: (i) not all committee members reviewed a draft of the OEA; (ii) the minutes of the September 26, 1995 compensation committee meeting do not recite any discussion of the grounds for which Ovitz could receive a non-fault termination; (iii) the committee members did not consider any comparable employment agreements or the economic impact of extending the exercisability of the options being granted to Ovitz; (iv) Crystal did not attend the September 26, 1995 committee meeting, nor was his letter distributed to or discussed with Poitier and Lozano; and (v) Poitier and Lozano did not review the spreadsheets generated by Watson. These contentions amount essentially to an attack upon underlying factual findings that will be upheld where they result from the Chancellor's assessment of live testimony.

Although the appellants have balkanized their due care claim into several fragmented parts, the overall thrust of that claim is that the compensation committee approved the OEA with NFT provisions that could potentially result in an enormous payout, without informing themselves of what the full magnitude of that payout could be. Rejecting that claim, the Court of Chancery found that the compensation committee members were adequately informed. The issue thus becomes whether that finding is supported by the evidence of record. We conclude that it is.

In our view, a helpful approach is to compare what actually happened here to what would have occurred had the committee followed a "best practices" (or "best case") scenario, from a process standpoint. In a "best case" scenario, all committee members would have received, before or at the committee's first meeting on September 26, 1995, a spreadsheet or similar document prepared by (or with the assistance of) a compensation expert (in this case, Graef Crystal). Making different, alternative assumptions, the spreadsheet would disclose the amounts that Ovitz could receive under the OEA in each circumstance that might foreseeably arise. One variable in that matrix of possibilities would be the cost to Disney of a non-fault termination for each of the five years of the initial term of the OEA. The contents of the spreadsheet would be explained to the committee members, either by the expert who prepared it or by a fellow committee member similarly knowledgeable about the subject. That spreadsheet, which ultimately would become an exhibit to the minutes of the compensation committee meeting, would form the basis of the committee's deliberations and decision.

Had that scenario been followed, there would be no dispute (and no basis for litigation) over what information was furnished to the committee members or when it was furnished. Regrettably, the committee's informational and decisionmaking process used here was not so tidy. That is one reason why the Chancellor found that although the committee's process did not fall below the level required for a proper exercise of due care, it did fall short of what best practices would have counseled.

The Disney compensation committee met twice: on September 26 and October 16, 1995. The minutes of the September 26 meeting reflect that the committee approved the terms of the OEA (at that time embodied in the form of a letter agreement), except for the option grants, which were not approved until October 16—after the Disney stock incentive plan had been amended to provide for those options. At the September 26 meeting, the compensation committee considered a "term sheet" which, in summarizing the material terms of the OEA, relevantly disclosed that in the event of a non-fault termination, Ovitz would receive: (i) the present value of his salary ($1 million per year) for the balance of the contract term, (ii) the present value of his annual bonus payments (computed at $7.5

million) for the balance of the contract term, (iii) a $10 million termination fee, and (iv) the acceleration of his options for 3 million shares, which would become immediately exercisable at market price.

Thus, the compensation committee knew that in the event of an NFT, Ovitz's severance payment alone could be in the range of $40 million cash, plus the value of the accelerated options. Because the actual payout to Ovitz was approximately $130 million, of which roughly $38.5 million was cash, the value of the options at the time of the NFT payout would have been about $91.5 million. Thus, the issue may be framed as whether the compensation committee members knew, at the time they approved the OEA, that the value of the option component of the severance package could reach the $92 million order of magnitude if they terminated Ovitz without cause after one year. The evidentiary record shows that the committee members were so informed.

On this question the documentation is far less than what best practices would have dictated. There is no exhibit to the minutes that discloses, in a single document, the estimated value of the accelerated options in the event of an NFT termination after one year. The information imparted to the committee members on that subject is, however, supported by other evidence, most notably the trial testimony of various witnesses about spreadsheets that were prepared for the compensation committee meetings.

The compensation committee members derived their information about the potential magnitude of an NFT payout from two sources. The first was the value of the "benchmark" options previously granted to Eisner and Wells and the valuations by Watson of the proposed Ovitz options. Ovitz's options were set at 75% of parity with the options previously granted to Eisner and to Frank Wells. Because the compensation committee had established those earlier benchmark option grants to Eisner and Wells and were aware of their value, a simple mathematical calculation would have informed them of the potential value range of Ovitz's options. Also, in August and September 1995, Watson and Russell met with Graef Crystal to determine (among other things) the value of the potential Ovitz options, assuming different scenarios. Crystal valued the options under the Black-Scholes method, while Watson used a different valuation metric. Watson recorded his calculations and the resulting values on a set of spreadsheets that reflected what option profits Ovitz might receive, based upon a range of different assumptions about stock market price increases. Those spreadsheets were shared with, and explained to, the committee members at the September meeting.

The committee's second source of information was the amount of "downside protection" that Ovitz was demanding. Ovitz required financial protection from the risk of leaving a very lucrative and secure position at CAA, of which he was a controlling partner, to join a publicly held corporation to which Ovitz was a stranger, and that had a very different culture and an environment which prevented him from completely controlling his destiny. The committee members knew that by leaving CAA and coming to Disney, Ovitz would be sacrificing "booked" CAA commissions of $150 to $200 million—an amount that Ovitz demanded as protection against the risk that his employment relationship with Disney might not work out. Ovitz wanted at least $50 million of that compensation to take the form of an "up-front" signing bonus. Had the $50 million bonus been paid, the size of the option grant would have been lower. Because it was contrary to Disney policy, the compensation committee rejected the up-front signing bonus demand, and elected instead to compensate Ovitz at the "back end," by awarding him options that would be phased in over the five-year term of the OEA.

It is on this record that the Chancellor found that the compensation committee was informed of the material facts relating to an NFT payout. If measured in terms of the documentation that would have been generated if "best practices" had been followed, that record leaves much to be desired. The Chancellor acknowledged that, and so do we. But, the Chancellor also found that despite its imperfections, the evidentiary record was sufficient to support the conclusion that the compensation committee had adequately informed itself of the potential magnitude of the entire severance package, including the options, that Ovitz would receive in the event of an early NFT.

The OEA was specifically structured to compensate Ovitz for walking away from $150 million to $200 million of anticipated commissions from CAA over the five-year OEA contract term. This meant that if Ovitz was terminated without cause, the earlier in the contract term the termination occurred the larger the severance amount would be to replace the lost commissions. Indeed, because Ovitz was terminated after only one year, the total amount of his severance payment (about $130 million) closely approximated the lower end of the range of Ovitz's forfeited commissions ($150 million), less the compensation Ovitz received during his first and only year as Disney's President. Accordingly, the Court of Chancery had a sufficient evidentiary basis in the record from which to find that, at the time they approved the OEA, the compensation committee members were adequately informed of the potential magnitude of an early. NFT severance payout.

Exposing the lack of merit in appellants' core due care claim enables us to address more cogently (and expeditiously) the appellants' fragmented subsidiary arguments. First, the appellants argue that not all members of the compensation committee reviewed the then-existing draft of the OEA. The Chancellor properly found that that was not required, because in this case the compensation committee was informed of the substance of the OEA.

Second, appellants point out that the minutes of the September 26 compensation committee meeting recite no discussion of the grounds for which Ovitz could receive a non-fault termination. But the term sheet did include a description of the consequences of a not-for-cause termination, and the Chancellor found that although "no one on the committee recalled any discussion concerning the meaning of gross negligence or malfeasance," those terms "were not foreign to the board of directors, as the language was standard, and could be found, for example, in Eisner's, Wells', Katzenberg's and Roth's employment contracts."

Third, contrary to the appellants' position, the compensation committee members did consider comparable employment agreements. The Chancellor found, as Russell's extensive notes demonstrated, that the comparable historical option grants that Russell analyzed at

123

the September 26 meeting were the grants to Eisner and Wells. The evidence also lays to rest the claim that the compensation committee members did not consider the economic impact of the extended exercisability of the options being granted to Ovitz. Russell and Crystal had assessed the value of those options using the Black-Scholes and other valuation methods during the two weeks preceding the September 26 compensation committee meeting. Russell summarized those analyses at that meeting, and (as earlier discussed) at the time the compensation committee members approved the OEA, they were informed of the magnitude of those values in the event of an NFT.

Fourth, the appellants stress that Crystal did not make a report in person to the compensation committee at its September 26 meeting. Although that is true, it is undisputed that Crystal was available by phone if the committee members had questions that could not be answered by those who were present. Moreover, Russell and Watson related the substance of Crystal's analysis and information to the committee. The Court of Chancery noted (and we agree) that although it might have been the better course of action, it was "not necessary for an expert to make a formal presentation at the committee meeting in order for the board to rely on that expert's analysis. . . ." Nor did the Chancellor find merit to the appellants' related argument that two committee members, Poitier and Lozano, were not entitled to rely upon the work performed by Russell, Watson and Crystal in August and September 1995, without having first seen all of the written materials generated during that process or having participated in the discussions held during that time. In reaching a contrary conclusion, the Chancellor found:

> The compensation committee reasonably believed that the analysis of the terms of the OEA was within Crystal's professional or expert competence, and together with Russell and Watson's professional competence in those same areas, the committee relied on the information, opinions, reports and statements made by Crystal, even if Crystal did not relay the information, opinions, reports and statements in person to the committee as a whole. Crystal's analysis was not so deficient that the compensation committee would have reason to question it. Furthermore, Crystal appears to have been selected with reasonable care, especially in light of his previous engagements with the Company in connection with past executive compensation contracts that were structurally, at least, similar to the OEA. For all these reasons, the compensation committee also is entitled to the protections of 8 *Del. C.* § 141(e) in relying upon Crystal.

The Chancellor correctly applied Section 141(e) in upholding the reliance of Lozano and Poitier upon the information that Crystal, Russell and Watson furnished to them. To accept the appellants' narrow reading of that statute would eviscerate its purpose, which is to protect directors who rely in good faith upon information presented to them from various sources, including "any other person as to matters the member reasonably believes are within such person's professional or expert competence and who has been selected with reasonable care by and on behalf of the corporation."

Finally, the appellants contend that Poitier and Lozano did not review the spreadsheets generated by Watson at the September 26 meeting. The short answer is that even if Poitier and Lozano did not review the spreadsheets themselves, Russell and Watson adequately informed them of the spreadsheets' contents. The Court of Chancery explicitly found, and the record supports, that Poitier and Lozano "were informed by Russell and Watson of all *material* information reasonably available, even though they were not privy to every conversation or document exchanged amongst Russell, Watson, Crystal, and Ovitz's representatives."

For these reasons, we uphold the Chancellor's determination that the compensation committee members did not breach their fiduciary duty of care in approving the OEA.

(e) HOLDING THAT THE REMAINING DISNEY DIRECTORS DID NOT FAIL TO EXERCISE DUE CARE IN APPROVING THE HIRING OF OVITZ AS THE PRESIDENT OF DISNEY

The appellants' final claim in this category is that the Court of Chancery erroneously held that the remaining members of the old Disney board had not breached their duty of care in electing Ovitz as President of Disney. This claim lacks merit, because the arguments appellants advance in this context relate to a different subject—the approval of the OEA, which was the responsibility delegated to the compensation committee, not the full board.

The appellants argue that the Disney directors breached their duty of care by failing to inform themselves of all material information reasonably available with respect to Ovitz's employment agreement. We need not dwell on the specifics of this argument, because in substance they repeat the gross negligence claims previously leveled at the compensation committee—claims that were rejected by the Chancellor and now also by this Court. The only properly reviewable action of the entire board was its decision to elect Ovitz as Disney's President. In that context the sole issue, as the Chancellor properly held, is "whether [the remaining members of the old board] properly exercised their business judgment and acted in accordance with their fiduciary duties when they elected Ovitz to the Company's presidency." The Chancellor determined that in electing Ovitz, the directors were informed of all information reasonably available and, thus, were not grossly negligent. We agree.

The Chancellor found and the record shows the following: well in advance of the September 26, 1995 board meeting the directors were fully aware that the Company needed—especially in light of Wells' death and Eisner's medical problems—to hire a "number two" executive and potential successor to Eisner. There had been many discussions about that need and about potential candidates who could fill that role even before Eisner decided to try to recruit Ovitz. Before the September 26 board meeting Eisner had individually discussed with each director the possibility of hiring Ovitz, and Ovitz's background and qualifications. The directors thus knew of Ovitz's skills, reputation and experience, all of which they believed would be highly valuable to the Company. The directors also knew that to accept a position at Disney, Ovitz would have to walk away from a very successful business—a reality that would lead a reasonable person to believe that Ovitz would likely succeed in similar pursuits elsewhere in the industry. The directors also knew of the public's highly positive reaction to the Ovitz announcement, and that Eisner and senior management had supported the Ovitz hiring. Indeed, Eisner, who had long desired to bring Ovitz within the Disney fold, consistently vouched for Ovitz's qualifications and told the directors that he could work well with Ovitz.

The board was also informed of the key terms of the OEA (including Ovitz's salary, bonus and options). Russell reported this information to them at the September 26, 1995 executive session, which was attended by Eisner and all non-executive directors. Russell also reported on the compensation committee meeting that had immediately preceded the executive session. And, both Russell and Watson responded to questions from the board. Relying upon the compensation committee's approval of the OEA and the other information furnished to them, the Disney directors, after further deliberating, unanimously elected Ovitz as President.

Based upon this record, we uphold the Chancellor's conclusion that, when electing Ovitz to the Disney presidency the remaining Disney directors were fully informed of all material facts, and that the appellants failed to establish any lack of due care on the directors' part.

2. The Good Faith Determinations

The Court of Chancery held that the business judgment rule presumptions protected the decisions of the compensation committee and the remaining Disney directors, not only because they had acted with due care but also because they had not acted in bad faith. That latter ruling, the appellants claim, was reversible error because the Chancellor formulated and then applied an incorrect definition of bad faith.

In its Opinion the Court of Chancery defined bad faith as follows:

> Upon long and careful consideration, I am of the opinion that the concept of *intentional dereliction of duty, a conscious disregard for one's responsibilities,* is an appropriate (although not the only) standard for determining whether fiduciaries have acted in good faith. Deliberate indifference and inaction *in the face of a duty to act* is, in my mind, conduct that is clearly disloyal to the corporation. It is the epitome of faithless conduct.

[...]

The appellants essentially concede that their proof of bad faith is insufficient to satisfy the standard articulated by the Court of Chancery. That is why they ask this Court to treat a failure to exercise due care as a failure to act in good faith. Unfortunately for appellants, that "rule," even if it were accepted, would not help their case. If we were to conflate these two duties and declare that a breach of the duty to be properly informed violates the duty to act in good faith, the outcome would be no different, because, as the Chancellor and we now have held, the appellants failed to establish any breach of the duty of care. To say it differently, even if the Chancellor's definition of bad faith were erroneous, the error would not be reversible because the appellants cannot satisfy the very test they urge us to adopt.

126

For that reason, our analysis of the appellants' bad faith claim could end at this point. In other circumstances it would. This case, however, is one in which the duty to act in good faith has played a prominent role, yet to date is not a well-developed area of our corporate fiduciary law. Although the good faith concept has recently been the subject of considerable scholarly writing, which includes articles focused on this specific case, the duty to act in good faith is, up to this point relatively uncharted. Because of the increased recognition of the importance of good faith, some conceptual guidance to the corporate community may be helpful. For that reason we proceed to address the merits of the appellants' second argument.

The precise question is whether the Chancellor's articulated standard for bad faith corporate fiduciary conduct—intentional dereliction of duty, a conscious disregard for one's responsibilities—is legally correct. In approaching that question, we note that the Chancellor characterized that definition as "*an* appropriate *(although not the only)* standard for determining whether fiduciaries have acted in good faith." That observation is accurate and helpful, because as a matter of simple logic, at least three different categories of fiduciary behavior are candidates for the "bad faith" pejorative label.

The first category involves so-called "subjective bad faith," that is, fiduciary conduct motivated by an actual intent to do harm. That such conduct constitutes classic, quintessential bad faith is a proposition so well accepted in the liturgy of fiduciary law that it borders on axiomatic. We need not dwell further on this category, because no such conduct is claimed to have occurred, or did occur, in this case.

The second category of conduct, which is at the opposite end of the spectrum, involves lack of due care—that is, fiduciary action taken solely by reason of gross negligence and without any malevolent intent. In this case, appellants assert claims of gross negligence to establish breaches not only of director due care but also of the directors' duty to act in good faith. Although the Chancellor found, and we agree, that the appellants failed to establish gross negligence, to afford guidance we address the issue of whether gross negligence (including a failure to inform one's self of available material facts), without more, can also constitute bad faith. The answer is clearly no.

From a broad philosophical standpoint, that question is more complex than would appear, if only because (as the Chancellor and others have observed) "issues of good faith are (to a certain degree) inseparably and necessarily intertwined with the duties of care and loyalty. . . ." But, in the pragmatic, conduct-regulating legal realm which calls for more precise conceptual line drawing, the answer is that grossly negligent conduct, without more, does not and cannot constitute a breach of the fiduciary duty to act in good faith. The conduct that is the subject of due care may overlap with the conduct that comes within the rubric of good faith in a psychological sense, but from a legal standpoint those duties are and must remain quite distinct. Both our legislative history and our common law jurisprudence distinguish sharply between the duties to exercise due care and to act in good faith, and highly significant consequences flow from that distinction.

The Delaware General Assembly has addressed the distinction between bad faith and a failure to exercise due care (*i.e.*, gross negligence) in two separate contexts. The first is Section 102(b)(7) of the DGCL, which authorizes Delaware corporations, by a provision in the certificate of incorporation, to exculpate their directors from monetary damage liability for a breach of the duty of care. That exculpatory provision affords significant protection to directors of Delaware corporations. The statute carves out several exceptions, however, including most relevantly, "for acts or omissions not in good faith. . . ." Thus, a corporation can exculpate its directors from monetary liability for a breach of the duty of care, but not for conduct that is not in good faith. To adopt a definition of bad faith that would cause a violation of the duty of care automatically to become an act or omission "not in good faith," would eviscerate the protections accorded to directors by the General Assembly's adoption of Section 102(b)(7).

A second legislative recognition of the distinction between fiduciary conduct that is grossly negligent and conduct that is not in good faith, is Delaware's indemnification statute, found at 8 *Del. C.* § 145. To oversimplify, subsections (a) and (b) of that statute permit a corporation to indemnify (*inter alia*) any person who is or was a director, officer, employee or agent of the corporation against expenses (including attorneys' fees), judgments, fines and amounts paid in settlement of specified actions, suits or proceedings, where (among other things): (i) that person is, was, or is threatened to be made a party to that action, suit or proceeding, and (ii) that person "acted in good faith and in a manner the person reasonably believed to be in or not opposed to the best interests of the corporation. . . ." Thus, under Delaware statutory law a director or officer of a corporation can be indemnified for liability (and litigation expenses) incurred by reason of a violation of the duty of care, but not for a violation of the duty to act in good faith.

Section 145, like Section 102(b)(7), evidences the intent of the Delaware General Assembly to afford significant protections to directors (and, in the case of Section 145, other fiduciaries) of Delaware corporations. To adopt a definition that conflates the duty of care with the duty to act in good faith by making a violation of the former an automatic violation of the latter, would nullify those legislative protections and defeat the General Assembly's intent. There is no basis in policy, precedent or common sense that would justify dismantling the distinction between gross negligence and bad faith.

That leaves the third category of fiduciary conduct, which falls in between the first two categories of (1) conduct motivated by subjective bad intent and (2) conduct resulting from gross negligence. This third category is what the Chancellor's definition of bad faith—intentional dereliction of duty, a conscious disregard for one's responsibilities—is intended to capture. The question is whether such misconduct is properly treated as a non-exculpable, non-indemnifiable violation of the fiduciary duty to act in good faith. In our view it must be, for at least two reasons.

First, the universe of fiduciary misconduct is not limited to either disloyalty in the classic sense (*i.e.*, preferring the adverse self-interest of the fiduciary or of a related person to the interest of the corporation) or gross negligence. Cases have arisen where corporate directors have no conflicting self-interest in a decision, yet engage in misconduct that is

128

more culpable than simple inattention or failure to be informed of all facts material to the decision. To protect the interests of the corporation and its shareholders, fiduciary conduct of this kind, which does not involve disloyalty (as traditionally defined) but is qualitatively more culpable than gross negligence, should be proscribed. A vehicle is needed to address such violations doctrinally, and that doctrinal vehicle is the duty to act in good faith. The Chancellor implicitly so recognized in his Opinion, where he identified different examples of bad faith as follows:

> The good faith required of a corporate fiduciary includes not simply the duties of care and loyalty, in the narrow sense that I have discussed them above, but all actions required by a true faithfulness and devotion to the interests of the corporation and its shareholders. A failure to act in good faith may be shown, for instance, where the fiduciary intentionally acts with a purpose other than that of advancing the best interests of the corporation, where the fiduciary acts with the intent to violate applicable positive law, or where the fiduciary intentionally fails to act in the face of a known duty to act, demonstrating a conscious disregard for his duties. There may be other examples of bad faith yet to be proven or alleged, but these three are the most salient.

Those articulated examples of bad faith are not new to our jurisprudence. Indeed, they echo pronouncements our courts have made throughout the decades.

Second, the legislature has also recognized this intermediate category of fiduciary misconduct, which ranks between conduct involving subjective bad faith and gross negligence. Section 102(b)(7)(ii) of the DGCL expressly denies money damage exculpation for "acts or omissions not in good faith or which involve intentional misconduct or a knowing violation of law." By its very terms that provision distinguishes between "intentional misconduct" and a "knowing violation of law" (both examples of subjective bad faith) on the one hand, and "acts...not in good faith," on the other. Because the statute exculpates directors only for conduct amounting to gross negligence, the statutory denial of exculpation for "acts...not in good faith" must encompass the intermediate category of misconduct captured by the Chancellor's definition of bad faith.

For these reasons, we uphold the Court of Chancery's definition as a legally appropriate, although not the exclusive, definition of fiduciary bad faith. We need go no further. To engage in an effort to craft (in the Court's words) "a definitive and categorical definition of the universe of acts that would constitute bad faith" would be unwise and is unnecessary to dispose of the issues presented on this appeal.

Having sustained the Chancellor's finding that the Disney directors acted in good faith when approving the OEA and electing Ovitz as President, we next address the claims arising out of the decision to pay Ovitz the amount called for by the NFT provisions of the OEA. . . .

VI. CONCLUSION

For the reasons stated above, the judgment of the Court of Chancery is affirmed.

[...]

Discussion Questions:

1. Did *Disney* overrule *Van Gorkom*, explicitly or implicitly? Or did the case present materially different facts? The *Disney* court certainly paints a more favorable picture of the board process than the *Van Gorkom* court. But were the processes substantively different? Imagine you are the plaintiffs' lawyer (or a judge in the *Van Gorkom* majority) and try to recast the *Disney* facts in a light less favorable to the defendants. You may find the following quote from a contemporaneous biography of Ovitz useful in your brief: "The two men [Eisner & Ovitz] had been close friends for 20 years. They and their wives often had vacationed together, and when Eisner had been hospitalized two summers earlier with serious heart problems, Ovitz had rarely left his hospital bedside."[15]

2. As a policy matter, why *shouldn't* the Disney board be liable for approving Ovitz's employment agreement? Note that the negligence standard governs most of our behavior (e.g., driving a car). Why should we have a "gross negligence" standard (*Van Gorkom*) or—even more deferential—a "lack of good faith" standard (*Disney*) for corporate directors? In other words, are there good policy reasons behind the fact that you are held to a higher standard when you are driving a car than when you are managing a company? Or is the deferential approach of corporate law just a manifestation of "capture" by the political and financial elites?

3. How does the court interpret "good faith"? How does "good faith" relate to the duty of care and the duty of loyalty? (Before you answer, see *Stone v. Ritter* below.)

The Duty to Monitor

The business judgment rule, as applied in *Disney*, should provide comfort to directors and officers even in the absence of a 102(b)(7) waiver (which does not cover officers). For a long time, however, directors and officers might have been worried by the following passage from *Aronson v. Lewis*: "However, it should be noted that the business judgment rule operates only in the context of director action. Technically speaking, it has no role where directors have either abdicated their functions, or absent a conscious decision, failed to act." 473 A.2d 805, at 813 (Del. 1984).

In general, boards have an obligation to respond to "red flags" if they come to the board's attention, but there is no affirmative obligation for boards to ferret out wrong-doing

---

[15] From Robert Slater, *Ovitz: The Inside Story of Hollywood's Most Controversial Power Broker* (1997).

wherever it might exist in the corporation. However, boards cannot put their head in the sane—they must have a reasonable control system that will bring problems to their attention. In the famous 1996 *Caremark* decision, Chancellor Allen mused that the absence of such a reporting system could give rise to liability. *Stone* affirmed this proposition but also clarified (and gave some comfort to directors) on what the duty to monitor requires.

Stone v. Ritter
911 A.2d 362 (Del. 2006)

HOLLAND, Justice:

This is an appeal from a final judgment of the Court of Chancery dismissing a derivative complaint against fifteen present and former directors of AmSouth Bancorporation ("AmSouth"), a Delaware corporation. The plaintiffs-appellants, William and Sandra Stone, are AmSouth shareholders [...]. The Court of Chancery held that the plaintiffs had failed to adequately plead [...] The Court, therefore, dismissed the derivative complaint [...].

The Court of Chancery characterized the allegations in the derivative complaint as a "classic *Caremark* claim," a claim that derives its name from *In re Caremark Int'l Deriv. Litig.* In *Caremark*, the Court of Chancery recognized that: "[g]enerally where a claim of directorial liability for corporate loss is predicated upon ignorance of liability creating activities within the corporation . . . only a sustained or systematic failure of the board to exercise oversight—such as an utter failure to attempt to assure a reasonable information and reporting system exists—will establish the lack of good faith that is a necessary condition to liability."

In this appeal, the plaintiffs acknowledge that the directors neither "knew [n]or should have known that violations of law were occurring," *i.e.,* that there were no "red flags" before the directors. Nevertheless, the plaintiffs argue that the Court of Chancery erred by dismissing the derivative complaint which alleged that "the defendants had utterly failed to implement any sort of statutorily required monitoring, reporting or information controls that would have enabled them to learn of problems requiring their attention." The defendants argue that the plaintiffs' assertions are contradicted by the derivative complaint itself and by the documents incorporated therein by reference.

Consistent with our opinion in *In re Walt Disney Co. Deriv Litig,* we hold that *Caremark* articulates the necessary conditions for assessing director oversight liability. We also conclude that the *Caremark* standard was properly applied to evaluate the derivative complaint in this case. Accordingly, the judgment of the Court of Chancery must be affirmed.

Facts

This derivative action is brought on AmSouth's behalf by William and Sandra Stone, who allege that they owned AmSouth common stock "at all relevant times." The nominal defendant, AmSouth, is a Delaware corporation with its principal executive offices in Birmingham, Alabama. During the relevant period, AmSouth's wholly-owned subsidiary, AmSouth Bank, operated about 600 commercial banking branches in six states throughout the southeastern United States and employed more than 11,600 people.

In 2004, AmSouth and AmSouth Bank paid $40 million in fines and $10 million in civil penalties to resolve government and regulatory investigations pertaining principally to the failure by bank employees to file "Suspicious Activity Reports" ("SARs"), as required by the federal Bank Secrecy Act ("BSA") and various anti-money-laundering ("AML") regulations. Those investigations were conducted by the United States Attorney's Office for the Southern District of Mississippi ("USAO"), the Federal Reserve, FinCEN and the Alabama Banking Department. No fines or penalties were imposed on AmSouth's directors, and no other regulatory action was taken against them.

The government investigations arose originally from an unlawful "Ponzi" scheme operated by Louis D. Hamric, II and Victor G. Nance. In August 2000, Hamric, then a licensed attorney, and Nance, then a registered investment advisor with Mutual of New York, contacted an AmSouth branch bank in Tennessee to arrange for custodial trust accounts to be created for "investors" in a "business venture." That venture (Hamric and Nance represented) involved the construction of medical clinics overseas. In reality, Nance had convinced more than forty of his clients to invest in promissory notes bearing high rates of return, by misrepresenting the nature and the risk of that investment. Relying on similar misrepresentations by Hamric and Nance, the AmSouth branch employees in Tennessee agreed to provide custodial accounts for the investors and to distribute monthly interest payments to each account upon receipt of a check from Hamric and instructions from Nance.

The Hamric-Nance scheme was discovered in March 2002, when the investors did not receive their monthly interest payments. Thereafter, Hamric and Nance became the subject of several civil actions brought by the defrauded investors in Tennessee and Mississippi (and in which AmSouth also was named as a defendant), and also the subject of a federal grand jury investigation in the Southern District of Mississippi. Hamric and Nance were indicted on federal money-laundering charges, and both pled guilty.

The authorities examined AmSouth's compliance with its reporting and other obligations under the BSA. On November 17, 2003, the USAO advised AmSouth that it was the subject of a criminal investigation. On October 12, 2004, AmSouth and the USAO entered into a Deferred Prosecution Agreement ("DPA") in which AmSouth agreed: first, to the filing by USAO of a one-count Information in the United States District Court for the Southern District of Mississippi, charging AmSouth with failing to file SARs; and second, to pay a $40 million fine. In conjunction with the DPA, the USAO issued a "Statement of Facts," which noted that although in 2000 "at least one" AmSouth employee suspected that Hamric was involved in a possibly illegal scheme, AmSouth failed to file SARs in a timely manner. In neither the Statement of Facts nor anywhere else did the USAO ascribe any blame to the Board or to any individual director.

On October 12, 2004, the Federal Reserve and the Alabama Banking Department concurrently issued a Cease and Desist Order against AmSouth, requiring it, for the first time, to improve its BSA/AML program. That Cease and Desist Order required AmSouth to (among other things) engage an independent consultant "to conduct a comprehensive review of the Bank's AML Compliance program and make recommendations, as appropriate, for new policies and procedures to be implemented by the Bank." KPMG Forensic Services ("KPMG") performed the role of independent consultant and issued its report on December 10, 2004 (the "KPMG Report").

Also on October 12, 2004, FinCEN and the Federal Reserve jointly assessed a $10 million civil penalty against AmSouth for operating an inadequate anti-money-laundering program and for failing to file SARs. In connection with that assessment, FinCEN issued a written Assessment of Civil Money Penalty (the "Assessment"), which included detailed "determinations" regarding AmSouth's BSA compliance procedures. FinCEN found that "AmSouth violated the suspicious activity reporting requirements of the Bank Secrecy Act," and that "[s]ince April 24, 2002, AmSouth has been in violation of the anti-money-laundering program requirements of the Bank Secrecy Act." Among FinCEN's specific determinations were its conclusions that "AmSouth's [AML compliance] program lacked adequate board and management oversight," and that "reporting to management for the purposes of monitoring and oversight of compliance activities was materially deficient." AmSouth neither admitted nor denied FinCEN's determinations in this or any other forum.

[...]

Critical to this [...] is the fact that the directors' potential personal liability depends upon whether or not their conduct can be exculpated by the section 102(b)(7) provision contained in the AmSouth certificate of incorporation. Such a provision can exculpate directors from monetary liability for a breach of the duty of care, but not for conduct that is not in good faith or a breach of the duty of loyalty. The standard for assessing a director's potential personal liability for failing to act in good faith in discharging his or her oversight responsibilities has evolved beginning with our decision in *Graham v. Allis-Chalmers Manufacturing Company,* through the Court of Chancery's *Caremark* decision to our most recent decision in *Disney.* A brief discussion of that evolution will help illuminate the standard that we adopt in this case.

Graham and *Caremark*

Graham was a derivative action brought against the directors of Allis-Chalmers for failure to prevent violations of federal anti-trust laws by Allis-Chalmers employees. There was no claim that the Allis-Chalmers directors knew of the employees' conduct that resulted in the corporation's liability. Rather, the plaintiffs claimed that the Allis-Chalmers directors *should have known* of the illegal conduct by the corporation's employees. In *Graham,* this Court held that "*absent cause for suspicion* there is no duty upon the directors to install and operate a corporate system of espionage to ferret out wrongdoing which they have no reason to suspect exists."

133

In *Caremark,* the Court of Chancery reassessed the applicability of our holding in *Graham* when called upon to approve a settlement of a derivative lawsuit brought against the directors of Caremark International, Inc. The plaintiffs claimed that the Caremark directors should have known that certain officers and employees of Caremark were involved in violations of the federal Anti-Referral Payments Law. That law prohibits health care providers from paying any form of remuneration to induce the referral of Medicare or Medicaid patients. The plaintiffs claimed that the *Caremark* directors breached their fiduciary duty for having "allowed a situation to develop and continue which exposed the corporation to enormous legal liability and that in so doing they violated a duty to be active monitors of corporate performance."

In evaluating whether to approve the proposed settlement agreement in *Caremark,* the Court of Chancery narrowly construed our holding in *Graham* "as standing for the proposition that, absent grounds to suspect deception, neither corporate boards nor senior officers can be charged with wrongdoing simply for assuming the integrity of employees and the honesty of their dealings on the company's behalf." The *Caremark* Court opined it would be a "mistake" to interpret this Court's decision in *Graham* to mean that:

> corporate boards may satisfy their obligation to be reasonably informed concerning the corporation, without assuring themselves that information and reporting systems exist in the organization that are reasonably designed to provide to senior management and to the board itself timely, accurate information sufficient to allow management and the board, each within its scope, to reach informed judgments concerning both the corporation's compliance with law and its business performance.

To the contrary, the *Caremark* Court stated, "it is important that the board exercise a good faith judgment that the corporation's information and reporting system is in concept and design adequate to assure the board that appropriate information will come to its attention in a timely manner as a matter of ordinary operations, so that it may satisfy its responsibility." The *Caremark* Court recognized, however, that "the duty to act in good faith to be informed cannot be thought to require directors to possess detailed information about all aspects of the operation of the enterprise." The Court of Chancery then formulated the following standard for assessing the liability of directors where the directors are unaware of employee misconduct that results in the corporation being held liable:

> Generally where a claim of directorial liability for corporate loss is predicated upon ignorance of liability creating activities within the corporation, as in *Graham* or in this case, . . . only a sustained or systematic failure of the board to exercise oversight—such as an utter failure to attempt to assure a reasonable information and reporting system exists—will establish the lack of good faith that is a necessary condition to liability.

Caremark **Standard Approved**

As evidenced by the language quoted above, the *Caremark* standard for so-called "oversight" liability draws heavily upon the concept of director failure to act in good faith. That is consistent with the definition(s) of bad faith recently approved by this Court in its recent *Disney* decision, where we held that a failure to act in good faith requires conduct that is qualitatively different from, and more culpable than, the conduct giving rise to a violation of the fiduciary duty of care (i.e., gross negligence). In *Disney*, we identified the following examples of conduct that would establish a failure to act in good faith:

> A failure to act in good faith may be shown, for instance, where the fiduciary intentionally acts with a purpose other than that of advancing the best interests of the corporation, where the fiduciary acts with the intent to violate applicable positive law, or where the fiduciary intentionally fails to act in the face of a known duty to act, demonstrating a conscious disregard for his duties. There may be other examples of bad faith yet to be proven or alleged, but these three are the most salient.

The third of these examples describes, and is fully consistent with, the lack of good faith conduct that the *Caremark* court held was a "necessary condition" for director oversight liability, i.e., "a sustained or systematic failure of the board to exercise oversight—such as an utter failure to attempt to assure a reasonable information and reporting system exists. . . ." Indeed, our opinion in *Disney* cited *Caremark* with approval for that proposition. Accordingly, the Court of Chancery applied the correct standard in assessing whether [...] in this case where failure to exercise oversight was the basis or theory of the plaintiffs' claim for relief.

It is important, in this context, to clarify a doctrinal issue that is critical to understanding fiduciary liability under *Caremark* as we construe that case. The phraseology used in *Caremark* and that we employ here—describing the lack of good faith as a "necessary condition to liability"—is deliberate. The purpose of that formulation is to communicate that a failure to act in good faith is not conduct that results, *ipso facto*, in the direct imposition of fiduciary liability. The failure to act in good faith may result in liability because the requirement to act in good faith "is a subsidiary element[,]" i.e., a condition, "of the fundamental duty of loyalty." It follows that because a showing of bad faith conduct, in the sense described in *Disney* and *Caremark*, is essential to establish director oversight liability, the fiduciary duty violated by that conduct is the duty of loyalty.

This view of a failure to act in good faith results in two additional doctrinal consequences. First, although good faith may be described colloquially as part of a "triad" of fiduciary duties that includes the duties of care and loyalty, the obligation to act in good faith does not establish an independent fiduciary duty that stands on the same footing as the duties of care and loyalty. Only the latter two duties, where violated, may directly result in liability, whereas a failure to act in good faith may do so, but indirectly. The second doctrinal consequence is that the fiduciary duty of loyalty is not limited to cases involving a financial or other cognizable fiduciary conflict of interest. It also encompasses cases where the fiduciary fails to act in good faith. As the Court of Chancery aptly put it in *Guttman,* "[a] director cannot act loyally towards the corporation unless she acts in the good faith belief that her actions are in the corporation's best interest."

We hold that *Caremark* articulates the necessary conditions predicate for director oversight liability: (a) the directors utterly failed to implement any reporting or information system or controls; *or* (b) having implemented such a system or controls, consciously failed to monitor or oversee its operations thus disabling themselves from being informed of risks or problems requiring their attention. In either case, imposition of liability requires a showing that the directors knew that they were not discharging their fiduciary obligations. Where directors fail to act in the face of a known duty to act, thereby demonstrating a conscious disregard for their responsibilities, they breach their duty of loyalty by failing to discharge that fiduciary obligation in good faith.

Chancery Court Decision

The plaintiffs contend that [...] AmSouth's directors breached their oversight duty [...] as a result of their "utter failure" to act in good faith to put into place policies and procedures to ensure compliance with BSA and AML obligations. The Court of Chancery found that the plaintiffs did not plead the existence of "red flags"—"facts showing that the board ever was aware that AmSouth's internal controls were inadequate, that these inadequacies would result in illegal activity, and that the board chose to do nothing about problems it allegedly knew existed." In dismissing the derivative complaint in this action, the Court of Chancery concluded:

> This case is not about a board's failure to carefully consider a material corporate decision that was presented to the board. This is a case where information was not reaching the board because of ineffective internal controls. . . . With the benefit of hindsight, it is beyond question that AmSouth's internal controls with respect to the Bank Secrecy Act and anti-money laundering regulations compliance were inadequate. Neither party disputes that the lack of internal controls resulted in a huge fine—$50 million, alleged to be the largest ever of its kind. The fact of those losses, however, is not alone enough [...].

This Court reviews *de novo* a Court of Chancery's decision to dismiss a derivative suit under Rule 23.1.

Reasonable Reporting System Existed

The KPMG Report evaluated the various components of AmSouth's longstanding BSA/AML compliance program. The KPMG Report reflects that AmSouth's Board dedicated considerable resources to the BSA/AML compliance program and put into place numerous procedures and systems to attempt to ensure compliance. According to KPMG, the program's various components exhibited between a low and high degree of compliance with applicable laws and regulations.

The KPMG Report describes the numerous AmSouth employees, departments and committees established by the Board to oversee AmSouth's compliance with the BSA and to report violations to management and the Board:

> BSA Officer. Since 1998, AmSouth has had a "BSA Officer" "responsible for all BSA/AML-related matters including employee training, general communications, CTR reporting and SAR reporting," and "presenting AML policy and program changes to the Board of Directors, the managers at the various lines of business, and participants in the annual training of security and audit personnel[;]"

> BSA/AML Compliance Department. AmSouth has had for years a BSA/AML Compliance Department, headed by the BSA Officer and comprised of nineteen professionals, including a BSA/AML Compliance Manager and a Compliance Reporting Manager;

> Corporate Security Department. AmSouth's Corporate Security Department has been at all relevant times responsible for the detection and reporting of suspicious activity as it relates to fraudulent activity, and William Burch, the head of Corporate Security, has been with AmSouth since 1998 and served in the U.S. Secret Service from 1969 to 1998; and

> Suspicious Activity Oversight Committee. Since 2001, the "Suspicious Activity Oversight Committee" and its predecessor, the "AML Committee," have actively overseen AmSouth's BSA/AML compliance program. The Suspicious Activity Oversight Committee's mission has for years been to "oversee the policy, procedure, and process issues affecting the Corporate Security and BSA/ AML Compliance Programs, to ensure that an effective program exists at AmSouth to deter, detect, and report money laundering, suspicious activity and other fraudulent activity."

The KPMG Report reflects that the directors not only discharged their oversight responsibility to establish an information and reporting system, but also proved that the system was designed to permit the directors to periodically monitor AmSouth's compliance with BSA and AML regulations. For example, as KPMG noted in 2004, AmSouth's designated BSA Officer "has made annual high-level presentations to the Board of Directors in each of the last five years." Further, the Board's Audit and Community Responsibility Committee (the "Audit Committee") oversaw AmSouth's BSA/AML compliance program on a quarterly basis. The KPMG Report states that "the BSA Officer presents BSA/AML training to the Board of Directors annually," and the "Corporate Security training is also presented to the Board of Directors."

The KPMG Report shows that AmSouth's Board at various times enacted written policies and procedures designed to ensure compliance with the BSA and AML regulations. For example, the Board adopted an amended bank-wide "BSA/AML Policy" on July 17, 2003—

four months before AmSouth became aware that it was the target of a government investigation. That policy was produced to plaintiffs in response to their demand to inspect AmSouth's books and records pursuant to section 220 and is included in plaintiffs' appendix. Among other things, the July 17, 2003, BSA/AML Policy directs all AmSouth employees to immediately report suspicious transactions or activity to the BSA/AML Compliance Department or Corporate Security.

Complaint Properly Dismissed

In this case, the adequacy of the plaintiffs' [...] depends on whether the complaint alleges facts sufficient to show that the defendant *directors* are potentially personally liable for the failure of non-director bank *employees* to file SARs. Delaware courts have recognized that "[m]ost of the decisions that a corporation, acting through its human agents, makes are, of course, not the subject of director attention." Consequently, a claim that directors are subject to personal liability for employee failures is "possibly the most difficult theory in corporation law upon which a plaintiff might hope to win a judgment."

For the plaintiffs' derivative complaint to withstand a motion to dismiss, "only a sustained or systematic failure of the board to exercise oversight—such as an utter failure to attempt to assure a reasonable information and reporting system exists—will establish the lack of good faith that is a necessary condition to liability." As the *Caremark* decision noted:

> Such a test of liability—lack of good faith as evidenced by sustained or systematic failure of a director to exercise reasonable oversight—is quite high. But, a demanding test of liability in the oversight context is probably beneficial to corporate shareholders as a class, as it is in the board decision context, since it makes board service by qualified persons more likely, while continuing to act as a stimulus to *good faith performance of duty* by such directors.

The KPMG Report—which the plaintiffs explicitly incorporated by reference into their derivative complaint—refutes the assertion that the directors "never took the necessary steps . . . to ensure that a reasonable BSA compliance and reporting system existed." KPMG's findings reflect that the Board received and approved relevant policies and procedures, delegated to certain employees and departments the responsibility for filing SARs and monitoring compliance, and exercised oversight by relying on periodic reports from them. Although there ultimately may have been failures by employees to report deficiencies to the Board, there is no basis for an oversight claim seeking to hold the directors personally liable for such failures by the employees.

With the benefit of hindsight, the plaintiffs' complaint seeks to equate a bad outcome with bad faith. The lacuna in the plaintiffs' argument is a failure to recognize that the directors' good faith exercise of oversight responsibility may not invariably prevent employees from violating criminal laws, or from causing the corporation to incur significant financial liability, or both, as occurred in *Graham, Caremark* and this very case. In the absence of red flags, good faith in the context of oversight must be measured by the directors' actions "to assure a reasonable information and reporting system exists" and not by second-guessing after the occurrence of employee conduct that results in an unintended adverse outcome. Accordingly, we hold that the Court of Chancery properly applied *Caremark* and dismissed the plaintiffs' derivative complaint for failure to [...] allege [...] particularized facts that created reason to doubt whether the directors had acted in good faith in exercising their oversight responsibilities.

Conclusion

The judgment of the Court of Chancery is affirmed.

[...]

Discussion Questions:

1. *Stone* confirmed the proposition in *Caremark* that boards have an affirmative obligation to put in control systems that will bring problems to their attention, but the Court also articulated a standard of review by which these control systems would be evaluated. What is this standard of review, and can you envision a scenario (in the real world) in which this standard would not be met?

2. As a conceptual matter, why should the business judgment rule only apply to director action and not director inaction? (Hint: recall the justifications for the business judgment rule that we discussed in the *Disney* case.)

In the case of *In re Puda Coal, Inc. Shareholder Litigation*, C.A. No. 6476-CS (Del. Ch., 2013), Puda Coal was a Delaware company with significant assets in China. One of the Chinese directors stole most of these assets from the company, and the theft had gone undetected for approximately two years (until a blogger started poking around). All of the other directors promptly resigned from the board, but shareholders nevertheless brought suit against them alleging breach of their *Caremark* responsibilities. In Chancellor Strine's bench ruling (which may be cited in legal briefs under Delaware rules), he refused to dismiss the claim against them:

> Even if it's just purely looked at as a *Caremark* case, drawing reasonable, rational inferences in favor of the plaintiffs, as I must . . . one possible inference you can draw from this complaint is that essentially somebody took hold of an American vehicle, filled it with assets, sold a large amount of stock to the American investing public that independent directors were willing to go on [the board] and get payments without understanding the duties they were taking on. . . .
>
> If you're going to have a company domiciled for purposes of its relations with investors in Delaware and the assets and operations of the company are situated in China that, in order for you to meet your obligation of good faith, you better have your physical body in China an awful lot. You better have in

place a system of controls to make sure that you know that you actually own the assets. You better have the language skills to navigate the environment in which the company is operating. You better have retained accountants and lawyers who are fit to the task of maintaining a system of controls over a public company…

This is a very troubling case in terms that, the use of a Delaware entity in something along these lines. Independent directors who step into these situations involving essentially the fiduciary oversight of assets in other parts of the world have a duty not to be dummy directors. I'm not mixing up care in the sense of negligence with loyalty here, in the sense of our duty of loyalty. I'm talking about the loyalty issue of understanding that if assets are in Russia, if they're in Nigeria, if they're in the Middle East, if they're in China, that you're not going to be able to sit in your home in the U.S. and do a conference call four times a year and discharge your duty of loyalty. That won't cut it. . . .

If it's a situation where, frankly, all the flow of information is in the language that I don't understand, in a culture where there's, frankly, not legal strictures or structures or ethical mores yet that may be advanced to the level where I'm comfortable? It would be very difficult if I didn't know the language, the tools. You better be careful there. You have a duty to think.

Discussion Questions:

1. Does Chancellor Strine's articulation of directors' duty to monitor in *Puda Coal* go beyond the articulation of the same duty in *Stone v. Ritter*?

2. As a practical matter, in the aftermath of *Puda Coal* many boards with significant overseas operations began holding at least one board meeting a year in an overseas location (no doubt creating great business class revenues for the major international airlines). Do you think this improves monitoring? Had the Puda Coal board held one or more of its meetings in China, do you think they would have detected the wrongdoing? (And more importantly, would the prospect thereof have deterred the wrongdoing?)

Indemnification and Insurance

Disney and *Stone* made it quite clear that the risk of liability for unconflicted directors is now modest at best even under the default rules: the business judgment rule provides robust protection to directors and officers. If the corporation's charter has a 102(b)(7) waiver, as most do, the risk of liability for directors (but not officers) is even less.

Nevertheless, directors and officers still face residual risk, in particular from litigation costs. Moreover, directors and officers may be the target of third-party litigation in relation to their corporate office: For example, the directors might be the target of an SEC enforcement action or an employee lawsuit as a result of their board service, whether or not such actions have a legally sound basis. For this reason, directors and officers should and do require that corporations indemnify and insure them extensively. Under DGCL 145, corporations are allowed (subsections a-b, e-f) and sometimes required (subsection c) to provide such indemnification and insurance. As a result, outside directors virtually never have to pay anything out of their own pockets in corporate lawsuits.

Discussion Questions:

1. Which liabilities and expenses are indemnifiable under DGCL 145? Which are insurable?

2. What does DGCL 145(f) add? Specifically, does it allow indemnification for actions not in good faith? Compare DGCL 145(f) with DGCL 145(a). What are the policy reasons for and against such a reading?

3. Why do directors and officers insist on insurance, i.e., why are they still worried in spite of the business judgment rule, 102(b)(7) waivers, and generous indemnification promises?

4. Does the belt-and-suspenders protection against out-of-pocket liability for corporate directors represent good public policy? Or would at least the possibility of out-of-pocket liability cause directors to "sit up straight" in the board room, and do a better job as corporate directors?

5. Regardless of your view for the third question, what is the point of the good faith carve-out? That is, if corporate directors can and do get protection against gross negligence, what is the point of making them liable for even grosser negligence?

Chapter 5 – The Protection of Creditors

Creditor protection is an important aspect of corporate law. The most basic, and perhaps the oldest, protection can be found in fraudulent conveyance doctrine: transfers out of the corporate entity that are intended to delay, hinder, or defraud creditors are voidable. Fraudulent conveyance doctrine protects the assets available to creditors: all of the corporation's assets, subject to normal wear and tear, but (due to limited liability) none of the shareholders' assets. When this reasonable expectation of creditors is violated (say, the corporate controller sells the key assets to his brother-in-law for a pittance), fraudulent conveyance doctrine steps in.

Another, more subtle, form of creditor protection is equitable subordination. As the name suggests, courts can equitably subordinate the claims of affiliated creditors to the corporation, for the purpose of protecting unaffiliated creditors. For example, if management loans the corporation $100, management might have to stand behind other creditors to the corporation in getting their $100 back, in the interest of fairness to outside creditors. As with fraudulent conveyance, the precise triggers of equitable subordination are murky. But the overall principle is to protect the reasonable expectations of creditors against opportunistic behavior by managers and the board.

A third form of creditor protection can be found implicitly in fiduciary duty. Directors and officers owe a duty to the corporation, which means that they have an obligation to maximize overall corporate value. Most of the time, maximizing corporate value is synonymous with maximizing shareholder value. Shareholders are the "residual claimants" on the corporation's cash flows, which means that they stand last in line, to claim whatever is left over after employees, creditors, and all other claims have been paid. Therefore, if boards maximize what shareholders receive, they must necessarily maximize what everyone before them receives as well.

This analysis changes, however, when the corporation is in the "zone of insolvency." Specifically, the board might have an incentive to "roll the dice" and take on risky projects, even if these projects have a negative expected value, because shareholders would receive the benefit if the project does well, and their downside is fixed (at zero) if the project goes poorly. A board that was focused solely on maximizing shareholder value in the zone of insolvency might knowingly take on projects that destroy value (in expected-value terms) for the corporation, but maximize value (again, in expected value terms) for the shareholders.

To mitigate this problem, Delaware case law from the 1980s created an amorphous "duty to creditors" that was triggered in the zone of insolvency. However, this new duty created problems of its own: How would directors know when they were in the zone of insolvency? And when they were, what precisely was triggered by the duty to creditors? More recent case law has cut back considerably on an affirmative duty to creditors. The current formulation can basically be boiled down to the proposition that boards have a fiduciary duty to maximize overall corporate value. Most of the time, that objective is the same as maximizing value for shareholders, but in the zone of insolvency that objective can mean maximizing value for the creditors.

Discussion Question:

1. Construct a quantitative example in which the board must choose between a risky project (say, pursuing litigation) and a safe alternative (say, settlement of litigation). Demonstrate how in the zone of insolvency the board might choose a value-destroying option (pursuing litigation) if the board's duty was solely to shareholders.

The granddaddy of creditor protection, however, is piercing the corporate veil. Unlike fraudulent conveyance and equitable subordination, which simply reverse or modify a particular transaction, piercing the corporate veil opens up an entirely new set of assets for the benefit of the corporation's creditors—namely, the assets of the shareholders themselves. Empirical studies suggest that veil-piercing is the most frequently litigated claim in all of corporate law, in terms of number of cases (though certainly not in terms of dollar value at stake).

Despite the voluminous case law, the doctrine of when a court will pierce the corporate veil is notoriously murky. "'Piercing' seems to happen freakishly. Like lightning, it is rare, severe, and unprincipled."[16] In general, piercing consists of two components: (1) evidence of "lack of separateness," e.g., shareholder domination, thin capitalization, no formalities/co-mingling of assets (sometimes called the "Tinkerbell test"—to be protected, a shareholder must believe in the separation); and (2) unfair or inequitable conduct—this is the wild-card in veil-piercing cases.

Some general contours are discernible. Veil-piercing is highly unlikely to be invoked against public corporations (even the shareholders of Enron did not receive a bill in the mail from Enron creditors after Enron went bankrupt); against passive shareholders or minority shareholders; and if corporate formalities are observed. Recognizing the benefits of asset partitioning, entity shielding, and limited liability as essential ingredients for the corporate form and drivers of economic growth, veil-piercing is invoked sparingly. The following cases provide some applications of veil-piercing doctrine.

Sea-Land Services, Inc. v. The Pepper Source
941 F.2d 519 (7th Cir. 1991)

BAUER, C.J.:

This spicy case finds its origin in several shipments of Jamaican sweet peppers. Appellee Sea-Land Services, Inc. ("Sea-Land"), an ocean carrier, shipped the peppers on behalf of The Pepper Source ("PS"), one of the appellants here. PS then stiffed Sea-Land on the

---

[16] Frank H. Easterbrook & Daniel R. Fischel, "Limited Liability and the Corporation," 52 U. CHI. L. REV. 89 (1985).

freight bill, which was rather substantial. Sea-Land filed a federal diversity action for the money it was owed. On December 2, 1987, the district court entered a default judgment in favor of Sea-Land and against PS in the amount of $86,767.70. But PS was nowhere to be found; it had been "dissolved" in mid-1987 for failure to pay the annual state franchise tax. Worse yet for Sea-Land, even had it not been dissolved, PS apparently had no assets. With the well empty, Sea-Land could not recover its judgment against PS. Hence the instant lawsuit.

In June 1988, Sea-Land brought this action against Gerald J. Marchese and five business entities he owns: PS, Caribe Crown, Inc., Jamar Corp., Salescaster Distributors, Inc., and Marchese Fegan Associates. Marchese also was named individually. Sea-Land sought by this suit to pierce PS's corporate veil and render Marchese personally liable for the judgment owed to Sea-Land, and then "reverse pierce" Marchese's other corporations so that they, too, would be on the hook for the $87,000. Thus, Sea-Land alleged in its complaint that all of these corporations "are alter egos of each other and hide behind the veils of alleged separate corporate existence for the purpose of defrauding plaintiff and other creditors." Not only are the corporations alter egos of each other, alleged Sea-Land, but also they are alter egos of Marchese, who should be held individually liable for the judgment because he created and manipulated these corporations and their assets for his own personal uses. Count III, PP 9-10. (Hot on the heels of the filing of Sea-Land's complaint, PS took the necessary steps to be reinstated as a corporation in Illinois.)

In early 1989, Sea-Land filed an amended complaint adding Tie-Net International, Inc., as a defendant. Unlike the other corporate defendants, Tie-Net is not owned solely by Marchese: he holds half of the stock, and an individual named George Andre owns the other half. Sea-Land alleged that, despite this shared ownership, Tie-Net is but another alter ego of Marchese and the other corporate defendants, and thus it also should be held liable for the judgment against PS.

Through 1989, Sea-Land pursued discovery in this case, including taking a two-day deposition from Marchese. In December 1989, Sea-Land moved for summary judgment. In that motion—which, with the brief in support and the appendices, was about three inches thick—Sea-Land argued that it was "entitled to judgment as a matter of law, since the evidence including deposition testimony and exhibits in the appendix will show that piercing the corporate veil and finding the status of an alter ego is merited in this case." Marchese and the other defendants filed brief responses.

In an order dated June 22, 1990, the court granted Sea-Land's motion. The court discussed and applied the test for corporate veil-piercing explicated in *Van Dorn Co. v. Future Chemical and Oil Corp.*, 753 F.2d 565 (7th Cir. 1985). Analyzing Illinois law, we held in *Van Dorn*:

> [A] corporate entity will be disregarded and the veil of limited liability pierced when two requirements are met: [F]irst, there must be such unity of interest and ownership that the separate personalities of the corporation and the individual [or other corporation] no longer exist; and second,

144

circumstances must be such that adherence to the fiction of separate corporate existence would sanction a fraud or promote injustice.

753 F.2d at 569-70 (quoting *Macaluso v. Jenkins,* 95 Ill. App. 3d 461, 420 N.E.2d 251, 255 (1981)) (other citations omitted). . . . As for determining whether a corporation is so controlled by another to justify disregarding their separate identities, the Illinois cases . . . focus on four factors: "(1) the failure to maintain adequate corporate records or to comply with corporate formalities, (2) the commingling of funds or assets, (3) under-capitalization, and (4) one corporation treating the assets of another corporation as its own." 753 F.2d at 570 (citations omitted). . . .

Following the lead of the parties, the district court in the instant case laid the template of *Van Dorn* over the facts of this case. The court concluded that both halves and all features of the test had been satisfied, and, therefore, entered judgment in favor of Sea-Land and against PS, Caribe Crown, Jamar, Salescaster, Tie-Net, and Marchese individually. These defendants were held jointly liable for Sea-Land's $87,000 judgment, as well as for post-judgment interest under Illinois law. From that judgment Marchese and the other defendants brought a timely appeal.

Because this is an appeal from a grant of summary judgment, our review is de novo. . . .

The first and most striking feature that emerges from our examination of the record is that these corporate defendants are, indeed, little but Marchese's playthings. Marchese is the sole shareholder of PS, Caribe Crown, Jamar, and Salescaster. He is one of the two shareholders of Tie-Net. Except for Tie-Net, none of the corporations ever held a single corporate meeting. (At the handful of Tie-Net meetings held by Marchese and Andre, no minutes were taken.) During his deposition, Marchese did not remember any of these corporations ever passing articles of incorporation, bylaws, or other agreements. As for physical facilities, Marchese runs all of these corporations (including Tie-Net) out of the same, single office, with the same phone line, the same expense accounts, and the like. And how he does "run" the expense accounts! When he fancies to, Marchese "borrows" substantial sums of money from these corporations—interest free, of course. The corporations also "borrow" money from each other when need be, which left at least PS completely out of capital when the Sea-Land bills came due. What's more, Marchese has used the bank accounts of these corporations to pay all kinds of personal expenses, including alimony and child support payments to his ex-wife, education expenses for his children, maintenance of his personal automobiles, health care for his pet—the list goes on and on. Marchese did not even have a personal bank account! (With "corporate" accounts like these, who needs one?)

And Tie-Net is just as much a part of this as the other corporations. On appeal, Marchese makes much of the fact that he shares ownership of Tie-Net, and that Sea-Land has not been able to find an example of funds flowing from PS to Tie-Net to the detriment of Sea-Land and PS's other creditors. So what? The record reveals that, in all material senses, Marchese treated Tie-Net like his other corporations: he "borrowed" over $30,000 from Tie-Net; money and "loans" flowed freely between Tie-Net and the other corporations; and

145

Marchese charged up various personal expenses (including $460 for a picture of himself with President Bush) on Tie-Net's credit card. Marchese was not deterred by the fact that he did not hold all of the stock of Tie-Net; why should his creditors be?

In sum, we agree with the district court that there can be no doubt that the "shared control/unity of interest and ownership" part of the *Van Dorn* test is met in this case: corporate records and formalities have not been maintained; funds and assets have been commingled with abandon; PS, the offending corporation, and perhaps others have been undercapitalized; and corporate assets have been moved and tapped and "borrowed" without regard to their source. Indeed, Marchese basically punted this part of the inquiry before the district court by coming forward with little or no evidence in response to Sea-Land's extensively supported argument on these points. That fact alone was enough to do him in; opponents to summary judgment motions cannot simply rest on their laurels, but must come forward with specific facts showing that there is a genuine issue for trial. . . . Regarding the elements that make up the first half of the *Van Dorn* test, Marchese and the other defendants have not done so. Thus, Sea-Land is entitled to judgment on these points.

The second part of the *Van Dorn* test is more problematic, however. "Unity of interest and ownership" is not enough; Sea-Land also must show that honoring the separate corporate existences of the defendants "would sanction a fraud or promote injustice." *Van Dorn*, 753 F.2d at 570. This last phrase truly is disjunctive:

> Although an intent to defraud creditors would surely play a part if established, the Illinois test does not require proof of such intent. Once the first element of the test is established, *either* the sanctioning of a fraud (intentional wrongdoing) or the promotion of injustice, will satisfy the second element.

Id. (emphasis in original). Seizing on this, Sea-Land has abandoned the language in its two complaints that make repeated references to "fraud" by Marchese, and has chosen not to attempt to prove that PS and Marchese intended to defraud it—which would be quite difficult on summary judgment. Instead, Sea-Land has argued that honoring the defendants' separate identities would "promote injustice."

But what, exactly, does "promote injustice" mean, and how does one establish it on summary judgment? These are the critical, troublesome questions in this case. To start with, as the above passage from *Van Dorn* makes clear, "promote injustice" means something less than an affirmative showing of fraud—but how much less? In its one-sentence treatment of this point, the district court held that it was enough that "Sea-Land would be denied a judicially-imposed recovery." Sea-Land defends this reasoning on appeal, arguing that "permitting the appellants to hide behind the shield of limited liability would clearly serve as an injustice against appellee" because it would "impermissibly deny appellee satisfaction." Appellee's Brief at 14-15. But that cannot be what is meant by "promote injustice." The prospect of an unsatisfied judgment looms in every veil-piercing action; why else would a plaintiff bring such an action? Thus, if an unsatisfied judgment is enough for the "promote injustice" feature of the test, then every plaintiff will pass on that score, and *Van Dorn* collapses into a one-step "unity of interest and ownership" test.

Because we cannot abide such a result we will undertake our own review of Illinois cases to determine how the "promote injustice" feature of the veil-piercing inquiry has been interpreted. In *Pederson* [*v. Paragon Enterprises,* 214 Ill. App. 3d 815, 158 Ill. Dec. 371, 373, 547 N.E.2d 165, 167 (1st Dist. 1991)], . . . the court offered the following summary: "Some element of unfairness, something akin to fraud or deception or the existence of a compelling public interest must be present in order to disregard the corporate fiction." 214 Ill. App. 3d at 821, 158 Ill. Dec. at 375, 574 N.E.2d at 169. (The court ultimately refused to pierce the corporate veil in *Pederson,* at least in part because "[n]othing in these facts provides evidence of scheming on the part of defendant to commit a fraud on potential creditors [of the two defendant corporations]." *Id.* at 823, 158 Ill. Dec. at 376, 574 N.E.2d at 169.)

The light shed on this point by other Illinois cases can be seen only if we examine the cases on their facts. . . .

Generalizing from these cases, we see that the courts that properly have pierced corporate veils to avoid "promoting injustice" have found that, unless it did so, some "wrong" beyond a creditor's inability to collect would result: the common sense rules of adverse possession would be undermined; former partners would be permitted to skirt the legal rules concerning monetary obligations; a party would be unjustly enriched; a parent corporation that caused a sub's liabilities and its inability to pay for them would escape those liabilities; or an intentional scheme to squirrel assets into a liability-free corporation while heaping liabilities upon an asset-free corporation would be successful. Sea-Land, although it alleged in its complaint the kind of intentional asset-and-liability-shifting found in *Van Dorn,* has yet to come forward with evidence akin to the "wrongs" found in these cases. Apparently, it believed as did the district court, that its unsatisfied judgment was enough. That belief was in error, and the entry of summary judgment premature. We, therefore, reverse the judgment and remand the case to the district court.

On remand, the court should require that Sea-Land produce, if it desires summary judgment, evidence and argument that would establish the kind of additional "wrong" present in the above cases. For example, perhaps Sea-Land could establish that Marchese, like Roth in *Van Dorn,* used these corporate facades to avoid its responsibilities to creditors; or that PS, Marchese, or one of the other corporations will be "unjustly enriched" unless liability is shared by all. Of course, Sea-Land is not required fully to prove intent to defraud, which it probably could not do on summary judgment anyway. But it is required to show the kind of injustice to merit the evocation of the court's essentially equitable power to prevent "injustice." It may well be that, after more of such evidence is adduced, no genuine issue of fact exists to prevent Sea-Land from reaching Marchese's other pet corporations for PS's debt. Or it may be that only a finder of fact will be able to determine whether fraud or "injustice" is involved here. In any event, the record as it currently stands is insufficient to uphold the entry of summary judgment.

REVERSED and REMANDED with instructions.

Discussion Questions:

1. Why does the plaintiff need to "reverse pierce"? (Isn't it good enough to gain recourse against Marchese's personal assets?) What policy concerns does reverse piercing raise, if it were to become a pervasive remedy?

2. On remand, the district court pierced the corporate veil against Marchese, on the grounds that maintaining the veil would "sanction a fraud or promote injustice" because Marchese had committed blatant tax fraud and had fraudulently represented that Sea-Land's bills would be paid while he was manipulating the corporate accounts (yet again) to ensure that they would not. Is this the kind of fraud that should satisfy the "fraud or injustice" prong of piercing doctrine?

Kinney Shoe Corp. v. Polan
939 F.2d 209 (4th Cir. 1991)

CHAPMAN, SENIOR CIR. J.:

Plaintiff-appellant Kinney Shoe Corporation ("Kinney") brought this action in the United States District Court for the Southern District of West Virginia against Lincoln M. Polan ("Polan") seeking to recover money owed on a sublease between Kinney and Industrial Realty Company ("Industrial"). Polan is the sole shareholder of Industrial. The district court found that Polan was not personally liable on the lease between Kinney and Industrial. Kinney appeals asserting that the corporate veil should be pierced, and we agree. . . .

The district court based its order on facts which were stipulated by the parties. In 1984 Polan formed two corporations, Industrial and Polan Industries, Inc., for the purpose of re-establishing an industrial manufacturing business. The certificate of incorporation for Polan Industries, Inc. was issued by the West Virginia Secretary of State in November 1984. The following month the certificate of incorporation for Industrial was issued. Polan was the owner of both corporations. Although certificates of incorporation were issued, no organizational meetings were held, and no officers were elected.

In November 1984 Polan and Kinney began negotiating the sublease of a building in which Kinney held a leasehold interest. The building was owned by the Cabell County Commission and financed by industrial revenue bonds issued in 1968 to induce Kinney to locate a manufacturing plant in Huntington, West Virginia. Under the terms of the lease, Kinney was legally obligated to make payments on the bonds on a semi-annual basis through January 1, 1993, at which time it had the right to purchase the property. Kinney had ceased using the building as a manufacturing plant in June 1983.

The term of the sublease from Kinney to Industrial commenced in December 1984, even though the written lease was not signed by the parties until April 5, 1985. On April 15, 1985, Industrial subleased part of the building to Polan Industries, for fifty percent of the rental amount due Kinney. Polan signed both subleases on behalf of the respective companies.

Other than the sublease with Kinney, Industrial had no assets, no income and no bank account. Industrial issued no stock certificates because nothing was ever paid in to this corporation. Industrial's only income was from its sublease to Polan Industries, Inc. The first rental payment to Kinney was made out of Polan's personal funds, and no further payments were made by Polan or by Polan Industries, Inc. to either Industrial or to Kinney.

Kinney filed suit against Industrial for unpaid rent and obtained a judgment in the amount of $166,400 on June 19, 1987. A writ of possession was issued, but because Polan Industries, Inc. had filed for bankruptcy, Kinney did not gain possession for six months. Kinney leased the building until it was sold on September 1, 1988. Kinney then filed this action against Polan individually to collect the amount owed by Industrial to Kinney. Since the amount to which Kinney is entitled is undisputed, the only issue is whether Kinney can pierce the corporate veil and hold Polan personally liable.

The district court held that Kinney had assumed the risk of Industrial's undercapitalization and was not entitled to pierce the corporate veil. Kinney appeals, and we reverse. . . .

We have long recognized that a corporation is an entity, separate and distinct from its officers and stockholders, and the individual stockholders are not responsible for the debts of the corporation. . . . This concept, however, is a fiction of the law "'and it is now well settled, as a general principle, that the fiction should be disregarded when it is urged with an intent not within its reason and purpose, and in such a way that its retention would produce injustices or inequitable consequences.'" *Laya v. Erin Homes, Inc.*, 352 S.E.2d 93, 97-98 (W. Va. 1986). . . . Piercing the corporate veil is an equitable remedy, and the burden rests with the party asserting such claim. A totality of the circumstances test is used in determining whether to pierce the corporate veil, and each case must be decided on its own facts. The district court's findings of facts may be overturned only if clearly erroneous.

Kinney seeks to pierce the corporate veil of Industrial so as to hold Polan personally liable on the sublease debt. The Supreme Court of Appeals of West Virginia has set forth a two-prong test to be used in determining whether to pierce the corporate veil in a breach of contract case. This test raises two issues. First, is the unity of interest and ownership such that the separate personalities of the corporation and the individual shareholder no longer exist; and second, would an inequitable result occur if the acts were treated as those of the corporation alone. In *Laya*, 352 S.E.2d at 99. Numerous factors have been identified as relevant in making this determination.

The district court found that the two prong test of *Laya* had been satisfied. The court concluded that Polan's failure to carry out the corporate formalities with respect to

Industrial, coupled with Industrial's gross undercapitalization, resulted in damage to Kinney. We agree.

It is undisputed that Industrial was not adequately capitalized. Actually, it had no paid in capital. Polan had put nothing into this corporation, and it did not observe any corporate formalities. As the West Virginia court stated in *Laya*, "[i]ndividuals who wish to enjoy limited personal liability for business activities under a corporate umbrella should be expected to adhere to the relatively simple formalities of creating and maintaining a corporate entity." *Laya*, 352 S.E.2d at 100, n.6 . . . . This, the court stated, is "a relatively small price to pay for limited liability." *Id.* Another important factor is adequate capitalization. "[G]rossly inadequate capitalization combined with disregard of corporate formalities, causing basic unfairness, are sufficient to pierce the corporate veil in order to hold the shareholder(s) actively participating in the operation of the business personally liable for a breach of contract to the party who entered into the contract with the corporation." *Laya*, 352 S.E.2d at 101-02.

In this case, Polan bought no stock, made no capital contribution, kept no minutes, and elected no officers for Industrial. In addition, Polan attempted to protect his assets by placing them in Polan Industries, Inc. and interposing Industrial between Polan Industries, Inc. and Kinney so as to prevent Kinney from going against the corporation with assets. Polan gave no explanation or justification for the existence of Industrial as the intermediary between Polan Industries, Inc. and Kinney. Polan was obviously trying to limit his liability and the liability of Polan Industries, Inc. by setting up a paper curtain constructed of nothing more than Industrial's certificate of incorporation. These facts present the classic scenario for an action to pierce the corporate veil so as to reach the responsible party and produce an equitable result. Accordingly, we hold that the district court correctly found that the two prong test in *Laya* had been satisfied. In *Laya*, the court also noted that when determining whether to pierce a corporate veil a third prong may apply in certain cases. The court stated:

> When, under the circumstances, it would be reasonable for that particular type of a party [those contract creditors capable of protecting themselves] entering into a contract with the corporation, for example, a bank or other lending institution, to conduct an investigation of the credit of the corporation prior to entering into the contract, such party will be charged with the knowledge that a reasonable credit investigation would disclose. If such an investigation would disclose that the corporation is grossly undercapitalized, based upon the nature and the magnitude of the corporate undertaking, such party will be deemed to have assumed the risk of the gross undercapitalization and will not be permitted to pierce the corporate veil.

Laya, 352 S.E.2d at 100. The district court applied this third prong and concluded that Kinney "assumed the risk of Industrial's defaulting" and that "the application of the doctrine of 'piercing the corporate veil' ought not and does not [apply]." While we agree that the two prong test of *Laya* was satisfied, we hold that the district court's conclusion that Kinney had assumed the risk is clearly erroneous.

150

Without deciding whether the third prong should be extended beyond the context of the financial institution lender mentioned in *Laya,* we hold that, even if it applies to creditors such as Kinney, it does not prevent Kinney from piercing the corporate veil in this case. The third prong is permissive and not mandatory. This is not a factual situation that calls for the third prong, if we are to seek an equitable result. Polan set up Industrial to limit his liability and the liability of Polan Industries, Inc. in their dealings with Kinney. A stockholder's liability is limited to the amount he has invested in the corporation, but Polan invested nothing in Industrial. This corporation was no more than a shell—a transparent shell. When nothing is invested in the corporation, the corporation provides no protection to its owner; nothing in, nothing out, no protection. If Polan wishes the protection of a corporation to limit his liability, he must follow the simple formalities of maintaining the corporation. This he failed to do, and he may not relieve his circumstances by saying Kinney should have known better....

For the foregoing reasons, we hold that Polan is personally liable for the debt of Industrial, and the decision of the district court is reversed and this case is remanded with instructions to enter judgment for the plaintiff.

REVERSED AND REMANDED WITH INSTRUCTIONS.

Discussion Questions:

1. What does it tell you that Kinney had ceased using the building as a manufacturing plant in June 1983, but the sublease did not begin until January 1984? (If this question seems abstruse, imagine a situation where you are trying to sublet your apartment for the summer, but a potential tenant only shows up in July—how much negotiation power do you think you would have?)

2. How do you compare Marchese's and Polan's behavior (the defendants in *Sea-Land Services* and *Kinney Shoe*)? Notice that the Seventh Circuit declined to pierce on the facts in *Sea-Land* (reversing the District Court), while the Fourth Circuit pierced in *Kinney Shoe* (also reversing the District Court). Which court(s) got it right?

Walkovszky v. Carlton
223 N.E.2d 6 (N.Y. 1966)

FULD, J.:

This case involves what appears to be a rather common practice in the taxicab industry of vesting the ownership of a taxi fleet in many corporations, each owning only one or two cabs.

The complaint alleges that the plaintiff was severely injured four years ago in New York City when he was run down by a taxicab owned by the defendant Seon Cab Corporation and negligently operated at the time by the defendant Marchese. The individual defendant, Carlton, is claimed to be a stockholder of 10 corporations, including Seon, each of which has but two cabs registered in its name, and it is implied that only the minimum automobile liability insurance required by law (in the amount of $10,000) is carried on any one cab. Although seemingly independent of one another, these corporations are alleged to be "operated . . . as a single entity, unit and enterprise" with regard to financing, supplies, repairs, employees and garaging, and all are named as defendants. The plaintiff asserts that he is also entitled to hold their stockholders personally liable for the damages sought because the multiple corporate structure constitutes an unlawful attempt "to defraud members of the general public" who might be injured by the cabs.

The defendant Carlton has moved . . . to dismiss the complaint on the ground that as to him it "fails to state a cause of action." The court at Special Term granted the motion but the Appellate Division, by a divided vote, reversed, holding that a valid cause of action was sufficiently stated. The defendant Carlton appeals to us, from the nonfinal order, by leave of the Appellate Division on a certified question.

The law permits the incorporation of a business for the very purpose of enabling its proprietors to escape personal liability . . . but, manifestly, the privilege is not without its limits. Broadly speaking, the courts will disregard the corporate form, or, to use accepted terminology, "pierce the corporate veil," whenever necessary "to prevent fraud or to achieve equity." . . . [W]henever anyone uses control of the corporation to further his own rather than the corporation's business, he will be liable for the corporation's acts "upon the principle of respondeat superior applicable even where the agent is a natural person." . . . Such liability, moreover, extends not only to the corporation's commercial dealings . . . but to its negligent acts as well.

In the *Mangan* case (247 App. Div. 853 . . .), the plaintiff was injured as a result of the negligent operation of a cab owned and operated by one of four corporations affiliated with the defendant Terminal. Although the defendant was not a stockholder of any of the operating companies, both the defendant and the operating companies were owned, for the most part, by the same parties. The defendant's name (Terminal) was conspicuously displayed on the sides of all the taxis used in the enterprise and, in point of fact, the defendant actually serviced, inspected, repaired and dispatched them. These facts were deemed to provide sufficient cause for piercing the corporate veil of the operating company—the nominal owner of the cab which injured the plaintiff—and holding the defendant liable. The operating companies were simple instrumentalities for carrying on the business of the defendant without imposing upon it financial and other liabilities incident to the actual ownership and operation of the cabs. . . .

In the case before us, the plaintiff has explicitly alleged that none of the corporations "had a separate existence of their own" and, as indicated above, all are named as defendants. However, it is one thing to assert that a corporation is a fragment of a larger corporate combine which actually conducts the business. (See Berle, "The Theory of Enterprise Entity," 47 Col. L. Rev. 343, 348-350.) It is quite another to claim that the corporation is a "dummy" for its individual stockholders who are in reality carrying on the business in their personal capacities for purely personal rather than corporate ends.... Either circumstance would justify treating the corporation as an agent and piercing the corporate veil to reach the principal but a different result would follow in each case. In the first, only a larger corporate entity would be held financially responsible . . . while, in the other, the stockholder would be personally liable....

At this stage in the present litigation, we are concerned only with the pleadings and, since CPLR §3014 permits causes of action to be stated "alternatively or hypothetically," it is possible for the plaintiff to allege both theories as the basis for his demand for judgment.... Reading the complaint in this case most favorably and liberally, we do not believe that there can be gathered from its averments the allegations required to spell out a valid cause of action against the defendant Carlton.

The individual defendant is charged with having "organized, managed, dominated and controlled" a fragmented corporate entity but there are no allegations that he was conducting business in his individual capacity. Had the taxicab fleet been owned by a single corporation, it would be readily apparent that the plaintiff would face formidable barriers in attempting to establish personal liability on the part of the corporation's stockholders. The fact that the fleet ownership has been deliberately split up among many corporations does not ease the plaintiff's burden in that respect. The corporate form may not be disregarded merely because the assets of the corporation, together with the mandatory insurance coverage of the vehicle which struck the plaintiff, are insufficient to assure him the recovery sought. If Carlton were to be held individually liable on those facts alone, the decision would apply equally to the thousands of cabs which are owned by their individual drivers who conduct their businesses through corporations organized pursuant to section 401 of the Business Corporation Law, ... and carry the minimum insurance.... These taxi owner-operators are entitled to form such corporations ... and we agree with the court at Special Term that, if the insurance coverage required by statute "is inadequate for the protection of the public, the remedy lies not with the courts but with the Legislature." It may very well be sound policy to require that certain corporations must take out liability insurance which will afford adequate compensation to their potential tort victims. However, the responsibility for imposing conditions on the privilege of incorporation has been committed by the Constitution to the Legislature....

This is not to say that it is impossible for the plaintiff to state a valid cause of action against the defendant Carlton. However, the simple fact is that the plaintiff has just not done so here. While the complaint alleges that the separate corporations were undercapitalized and that their assets have been intermingled, it is barren of any "sufficiently particular(ized) statements" ... that the defendant Carlton and his associates are actually doing business in their individual capacities, shuttling their personal funds in and out of the corporations "without regard to formality and to suit their immediate convenience." *Weisser v. Mursam Shoe Corp.,* 127 F.2d 344 .... Nothing of the sort has in fact been charged, and it cannot reasonably or logically be inferred from the happenstance that the business of Seon Cab Corporation may actually be carried on by a large corporate entity composed of many corporations which, under general principles of agency, would be liable to each other's creditors in contract and in tort.

In point of fact, the principle relied upon in the complaint to sustain the imposition of personal liability is not agency but fraud. Such a cause of action cannot withstand analysis. If it is not fraudulent for the owner-operator of a single cab corporation to take out only the minimum required liability insurance, the enterprise does not become either illicit or fraudulent merely because it consists of many corporations. The plaintiff's injuries are the same regardless of whether the cab which strikes him is owned by a single corporation or part of a fleet with ownership fragmented among many corporations. Whatever rights he may be able to assert against parties other than the registered owner of the vehicle come into being not because he has been defrauded but because, under the principle of respondeat superior, he is entitled to hold the whole enterprise responsible for the acts of its agents.

In sum, then, the complaint falls short of adequately stating a cause of action against the defendant Carlton in his individual capacity.

The order of the Appellate Division should be reversed, with . . . leave to serve an amended complaint.

KEATING, J. (dissenting):

The defendant Carlton, the shareholder here sought to be held for the negligence of the driver of a taxicab, was a principal shareholder and organizer of the defendant corporation which owned the taxicab. The corporation was one of 10 organized by the defendant, each containing two cabs and each cab having the "minimum liability" insurance coverage mandated by section 370 of the Vehicle and Traffic Law. The sole assets of these operating corporations are the vehicles themselves and they are apparently subject to mortgages.

From their inception these corporations were intentionally undercapitalized for the purpose of avoiding responsibility for acts which were bound to arise as a result of the operation of a large taxi fleet having cars out on the street 24 hours a day and engaged in public transportation. And during the course of the corporations' existence all income was continually drained out of the corporations for the same purpose.

The issue presented by this action is whether the policy of this State, which affords those desiring to engage in a business enterprise the privilege of limited liability through the use of the corporate device, is so strong that it will permit that privilege to continue no matter how much it is abused, no matter how irresponsibly the corporation is operated, no matter what the cost to the public. I do not believe that it is.

Under the circumstances of this case the shareholders should all be held individually liable to this plaintiff for the injuries he suffered. . . . At least, the matter should not be disposed of on the pleadings by a dismissal of the complaint. . . .

The policy of this State has always been to provide and facilitate recovery for those injured through the negligence of others. The automobile, by its very nature, is capable of causing severe and costly injuries when not operated in a proper manner. The great increase in the number of automobile accidents combined with the frequent financial irresponsibility of the individual driving the car led to the adoption of section 388 of the Vehicle and Traffic law which had the effect of imposing upon the owner of the vehicle the responsibility for its negligent operation. It is upon this very statute that the cause of action against both the corporation and the individual defendant is predicated.

In addition the Legislature, still concerned with the financial irresponsibility of those who owned and operated motor vehicles, enacted a statute requiring minimum liability coverage for all owners of automobiles. The important public policy represented by both these statutes is outlined in section 310 of the Vehicle and Traffic Law. That section provides that: "The legislature is concerned over the rising toll of motor vehicle accidents and the suffering and loss thereby afflicted. . . . "

The defendant Carlton claims that, because the minimum amount of insurance required by the statute was obtained, the corporate veil cannot and should not be pierced despite the fact that the assets of the corporation which owned the cab were "trifling compared with the business to be done and the risks of loss" which were certain to be encountered. I do not agree.

The Legislature is requiring minimum liability insurance of $10,000, no doubt intended to provide at least some small fund for recovery against those individuals and corporations who just did not have and were not able to raise or accumulate assets sufficient to satisfy the claims of those who were injured as a result of their negligence. It certainly could not have intended to shield those individuals who organized corporations, with the specific intent of avoiding responsibility to the public, where the operation of the corporate enterprise yielded profits sufficient to purchase additional insurance. . . .

The defendant contends that a decision holding him personally liable would discourage people from engaging in corporate enterprise.

What I would merely hold is that a participating shareholder of a corporation vested with a public interest, organized with capital insufficient to meet liabilities which are certain to arise in the ordinary course of the corporation's business, may be held personally responsible for such liabilities. Where corporate income is not sufficient to cover the cost of insurance premiums above the statutory minimum or where initially adequate finances dwindle under the pressure of competition, bad times or extraordinary and unexpected liability, obviously the shareholder will not be held liable. . . .

The only type of corporate enterprises that will be discouraged as a result of a decision allowing the individual shareholder to be sued will be those such as the one in question, designed solely to abuse the corporate privilege at the expense of the public interest.

For these reasons I would vote to affirm the order of the Appellate Division.

DESMOND, C.J., and VAN VOORHIS, BURKE and SCILEPPI, JJ., concur with FULD, J.

KEATING, J., dissents and votes to affirm in an opinion in which BERGAN, J., concurs.

Order reversed, etc.

Discussion Questions:

1. Notice that the plaintiff in *Walkovszky* was a tort victim. Unlike the contracting parties in *Sea-Land Services* and *Kinney Shoe*, tort victims cannot contract around the limited liability feature, and they never agreed to it. Doesn't limited liability externalize risks, and therefore encourage corporations to engage in excessively risky behavior?

2. Even worse, how did Carlton structure his corporations to make maximum use of the limited liability shield? Doesn't this kind of corporate structure really encourage corporations to engage in excessively risky behavior? Shouldn't we consolidate all of Carlton's assets in order to satisfy tort claims?

3. What features of the business or regulatory landscape might mitigate the concern of excessive risk-taking due to limited liability of corporations?

There is a happ(ier) ending to the story in *Walkovszky*, in two respects. First, the plaintiff amended his complaint, and this time the Appellate Division held that "the amended complaint successfully alleges a cause of action against appellant, i.e., that he and the other individual defendants were conducting the business of the taxicab fleet in their individual capacities." *Walkovszky v. Carlton*, 29 A.D.2d 763 (1968). Second, Walkovszky would have better recourse today—taxicab medallions, which are extremely valuable, are no longer judgment proof in New York City; and a new owner of a medallion in an execution sale must pay off any tort victims of the former owner.

Chapter 6 – Fiduciary Duties of Controlling Shareholders

Corporate law imposes fiduciary duties on controlling shareholders. The reason is the same as for directors and officers: controlling shareholders might use their power over the corporation in ways that defeat the reasonable expectations of the minority shareholders. Without imposing a fiduciary duty on controlling shareholders to treat minority shareholders fairly, minority shareholders will decline to invest, or will insist on more favorable terms. A long line of research (known as the "law and finance" literature) finds an empirical connection between protections for minority shareholders and the development of capital markets around the world. In certain developing parts of the world (e.g., Turkey, India) the largest corporations are still privately held by extremely wealthy families. This might be due, at least in part, to the unwillingness of the controlling family to give up control combined with the inability for that family to attract minority capital in the absence of adequate procedural protections. Without access to public capital, these companies are likely to grow more slowly than they otherwise might.

In general, the U.S. provides the most substantial protections for minority shareholders around the world. Still, there are regular allegations of abuse by controlling shareholders, as the following article illustrates.

Holman W. Jenkins, Jr., *Minority Shareholders Wise Up in 2016*
Wall Street Journal **(Dec. 26, 2016)**

"There ought to be a law" is always somebody's idea of a solution when corporate governance problems crop up. It's usually a bad idea, even with the past year's excess supply of aggrieved minority shareholders.

The great virtue of our corporate system is that investors have thousands of companies to choose from. If a company's governance or ownership structure aren't what you think they should be, don't buy its shares. Caveat emptor, in most cases, is a better regulator than any regulator.

That's true even in a case like Viacom's, where the problem was a prolonged squabble over a successor to a possibly incapacitated controlling shareholder. Sumner Redstone, the aged founder, had every incentive to avoid such a problem in the first place. He didn't. And as uncertainty over his leadership dragged out, Viacom failed to adapt its mediocre and dispensable cable TV networks to the digital age.

Now his daughter, Shari Redstone, is in charge. Shareholders of CBS, another company in which she has an influential stake, have lately worried about being railroaded into a merger with Viacom to suit Ms. Redstone.

To those who say law and regulation should provide a solution, there is one: It's called steering clear of companies with controlling shareholders if you don't like the risk.

This applies also to Michael Dell of Dell Computer, whose 2013 management buyout left many shareholders feeling shortchanged. This year he lost a mostly symbolic shareholder lawsuit on the matter, but the case also reaffirmed our basic judgment at the time: Mr. Dell legitimately had his shareholders over a barrel.

Another buyer could have offered a higher price, but Carl Icahn, Mr. Dell's chief critic, didn't and neither did anyone else. Maybe potential buyers feared that outbidding a charismatic founder would win them a demoralized and devalued company. Who knows? But it's not obvious what the solution would be except for investors to be careful when getting in bed with a charismatic founder in the first place.

Shareholders of Tesla last month didn't like their money being used to bail out another Elon Musk-backed company, Solar City. But Tesla's share value inordinately depends on Mr. Musk's reputation as a genius and capitalist conjurer. Now those investors who bought into this story were being asked to chip in for Solar City if that's what it takes to maintain the Musk bubble. We'd say that's their lookout.

Ditto a recent lawsuit charging that Facebook founder Mark Zuckerberg was improperly coached when cajoling his board this year to let him maintain voting control as he sells shares to fund his philanthropic efforts. So what? Mr. Zuckerberg already has control so never was going to settle for any terms that don't leave him in control....

Some bits of advice become clichés because they have to be repeated over and over: Trust but verify. Fool me twice, shame on me. These are elements of eternal wisdom that investors can console themselves with when they get on the wrong side of highhanded controlling shareholders.

This chapter explores the contours of the fiduciary duty that controlling shareholders owe minority shareholders. Before jumping in, it is useful to understand the three ways that a control stake can be created.

First, and most simply, a control stake can be bought in a private transaction. Under Delaware law, a control stake can be sold for a premium (the so-called "market rule"), though the seller has an obligation to not sell to a known "looter" (i.e., someone who will take assets out of the company) and the seller cannot "sell" their corporate office (in the form of an even higher premium) along with the control stake. Of course, violations of these principles are hard to detect, and the Delaware doctrine governing these prohibitions is murky. There is an even more inchoate exception to the market rule, that the seller cannot sell a corporate opportunity (see *Perlman v. Feldmann*, below).

Second, a 100% shareholder can sell a minority stake, e.g., to friends and family, "angel" investors (usually a slightly broader group than friends and family), to a venture capitalist, and or to the public (the last in the form of an initial public offering, or IPO). Although fiduciary duty claims could theoretically arise with respect to a 100% shareholder (for example, acting opportunistically against creditors), the fiduciary duties of controlling shareholders generally become more salient as the size of the control block gets smaller.

Third, a third-party can assemble a control block—either by buying shares over time, or (in the case of a public company) through a tender offer to all shareholders. The Williams Act, promulgated in 1968, and its accompanying SEC rules provide strict guidelines on how a tender offer must be conducted. (See 1934 Act §14(d) and accompanying Rules) For example, the offeror must disclose its identity and future plans, including any intention to take the company private ((§14(d)(1)). And there is a general anti-fraud provision, which prohibits any "fraudulent, deceptive, or manipulative" practices in connection with a tender offer. (§14(e))

Certain SEC Rules also govern the substantive terms of the tender offer. For example, the buyer must leave the tender offer open for at least 20 business days (Rule 14e-1), the buyer cannot buy shares "outside" the tender offer during this period (Rule 14e-5), and the offer must be made to all shareholders, and all purchases must be made at the best price (Rule 14d-10). If the offer is over-subscribed (for example, 80% of shares are tendered but the buyer only wants 51%), the buyer must buy shares on a pro rata basis (not first-come, first-served).

While the Williams Act and accompanying rules heavily regulate tender offers, they do not define what a tender offer actually is. To fill this gap, case law has developed the proposition that a tender offer, roughly speaking, is an offer for a substantial percentage of the corporation's stock, at a premium over the prevailing market price, with fixed (not negotiable) terms, and is open only for a limited period of time.

Discussion Questions:

1. Why do you think that control blocks trade at a premium? (Or put differently, why is owning 51% of a corporation not just worth 51 times more than owning 1%?)

2. The Delaware courts have held that a control block can be as small as 30-35% of the outstanding shares, particularly if the other shares are widely-held, because less than 51% could still constitute effective control of the corporation. Why are Delaware courts more suspicious of these smaller controlling shareholders? (Shouldn't it be the opposite, i.e., the bigger the gorilla the more you should be afraid of them?)

3. Until recently, any group looking to buy a National Football League team had to be led by a single individual who owned at least 30% of the team. Why do you think the NFL would require a (close to) controlling shareholder in every NFL team? Extra credit: there is one NFL team that is widely-held; it was grandfathered in when the rule was put into place. Which team is it? Extra extra credit: why do you think the NFL is loosening its 30% requirement?

4. Prior to the Williams Act, aggressive acquirors used to make "Saturday Night Special" tender offers, which were open for an extremely short window; or "cascading" tender offers, which would offer a high price for those who tendered early and lower prices for those who tendered later. What was so bad about such offers that the Williams Act prohibited them? (Department stores often advertise "One-Day Only" sales—what is different about a tender offer?)

Perlman v. Feldmann
219 F.2d 173 (2d Cir. 1955), cert denied, 349 U.S. 952 (1955)

CLARK, C.J.:

This is a derivative action brought by minority stockholders of Newport Steel Corporation to compel accounting for, and restitution of, allegedly illegal gains which accrued to defendants as a result of the sale in August, 1950, of their controlling interest in the corporation. The principal defendant, C. Russell Feldmann, who represented and acted for the others, members of his family, was at that time not only the dominant stockholder, but also the chairman of the board of directors and the president of the corporation. Newport, an Indiana corporation, operated mills for the production of steel sheets for sale to manufacturers of steel products, first at Newport, Kentucky, and later also at other places in Kentucky and Ohio. The buyers, a syndicate organized as Wilport Company, a Delaware corporation, consisted of end-users of steel who were interested in securing a source of supply in a market becoming ever tighter in the Korean War.

Plaintiffs contend that the consideration paid for the stock included compensation for the sale of a corporate asset, a power held in trust for the corporation by Feldmann as its fiduciary. This power was the ability to control the allocation of the corporate product in a time of short supply, through control of the board of directors; and it was effectively transferred in this sale by having Feldmann procure the resignation of his own board and the election of Wilport's nominees immediately upon consummation of the sale.

... Jurisdiction below was based upon the diverse citizenship of the parties. Plaintiffs argue ... that in the situation here disclosed the vendors must account to the non-participating minority stockholders for that share of their profit which is attributable to the sale of the corporate power. Judge Hincks denied the validity of the premise, holding that the rights involved in the sale were only those normally incident to the possession of a controlling block of shares, with which a dominant stockholder, in the absence of fraud or foreseeable looting, was entitled to deal according to his own best interests. Furthermore, he held that plaintiffs had failed to satisfy their burden of proving that the sales price was not a fair price for the stock per se. ...

The essential facts found by the trial judge are not in dispute. Newport was a relative newcomer in the steel industry with predominantly old installations which were in the process of being supplemented by more modern facilities. Except in times of extreme shortage Newport was not in a position to compete profitably with other steel mills for customers not in its immediate geographical area. Wilport, the purchasing syndicate, consisted of geographically remote end-users of steel who were interested in buying more steel from Newport than they had been able to obtain during recent periods of tight supply. The price of $20 per share was found by Judge Hincks to be a fair one for a control block of stock, although the over-the-counter market price had not exceeded $12 and the book value per share was $17.03. But this finding was limited by Judge Hincks' statement that "[what] value the block would have had if shorn of its appurtenant power to control distribution of the corporate product, the evidence does not show." It was also conditioned by his earlier ruling that the burden was on plaintiffs to prove a lesser value for the stock.

Both as director and as dominant stockholder, Feldmann stood in a fiduciary relationship to the corporation and to the minority stockholders as beneficiaries thereof. . . . Although there is no Indiana case directly in point, the most closely analogous one emphasizes the close scrutiny to which Indiana subjects the conduct of fiduciaries when personal benefit may stand in the way of fulfillment of trust obligations. . . . Directors of a corporation are its agents, and they are governed by the rules of law applicable to other agents, and, as between themselves and their principal, the rules relating to honesty and fair dealing in the management of the affairs of their principal are applicable. They must not, in any degree, allow their official conduct to be swayed by their private interest, which must yield to official duty.

In Indiana, then as elsewhere, the responsibility of the fiduciary is not limited to a proper regard for the tangible balance sheet assets of the corporation, but includes the dedication of his uncorrupted business judgment for the sole benefit of the corporation, in any dealings which may adversely affect it. *Meinhard v. Salmon,* . . . 164 N.E. 545. . . . Although the Indiana case is particularly relevant to Feldmann as a director, the same rule should apply to his fiduciary duties as majority stockholder, for in that capacity he chooses and controls the directors, and thus is held to have assumed their liability. *Pepper v. Litton,* supra, 308 U.S. 295, 60 S. Ct. 238. This, therefore, is the standard to which Feldmann was by law required to conform in his activities here under scrutiny.

It is true . . . that this is not the ordinary case of breach of fiduciary duty. We have here no fraud, no misuse of confidential information, no outright looting of a helpless corporation. But on the other hand, we do not find compliance with that high standard which we have just stated and which we and other courts have come to expect and demand of corporate fiduciaries. In the often-quoted words of Judge Cardozo: "Many forms of conduct permissible in a workaday world for those acting at arm's length, are forbidden to those bound by fiduciary ties. A trustee is held to something stricter than the morals of the market place. Not honesty alone, but the punctilio of an honor the most sensitive, is then the standard of behavior. As to this there has developed a tradition that is unbending and inveterate. Uncompromising rigidity has been the attitude of courts of equity when petitioned to undermine the rule of undivided loyalty by the 'disintegrating erosion' of particular exceptions." *Meinhard v. Salmon,* supra, . . . 164 N.E. 545, 546. . . . The actions of defendants in siphoning off for personal gain corporate advantages to be derived from a favorable market situation do not betoken the necessary undivided loyalty owed by the fiduciary to his principal.

The corporate opportunities of whose misappropriation the minority stockholders complain need not have been an absolute certainty in order to support this action against Feldmann. If there was possibility of corporate gain, they are entitled to recover. . . . [I]n *Irving Trust Co. v. Deutsch,* supra, 2 Cir., 73 F.2d 121, 124, an accounting was required of corporate directors who bought stock for themselves for corporate use, even though there was an affirmative showing that the corporation did not have the finances itself to acquire the stock. . . .

This rationale is equally appropriate to a consideration of the benefits which Newport might have derived from the steel shortage. In the past Newport had used and profited by its market leverage by operation of what the industry had come to call the "Feldmann Plan." This consisted of securing interest-free advances from prospective purchasers of steel in return for firm commitments to them from future production. The funds thus acquired were used to finance improvements in existing plants and to acquire new installations. In the summer of 1950 Newport had been negotiating for cold-rolling facilities which it needed for a more fully integrated operation and a more marketable product, and Feldmann plan funds might well have been used toward this end.

Further, as plaintiffs alternatively suggest, Newport might have used the period of short supply to build up patronage in the geographical area in which it could compete profitably even when steel was more abundant. Either of these opportunities was Newport's, to be used to its advantage only. Only if defendants had been able to negate completely any possibility of gain by Newport could they have prevailed. It is true that a trial court finding states: "Whether or not, in August, 1950, Newport's position was such that it could have entered into 'Feldmann Plan' type transactions to procure funds and financing for the further expansion and integration of its steel facilities and whether such expansion would have been desirable for Newport, the evidence does not show." This, however, cannot avail the defendants, who—contrary to the ruling below—had the burden of proof on this issue, since fiduciaries always have the burden of proof in establishing the fairness of their dealings with trust property. . . .

Defendants seek to categorize the corporate opportunities which might have accrued to Newport as too unethical to warrant further consideration. It is true that reputable steel producers were not participating in the gray market brought about by the Korean War and were refraining from advancing their prices, although to do so would not have been illegal. But Feldmann Plan transactions were not considered within this self-imposed interdiction; the trial court found that around the time of the Feldmann sale Jones & Laughlin Steel Corporation, Republic Steel Company, and Pittsburgh Steel Corporation were all participating in such arrangements. In any event, it ill becomes the defendants to disparage as unethical the market advantages from which they themselves reaped rich benefits.

We do not mean to suggest that a majority stockholder cannot dispose of his controlling block of stock to outsiders without having to account to his corporation for profits or even never do this with impunity when the buyer is an interested customer, actual or potential, for the corporation's product. But when the sale necessarily results in a sacrifice of this element of corporate good will and consequent unusual profit to the fiduciary who has caused the sacrifice, he should account for his gains. So in a time of market shortage, where a call on a corporation's product commands an unusually large premium, in one form or another, we think it sound law that a fiduciary may not appropriate to himself the value of this premium. Such personal gain at the expense of his coventurers seems particularly reprehensible when made by the trusted president and director of his company. In this case the violation of duty seems to be all the clearer because of this triple role in which Feldmann appears, though we are unwilling to say, and are not to be understood as saying, that we should accept a lesser obligation for any one of his roles alone.

Hence to the extent that the price received by Feldmann and his codefendants included such a bonus, he is accountable to the minority stockholders who sue here. . . . And plaintiffs, as they contend, are entitled to a recovery in their own right, instead of in right of the corporation (as in the usual derivative actions), since neither Wilport nor their successors in interest should share in any judgment which may be rendered. . . . Defendants cannot well object to this form of recovery, since the only alternative, recovery for the corporation as a whole, would subject them to a greater total liability.

The case will therefore be remanded to the district court for a determination of the question expressly left open below, namely, the value of defendants' stock without the appurtenant control over the corporation's output of steel. We reiterate that on this issue, as on all others relating to a breach of fiduciary duty, the burden of proof must rest on the defendants. . . .

SWAN, CIR. J. (dissenting).

. . . My brothers' opinion does not specify precisely what fiduciary duty Feldmann is held to have violated or whether it was a duty imposed upon him as the dominant stockholder or as a director of Newport. Without such specification I think that both the legal profession and the business world will find the decision confusing and will be unable to foretell the extent of its impact upon customary practices in the sale of stock.

The power to control the management of a corporation, that is, to elect directors to manage its affairs, is an inseparable incident to the ownership of a majority of its stock, or sometimes, as in the present instance, to the ownership of enough shares, less than a majority, to control an election. Concededly a majority or dominant shareholder is ordinarily privileged to sell his stock at the best price obtainable from the purchaser. In so doing he acts on his own behalf, not as an agent of the corporation. If he knows or has reason to believe that the purchaser intends to exercise to the detriment of the corporation the power of management acquired by the purchase, such knowledge or reasonable suspicion will terminate the dominant shareholders' privilege to sell and will create a duty not to transfer the power of management to such purchaser. The duty seems to me to resemble the obligation which everyone is under not to assist another to commit a tort rather than the obligation of a fiduciary. But whatever the nature of the duty, a violation of it will subject the violator to liability for damages sustained by the corporation. Judge Hincks found that Feldmann had no reason to think that Wilport would use the power of management it would acquire by the purchase to injure Newport, and that there was no proof that it ever was so used. Feldmann did know, it is true, that the reason Wilport wanted the stock was to put in a board of directors who would be likely to permit Wilport's members to purchase more of Newport's steel than they might otherwise be able to get. But there is nothing illegal in a dominant shareholder purchasing from his own corporation at the same prices it offers to other customers. That is what the members of Wilport did, and there is no proof that Newport suffered any detriment therefrom.

My brothers say that "the consideration paid for the stock included compensation for the sale of a corporate asset," which they describe as "the ability to control the allocation of the corporate product in a time of short supply, through control of the board of directors; and it was effectively transferred in this sale by having Feldmann procure the resignation of his own board and the election of Wilport's nominees immediately upon consummation of the sale." The implications of this are not clear to me. If it means that when market conditions are such as to induce users of a corporation's product to wish to buy a controlling block of stock in order to be able to purchase part of the corporation's output at the same mill list prices as are offered to other customers, the dominant stockholder is under a fiduciary duty not to sell his stock, I cannot agree. For reasons already stated, in my opinion Feldmann was not proved to be under any fiduciary duty as a stockholder not to sell the stock he controlled.

Feldmann was also a director of Newport. Perhaps the quoted statement means that as a director he violated his fiduciary duty in voting to elect Wilport's nominees to fill the vacancies created by the resignations of the former directors of Newport. As a director Feldmann was under a fiduciary duty to use an honest judgment in acting on the corporation's behalf. A director is privileged to resign, but so long as he remains a director he must be faithful to his fiduciary duties and must not make a personal gain from performing them. Consequently, if the price paid for Feldmann's stock included a payment for voting to elect the new directors, he must account to the corporation for such payment, even though he honestly believed that the men he voted to elect were well qualified to serve as directors. He can not take pay for performing his fiduciary duty. There is no suggestion that he did do so, unless the price paid for his stock was more than its value. So it seems to me that decision must turn on whether finding 120 and conclusion 5 of the district judge are supportable on the evidence. They are set out in the margin.

Judge Hincks went into the matter of valuation of the stock with his customary care and thoroughness. He made no error of law in applying the principles relating to valuation of stock. Concededly a controlling block of stock has greater sale value than a small lot. While the spread between $10 per share for small lots and $20 per share for the controlling block seems rather extraordinarily wide, the $20 valuation was supported by the expert testimony of Dr. Badger, whom the district judge said he could not find to be wrong. I see no justification for upsetting the valuation as clearly erroneous. Nor can I agree with my brothers that the $20 valuation "was limited" by the last sentence in finding 120. The controlling block could not by any possibility be shorn of its appurtenant power to elect

164

directors and through them to control distribution of the corporate product. It is this "appurtenant power" which gives a controlling block its value as such block. What evidence could be adduced to show the value of the block "if shorn" of such appurtenant power, I cannot conceive, for it cannot be shorn of it.

The opinion also asserts that the burden of proving a lesser value than $20 per share was not upon the plaintiffs but the burden was upon the defendants to prove that the stock was worth that value. Assuming that this might be true as to the defendants who were directors of Newport, they did show it, unless finding 120 be set aside. Furthermore, not all the defendants were directors; upon what theory the plaintiffs should be relieved from the burden of proof as to defendants who were not directors, the opinion does not explain.

The final conclusion of my brothers is that the plaintiffs are entitled to recover in their own right instead of in the right of the corporation. This appears to be completely inconsistent with the theory advanced at the outset of the opinion, namely, that the price of the stock "included compensation for the sale of a corporate asset." If a corporate asset was sold, surely the corporation should recover the compensation received for it by the defendants. . . .

Discussion Questions:[17]

1. Feldmann sold his control stake for $20/share when the market price was $12/share. Upon remand, the district court determined that the pro rata value of Newport's stock, based on the underlying value of the company's assets, was $14.67/share. This left Feldmann with a premium of $5.33/share, which he was ordered to share pro rata with his fellow shareholders. Does *Perlman* support a general rule of equal sharing in sales of control blocks, as some have argued, or does its holding turn on the unique circumstances of the case? Put differently, can *Perlman* be reconciled with the market rule?

2. In the district court's opinion in *Perlman*, written almost two years after the sale of Feldmann's stock, the court found that the Wilport Group had made substantial improvements in Newport's facilities, that Newport had sold substantial quantities of steel to Wilport at the same prices at which it had sold steel to other customers, and that there was simply no evidence of any sort that Wilport had inflicted economic harm on Newport. Does this finding alter your view of the case?

3. What would be so bad about expanding the holding in *Perlman* to impose an "equal opportunity" rule (minority shareholders would be entitled to sell their shares to a buyer of control at the same price as the seller of control) rather than the "market rule," with exceptions?

---

[17] The first two discussion questions come from Allen, Kraakman & Subramanian, *Commentaries and Cases on the Law of Business Organizations* (4th ed. 2012) at 426-427.

Sinclair Oil Corp. v. Levien
280 A.2d 717 (Del. 1971)

WOLCOTT, Chief Justice.

This is an appeal by the defendant, Sinclair Oil Corporation (hereafter Sinclair), from an order of the Court of Chancery, 261 A.2d 911 in a derivative action requiring Sinclair to account for damages sustained by its subsidiary, Sinclair Venezuelan Oil Company (hereafter Sinven), organized by Sinclair for the purpose of operating in Venezuela, as a result of dividends paid by Sinven, the denial to Sinven of industrial development, and a breach of contract between Sinclair's wholly-owned subsidiary, Sinclair International Oil Company, and Sinven.

Sinclair, operating primarily as a holding company, is in the business of exploring for oil and of producing and marketing crude oil and oil products. At all times relevant to this litigation, it owned about 97% of Sinven's stock. The plaintiff owns about 3000 of 120,000 publicly held shares of Sinven. Sinven, incorporated in 1922, has been engaged in petroleum operations primarily in Venezuela and since 1959 has operated exclusively in Venezuela.

Sinclair nominates all members of Sinven's board of directors. The Chancellor found as a fact that the directors were not independent of Sinclair. Almost without exception, they were officers, directors, or employees of corporations in the Sinclair complex. By reason of Sinclair's domination, it is clear that Sinclair owed Sinven a fiduciary duty. Getty Oil Company v. Skelly Oil Co., 267 A.2d 883 (Del.Supr. 1970); Cottrell v. Pawcatuck Co., 35 Del. Ch. 309, 116 A.2d 787 (1955). Sinclair concedes this.

The Chancellor held that because of Sinclair's fiduciary duty and its control over Sinven, its relationship with Sinven must meet the test of intrinsic fairness. The standard of intrinsic fairness involves both a high degree of fairness and a shift in the burden of proof. Under this standard the burden is on Sinclair to prove, subject to careful judicial scrutiny, that its transactions with Sinven were objectively fair. Guth v. Loft, Inc., 23 Del.Ch. 255, 5 A.2d 503 (1939); Sterling v. Mayflower Hotel Corp., 33 Del.Ch. 293, 93 A.2d 107, 38 A. L.R.2d 425 (Del.Supr.1952); Getty Oil Co. v. Skelly Oil Co., supra.

Sinclair argues that the transactions between it and Sinven should be tested, not by the test of intrinsic fairness with the accompanying shift of the burden of proof, but by the business judgment rule under which a court will not interfere with the judgment of a board of directors unless there is a showing of gross and palpable overreaching. Meyerson v. El Paso Natural Gas Co., 246 A.2d 789 (Del.Ch. 1967). A board of directors enjoys a presumption of sound business judgment, and its decisions will not be disturbed if they can be attributed to any rational business purpose. A court under such circumstances will not substitute its own notions of what is or is not sound business judgment.

We think, however, that Sinclair's argument in this respect is misconceived. When the situation involves a parent and a subsidiary, with the parent controlling the transaction and fixing the terms, the test of intrinsic fairness, with its resulting shifting of the burden of proof, is applied. Sterling v. Mayflower Hotel Corp., supra; David J. Greene & Co. v. Dunhill International, Inc., 249 A.2d 427 (Del.Ch.1968); Bastian v. Bourns, Inc., 256 A.2d 680 (Del.Ch.1969) aff'd. Per Curiam (unreported) (Del.Supr.1970). The basic situation for the application of the rule is the one in which the parent has received a benefit to the exclusion and at the expense of the subsidiary.

Recently, this court dealt with the question of fairness in parent-subsidiary dealings in Getty Oil Co. v. Skelly Oil Co., supra. In that case, both parent and subsidiary were in the business of refining and marketing crude oil and crude oil products. The Oil Import Board ruled that the subsidiary, because it was controlled by the parent, was no longer entitled to a separate allocation of imported crude oil. The subsidiary then contended that it had a right to share the quota of crude oil allotted to the parent. We ruled that the business judgment standard should be applied to determine this contention. Although the subsidiary suffered a loss through the administration of the oil import quotas, the parent gained nothing. The parent's quota was derived solely from its own past use. The past use of the subsidiary did not cause an increase in the parent's quota. Nor did the parent usurp a quota of the subsidiary. Since the parent received nothing from the subsidiary to the exclusion of the minority stockholders of the subsidiary, there was no self-dealing. Therefore, the business judgment standard was properly applied.

A parent does indeed owe a fiduciary duty to its subsidiary when there are parent-subsidiary dealings. However, this alone will not evoke the intrinsic fairness standard. This standard will be applied only when the fiduciary duty is accompanied by self-dealing—the situation when a parent is on both sides of a transaction with its subsidiary. Self-dealing occurs when the parent, by virtue of its domination of the subsidiary, causes the subsidiary to act in such a way that the parent receives something from the subsidiary to the exclusion of, and detriment to, the minority stockholders of the subsidiary.

We turn now to the facts. The plaintiff argues that, from 1960 through 1966, Sinclair caused Sinven to pay out such excessive dividends that the industrial development of Sinven was effectively prevented, and it became in reality a corporation in dissolution.

From 1960 through 1966, Sinven paid out $108,000,000 in dividends ($38,000,000 in excess of Sinven's earnings during the same period). The Chancellor held that Sinclair caused these dividends to be paid during a period when it had a need for large amounts of cash. Although the dividends paid exceeded earnings, the plaintiff concedes that the payments were made in compliance with 8 Del.C. § 170, authorizing payment of dividends out of surplus or net profits. However, the plaintiff attacks these dividends on the ground that they resulted from an improper motive—Sinclair's need for cash. The Chancellor, applying the intrinsic fairness standard, held that Sinclair did not sustain its burden of proving that these dividends were intrinsically fair to the minority stockholders of Sinven.

Since it is admitted that the dividends were paid in strict compliance with 8 Del.C. § 170, the alleged excessiveness of the payments alone would not state a cause of action. Nevertheless, compliance with the applicable statute may not, under all circumstances, justify all dividend payments. If a plaintiff can meet his burden of proving that a dividend cannot be grounded on any reasonable business objective, then the courts can and will interfere with the board's decision to pay the dividend.

Sinclair contends that it is improper to apply the intrinsic fairness standard to dividend payments even when the board which voted for the dividends is completely dominated. In support of this contention, Sinclair relies heavily on American District Telegraph Co. [ADT] v. Grinnell Corp., (N.Y.Sup.Ct.1969) aff'd. 33 A.D.2d 769, 306 N.Y.S.2d 209 (1969). Plaintiffs were minority stockholders of ADT, a subsidiary of Grinnell. The plaintiffs alleged that Grinnell, realizing that it would soon have to sell its ADT stock because of a pending anti-trust action, caused ADT to pay excessive dividends. Because the dividend payments conformed with applicable statutory law, and the plaintiffs could not prove an abuse of discretion, the court ruled that the complaint did not state a cause of action. Other decisions seem to support Sinclair's contention. In Metropolitan Casualty Ins. Co. v. First State Bank of Temple, 54 S.W.2d 358 (Tex.Civ.App.1932), rev'd. on other grounds, 79 S.W.2d 835 (Sup.Ct. 1935), the court held that a majority of interested directors does not void a declaration of dividends because all directors, by necessity, are interested in and benefited by a dividend declaration. See, also, Schwartz v. Kahn, 183 Misc. 252, 50 N.Y.S. 2d 931 (1944); Weinberger v. Quinn, 264 A.D. 405, 35 N.Y.S.2d 567 (1942).

We do not accept the argument that the intrinsic fairness test can never be applied to a dividend declaration by a dominated board, although a dividend declaration by a dominated board will not inevitably demand the application of the intrinsic fairness standard. Moskowitz v. Bantrell, 41 Del.Ch. 177, 190 A.2d 749 (Del.Supr. 1963). If such a dividend is in essence self-dealing by the parent, then the intrinsic fairness standard is the proper standard. For example, suppose a parent dominates a subsidiary and its board of directors. The subsidiary has outstanding two classes of stock, X and Y. Class X is owned by the parent and Class Y is owned by minority stockholders of the subsidiary. If the subsidiary, at the direction of the parent, declares a dividend on its Class X stock only, this might well be self-dealing by the parent. It would be receiving something from the subsidiary to the exclusion of and detrimental to its minority stockholders. This self-dealing, coupled with the parent's fiduciary duty, would make intrinsic fairness the proper standard by which to evaluate the dividend payments.

Consequently it must be determined whether the dividend payments by Sinven were, in essence, self-dealing by Sinclair. The dividends resulted in great sums of money being transferred from Sinven to Sinclair. However, a proportionate share of this money was received by the minority shareholders of Sinven. Sinclair received nothing from Sinven to the exclusion of its minority stockholders. As such, these dividends were not self-dealing. We hold therefore that the Chancellor erred in applying the intrinsic fairness test as to these dividend payments. The business judgment standard should have been applied.

We conclude that the facts demonstrate that the dividend payments complied with the business judgment standard and with 8 Del.C. § 170. The motives for causing the declaration of dividends are immaterial unless the plaintiff can show that the dividend payments resulted from improper motives and amounted to waste. The plaintiff contends only that the dividend payments drained Sinven of cash to such an extent that it was prevented from expanding.

The plaintiff proved no business opportunities which came to Sinven independently and which Sinclair either took to itself or denied to Sinven. As a matter of fact, with two minor exceptions which resulted in losses, all of Sinven's operations have been conducted in Venezuela, and Sinclair had a policy of exploiting its oil properties located in different countries by subsidiaries located in the particular countries.

From 1960 to 1966 Sinclair purchased or developed oil fields in Alaska, Canada, Paraguay, and other places around the world. The plaintiff contends that these were all opportunities which could have been taken by Sinven. The Chancellor concluded that Sinclair had not proved that its denial of expansion opportunities to Sinven was intrinsically fair. He based this conclusion on the following findings of fact. Sinclair made no real effort to expand Sinven. The excessive dividends paid by Sinven resulted in so great a cash drain as to effectively deny to Sinven any ability to expand. During this same period Sinclair actively pursued a company-wide policy of developing through its subsidiaries new sources of revenue, but Sinven was not permitted to participate and was confined in its activities to Venezuela.

However, the plaintiff could point to no opportunities which came to Sinven. Therefore, Sinclair usurped no business opportunity belonging to Sinven. Since Sinclair received nothing from Sinven to the exclusion of and detriment to Sinven's minority stockholders, there was no self-dealing. Therefore, business judgment is the proper standard by which to evaluate Sinclair's expansion policies.

Since there is no proof of self-dealing on the part of Sinclair, it follows that the expansion policy of Sinclair and the methods used to achieve the desired result must, as far as Sinclair's treatment of Sinven is concerned, be tested by the standards of the business judgment rule. Accordingly, Sinclair's decision, absent fraud or gross overreaching, to achieve expansion through the medium of its subsidiaries, other than Sinven, must be upheld.

Even if Sinclair was wrong in developing these opportunities as it did, the question arises, with which subsidiaries should these opportunities have been shared? No evidence indicates a unique need or ability of Sinven to develop these opportunities. The decision of which subsidiaries would be used to implement Sinclair's expansion policy was one of business judgment with which a court will not interfere absent a showing of gross and palpable overreaching. Meyerson v. El Paso Natural Gas Co., 246 A.2d 789 (Del.Ch.1967). No such showing has been made here.

Next, Sinclair argues that the Chancellor committed error when he held it liable to Sinven for breach of contract.

In 1961 Sinclair created Sinclair International Oil Company (hereafter International), a wholly owned subsidiary used for the purpose of coordinating all of Sinclair's foreign operations. All crude purchases by Sinclair were made thereafter through International.

On September 28, 1961, Sinclair caused Sinven to contract with International whereby Sinven agreed to sell all of its crude oil and refined products to International at specified prices. The contract provided for minimum and maximum quantities and prices. The plaintiff contends that Sinclair caused this contract to be breached in two respects. Although the contract called for payment on receipt, International's payments lagged as much as 30 days after receipt. Also, the contract required International to purchase at least a fixed minimum amount of crude and refined products from Sinven. International did not comply with this requirement.

Clearly, Sinclair's act of contracting with its dominated subsidiary was self-dealing. Under the contract Sinclair received the products produced by Sinven, and of course the minority shareholders of Sinven were not able to share in the receipt of these products. If the contract was breached, then Sinclair received these products to the detriment of Sinven's minority shareholders. We agree with the Chancellor's finding that the contract was breached by Sinclair, both as to the time of payments and the amounts purchased.

Although a parent need not bind itself by a contract with its dominated subsidiary, Sinclair chose to operate in this manner. As Sinclair has received the benefits of this contract, so must it comply with the contractual duties.

Under the intrinsic fairness standard, Sinclair must prove that its causing Sinven not to enforce the contract was intrinsically fair to the minority shareholders of Sinven. Sinclair has failed to meet this burden. Late payments were clearly breaches for which Sinven should have sought and received adequate damages. As to the quantities purchased, Sinclair argues that it purchased all the products produced by Sinven. This, however, does not satisfy the standard of intrinsic fairness. Sinclair has failed to prove that Sinven could not possibly have produced or someway have obtained the contract minimums. As such, Sinclair must account on this claim.

Finally, Sinclair argues that the Chancellor committed error in refusing to allow it a credit or setoff of all benefits provided by it to Sinven with respect to all the alleged damages. The Chancellor held that setoff should be allowed on specific transactions, e. g., benefits to Sinven under the contract with International, but denied an overall setoff against all damages claimed. We agree with the Chancellor, although the point may well be moot in view of our holding that Sinclair is not required to account for the alleged excessiveness of the dividend payments.

We will therefore reverse that part of the Chancellor's order that requires Sinclair to account to Sinven for damages sustained as a result of dividends paid between 1960 and

1966, and by reason of the denial to Sinven of expansion during that period. We will affirm the remaining portion of that order and remand the cause for further proceedings.

Discussion Questions:

1. As we will see in more detail in *Weinberger*, the standard of review for self-dealing—"utmost good faith" or "intrinsic fairness" or, nowadays, "entire fairness"—is demanding. It is, thus, extremely important to determine which transactions count as self-dealing. What is *Sinclair's* answer? Can you envision situations where the *Sinclair* rule does not adequately protect minority shareholders?

2. As an alternative to the rule articulated in *Sinclair*, a court could simply impose entire fairness review on all actions taken by a controlling shareholder. What would be the pros and cons of this approach?

In re Delphi Financial Group Shareholder Litigation
2012 WL 729232 (Del. Ch. Mar. 6, 2012)

GLASSCOCK, Vice Chancellor.

This matter involves the proposed takeover of Delphi Financial Group, Inc. ("Delphi" or the "Company"), by Tokio Marine Holdings, Inc. ("TMH"). Delphi is an insurance holding company founded by Defendant Robert Rosenkranz. Rosenkranz took Delphi public in 1990. In so doing, he created two classes of stock, Class A, largely held by the public, and Class B, retained by Rosenkranz. Although Rosenkranz retained less than 13% of the shares outstanding, each share of Class B stock represented the right to ten votes in stockholder matters, while each share of Class A stock entitled the holder to one vote. In other words, Rosenkranz retained control of Delphi. Among the rights associated with control is the ability to seek a control premium should Delphi be sold. Rosenkranz could retain or bargain away that right; he chose to sell it to the Class A stockholders. This was accomplished by a charter provision, which directed that, on sale of the company, each share of Class B stock would be converted to Class A, entitled to the same consideration as any other Class A stock. This concession to the Class A stockholders resulted, presumably, in a higher purchase price for Class A stock than would have been the case without the provision.

In 2011, TMH, through an intermediary, contacted Rosenkranz about the possible purchase of Delphi. While negotiating with TMH on behalf of Delphi, Rosenkranz at the same time made it clear to Delphi's board that, notwithstanding the charter provision, he would not consent to the sale without a premium paid for his Class B stock. Although the Delphi board was reluctant to recommend a differential for the Class B stock, it also recognized that the premium TMH was willing to pay over market was very large, and would probably be attractive to the stockholders. It therefore set up a committee of independent directors to negotiate a differential for the Class B stock. The committee was ultimately able to negotiate the per share price demanded by Rosenkranz from $59 down to $53.875.[1]

Meanwhile, Rosenkranz continued to negotiate with TMH on behalf of Delphi. TMH ultimately agreed to pay $46 per share for Delphi. TMH was then informed that the deal would be structured to provide a differential: $44.875 per share for the Class A shares; $53.875 per share for the Class B shares. The deal was conditioned on a majority of the publicly held Class A shares being voted in favor, and a successful vote to amend the Delphi Charter to allow Rosenkranz to receive the differential.

Before creating Delphi, Rosenkranz had established an investment advising firm, Acorn Advisory Capital L.P. ("Acorn"), which provided investment services to third parties. After Rosenkranz founded Delphi, Delphi established a contractual relationship with Acorn under which Acorn would use Delphi employees and resources to provide services both to third parties and to Delphi. Acorn would then reimburse Delphi for the use of its employees, office facilities, and the like. Acorn provided investment advisory services to Delphi pursuant to contractual agreements (the "RAM Contracts"), under which Acorn would bill Delphi through another Rosenkranz entity, Rosenkranz Asset Management, LLC ("RAM"). The RAM Contracts are terminable upon thirty days' notice from either party. The revenue from the sale of Acorn's services to third parties and to Delphi went to Rosenkranz.

During the negotiation of the Delphi/TMH deal, Rosenkranz discussed with TMH the retention of the RAM Contracts by TMH for a period of years, or, alternatively, the purchase of RAM by TMH. While Rosenkranz and TMH deny that any agreement was reached, Rosenkranz testified that he expects the parties to complete such an agreement shortly after the Delphi/TMH deal closes.

The Plaintiff stockholders argue that Rosenkranz is not entitled to the stock price differential, that the Delphi Board breached its duty to the stockholders in structuring the deal to include such a differential at the Class A stockholders' expense, and that the fiduciary breaches of Rosenkranz and the Board were aided wrongfully by TMH. They also argue that the RAM Contract was nothing but a device for Rosenkranz to skim money from Delphi for work Delphi could have provided for itself at lower cost, and that the Acorn services sold to third parties represented an opportunity of Delphi's usurped by Rosenkranz. They argue that the agreement discussed between TMH and Rosenkranz to retain the RAM Contracts for a term of years, or to buy RAM outright, really involved disguised consideration for Rosenkranz's assent to the Delphi/TMH deal, which therefore constituted additional consideration that should belong to the stockholders. The Plaintiffs seek to enjoin the stockholders' vote on the Delphi/TMH merger.

Based upon the record developed through expedited discovery and presented at the preliminary injunction hearing, I find that the Plaintiffs have demonstrated a likelihood of

---

[1] The latter amount includes a $1 special dividend agreed to by TMH to be paid around the closing of the merger.

success on the merits at least with respect to the allegations against Rosenkranz. However, because the deal represents a large premium over market price, because damages are available as a remedy, and because no other potential purchaser has come forth or seems likely to come forth to match, let alone best, the TMH offer, I cannot find that the balance of the equities favors an injunction over letting the stockholders exercise their franchise, and allowing the Plaintiffs to pursue damages. Therefore, the Plaintiffs' request for a preliminary injunction is denied.

I. BACKGROUND

A. Parties

Delphi is a financial services holding company incorporated in Delaware. Delphi's subsidiaries are insurance and insurance-related businesses that provide small-to mid-sized businesses with employee benefit services, including group coverage for long term and short term disability, life, travel accident, dental, and health insurance, and workers' compensation. Delphi was founded in 1987 by Defendant Robert Rosenkranz, who is Delphi's current CEO and Chairman.

Delphi's board comprises nine directors, all of whom are Defendants in this action. Seven of the directors are independent and do not hold officer positions within Delphi. They are Kevin R. Brine, Edward A. Fox, Steven A. Hirsh, James M. Litvack, James N. Meehan, Philip R. O'Connor, and Robert F. Wright. The Complaint also names Harold F. Ilg, a former director whose retirement was announced in January 2012, as a Defendant (together with Brine, Fox, Hirsh, Litvack, Meehan, O'Connor, and Wright, the "Director Defendants").

Delphi's board also includes two directors who hold officer positions in the Company: Rosenkranz, who is Chairman of the Board and CEO, and Donald A. Sherman, who has served as President and COO of Delphi since 2006 and as a director since 2002. Sherman also serves as a director of Delphi's principal subsidiaries and as President and COO of Delphi Capital Management, Inc. ("DCM"), a wholly owned subsidiary of Delphi through which Delphi conducts its New York activities and which is involved in an expense allocation agreement, discussed below, with certain Rosenkranz-affiliated entities.

The Complaint also names several of Delphi's non-director officers: Defendant Stephan A. Kiratsous, Executive Vice President and CFO of Delphi since June 2011, and Chad W. Coulter, General Counsel of Delphi since January 1998, Secretary since May 2003, and Senior Vice President since February 2007 (together with Rosenkranz, Sherman, and Kiratsous, the "Executive Defendants").

Defendant TMH is a Japanese holding company whose subsidiaries offer products and services in the global property and casualty insurance, reinsurance, and life insurance markets. TMH has no affiliation with Rosenkranz, Delphi, or any of the Director or Executive Defendants.

B. Delphi's Capital Structure and Relevant Charter Provisions

Delphi first issued shares to the public in 1990. Following this IPO, Delphi's ownership was divided between holders of Class A common stock and Class B common stock. Delphi Class A shares are widely held, publicly traded, and entitled by the Delphi Charter to one vote per share. Class B shares are held entirely by Rosenkranz and his affiliates and are entitled to ten votes per share; however, the Delphi Charter caps the aggregate voting power of the Class B shares at 49.9%. Rosenkranz also owns Class A shares, but a voting agreement with Delphi caps Rosenkranz's total voting power, regardless of his stock ownership, at 49.9%. Although Rosenkranz possesses 49.9% of the Delphi stockholder voting power due to his Class B shares, his stock ownership accounts for roughly 12.9% of Delphi's equity.

In addition to the cap the Delphi Charter places on Class B voting power and the cap placed on Rosenkranz's total voting power by voting agreement, the Delphi Charter contains other restrictions on the Class B shares and Rosenkranz's rights as the holder of those shares. Except for transfers to certain affiliates, the Delphi Charter provides that the transfer of any Class B shares first effects a share-for-share conversion of those shares into Class A stock; thus, while Rosenkranz exercises with his Class B voting power an effective veto right over any action requiring stockholder approval, he is unable to transfer that voting power. Moreover, the Delphi Charter contains a provision prohibiting disparate consideration between Class A and B stock in the event of a merger:

> [I]n the case of any distribution or payment . . . on Class A Common Stock or Class B Common Stock upon the consolidation or merger of the Corporation with or into any other corporation . . . such distribution payment shall be made ratably on a per share basis among the holders of the Class A Common Stock and Class B Common Stock as a single class.

These Charter provisions were in force at Delphi's IPO, and while they preserve Rosenkranz's voting power and effective right of approval over all Delphi actions requiring a majority stockholder vote, they severely limit Rosenkranz's ability to realize any other benefits by means of his Class B stock ownership, beyond those he of course possesses as a 12.9% equity holder in Delphi.

C. Delphi's Consulting Contracts with Rosenkranz-Affiliated Entities

Before founding Delphi in 1987, Rosenkranz created in 1982 a group of private investment funds to construct and manage investment portfolios. One such fund was Acorn Partners, L.P., which is managed by Acorn, a financial advisory firm registered with the U.S. Securities and Exchange Commission under the Investment Advisers Act of 1940. Since 1982, Acorn has provided consulting services to third parties.

Pursuant to two contracts entered into in 1987 and 1988, Delphi and its largest subsidiary, Reliance Standard, receive investment consulting services from Acorn under the RAM Contracts. Although Acorn provides the services under these contracts, payment under the contracts is made by Delphi to RAM, another Rosenkranz-affiliated entity, in order to segregate the fees Acorn receives from Delphi from those it receives from other parties to which it provides services. This payment arrangement is purportedly for accounting purposes and does not affect the economics of the contracts, as Rosenkranz is the beneficial owner of both Acorn and RAM. The RAM Contracts have been publicly disclosed in Delphi's SEC filings since the Company's 1990 IPO. Additionally, they are terminable by either RAM or Delphi upon thirty days' notice.

For the consulting services it provides to Delphi, Acorn operates through an Expense Allocation Agreement ("EAA") with DCM, a wholly owned subsidiary of Delphi and the entity through which Delphi conducts its New York activities. Under the EAA, DCM provides Acorn with office space, facilities, and personnel; in fact, Acorn's "employees" are on the DCM payroll. Acorn then reimburses DCM for these personnel, facility, and office space costs. Acorn itself does not actually own any assets beyond, according to Rosenkranz, proprietary trading systems and models developed by him that Acorn uses for its business. At oral argument, Defendants' counsel seemed unclear as to exactly what tangible value the RAM Contracts bring to Delphi that Delphi could not provide to itself at cost. The nature of the benefit of the RAM Contracts to Delphi remains unclear to me, perhaps because the contracts are, as the Plaintiffs allege, sham agreements through which Rosenkranz has being skimming money from Delphi since the Company's inception. That theory, however, awaits factual development on a full record.

D. TMH Approaches Delphi Regarding an Acquisition

On July 20, 2011, TMH made an unsolicited approach, through its investment banker MacQuarie Capital ("MacQuarie"), to Delphi to express its interest in acquiring the Company. TMH had plans to expand internationally and enter the property, casualty, and life insurance markets, and it had identified Delphi as a potential acquisition target in pursuit of that strategy. A MacQuarie representative called Rosenkranz to request a preliminary meeting between the senior management of Delphi and TMH. Rosenkranz's initial response was that he did not think Delphi was for sale. Eventually, however, Rosenkranz called the MacQuarie representative back and indicated that he would report TMH's interest to Delphi's Board at the upcoming quarterly meeting. Rosenkranz also tentatively scheduled a meeting between Delphi and TMH representatives for the day after the board meeting.[14]

---

[14] In the Plaintiffs' version of these events, Rosenkranz scheduled the meeting with TMH during the initial phone call with MacQuarie, rather than sometime thereafter, thus setting up the Plaintiffs' argument that Rosenkranz waited weeks before informing Delphi's Board of the meeting and implying that Rosenkranz intended to keep the Board in the dark until it was too late for it to have any input. *See* POB at 13. Although Plaintiffs' counsel's recounting of these initial phone calls certainly fits their preferred narrative of a merger negotiation dominated from the outset by an autarchic controller, it is not supported by the current record. *See* Rosenkranz Dep. 212:9-15 ("I don't think the meeting was set up on July 20th, but somewhere in the interim [between Anderson's initial phone call and the August 3rd board meeting] it was set up."); James M. Anderson Dep. 72:17-23 (Feb. 9, 2012) ("[Rosenkranz's] initial reaction was that Delphi was not for sale, but he would think about it and call me back.").

At the Delphi Board's August 3rd meeting, Rosenkranz informed the other directors of the Delphi Board of TMH's interest in acquiring Delphi. The Director Defendants authorized preliminary discussions and disclosures with TMH. The directors also discussed the seriousness of TMH's interest, and Rosenkranz suggested 1.5-2.0 times book value as a reference point for an attractive deal, or $45-$60 per share, approximately an 80-140% premium over the Class A stock price at the time.

For most of August, senior management from Delphi and TMH had general discussions regarding a potential merger, with Rosenkranz representing Delphi with assistance from Delphi COO Sherman and CFO Kiratsous. Delphi began providing due diligence materials in late August and continued to discuss potential synergies with TMH; however, no discussions of price or other specific terms occurred.

During this time, Rosenkranz considered how he might receive a premium on his Class B shares above what the Class A stockholders would receive in the Merger. Because the Delphi Charter prohibits disparate distributions of merger consideration through a provision that was in place when Delphi went public in 1990, Rosenkranz knew that any premium would require a charter amendment. Apparently undeterred by the fact that Section 7 of Delphi's Charter would likely be viewed by Delphi's public stockholders as expressly prohibiting the differential consideration he sought, and that the Delphi stock price paid by these investors likely reflected a company in which the controlling stockholder, though retaining voting control, had bargained away his right to be compensated disparately for his shares, Rosenkranz discussed with Sherman, Kiratsous, and Coulter, Delphi's General Counsel, how such a division of the merger proceeds might be accomplished. The Executive Defendants obtained data on acquisitions of corporations with dual-class stock, and Coulter advised Rosenkranz that a special committee should be formed and that the transaction should be conditioned on approval by a majority vote of the disinterested Class A stockholders. Despite using Delphi resources in procuring this advice, Rosenkranz did not inform the Board of his desire for disparate consideration until a Board meeting in mid September.

On September 7, 2011, at a meeting attended by the Executive Defendants, Brimecome conveyed TMH's interest in acquiring Delphi at a price between $33-$35 per share (a 50-59% premium over Delphi's then-market price of $21.98). After initially responding that TMH's offer was inadequate, Rosenkranz later contacted Brimecome to reiterate his disappointment and convey his expectation of an opening offer in the range of 1.5-2.0 times book value, or $45-$60 per share, which was consistent with the price he had suggested to Delphi's Board in early August. Rosenkranz countered with this range despite the fact that he knew at the time that he was unwilling to sell at $45. Nevertheless, he thought $45 per share might be attractive to the Class A stockholders, as Delphi's stock was at the time trading around the low twenties, and he suspected that demanding his own desired price of $55-$60 at that stage of the negotiations would have turned off TMH and killed the discussions. Several days later, Brimecome called and informed Rosenkranz that TMH, after hearing that $40 was a nonstarter for Delphi's controlling stockholder, was raising its offer to $45 per share, then a 106% premium over market. Rosenkranz advised Brimecome that he would take the offer to Delphi's Board.

E. The Board Forms a Special Committee and Sub-Committee

On September 16, 2011, Rosenkranz presented TMH's $45 per share offer to the Board. Rosenkranz acknowledged the offer's substantial premium over Delphi's stock price, but he disclosed to the Board that he nonetheless found it inadequate from his perspective as controlling stockholder, and that he would be unlikely to vote his Class B shares in favor of Merger at that price. Because of the conflict of interest Rosenkranz's position created between him and Delphi's public stockholders, Rosenkranz suggested, and the Board agreed, to form a Special Committee, comprising the Board's seven independent directors (the Director Defendants), to evaluate the proposal from TMH, direct further discussions with TMH, and consider alternatives to the TMH proposal. The members of the Special Committee held Class A shares only, aligning their financial interests with those of the public stockholders.

The Special Committee retained Cravath, Swaine & Moore LLP ("Cravath") as legal advisor and Lazard Frères & Co. LLC ("Lazard") as financial advisor. Cravath advised the Special Committee of its fiduciary obligations, including its mandate to represent only the Class A stockholders, and interviewed the directors about their connections to Rosenkranz. Based on these interviews and per Cravath's advice, the Special Committee limited its membership to five directors—Fox, Hirsh, Litvack, Meehan, and O'Connor—each chosen for his relative business and industry experience and his lack of any connection, economic or social, to Rosenkranz.

At a later board meeting, the full Delphi Board formally established the Special Committee and set forth its mandate. The Board charged the Special Committee with representing the best interests of the Class A stockholders, granted the Special Committee full authority to take any action that would be available to the Board in connection with the transaction, and authorized the Special Committee to pursue and consider alternative transactions to the TMH bid if it deemed such alternatives to be of interest to the Class A stockholders. Additionally, the Board conditioned its approval or recommendation of the potential transaction on the Special Committee's affirmative recommendation thereof. The Special Committee then met and created a Sub-Committee—comprising Fox, Meehan, and O'Connor—to act on the Special Committee's behalf with respect to any matters related to Rosenkranz and differential merger consideration. The Sub-Committee was given full authority with respect to these matters. Finally, just as the Board conditioned its approval of any transaction on a favorable recommendation by the Special Committee, the Special Committee conditioned its approval on the favorable recommendation of the Sub-Committee.

The Special Committee then sought advice from its legal and financial advisors on its obligations and the valuation of the Company. Lazard advised the Special Committee that the premium offered by the TMH proposal—more than 100% over Delphi's stock price at the time—was a tremendous deal, and that in light of the significant premium offered, Delphi was unlikely to see a comparable proposal from another buyer. The Special Committee discussed Lazard's advice and considered whether to solicit additional offers, such as through an auction or a quiet shopping of the Company. Ultimately, the Special Committee concluded that since TMH was the acquirer most likely to be interested in acquiring Delphi and had already offered a colossal premium over market price, shopping Delphi was not worth the impact such a course of action would have on negotiations with TMH or the risk of a potential leak disrupting Delphi's ongoing business.

F. Price Differential Negotiations

Leading up to and simultaneously with the negotiations with TMH, the Sub-Committee negotiated with Rosenkranz regarding whether there would be any disparate allocation of the Merger consideration and, if so, what the differential would be. Rosenkranz opened the discussion with a request of $59 per Class B share and $43 per Class A share, asserting to the Special Committee that he did not expect TMH to raise its offer price; that if TMH did raise its price, Rosenkranz expected that increase to be allocated evenly dollar-for-dollar on top of the $59/$43 split; that he was unequivocally not a seller at $45; and that if his demands were not met, he would have no qualms about walking away from the deal and continuing the status quo of running Delphi on a standalone basis. The Sub-Committee reviewed comparable acquisitions of companies with dual-class stock, and, after hearing from its financial and legal advisors that disparate consideration in such cases is unusual and problematic, attempted to persuade Rosenkranz, over a number of meetings and phone conversations, to accept the same price as the Class A stockholders. Nevertheless, Rosenkrantz remained obstinate, refusing to back down on his demand for some level of disparate consideration.

The Sub-Committee considered whether Rosenkrantz was truly willing to walk away from the merger rather than accept $45 per share, and it concluded, for several reasons, including Rosenkranz's plans for Delphi's expansion, that Rosenkranz was prepared to jettison the deal if he did not get his way. Thus, not wanting to deprive the Class A stockholders of the opportunity to realize a circa-100% premium on their shares, the Special Committee decided to accept the idea of differential consideration but to fight for a reduction in the consideration differential.

The Sub-Committee engaged in a back-and-forth with Rosenkranz in the days leading up to an October 14, 2011, meeting with TMH representatives. The Sub-Committee informed Rosenkranz that it was willing to permit him differential consideration, but only if Rosenkranz's per share incremental premium was limited to less than 10%, to which Rosenkranz replied by reducing his request for disparate consideration to $55.50 per share for Class B shares and $43.50 per share for the Class A shares. Just days before the October 14th meeting with TMH, the Sub-Committee and Rosenkranz remained far apart on the magnitude of the differential. Still, neither side wanted to lose momentum in the negotiations with TMH or insult the TMH representatives who were flying in from Japan, and so both sides felt that it was important to keep the October 14th meeting date.

There was also the issue of what role Rosenkranz should have in the upcoming meeting, given his and the Sub-Committee's concurrent sparring over the differential consideration. After consulting with Cravath, the Sub-Committee decided that it was best to allow

Rosenkranz to remain the point person, subject to direction and oversight by the Special Committee and Sub-Committee. The Sub-Committee reasoned that Rosenkranz would be an effective negotiatior because, as Chairman, CEO, and founder of Delphi, Rosenkranz had intimate knowledge of the business, and that while Rosenkranz's interests were adverse to the Class A stockholders', both Classes' interests were aligned with respect to securing the highest *total* offer from TMH. Moreover, as TMH did not at that point know of the potential for differential consideration, the Special Committee did not want to spook TMH by replacing Rosenkranz, who had theretofore represented Delphi in the negotiations. The Special Committee thus agreed that Rosenkranz would remain the face of the negotiations and would attend the October 14th meeting with TMH. Apparently not trusting Rosenkranz to act solely as a fiduciary for the stockholders, the Special Committee also directed Lazard to attend the meeting.

G. Merger Price Negotiations

The morning before the October 14th meeting, the Special Committee met to decide on Delphi's position with respect to price. After a discussion with Lazard, the Special Committee directed Rosenkranz to request that TMH increase its offer to $48.50 and authorized Rosenkranz to convey to TMH that he would take a price of $47 or higher back to the Special Committee if the circumstances warranted. At the meeting with TMH, Rosenkranz requested $48.50 per share, and TMH responded that it would consider whether it could increase its offer, although it expressed surprise that Delphi was asking for more money given that TMH had previously indicated that $45 was its maximum price.

Several days later, Brimecome of TMH called Rosenkranz to inform him that $45 was TMH's best and final offer. Authorized by the Special Committee to drop Delphi's ask to $47 per share, Rosenkranz responded by proposing a $2 special dividend per share at or around the time of the closing (which would effectively increase the merger consideration to $47). Brimecome then informed Rosenkranz that TMH would respond to this offer shortly. The next day, TMH contacted Rosenkranz to counter with a $1 special dividend; Rosenkranz agreed to take the offer to the Special Committee.

Rosenkranz immediately called Fox, the Chairman of the Special Committee, and informed him of the call with TMH. Rosenkranz relayed TMH's offer and indicated that he would not support a transaction based on TMH's revised offer unless the $1 special dividend was split evenly between Class A and Class B shares. Rosenkranz also warned Fox that he would refuse to entertain further negotiations regarding the differential consideration, and that he would walk away from the transaction if he did not receive $56.50 for each of his Class B shares (with the Class A consideration being $44.50 per share).[40] The Special Committee and the Sub-Committee thus decided to finish negotiating the terms of the differential consideration before responding to TMH's revised offer.

---

[40] These amounts include the $1 special dividend.

H. Agreement on Price and Remaining Merger Terms

With TMH's offer of $46 per share ($45 plus the $1 special dividend) on the table, the Sub-Committee and Rosenkranz continued their negotiations regarding the division of the Merger consideration. Fox and Rosenkranz engaged in extensive back-and-forth discussions, with Rosenkranz refusing to accept less than $56.50 for his Class B shares and Fox holding fast to his demand for $45.25 for the Class A shares, which would have left $51.25 per Class B share. Over the course of this back-and-forth, Rosenkranz's gamut of emotions confirmed that the Kübler-Ross Model[41] indeed applies to corporate controllers whose attempts to divert merger consideration to themselves at the expense of the minority stockholders are rebuked by intractable special committees. Rosenkranz began in denial of the fact that he might not receive his original request of $59 per share and was isolated with the formation of the Special Committee, grew angry as the Sub-Committee held firm to its original demand of $45.25 for the Class A shares, began to bargain and revised his proposal to $44.75 for the Class A shares, plunged into depression when the Sub-Committee only reduced its demand to $45 per Class A share,[44] and finally arrived at "acceptance" when Fox, believing the deal to be in jeopardy, proposed $44.875 for Class A and $53.875 for Class B.

Fox brought this proposal to the Sub-Committee, which approved the differential consideration of $53.875 and $44.875, which fell on the low end of the range of differential consideration transactions presented by Lazard. The Sub-Committee brought the proposal to the Special Committee, which upon hearing Fox's report approved the differential and agreed to accept TMH's $46 offer and move forward with the remaining terms of the transaction. On October 21, 2011, Rosenkranz relayed the Special Committee's acceptance to TMH and informed TMH for the first time of the differential consideration, toward which TMH reportedly did not express any concern.

In the months following the agreement on price, the Special Committee and TMH negotiated the remaining terms of the Merger. One of the key provisions obtained by the Special Committee was the non-waivable conditioning of the Merger on the affirmative vote of a majority of the disinterested Class A stockholders. In other words, the Merger must receive majority approval from a group of Class A shares that excludes Class A shares owned directly or indirectly by Class B stockholders (Rosenkranz), Delphi officers or directors, TMH, or any of their affiliates.

In addition, since Section 7 of Delphi's Charter prohibits the unequal distribution of merger consideration, the parties agreed to condition the Merger on the approval of a charter amendment that explicitly excludes the Merger from that prohibition (the "Charter

---

[41] *See generally* Elisabeth Kübler-Ross, *ON DEATH AND DYING* 51-146 (Scribner 1997) (1969) (discussing the Kübler-Ross Model, or as it is commonly known, the Five Stages of Grief).

[44] *See id.* Ex. 40, at DEL_SCP00000182 ("Mr. Rosenkranz sounded depressed" and told Fox that he "could not believe that the Sub-Committee was willing to threaten the deal and that the negotiation process had to be this financially painful for him." Rosenkranz also told Fox that "he felt beaten up and that the Sub-Committee had handled him harshly.").

Amendment"). The Sub-Committee found such an amendment to be in the best interests of the Class A stockholders as it was, in the view of the Sub-Committee and in light of Rosenkranz's demands, the only way to enable the Class A stockholders to obtain a substantial premium on their shares. The differential was necessary to secure Rosenkranz's approval of the deal, and the Charter Amendment was necessary to allow that differential.

I. Rosenkranz Tries to Hustle the RAM Contracts

On December 12, 2011, shortly before the signing of the Merger Agreement, Rosenkranz informed Cravath that he and TMH had been discussing the possibility of having TMH acquire RAM, Rosenkranz's investment advising company that provides services to Delphi, immediately before the closing for a price around $57 million. This development concerned the Sub-Committee, as it realized that the $57 million could be seen as additional Merger consideration being allocated to Rosenkranz, rather than as compensation for investment consulting services, if the transaction were structured as an up-front payment with no obligation for RAM or Acorn to continue to perform.

As an alternative, TMH proposed an agreement to keep the RAM Contracts in place for five years. This alternative also concerned the Sub-Committee because the RAM Contracts are terminable by Delphi on thirty days' notice, and an agreement by TMH to continue those contracts for five years would guarantee additional payments to Rosenkranz that might otherwise be unavailable. Moreover, the Sub-Committee questioned the value of RAM's consulting services to TMH, which gave the Sub-Committee concern that TMH was purchasing the RAM Contracts to secure Rosenkranz's consent to the merger and not to obtain the services themselves.

Addressing its concerns, the Sub-Committee decided to push Rosenkranz and TMH to postpone their negotiations regarding the RAM Contracts until after the Merger Agreement was signed, at which point Rosenkranz would be contractually obligated through a voting agreement to support the merger. The Sub-Committee reasoned that such a postponement would effectively ensure that the RAM Contracts purchase negotiations were based on the actual value TMH saw in RAM's services, rather than a need to induce Rosenkranz to support the merger.

Although the Sub-Committee's proposition agitated Rosenkranz, he told the Sub-Committee that he would postpone any renegotiation of the RAM Contracts until after the merger and voting agreement were signed. The Sub-Committee also obtained the inclusion in the Merger Agreement of a contractual representation by TMH that there were no agreements or understandings between TMH and Rosenkranz other than those expressly set forth in the transaction documents. Additionally, the Special Committee used this incident in an attempt to obtain a higher price from TMH, but TMH quickly rejected the Special Committee's request and made clear that it was unwilling to reopen the issue of price.

J. Merger Signing and the Purported "Gentlemen's Agreement"

On December 20, 2011, the Sub-Committee, Special Committee, and the full Board held meetings to discuss the finalized terms of the Merger Agreement. Lazard advised that the overall merger consideration was fair and represented a significant premium over market price.[52] Also, the Special Committee, considering data provided to it by Lazard, concluded that the consideration differential was well within and potentially at the low end of comparable precedent transactions. The Sub-Committee, Special Committee, and the Board then approved the transaction, and Delphi and TMH executed the Merger Agreement on December 21, 2011.

Despite Rosenkranz's representations to the Sub-Committee and TMH's contractual representations in the Merger Agreement, it became apparent during discovery for this action that there had been a non-binding understanding, or "Gentlemen's Agreement," between TMH and Rosenkranz that TMH would continue to pay Rosenkranz for five years of investment consulting services, either under the RAM Contracts or, if TMH terminated the contracts, directly to Rosenkranz. After reviewing a series of emails that revealed this Gentlemen's Agreement, the Sub-Committee decided to revise Delphi's Preliminary Proxy filed on January 13, 2012, to disclose the content of the emails and the Sub-Committee's conclusion that they indicated the existence of a non-binding agreement between Rosenkranz and TMH that existed before the signing of the Merger. The Sub-Committee also informed TMH and Rosenkranz that it was considering exercising its termination rights due to TMH's breach of a contractual representation or changing its recommendation of the Merger to the stockholders.

TMH and Rosenkranz responded by providing the Special Committee with a letter agreement denying that any "Gentlemen's Agreement" existed and stating that, if there had been such an agreement regarding the RAM Contracts, TMH and Rosenkranz "expressly and irrevocably repudiate, and waive any and all rights that [they] may have pursuant to, any such Contract or understanding." After receiving the letter, the Sub-Committee met again to decide on a course of action. The Sub-Committee determined that, despite the denial in the letter agreement, a non-binding understanding had existed between TMH and Rosenkranz, but that TMH and Rosenkranz had repudiated the Gentlemen's Agreement with their letter. The Sub-Committee's conclusions were disclosed in Delphi's February 21, 2012, Definitive Proxy.

The Special Committee and Sub-Committee then reviewed anew whether they considered the proposed Merger and the differential consideration to be fair to the Class A stockholders. They determined that the Merger was fair on both counts and thus decided against changing their recommendation to the stockholders, obviating the need to

---

[52] The unadjusted closing price of Delphi's publicly traded stock on December 20, 2011, the day before the merger was announced, was $25.43. *See* Yahoo! Finance, Delphi Financial Group Inc. Co. Historical Prices, (last visited Mar. 5, 2012). The consideration of $44.875 per Class A share offered by the Merger thus represents a 76% premium over market price.

determine whether Delphi had the right to terminate the Merger Agreement on the basis of TMH's alleged breach.

II. THE PLAINTIFFS' CLAIMS

The wrongdoing alleged by the Plaintiff essentially falls under two areas. The Plaintiffs first challenge the negotiation process used with TMH, arguing that the Executive and Director Defendants breached their fiduciary duties in their efforts to obtain the best price reasonably available to the stockholders, in violation of their fiduciary duties [...]. Second, the Plaintiffs attack the negotiations between the Director Defendants (through the Sub-Committee) and Rosenkranz with respect to differential consideration. The Plaintiffs allege that the Director Defendants and Rosenkranz breached their fiduciary duties to the Class A stockholders in approving the consideration differential. Additionally, the Plaintiffs assert that Rosenkranz breached his fiduciary and contractual obligations in seeking such a differential in the first instance because the Delphi Charter prohibits the unequal distribution of merger consideration. Finally, the Plaintiffs contend—without, however, much enthusiasm—that Delphi's February 2012 Proxy Statement omits or misrepresents material information in violation of the Board's disclosure obligations.

With respect to the negotiations with TMH, the Plaintiffs point to several instances of wrongdoing on the part of Rosenkranz, the Executive and Director Defendants, and TMH. They contend that Rosenkranz, who holds a fiduciary position as Board member, CEO, and controlling stockholder, dominated the negotiation process with TMH against the interests of the Class A stockholders. The Plaintiffs assert that Rosenkranz's interests were not aligned with the stockholders' when he negotiated with TMH because he knew that he would collect a higher price per share than the Class A stockholders. The Plaintiffs contend that Rosenkranz intended from the outset to receive a premium on his Class B shares at the expense of the Class A shares, and is attempting, by tying the vote on the Charter Amendment with the vote on the Merger, to coerce the Class A stockholders into amending the provisions of Delphi's Charter that prohibit such disparate consideration, in violation of his fiduciary and contractual obligations. The Plaintiffs allege that the Board went along with this plan by allowing Rosenkranz to remain the face of Delphi in negotiations with TMH even after Rosenkranz disclosed his intent to procure disparate consideration and by allowing the Merger to be predicated on a coercive vote on the Charter Amendment.

Related to Rosenkranz's and the Director Defendants' failure to secure the best price available, the Plaintiffs present several allegations concerning Acorn and the RAM Contracts. The Plaintiffs contend that Rosenkranz has funneled money to himself through the RAM Contracts, thereby depressing Delphi's share price, which caused Lazard to value Delphi at too low a price in its Fairness Opinion. Additionally, the Plaintiffs accuse Rosenkranz of usurping a corporate opportunity belonging to Delphi by using Delphi employees and resources to provide lucrative investment consulting services through Acorn to third parties, diverting a revenue stream that should have flowed to Delphi and that would have increased Delphi's value to potential bidders. The Plaintiffs also allege that Rosenkranz has obtained, or attempted to obtain, through negotiations with and aided and abetted by TMH, disparate consideration by preserving the income stream flowing from the RAM Contracts.

In addition to attacking the negotiation process with TMH, the Plaintiffs assert that the Sub-Committee did not achieve a fair result with respect to the differential consideration. The Plaintiffs argue that Rosenkranz breached his fiduciary and contractual obligations to the stockholders by seeking disparate consideration in the first place, as the Delphi Charter requires equal treatment of Class A and Class B shares in the distribution of merger consideration. For the same reasons, argue the Plaintiffs, the Director and Executive Defendants breached their fiduciary duties in facilitating and approving the consideration differential. The Plaintiffs also contend that, even assuming that some level of disparate consideration is permissible, the Sub-Committee members, in breach of their fiduciary duties, failed to negotiate a fair price for the Class A stockholders.

III. ANALYSIS

I may issue a preliminary injunction only where I find that the moving party has demonstrated a reasonable likelihood of success on the merits, that failure to enjoin will result in irreparable harm to the moving party, and that a balancing of the equities discloses that any harm likely to result from the injunctive relief is outweighed by the benefit conferred thereby. Although I find that the Plaintiffs have demonstrated a reasonable probability of success on the merits of some of their claims, I nonetheless find that injunctive relief here is inappropriate. The threatened harm here is largely, if not completely, remediable by damages, and because the value of injunctive relief to the stockholder class seems likely to be overwhelmed by the concomitant loss, I must deny the Plaintiffs' request for a preliminary injunction.

A. Reasonable Probability of Success

As discussed above, the Plaintiffs' allegations essentially fall under two categories: those attacking the negotiation of the Merger price, and those attacking the differential consideration. Under the former category, the Plaintiffs challenge the negotiations with TMH and Rosenkranz's involvement therein, as well as the effect of the Acorn business and RAM Contracts on Delphi's value to potential bidders. Under the latter category, the Plaintiffs challenge Rosenkranz's entitlement to disparate consideration, the effectiveness of the Sub-Committee's negotiations with Rosenkranz, and Rosenkranz's potential receipt of additional consideration not shared with the Class A stockholders through an alleged agreement with TMH to maintain the RAM Contracts. I address below the Plaintiffs' likelihood of success on these arguments and their allegations regarding disclosure violations.

1. Challenges to the Negotiations with TMH and the Price Approved by the Special Committee

[...]

184

The Plaintiffs argue that the Special Committee faltered when it allowed Rosenkranz to take the lead in negotiations despite his conflict of interest with the Class A stockholders. The Plaintiffs contend that Rosenkranz was content to eschew the highest price per share because his personal interest was to ensure that the Merger was realized; he could then turn and negotiate for disparate consideration for his shares. The Plaintiffs point out that the Board used Rosenkranz to negotiate the deal with TMH even after he disclosed his intention to demand additional compensation for his Class B shares as a condition of his supporting the Merger. The Director Defendants explain that they kept Rosenkranz as lead negotiator because, as CEO, he was the natural choice, and because replacing Rosenkranz with another negotiator might have tipped TMH to the internal conflict or otherwise alarmed TMH, potentially spawning negotiation difficulties or even jeopardizing the entire deal.

As a negotiator, however, Rosenkranz's interests may not have been entirely aligned with those of the Class A stockholders. Rosenkranz was a fiduciary for Delphi, seeking to extract as much value for the Company as possible for the public shareholders. Nevertheless, though he was the holder of a class of stock relegated by the Charter to receiving, upon the merger, the same price per share as the publicly held stock, he firmly believed he was entitled to a control premium. Throughout the negotiations, he knew he was negotiating a price which he, as controlling stockholder, would not accept for his stock. Finally, Rosenkranz was the owner of a business, Acorn, which had a contractual relationship with Delphi. Thus, throughout the negotiations, Rosenkranz knew that he would also be negotiating the futures of those contracts with TMH.

In addition to his conflicted roles, Rosenkranz's actions, and those of the other Executive Defendants, are troubling. Upon being approached by TMH, Rosenkranz did not immediately inform the Board that he would insist on differential consideration for his Class B stock. Instead, Rosenkranz consulted with Coulter, Sherman, and Kiratsous to formulate a plan, not to maximize, via the Merger, return to the stockholders, for whom they are fiduciaries, but to maximize return to Rosenkranz himself.

I am not persuaded, however, by the Plaintiffs' theory that because Rosenkranz knew he was going to receive disparate consideration, he lacked an incentive to extract the highest price from TMH. Regardless of whether he was able to achieve a premium for his shares, to the extent that Rosenkranz secured a higher overall price, there would be a bigger pie from which Rosenkranz could cut an outsized slice. The Plaintiffs make the argument that Rosenkranz perhaps had an incentive to accept a smaller merger price so that TMH would have more funds available for the renegotiation of the RAM Contracts, in which only Rosenkranz holds an interest. The Special Committee made an attempt to achieve a higher price from TMH after it learned of the side negotiations between Rosenkranz and TMH regarding the RAM Contracts, but was unsuccessful. On the current record, it seems unlikely that money was left on the table by Rosenkranz in anticipation of a lucrative renegotiation of the RAM Contracts.

The Plaintiffs also allege that the existence of Acorn and the RAM Contracts poisoned the sale process. As discussed earlier, after Rosenkranz formed Delphi, Delphi entered into contracts to purchase investment advising services from Acorn through RAM, both of which are Rosenkranz-affiliated entities. These contracts continued after Delphi went public and have been disclosed continuously. Under the Expense Allocation Agreement, Acorn would reimburse Delphi for Acorn's use of Delphi's employees, facilities, and other resources to provide services to third parties as well as Delphi. When providing services to Delphi, Acorn would bill the Company through RAM, pursuant to the RAM Contracts. These contracts were terminable at thirty days' notice by either party.

The Plaintiffs contend that the RAM Contracts were a sham device through which Rosenkranz used Delphi employees and Delphi resources in order to charge Delphi for services that the Company could have provided in house, and to usurp an opportunity which Delphi could have seized to provide similar services to third parties. The Plaintiffs allege that Delphi's stock price was depressed as a result of this diverted income stream and that the stockholders will be misled by Lazard's Fairness Opinion, which does not take this into account. The Director Defendants and Rosenkranz argue that the RAM Contracts provided value for Delphi. The record regarding the RAM Contracts remains largely undeveloped at this stage; such evidence as exists warrants further consideration, but it is insufficient to convince me that the Plaintiffs are likely to be able to demonstrate at trial that the existence of Acorn and the RAM Contracts depressed Delphi's stock price.

2. Challenges to the Negotiations with Rosenkranz and the Sub-Committee's Approval of Disparate Consideration

The Plaintiffs' most persuasive argument, based on the preliminary record before me, is that despite a contrary provision in the Delphi Charter, Rosenkranz, in breach of his contractual and fiduciary duties, sought and obtained a control premium for his shares, an effort that was facilitated by the Executive and Director Defendants. As discussed above, Delphi's Charter contains two classes of stock: Class A, entitled to one vote per share, and Class B, entitled to ten votes per share. Rosenkranz holds all of the Class B shares; thus, even though he only owns 12.9% of Delphi's equity, he controls 49.9% of the stockholders' voting power. As a result, Rosenkranz can effectively block any merger or similar transaction that is not to his liking.

Nevertheless, the Delphi Charter contains certain restrictions on Rosenkranz's power. Though Rosenkranz can act as a controlling stockholder, the Charter provides that, in a merger, the Class A stockholders and the Class B stockholders must be treated equally. Additionally, if Rosenkranz attempts to transfer his Class B stock to anyone besides an affiliate of his, the Class B stock converts into Class A stock. The Merger here is conditioned, at Rosenkranz's insistence, on a Charter Amendment removing the requirement of equal distribution of merger consideration. Once the Charter is amended, Rosenkranz can receive a higher payment for his shares than the Class A stockholders. At the same time the disinterested Sub-Committee negotiated these provisions with Rosenkranz, Rosenkranz took the lead in the negotiations with TMH, despite this apparent conflict with Delphi's public stockholders.

Rosenkranz, in taking Delphi public, created, via the Charter, a mechanism whereby he retained voting control of Delphi as the holder of the high-vote Class B stock. As Rosenkranz points out, a controlling stockholder is, with limited exceptions, entitled under Delaware law to negotiate a control premium for its shares. Moreover, a controlling stockholder is free to consider its interests alone in weighing the decision to sell its shares or, having made such a decision, evaluating the adequacy of a given price. Rosenkranz contends that as a stockholder he has the right to control and vote his shares in his best interest, which generally includes the right to sell a controlling share for a premium at the expense of the minority stockholders.

The Plaintiffs argue that by including a provision in Delphi's Charter providing that Class B stockholders would accept the same consideration as Class A stockholders in the case of a sale, Rosenkranz gave up his right to a control premium. They argue that by approving a merger conditioned on the Charter Amendment, which restores Rosenkranz's right to obtain disparate consideration for his shares, the Board and Rosenkranz are coercing the stockholders into choosing between approving the Merger at the cost of a substantial premium to Rosenkranz or voting against the Merger and forgoing an otherwise attractive deal (that could nevertheless be more attractive sans the Rosenkranz premium). The Plaintiffs allege that the Charter Amendment is coercive because in order to realize the benefits of the merger, the stockholders must induce Rosenkranz's consent by repealing a Charter provision that exists to protect them from exactly this situation. In other words, the Plaintiffs contend that although Rosenkranz may sell his stock generally free of fiduciary concerns for the minority stockholders, he may not do so in a way that coerces the stockholders' concession of a right guaranteed under the Charter.

Rosenkranz and the Board counter that the Charter specifically provides for amendment. The Director Defendants also argue that, notwithstanding the Charter provision requiring the equal distribution of consideration to Class A and Class B stockholders in the event of a sale, the sale to TMH involves a substantial premium over market and is a compelling transaction—one which the stockholders ought to have the opportunity to accept, even if they must also approve the Charter Amendment to consummate the Merger. The Director Defendants state:

> [I]f stockholders like the transaction, they will support the Certificate Amendment, and if they don't like the transaction, they won't. Amazingly, the supposed source of "coercion" is that the price being offered by [TMH] is so *high* that stockholders might actually want to accept it. By this definition, every good deal is "coercive."

The argument of the Director Defendants and Rosenkranz reduces to this syllogism: Rosenkranz, in taking Delphi public in 1990, retained control. Notwithstanding his retention of control, he gave up, through Section 7 of the Delphi Charter, the right to receive a control premium. Consistent with Delaware law, however, the Charter provided for its own amendment by majority vote of the stockholders. Thus, since Rosenkranz is, as a controlling stockholder, generally unconstrained by fiduciary duties when deciding whether to sell his stock, he is permitted to condition his approval of a sale on both a restoration of his right to receive a control premium and on actually receiving such a premium. I find this argument unpersuasive.

Section 7 of the Charter gives the stockholders the right to receive the same consideration, in a merger, as received by Rosenkranz. I assume that the stockholders, in return for the protection against differential merger consideration found in the Charter, paid a higher price for their shares.[68] In other words, though Rosenkranz retained voting control, he sold his right to a control premium to the Class A stockholders via the Charter. The Charter provision, which prevents disparate consideration, exists so that if a merger is proposed, Rosenkranz cannot extract a *second* control premium for himself at the expense of the Class A stockholders.

Of course, the Charter provided for its own amendment. Presumably, Rosenkranz, clear of any impending sale, could have purchased the right to a control premium back from the stockholders through a negotiated vote in favor of a charter amendment. But to accept Rosenkranz's argument and to allow him to coerce such an amendment here would be to render the Charter rights illusory and would permit Rosenkranz, who benefited by selling his control premium to the Class A stockholders at Delphi's IPO, to sell the same control premium again in connection with this Merger. That would amount to a wrongful transfer of merger consideration from the Class A stockholders to Rosenkranz.

What would have happened if Rosenkranz had respected the Charter provision? He would still have had voting control. He may have insisted that no merger occur without consideration for all shares of at least $53.875, which likely would have killed the deal and restored the status quo. Or, without his steadfast belief that he was entitled to a differential,

Rosenkranz may have agreed to a deal for all shares at $46, representing as it does a substantial premium over market. Because Rosenkranz sought instead to exact a control premium he had already bargained away, the answer to the question posed above is unknowable.

Our Supreme Court has stated that a corporate charter, along with its accompanying bylaws, is a contract between the corporation's stockholders. Inherent in any contractual relationship is the implied covenant of good faith and fair dealing. This implied covenant "embodies the law's expectation that each party to a contract will act with good faith

---

[68] At oral argument, neither Rosenkranz nor the Director Defendants provided a convincing explanation as to why a prohibition on disparate consideration would have been included other than to improve the marketability of Delphi's public shares. In his deposition, Rosenkranz claimed that the primary reason for having two stock classes was "to avoid the risk that Delphi would be sold at an inadequate price at an inopportune time, once it was publicly traded" and that he wanted to exit Delphi "at a time and on terms that were acceptable to [him]." Rosenkranz Dep. 58:10-59:21. With respect to the Charter Amendment, Rosenkranz argued that he was simply controlling when the stock was to be sold and that the Charter Amendment was really just an altruistic act that would give the Class A stockholders "an opportunity to accept a proposal which [Rosenkranz would] otherwise . . . reject." *Id.* at 80:8-16.

toward the other with respect to the subject matter of the contract." A party breaches the covenant "by taking advantage of [its] position to control implementation of the agreement's terms," such that "[its] conduct frustrates the `overarching purpose' of the contract."

The Plaintiffs argue that Rosenkranz has breached the implied covenant of good faith and fair dealing. They assert that the stockholders, therefore, have a remedy for breach of contract as well as fiduciary duty. They point out that, following the Defendants' logic, the existence of the amendment procedure rendered the provision mandating equal price on sale for the Class A and B shares a sham, since Rosenkranz retained the ability to coerce a charter amendment, and thus a control premium, in connection with any favorable merger offer. Implicit in the Plaintiffs' argument is that, had the purchasers of Delphi's public stock realized this, they may not have purchased the stock, at least at the price paid.

I need not decide at this preliminary stage whether the rights of the stockholder class here sound in breach of contract as well as breach of fiduciary duty. It suffices that I find on the present record that the Plaintiffs bought Delphi's stock with the understanding that the Charter structured the corporation in such a way that denied Rosenkranz a control premium, and that as a result, Rosenkranz effectively extracted a control premium from the initial sale of the Class A shares, while at the same time retaining his voting majority. I therefore find that the Plaintiffs are reasonably likely to be able to demonstrate at trial that in negotiating for disparate consideration and only agreeing to support the merger if he received it, Rosenkranz violated duties to the stockholders.

Next, the Plaintiffs argue that Rosenkranz's attempts to preserve the RAM Contracts after the Merger will result in a form of disparate consideration that would contravene the Charter, to the detriment of the Class A stockholders. As described below, the process by which Rosenkranz negotiated both as a fiduciary for Delphi and, at the same time, for himself as a controlling stockholder, is troubling. I note, however, that these contracts can be canceled at thirty days' notice. Despite the Plaintiffs' arguments to the contrary, TMH has little incentive to pay more to Rosenkranz than the actual value of Acorn's services to TMH: Rosenkranz is contractually obligated to vote in favor of the Merger per a voting agreement, thus obviating any reason for TMH to induce Rosenkranz's support through overpayment for Acorn's services. Therefore, despite Rosenkranz's potential conflict in negotiating both for Delphi and for Acorn, I do not find that the Plaintiffs have demonstrated a reasonable probability that a post-Merger contract involving RAM or Acorn will net Rosenkranz any disparate consideration in violation of Delphi's Charter. . . .

B. Irreparable Harm and the Balance of the Equities

A preliminary injunction is an "extraordinary remedy . . . [and] is granted sparingly and only upon a persuasive showing that it is urgently necessary, that it will result in comparatively less harm to the adverse party, and that, in the end, it is unlikely to be shown to have been issued improvidently." To demonstrate irreparable harm, a plaintiff must show harm "of such a nature that no fair and reasonable redress may be had in a court of law and must show that to refuse the injunction would be a denial of justice." A harm that can be remedied by money damages is not irreparable.

Additionally, in the context of a single-bidder merger, the Court when balancing the equities must be cognizant that if the merger is enjoined, the deal may be lost forever, a concern of particular gravity where, as here, the proposed deal offers a substantial premium over market price. In evaluating the appropriateness of enjoining a given merger, this Court has noted the difference between a single bidder situation and a situation where there exists a competing, potentially superior, rival bid.

This Court recently addressed a situation similar to the present action in *In re El Paso Corp. Shareholder Litigation.* In that case, the Chancellor identified numerous "debatable negotiating and tactical choices made by El Paso fiduciaries and advisors," which were compounded by a lead negotiator and financial advisor with interests in conflict with those of the El Paso stockholders. The proposed transaction offered a premium of 37% over El Paso's stock price, however, and was the only bid on the table. The Chancellor, though troubled by the conduct of the El Paso fiduciaries and advisors, declined to enjoin the merger, finding that the stockholders were "well positioned to turn down the [offeror's] price if they [did] not like it," noting that while damages were not a perfect remedy, the "stockholders should not be deprived of the chance to decide for themselves about the Merger."

Here, the 76% premium offered by TMH dwarfs the premium percentage in *El Paso.* Moreover, although I have found it reasonably likely that Rosenkranz violated a duty in his role as lead negotiator, his interests were at least in some respects aligned with those of the Class A stockholders. Given these considerations, and the fact that, as explained below, money damages can largely remedy the threatened harm, the stockholders' potential loss of a substantial premium on their shares outweighs the value of an injunction; therefore, I must deny the Plaintiffs' request for injunctive relief.

Much of the alleged misconduct of which the Plaintiffs complain is remediable by readily ascertainable damages. The Plaintiffs argue that the differential consideration negotiated between Rosenkranz and the Sub-Committee is improper. If so, I may order disgorgement of the improper consideration. The Plaintiffs allege that any post-Merger contract between RAM/Acorn and TMH would constitute additional merger consideration flowing to Rosenkranz, when such consideration rightly belongs to all of the stockholders. If so, such an amount would be recoverable in damages as well. In other words, if these factors constitute harm to the Class A stockholders, it is not irreparable harm.

The Plaintiffs' allegations regarding past losses to the Company arising from Rosenkranz's operation of Acorn are more problematic. As described above, the Plaintiffs argue that Acorn, operated with borrowed Delphi employees, facilities, and resources, was a sham; that the investment advice it sold to Delphi under the RAM Contracts could have been produced "in house" for a fraction of what Delphi paid for it; and that its third-party business was a corporate opportunity belonging to Delphi and usurped by Rosenkranz. According to the Plaintiffs, this activity depressed Delphi's stock price, causing the Lazard

Fairness Opinion to be of limited value, since Delphi was worth more than the analysis assumed. Stockholders, under this theory, may be misled by the fairness opinion, and the recommendation of the Board based on that opinion, when choosing whether to vote for the Merger. Moreover, the Plaintiffs argue, TMH may have been willing to pay more for a Delphi unencumbered by the RAM Contracts, in an amount unknowable and thus irremediable by damages, and Rosenkranz may have been willing to forgo the highest merger price in favor of maximizing the value available in the negotiations of the RAM Contracts.

While the concerns above appear irreparable absent an injunction, I give the possibility of such harm little weight. First, it seems unlikely that TMH will feel itself significantly encumbered, let alone bound, by contracts terminable upon thirty days' notice with a sham entity returning no actual value to Delphi or TMH. It is clear from the record that TMH has no legal obligation to keep such contracts in place, and thus it is unlikely that the existence of the RAM Contracts has depressed the price TMH is willing to pay for Delphi.

Similarly, the risk that the stockholders will be misled by Lazard's Fairness Opinion because Delphi's stock price was depressed due to the RAM Contracts is only speculative. The record is insufficient to demonstrate that those contracts, in place since Delphi's IPO and disclosed continuously thereafter, were wrongful, and if so, to what extent they may have affected Delphi's stock price, if at all. To the extent they have, they have similarly decreased the price each stockholder *paid* for his shares. Moreover, the existence of the RAM Contracts, the Board's concern that negotiations over those contracts between Rosenkranz and TMH might have involved hidden additional compensation for Rosenkranz, as well as the other circumstances I have set out above, are all disclosed in the February 2012 Proxy available to each stockholder.

In that vein, I also find that the alleged disclosure violations provide no basis for injunctive relief. The February 2012 Proxy fully informs the stockholders about the concerns detailed above. With respect to the differential consideration, which I view as the issue raised by Plaintiffs most likely to be successful, any recovery in damages will be on top of the amount at which the stockholders are being asked to tender their shares. In light of all the issues raised above, the stockholders have a fair if not perfect ability to decide whether to tender their shares or seek appraisal rights under 8 *Del. C.* § 262.

I find the opportunity to exercise that franchise particularly important here. The price offered by TMH for the Class A shares, even though less than what Rosenkranz will receive in the Merger, is 76% above Delphi's stock price on the day before the Merger was announced. No party has suggested that another suitor is in the wings or is likely to be developed at a greater, or even equal, price. Nothing beyond the Plaintiffs' speculation about the effects of the Acorn business and RAM Contracts indicates that injunctive relief would lead to negotiation of a significant increase in price. In fact, it seems at least as likely that a renegotiated deal may yield a lower price, or a loss of the Merger entirely and a return to the status quo ante, including regarding stock price. Having determined that a judicial intervention at this point is unlikely to prove a net benefit to the plaintiff class, and may cause substantial harm, it is preferable to allow the stockholders to decide whether they wish to go forward with the Merger despite the imperfections of the process leading to its formulation.

The Plaintiffs make a final argument that injunctive relief must be afforded here, based upon the deterrent effect of an injunction: they argue that if I decide that the proffered deal is "good enough" to cause this Court to deny injunctive relief despite the wrongful differential they see Rosenkranz as extorting from the stockholders, I will be, to paraphrase Chairman Mao, letting a thousand little Rosenkranzes bloom. It is obvious to me, however, that the available damages remedies, particularly in this case where damages may be easily calculated, will serve as a sufficient deterrent for the behavior the Plaintiffs allege here.

CONCLUSION

Robert Rosenkranz founded Delphi, built its value, and took the Company public. The complaints about the RAM Contracts notwithstanding, the Plaintiffs concede that, as a public company, Delphi has been well-run by Rosenkranz and the Board. Having built Delphi, and having retained control of the Company throughout, Rosenkranz clearly feels morally entitled to a premium for his stock. The Plaintiffs have demonstrated a reasonable likelihood that they will be able to prove at trial that Rosenkranz is not so entitled, however.

Nonetheless, given that the meritorious allegations discussed above are remediable by damages, I find it in the best interests of the stockholders that they be given the opportunity to decide for themselves whether the Merger negotiated by Rosenkranz and the Director Defendants offers an acceptable price for their shares. For the foregoing reasons, the Motion for Preliminary Injunction is denied.

IT IS SO ORDERED.

[...]

Discussion Questions:

1. What rule would have governed in the absence of an explicit charter provision? See DGCL 251(c).

2. Could Rosenkranz have amended the charter provision in question without the approval of the minority shareholders? *Cf.* DGCL 242(b)(2).

3. What did Rosenkranz promise to do in a future sale, according to the court? Why do you think he would have made this promise? Was this promise economically enforceable? (In particular, could Rosenkranz be forced to agree to a sale in the first place?) Note that the deal was approved by shareholders, plaintiff shareholders unsurprisingly brought suit challenging the differential consideration, and the case eventually settled for $49 million (out of the $70 million that Rosenkranz extracted from the differential consideration).

4. The plaintiffs alleged that failure to grant an injunction would be (in the words of the court) "letting a thousand little Rosenkranzes bloom." In 2016, Facebook founder Mark Zuckerberg, in order to facilitate the charitable donation of most of his Facebook shares over the course of his lifetime, proposed a new Class C share to replace his high-vote Class B shares. In exchange for this recapitalization, Facebook proposed the following "Equal Treatment Provision:"

> Except as expressly provided in the New Certificate, shares of Class A common stock, Class B common stock, and Class C capital stock have the same rights and privileges and rank equally, share ratably, and are identical in all respects as to all matters. In the event of a consolidation or merger of us with or into any other entity, or in the case of any other transaction having an effect on stockholders substantially similar to that resulting from a consolidation or merger, such as a sale of substantially all of our assets, the holders of Class A common stock, Class B common stock, and Class C capital stock shall share ratably on a per share basis in any distribution or payment in connection with such transaction. In the event of any tender offer or exchange offer by any third party pursuant to an agreement to which we are a party or that we recommend, the holders of Class A common stock, Class B common stock, and Class C capital stock will be entitled to receive, or to elect to receive, the same form of consideration and the same amount of consideration on a per share basis.[18]

In view of *In re Delphi*, does this proposed Equal Treatment Provision have substantive bite? Or could Mark Zuckerberg threaten to do the same thing as Rosenkranz did in this case?

---

[18] Facebook Proxy Statement (June 2, 2016) at 69.

Chapter 7 – Mergers & Acquisitions

Mergers & Acquisitions have become an important piece of the corporate board's overall toolkit. The following chart is useful in providing a historical perspective on M&A[19]:

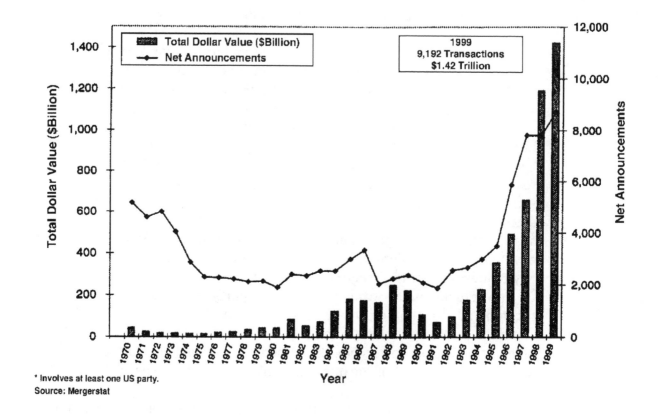

* Involves at least one US party.
Source: Mergerstat

In the old days (through the 1970s), most companies grew organically. As shown on the chart, the first merger "wave" occurred in the 1980s. While this wave attracted considerable popular and political attention because of the emergence of hostile takeovers (more on this in the next chapter), it was swamped—in dollar volume—by the 1990s, which in turn was swamped by the merger wave of the mid-2000s (not shown). Each of these waves was distinctive: while the 1980s featured hostile takeovers, the 1990s wave was driven by "synergies" between strategic partners, and the 2000s merger wave was known for its massive private equity deals.

Today, every board of directors of every significant corporation regularly talks about M&A. What businesses should we sell? What businesses should we buy? In effect, M&A is the operationalization of the ideas of economic theorists such as Ronald Coase and Oliver Williamson regarding the "Theory of the Firm:" firm boundaries will expand or contract to allow the firm to achieve the optimal scale and scope.

---

[19] Chart from Joseph H. Flom, *Mergers & Acquisitions: The Decade in Review*, 54 U. Miami L. Rev., 753 (2000).

Delaware provides two mechanisms for M&A: asset acquisitions (see DGCL 271) and statutory mergers (see DGCL 251). An asset acquisition (as the name suggests) involves the acquisition of the assets of the selling company, in exchange for cash, the acquirer's stock, or other consideration. If the sale involves "all or substantially all" of the selling company's assets, the selling company must gain approval from a majority of the outstanding shares. DGCL 271(a). In theory, the liabilities stay with the target company, because the acquirer is only buying the assets. However, certain environmental liabilities and subsequent tort claims against the selling company cannot be shed so easily, under the doctrine of "successor liability."

Delaware's second mechanism for M&A is the statutory merger, which legally collapses one corporation into the other. The boards of both companies must approve the merger. DGCL 251(b). Target shareholders always must approve the merger as well. DGCL 251(c). Acquiring shareholders must also approve the merger, unless three conditions are met: (1) the surviving company's charter is not modified; (2) the shares held by the surviving corporation's shareholders remain unchanged; and (3) the surviving company's outstanding common stock is not increased by more than 20%. DGCL 251(f).

Unlike an asset acquisition, which transfers only the assets of the target company, a statutory merger transfers both the assets and the liabilities. But what if some of these liabilities are unknown at the time of the merger? Consider the case of Bank of America buying Countrywide Home Loans, Inc., just as the financial crisis was beginning to gather steam in 2008. BofA knew that Countrywide held a certain share of "toxic" mortgages on its portfolio, but how much? If BofA executed a simple merger with Countrywide, it would expose BofA's $2 *trillion* in assets to claims of Countrywide's creditors—claims that preceded BofA's rescue, and claims that BofA had nothing to do with. Or consider Dow Chemical's acquisition of Union Carbide Corp. (UCC) in 2001. In 1984, a terrible tragedy occurred when Methyl Isocynate, an ingredient used to make pesticides, leaked from a plant in Bhopal, India that was owned by a UCC subsidiary. Thousands of people died or were injured, and claims were still playing out in the Indian courts seventeen year later. Did Dow want to expose its balance sheet to tort claims against UCC? Without some mechanism to protect the acquirer's balance sheet from the (imperfectly known) claims against the target company, potential target companies such as Countrywide and UCC would become untouchable in the M&A marketplace. This would be unfortunate as a policy matter, because companies like Countrywide and UCC are often in most need of help from a most established player such as BofA or Dow Chemical.

Enter the triangular merger mechanism. The vast majority (90+%) of mergers today are done as either a "forward" or a "reverse" triangular merger. In both cases, the acquiring company creates a wholly-owned subsidiary (often called, in M&A parlance, a "drop-down subsidiary"). In a forward triangular merger, the target company merges into the drop-down subsidiary. In a reverse triangular merger, the drop-down subsidiary merges into the target. BofA-Countrywide was structured as a forward triangular merger, while Dow Chemical-UCC was structured as a reverse triangular merger. The reasons for choosing one or the other are often idiosyncratic, pertaining to regulatory and tax factors, and are beyond the scope of the course.

It is universally accepted among practitioners and academics that a triangular merger, if properly executed, preserves the liability shield of the acquirer against the target's liabilities. Of course, this does not prevent former creditors to the target company from attempting to gain access to the acquirer's assets through piercing the corporate veil, *de facto* merger doctrine (discussed below), or other equitable claims (creditors to UCC and Countrywide both did); but the acquiring company will have strong claims that the form of the transaction should be respected. Note that in a stock-for-stock deal, preserving the liability shield works in the other direction too: creditors to the parent must stand behind creditors to the subsidiary, thereby protecting the target's creditors.

The merger agreement below illustrates the triangular merger mechanism.

3G / Burger King Merger Agreement (2010)

The following is an excerpt from the acquisition agreement whereby 3G Capital, a private equity fund, acquired Burger King.

AGREEMENT AND PLAN OF MERGER

This AGREEMENT AND PLAN OF MERGER (this "Agreement"), dated as of September 2, 2010, is entered into by and among Blue Acquisition Holding Corporation, a Delaware corporation ("Parent"), Blue Acquisition Sub, Inc., a Delaware corporation and a wholly owned Subsidiary of Parent ("Sub"), and Burger King Holdings, Inc., a Delaware corporation (the "Company"). Each of Parent, Sub and the Company are referred to herein as a "Party" and together as "Parties". Capitalized terms used and not otherwise defined herein have the meanings set forth in Article X.

RECITALS

WHEREAS, the respective boards of directors of each of Parent, Sub and the Company have unanimously (i) determined that this Agreement and the transactions contemplated hereby, including the Offer and the Merger, are advisable, fair to and in the best interests of their respective stockholders and (ii) approved this Agreement and the transactions contemplated hereby, including the Offer and the Merger, on the terms and subject to the conditions set forth in this Agreement;

WHEREAS, Parent proposes to cause Sub to commence a tender offer (as it may be amended from time to time as permitted under this Agreement, the "Offer") to purchase all the outstanding shares of common stock, par value $0.01 per share, of the Company (the "Company Common Stock") at a price per share of Company Common Stock of $24.00, without interest (such amount, or any other amount per share paid pursuant to the Offer and this Agreement, the "Offer Price"), net to the seller thereof in cash, on the terms and subject to the conditions set forth in this Agreement;

WHEREAS, concurrently with the execution and delivery of this Agreement, the Company has entered into a Sponsor Tender Agreement with certain investment funds affiliated with Bain Capital Investors, LLC, TPG Capital, L.P. and The Goldman Sachs Group, Inc. and their respective Affiliates set forth therein (collectively, the "Sponsor Tender Agreements"), pursuant to which, among other things, such investment funds have irrevocably agreed to tender shares of Company Common Stock beneficially owned by them in the Offer (the shares subject to such agreements constituting, in the aggregate, approximately 31% of the Company Common Stock as of the date hereof) and to take certain actions and exercise certain rights, and to refrain from taking other actions or exercising other rights, in each case, as set forth therein;

WHEREAS, regardless of whether the Offer Closing occurs, Sub will merge with and into the Company, with the Company continuing as the surviving corporation in the merger (the "Merger"), upon the terms and subject to the conditions set forth in this Agreement, whereby, except as expressly provided in Section 3.01, each issued and outstanding share of Company Common Stock immediately prior to the effective time of the Merger will be cancelled and converted into the right to receive the Offer Price; and

WHEREAS Parent, Sub and the Company desire to make certain representations, warranties, covenants and agreements in connection with the Offer and the Merger and also to prescribe various conditions to the Offer and the Merger.

NOW, THEREFORE, in consideration of the foregoing premises and the representations, warranties, covenants and agreements contained in this Agreement, and subject to the conditions set forth herein, as well as other good and valuable consideration, the receipt and sufficiency of which are hereby acknowledged, and intending to be legally bound hereby, the Parties agree as follows:

Article I: The Offer

Section 1.01 The Offer.

(a) Commencement of the Offer. As promptly as reasonably practicable (and, in any event, within 10 business days) after the date of this Agreement, Sub shall, and Parent shall cause Sub to, commence (within the meaning of Rule 14d-2 under the Securities Exchange Act of 1934, as amended (together with the rules and regulations promulgated thereunder, the "Exchange Act")) the Offer to purchase all of the outstanding shares of Company Common Stock at a price per share equal to the Offer Price (as adjusted as provided in Section 1.01(c), if applicable).

(b) Terms and Conditions of the Offer. The obligations of Sub to, and of Parent to cause Sub to, accept for payment, and pay for, any shares of Company Common Stock tendered pursuant to the Offer are subject only to the conditions set forth in Annex I (the "Offer Conditions"). The Offer Conditions are for the sole benefit of Parent and Sub, and Parent and Sub may waive, in whole or in part, any Offer Condition at any time and from time to time, in their sole discretion, other than the Minimum Tender Condition, which may be waived by Parent and Sub only with the prior written consent of the Company. Parent and Sub expressly reserve the right to increase the Offer Price or to waive or make any other changes in the terms and conditions of the Offer; provided, however, that unless otherwise provided in this Agreement or previously approved by the Company in writing, Sub shall not, and Parent shall not permit Sub to, (i) reduce the number of shares of Company Common Stock sought to be purchased in the Offer, (ii) reduce the Offer Price, (iii) change the form of consideration payable in the Offer, (iv) amend, modify or waive the Minimum Tender Condition, (v) add to the Offer Conditions or amend, modify or supplement any Offer Condition, or (vi) extend the expiration date of the Offer in any manner other than in accordance with the terms of Section 1.01(d).

(c) Adjustments to Offer Price. The Offer Price shall be adjusted appropriately to reflect the effect of any stock split, reverse stock split, stock dividend (including any dividend or distribution of securities convertible into Company Common Stock), cash dividend (other than the First Quarter Dividend), reorganization, recapitalization, reclassification, combination, exchange of shares or other like change with respect to Company Common Stock occurring on or after the date hereof and prior to Sub's acceptance for payment of, and payment for, Company Common Stock tendered in the Offer.

(d) Expiration and Extension of the Offer. The Offer shall initially be scheduled to expire at midnight, New York City time, on the later of (x) the 20th business day following the commencement of the Offer (determined using Rule 14d-1(g)(3) under the Exchange Act) and (y) the second business day following the No-Shop Period Start Date (such later date being the "Initial Offer Expiration Date"), provided, however, if at the Initial Offer Expiration Date, any Offer Condition is not satisfied or waived, Sub shall, and Parent shall cause Sub to, extend the Offer for ten (10) business days; provided, further, that if the only Offer Condition not satisfied at such time is the Financing Proceeds Condition, then such Initial Offer Expiration Date may be extended, at Parent's option, for less than ten (10) business days. Thereafter, if at any then scheduled expiration of the Offer, any Offer Condition is not satisfied or waived, Sub shall, and Parent shall cause Sub to, extend the Offer on one or more occasions, in consecutive increments of up to five (5) business days (or such longer period as the Parties may agree) each; provided, however, if the Proxy Statement Clearance Date has occurred on or prior to November 24, 2010, then no such extension shall be required after November 24, 2010; provided, further, however, if the Proxy Statement Clearance Date has not occurred on or prior to November 24, 2010, then either Parent or the Company may request, and upon such request, Sub shall extend the Offer in increments of up to five (5) business days (or such longer period as the Parties may agree) each until the Proxy Statement Clearance Date; it being understood that nothing contained herein shall limit or otherwise affect the Company's right to terminate this Agreement pursuant to Section 9.01(g) in accordance with the terms thereof. "Proxy Statement Clearance Date" means the date on which the SEC has, orally or in writing, confirmed that it has no further comments on the Proxy Statement, including the first date following the tenth calendar day following the filing of the preliminary Proxy Statement if the SEC has not informed the Company that it intends to review the Proxy Statement. In addition, Sub shall, and Parent shall cause Sub to, extend the Offer on one or more occasions for the minimum period required by any rule, regulation, interpretation or position of the Securities and Exchange Commission (the "SEC") or the staff thereof applicable to the Offer; provided, however, that Sub shall not be required to extend the Offer beyond the Outside Date and such extension shall be subject to the right to terminate the Offer in accordance with Section 1.01(f). The last date on which the Offer is required to be extended pursuant to this Section 1.01(d) is referred to as the "Offer End Date" (it being understood that under no circumstances shall the Offer End Date occur prior to November 24, 2010).

(e) Payment. On the terms and subject to the conditions of the Offer and this Agreement, Sub shall, and Parent shall cause Sub to, accept for payment, and pay for, all shares of Company Common Stock validly tendered and not withdrawn pursuant to the Offer promptly (and in any event within 3 business days) after the applicable expiration date of the Offer (as it may be extended in accordance with Section 1.01(d)) and in any event in compliance with Rule 14e-1(c) promulgated under the Exchange Act. The date of payment for shares of Company Common Stock accepted for payment pursuant to and subject to the conditions of the Offer is referred to in this Agreement as the "Offer Closing", and the date on which the Offer Closing occurs is referred to in this Agreement as the "Offer Closing Date".

[...]

(h) Funds. Subject to the other terms and conditions of this Agreement and the Offer Conditions, Parent shall provide or cause to be provided to Sub on a timely basis the funds necessary to purchase any shares of Company Common Stock that Sub becomes obligated to purchase pursuant to the Offer.

[...]

Section 1.03 Top-Up.

(a) Top-Up. The Company hereby grants to Sub an irrevocable right (the "Top-Up"), exercisable on the terms and conditions set forth in this Section 1.03, to purchase at a price per share equal to the Offer Price that number of newly issued, fully paid and nonassessable shares of Company Common Stock (the "Top-Up Shares") equal to the lowest number of shares of Company Common Stock that, when added to the number of shares of Company Common Stock directly or indirectly owned by Parent and Sub at the time of the Top-Up Closing (after giving effect to the Offer Closing), shall constitute one share more than 90% of the shares of the Company Common Stock outstanding immediately after the issuance of the Top-Up Shares; provided, however, that the Top-Up may not be exercised to purchase an amount of Top-Up Shares in excess of the number of shares of Company Common Stock authorized and unissued (treating shares owned by the Company as treasury stock as unissued) and not reserved for issuance at the time of exercise of the Top-Up. The Top-Up shall be exercisable only once, in whole but not in part.

(b) Exercise of Top-Up; Top-Up Closing. If there shall have not been validly tendered and not validly withdrawn that number of shares of Company Common Stock which, when added to the shares of Company Common Stock owned by Parent and its Affiliates, would represent at least 90% of the shares of the Company Common Stock outstanding on the Offer Closing Date, Sub shall be deemed to have exercised the Top-Up and on such date shall give the Company prior written notice specifying the number of shares of Company Common Stock directly or indirectly owned by Parent and its Subsidiaries at the time of such notice (giving effect to the Offer Closing). The Company shall, as soon as practicable following receipt of such notice (and in any event no later than the Offer Closing), deliver written notice to Sub specifying, based on the information provided by Sub in its notice, the number of Top-Up Shares. At the closing of the purchase of the Top-Up Shares (the "Top-Up Closing"), which shall take place at the location of the Merger Closing specified in Section 2.02, and shall take place simultaneously with the Offer Closing, the purchase price owed by Sub to the Company to purchase the Top-Up Shares shall be paid to the Company, at Sub's option, (i) in cash, by wire transfer of same-day funds, or (ii) by (x) paying in cash, by wire transfer of same-day funds, an amount equal to not less than the aggregate par value of the Top-Up Shares and (y) executing and delivering to the Company a promissory note having a principal amount equal to the aggregate purchase price pursuant to the Top-Up less the amount paid in cash pursuant to the preceding clause (x) (the "Promissory Note"). The Promissory Note (i) shall be due on the first anniversary of the Top-Up Closing, (ii) shall bear simple interest of 5% per annum, (iii) shall be full recourse to Parent and Sub, (iv) may be prepaid, in whole or in part, at any time without premium or penalty, and (v) shall have no other material terms. At the Top-Up Closing, the Company shall cause to be issued to Sub a certificate representing the Top-Up Shares.

[...]

Article II: The Merger

Section 2.01 The Merger. Upon the terms and subject to the conditions set forth in this Agreement, and in accordance with the General Corporation Law of the State of Delaware (the "DGCL"), Sub shall be merged with and into the Company at the Effective Time. Following the Effective Time, the separate corporate existence of Sub shall cease, and the Company shall continue as the surviving corporation in the Merger (the "Surviving Corporation").

Section 2.02 Closing. The closing of the Merger (the "Merger Closing") will take place at (a) if the Offer Closing shall have not occurred at or prior to the Merger Closing, 10:00 a.m., New York City time, on the second business day after satisfaction or (to the extent permitted by Law) waiver of the conditions set forth in Article VIII (other than those conditions that by their terms are to be satisfied at the Merger Closing, but subject to the satisfaction or (to the extent permitted by Law) waiver of those conditions), or (b) if the Offer Closing shall have occurred on or prior to the Merger Closing, on the date of, and immediately following the Offer Closing (or the Top-Up Closing if the Top-Up has been exercised), in either case at the offices of Kirkland & Ellis LLP, located at 601 Lexington Avenue, New York, New York 10022, unless another time, date or place is agreed to in writing by Parent and the Company. The date on which the Merger Closing occurs is referred to in this Agreement as the "Merger Closing Date".

Section 2.03 Effective Time. Subject to the provisions of this Agreement, as promptly as reasonably practicable on the Merger Closing Date, the Parties shall file a certificate of merger (the "Certificate of Merger") in such form as is required by, and executed and acknowledged in accordance with, the relevant provisions of the DGCL, and shall make all other filings and recordings required under the DGCL. The Merger shall become effective on such date and time as the Certificate of Merger is filed with the Secretary of State of the State of Delaware or at such other date and time as Parent and the Company shall agree and specify in the Certificate of Merger. The date and time at which the Merger becomes effective is referred to in this Agreement as the "Effective Time".

Section 2.04 Effects of the Merger. The Merger shall have the effects set forth in the applicable provisions of the DGCL. Without limiting the generality of the foregoing, from and after the Effective Time, the Surviving Corporation shall possess all properties, rights, privileges, powers and franchises of the Company and Sub, and all of the claims, obligations, liabilities, debts and duties of the Company and Sub shall become the claims, obligations, liabilities, debts and duties of the Surviving Corporation.

Section 2.05 Certificate of Incorporation and By-Laws.

(a) At the Effective Time, the certificate of incorporation of Sub as in effect immediately prior to the Effective Time (which shall not be amended by Sub from the date hereof until such time except as otherwise contemplated hereby) shall be the certificate of incorporation of the Surviving Corporation until thereafter changed or amended (subject to Section 7.06(a)) as provided therein or by applicable Law; provided, however, that at the Effective Time the certificate of incorporation of the Surviving Corporation shall be amended so that the name of the Surviving Corporation shall be "Burger King Holdings, Inc."

(b) The by-laws of Sub as in effect immediately prior to the Effective Time shall be the by-laws of the Surviving Corporation until thereafter changed or amended (subject to Section 7.06(a)) as provided therein or by applicable Law.

Section 2.06 Directors. The directors of Sub immediately prior to the Effective Time shall be the directors of the Surviving Corporation until the earlier of their resignation or removal or until their respective successors are duly elected and qualified, as the case may be.

Section 2.07 Officers. The officers of the Company immediately prior to the Effective Time shall be the officers of the Surviving Corporation, until the earlier of their resignation or removal or until their respective successors are duly elected and qualified, as the case may be.

Section 2.08 Taking of Necessary Action. If at any time after the Effective Time any further action is necessary or desirable to carry out the purposes of this Agreement and to vest the Surviving Corporation with full right, title and possession to all assets, property, rights, privileges, powers and franchises of the Company and Sub, the Surviving Corporation, the board of directors of the Surviving Corporation and officers of the Surviving Corporation shall take all such lawful and necessary action, consistent with this Agreement, on behalf of the Company, Sub and the Surviving Corporation.

Article III: Effect of the Merger on the Capital Stock of the Constituent Corporations

Section 3.01 Effect on Capital Stock. At the Effective Time, by virtue of the Merger and without any action on the part of the holder of any shares of Company Common Stock or any shares of capital stock of Parent or Sub:

(a) Capital Stock of Sub. Each share of capital stock of Sub issued and outstanding immediately prior to the Effective Time shall be converted into and become one validly issued, fully paid and nonassessable share of common stock, par value $0.01 per share, of the Surviving Corporation.

(b) Cancellation of Treasury Stock and Parent-Owned Stock. Each share of Company Common Stock issued and outstanding immediately prior to the Effective Time that is directly owned by the Company as treasury stock, or by Parent or Sub at such time, shall automatically be canceled and shall cease to exist, and no consideration shall be delivered in exchange therefor.

(c) Conversion of Company Common Stock. Each share of Company Common Stock issued and outstanding immediately prior to the Effective Time (excluding shares to be canceled in accordance with Section 3.01(b)and, except as provided in Section 3.01(d), the Appraisal Shares) shall be converted into the right to receive the Offer Price in cash, without interest (the "Merger Consideration"). At the Effective Time, all such shares of Company Common Stock shall no longer be outstanding and shall automatically be canceled and shall cease to exist, and each holder of a certificate (or evidence of shares in book-entry form) that immediately prior to the Effective Time represented any such shares of Company Common Stock (each, a "Certificate") shall cease to have any rights with respect thereto, except the right to receive the Merger Consideration and any dividends declared from and after the date hereof in accordance with Section 6.01(a) with a record date prior to the Effective Time that remain unpaid at the Effective Time and that are due to such holder.

(d) Appraisal Rights. Notwithstanding anything in this Agreement to the contrary, shares of Company Common Stock issued and outstanding immediately prior to the Effective Time that are held by any holder who is entitled to demand and properly demands appraisal of such shares pursuant to, and who complies in all respects with, the provisions of Section 262 of the DGCL (the "Appraisal Shares") shall not be converted into the right to receive the Merger Consideration as provided in Section 3.01(c), but instead such holder shall be entitled to payment of the fair value of such shares in accordance with the provisions of Section 262 of the DGCL. At the Effective Time, the Appraisal Shares shall no longer be outstanding and shall automatically be canceled and shall cease to exist, and each holder of Appraisal Shares shall cease to have any rights with respect thereto, except the right to receive the fair value of such Appraisal Shares in accordance with the provisions of Section 262 of the DGCL. Notwithstanding the foregoing, if any such holder shall fail to perfect or otherwise shall waive, withdraw or lose the right to appraisal under Section 262 of the DGCL or a court of competent jurisdiction shall determine that such holder is not entitled to the relief provided by Section 262 of the DGCL, then the right of such holder to be paid the fair value of such holder's Appraisal Shares under Section 262 of the DGCL shall cease and such Appraisal Shares shall be deemed to have been converted at the Effective Time into, and shall have become, the right to receive the Merger Consideration as provided in Section 3.01(c), without any interest thereon. The Company shall give prompt notice to Parent of any demands for appraisal of any shares of Company Common Stock or written threats thereof, withdrawals of such demands and any other instruments served pursuant to the DGCL received by the Company, and Parent shall have the right to participate in and direct all negotiations and proceedings with respect to such demands. Prior to the Effective Time, the Company shall not, without the prior written consent of Parent (which consent shall not be unreasonably withheld or delayed), voluntarily make any payment with respect to, or settle or offer to settle, any such demands, or agree to do or commit to do any of the foregoing.

[...]

Article V: Representations and Warranties of Parent and Sub

Parent and Sub jointly and severally represent and warrant to the Company as follows:

[...]

Section 5.04 Financing. Parent has delivered to the Company true and complete copies of (i) the executed equity commitment letter, dated as of the date of this Agreement (the "Equity Financing Commitment"), pursuant to which 3G Special Situations Fund II L.P. ("Sponsor") has committed, upon the terms and subject to the conditions thereof, to invest in Parent the cash amount set forth therein (the "Equity Financing"), and (ii) the executed commitment letter, dated as of the date hereof, among Parent, J.P. Morgan Chase Bank, N.A., J.P. Morgan Securities LLC, and Barclays Bank PLC (the "Debt Commitment Letter"), pursuant to which the lenders party thereto have agreed, upon the terms and subject to the conditions thereof, to lend the amounts (which includes up to $900,000,000.00 in bridge financing (the "Bridge Financing") to be utilized in the event the placement of senior notes (the "High Yield Financing") is not consummated) set forth therein for the purposes of financing the transactions contemplated by this Agreement and related fees and expenses and the refinancing of any outstanding indebtedness of the Company (including under the Existing Credit Agreement) (the "Debt Financing" and, together with the Equity Financing, the "Financing"). The Debt Commitment Letter and the related Fee Letter and the Equity Financing Commitment are referred to collectively in this Agreement as the "Financing Agreements". None of the Financing Agreements has been amended or modified prior to the date of this Agreement, no such amendment or modification is contemplated and none of the respective commitments contained in the Financing Agreements have been withdrawn or rescinded in any respect. As of the date of this Agreement, the Financing Agreements are in full force and effect. Except for a fee letter and fee credit letter relating to fees with respect to the Debt Financing and an engagement letter (complete copies of which have been provided to the Company, with only the fee amounts and certain economic terms of the market flex (none of which would adversely effect the amount or availability of the Debt Financing) redacted), as of the date of this Agreement there are no side letters or other agreements, Contracts or arrangements related to the funding or investment, as applicable, of the Financing other than as expressly set forth in the Financing Agreements delivered to the Company prior to the date hereof. Parent has fully paid any and all commitment fees or other fees in connection with the Financing Agreements that are payable on or prior to the date hereof. The only conditions precedent or other contingencies related to the obligations of the Sponsor to fund the full amount of the Equity Financing and lenders to fund the full amount of Debt Financing are those expressly set forth in the Equity Financing Commitment and the Debt Commitment Letter, respectively. As of the date of this Agreement, no event has occurred which, with or without notice, lapse of time or both, would constitute a default or breach on the part of Parent, Sub or any direct investor in Parent under any term, or a failure of any condition, of the Financing Agreements or otherwise be reasonably likely to result in any portion of the Financing contemplated thereby to be unavailable. As of the date of this Agreement, neither Parent nor Sub has any reason to believe that it will be unable to satisfy on a timely basis any term or condition of the Financing Agreements required to be satisfied by it. Based on the terms and conditions of this Agreement, the proceeds from the Financing will be sufficient to provide Parent and Sub with the funds necessary to pay the aggregate Offer Price and Merger Consideration, the Equity Awards Amount, any repayment or refinancing of debt contemplated in this Agreement or the Financing Agreements (including repayment of indebtedness under the Existing Credit Agreement), the payment of all other amounts required to be paid in connection with the consummation of the transactions contemplated by this Agreement and to allow Parent and Sub to perform all of their obligations under this Agreement and pay all fees and expenses to be paid by Parent or Sub related to the transactions contemplated by this Agreement.

[...]

Article VII: Additional Agreements

Section 7.01 Preparation of the Proxy Statement; Stockholders' Meeting.

(a) Preparation of Proxy Statement. As soon as practicable after the date hereof (and in any event, but subject to Parent's timely performance of its obligations under Section 7.01(b), within 15 business days hereof), the Company shall prepare and shall cause to be filed with the SEC in preliminary form a proxy statement relating to the Stockholders' Meeting (together with any amendments thereof or supplements thereto, the "Proxy Statement"). Except as expressly contemplated by Section 6.02(f), the Proxy Statement shall include the Recommendation with respect to the Merger, the Fairness Opinions and a copy of Section 262 of the DGCL. The Company will cause the Proxy Statement, at the time of the mailing of the Proxy Statement or any amendments or supplements thereto, and at the time of the Stockholders' Meeting, to not contain any untrue statement of a material fact or omit to state any material fact required to be stated therein or necessary in order to make the statements therein, in light of the circumstances under which they were made, not misleading; provided, however, that no representation or warranty is made by the Company with respect to information supplied by Parent or Sub for inclusion or incorporation by reference in the Proxy Statement. The Company shall cause the Proxy Statement to comply as to form in all material respects with the provisions of the Exchange Act and the rules and regulations promulgated thereunder and to satisfy all rules of the NYSE. The Company shall promptly notify Parent and Sub upon the receipt of any comments from the SEC or the staff of the SEC or any request from the SEC or the staff of the SEC for amendments or supplements to the Proxy Statement, and shall provide Parent and Sub with copies of all correspondence between the Company and its Representatives, on the one hand, and the SEC or the staff of the SEC, on the other hand. The Company shall use reasonable best efforts to respond as promptly as reasonably practicable to any comments of the SEC or the staff of the SEC with respect to the Proxy Statement, and the Company shall provide Parent and Sub and their respective counsel a reasonable opportunity to participate in the formulation of any written response to any such written comments of the SEC or its staff. Prior to the filing of the Proxy Statement or the dissemination thereof to the holders of Company Common Stock, or responding to any comments of the SEC or the staff of the SEC with respect thereto, the Company shall provide Parent and Sub a reasonable opportunity to review and to propose comments on such document or response.

[...]

(c) Mailing of Proxy Statement; Stockholders' Meeting. If the adoption of this Agreement by the Company's stockholders is required by applicable Law, then the Company shall have the right at any time after the Proxy Statement Clearance Date to (and Parent and Sub shall have the right, at any time after the later of the Proxy Statement Clearance Date and November 1, 2010, to request in writing that the Company, and upon receipt of such written request, the Company shall, as promptly as practicable and in any event within ten (10) business days), (x) establish a record date for and give notice of a meeting of its stockholders, for the purpose of voting upon the adoption of this Agreement (the "Stockholders' Meeting"), and (y) mail to the holders of Company Common Stock as of the record date established for the Stockholders' Meeting a Proxy Statement (the date the Company elects to take such action or is required to take such action, the "Proxy Date"). The Company shall duly call, convene and hold the Stockholders' Meeting as promptly as reasonably practicable after the Proxy Date; provided, however, that in no event shall such meeting be held later than 35 calendar days following the date the Proxy Statement is mailed to the Company's stockholders and any adjournments of such meetings shall require the prior written consent of the Parent other than in the case it is required to allow reasonable additional time for the filing and mailing of any supplemental or amended disclosure which the SEC or its staff has instructed the Company is necessary under applicable Law and for such supplemental or amended disclosure to be disseminated and reviewed by the Company's stockholders prior to the Stockholders' Meeting.

Notwithstanding the foregoing, Parent may require the Company to adjourn or postpone the Stockholders' Meeting one (1) time (for a period of not more than 30 calendar days but not past 2 business days prior to the Outside Date), unless prior to such adjournment the Company shall have received an aggregate number of proxies voting for the adoption of this Agreement and the transactions contemplated hereby (including the Merger), which have not been withdrawn, such that the condition in Section 8.01(a) will be satisfied at such meeting. Once the Company has established a record date for the Stockholders' Meeting, the Company shall not change such record date or establish a different record date for the Stockholders' Meeting without the prior written consent of Parent, unless required to do so by applicable Law or the Company's By-Laws. Unless the Company Board shall have withdrawn, modified or qualified its recommendation thereof or otherwise effected an Adverse Recommendation Change, the Company shall use reasonable best efforts to solicit proxies in favor of the adoption of this Agreement and shall ensure that all proxies solicited in connection with the Stockholders' Meeting are solicited in compliance with all applicable Laws and all rules of the NYSE. Unless this Agreement is validly terminated in accordance with Section 9.01, the Company shall submit this Agreement to its stockholders at the Stockholders' Meeting even if the Company Board shall have effected an Adverse Recommendation Change or proposed or announced any intention to do so. The Company shall, upon the reasonable request of Parent, advise Parent at least on a daily basis on each of the last seven business days prior to the date of the Stockholders' Meeting as to the aggregate tally of proxies received by the Company with respect to the Stockholder Approval. Without the prior written consent of Parent, the adoption of this Agreement and the transactions contemplated hereby (including the Merger) shall be the only matter (other than procedure matters) which the Company shall propose to be acted on by the stockholders of the Company at the Stockholders' Meeting.

[...]

(e) Short Form Merger. Notwithstanding the foregoing, if, following the Offer Closing and the exercise, if any, of the Top-Up, Parent and its Affiliates shall own at least 90% of the outstanding shares of the Company Common Stock, the Parties shall take all necessary and appropriate action, including with respect to the transfer to Sub of any shares of Company Common Stock held by Parent or its Affiliates, to cause the Merger to become effective as soon as practicable after the Offer Closing without the Stockholders' Meeting in accordance with Section 253 of the DGCL.

[...]

Section 7.08 Financing.

(a) Each of Parent and Sub shall use, and cause its Affiliates to use, its reasonable best efforts (unless, with respect to any action, another standard for performance is expressly provided for herein) to take, or cause to be taken, all actions and to do, or cause to be done, all things necessary, proper or advisable to consummate and obtain the Financing on the terms and conditions (including the flex provisions) set forth in the Financing Agreements and any related Fee Letter (taking into account the anticipated timing of the Marketing

Period), including using reasonable best efforts to seek to enforce (including through litigation) its rights under the Debt Commitment Letter in the event of a material breach thereof by the Financing sources thereunder, and shall not permit any amendment or modification to be made to, or consent to any waiver of any provision or remedy under, the Financing Agreements or any related Fee Letter, if such amendment, modification or waiver (i) reduces the aggregate amount of the Financing (including by changing the amount of fees to be paid or original issue discount) from that contemplated in the Financing Agreements, (ii) imposes new or additional conditions or otherwise expands, amends or modifies any of the conditions to the receipt of the Financing in a manner adverse to Parent or the Company, (iii) decreases the aggregate Equity Financing as set forth in the Equity Financing Commitment delivered on the date hereof, (iv) amends or modifies any other terms in a manner that would reasonably be expected to (x) delay or prevent the Offer Closing or the Merger Closing Date or (y) make the timely funding of the Financing or satisfaction of the conditions to obtaining the Financing less likely to occur or (v) adversely impact the ability of Parent or Sub to enforce its rights against the other parties to the Financing Agreements. For purposes of clarification, the foregoing shall not prohibit Parent from amending the Debt Commitment Letter and any related Fee Letter to add additional lender(s) (and Affiliates of such additional lender(s)) as a party thereto. Any reference in this Agreement to (A) "Financing" shall include the financing contemplated by the Financing Agreements as amended or modified in compliance with this Section 7.08(a), and (B) "Financing Agreements" or "Debt Commitment Letter" shall include such documents as amended or modified in compliance with this Section 7.08(a).

[...]

Article VIII: Conditions Precedent

Section 8.01 Conditions to Each Party's Obligation to Effect the Merger. The respective obligation of each party to effect the Merger is subject to the satisfaction or (to the extent permitted by Law) waiver at or prior to the Effective Time of the following conditions:

(a) Stockholder Approval. If required by applicable Law, the Stockholder Approval shall have been obtained.

(b) Regulatory Approvals. The waiting period applicable to the consummation of the Merger and, unless the Offer Termination shall have occurred, the Offer under the HSR Act (or any extension thereof) shall have expired or early termination thereof shall have been granted. In addition, the consummation of the Merger and, unless the Offer Termination shall have occurred, the Offer, is not unlawful under any Foreign Merger Control Law of any jurisdiction set forth in Section 8.01(b) of the Company Disclosure Letter.

(c) No Injunctions or Restraints. No temporary restraining order, preliminary or permanent injunction, Law or other Judgment issued by any court of competent jurisdiction (collectively, "Restraints") shall be in effect enjoining or otherwise preventing or prohibiting the consummation of the Merger.

(d) Purchase of Company Common Stock in the Offer. Unless the Offer Termination shall have occurred, Sub shall have accepted for payment all shares of Company Common Stock validly tendered and not validly withdrawn pursuant to the Offer.

Section 8.02 Conditions to Obligations of Parent and Sub to Effect the Merger. Solely if the Offer Termination shall have occurred or the Offer Closing shall not have occurred, the obligations of Parent and Sub to effect the Merger are further subject to the satisfaction or (to the extent permitted by Law) waiver at or prior to the Effective Time of the following conditions:

(a) Representations and Warranties. The representations and warranties of the Company (i) set forth in Section 4.03, Section 4.04, Section 4.26 and Section 4.27 shall be true and correct in all material respects as of the date of this Agreement and as of the Merger Closing Date as though made on the Merger Closing Date, (ii) set forth in Section 4.07 shall be true and correct as of the date of this Agreement and as of the Merger Closing Date as though made on the Merger Closing Date without disregarding the "Material Adverse Effect" qualification set forth therein and (iii) set forth in this Agreement, other than those described in clauses (i) and (ii) above, shall be true and correct (disregarding all qualifications or limitations as to "materiality", "Material Adverse Effect" and words of similar import set forth therein) as of the date of this Agreement and as of the Merger Closing Date as though made on the Merger Closing Date, except, in the case of this clause (iii), where the failure of such representations and warranties to be so true and correct would not, individually or in the aggregate, reasonably be expected to have a Material Adverse Effect; provided in each case that representations and warranties made as of a specific date shall be required to be so true and correct (subject to such qualifications) as of such date only. Parent shall have received a certificate signed on behalf of the Company by the chief executive officer or chief financial officer thereof to such effect.

(b) Performance of Obligations of the Company. The Company shall have performed or complied in all material respects with its obligations required to be performed or complied with by it under this Agreement at or prior to the Merger Closing, and Parent shall have received a certificate signed on behalf of the Company by the chief executive officer or chief financial officer thereof to such effect.

(c) No Material Adverse Effect. Since the date of this Agreement, there shall not have occurred any change, event or occurrence that has had or would reasonably be expected to have a Material Adverse Effect, and Parent shall have received a certificate signed on behalf of the Company the chief executive officer or chief financial officer thereof to such effect.

(d) Pre-Closing Solvency. As of immediately prior to the Merger Closing Date (and, for the avoidance of doubt, before giving effect to the incurrence of the Debt Financing and the consummation of the transactions contemplated by this Agreement and such Debt Financing), the Company is Solvent, and Parent shall have received a certificate signed on behalf of the Company by the chief executive officer or chief financial officer thereof to such effect.

Section 8.03 Conditions to Obligation of the Company to Effect the Merger. Solely if the Offer Termination shall have occurred or the Offer Closing shall not have occurred, then the obligation of the Company to effect the Merger is further subject to the satisfaction or (to the extent permitted by Law) waiver at or prior to the Effective Time of the following conditions:

(a) Representations and Warranties. The representations and warranties of Parent and Sub set forth in this Agreement shall be true and correct (disregarding all qualifications or limitations as to "materiality", "Parent Material Adverse Effect" and words of similar import set forth therein) as of the date of this Agreement and as of the Merger Closing Date as though made on the Merger Closing Date (except to the extent such representations and warranties expressly relate to an earlier date, in which case as of such earlier date), except where the failure of such representations and warranties to be so true and correct would not, individually or in the aggregate, reasonably be expected to have a Parent Material Adverse Effect. The Company shall have received a certificate signed on behalf of Parent by an executive officer thereof to such effect.

(b) Performance of Obligations of Parent and Sub. Parent and Sub shall have performed or complied in all material respects with its obligations required to be performed or complied with by it under this Agreement at or prior to the Merger Closing, and the Company shall have received a certificate signed on behalf of Parent by an executive officer thereof to such effect.

Section 8.04 Frustration of Closing Conditions. Neither Parent nor Sub may rely on the failure of any condition set forth in Sections 8.01 or 8.02 to be satisfied if such failure was caused by the failure of Parent or Sub to perform any of its obligations under this Agreement. The Company may not rely on the failure of any condition set forth in Sections 8.01 or 8.03 to be satisfied if such failure was caused by its failure to perform any of its obligations under this Agreement.

[...]

Annex I: Conditions to the Offer

Notwithstanding any other term of the Offer or this Agreement, Sub shall not be required to, and Parent shall not be required to cause Sub to, accept for payment or, subject to any applicable rules and regulations of the SEC, including Rule 14e-1(c) under the Exchange Act (relating to Sub's obligation to pay for or return tendered shares of Company Common Stock promptly after the termination or withdrawal of the Offer), pay for any shares of Company Common Stock tendered pursuant to the Offer if: (a) there shall have not been validly tendered and not validly withdrawn prior to the expiration of the Offer that number of shares of Company Common Stock which, when added to the shares of Company Common Stock owned by Parent and its Affiliates, would represent at least 79.1% of the shares of the Company Common Stock outstanding as of the expiration of the Offer (the "Minimum Tender Condition"); (b) the waiting period applicable to the purchase of shares of Company Common Stock pursuant to the Offer and the consummation of the Merger under the HSR Act (or any extension thereof) shall have neither expired nor terminated; (c) Parent (either directly or through its Subsidiaries) shall not have received the proceeds of the Debt Financing (or any Alternative Debt Financing) and/or the lenders party to the Debt Financing Letter (or New Debt Commitment Letter for any Alternative Debt Financing) shall not have confirmed to Parent or Sub that the Debt Financing (or any Alternative Debt Financing) in an amount sufficient to consummate the Offer and the Merger will be available at the Offer Closing on the terms and conditions set forth in the Debt Financing Letter (or New Debt Commitment Letter for any Alternative Debt Financing) ("Financing Proceeds Condition"), or (d) any of the following conditions shall have occurred and be continuing as of the expiration of the Offer:

(i) there shall be any Restraint in effect enjoining or otherwise preventing or prohibiting the making of the Offer or the consummation of the Merger or the Offer;

(ii) the consummation of the Offer is unlawful under any Foreign Merger Control Law of any jurisdiction set forth in Section 8.01(b) of the Company Disclosure Letter;

(iii) any of the representations and warranties of the Company (A) set forth in Section 4.03, Section 4.04, Section 4.26 and Section 4.27 shall not be true and correct in all material respects, (B) set forth in Section 4.07 shall not be true and correct without disregarding the "Material Adverse Effect" qualification set forth therein and (C) set forth in this Agreement, other than those described in clauses (A) and (B) above, shall not be true and correct (disregarding all qualifications or limitations as to "materiality", "Material Adverse Effect" and words of similar import set forth therein), except, in the case of this clause (C), where the failure of such representations and warranties to be so true and correct would not, individually or in the aggregate, reasonably be expected to have a Material Adverse Effect and except, in each case, to the extent such representations and warranties are made as of a specific date (in which case such representations and warranties shall not be true and correct (subject to such qualifications) as of such specific date only);

(iv) the Company shall have failed to perform or comply in all material respects with its obligations required to be performed or complied with by it under this Agreement;

(v) since the date of this Agreement, there shall have occurred any change, event or occurrence that has had or would reasonably be expected to have a Material Adverse Effect;

(vi) as of immediately prior to the Offer Closing Date (and, for the avoidance of doubt, before giving effect to the incurrence of the Debt Financing and the consummation of the transactions contemplated by this Agreement and such Debt Financing), the Company is not Solvent;

(vii) in the event that the exercise of the Top-Up is necessary to ensure that Parent or Sub owns at least 90% of the outstanding shares of Company Common Stock immediately after the Acceptance Time, there shall exist under applicable Law or other Restraint any restriction or legal impediment on Sub's ability and right to exercise the Top-Up, or the shares of Company Common Stock issuable upon exercise of the Top-Up together with the shares of Company Common Stock validly tendered in the Offer and not properly withdrawn are insufficient for Sub to owns at least 90% of the outstanding shares of Company Common Stock;

(viii) a Triggering Event shall have occurred; and

(ix) this Agreement shall have been terminated in accordance with its terms.

At the request of Parent, the Company shall deliver to Parent a certificate executed on behalf of the Company by the chief executive officer or the chief financial officer of the Company certifying that none of the conditions set forth in clauses (d)(iii), (d)(iv), (d)(v) and (d)(vi) above shall have occurred and be continuing as of the expiration of the Offer.

For purposes of determining whether the Minimum Tender Condition and the condition set forth in clause (d)(vii) have been satisfied, Parent and Sub shall have the right to include or exclude for purposes of its determination thereof shares tendered in the Offer pursuant to guaranteed delivery procedures. [NB: These are shares that are promised to be delivered pursuant to some pre-agreed form but that are not available for delivery immediately. This is not the same as the shares committed to be tendered under the Sponsor Tender Agreements, which presumably are available for delivery.]

The foregoing conditions shall be in addition to, and not a limitation of, the rights and obligations of Parent and Sub to extend, terminate or modify the Offer pursuant to the terms and conditions of this Agreement.

The foregoing conditions are for the sole benefit of Parent and Sub and, subject to the terms and conditions of this Agreement and the applicable rules and regulations of the SEC, may be waived by Parent and Sub in whole or in part at any time and from time to time in their sole discretion (other than the Minimum Tender Condition). The failure by Parent or Sub at any time to exercise any of the foregoing rights shall not be deemed a waiver of any such right and each such right shall be deemed an ongoing right that may be asserted at any time and from time to time.

The capitalized terms used in this Annex I and not defined in this Annex I shall have the meanings set forth in the Agreement and Plan of Merger, dated as of September 2, 2010, by and among Blue Acquisition Holding Corporation, Blue Acquisition Sub, Inc. and Burger King Holdings, Inc.

Discussion Questions:

1. What is the sequence of events mapped out in this agreement?

2. What are the main economic terms?

3. What will happen to Burger King Holdings, Inc. (its shares, its board, etc.) in the merger?

4. A technical point: Section 1.03 ("Top Up") would not be needed today because of DGCL 251(h), which was adopted in 2013. What does 251(h) do? Specifically, how does it resolve a prior disparity between the shareholder approval required in a statutory merger versus a deal executed pursuant to a tender offer?

Appraisal Rights

Appraisal rights are an ancient remedy in corporate law. They are thought to be part of the grand compromise that arose in corporate codes around the turn of the century: in exchange for the right to merge two corporations for less than a unanimous vote (today, of course, a simple majority vote) shareholders who dissented from the merger would have the right to seek a judicial appraisal of the "fair value" of their shares. DGCL 262(h) specifies that the Delaware Chancery Court "shall appraise the shares, determining their fair value exclusive of any element of value arising from the accomplishment or expectation of the merger or consolidation, together with a fair rate of interest, if any, to be paid upon the amount determined to be the fair value."

Through the early 2000s, appraisal was time-consuming and expensive, and therefore rarely invoked. All of this changed with the rise of appraisal arbitrage: hedge funds that would buy shares *after* the deal was announced but *before* the "record date" to determine who gets to vote for the merger. These firms would then perfect their appraisal rights— most importantly, by dissenting from the merger and giving notice to the corporation of their intention to seek appraisal. Hedge funds that devoted significant capital to appraisal arbitrage (for example, Merion Capital and Magnetar Financial) had the sophistication, patience, and financial firepower to make appraisal into a very powerful weapon.

The question of when shareholders have appraisal rights is, unfortunately, a complicated one. DGCL 262(b) provides the statutory language that answers this question, but given the complexity of the language some paraphrasing is appropriate. First, shareholders do not get appraisal rights in asset acquisitions. Second, shareholders do get appraisal rights in all other cases, unless the so-called "stock market exception" applies.

Okay, so what is the stock market exception? Simplifying a little bit, shareholders do not get appraisal rights if the shares are market-traded, DGCL 262(b)(1), but they do get appraisal rights if the merger consideration is anything other than shares in the surviving corporation. DGCL 262(b)(2).

In the end, without too much loss of generality: shareholders get appraisal rights in statutory mergers but not in asset acquisitions; and within statutory mergers, shareholders get appraisal rights in cash deals but not stock-for-stock deals.

This construction of appraisal rights raises a question: what happens when an asset acquisition is the functional equivalent of a statutory merger? Should the deal be declared a "de facto merger," which therefore triggers appraisal rights? The following case answers this question.

Hariton v. Arco Electronics, Inc.
188 A.2d 123 (1963)

SOUTHERLAND, Chief Justice.

This case involves a sale of assets under § 271 of the corporation law, 8 Del.C. It presents for decision the question presented, but not decided, in Heilbrunn v. Sun Chemical Corporation, Del., 150 A.2d 755. It may be stated as follows:

A sale of assets is effected under § 271 in consideration of shares of stock of the purchasing corporation. The agreement of sale embodies also a plan to dissolve the selling corporation and distribute the shares so received to the stockholders of the seller, so as to accomplish the same result as would be accomplished by a merger of the seller into the purchaser. Is the sale legal?

The facts are these:

The defendant Arco and Loral Electronics Corporation, a New York corporation, are both engaged, in somewhat different forms, in the electronic equipment business. In the summer of 1961 they negotiated for an amalgamation of the companies. As of October 27, 1961, they entered into a "Reorganization Agreement and Plan." The provisions of this Plan pertinent here are in substance as follows:

1. Arco agrees to sell all its assets to Loral in consideration (inter alia) of the issuance to it of 283,000 shares of Loral.

2. Arco agrees to call a stockholders meeting for the purpose of approving the Plan and the voluntary dissolution.

3. Arco agrees to distribute to its stockholders all the Loral shares received by it as a part of the complete liquidation of Arco.

At the Arco meeting all the stockholders voting (about 80%) approved the Plan. It was thereafter consummated.

Plaintiff, a stockholder who did not vote at the meeting, sued to enjoin the consummation of the Plan on the grounds (1) that it was illegal, and (2) that it was unfair. The second ground was abandoned. Affidavits and documentary evidence were filed, and defendant moved for summary judgment and dismissal of the complaint. The Vice Chancellor granted the motion and plaintiff appeals.

The question before us we have stated above. Plaintiff's argument that the sale is illegal runs as follows:

The several steps taken here accomplish the same result as a merger of Arco into Loral. In a "true" sale of assets, the stockholder of the seller retains the right to elect whether the selling company shall continue as a holding company. Moreover, the stockholder of the selling company is forced to accept an investment in a new enterprise without the right of appraisal granted under the merger statute. § 271 cannot therefore be legally combined with a dissolution proceeding under § 275 and a consequent distribution of the purchaser's stock. Such a proceeding is a misuse of the power granted under § 271, and a *de facto* merger results.

The foregoing is a brief summary of plaintiff's contention.

Plaintiff's contention that this sale has achieved the same result as a merger is plainly correct. The same contention was made to us in Heilbrunn v. Sun Chemical Corporation, Del., 150 A.2d 755. Accepting it as correct, we noted that this result is made possible by the overlapping scope of the merger statute and section 271, mentioned in Sterling v. Mayflower Hotel Corporation, 33 Del.Ch. 293, 93 A.2d 107, 38 A. L.R.2d 425. We also adverted to the increased use, in connection with corporate reorganization plans, of § 271 instead of the merger statute. Further, we observed that no Delaware case has held such procedure to be improper, and that two cases appear to assume its legality. Finch v. Warrior Cement Corporation, 16 Del.Ch. 44, 141 A. 54, and Argenbright v. Phoenix Finance Co., 21 Del.Ch. 288, 187 A. 124. But we were not required in the Heilbrunn case to decide the point.

We now hold that the reorganization here accomplished through § 271 and a mandatory plan of dissolution and distribution is legal. This is so because the sale-of-assets statute and the merger statute are independent of each other. They are, so to speak, of equal dignity, and the framers of a reorganization plan may resort to either type of corporate mechanics to achieve the desired end. This is not an anomalous result in our corporation law. As the Vice Chancellor pointed out, the elimination of accrued dividends, though forbidden under a charter amendment (Keller v. Wilson & Co., 21 Del.Ch. 391, 190 A. 115) may be accomplished by a merger. Federal United Corporation v. Havender, 24 Del.Ch. 318, 11 A.2d 331.

In Langfelder v. Universal Laboratories, D.C., 68 F.Supp. 209, Judge Leahy commented upon "the general theory of the Delaware Corporation Law that action taken pursuant to the authority of the various sections of that law constitute acts of independent legal significance and their validity is not dependent on other sections of the Act." 68 F.Supp. 211, footnote.

In support of his contentions of a *de facto* merger plaintiff cites Finch v. Warrior Cement Corporation, 16 Del.Ch. 44, 141 A. 54, and Drug Inc. v. Hunt, 5 W.W.Harr. 339, 35 Del. 339, 168 A. 87. They are patently inapplicable. Each involved a disregard of the statutory provisions governing sales of assets. Here it is admitted that the provisions of the statute were fully complied with.

Plaintiff concedes, as we read his brief, that if the several steps taken in this case had been taken separately they would have been legal. That is, he concedes that a sale of assets, followed by a separate proceeding to dissolve and distribute, would be legal, even though the same result would follow. This concession exposes the weakness of his contention. To attempt to make any such distinction between sales under § 271 would be to create uncertainty in the law and invite litigation.

We are in accord with the Vice Chancellor's ruling, and the judgment below is affirmed.

Discussion Questions:

1. Why did the defendant structure the deal as an asset sale rather than a merger?

2. How would you articulate the Delaware Supreme Court's position on the de *facto* merger theory? (NB: This position is still good law in Delaware.)

3. *Hariton* illustrates Delaware's generally formalistic approach to corporate law. Other states, at least historically, have taken a "substance over form" approach (or, equivalently, "if it walks like a duck, it is a duck.") In *Farris v. Glen Alden Corp.*, 393 Pa. 427 (1958), for example, the Pennsylvania Supreme Court accepted *de facto* merger doctrine, stating that: "[T]o determine properly the nature of a corporate transaction, we must refer not only to all the provisions of the agreement, but also to the consequences of the transaction and to the purposes of the provisions of the corporation law said to be applicable." However, just one year later, the Pennsylvania legislature explicitly overruled this decision, abolishing *de facto* merger doctrine "in the absence of fraud or fundamental unfairness." 15 Pa. C.S.A. § 1105. In 1988, the Pennsylvania legislature further clarified that: "Structuring a plan or transaction for the purpose or with the effect of eliminating or avoiding the application of dissenters rights [a.k.a. appraisal rights] is not a fraud or fundamental unfairness within the meaning of this section." The Committee Comment notes that: "[These amendments] are intended to make Pennsylvania an attractive situs for business organization by assuring the incorporators that the Pennsylvania courts will not be authorized to recharacterize a transaction on a form-over-substance basis. The goal of the 1988 BCL is to reject as emphatically as possible that practice of the 1940's and 1950's, which gave Pennsylvania law a reputation of unpredictability and which was incompatible with modern business and financial practices."

Pennsylvania's trajectory is extreme, but representative. Why do you think corporate law has generally moved more toward the Delaware (formalistic) approach, rather than a "substance over form" approach?

Chapter 8 – Takeover Defense

While proxy contests for control date back to the 1960s, hostile takeovers emerged in numbers only in the 1970s and entered the mainstream press and political debate in the 1980s. They were a new deal technology: a tender offer for the company's shares, launched by a third-party and unwanted by the incumbent board. Advocates of hostile takeovers claimed that they "cleansed" corporate America of inefficiencies. If the "takeover artists" such as T. Boone Pickens, Ron Perelman, Michael Milken, Carl Icahn, and Sir James Goldsmith (all of whom feature in the cases below) became wildly rich because of hostile takeovers, it was only because they were doing a good deed for shareholders and (in the long-term) corporate America. This viewpoint was famously summarized in Oliver Stone's 1987 movie *Wall Street*, where the quintessential corporate raider Gordon Gekko (played by Michael Douglas), in his iconic speech at the Teldar Paper annual shareholders' meeting, offered the mantra: "Greed is Good."

On the other side of the debate were politicians and managers in corporate America, who argued that corporate raiders focused on short-term profits at the expense of long-term investment and U.S. jobs. Under this view, it was nothing less than American capitalism that was under attack from these corporate raiders. *Pretty Woman*, yet another iconic movie from this era, illustrated this viewpoint when the other lead character[20] Edward Lewis (played by Richard Gere) turns from a bad guy who only mounts hostile takeovers into a good guy who wants to "build things" in the final scene of the movie (extra credit for remembering what it was that he planned to build).

Viewpoints in this debate had direct corporate law implications. Those in the "Greed is Good" camp believed that a wide open market for corporate control was desirable. Corporate raiders would hunt for underperforming targets, launch hostile takeovers, and cleanse corporate America of underperforming management. In this view, corporate takeover defenses, which dampened or potentially shut down a wide open "market for corporate control," should be categorically prohibited. Those in the "America is Under Attack" camp believed that corporate America should be given the tools to protect the corporate bastion from the "Barbarians at the Gate." The "poison pill" takeover defense was a critical tool in the arsenal, and courts should give leeway to board that wanted to use "the pill."

This debate—perhaps the fiercest debate in all of corporate law—came to a head in a series of Delaware Supreme Court decisions in the 1980s. We focus in this chapter on the "Big Three": *Unocal*, *Moran*, and *Revlon*. These cases can be considered as three acts in a play.[21]

---

[20] If you don't know who the main lead character was in this movie, you were probably not alive in 1990. For this crowd, we can offer the Disney movie *Cars*, in which the good guy race car (Lightning McQueen) was sponsored by Rust-Eze, while the bad guy race car (Chick Hicks) was sponsored by Hostile Takeover Bank. Of course, as the Disney writers surely knew, banks are highly regulated and it would be virtually impossible to execute a truly hostile takeover of a bank.

[21] Thanks to Professors Reinier Kraakman and William Allen for this formulation.

Act I is *Unocal*: what can you do before a hostile takeover bid is launched? Act II is *Moran*: what can you do while a hostile takeover bid is underway? And Act III is *Revlon*: what do you need to do in an "end game" situation, when there is competition among multiple bidders? We examine them in this order, with commentary and other cases along the way.

Unocal Corp. v. Mesa Petroleum Co.
493 A.2d 946 (1985)

MOORE, Justice.

We confront an issue of first impression in Delaware—the validity of a corporation's self-tender for its own shares which excludes from participation a stockholder making a hostile tender offer for the company's stock.

The Court of Chancery granted a preliminary injunction to the plaintiffs, Mesa Petroleum Co., Mesa Asset Co., Mesa Partners II, and Mesa Eastern, Inc. (collectively "Mesa")[1], enjoining an exchange offer of the defendant, Unocal Corporation (Unocal) for its own stock. The trial court concluded that a selective exchange offer, excluding Mesa, was legally impermissible. We cannot agree with such a blanket rule. The factual findings of the Vice Chancellor, fully supported by the record, establish that Unocal's board, consisting of a majority of independent directors, acted in good faith, and after reasonable investigation found that Mesa's tender offer was both inadequate and coercive. Under the circumstances the board had both the power and duty to oppose a bid it perceived to be harmful to the corporate enterprise. On this record we are satisfied that the device Unocal adopted is reasonable in relation to the threat posed, and that the board acted in the proper exercise of sound business judgment. We will not substitute our views for those of the board if the latter's decision can be "attributed to any rational business purpose." *Sinclair Oil Corp. v. Levien,* Del.Supr., 280 A.2d 717, 720 (1971). Accordingly, we reverse the decision of the Court of Chancery and order the preliminary injunction vacated.

I.

The factual background of this matter bears a significant relationship to its ultimate outcome.

On April 8, 1985, Mesa, the owner of approximately 13% of Unocal's stock, commenced a two-tier "front loaded" cash tender offer for 64 million shares, or approximately 37%, of Unocal's outstanding stock at a price of $54 per share. The "back-end" was designed to eliminate the remaining publicly held shares by an exchange of securities purportedly worth $54 per share. However, pursuant to an order entered by the United States District Court for the Central District of California on April 26, 1985, Mesa issued a supplemental proxy statement to Unocal's stockholders disclosing that the securities offered in the second-step merger would be highly subordinated, and that Unocal's capitalization would

---

[1] T. Boone Pickens, Jr., is President and Chairman of the Board of Mesa Petroleum and President of Mesa Asset and controls the related Mesa entities.

differ significantly from its present structure. Unocal has rather aptly termed such securities "junk bonds".

Unocal's board consists of eight independent outside directors and six insiders. It met on April 13, 1985, to consider the Mesa tender offer. Thirteen directors were present, and the meeting lasted nine and one-half hours. The directors were given no agenda or written materials prior to the session. However, detailed presentations were made by legal counsel regarding the board's obligations under both Delaware corporate law and the federal securities laws. The board then received a presentation from Peter Sachs on behalf of Goldman Sachs & Co. (Goldman Sachs) and Dillon, Read & Co. (Dillon Read) discussing the bases for their opinions that the Mesa proposal was wholly inadequate. Mr. Sachs opined that the minimum cash value that could be expected from a sale or orderly liquidation for 100% of Unocal's stock was in excess of $60 per share. In making his presentation, Mr. Sachs showed slides outlining the valuation techniques used by the financial advisors, and others, depicting recent business combinations in the oil and gas industry. The Court of Chancery found that the Sachs presentation was designed to apprise the directors of the scope of the analyses performed rather than the facts and numbers used in reaching the conclusion that Mesa's tender offer price was inadequate.

Mr. Sachs also presented various defensive strategies available to the board if it concluded that Mesa's two-step tender offer was inadequate and should be opposed. One of the devices outlined was a self-tender by Unocal for its own stock with a reasonable price range of $70 to $75 per share. The cost of such a proposal would cause the company to incur $6.1-6.5 billion of additional debt, and a presentation was made informing the board of Unocal's ability to handle it. The directors were told that the primary effect of this obligation would be to reduce exploratory drilling, but that the company would nonetheless remain a viable entity.

The eight outside directors, comprising a clear majority of the thirteen members present, then met separately with Unocal's financial advisors and attorneys. Thereafter, they unanimously agreed to advise the board that it should reject Mesa's tender offer as inadequate, and that Unocal should pursue a self-tender to provide the stockholders with a fairly priced alternative to the Mesa proposal. The board then reconvened and unanimously adopted a resolution rejecting as grossly inadequate Mesa's tender offer. Despite the nine and one-half hour length of the meeting, no formal decision was made on the proposed defensive self-tender.

On April 15, the board met again with four of the directors present by telephone and one member still absent. This session lasted two hours. Unocal's Vice President of Finance and its Assistant General Counsel made a detailed presentation of the proposed terms of the exchange offer. A price range between $70 and $80 per share was considered, and ultimately the directors agreed upon $72. The board was also advised about the debt securities that would be issued, and the necessity of placing restrictive covenants upon certain corporate activities until the obligations were paid. The board's decisions were made in reliance on the advice of its investment bankers, including the terms and conditions upon which the securities were to be issued. Based upon this advice, and the board's own deliberations, the directors unanimously approved the exchange offer. Their resolution provided that if Mesa acquired 64 million shares of Unocal stock through its own offer (the Mesa Purchase Condition), Unocal would buy the remaining 49% outstanding for an exchange of debt securities having an aggregate par value of $72 per share. The board resolution also stated that the offer would be subject to other conditions that had been described to the board at the meeting, or which were deemed necessary by Unocal's officers, including the exclusion of Mesa from the proposal (the Mesa exclusion). Any such conditions were required to be in accordance with the "purport and intent" of the offer.

Unocal's exchange offer was commenced on April 17, 1985, and Mesa promptly challenged it by filing this suit in the Court of Chancery. On April 22, the Unocal board met again and was advised by Goldman Sachs and Dillon Read to waive the Mesa Purchase Condition as to 50 million shares. This recommendation was in response to a perceived concern of the shareholders that, if shares were tendered to Unocal, no shares would be purchased by either offeror. The directors were also advised that they should tender their own Unocal stock into the exchange offer as a mark of their confidence in it.

Another focus of the board was the Mesa exclusion. Legal counsel advised that under Delaware law Mesa could only be excluded for what the directors reasonably believed to be a valid corporate purpose. The directors' discussion centered on the objective of adequately compensating shareholders at the "back-end" of Mesa's proposal, which the latter would finance with "junk bonds". To include Mesa would defeat that goal, because under the proration aspect of the exchange offer (49%) every Mesa share accepted by Unocal would displace one held by another stockholder. Further, if Mesa were permitted to tender to Unocal, the latter would in effect be financing Mesa's own inadequate proposal.

On April 24, 1985 Unocal issued a supplement to the exchange offer describing the partial waiver of the Mesa Purchase Condition. On May 1, 1985, in another supplement, Unocal extended the withdrawal, proration and expiration dates of its exchange offer to May 17, 1985.

Meanwhile, on April 22, 1985, Mesa amended its complaint in this action to challenge the Mesa exclusion. A preliminary injunction hearing was scheduled for May 8, 1985. However, on April 23, 1985, Mesa moved for a temporary restraining order in response to Unocal's announcement that it was partially waiving the Mesa Purchase Condition. After expedited briefing, the Court of Chancery heard Mesa's motion on April 26.

On April 29, 1985, the Vice Chancellor temporarily restrained Unocal from proceeding with the exchange offer unless it included Mesa. . . .

On May 13, 1985 the Court of Chancery certified this interlocutory appeal to us as a question of first impression, and we accepted it on May 14. The entire matter was scheduled on an expedited basis. . . .

We begin with the basic issue of the power of a board of directors of a Delaware corporation to adopt a defensive measure of this type. Absent such authority, all other questions are moot. Neither issues of fairness nor business judgment are pertinent without the basic underpinning of a board's legal power to act.

The board has a large reservoir of authority upon which to draw. Its duties and responsibilities proceed from the inherent powers conferred by 8 *Del.C.* § 141(a), respecting management of the corporation's "business and affairs". Additionally, the powers here being exercised derive from 8 *Del.C.* § 160(a), conferring broad authority upon a corporation to deal in its own stock. From this it is now well established that in the acquisition of its shares a Delaware corporation may deal selectively with its stockholders, provided the directors have not acted out of a sole or primary purpose to entrench themselves in office. *Cheff v. Mathes,* Del.Supr., 199 A.2d 548, 554 (1964); *Bennett v. Propp,* Del.Supr., 187 A.2d 405, 408 (1962); *Martin v. American Potash & Chemical Corporation,* Del.Supr., 92 A.2d 295, 302 (1952); *Kaplan v. Goldsamt,* Del.Ch., 380 A.2d 556, 568-569 (1977); *Kors v. Carey,* Del. Ch., 158 A.2d 136, 140-141 (1960).

Finally, the board's power to act derives from its fundamental duty and obligation to protect the corporate enterprise, which includes stockholders, from harm reasonably perceived, irrespective of its source. *See e.g. Panter v. Marshall Field & Co.,* 646 F.2d 271, 297 (7th Cir.1981); *Crouse-Hinds Co. v. Internorth, Inc.,* 634 F.2d 690, 704 (2d Cir.1980); *Heit v. Baird,* 567 F.2d 1157, 1161 (1st Cir.1977); *Cheff v. Mathes,* 199 A.2d at 556; *Martin v. American Potash & Chemical Corp.,* 92 A.2d at 302; *Kaplan v. Goldsamt,* 380 A.2d at 568-69; *Kors v. Carey,* 158 A.2d at 141; *Northwest Industries, Inc. v. B.F. Goodrich Co.,* 301 F.Supp. 706, 712 (M.D.Ill. 1969). Thus, we are satisfied that in the broad context of corporate governance, including issues of fundamental corporate change, a board of directors is not a passive instrumentality.

Given the foregoing principles, we turn to the standards by which director action is to be measured. In *Pogostin v. Rice,* Del.Supr., 480 A.2d 619 (1984), we held that the business judgment rule, including the standards by which director conduct is judged, is applicable in the context of a takeover. *Id.* at 627. The business judgment rule is a "presumption that in making a business decision the directors of a corporation acted on an informed basis, in good faith and in the honest belief that the action taken was in the best interests of the company." *Aronson v. Lewis,* Del.Supr., 473 A.2d 805, 812 (1984) (citations omitted). A hallmark of the business judgment rule is that a court will not substitute its judgment for that of the board if the latter's decision can be "attributed to any rational business purpose." *Sinclair Oil Corp. v. Levien,* Del.Supr., 280 A.2d 717, 720 (1971).

When a board addresses a pending takeover bid it has an obligation to determine whether the offer is in the best interests of the corporation and its shareholders. In that respect a board's duty is no different from any other responsibility it shoulders, and its decisions should be no less entitled to the respect they otherwise would be accorded in the realm of business judgment.[9] *See also Johnson v. Trueblood,* 629 F.2d 287, 292-293 (3d Cir.1980).

---

[9] This is a subject of intense debate among practicing members of the bar and legal scholars. Excellent examples of these contending views are: Block & Miller, *The Responsibilities and Obligations of Corporate Directors in Takeover Contests,* 11 Sec.Reg. L.J. 44 (1983); Easterbrook &

There are, however, certain caveats to a proper exercise of this function. Because of the omnipresent specter that a board may be acting primarily in its own interests, rather than those of the corporation and its shareholders, there is an enhanced duty which calls for judicial examination at the threshold before the protections of the business judgment rule may be conferred.

This Court has long recognized that:

> We must bear in mind the inherent danger in the purchase of shares with corporate funds to remove a threat to corporate policy when a threat to control is involved. The directors are of necessity confronted with a conflict of interest, and an objective decision is difficult.

Bennett v. Propp, Del.Supr., 187 A.2d 405, 409 (1962). In the face of this inherent conflict directors must show that they had reasonable grounds for believing that a danger to corporate policy and effectiveness existed because of another person's stock ownership. *Cheff v. Mathes,* 199 A.2d at 554-55. However, they satisfy that burden "by showing good faith and reasonable investigation...." *Id.* at 555. Furthermore, such proof is materially enhanced, as here, by the approval of a board comprised of a majority of outside independent directors who have acted in accordance with the foregoing standards. *See Aronson v. Lewis,* 473 A.2d at 812, 815; *Puma v. Marriott,* Del.Ch., 283 A.2d 693, 695 (1971); *Panter v. Marshall Field & Co.,* 646 F.2d 271, 295 (7th Cir.1981).

IV.

A.

In the board's exercise of corporate power to forestall a takeover bid our analysis begins with the basic principle that corporate directors have a fiduciary duty to act in the best interests of the corporation's stockholders. *Guth v. Loft, Inc.,* Del. Supr., 5 A.2d 503, 510 (1939). As we have noted, their duty of care extends to protecting the corporation and its owners from perceived harm whether a threat originates from third parties or other shareholders.[10] But such powers are not absolute. A corporation does not have unbridled discretion to defeat any perceived threat by any Draconian means available.

Fischel, *Takeover Bids, Defensive Tactics, and Shareholders' Welfare,* 36 Bus.Law. 1733 (1981); Easterbrook & Fischel, *The Proper Role of a Target's Management In Responding to a Tender Offer,* 94 Harv.L.Rev. 1161 (1981). Herzel, Schmidt & Davis, *Why Corporate Directors Have a Right To Resist Tender Offers,* 3 Corp.L.Rev. 107 (1980); Lipton, *Takeover Bids in the Target's Boardroom,* 35 Bus.Law. 101 (1979).

[10] It has been suggested that a board's response to a takeover threat should be a passive one. Easterbrook & Fischel, *supra,* 36 Bus.Law. at 1750. However, that clearly is not the law of Delaware, and as the proponents of this rule of passivity readily concede, it has not been adopted either by courts or state legislatures. Easterbrook & Fischel, *supra,* 94 Harv.L.Rev. at 1194.

The restriction placed upon a selective stock repurchase is that the directors may not have acted solely or primarily out of a desire to perpetuate themselves in office. *See Cheff v. Mathes,* 199 A.2d at 556; *Kors v. Carey,* 158 A.2d at 140. Of course, to this is added the further caveat that inequitable action may not be taken under the guise of law. *Schnell v. Chris-Craft Industries, Inc.,* Del.Supr., 285 A.2d 437, 439 (1971). The standard of proof established in *Cheff v. Mathes* and discussed *supra* at page 16, is designed to ensure that a defensive measure to thwart or impede a takeover is indeed motivated by a good faith concern for the welfare of the corporation and its stockholders, which in all circumstances must be free of any fraud or other misconduct. *Cheff v. Mathes,* 199 A.2d at 554-55. However, this does not end the inquiry.

B.

A further aspect is the element of balance. If a defensive measure is to come within the ambit of the business judgment rule, it must be reasonable in relation to the threat posed. This entails an analysis by the directors of the nature of the takeover bid and its effect on the corporate enterprise. Examples of such concerns may include: inadequacy of the price offered, nature and timing of the offer, questions of illegality, the impact on "constituencies" other than shareholders (i.e., creditors, customers, employees, and perhaps even the community generally), the risk of nonconsummation, and the quality of securities being offered in the exchange. *See* Lipton and Brownstein, *Takeover Responses and Directors' Responsibilities: An Update,* p. 7, ABA National Institute on the Dynamics of Corporate Control (December 8, 1983). While not a controlling factor, it also seems to us that a board may reasonably consider the basic stockholder interests at stake, including those of short term speculators, whose actions may have fueled the coercive aspect of the offer at the expense of the long term investor.[11] Here, the threat posed was viewed by the Unocal board as a grossly inadequate two-tier coercive tender offer coupled with the threat of greenmail.

Specifically, the Unocal directors had concluded that the value of Unocal was substantially above the $54 per share offered in cash at the front end. Furthermore, they determined that the subordinated securities to be exchanged in Mesa's announced squeeze out of the remaining shareholders in the "back-end" merger were "junk bonds" worth far less than

---

[11] There has been much debate respecting such stockholder interests. One rather impressive study indicates that the stock of over 50 percent of target companies, who resisted hostile takeovers, later traded at higher market prices than the rejected offer price, or were acquired after the tender offer was defeated by another company at a price higher than the offer price. *See* Lipton, *supra* 35 Bus.Law. at 106-109, 132-133. Moreover, an update by Kidder Peabody & Company of this study, involving the stock prices of target companies that have defeated hostile tender offers during the period from 1973 to 1982 demonstrates that in a majority of cases the target's shareholders benefited from the defeat. The stock of 81% of the targets studied has, since the tender offer, sold at prices higher than the tender offer price. When adjusted for the time value of money, the figure is 64%. *See* Lipton & Brownstein, *supra* ABA Institute at 10. The thesis being that this strongly supports application of the business judgment rule in response to takeover threats. There is, however, a rather vehement contrary view. *See* Easterbrook & Fischel, *supra* 36 Bus.Law. at 1739-1745.

$54. It is now well recognized that such offers are a classic coercive measure designed to stampede shareholders into tendering at the first tier, even if the price is inadequate, out of fear of what they will receive at the back end of the transaction.[12] Wholly beyond the coercive aspect of an inadequate two-tier tender offer, the threat was posed by a corporate raider with a national reputation as a "greenmailer".[13]

In adopting the selective exchange offer, the board stated that its objective was either to defeat the inadequate Mesa offer or, should the offer still succeed, provide the 49% of its stockholders, who would otherwise be forced to accept "junk bonds", with $72 worth of senior debt. We find that both purposes are valid.

However, such efforts would have been thwarted by Mesa's participation in the exchange offer. First, if Mesa could tender its shares, Unocal would effectively be subsidizing the former's continuing effort to buy Unocal stock at $54 per share. Second, Mesa could not, by definition, fit within the class of shareholders being protected from its own coercive and inadequate tender offer.

Thus, we are satisfied that the selective exchange offer is reasonably related to the threats posed. It is consistent with the principle that "the minority stockholder shall receive the substantial equivalent in value of what he had before." *Sterling v. Mayflower Hotel Corp.,* Del.Supr., 93 A.2d 107, 114 (1952). *See also Rosenblatt v. Getty Oil Co.,* Del.Supr., 493 A.2d 929, 940 (1985). This concept of fairness, while stated in the merger context, is also relevant in the area of tender offer law. Thus, the board's decision to offer what it determined to be the fair value of the corporation to the 49% of its shareholders, who would otherwise be forced to accept highly subordinated "junk bonds", is reasonable and consistent with the directors' duty to ensure that the minority stockholders receive equal value for their shares.

V.

Mesa contends that it is unlawful, and the trial court agreed, for a corporation to discriminate in this fashion against one shareholder. It argues correctly that no case has ever sanctioned a device that precludes a raider from sharing in a benefit available to all

---

[12] For a discussion of the coercive nature of a two-tier tender offer see e.g., Brudney & Chirelstein, *Fair Shares in Corporate Mergers and Takeovers,* 88 Harv.L.Rev. 297, 337 (1974); Finkelstein, *Antitakeover Protection Against Two-Tier and Partial Tender Offers: The Validity of Fair Price, Mandatory Bid, and Flip-Over Provisions Under Delaware Law,* 11 Sec.Reg. L.J. 291, 293 (1984); Lipton, *supra,* 35 Bus.Law at 113-14; Note, *Protecting Shareholders Against Partial and Two-Tiered Takeovers: The Poison Pill Preferred,* 97 Harv.L.Rev. 1964, 1966 (1984).

[13] The term "greenmail" refers to the practice of buying out a takeover bidder's stock at a premium that is not available to other shareholders in order to prevent the takeover. The Chancery Court noted that "Mesa has made tremendous profits from its takeover activities although in the past few years it has not been successful in acquiring any of the target companies on an unfriendly basis." Moreover, the trial court specifically found that the actions of the Unocal board were taken in good faith to eliminate both the inadequacies of the tender offer and to forestall the payment of "greenmail".

other stockholders. However, as we have noted earlier, the principle of selective stock repurchases by a Delaware corporation is neither unknown nor unauthorized. *Cheff v. Mathes,* 199 A.2d at 554; *Bennett v. Propp,* 187 A.2d at 408; *Martin v. American Potash & Chemical Corporation,* 92 A.2d at 302; *Kaplan v. Goldsamt,* 380 A.2d at 568-569; *Kors v. Carey,* 158 A.2d at 140-141; 8 *Del. C.* § 160. The only difference is that heretofore the approved transaction was the payment of "greenmail" to a raider or dissident posing a threat to the corporate enterprise. All other stockholders were denied such favored treatment, and given Mesa's past history of greenmail, its claims here are rather ironic.

However, our corporate law is not static. It must grow and develop in response to, indeed in anticipation of, evolving concepts and needs. Merely because the General Corporation Law is silent as to a specific matter does not mean that it is prohibited. *See Providence and Worcester Co. v. Baker,* Del.Supr., 378 A.2d 121, 123-124 (1977). In the days when *Cheff, Bennett, Martin* and *Kors* were decided, the tender offer, while not an unknown device, was virtually unused, and little was known of such methods as two-tier "front-end" loaded offers with their coercive effects. Then, the favored attack of a raider was stock acquisition followed by a proxy contest. Various defensive tactics, which provided no benefit whatever to the raider, evolved. Thus, the use of corporate funds by management to counter a proxy battle was approved. *Hall v. Trans-Lux Daylight Picture Screen Corp.,* Del.Supr., 171 A. 226 (1934); *Hibbert v. Hollywood Park, Inc.,* Del.Supr., 457 A.2d 339 (1983). Litigation, supported by corporate funds, aimed at the raider has long been a popular device.

More recently, as the sophistication of both raiders and targets has developed, a host of other defensive measures to counter such ever mounting threats has evolved and received judicial sanction. These include defensive charter amendments and other devices bearing some rather exotic, but apt, names: Crown Jewel, White Knight, Pac Man, and Golden Parachute. Each has highly selective features, the object of which is to deter or defeat the raider.

Thus, while the exchange offer is a form of selective treatment, given the nature of the threat posed here the response is neither unlawful nor unreasonable. If the board of directors is disinterested, has acted in good faith and with due care, its decision in the absence of an abuse of discretion will be upheld as a proper exercise of business judgment.

To this Mesa responds that the board is not disinterested, because the directors are receiving a benefit from the tender of their own shares, which because of the Mesa exclusion, does not devolve upon *all* stockholders equally. *See Aronson v. Lewis,* Del.Supr., 473 A.2d 805, 812 (1984). However, Mesa concedes that if the exclusion is valid, then the directors and all other stockholders share the same benefit. The answer of course is that the exclusion is valid, and the directors' participation in the exchange offer does not rise to the level of a disqualifying interest. The excellent discussion in *Johnson v. Trueblood,* 629 F.2d at 292-293, of the use of the business judgment rule in takeover contests also seems pertinent here.

Nor does this become an "interested" director transaction merely because certain board members are large stockholders. As this Court has previously noted, that fact alone does

224

not create a disqualifying "personal pecuniary interest" to defeat the operation of the business judgment rule. *Cheff v. Mathes,* 199 A.2d at 554.

Mesa also argues that the exclusion permits the directors to abdicate the fiduciary duties they owe it. However, that is not so. The board continues to owe Mesa the duties of due care and loyalty. But in the face of the destructive threat Mesa's tender offer was perceived to pose, the board had a supervening duty to protect the corporate enterprise, which includes the other shareholders, from threatened harm.

Mesa contends that the basis of this action is punitive, and solely in response to the exercise of its rights of corporate democracy. Nothing precludes Mesa, as a stockholder, from acting in its own self-interest. *See e.g., DuPont v. DuPont,* 251 Fed. 937 (D.Del.1918), *aff'd* 256 Fed. 129 (3d Cir.1918); *Ringling Bros.-Barnum & Bailey Combined Shows, Inc. v. Ringling,* Del.Supr., 53 A.2d 441, 447 (1947); *Heil v. Standard Gas & Electric Co.,* Del.Ch., 151 A. 303, 304 (1930). *But see, Allied Chemical & Dye Corp. v. Steel & Tube Co. of America,* Del.Ch., 120 A. 486, 491 (1923) (majority shareholder owes a fiduciary duty to the minority shareholders). However, Mesa, while pursuing its own interests, has acted in a manner which a board consisting of a majority of independent directors has reasonably determined to be contrary to the best interests of Unocal and its other shareholders. In this situation, there is no support in Delaware law for the proposition that, when responding to a perceived harm, a corporation must guarantee a benefit to a stockholder who is deliberately provoking the danger being addressed. There is no obligation of self-sacrifice by a corporation and its shareholders in the face of such a challenge.

Here, the Court of Chancery specifically found that the "directors' decision [to oppose the Mesa tender offer] was made in the good faith belief that the Mesa tender offer is inadequate." Given our standard of review under *Levitt v. Bouvier,* Del. Supr., 287 A.2d 671, 673 (1972), and *Application of Delaware Racing Association,* Del.Supr., 213 A.2d 203, 207 (1965), we are satisfied that Unocal's board has met its burden of proof. *Cheff v. Mathes,* 199 A.2d at 555.

VI.

In conclusion, there was directorial power to oppose the Mesa tender offer, and to undertake a selective stock exchange made in good faith and upon a reasonable investigation pursuant to a clear duty to protect the corporate enterprise. Further, the selective stock repurchase plan chosen by Unocal is reasonable in relation to the threat that the board rationally and reasonably believed was posed by Mesa's inadequate and coercive two-tier tender offer. Under those circumstances the board's action is entitled to be measured by the standards of the business judgment rule. Thus, unless it is shown by a preponderance of the evidence that the directors' decisions were primarily based on perpetuating themselves in office, or some other breach of fiduciary duty such as fraud, overreaching, lack of good faith, or being uninformed, a Court will not substitute its judgment for that of the board.

In this case that protection is not lost merely because Unocal's directors have tendered their shares in the exchange offer. Given the validity of the Mesa exclusion, they are receiving a benefit shared generally by all other stockholders except Mesa. In this circumstance the test of *Aronson v. Lewis*, 473 A.2d at 812, is satisfied. *See also Cheff v. Mathes*, 199 A.2d at 554. If the stockholders are displeased with the action of their elected representatives, the powers of corporate democracy are at their disposal to turn the board out. *Aronson v. Lewis*, Del.Supr., 473 A.2d 805, 811 (1984). *See also 8 Del.C.* §§ 141(k) and 211(b).

With the Court of Chancery's findings that the exchange offer was based on the board's good faith belief that the Mesa offer was inadequate, that the board's action was informed and taken with due care, that Mesa's prior activities justify a reasonable inference that its principle objective was greenmail, and implicitly, that the substance of the offer itself was reasonable and fair to the corporation and its stockholders if Mesa were included, we cannot say that the Unocal directors have acted in such a manner as to have passed an "unintelligent and unadvised judgment". *Mitchell v. Highland-Western Glass Co.*, Del. Ch., 167 A. 831, 833 (1933). The decision of the Court of Chancery is therefore REVERSED, and the preliminary injunction is VACATED.

[...]

Discussion Questions:

1. How could Pickens have acquired 13% of Unocal before having to disclose his stake? See Rule 13D.

2. Does Pickens' offer create a "pressure to tender"? If so, does the board's response eliminate this pressure to tender? Consider the Unocal shareholder's choice in view of: (1) Pickens' original offer; (2) Unocal's initial response; (3) Unocal's revised response.

3. What is the standard of review for the board's defensive tactics, and how is that standard applied here? How does it relate to our two old friends: the business judgment rule and entire fairness?

The next act in our three-act play, *Moran v. Household International* (1985), endorsed the "rights plan" a/k/a "poison pill" invented by Martin Lipton. "Rights plan" may sound innocuous. But it completely transformed US takeover law and practice.

The pill has only one goal: to deter the acquisition of a substantial block of shares by anyone not approved by the board. It does so by diluting, or rather threatening to dilute, the acquired block. If anyone "triggers" the pill by acquiring more than the threshold percentage of shares (usually 15%), the corporation issues additional shares to all *other* shareholders. The number of additional shares is generally chosen so as to reduce the acquirer's stake by about half. Needless to say, that would be painful—arguably prohibitively painful—to any would-be acquirer.

226

The pill ingeniously obscures this discriminatory mechanism in complicated warrants. The corporation declares a dividend of warrants to purchase additional stock or preferred stock. Initially, these warrants are neither tradeable nor exercisable. If anybody becomes an "acquiring person" by acquiring more than the threshold percentage, however, the warrants grant the right to buy corporate stock for prices below value. Of course, all shareholders will then rationally choose to exercise the warrant. So what is the point? The point is that by their terms, the *warrants held by the acquiring person* are automatically void.

The pill is extraordinarily powerful. In the 30 years since *Moran*, only one bidder has dared triggering the pill, and that was one with a particularly low trigger of 5% (chosen to preserve a tax advantage). The exercise of the rights did not only dilute the acquirer but caused massive administrative problems (a lot of new stock had to be issued!), leading to a suspension of issuer stock from trading. The issuer, Selectica, also violated the listing rules. What this shows is that the pill really is designed purely as a deterrent—it is intended never to be triggered. It's MAD (Mutually Assured Destruction) intended to keep out the unwanted acquirer, nothing else.

The upshot is that nowadays no Delaware corporation can be acquired unless the board agrees to sell. The pill has stopped not only hostile two-tier bids, but all hostile bids. To be sure, a would-be acquirer could attempt to replace a reluctant board through a proxy fight. But one proxy fight may not be enough, if and because the corporation has a staggered board in its charter (cf. *Airgas* below). In any event, the point is that board acquiescence is ultimately indispensable. The acceptance of the pill was thus a fundamental power shift from shareholders to boards in dealing with "hostile" offers.

Perhaps understandably, the *Moran* court did not fully understand these implications. Or perhaps it didn't want to? The SEC's amicus brief certainly predicted as much. As it were, the Court gives mainly technical, statutory reasons for approving the pill. But in *Schnell v. Chris-Craft Industries*, 285 A.2d 437 (Del. 1971), for example, the Court *could* have brushed those aside since "[t]he answer to that contention, of course, is that inequitable action does not become permissible simply because it is legally possible." Why didn't it? Should it have?

Moran v. HouseHold International, Inc.
500 A.2d 1346 (1985)

McNEILLY, Justice:

This case presents to this Court for review the most recent defensive mechanism in the arsenal of corporate takeover weaponry—the Preferred Share Purchase Rights Plan ("Rights Plan" or "Plan"). The validity of this mechanism has attracted national attention. *Amici curiae* briefs have been filed in support of appellants by the Security and Exchange

Commission ("SEC")[1] and the Investment Company Institute. An *amicus curiae* brief has been filed in support of appellees ("Household") by the United Food and Commercial Workers International Union.

In a detailed opinion, the Court of Chancery upheld the Rights Plan as a legitimate exercise of business judgment by Household. *Moran v. Household International, Inc.*, Del.Ch., 490 A.2d 1059 (1985). We agree, and therefore, affirm the judgment below.

I.

The facts giving rise to this case have been carefully delineated in the Court of Chancery's opinion. *Id.* at 1064-69. A review of the basic facts is necessary for a complete understanding of the issues.

On August 14, 1984, the Board of Directors of Household International, Inc. adopted the Rights Plan by a fourteen to two vote.[2] The intricacies of the Rights Plan are contained in a 48-page document entitled "Rights Agreement". Basically, the Plan provides that Household common stockholders are entitled to the issuance of one Right per common share under certain triggering conditions. There are two triggering events that can activate the Rights. The first is the announcement of a tender offer for 30 percent of Household's shares ("30% trigger") and the second is the acquisition of 20 percent of Household's shares by any single entity or group ("20% trigger").

If an announcement of a tender offer for 30 percent of Household's shares is made, the Rights are issued and are immediately exercisable to purchase 1/100 share of new preferred stock for $100 and are redeemable by the Board for $.50 per Right. If 20 percent of Household's shares are acquired by anyone, the Rights are issued and become non-redeemable and are exercisable to purchase 1/100 of a share of preferred. If a Right is not exercised for preferred, and thereafter, a merger or consolidation occurs, the Rights holder can exercise each Right to purchase $200 of the common stock of the tender offeror for $100. This "flip-over" provision of the Rights Plan is at the heart of this controversy.

Household is a diversified holding company with its principal subsidiaries engaged in financial services, transportation and merchandising. HFC, National Car Rental and Vons Grocery are three of its wholly-owned entities.

Household did not adopt its Rights Plan during a battle with a corporate raider, but as a preventive mechanism to ward off future advances. The Vice-Chancellor found that as early

---

[1] The SEC split 3-2 on whether to intervene in this case. The two dissenting Commissioners have publicly disagreed with the other three as to the merits of the Rights Plan. 17 Securities Regulation & Law Report 400; The Wall Street Journal, March 20, 1985, at 6.

[2] Household's Board has ten outside directors and six who are members of management. Messrs. Moran (appellant) and Whitehead voted against the Plan. The record reflects that Whitehead voted against the Plan not on its substance but because he thought it was novel and would bring unwanted publicity to Household.

as February 1984, Household's management became concerned about the company's vulnerability as a takeover target and began considering amending its charter to render a takeover more difficult. After considering the matter, Household decided not to pursue a fair price amendment.

In the meantime, appellant Moran, one of Household's own Directors and also Chairman of the Dyson-Kissner-Moran Corporation, ("D-K-M") which is the largest single stockholder of Household, began discussions concerning a possible leveraged buyout of Household by D-K-M. D-K-M's financial studies showed that Household's stock was significantly undervalued in relation to the company's break-up value. It is uncontradicted that Moran's suggestion of a leveraged buy-out never progressed beyond the discussion stage.

Concerned about Household's vulnerability to a raider in light of the current takeover climate, Household secured the services of Wachtell, Lipton, Rosen and Katz ("Wachtell, Lipton") and Goldman, Sachs & Co. ("Goldman, Sachs") to formulate a takeover policy for recommendation to the Household Board at its August 14 meeting. After a July 31 meeting with a Household Board member and a pre-meeting distribution of material on the potential takeover problem and the proposed Rights Plan, the Board met on August 14, 1984.

Representatives of Wachtell, Lipton and Goldman, Sachs attended the August 14 meeting. The minutes reflect that Mr. Lipton explained to the Board that his recommendation of the Plan was based on his understanding that the Board was concerned about the increasing frequency of "bust-up"[4] takeovers, the increasing takeover activity in the financial service industry, such as Leucadia's attempt to take over Arco, and the possible adverse effect this type of activity could have on employees and others concerned with and vital to the continuing successful operation of Household even in the absence of any actual bust-up takeover attempt. Against this factual background, the Plan was approved.

Thereafter, Moran and the company of which he is Chairman, D-K-M, filed this suit. On the eve of trial, Gretl Golter, the holder of 500 shares of Household, was permitted to intervene as an additional plaintiff. The trial was held, and the Court of Chancery ruled in favor of Household. Appellants now appeal from that ruling to this Court.

II.

The primary issue here is the applicability of the business judgment rule as the standard by which the adoption of the Rights Plan should be reviewed. Much of this issue has been decided by our recent decision in *Unocal Corp. v. Mesa Petroleum Co.*, Del.Supr., 493 A.2d 946 (1985). In *Unocal*, we applied the business judgment rule to analyze Unocal's discriminatory self-tender. We explained:

---

[4] "Bust-up" takeover generally refers to a situation in which one seeks to finance an acquisition by selling off pieces of the acquired company.

229

When a board addresses a pending takeover bid it has an obligation to determine whether the offer is in the best interests of the corporation and its shareholders. In that respect a board's duty is no different from any other responsibility it shoulders, and its decisions should be no less entitled to the respect they otherwise would be accorded in the realm of business judgment.

Id. at 954 (citation and footnote omitted).

Other jurisdictions have also applied the business judgment rule to actions by which target companies have sought to forestall takeover activity they considered undesirable. *See Gearhart Industries, Inc. v. Smith International,* 5th Cir., 741 F.2d 707 (1984) (sale of discounted subordinate debentures containing springing warrants); *Treco, Inc. v. Land of Lincoln Savings and Loan,* 7th Cir., 749 F.2d 374 (1984) (amendment to by-laws); *Panter v. Marshall Field,* 7th Cir., 646 F.2d 271 (1981) (acquisitions to create antitrust problems); *Johnson v. Trueblood,* 3d Cir., 629 F.2d 287 (1980), *cert. denied,* 450 U.S. 999, 101 S.Ct. 1704, 68 L.Ed.2d 200 (1981) (refusal to tender); *Crouse-Hinds Co. v. InterNorth, Inc.,* 2d Cir., 634 F.2d 690 (1980) (sale of stock to favored party); *Treadway v. Cane Corp.,* 2d Cir., 638 F.2d 357 (1980) (sale to White Knight), *Enterra Corp. v. SGS Associates,* E.D.Pa., 600 F.Supp. 678 (1985) (standstill agreement); *Buffalo Forge Co. v. Ogden Corp.,* W.D.N.Y., 555 F.Supp. 892, *aff'd,* (2d Cir.) 717 F.2d 757, *cert. denied,* 464 U.S. 1018, 104 S.Ct. 550, 78 L.Ed.2d 724 (1983) (sale of treasury shares and grant of stock option to White Knight); *Whittaker Corp. v. Edgar,* N.D.Ill., 535 F.Supp. 933 (1982) (disposal of valuable assets); *Martin Marietta Corp. v. Bendix Corp.,* D.Md., 549 F.Supp. 623 (1982) (PacMan defense).[6]

This case is distinguishable from the ones cited, since here we have a defensive mechanism adopted to ward off possible future advances and not a mechanism adopted in reaction to a specific threat. This distinguishing factor does not result in the Directors losing the protection of the business judgment rule. To the contrary, pre-planning for the contingency of a hostile takeover might reduce the risk that, under the pressure of a takeover bid, management will fail to exercise reasonable judgment. Therefore, in reviewing a pre-planned defensive mechanism it seems even more appropriate to apply the business judgment rule. *See Warner Communications v. Murdoch,* D.Del., 581 F.Supp. 1482, 1491 (1984).

Of course, the business judgment rule can only sustain corporate decision making or transactions that are within the power or authority of the Board. Therefore, before the business judgment rule can be applied it must be determined whether the Directors were authorized to adopt the Rights Plan.

---

[6] The "Pac-Man" defense is generally a target company countering an unwanted tender offer by making its own tender offer for stock of the would-be acquirer. Block & Miller, *The Responsibilities and Obligations of Corporate Directors in Takeover Contests,* 11 Sec.Reg.L.J. 44, 64 (1983).

III.

Appellants vehemently contend that the Board of Directors was unauthorized to adopt the Rights Plan. First, appellants contend that no provision of the Delaware General Corporation Law authorizes the issuance of such Rights. Secondly, appellants, along with the SEC, contend that the Board is unauthorized to usurp stockholders' rights to receive hostile tender offers. Third, appellants and the SEC also contend that the Board is unauthorized to fundamentally restrict stockholders' rights to conduct a proxy contest. We address each of these contentions in turn.

A.

While appellants contend that no provision of the Delaware General Corporation Law authorizes the Rights Plan, Household contends that the Rights Plan was issued pursuant to 8 *Del.C.* §§ 151(g) and 157. It explains that the Rights are authorized by § 157[7] and the issue of preferred stock underlying the Rights is authorized by § 151.[8] Appellants respond by making several attacks upon the authority to issue the Rights pursuant to § 157.

Appellants begin by contending that § 157 cannot authorize the Rights Plan since § 157 has never served the purpose of authorizing a takeover defense. Appellants contend that § 157 is a corporate financing statute, and that nothing in its legislative history suggests a purpose that has anything to do with corporate control or a takeover defense. Appellants are unable to demonstrate that the legislature, in its adoption of § 157, meant to limit the applicability of § 157 to only the issuance of Rights for the purposes of corporate financing. Without such affirmative evidence, we decline to impose such a limitation upon the section that the legislature has not. *Compare Providence & Worchester Co. v. Baker,* Del.Supr., 378 A.2d 121, 124 (1977) (refusal to read a bar to protective voting provisions into 8 *Del.C.* § 212(a)).

---

[7] The power to issue rights to purchase shares is conferred by 8 *Del.C.* § 157 which provides in relevant part: Subject to any provisions in the certificate of incorporation, every corporation may create and issue, whether or not in connection with the issue and sale of any shares of stock or other securities of the corporation, rights or options entitling the holders thereof to purchase from the corporation any shares of its capital stock of any class or classes, such rights or options to be evidenced by or in such instrument or instruments as shall be approved by the board of directors.

[8] 8 *Del.C.* § 151(g) provides in relevant part: When any corporation desires to issue any shares of stock of any class or of any series of any class of which the voting powers, designations, preferences and relative, participating, optional or other rights, if any, or the qualifications, limitations or restrictions thereof, if any, shall not have been set forth in the certificate of incorporation or in any amendment thereto but shall be provided for in a resolution or resolutions adopted by the board of directors pursuant to authority expressly vested in it by the provisions of the certificate of incorporation or any amendment thereto, a certificate setting forth a copy of such resolution or resolutions and the number of shares of stock of such class or series shall be executed, acknowledged, filed, recorded, and shall become effective, in accordance with § 103 of this title.

As we noted in *Unocal:*

> [O]ur corporate law is not static. It must grow and develop in response to, indeed in anticipation of, evolving concepts and needs. Merely because the General Corporation Law is silent as to a specific matter does not mean that it is prohibited.

493 A.2d at 957. *See also Cheff v. Mathes,* Del.Supr., 199 A.2d 548 (1964).

Secondly, appellants contend that § 157 does not authorize the issuance of sham rights such as the Rights Plan. They contend that the Rights were designed never to be exercised, and that the Plan has no economic value. In addition, they contend the preferred stock made subject to the Rights is also illusory, citing *Telvest, Inc. v. Olson,* Del.Ch., C.A. No. 5798, Brown, V.C. (March 8, 1979).

Appellants' sham contention fails in both regards. As to the Rights, they can and will be exercised upon the happening of a triggering mechanism, as we have observed during the current struggle of Sir James Goldsmith to take control of Crown Zellerbach. *See* Wall Street Journal, July 26, 1985, at 3, 12. As to the preferred shares, we agree with the Court of Chancery that they are distinguishable from sham securities invalidated in *Telvest, supra.* The Household preferred, issuable upon the happening of a triggering event, have superior dividend and liquidation rights.

Third, appellants contend that § 157 authorizes the issuance of Rights "entitling holders thereof to purchase from the corporation any shares of *its* capital stock of any class ..." (emphasis added). Therefore, their contention continues, the plain language of the statute does not authorize Household to issue rights to purchase another's capital stock upon a merger or consolidation.

Household contends, *inter alia,* that the Rights Plan is analogous to "anti-destruction" or "anti-dilution" provisions which are customary features of a wide variety of corporate securities. While appellants seem to concede that "anti-destruction" provisions are valid under Delaware corporate law, they seek to distinguish the Rights Plan as not being incidental, as are most "anti-destruction" provisions, to a corporation's statutory power to finance itself. We find no merit to such a distinction. We have already rejected appellants' similar contention that § 157 could only be used for financing purposes. We also reject that distinction here.

"Anti-destruction" clauses generally ensure holders of certain securities of the protection of their right of conversion in the event of a merger by giving them the right to convert their securities into whatever securities are to replace the stock of their company. *See Broad v. Rockwell International Corp.,* 5th Cir., 642 F.2d 929, 946, *cert. denied,* 454 U.S. 965, 102 S.Ct. 506, 70 L.Ed.2d 380 (1981); *Wood v. Coastal States Gas Corp.,* Del.Supr., 401 A.2d 932, 937-39 (1979); *B.S.F. Co. v. Philadelphia National Bank,* Del.Supr., 204 A.2d 746, 750-51 (1964). The fact that the rights here have as their purpose the prevention of coercive two-tier tender offers does not invalidate them.

Fourth, appellants contend that Household's reliance upon § 157 is contradictory to 8 *Del.C.* § 203.[9] [*The decision refers to the old version of DGCL 203, which was completely overhauled in 1988. – eds.*] Section 203 is a "notice" statute which generally requires that timely notice be given to a target of an offeror's intention to make a tender offer. Appellants contend that the lack of stronger regulation by the State indicates a legislative intent to reject anything which would impose an impediment to the tender offer process. Such a contention is a *non sequitur*. The desire to have little state regulation of tender offers cannot be said to also indicate a desire to also have little private regulation. Furthermore, as we explain *infra*, we do not view the Rights Plan as much of an impediment on the tender offer process.

Fifth, appellants contend that if § 157 authorizes the Rights Plan it would be unconstitutional pursuant to the Commerce Clause and Supremacy Clause of the United States Constitution. Household counters that appellants have failed to properly raise the issues in the Court of Chancery and are, therefore, precluded from raising them. Moreover, Household counters that appellants' contentions are without merit since the conduct complained of here is private conduct of corporate directors and not state regulation.

It is commonly known that issues not properly raised in the trial court will not be considered in the first instance by this Court. Supreme Court Rule 8. We cannot conclude here that appellants have failed to adequately raise their constitutional issues in the Court of Chancery. Appellants raised the Commerce Clause and Supremacy Clause contentions in their "pretrial memo of points and authorities" and in their opening argument at trial. The fact that they did not again raise the issues in their post-trial briefing will not preclude them from raising the issues before this Court.

Appellants contend that § 157 authorization for the Rights Plan violates the Commerce Clause and is void under the Supremacy Clause, since it is an obstacle to the

---

[9] 8 *Del.C.* § 203 provides in relevant part: (a) No offeror shall make a tender offer unless: (1) Not less than 20 nor more than 60 days before the date the tender offer is to be made, the offeror shall deliver personally or by registered or certified mail to the corporation whose equity securities are to be subject to the tender offer, at its registered office in this State or at its principal place of business, a written statement of the offeror's intention to make the tender offer.... (2) The tender offer shall remain open for a period of at least 20 days after it is first made to the holders of the equity securities, during which period any stockholder may withdraw any of the equity securities tendered to the offeror, and any revised or amended tender offer which changes the amount or type of consideration offered or the number of equity securities for which the offer is made shall remain open at least 10 days following the amendment; and (3) The offeror and any associate of the offeror will not purchase or pay for any tendered equity security for a period of at least 20 days after the tender offer is first made to the holders of the equity securities, and no such purchase or payment shall be made within 10 days after an amended or revised tender offer if the amendment or revision changes the amount or type of consideration offered or the number of equity securities for which the offer is made. If during the period the tender offer must remain open pursuant to this section, a greater number of equity securities is tendered than the offeror is bound or willing to purchase, the equity securities shall be purchased pro rata, as nearly as may be, according to the number of shares tendered during such period by each equity security holder.

accomplishment of the policies underlying the Williams Act. Appellants put heavy emphasis upon the case of *Edgar v. MITE Corp.,* 457 U.S. 624, 102 S.Ct. 2629, 73 L.Ed.2d 269 (1982), in which the United States Supreme Court held that the Illinois Business Takeover Act was unconstitutional, in that it unduly burdened interstate commerce in violation of the Commerce Clause.[10] We do not read the analysis in *Edgar* as applicable to the actions of private parties. The fact that directors of a corporation act pursuant to a state statute provides an insufficient nexus to the state for there to be state action which may violate the Commerce Clause or Supremacy Clause. *See Data Probe Acquisition Corp. v. Datatab, Inc.,* 2d Cir., 722 F.2d 1, 5 (1983).

Having concluded that sufficient authority for the Rights Plan exists in 8 *Del.C.* § 157, we note the inherent powers of the Board conferred by 8 *Del.C.* § 141(a), concerning the management of the corporation's "business and *affairs*" (emphasis added), also provides the Board additional authority upon which to enact the Rights Plan. *Unocal,* 493 A.2d at 953.

B.

Appellants contend that the Board is unauthorized to usurp stockholders' rights to receive tender offers by changing Household's fundamental structure. We conclude that the Rights Plan does not prevent stockholders from receiving tender offers, and that the change of Household's structure was less than that which results from the implementation of other defensive mechanisms upheld by various courts.

Appellants' contention that stockholders will lose their right to receive and accept tender offers seems to be premised upon an understanding of the Rights Plan which is illustrated by the SEC *amicus* brief which states: "The Chancery Court's decision seriously understates the impact of this plan. In fact, as we discuss below, the Rights Plan will deter not only two-tier offers, but virtually all hostile tender offers."

The fallacy of that contention is apparent when we look at the recent takeover of Crown Zellerbach, which has a similar Rights Plan, by Sir James Goldsmith. The evidence at trial also evidenced many methods around the Plan ranging from tendering with a condition that the Board redeem the Rights, tendering with a high minimum condition of shares and Rights, tendering and soliciting consents to remove the Board and redeem the Rights, to acquiring 50% of the shares and causing Household to self-tender for the Rights. One could also form a group of up to 19.9% and solicit proxies for consents to remove the Board and redeem the Rights. These are but a few of the methods by which Household can still be acquired by a hostile tender offer.

In addition, the Rights Plan is not absolute. When the Household Board of Directors is faced with a tender offer and a request to redeem the Rights, they will not be able to arbitrarily

---

[10] Justice White, joined by Chief Justice Burger and Justice Blackman also concluded that the Illinois Business Takeover Act was pre-empted by the Williams Act. *Edgar,* 457 U.S. at 630, 102 S.Ct. at 2634.

reject the offer. They will be held to the same fiduciary standards any other board of directors would be held to in deciding to adopt a defensive mechanism, the same standard as they were held to in originally approving the Rights Plan. *See Unocol,* 493 A.2d at 954-55, 958.

In addition, appellants contend that the deterence *[sic]* of tender offers will be accomplished by what they label "a fundamental transfer of power from the stockholders to the directors." They contend that this transfer of power, in itself, is unauthorized.

The Rights Plan will result in no more of a structural change than any other defensive mechanism adopted by a board of directors. The Rights Plan does not destroy the assets of the corporation. The implementation of the Plan neither results in any outflow of money from the corporation nor impairs its financial flexibility. It does not dilute earnings per share and does not have any adverse tax consequences for the corporation or its stockholders. The Plan has not adversely affected the market price of Household's stock.

Comparing the Rights Plan with other defensive mechanisms, it does less harm to the value structure of the corporation than do the other mechanisms. Other mechanisms result in increased debt of the corporation. *See Whittaker Corp. v. Edgar, supra* (sale of "prize asset"), *Cheff v. Mathes, supra,* (paying greenmail to eliminate a threat), *Unocal Corp. v. Mesa Petroleum Co., supra,* (discriminatory self-tender).

There is little change in the governance structure as a result of the adoption of the Rights Plan. The Board does not now have unfettered discretion in refusing to redeem the Rights. The Board has no more discretion in refusing to redeem the Rights than it does in enacting any defensive mechanism.

The contention that the Rights Plan alters the structure more than do other defensive mechanisms because it is so effective as to make the corporation completely safe from hostile tender offers is likewise without merit. As explained above, there are numerous methods to successfully launch a hostile tender offer.

C.

Appellants' third contention is that the Board was unauthorized to fundamentally restrict stockholders' rights to conduct a proxy contest. Appellants contend that the "20% trigger" effectively prevents any stockholder from first acquiring 20% or more shares before conducting a proxy contest and further, it prevents stockholders from banding together into a group to solicit proxies if, collectively, they own 20% or more of the stock. In addition, at trial, appellants contended that read literally, the Rights Agreement triggers the Rights upon the mere acquisition of the right to vote 20% or more of the shares through a proxy solicitation, and thereby precludes any proxy contest from being waged.[13]

---

[13] The SEC still contends that the mere acquisition of the right to vote 20% of the shares through a proxy solicitation triggers the rights. We do not interpret the Rights Agreement in that manner.

Appellants seem to have conceded this last contention in light of Household's response that the receipt of a proxy does not make the recipient the "beneficial owner" of the shares involved which would trigger the Rights. In essence, the Rights Agreement provides that the Rights are triggered when someone becomes the "beneficial owner" of 20% or more of Household stock. Although a literal reading of the Rights Agreement definition of "beneficial owner" would seem to include those shares which one has the right to vote, it has long been recognized that the relationship between grantor and recipient of a proxy is one of agency, and the agency is revocable by the grantor at any time. Henn, *Corporations* § 196, at 518. Therefore, the holder of a proxy is not the "beneficial owner" of the stock. As a result, the mere acquisition of the right to vote 20% of the shares does not trigger the Rights.

The issue, then, is whether the restriction upon individuals or groups from first acquiring 20% of shares before waging a proxy contest fundamentally restricts stockholders' right to conduct a proxy contest. Regarding this issue the Court of Chancery found:

> Thus, while the Rights Plan does deter the formation of proxy efforts of a certain magnitude, it does not limit the voting power of individual shares. On the evidence presented it is highly conjectural to assume that a particular effort to assert shareholder views in the election of directors or revisions of corporate policy will be frustrated by the proxy feature of the Plan. Household's witnesses, Troubh and Higgins described recent corporate takeover battles in which insurgents holding less than 10% stock ownership were able to secure corporate control through a proxy contest or the threat of one.

Moran, 490 A.2d at 1080.

We conclude that there was sufficient evidence at trial to support the Vice-Chancellor's finding that the effect upon proxy contests will be minimal. Evidence at trial established that many proxy contests are won with an insurgent ownership of less than 20%, and that very large holdings are no guarantee of success. There was also testimony that the key variable in proxy contest success is the merit of an insurgent's issues, not the size of his holdings.

IV.

Having concluded that the adoption of the Rights Plan was within the authority of the Directors, we now look to whether the Directors have met their burden under the business judgment rule.

The business judgment rule is a "presumption that in making a business decision the directors of a corporation acted on an informed basis, in good faith and in the honest belief that the action taken was in the best interests of the company." *Aronson v. Lewis,* Del.Supr., 473 A.2d 805, 812 (1984) (citations omitted). Notwithstanding, in *Unocal* we held that when the business judgment rule applies to adoption of a defensive mechanism, the initial burden will lie with the directors. The "directors must show that they had reasonable grounds for believing that a danger to corporate policy and effectiveness existed. . . . [T]hey satisfy that burden 'by showing good faith and reasonable investigation. . . .'" *Unocal*, 493 A.2d at 955 (citing *Cheff v. Mathes*, 199 A.2d at 554-55). In addition, the directors must show that the defensive mechanism was "reasonable in relation to the threat posed." *Unocal*, 493 A.2d at 955. Moreover, that proof is materially enhanced, as we noted in *Unocal*, where, as here, a majority of the board favoring the proposal consisted of outside independent directors who have acted in accordance with the foregoing standards. *Unocal*, 493 A.2d at 955; *Aronson*, 473 A.2d at 815. Then, the burden shifts back to the plaintiffs who have the ultimate burden of persuasion to show a breach of the directors' fiduciary duties. *Unocal*, 493 A.2d at 958.

There are no allegations here of any bad faith on the part of the Directors' action in the adoption of the Rights Plan. There is no allegation that the Directors' action was taken for entrenchment purposes. Household has adequately demonstrated, as explained above, that the adoption of the Rights Plan was in reaction to what it perceived to be the threat in the market place of coercive two-tier tender offers. Appellants do contend, however, that the Board did not exercise informed business judgment in its adoption of the Plan.

Appellants contend that the Household Board was uninformed since they were, *inter alia*, told the Plan would not inhibit a proxy contest, were not told the plan would preclude all hostile acquisitions of Household, and were told that Delaware counsel opined that the plan was within the business judgment of the Board.

As to the first two contentions, as we explained above, the Rights Plan will not have a severe impact upon proxy contests and it will not preclude all hostile acquisitions of Household. Therefore, the Directors were not misinformed or uninformed on these facts.

Appellants contend the Delaware counsel did not express an opinion on the flip-over provision of the Rights, rather only that the Rights would constitute validly issued and outstanding rights to subscribe to the preferred stock of the company.

To determine whether a business judgment reached by a board of directors was an informed one, we determine whether the directors were grossly negligent. *Smith v. Van Gorkom,* Del.Supr., 488 A.2d 858, 873 (1985). Upon a review of this record, we conclude the Directors were not grossly negligent. The information supplied to the Board on August 14 provided the essentials of the Plan. The Directors were given beforehand a notebook which included a three-page summary of the Plan along with articles on the current takeover environment. The extended discussion between the Board and representatives of Wachtell, Lipton and Goldman, Sachs before approval of the Plan reflected a full and candid evaluation of the Plan. Moran's expression of his views at the meeting served to place before the Board a knowledgeable critique of the Plan. The factual happenings here are clearly distinguishable from the actions of the directors of Trans Union Corporation who displayed gross negligence in approving a cash-out merger. *Id.*

In addition, to meet their burden, the Directors must show that the defensive mechanism was "reasonable in relation to the threat posed". The record reflects a concern on the part of the Directors over the increasing frequency in the financial services industry of "boot-strap" and "bust-up" takeovers. The Directors were also concerned that such takeovers may take the form of two-tier offers.[14] In addition, on August 14, the Household Board was aware of Moran's overture on behalf of D-K-M. In sum, the Directors reasonably believed Household was vulnerable to coercive acquisition techniques and adopted a reasonable defensive mechanism to protect itself.

V.

In conclusion, the Household Directors receive the benefit of the business judgment rule in their adoption of the Rights Plan.

The Directors adopted the Plan pursuant to statutory authority in 8 *Del.C.* §§ 141, 151, 157. We reject appellants' contentions that the Rights Plan strips stockholders of their rights to receive tender offers, and that the Rights Plan fundamentally restricts proxy contests.

The Directors adopted the Plan in the good faith belief that it was necessary to protect Household from coercive acquisition techniques. The Board was informed as to the details of the Plan. In addition, Household has demonstrated that the Plan is reasonable in relation to the threat posed. Appellants, on the other hand, have failed to convince us that the Directors breached any fiduciary duty in their adoption of the Rights Plan.

While we conclude for present purposes that the Household Directors are protected by the business judgment rule, that does not end the matter. The ultimate response to an actual takeover bid must be judged by the Directors' actions at that time, and nothing we say here relieves them of their basic fundamental duties to the corporation and its stockholders. *Unocal,* 493 A.2d at 954-55, 958; *Smith v. Van Gorkom,* 488 A.2d at 872-73; *Aronson,* 473 A.2d at 812-13; *Pogostin v. Rice,* Del.Supr., 480 A.2d 619, 627 (1984). Their use of the Plan will be evaluated when and if the issue arises.

* * *

AFFIRMED.

[...]

Discussion Questions:

1. What do you make of the Court's statutory interpretation exercise? Is there a potential political explanation for the Court's reading?

---

[14] We have discussed the coercive nature of two-tier tender offers in *Unocal,* 493 A.2d at 956, n. 12. We explained in *Unocal* that a discriminatory self-tender was reasonably related to the threat of two-tier tender offers and possible greenmail.

2. How does the Court apply the Unocal two-part test? (What is the threat, and is the response reasonable in relation to the threat posed?)

3. The Rights Plan that was at issue in Moran was a "flip-over" poison pill, which gave target shareholders (except the bidder) the right to buy shares of the bidder at a significantly discounted price. Modern poison pills typically have a flip-over feature and a "flip-in" feature, which gives target shareholders (except the bidder) the right to buy shares of the target company at a discounted price. Is the statutory authority for a flip-over pill any stronger or weaker than the statutory authority for a flip-in pill?

4. Today, poison pills often have bells and whistles: e.g., "chewable pills" (i.e., pills that disappear against a fully-financed high-premium offer), and "sunset pills" (i.e., pills that disappear after one year or longer, unless shareholders approve) are quite common today. Why do you think these kinds of pills are more popular with shareholders than plain-vanilla pills?

5. In the 1990s, transactional planners attempted to create more potent pills, such as "dead hand pills" (i.e., pills that could only be redeemed by the "continuing directors," defined as the directors who were then in office when the pill was installed or their approved successors) and "slow hand pills" (i.e., pills that could not be redeemed by anyone for a specified period of time, e.g., six months). What additional takeover protection do these pills provide that plain-vanilla pills do not? (And in view of your answer, what kinds of companies would particularly benefit from this protection?) These pills were invalidated under Delaware law in *Carmody v. Toll Brothers, Inc.*, 723 A.2d 1180 (Del. Ch. 1998) (invalidating dead hand pills) and *Mentor Graphics Corp. v. Quickturn Design Systems, Inc.*, 728 A.2d 25 (Del. Ch. 1998) (invalidating no hand pills), under *Unocal* proportionality analysis, and because these pills created distinctions between current and future directors (dead hand pills) and attempted to bind future boards (no hand pills). Dead hand and no hand pills continue to be valid in some other states, such as Georgia, Maryland, Pennsylvania, and Virginia.

Revlon, Inc. v. MacAndrews & Forbes Holdings, Inc.
506 A.2d 173 (1986)

MOORE, Justice:

In this battle for corporate control of Revlon, Inc. (Revlon), the Court of Chancery enjoined certain transactions designed to thwart the efforts of Pantry Pride, Inc. (Pantry Pride) to acquire Revlon. The defendants are Revlon, its board of directors, and Forstmann Little & Co. and the latter's affiliated limited partnership (collectively, Forstmann). The injunction barred consummation of an option granted Forstmann to purchase certain Revlon assets (the lockup option), a promise by Revlon to deal exclusively with Forstmann in the face of a takeover (the no-shop provision), and the payment of a $25 million cancellation fee to

Forstmann if the transaction was aborted. The Court of Chancery found that the Revlon directors had breached their duty of care by entering into the foregoing transactions and effectively ending an active auction for the company. The trial court ruled that such arrangements are not illegal *per se* under Delaware law, but that their use under the circumstances here was impermissible. We agree. *See MacAndrews & Forbes Holdings, Inc. v. Revlon, Inc.,* Del. Ch., 501 A.2d 1239 (1985). Thus, we granted this expedited interlocutory appeal to consider for the first time the validity of such defensive measures in the face of an active bidding contest for corporate control. Additionally, we address for the first time the extent to which a corporation may consider the impact of a takeover threat on constituencies other than shareholders. *See Unocal Corp. v. Mesa Petroleum Co.,* Del.Supr., 493 A.2d 946, 955 (1985).

In our view, lock-ups and related agreements are permitted under Delaware law where their adoption is untainted by director interest or other breaches of fiduciary duty. The actions taken by the Revlon directors, however, did not meet this standard. Moreover, while concern for various corporate constituencies is proper when addressing a takeover threat, that principle is limited by the requirement that there be some rationally related benefit accruing to the stockholders. We find no such benefit here.

Thus, under all the circumstances we must agree with the Court of Chancery that the enjoined Revlon defensive measures were inconsistent with the directors' duties to the stockholders. Accordingly, we affirm.

I.

The somewhat complex maneuvers of the parties necessitate a rather detailed examination of the facts. The prelude to this controversy began in June 1985, when Ronald O. Perelman, chairman of the board and chief executive officer of Pantry Pride, met with his counterpart at Revlon, Michel C. Bergerac, to discuss a friendly acquisition of Revlon by Pantry Pride. Perelman suggested a price in the range of $40-50 per share, but the meeting ended with Bergerac dismissing those figures as considerably below Revlon's intrinsic value. All subsequent Pantry Pride overtures were rebuffed, perhaps in part based on Mr. Bergerac's strong personal antipathy to Mr. Perelman.

Thus, on August 14, Pantry Pride's board authorized Perelman to acquire Revlon, either through negotiation in the $42-$43 per share range, or by making a hostile tender offer at $45. Perelman then met with Bergerac and outlined Pantry Pride's alternate approaches. Bergerac remained adamantly opposed to such schemes and conditioned any further discussions of the matter on Pantry Pride executing a standstill agreement prohibiting it from acquiring Revlon without the latter's prior approval.

On August 19, the Revlon board met specially to consider the impending threat of a hostile bid by Pantry Pride. At the meeting, Lazard Freres, Revlon's investment banker, advised the directors that $45 per share was a grossly inadequate price for the company. Felix Rohatyn and William Loomis of Lazard Freres explained to the board that Pantry Pride's financial strategy for acquiring Revlon would be through "junk bond" financing followed by a break-up of Revlon and the disposition of its assets. With proper timing, according to the experts, such transactions could produce a return to Pantry Pride of $60 to $70 per share, while a sale of the company as a whole would be in the "mid 50" dollar range. Martin Lipton, special counsel for Revlon, recommended two defensive measures: first, that the company repurchase up to 5 million of its nearly 30 million outstanding shares; and second, that it adopt a Note Purchase Rights Plan. Under this plan, each Revlon shareholder would receive as a dividend one Note Purchase Right (the Rights) for each share of common stock, with the Rights entitling the holder to exchange one common share for a $65 principal Revlon note at 12% interest with a one-year maturity. The Rights would become effective whenever anyone acquired beneficial ownership of 20% or more of Revlon's shares, unless the purchaser acquired all the company's stock for cash at $65 or more per share. In addition, the Rights would not be available to the acquiror, and prior to the 20% triggering event the Revlon board could redeem the rights for 10 cents each. Both proposals were unanimously adopted.

Pantry Pride made its first hostile move on August 23 with a cash tender offer for any and all shares of Revlon at $47.50 per common share and $26.67 per preferred share, subject to (1) Pantry Pride's obtaining financing for the purchase, and (2) the Rights being redeemed, rescinded or voided.

The Revlon board met again on August 26. The directors advised the stockholders to reject the offer. Further defensive measures also were planned. On August 29, Revlon commenced its own offer for up to 10 million shares, exchanging for each share of common stock tendered one Senior Subordinated Note (the Notes) of $47.50 principal at 11.75% interest, due 1995, and one-tenth of a share of $9.00 Cumulative Convertible Exchangeable Preferred Stock valued at $100 per share. Lazard Freres opined that the notes would trade at their face value on a fully distributed basis. Revlon stockholders tendered 87 percent of the outstanding shares (approximately 33 million), and the company accepted the full 10 million shares on a pro rata basis. The new Notes contained covenants which limited Revlon's ability to incur additional debt, sell assets, or pay dividends unless otherwise approved by the "independent" (nonmanagement) members of the board.

At this point, both the Rights and the Note covenants stymied Pantry Pride's attempted takeover. The next move came on September 16, when Pantry Pride announced a new tender offer at $42 per share, conditioned upon receiving at least 90% of the outstanding stock. Pantry Pride also indicated that it would consider buying less than 90%, and at an increased price, if Revlon removed the impeding Rights. While this offer was lower on its face than the earlier $47.50 proposal, Revlon's investment banker, Lazard Freres, described the two bids as essentially equal in view of the completed exchange offer.

The Revlon board held a regularly scheduled meeting on September 24. The directors rejected the latest Pantry Pride offer and authorized management to negotiate with other parties interested in acquiring Revlon. Pantry Pride remained determined in its efforts and continued to make cash bids for the company, offering $50 per share on September 27, and raising its bid to $53 on October 1, and then to $56.25 on October 7.

In the meantime, Revlon's negotiations with Forstmann and the investment group Adler & Shaykin had produced results. The Revlon directors met on October 3 to consider Pantry Pride's $53 bid and to examine possible alternatives to the offer. Both Forstmann and Adler & Shaykin made certain proposals to the board. As a result, the directors unanimously agreed to a leveraged buyout by Forstmann. The terms of this accord were as follows: each stockholder would get $56 cash per share; management would purchase stock in the new company by the exercise of their Revlon "golden parachutes";[5] Forstmann would assume Revlon's $475 million debt incurred by the issuance of the Notes; and Revlon would redeem the Rights and waive the Notes covenants for Forstmann or in connection with any other offer superior to Forstmann's. The board did not actually remove the covenants at the October 3 meeting, because Forstmann then lacked a firm commitment on its financing, but accepted the Forstmann capital structure, and indicated that the outside directors would waive the covenants in due course. Part of Forstmann's plan was to sell Revlon's Norcliff Thayer and Reheis divisions to American Home Products for $335 million. Before the merger, Revlon was to sell its cosmetics and fragrance division to Adler & Shaykin for $905 million. These transactions would facilitate the purchase by Forstmann or any other acquiror of Revlon.

When the merger, and thus the waiver of the Notes covenants, was announced, the market value of these securities began to fall. The Notes, which originally traded near par, around 100, dropped to 87.50 by October 8. One director later reported (at the October 12 meeting) a "deluge" of telephone calls from irate noteholders, and on October 10 the Wall Street Journal reported threats of litigation by these creditors.

Pantry Pride countered with a new proposal on October 7, raising its $53 offer to $56.25, subject to nullification of the Rights, a waiver of the Notes covenants, and the election of three Pantry Pride directors to the Revlon board. On October 9, representatives of Pantry Pride, Forstmann and Revlon conferred in an attempt to negotiate the fate of Revlon, but could not reach agreement. At this meeting Pantry Pride announced that it would engage in fractional bidding and top any Forstmann offer by a slightly higher one. It is also significant that Forstmann, to Pantry Pride's exclusion, had been made privy to certain Revlon financial data. Thus, the parties were not negotiating on equal terms.

Again privately armed with Revlon data, Forstmann met on October 11 with Revlon's special counsel and investment banker. On October 12, Forstmann made a new $57.25 per share offer, based on several conditions.[6] The principal demand was a lock-up option to purchase Revlon's Vision Care and National Health Laboratories divisions for $525 million,

---

[5] In the takeover context "golden parachutes" generally are understood to be termination agreements providing substantial bonuses and other benefits for managers and certain directors upon a change in control of a company.

[6] Forstmann's $57.25 offer ostensibly is worth $1 more than Pantry Pride's $56.25 bid. However, the Pantry Pride offer was immediate, while the Forstmann proposal must be discounted for the time value of money because of the delay in approving the merger and consummating the transaction. The exact difference between the two bids was an unsettled point of contention even at oral argument.

some $100-$175 million below the value ascribed to them by Lazard Freres, if another acquiror got 40% of Revlon's shares. Revlon also was required to accept a no-shop provision. The Rights and Notes covenants had to be removed as in the October 3 agreement. There would be a $25 million cancellation fee to be placed in escrow, and released to Forstmann if the new agreement terminated or if another acquiror got more than 19.9% of Revlon's stock. Finally, there would be no participation by Revlon management in the merger. In return, Forstmann agreed to support the par value of the Notes, which had faltered in the market, by an exchange of new notes. Forstmann also demanded immediate acceptance of its offer, or it would be withdrawn. The board unanimously approved Forstmann's proposal because: (1) it was for a higher price than the Pantry Pride bid, (2) it protected the noteholders, and (3) Forstmann's financing was firmly in place.[7] The board further agreed to redeem the rights and waive the covenants on the preferred stock in response to any offer above $57 cash per share. The covenants were waived, contingent upon receipt of an investment banking opinion that the Notes would trade near par value once the offer was consummated.

Pantry Pride, which had initially sought injunctive relief from the Rights plan on August 22, filed an amended complaint on October 14 challenging the lock-up, the cancellation fee, and the exercise of the Rights and the Notes covenants. Pantry Pride also sought a temporary restraining order to prevent Revlon from placing any assets in escrow or transferring them to Forstmann. Moreover, on October 22, Pantry Pride again raised its bid, with a cash offer of $58 per share conditioned upon nullification of the Rights, waiver of the covenants, and an injunction of the Forstmann lock-up.

On October 15, the Court of Chancery prohibited the further transfer of assets, and eight days later enjoined the lock-up, no-shop, and cancellation fee provisions of the agreement. The trial court concluded that the Revlon directors had breached their duty of loyalty by making concessions to Forstmann, out of concern for their liability to the noteholders, rather than maximizing the sale price of the company for the stockholders' benefit. *MacAndrews & Forbes Holdings, Inc. v. Revlon, Inc.,* 501 A.2d at 1249-50.

II.

To obtain a preliminary injunction, a plaintiff must demonstrate both a reasonable probability of success on the merits and some irreparable harm which will occur absent the injunction. *Gimbel v. Signal Companies,* Del.Ch., 316 A.2d 599, 602 (1974), *aff'd,* Del.Supr., 316 A.2d 619 (1974). Additionally, the Court shall balance the conveniences of and possible injuries to the parties. *Id.*

---

[7] Actually, at this time about $400 million of Forstmann's funding was still subject to two investment banks using their "best efforts" to organize a syndicate to provide the balance. Pantry Pride's entire financing was not firmly committed at this point either, although Pantry Pride represented in an October 11 letter to Lazard Freres that its investment banker, Drexel Burnham Lambert, was highly confident of its ability to raise the balance of $350 million. Drexel Burnham had a firm commitment for this sum by October 18.

A.

We turn first to Pantry Pride's probability of success on the merits. The ultimate responsibility for managing the business and affairs of a corporation falls on its board of directors. 8 *Del.C.* § 141(a). In discharging this function the directors owe fiduciary duties of care and loyalty to the corporation and its shareholders. *Guth v. Loft, Inc.,* 23 Del.Supr. 255, 5 A.2d 503, 510 (1939); *Aronson v. Lewis,* Del.Supr., 473 A.2d 805, 811 (1984). These principles apply with equal force when a board approves a corporate merger pursuant to 8 *Del.C.* § 251(b); *Smith v. Van Gorkom,* Del.Supr., 488 A.2d 858, 873 (1985); and of course they are the bedrock of our law regarding corporate takeover issues. *Pogostin v. Rice,* Del.Supr., 480 A.2d 619, 624 (1984); *Unocal Corp. v. Mesa Petroleum Co.,* Del.Supr., 493 A.2d 946, 953, 955 (1985); *Moran v. Household International, Inc.,* Del.Supr., 500 A.2d 1346, 1350 (1985). While the business judgment rule may be applicable to the actions of corporate directors responding to takeover threats, the principles upon which it is founded—care, loyalty and independence—must first be satisfied. *Aronson v. Lewis,* 473 A.2d at 812.

If the business judgment rule applies, there is a "presumption that in making a business decision the directors of a corporation acted on an informed basis, in good faith and in the honest belief that the action taken was in the best interests of the company." *Aronson v. Lewis,* 473 A.2d at 812. However, when a board implements anti-takeover measures there arises "the omnipresent specter that a board may be acting primarily in its own interests, rather than those of the corporation and its shareholders ..." *Unocal Corp. v. Mesa Petroleum Co.,* 493 A.2d at 954. This potential for conflict places upon the directors the burden of proving that they had reasonable grounds for believing there was a danger to corporate policy and effectiveness, a burden satisfied by a showing of good faith and reasonable investigation. *Id.* at 955. In addition, the directors must analyze the nature of the takeover and its effect on the corporation in order to ensure balance—that the responsive action taken is reasonable in relation to the threat posed. *Id.*

B.

The first relevant defensive measure adopted by the Revlon board was the Rights Plan, which would be considered a "poison pill" in the current language of corporate takeovers— a plan by which shareholders receive the right to be bought out by the corporation at a substantial premium on the occurrence of a stated triggering event. *See generally Moran v. Household International, Inc.,* Del.Supr., 500 A.2d 1346 (1985). By 8 *Del.C.* §§ 141 and 122(13), the board clearly had the power to adopt the measure. *See Moran v. Household International, Inc.,* 500 A.2d at 1351. Thus, the focus becomes one of reasonableness and purpose.

The Revlon board approved the Rights Plan in the face of an impending hostile takeover bid by Pantry Pride at $45 per share, a price which Revlon reasonably concluded was grossly inadequate. Lazard Freres had so advised the directors, and had also informed them that Pantry Pride was a small, highly leveraged company bent on a "bust-up" takeover by using "junk bond" financing to buy Revlon cheaply, sell the acquired assets to pay the debts incurred, and retain the profit for itself.[12] In adopting the Plan, the board protected the shareholders from a hostile takeover at a price below the company's intrinsic value, while retaining sufficient flexibility to address any proposal deemed to be in the stockholders' best interests.

To that extent the board acted in good faith and upon reasonable investigation. Under the circumstances it cannot be said that the Rights Plan as employed was unreasonable, considering the threat posed. Indeed, the Plan was a factor in causing Pantry Pride to raise its bids from a low of $42 to an eventual high of $58. At the time of its adoption the Rights Plan afforded a measure of protection consistent with the directors' fiduciary duty in facing a takeover threat perceived as detrimental to corporate interests. *Unocal*, 493 A.2d at 954-55. Far from being a "show-stopper," as the plaintiffs had contended in *Moran*, the measure spurred the bidding to new heights, a proper result of its implementation. *See Moran*, 500 A.2d at 1354, 1356-67.

Although we consider adoption of the Plan to have been valid under the circumstances, its continued usefulness was rendered moot by the directors' actions on October 3 and October 12. At the October 3 meeting the board redeemed the Rights conditioned upon consummation of a merger with Forstmann, but further acknowledged that they would also be redeemed to facilitate any more favorable offer. On October 12, the board unanimously passed a resolution redeeming the Rights in connection with any cash proposal of $57.25 or more per share. Because all the pertinent offers eventually equalled or surpassed that amount, the Rights clearly were no longer any impediment in the contest for Revlon. This mooted any question of their propriety under *Moran* or *Unocal*.

C.

The second defensive measure adopted by Revlon to thwart a Pantry Pride takeover was the company's own exchange offer for 10 million of its shares. The directors' general broad powers to manage the business and affairs of the corporation are augmented by the specific authority conferred under 8 *Del.C.* § 160(a), permitting the company to deal in its own stock. *Unocal*, 493 A.2d at 953-54; *Cheff v. Mathes*, 41 Del.Supr. 494, 199 A.2d 548, 554 (1964); *Kors v. Carey*, 39 Del.Ch. 47, 158 A.2d 136, 140 (1960). However, when exercising that power in an effort to forestall a hostile takeover, the board's actions are strictly held to the fiduciary standards outlined in *Unocal*. These standards require the directors to determine the best interests of the corporation and its stockholders, and impose an enhanced duty to abjure any action that is motivated by considerations other than a good faith concern for such interests. *Unocal*, 493 A.2d at 954-55; *see Bennett v. Propp*, 41 Del.Supr. 14, 187 A.2d 405, 409 (1962).

The Revlon directors concluded that Pantry Pride's $47.50 offer was grossly inadequate. In that regard the board acted in good faith, and on an informed basis, with reasonable

---

[12] As we noted in *Moran*, a "bust-up" takeover generally refers to a situation in which one seeks to finance an acquisition by selling off pieces of the acquired company, presumably at a substantial profit. *See Moran*, 500 A.2d at 1349, n. 4.

grounds to believe that there existed a harmful threat to the corporate enterprise. The adoption of a defensive measure, reasonable in relation to the threat posed, was proper and fully accorded with the powers, duties, and responsibilities conferred upon directors under our law. *Unocal,* 493 A.2d at 954; *Pogostin v. Rice,* 480 A.2d at 627.

D.

However, when Pantry Pride increased its offer to $50 per share, and then to $53, it became apparent to all that the break-up of the company was inevitable. The Revlon board's authorization permitting management to negotiate a merger or buyout with a third party was a recognition that the company was for sale. The duty of the board had thus changed from the preservation of Revlon as a corporate entity to the maximization of the company's value at a sale for the stockholders' benefit. This significantly altered the board's responsibilities under the *Unocal* standards. It no longer faced threats to corporate policy and effectiveness, or to the stockholders' interests, from a grossly inadequate bid. The whole question of defensive measures became moot. The directors' role changed from defenders of the corporate bastion to auctioneers charged with getting the best price for the stockholders at a sale of the company.

III.

This brings us to the lock-up with Forstmann and its emphasis on shoring up the sagging market value of the Notes in the face of threatened litigation by their holders. Such a focus was inconsistent with the changed concept of the directors' responsibilities at this stage of the developments. The impending waiver of the Notes covenants had caused the value of the Notes to fall, and the board was aware of the noteholders' ire as well as their subsequent threats of suit. The directors thus made support of the Notes an integral part of the company's dealings with Forstmann, even though their primary responsibility at this stage was to the equity owners.

The original threat posed by Pantry Pride—the break-up of the company—had become a reality which even the directors embraced. Selective dealing to fend off a hostile but determined bidder was no longer a proper objective. Instead, obtaining the highest price for the benefit of the stockholders should have been the central theme guiding director action. Thus, the Revlon board could not make the requisite showing of good faith by preferring the noteholders and ignoring its duty of loyalty to the shareholders. The rights of the former already were fixed by contract. *Wolfensohn v. Madison Fund, Inc.,* Del.Supr., 253 A.2d 72, 75 (1969); *Harff v. Kerkorian,* Del.Ch., 324 A.2d 215 (1974). The noteholders required no further protection, and when the Revlon board entered into an auction-ending lock-up agreement with Forstmann on the basis of impermissible considerations at the expense of the shareholders, the directors breached their primary duty of loyalty.

The Revlon board argued that it acted in good faith in protecting the noteholders because *Unocal* permits consideration of other corporate constituencies. Although such considerations may be permissible, there are fundamental limitations upon that prerogative. A board may have regard for various constituencies in discharging its responsibilities, provided there are rationally related benefits accruing to the stockholders. *Unocal*, 493 A.2d at 955. However, such concern for non-stockholder interests is inappropriate when an auction among active bidders is in progress, and the object no longer is to protect or maintain the corporate enterprise but to sell it to the highest bidder.

Revlon also contended that by *Gilbert v. El Paso Co.*, Del. Ch., 490 A.2d 1050, 1054-55 (1984), it had contractual and good faith obligations to consider the noteholders. However, any such duties are limited to the principle that one may not interfere with contractual relationships by improper actions. Here, the rights of the noteholders were fixed by agreement, and there is nothing of substance to suggest that any of those terms were violated. The Notes covenants specifically contemplated a waiver to permit sale of the company at a fair price. The Notes were accepted by the holders on that basis, including the risk of an adverse market effect stemming from a waiver. Thus, nothing remained for Revlon to legitimately protect, and no rationally related benefit thereby accrued to the stockholders. Under such circumstances we must conclude that the merger agreement with Forstmann was unreasonable in relation to the threat posed.

A lock-up is not *per se* illegal under Delaware law. Its use has been approved in an earlier case. *Thompson v. Enstar Corp.*, Del. Ch., __ A.2d __ (1984). Such options can entice other bidders to enter a contest for control of the corporation, creating an auction for the company and maximizing shareholder profit. Current economic conditions in the takeover market are such that a "white knight" like Forstmann might only enter the bidding for the target company if it receives some form of compensation to cover the risks and costs involved. Note, *Corporations-Mergers—"Lock-up" Enjoined Under Section 14(e) of Securities Exchange Act—Mobil Corp. v. Marathon Oil Co., 669 F.2d 366 (6th Cir.1981)*, 12 Seton Hall L.Rev. 881, 892 (1982). However, while those lock-ups which draw bidders into the battle benefit shareholders, similar measures which end an active auction and foreclose further bidding operate to the shareholders' detriment. Note, *Lock-up Options: Toward a State Law Standard,* 96 Harv. L. Rev. 1068, 1081 (1983).

Recently, the United States Court of Appeals for the Second Circuit invalidated a lock-up on fiduciary duty grounds similar to those here. *Hanson Trust PLC, et al. v. ML SCM Acquisition Inc., et al.,* 781 F.2d 264 (2nd Cir.1986). Citing *Thompson v. Enstar Corp., supra,* with approval, the court stated:

> In this regard, we are especially mindful that some lock-up options may be beneficial to the shareholders, such as those that induce a bidder to compete for control of a corporation, while others may be harmful, such as those that effectively preclude bidders from competing with the optionee bidder. 781 F.2d at 274.

In *Hanson Trust,* the bidder, Hanson, sought control of SCM by a hostile cash tender offer. SCM management joined with Merrill Lynch to propose a leveraged buy-out of the company at a higher price, and Hanson in turn increased its offer. Then, despite very little improvement in its subsequent bid, the management group sought a lock-up option to purchase SCM's two main assets at a substantial discount. The SCM directors granted the lock-up without adequate information as to the size of the discount or the effect the transaction would have on the company. Their action effectively ended a competitive bidding situation. The Hanson Court invalidated the lock-up because the directors failed to fully inform themselves about the value of a transaction in which management had a strong self-interest. "In short, the Board appears to have failed to ensure that negotiations for alternative bids were conducted by those whose only loyalty was to the shareholders." *Id.* at 277.

The Forstmann option had a similar destructive effect on the auction process. Forstmann had already been drawn into the contest on a preferred basis, so the result of the lock-up was not to foster bidding, but to destroy it. The board's stated reasons for approving the transactions were: (1) better financing, (2) noteholder protection, and (3) higher price. As the Court of Chancery found, and we agree, any distinctions between the rival bidders' methods of financing the proposal were nominal at best, and such a consideration has little or no significance in a cash offer for any and all shares. The principal object, contrary to the board's duty of care, appears to have been protection of the noteholders over the shareholders' interests.

While Forstmann's $57.25 offer was objectively higher than Pantry Pride's $56.25 bid, the margin of superiority is less when the Forstmann price is adjusted for the time value of money. In reality, the Revlon board ended the auction in return for very little actual improvement in the final bid. The principal benefit went to the directors, who avoided personal liability to a class of creditors to whom the board owed no further duty under the circumstances. Thus, when a board ends an intense bidding contest on an insubstantial basis, and where a significant by-product of that action is to protect the directors against a perceived threat of personal liability for consequences stemming from the adoption of previous defensive measures, the action cannot withstand the enhanced scrutiny which *Unocal* requires of director conduct. *See Unocal,* 493 A.2d at 954-55.

In addition to the lock-up option, the Court of Chancery enjoined the no-shop provision as part of the attempt to foreclose further bidding by Pantry Pride. *MacAndrews & Forbes Holdings, Inc. v. Revlon, Inc.,* 501 A.2d at 1251. The no-shop provision, like the lock-up option, while not *per se* illegal, is impermissible under the *Unocal* standards when a board's primary duty becomes that of an auctioneer responsible for selling the company to the highest bidder. The agreement to negotiate only with Forstmann ended rather than intensified the board's involvement in the bidding contest.

It is ironic that the parties even considered a no-shop agreement when Revlon had dealt preferentially, and almost exclusively, with Forstmann throughout the contest. After the directors authorized management to negotiate with other parties, Forstmann was given every negotiating advantage that Pantry Pride had been denied: cooperation from management, access to financial data, and the exclusive opportunity to present merger proposals directly to the board of directors. Favoritism for a white knight to the total exclusion of a hostile bidder might be justifiable when the latter's offer adversely affects shareholder interests, but when bidders make relatively similar offers, or dissolution of the company becomes inevitable, the directors cannot fulfill their enhanced *Unocal* duties by playing favorites with the contending factions. Market forces must be allowed to operate freely to bring the target's shareholders the best price available for their equity.[16] Thus, as the trial court ruled, the shareholders' interests necessitated that the board remain free to negotiate in the fulfillment of that duty.

The court below similarly enjoined the payment of the cancellation fee, pending a resolution of the merits, because the fee was part of the overall plan to thwart Pantry Pride's efforts. We find no abuse of discretion in that ruling.

IV.

Having concluded that Pantry Pride has shown a reasonable probability of success on the merits, we address the issue of irreparable harm. The Court of Chancery ruled that unless the lock-up and other aspects of the agreement were enjoined, Pantry Pride's opportunity to bid for Revlon was lost. The court also held that the need for both bidders to compete in the marketplace outweighed any injury to Forstmann. Given the complexity of the proposed transaction between Revlon and Forstmann, the obstacles to Pantry Pride obtaining a meaningful legal remedy are immense. We are satisfied that the plaintiff has shown the need for an injunction to protect it from irreparable harm, which need outweighs any harm to the defendants.

V.

In conclusion, the Revlon board was confronted with a situation not uncommon in the current wave of corporate takeovers. A hostile and determined bidder sought the company at a price the board was convinced was inadequate. The initial defensive tactics worked to the benefit of the shareholders, and thus the board was able to sustain its *Unocal* burdens in justifying those measures. However, in granting an asset option lock-up to Forstmann, we must conclude that under all the circumstances the directors allowed considerations other than the maximization of shareholder profit to affect their judgment, and followed a course that ended the auction for Revlon, absent court intervention, to the ultimate detriment of its shareholders. No such defensive measure can be sustained when it represents a breach of the directors' fundamental duty of care. *See Smith v. Van Gorkom*, Del.Supr., 488 A.2d 858, 874 (1985). In that context the board's action is not entitled to the deference accorded it by the business judgment rule. The measures were properly enjoined. The decision of the Court of Chancery, therefore, is

AFFIRMED.

[...]

---

[16] By this we do not embrace the "passivity" thesis rejected in *Unocal. See* 493 A.2d at 954-55, nn. 8-10. The directors' role remains an active one, changed only in the respect that they are charged with the duty of selling the company at the highest price attainable for the stockholders' benefit.

Discussion Questions:

1. According to the Delaware Supreme Court, what should the Revlon board have done when faced with the competing offers from Ted Forstmann and Ron Perelman?

2. Compare these divergent viewpoints on the wisdom of so-called "Revlon duties," from two of the most prominent corporate law practitioners in the modern era of corporations:[22]

   > *Joe Flom, former Managing Partner, Skadden, Arps, Slate, Meagher & Flom*: "I'm comfortable with *Revlon*. The way I look at it is very simple. If you're selling the company, you've got to make sure that the premium is realized for your shareholders, because they're not going to have another chance. So you have to adopt a process, and your judgment is completely critical as to how you're going to structure it to try to get the best price."

   > *Martin Lipton, Managing Partner, Wachtell, Lipton, Rosen & Katz*: "The ability to bring somebody into a situation is far more important than the extra dollar a share at the back end. In other words, at the front end you're probably talking about 50%. At the back end you're talking about one or two percent. By saying that you have to be open to the last dollar at the back end, maybe you'd better not start on the front end. And to me that's the key to all of this. That's what I argued in *Revlon*. Remember, though, I lost *Revlon*, so I'm prejudiced."

   Do Flom and Lipton accurately characterize what *Revlon* means? Which, if either, do you agree with?

3. Lipton's comment foreshadows a broader concern with the "free-rider" problem introduced in *Revlon*. This concern was illustrated by commentary from Stephen Fraidin who at the time was Forstmann Little's lawyer:

   > I was involved in the *Revlon* case—I represented Forstmann Little. At one point there was a negotiation between the parties to try to settle the situation, and my client tells Perelman, 'We have a big advantage—we have confidential information, you don't have any. We know what to bid and you do not.' Perelman, who is a smart man, said, 'Actually, I have even better information than you have because I know what you're bidding. And once I know what you're bidding and I know how smart you are and I know that you have all the confidential information, I know I can bid a nickel more and still have a good deal.' And he was absolutely right.

---

[22] Quoted in Guhan Subramanian, *The Drivers of Market Efficiency in Revlon Transactions*, 28 J. Corp. L. 691 (2000).

If Perelman's tactic (known as "incremental bidding") became pervasive, what implications would it have for the wisdom of Revlon duties, and for the takeover marketplace overall? (In law & economics terms, if Revlon seeks to achieve *ex post* allocational efficiency, what might it do for *ex ante* incentives?)

In the aftermath of *Revlon*, some practitioners expressed concern that the decision would require a full-blown, put-out-the-gavel auction in the sale of a company. Subsequent Delaware case law clarified that there is no "single blueprint" for achieving the highest price for shareholders. *See, e.g., In C&J Energy Services, Inc. v. City of Miami General Employees' and Sanitation Employees' Retirement Trust*, 107 A.3d 1049 (Del. 2014). The following case provides a significant articulation of what *Revlon* does (and does not) require.

Lyondell Chemical Co. v. Ryan
970 A.2d 235 (Del. 2009)

BERGER, Justice.

We accepted this interlocutory appeal to consider a claim that directors failed to act in good faith in conducting the sale of their company. The Court of Chancery [on defendants' motion for summary judgment] decided that "unexplained inaction" permits a reasonable inference that the directors may have consciously disregarded their fiduciary duties [thus requiring a trial of the issue]. The trial court expressed concern about the speed with which the transaction was consummated; the directors' failure to negotiate better terms; and their failure to seek potentially superior deals. But the record establishes that the directors were disinterested and independent; that they were generally aware of the company's value and its prospects; and that they considered the offer, under the time constraints imposed by the buyer, with the assistance of financial and legal advisors. At most, this record creates a triable issue of fact on the question of whether the directors exercised due care. There is no evidence, however, from which to infer that the directors knowingly ignored their responsibilities, thereby breaching their duty of loyalty. Accordingly, [since the company has a waiver provision of the kind authorized by §102(b)(7) of the DGCL] the directors are entitled to the entry of summary judgment.

FACTUAL AND PROCEDURAL BACKGROUND

Before the merger at issue, Lyondell Chemical Company ("Lyondell") was the third largest independent, publicly traded chemical company in North America. Dan Smith ("Smith") was Lyondell's Chairman and CEO. Lyondell's other ten directors were independent and many were, or had been, CEOs of other large, publicly traded companies. Basell AF ("Basell") is a privately held Luxembourg company owned by Leonard Blavatnik ("Blavatnik") through his ownership of Access Industries. Basell is in the business of polyolefin technology, production and marketing.

In April 2006, Blavatnik told Smith that Basell was interested in acquiring Lyondell. A few months later, Basell sent a letter to Lyondell's board offering $26.50-$28.50 per share. Lyondell determined that the price was inadequate and that it was not interested in selling. During the next year, Lyondell prospered and no potential acquirors expressed interest in the company. In May 2007, an Access affiliate filed a Schedule 13D with the Securities and Exchange Commission disclosing its right to acquire an 8.3% block of Lyondell stock owned by Occidental Petroleum Corporation. The Schedule 13D also disclosed Blavatnik's interest in possible transactions with Lyondell.

In response to the Schedule 13D, the Lyondell board immediately convened a special meeting. The board recognized that the 13D signaled to the market that the company was "in play," but the directors decided to take a "wait and see" approach. A few days later, Apollo Management, L.P. contacted Smith to suggest a management-led LBO, but Smith rejected that proposal. In late June 2007, Basell announced that it had entered into a $9.6 billion merger agreement with Huntsman Corporation ("Huntsman"), a specialty chemical company. Basell apparently reconsidered, however, after Hexion Specialty Chemicals, Inc. made a topping bid for Huntsman. Faced with competition for Huntsman, Blavatnik returned his attention to Lyondell.

On July 9, 2007, Blavatnik met with Smith to discuss an all-cash deal at $40 per share. Smith responded that $40 was too low, and Blavatnik raised his offer to $44-$45 per share. Smith told Blavatnik that he would present the proposal to the board, but that he thought the board would reject it. Smith advised Blavatnik to give Lyondell his best offer, since Lyondell really was not on the market. The meeting ended at that point, but Blavatnik asked Smith to call him later in the day. When Smith called, Blavatnik offered to pay $48 per share. Under Blavatnik's proposal, Basell would require no financing contingency, but Lyondell would have to agree to a $400 million break-up fee and sign a merger agreement by July 16, 2007.

Smith called a special meeting of the Lyondell board on July 10, 2007 to review and consider Basell's offer. The meeting lasted slightly less than one hour, during which time the board reviewed valuation material that had been prepared by Lyondell management for presentation at the regular board meeting, which was scheduled for the following day. The board also discussed the Basell offer, the status of the Huntsman merger, and the likelihood that another party might be interested in Lyondell. The board instructed Smith to obtain a written offer from Basell and more details about Basell's financing.

Blavatnik agreed to the board's request, but also made an additional demand. Basell had until July 11 to make a higher bid for Huntsman, so Blavatnik asked Smith to find out whether the Lyondell board would provide a firm indication of interest in his proposal by the end of that day. The Lyondell board met on July 11, again for less than one hour, to consider the Basell proposal and how it compared to the benefits of remaining independent. The board decided that it was interested, authorized the retention of Deutsche Bank Securities, Inc. ("Deutsche Bank") as its financial advisor, and instructed Smith to negotiate with Blavatnik.

Basell then announced that it would not raise its offer for Huntsman, and Huntsman terminated the Basell merger agreement. From July 12-July 15 the parties negotiated the terms of a Lyondell merger agreement; Basell conducted due diligence; Deutsche Bank prepared a "fairness" opinion; and Lyondell conducted its regularly scheduled board meeting. The Lyondell board discussed the Basell proposal again on July 12, and later instructed Smith to try to negotiate better terms. Specifically, the board wanted a higher price, a go-shop provision, and a reduced break-up fee. As the trial court noted, Blavatnik was "incredulous." He had offered his best price, which was a substantial premium, and the deal had to be concluded on his schedule. As a sign of good faith, however, Blavatnik agreed to reduce the break-up fee from $400 million to $385 million.

On July 16, 2007, the board met to consider the Basell merger agreement. Lyondell's management, as well as its financial and legal advisers, presented reports analyzing the merits of the deal. The advisors explained that, notwithstanding the no-shop provision in the merger agreement, Lyondell would be able to consider any superior proposals that might be made because of the "fiduciary out" provision. In addition, Deutsche Bank reviewed valuation models derived from "bullish" and more conservative financial projections. Several of those valuations yielded a range that did not even reach $48 per share, and Deutsche Bank opined that the proposed merger price was fair. . . . Deutsche Bank also identified other possible acquirors and explained why it believed no other entity would top Basell's offer. After considering the presentations, the Lyondell board voted to approve the merger and recommend it to the stockholders. At a special stockholders' meeting held on November 20, 2007, the merger was approved by more than 99% of the voted shares.

***

[Walter E. Ryan, Jr. filed suit in Delaware on August 20, 2007. The claims he asserted are summarized by the court below. Defendants moved for summary judgment and on July 29, 2008 the Court of Chancery issued its opinion denying summary judgment as to the *Revlon* and deal protection claims, holding that the facts as alleged allowed room for a possible finding at trial that the Lyondell directors had violated their duty of loyalty by not acting in "good faith." The Delaware Supreme Court accepted an application for interlocutory appeal on September 15, 2008.]

DISCUSSION

The class action complaint challenging this $13 billion cash merger alleges that the Lyondell directors breached their "fiduciary duties of care, loyalty and candor . . . and . . . put their personal interests ahead of the interests of the Lyondell shareholders." Specifically, the complaint alleges that: 1) the merger price was grossly insufficient; 2) the directors were motivated to approve the merger for their own self-interest; 3) the process by which the merger was negotiated was flawed; 4) the directors agreed to unreasonable deal protection provisions; and 5) the preliminary proxy statement omitted numerous material facts. The trial court rejected all claims except those directed at the process by which the directors sold the company and the deal protection provisions in the merger agreement.

The remaining claims are but two aspects of a single claim, under *Revlon v. MacAndrews & Forbes Holdings, Inc.*, that the directors failed to obtain the best available price in selling the company. As the trial court correctly noted, *Revlon* did not create any new fiduciary duties. It simply held that the "board must perform its fiduciary duties in the service of a specific objective: maximizing the sale price of the enterprise." The trial court reviewed the record, and found that Ryan might be able to prevail at trial on a claim that the Lyondell directors breached their duty of care. But Lyondell's charter includes an exculpatory provision, pursuant to 8 Del. C. §102(b)(7), protecting the directors from personal liability for breaches of the duty of care. Thus, this case turns on whether any arguable short comings on the part of the Lyondell directors also implicate their duty of loyalty, a breach of which is not exculpated. Because the trial court determined that the board was independent and was not motivated by self-interest or ill will, the sole issue is whether the directors are entitled to summary judgment on the claim that they breached their duty of loyalty by failing to act in good faith.

This Court examined "good faith" in two recent decisions. In *In re Walt Disney Co. Deriv. Litig.*, the Court discussed the range of conduct that might be characterized as bad faith, and concluded that bad faith encompasses not only an intent to harm but also intentional dereliction of duty:

> [A]t least three different categories of fiduciary behavior are candidates for the "bad faith" pejorative label. The first category involves so-called "subjective bad faith," that is, fiduciary conduct motivated by an actual intent to do harm.... [S]uch conduct constitutes classic, quintessential bad faith....

The second category of conduct, which is at the opposite end of the spectrum, involves lack of due care—that is, fiduciary action taken solely by reason of gross negligence and without any malevolent intent....

[W]e address the issue of whether gross negligence (including failure to inform one's self of available material facts), without more, can also constitute bad faith. The answer is clearly no.

***

That leaves the third category of fiduciary conduct, which falls in between the first two categories. . . . This third category is what the Chancellor's definition of bad faith—intentional dereliction of duty, a conscious disregard for one's responsibilities—is intended to capture. The question is whether such misconduct is properly treated as a non-exculpable, nonindemnifiable violation of the fiduciary duty to act in good faith. In our view, it must be . . . .

254

The Court of Chancery recognized [the legal principles announced in the *Disney* case and *Stone v. Ritter*] . . . , but it denied summary judgment in order to obtain a more complete record before deciding whether the directors had acted in bad faith. Under other circumstances, deferring a decision to expand the record would be appropriate. Here, however, the trial court reviewed the existing record under a mistaken view of the applicable law. . . .

Summary judgment may be granted if there are no material issues of fact in dispute and the moving party is entitled to judgment as a matter of law. . . . The Court of Chancery identified several undisputed facts that would support the entry of judgment in favor of the Lyondell directors: the directors were "active, sophisticated, and generally aware of the value of the Company and the conditions of the markets in which the Company operated." They had reason to believe that no other bidders would emerge, given the price Basell had offered and the limited universe of companies that might be interested in acquiring Lyondell's unique assets. Smith negotiated the price up from $40 to $48 per share—a price that Deutsche Bank opined was fair. Finally, no other acquiror expressed interest during the four months between the merger announcement and the stockholder vote.

Other facts, however, led the trial court to "question the adequacy of the Board's knowledge and efforts. . . ." After the Schedule 13D was filed in May, the directors apparently took no action to prepare for a possible acquisition proposal. The merger was negotiated and finalized in less than one week, during which time the directors met for a total of only seven hours to consider the matter. The directors did not seriously press Blavatnik for a better price, nor did they conduct even a limited market check. Moreover, although the deal protections were not unusual or preclusive, the trial court was troubled by "the Board's decision to grant considerable protection to a deal that may not have been adequately vetted under *Revlon*."

The trial court found the directors' failure to act during the two months after the filing of the Basell Schedule 13D critical to its analysis of their good faith. The court pointedly referred to the directors' "two months of slothful indifference despite knowing that the Company was in play," and the fact that they "languidly awaited overtures from potential suitors. . . ." In the end, the trial court found that it was this "failing" that warranted denial of their motion for summary judgment:

[T]he Opinion clearly questions whether the Defendants "engaged" [that] is, were properly or adequately engaged – EDS.] in the sale process. . . .

> This is where the 13D filing in May 2007 and the subsequent two months of (apparent) Board inactivity become critical. . . . [T]he Directors made no apparent effort to arm themselves with specific knowledge about the present value of the Company in the May through July 2007 time period, despite admittedly knowing that the 13D filing . . . effectively put the Company "in play," and, therefore, presumably, also knowing that an offer for the sale of the Company could occur at any time. It is these facts that raise the specter of "bad faith" in the present summary judgment record. . . .

. . . . Basell's Schedule 13D did put the Lyondell directors, and the market in general, on notice that Basell was interested in acquiring Lyondell. The directors responded by promptly holding a special meeting to consider whether Lyondell should take any action. The directors decided that they would neither put the company up for sale nor institute defensive measures to fend off a possible hostile offer. Instead, they decided to take a "wait and see" approach. That decision was an entirely appropriate exercise of the directors' business judgment. The time for action under *Revlon* did not begin until July 10, 2007, when the directors began negotiating the sale of Lyondell.

The Court of Chancery focused on the directors' two months of inaction, when it should have focused on the one week during which they considered Basell's offer. During that one week, the directors met several times; their CEO tried to negotiate better terms; they evaluated Lyondell's value, the price offered and the likelihood of obtaining a better price; and then the directors approved the merger. The trial court acknowledged that the directors' conduct during those seven days might not demonstrate anything more than lack of due care. But the court remained skeptical about the directors' good faith. . . . That lingering concern was based on the trial court's synthesis of the *Revlon* line of cases, which led it to the erroneous conclusion that directors must follow one of several courses of action to satisfy their *Revlon* duties.

There is only one *Revlon* duty—to "[get] the best price for the stockholders at a sale of the company." No court can tell directors exactly how to accomplish that goal, because they will be facing a unique combination of circumstances, many of which will be outside their control. As we noted in *Barkan v. Amsted Industries, Inc.*, "there is no single blueprint that a board must follow to fulfill its duties.". . . The trial court drew several principles from those cases: directors must "engage actively in the sale process," and they must confirm that they have obtained the best available price either by conducting an auction, by conducting a market check, or by demonstrating "an impeccable knowledge of the market."

The Lyondell directors did not conduct an auction or a market check, and they did not satisfy the trial court that they had the "impeccable" market knowledge that the court believed was necessary to excuse their failure to pursue one of the first two alternatives. As a result, the Court of Chancery was unable to conclude that the directors had met their burden under *Revlon*. In evaluating the totality of the circumstances, even on this limited record, we would be inclined to hold otherwise. But we would not question the trial court's decision to seek additional evidence if the issue were whether the directors had exercised due care. Where, as here, the issue is whether the directors failed to act in good faith, the analysis is very different, and the existing record mandates the entry of judgment in favor of the directors.

* * *

Directors' decisions [when *Revlon* duties are triggered] must be reasonable, not perfect. "In the transactional context, [an] extreme set of facts [is] required to sustain a disloyalty claim premised on the notion that disinterested directors were intentionally disregarding their duties." The trial court denied summary judgment because the Lyondell directors' "un-explained inaction" prevented the court from determining that they had acted in good faith. But, if the directors failed to do all that they should have under the circumstances, they breached their duty of care. Only if they knowingly and completely failed to undertake their responsibilities would they breach their duty of loyalty. The trial court approached the record from the wrong perspective. Instead of questioning whether disinterested, independent directors did everything that they (arguably) should have done to obtain the best sale price, the inquiry should have been whether those directors utterly failed to attempt to obtain the best sale price.

. . . [T]his record clearly establishes that the Lyondell directors did not breach their duty of loyalty by failing to act in good faith. In concluding otherwise, the Court of Chancery reversibly erred.

CONCLUSION

Based on the foregoing, the decision of the Court of Chancery is reversed and this matter is remanded for entry of judgment in favor of the Lyondell directors. Jurisdiction is not retained.

Discussion Questions:

1. How does the *Lyondell* Court articulate the board's duties under *Revlon*? (Extra credit: does the language have a familiar ring to it?)

2. Can you reconcile *Lyondell* with *Van Gorkom*, or does the *Lyondell* case represent the completion of a trajectory (beginning with *Disney*) that fully rejects the principle of some kind of enhanced scrutiny in sale-of-the-company situations?

3G / Burger King Merger Agreement § 6.02 ("Go-Shop")

In reading *Revlon*, did you wonder how the Burger King board discharged its duty of "getting the best price for the stockholders" in its acquisition by 3G? Section 6.02 of the Merger Agreement tells you how. Such a "go-shop" provision is now a standard feature in merger agreements with Delaware corporations.

Section 6.02 *Solicitation; Takeover Proposals; Change of Recommendation.*

(a) *Solicitation.* Notwithstanding any other provision of this Agreement to the contrary, during the period beginning on the date of this Agreement and continuing until 11:59 p.m., New York City time, on October 12, 2010 (the "No-Shop Period Start Date"), the Company may, directly or through its Representatives: (i) solicit, initiate or encourage, whether publicly or otherwise, any Takeover Proposals, including by way of providing access to non-public information; provided, however, that the Company shall only permit such non-public information related to the Company to be provided pursuant to an Acceptable

Confidentiality Agreement, and provided further that (A) the Company shall promptly provide to Parent any non-public information concerning the Company or its Subsidiaries to which any person is provided such access and which was not previously provided to Parent, and (B) the Company shall withhold such portions of documents or information, or provide pursuant to customary "clean-room" or other appropriate procedures, to the extent relating to any pricing or other matters that are highly sensitive or competitive in nature if the exchange of such information (or portions thereof) could reasonably be likely to be harmful to the operation of the Company in any material respect; and (ii) engage in and maintain discussions or negotiations with respect to any inquiry, proposal or offer that constitutes or may reasonably be expected to lead to any Takeover Proposal or otherwise cooperate with or assist or participate in, or facilitate any such inquiries, proposals, offers, discussions or negotiations or the making of any Takeover Proposal.

The term "Takeover Proposal" means any inquiry, proposal or offer from any person or group providing for (a) any direct or indirect acquisition or purchase, in a single transaction or a series of related transactions, of (1) 20% or more (based on the fair market value, as determined in good faith by the Company Board) of assets (including capital stock of the Subsidiaries of the Company) of the Company and its Subsidiaries, taken as a whole, or (2)(A) shares of Company Common Stock, which together with any other shares of Company Common Stock beneficially owned by such person or group, would equal to 20% or more of the outstanding shares of Company Common Stock, or (B) any other equity securities of the Company or any of its Subsidiaries, (b) any tender offer or exchange offer that, if consummated, would result in any person or group owning, directly or indirectly, 20% or more of the outstanding shares of Company Common Stock or any other equity securities of the Company or any of its Subsidiaries, (c) any merger, consolidation, business combination, binding share exchange or similar transaction involving the Company or any of its Subsidiaries pursuant to which any person or group (or the shareholders of any person) would own, directly or indirectly, 20% or more of the aggregate voting power of the Company or of the surviving entity in a merger or the resulting direct or indirect parent of the Company or such surviving entity, or (d) any recapitalization, liquidation, dissolution or any other similar transaction involving the Company or any of its material operating Subsidiaries, other than, in each case, the transactions contemplated by this Agreement.

Wherever the term "group" is used in this Section 6.02, it is used as defined in Rule 13d-3 under the Exchange Act.

(b) *No Solicitation.* From the No-Shop Period Start Date until the Effective Time, or, if earlier, the termination of this Agreement in accordance with Section 9.01, the Company shall not, nor shall it permit any Representative of the Company to, directly or indirectly, (i) solicit, initiate or knowingly encourage (including by way of providing information) the submission or announcement of any inquiries, proposals or offers that constitute or would reasonably be expected to lead to any Takeover Proposal, (ii) provide any non-public information concerning the Company or any of its Subsidiaries related to, or to any person or group who would reasonably be expected to make, any Takeover Proposal, (iii) engage in any discussions or negotiations with respect thereto, (iv) approve, support, adopt, endorse or recommend any Takeover Proposal, or (v) otherwise cooperate with or assist or participate in, or knowingly facilitate any such inquiries, proposals, offers, discussions or negotiations. Subject to Section 6.02(c), at the No-Shop Period Start Date, the Company shall immediately cease and cause to be terminated any solicitation, encouragement, discussion or negotiation with any person or groups (other than a Qualified Go-Shop Bidder) conducted theretofore by the Company, its Subsidiaries or any of their respective Representatives with respect to any Takeover Proposal and shall use reasonable best efforts to require any other parties (other than a Qualified Go-Shop Bidder) who have made or have indicated an intention to make a Takeover Proposal to promptly return or destroy any confidential information previously furnished by the Company, any of its Subsidiaries or any of their respective Representatives.

The term "Qualified Go-Shop Bidder" means any person or group from whom the Company or any of its Representatives has received a Takeover Proposal after the execution of this Agreement and prior to the No-Shop Period Start Date that the Company Board determines, prior to or as of the No-Shop Period Start Date, in good faith, after consultation with its financial advisor and outside legal counsel, constitutes or could reasonably be expected to result in a Superior Proposal.

The term "Superior Proposal" means any *bona fide*, written Takeover Proposal that if consummated would result in a person or group (or the shareholders of any person) owning, directly or indirectly, (a) 75% or more of the outstanding shares of Company Common Stock or (b) 75% or more of the assets of the Company and its Subsidiaries, taken as a whole, in either case which the Company Board determines in good faith (after consultation with its financial advisor and outside legal counsel) (x) is reasonably likely to be consummated in accordance with its terms, and (y) if consummated, would be more favorable to the stockholders of the Company from a financial point of view than the Offer and the Merger, in each case taking into account all financial, legal, financing, regulatory and other aspects of such Takeover Proposal (including the person or group making the Takeover Proposal) and of this Agreement (including any changes to the terms of this Agreement proposed by Parent pursuant to Section 6.02(f).

(c) *Response to Takeover Proposals.* Notwithstanding anything to the contrary contained in Section 6.02(b) or any other provisions of this Agreement, if at any time following the No-Shop Period Start Date and prior to the earlier to occur of the Offer Closing and obtaining the Stockholder Approval, (i) the Company has received a *bona fide*, written Takeover Proposal from a third party that did not result from a breach of this Section 6.02, and (ii) the Company Board determines in good faith, after consultation with its financial advisor and outside legal counsel, that such Takeover Proposal constitutes or could reasonably be expected to result in a Superior Proposal, then the Company may (A) furnish information with respect to the Company and its Subsidiaries to the person making such Takeover Proposal pursuant to an Acceptable Confidentiality Agreement and the other restrictions imposed by clause (A) and (B) of Section 6.02(a)related to the sharing of information, or (B) engage in discussions or negotiations with the person making such Takeover Proposal regarding such Takeover Proposal. The Company shall be permitted prior to the earlier to occur of the Offer Closing and obtaining the Stockholder Approval to take the actions described in clauses (A) and (B) above with respect to any Qualified Go-Shop Bidder.

(d) *Notice to Parent of Takeover Proposals.* The Company shall promptly (and, in any event, within one (1) business day) notify Parent in the event that the Company or any of its Representatives receives any Takeover Proposal, or any initial request for non-public information concerning the Company or any of its Subsidiaries related to, or from any person or group who would reasonably be expected to make any Takeover Proposal, or any initial request for discussions or negotiations related to any Takeover Proposal (including any material changes related to the foregoing), and in connection with such notice, provide the identity of the person or group making such Takeover Proposal or request and the material terms and conditions thereof (including, if applicable, copies of any written requests, proposals or offers, including proposed agreements), and thereafter the Company shall keep Parent reasonably informed of any material changes to the terms thereof.

(e) *Prohibited Activities.* Neither the Company Board nor any committee thereof shall (i) withdraw or rescind (or modify in a manner adverse to Parent), or publicly propose to withdraw (or modify in a manner adverse to Parent), the Recommendation or the findings or conclusions of the Company Board referred to in Section 4.04(b), (ii) approve or recommend the adoption of, or publicly propose to approve, declare the advisability of or recommend the adoption of, any Takeover Proposal, (iii) or cause or permit the Company or any of its Subsidiaries to execute or enter into, any letter of intent, memorandum of understanding, agreement in principle, merger agreement, acquisition agreement or other similar agreement related to any Takeover Proposal, other than any Acceptable Confidentiality Agreement referred to in Section 6.02(a) or 6.02(c) (an "Acquisition Agreement"), or (iv) publicly proposed or announced an intention to take any of the foregoing actions (any action described in clauses (i), (ii), (iii) or (iv) being referred to as an "Adverse Recommendation Change").

(f) *Change of Recommendation.* Notwithstanding any provision of Section 6.02(e), at any time prior to the earlier to occur of the Offer Closing and obtaining the Stockholder Approval, the Company Board may effect an Adverse Recommendation Change only if the Company Board determines in good faith (after consultation with its outside legal counsel) that the failure to take such action would be inconsistent with its fiduciary duties under applicable Law. Notwithstanding anything to the contrary, the Company Board shall not be entitled to exercise its right to make an Adverse Recommendation Change or, solely with regards to a Superior Proposal, terminate this Agreement pursuant to Section 9.01(f) (x) unless the Company shall have provided prior written notice to Parent and Sub, at least three (3) business days in advance, that it will effect an Adverse Recommendation Change or terminate this Agreement pursuant to Section 9.01(f) and specifying the reasons therefor (a "Notice of Intended Recommendation Change") and (y):

(i) if such Adverse Recommendation Change is not being made as a result of a Superior Proposal, during such three (3) business day period, if requested by Parent, the Company shall have engaged in good faith negotiations with Parent to amend this Agreement in such a manner that would otherwise obviate the need for such Adverse Recommendation Change; or

(ii) if such Adverse Recommendation Change or termination is being made as a result of a Superior Proposal:

(1) the Notice of Intended Recommendation Change shall specify the identity of the party making such Superior Proposal and the material terms thereof and copies of all relevant documents relating to such Superior Proposal (it being understood and agreed that any material amendment to the terms of any such Superior Proposal (and in any event including any amendment to any price term thereof), shall require a new Notice of Intended Recommendation Change and compliance with the requirements of this Section 6.02(f), except that the prior written notice period and corresponding references to a three (3) business day period shall be reduced to a one (1) business day for any such new Notice of Intended Recommendation Change); (2) after providing any such Notice of Intended Recommendation Change, the Company shall, and shall cause its Representatives to, negotiate with Parent and Sub in good faith (to the extent Parent and Sub desire to negotiate) during such three (3) business day period (or one business day period in the case of a new Notice of Intended Recommendation Change) to make such adjustments in the terms and conditions of this Agreement and the other agreements contemplated hereby; and

(iii) in the case of either clause (i) or clause (ii), the Company Board shall have considered in good faith any adjustments to this Agreement (including a change to the price terms hereof) and the other agreements contemplated hereby that may be offered in writing by Parent no later than 5:00 p.m., New York City time, on the third business day of such three (3) business day period (or the first business day of such one (1) business day period for any such new Notice of Intended Recommendation Change) and shall have determined that (x) in the case of a Superior Proposal, the Superior Proposal would continue to constitute a Superior Proposal if such adjustments were to be given effect, or (y) in the case of an Adverse Recommendation Change not being made as a result of a Superior Proposal, no adjustment has been made that would obviate the need for such Adverse Recommendation Change, and (y) the findings contemplated by clause (i) above continue to be applicable such that an Adverse Recommendation Change should be made the Superior Proposal would continue to constitute a Superior Proposal if such adjustments were to be given effect.

Discussion Questions:

1. Delaware courts have consistently held that an appropriately structured go-shop provision satisfies the seller's *Revlon* duties. Do you think this is the correct conclusion? If so, what features should an appropriately structured go-shop have, to ensure a meaningful market check?

2. The 3G/Burger King go-shop process contains "information rights," *see* Section 6.02(d) above, and "matching rights," *see* Section 6.02(f). What do these sections of

the merger agreement require the parties to do? Who benefits (3G or Burger King)? What effect should these information rights and match rights have on the willingness of prospective third-party bidders to bid? (NB: Game theorists will have a special advantage in answering this last part.)

Summarizing the Delaware Takeover Trilogy (*Unocal, Moran & Revlon*)

Unocal established the principle that "the board ha[s] both the power and duty to oppose a bid it perceive[s] to be harmful to the corporate enterprise." In recognition of the possibility of board entrenchment, however, the Delaware Supreme Court formulated an "intermediate scrutiny" standard of review for defensive actions:

> "Because of the *omnipresent specter* that a board [defending against a takeover] may be acting primarily in its own interests [of keeping its job], rather than those of the corporation and its shareholders, there is an *enhanced duty* which calls for judicial examination at the threshold before the protections of the business judgment rule may be conferred. . . . If a defensive measure is to come within the ambit of the business judgment rule, it must be *reasonable in relation to the threat posed.*" (Emphasis added)

Unocal explicitly blessed discriminatory defensive measures—measures that treat the bidder differently from other shareholders. *Moran* approved the one discriminatory defensive device that made all others unnecessary: the "rights plan," a/k/a the "poison pill."

Revlon announced the main limit to these defenses. If the board is set to sell, it must simply get the highest price for shareholders; it cannot use defenses to play favorites between bidders or to protect some non-shareholder constituency. In the words of the Court:

> "[W]hen . . . it became apparent to all that the *break-up* of the company was inevitable [and] that *the company was for sale* . . . [t]he duty of the board . . . changed from the preservation of [the] corporate entity to the *maximization of the company's value at a sale for the stockholders' benefit.* This significantly altered the board's responsibilities under the Unocal standards. It no longer faced threats to corporate policy and effectiveness, or to the stockholders' interests, from a grossly inadequate bid. The whole question of defensive measures became moot. *The directors' role changed from defenders of the corporate bastion to auctioneers charged with getting the best price for the stockholders at a sale of the company.*" (Emphasis added)

In particular, the Court explicitly held that the board breached its duty of loyalty to shareholders when it favored one bidder over another out of concern for certain non-shareholder constituents—the note-holders. "Instead, obtaining the highest price for the benefit of the stockholders should have been the central theme guiding director action."

Importantly, *Unocal* and *Revlon* are not generally available to support a claim for monetary damages. Under *Corwin v. KKR Financial Holdings LLC* (Del. 2015), "when a transaction not subject to the entire fairness standard is approved by a fully informed, uncoerced vote of the disinterested stockholders, the business judgment rule applies." According to Chief Justice Strine's opinion:

> "*Unocal* and *Revlon* are primarily designed to give stockholders and the Court of Chancery the tool of injunctive relief to address important M & A decisions in real time, before closing. They were not tools designed with post-closing money damages claims in mind, the standards they articulate do not match the gross negligence standard for director due care liability under *Van Gorkom*, and with the prevalence of exculpatory charter provisions, due care liability is rarely even available. ... [W]hen a transaction is not subject to the entire fairness standard, the long-standing policy of our law has been to avoid the uncertainties and costs of judicial second-guessing when the disinterested stockholders have had the free and informed chance to decide on the economic merits of a transaction for themselves."

A Brief Intermission

The Delaware trilogy is now firmly established law, and fundamental change is highly unlikely. Nevertheless, it is worth pausing for a brief moment to note some irony in the Delaware Supreme Court's reasoning.

Both *Unocal* and *Moran* find that defenses are necessary to protect shareholders from the coercive nature of front-loaded two-tiered bids. But the defenses that the Court endorses are themselves coercive. In *Unocal*, the Court approved a partial self-tender that any individual shareholder will rationally tender into (because the price offered is higher than the share value) even if that shareholder believes the self-tender is a bad idea for the shareholders collectively. Similarly, the poison pill approved in *Moran* relies on the fact that all shareholders will rationally exercise their rights once they become exercisable, regardless of the collective effect of such exercise. Additionally, the board adopts the pill unilaterally without approval from the shareholders.

Moreover, the Delaware Supreme Court could have easily shut down coercive two-tiered bids. All it had to do was remind shareholders and deal-makers that the demanding "entire fairness" standard also applied to the consideration offered in the second tier squeeze-out merger. Recall that "coercion" emanates from the lower consideration expected in the second tier squeeze-out: shareholders tender in the first tier because they fear they will otherwise only receive low value in the second tier squeeze-out. But the merger consideration in the squeeze-out is subject to fiduciary duty review. In fact, it is subject to the exacting "entire fairness" standard because the bidder will be a controlling stockholder at the time of the squeeze-out. It seems quite straightforward to argue that any second tier (merger) consideration less than the first tier (tender) consideration is presumptively unfair.

Finally, coercive two-tiered bids entirely disappeared after the 1980s. As we will see in the next section, however, the Court's attitude towards defenses became, if anything, more permissive. As a result, Delaware boards are now allowed to deploy unilateral, coercive defenses against even non-coercive bids.

Rather than allowing coercive defenses against coercive bids, the Court *could have* attempted to suppress all coercive devices, no matter who deploys them. It could have attempted to facilitate uncoerced shareholder choice to decide the merits of a takeover bid. However, that is not Delaware law and presumably never will be.

The Power of the Pill

The poison pill is now all but ubiquitous and defines the playing field for any takeover contest. It is not necessary for a corporation to formally adopt a "rights plan" because such a plan can be adopted on very short notice in the face of a threat. Thus, all Delaware corporations have a "shadow pill," and a bidder must plan accordingly.

While some technical details have changed over time, the basic design and idea of the pill has remained the same, and it is as deadly as ever. In the 30 years since *Moran*, only one bidder has dared to trigger the pill. Thus, practically speaking, the only way to take over a Delaware corporation is by replacing the board.

Unocal could have placed important limits on the use of the pill. But subsequent decisions interpreted both cognizable "threats" and "reasonable" defensive measures extremely broadly. In *Paramount v. Time* (1989) (a.k.a. "Time-Warner") and even more clearly in *Unitrin v. American General* (1995), the Delaware Supreme Court confirmed that inadequacy of price was a sufficient threat, at least in conjunction with the risk that "shareholders might elect to tender into [the] offer in ignorance or a mistaken belief" about the alternative. Such threats have been labeled "substantive coercion." As a practical matter, the endorsement of substantive coercion as a cognizable threat under *Unocal* means that boards have substantial (maybe infinite) discretion in maintaining a poison pill.

Deal Protections

"Deal protections" are contractual arrangements related to a merger agreement (and sometimes provided in a merger agreement) that protect the initial bidder from third-party competition. Deal protections are useful to buyers because of the inevitable 3-6 month window between the signing/announcement of the deal and the closing of the deal, during which the target and buyer will need to get shareholder and regulatory approvals. During this 3-6 month period, the deal is vulnerable to "jumping" from a higher-value bidder. Deal protections put some "furniture against the door" that deters third-party bids; and, in the event that a third-party bidder appears, tilts the playing field slightly in favor of the first bidder.

There are three kinds of deal protections: (1) asset lockups (which you saw in the *Revlon* case above), which give the buyer the right to buy certain assets of the target company at a specified price; (2) stock option agreements (which you will see in the Paramount-Viacom-QVC contest below), which give the buyer the right to buy a certain percentage of the shares of the target company (typically 19.9%) at a specified price (typically the deal price); and (3) by far the most common and cleanest form of deal protection, a breakup fee (or termination fee), which is simply a cash payment from the target to the buyer in the event of a higher-value third-party bid.

Deal protections are subject to *Unocal* scrutiny, because they are a defensive mechanism against third-party bids. In general, Delaware courts have usually tolerated deal protections in the range of 3-4% of deal value, though in recent decisions the courts have signaled that 4-5% stretches the range of reasonableness. Delaware courts have rarely struck down deal protections, although the Paramount-QVC case below represents an important exception.

Revlon Duties

With *Unocal* review weak at best, the boundary to "Revlon land" assumes great importance. When does the board's duty shift to maximization of the sale price?

Revlon duties are clearly triggered in a break-up or sale for cash. But what about "stock-for-stock deals," i.e., deals in which the shareholders of both merging corporations become shareholders of the surviving corporation? In these situations, it may not even be obvious who is "the buyer" and who is "the seller."

In the *Time-Warner* and *Paramount-QVC* cases excerpted below, the Delaware Supreme Court ruled that a stock deal triggered *Revlon* duties only if there was a change of control. In particular, *Time-Warner* held that *Revlon* duties were not triggered if the corporation is not broken up and was widely held both before and after the merger. By contrast, the Court found a change of control in *Paramount v. QVC* because the other constituent corporation had a controlling stockholder who would also control the surviving corporation. Control of the corporation would thus pass from the "fluid aggregation of unaffiliated stockholders" to the controlling stockholder of the merger partner.

Paramount Communications, Inc. v. Time, Inc.
571 A.2d (Del. 1989)

Horsey, J.:

. . . Time is a Delaware corporation with its principal offices in New York City. Time's traditional business is publication of magazines and books; however, Time also provides pay television programming through its Home Box Office, Inc. and Cinemax subsidiaries. In addition, Time owns and operates cable television franchises through its subsidiary, American Television and Communication Corporation. During the relevant time period,

Time's board consisted of sixteen directors. Twelve of the directors were "outside," nonemployee directors. Four of the directors were also officers of the company. . . . The inside officer directors were: J. Richard Munro, Time's chairman and CEO since 1980: N.J. Nicholas, Jr., president and chief operating officer of the company since 1986; Gerald M. Levin, vice chairman of the board; and Jason D. McManus, editor-in-chief of Time magazine and a board member since 1988.

As early as 1983 and 1984, Time's executive board began considering expanding Time's operations into the entertainment industry. In 1987, Time established a special committee of executives to consider and propose corporate strategies for the 1990s. The consensus of the committee was that Time should move ahead in the area of ownership and creation of video programming. This expansion, as the Chancellor noted, was predicated upon two considerations: first, Time's desire to have greater control, in terms of quality and price, over the film products delivered by way of its cable network and franchises; and second, Time's concern over the increasing globalization of the world economy. Some of Time's outside directors, especially Luce and Temple, had opposed this move as a threat to the editorial integrity and journalistic focus of Time. Despite this concern, the board recognized that a vertically integrated video enterprise to complement Time's existing HBO and cable networks would better enable it to compete on a global basis.

In late spring of 1987, a meeting took place between Steve Ross, CEO of Warner Brothers, and Nicholas of Time. Ross and Nicholas discussed the possibility of a joint venture between the two companies through the creation of a jointly-owned cable company. Time would contribute its cable system and HBO. Warner would contribute its cable system and provide access to Warner Brothers Studio. The resulting venture would be a larger, more efficient cable network, able to produce and distribute its own movies on a worldwide basis. Ultimately the parties abandoned this plan, determining that it was impractical for several reasons, chief among them being tax considerations.

On August 11, 1987, Gerald M. Levin, Time's vice chairman and chief strategist, wrote J. Richard Munro a confidential memorandum in which he strongly recommended a strategic consolidation with Warner. In June 1988, Nicholas and Munro sent to each outside director a copy of the "comprehensive long-term planning document" prepared by the committee of Time executives that had been examining strategies for the 1990s. The memo included reference to and a description of Warner as a potential acquisition candidate.

Thereafter, Munro and Nicholas held meetings with Time's outside directors to discuss, generally, long-term strategies for Time and, specifically, a combination with Warner. Nearly a year later, Time's board reached the point of serious discussion of the "nuts and bolts" of a consolidation with an entertainment company. On July 21, 1988, Time's board met, with all outside directors present. The meeting's purpose was to consider Time's expansion into the entertainment industry on a global scale. Management presented the board with a profile of various entertainment companies in addition to Warner, including Disney, 20th Century Fox, Universal, and Paramount.

Without any definitive decision on choice of a company, the board approved in principle a strategic plan for Time's expansion. The board gave management the "go-ahead" to continue discussions with Warner concerning the possibility of a merger. With the exception of Temple and Luce, most of the outside directors agreed that a merger involving expansion into the entertainment field promised great growth opportunity for Time. Temple and Luce remained unenthusiastic about Time's entry into the entertainment field.

The board's consensus was that a merger of Time and Warner was feasible, but only if Time controlled the board of the resulting corporation and thereby preserved a management committed to Time's journalistic integrity. To accomplish this goal, the board stressed the importance of carefully defining in advance the corporate governance provisions that would control the resulting entity. Some board members expressed concern over whether such a business combination would place Time "in play." The board discussed the wisdom of adopting further defensive measures to lessen such a possibility.

Of a wide range of companies considered by Time's board as possible merger candidates, Warner Brothers, Paramount, Columbia, M.C.A., Fox, MGM, Disney, and Orion, the board, in July 1988, concluded that Warner was the superior candidate for a consolidation. Warner stood out on a number of counts. Warner had just acquired Lorimar and its film studios. Time–Warner could make movies and television shows for use on HBO. Warner had an international distribution system, which Time could use to sell films, videos, books and magazines. Warner was a giant in the music and recording business, an area into which Time wanted to expand. None of the other companies considered had the musical clout of Warner. Time and Warner's cable systems were compatible and could be easily integrated; none of the other companies considered presented such a compatible cable partner. Together, Time and Warner would control half of New York City's cable system; Warner had cable systems in Brooklyn and Queens; and Time controlled cable systems in Manhattan and Queens. Warner's publishing company would integrate well with Time's established publishing company. Time sells hardcover books and magazines, and Warner sells softcover books and comics. Time–Warner could sell all of these publications and Warner's videos by using Time's direct mailing network and Warner's international distribution system. Time's network could be used to promote and merchandise Warner's movies.

In August 1988, Levin, Nicholas, and Munro, acting on instructions from Time's board, continued to explore a business combination with Warner. By letter dated August 4, 1988, management informed the outside directors of proposed corporate governance provisions to be discussed with Warner. The provisions incorporated the recommendations of several of Time's outside directors.

From the outset, Time's board favored an all-cash or cash and securities acquisition of Warner as the basis for consolidation. Bruce Wasserstein, Time's financial advisor, also favored an outright purchase of Warner. However, Steve Ross, Warner's CEO, was adamant that a business combination was only practicable on a stock-for-stock basis. Warner insisted on a stock swap in order to preserve its shareholders' equity in the resulting corporation. Time's officers, on the other hand, made it abundantly clear that Time would be the acquiring corporation and that Time would control the resulting board. Time refused to permit itself to be cast as the "acquired" company.

Eventually Time acquiesced in Warner's insistence on a stock-for-stock deal, but talks broke down over corporate governance issues. Time wanted Ross' position as a co-CEO to be temporary and wanted Ross to retire in five years. Ross, however, refused to set a time for his retirement and viewed Time's proposal as indicating a lack of confidence in his leadership. Warner considered it vital that their executives and creative staff not perceive Warner as selling out to Time. Time's request of a guarantee that Time would dominate the CEO succession was objected to as inconsistent with the concept of a Time–Warner merger "of equals." Negotiations ended when the parties reached an impasse. Time's board refused to compromise on its position on corporate governance. Time, and particularly its outside directors, viewed the corporate governance provisions as critical for preserving the "Time Culture" through a pro-Time management at the top.

Throughout the fall of 1988 Time pursued its plan of expansion into the entertainment field; Time held informal discussions with several companies, including Paramount. Capital Cities/ABC approached Time to propose a merger. Talks terminated, however, when Capital Cities/ABC suggested that it was interested in purchasing Time or in controlling the resulting board. Time steadfastly maintained it was not placing itself up for sale.

Warner and Time resumed negotiations in January 1989. The catalyst for the resumption of talks was a private dinner between Steve Ross and Time outside director, Michael Dingman. Dingman was able to convince Ross that the transitional nature of the proposed co-CEO arrangement did not reflect a lack of confidence in Ross. Ross agreed that this course was best for the company and a meeting between Ross and Munro resulted. Ross agreed to retire in five years and let Nicholas succeed him. Negotiations resumed and many of the details of the original stock-for-stock exchange agreement remained intact. In addition, Time's senior management agreed to long-term contracts.

Time insider directors Levin and Nicholas met with Warner's financial advisors to decide upon a stock exchange ratio. Time's board had recognized the potential need to pay a premium in the stock ratio in exchange for dictating the governing arrangement of the new Time–Warner. Levin and outside director Finkelstein were the primary proponents of paying a premium to protect the "Time Culture." The board discussed premium rates of 10%, 15% and 20%. Wasserstein also suggested paying a premium for Warner due to Warner's rapid growth rate. The market exchange ratio of Time stock for Warner stock was .38 in favor of Warner. Warner's financial advisors informed its board that any exchange rate over .400 was a fair deal and any exchange rate over .450 was "one hell of a deal." The parties ultimately agreed upon an exchange rate favoring Warner of .465. On that basis, Warner stockholders would have owned approximately 62% of the common stock of Time–Warner.

On March 3, 1989, Time's board, with all but one director in attendance, met and unanimously approved the stock-for-stock merger with Warner. Warner's board likewise approved the merger. The agreement called for Warner to be merged into a wholly-owned

Time subsidiary with Warner becoming the surviving corporation. The common stock of Warner would then be converted into common stock of Time at the agreed upon ratio. Thereafter, the name of Time would be changed to Time–Warner, Inc.

The rules of the New York Stock Exchange required that Time's issuance of shares to effectuate the merger be approved by a vote of Time's stockholders. The Delaware General Corporation Law required approval of the merger by a majority of the Warner stockholders. Delaware law did not require any vote by Time stockholders. The Chancellor concluded that the agreement was the product of "an arms-length negotiation between two parties seeking individual advantage through mutual action."

The resulting company would have a 24–member board, with 12 members representing each corporation. The company would have co-CEO's, at first Ross and Munro, then Ross and Nicholas, and finally, after Ross' retirement, by Nicholas alone. The board would create an editorial committee with a majority of members representing Time. A similar entertainment committee would be controlled by Warner board members. A two-thirds supermajority vote was required to alter CEO successions but an earlier proposal to have supermajority protection for the editorial committee was abandoned. Warner's board suggested raising the compensation levels for Time's senior management under the new corporation. Warner's management, as with most entertainment executives, received higher salaries than comparable executives in news journalism. Time's board, however, rejected Warner's proposal to equalize the salaries of the two management teams.

At its March 3, 1989 meeting, Time's board adopted several defensive tactics. Time entered an automatic share exchange agreement with Warner. Time would receive 17,292,747 shares of Warner's outstanding common stock (9.4%) and Warner would receive 7,080,016 shares of Time's outstanding common stock (11.1%). Either party could trigger the exchange. Time sought out and paid for "confidence" letters from various banks with which it did business. In these letters, the banks promised not to finance any third-party attempt to acquire Time. Time argues these agreements served only to preserve the confidential relationship between itself and the banks. The Chancellor found these agreements to be inconsequential and futile attempts to "dry up" money for a hostile takeover. Time also agreed to a "no-shop" clause, preventing Time from considering any other consolidation proposal, thus relinquishing its power to consider other proposals, regardless of their merits. Time did so at Warner's insistence. Warner did not want to be left "on the auction block" for an unfriendly suitor, if Time were to withdraw from the deal.

Time's board simultaneously established a special committee of outside directors, Finkelstein, Kearns, and Opel, to oversee the merger. The committee's assignment was to resolve any impediments that might arise in the course of working out the details of the merger and its consummation.

Time representatives lauded the lack of debt to the United States Senate and to the President of the United States. Public reaction to the announcement of the merger was positive. Time–Warner would be a media colossus with international scope. The board scheduled the stockholder vote for June 23; and a May 1 record date was set. On May 24,

1989, Time sent out extensive proxy statements to the stockholders regarding the approval vote on the merger. In the meantime, with the merger proceeding without impediment, the special committee had concluded, shortly after its creation, that it was not necessary either to retain independent consultants, legal or financial, or even to meet. Time's board was unanimously in favor of the proposed merger with Warner; and, by the end of May, the Time–Warner merger appeared to be an accomplished fact.

On June 7, 1989, these wishful assumptions were shattered by Paramount's surprising announcement of its all-cash offer to purchase all outstanding shares of Time for $175 per share. The following day, June 8, the trading price of Time's stock rose from $126 to $170 per share. Paramount's offer was said to be "fully negotiable." . . .

On June 8, 1989, Time formally responded to Paramount's offer. Time's chairman and CEO, J. Richard Munro, sent an aggressively worded letter to Paramount's CEO, Martin Davis. Munro's letter attacked Davis' personal integrity and called Paramount's offer "smoke and mirrors." Time's nonmanagement directors were not shown the letter before it was sent. However, at a board meeting that same day, all members endorsed management's response as well as the letter's content.

Over the following eight days, Time's board met three times to discuss Paramount's $175 offer. The board viewed Paramount's offer as inadequate and concluded that its proposed merger with Warner was the better course of action. Therefore, the board declined to open any negotiations with Paramount and held steady its course toward a merger with Warner.

In June, Time's board of directors met several times. During the course of their June meetings, Time's outside directors met frequently without management, officers or directors being present. At the request of the outside directors, corporate counsel was present during the board meetings and, from time to time, the management directors were asked to leave the board sessions. During the course of these meetings, Time's financial advisors informed the board that, on an auction basis, Time's per share value was materially higher than Warner's $175 per share offer. After this advice, the board concluded that Paramount's $175 offer was inadequate.

At these June meetings, certain Time directors expressed their concern that Time stockholders would not comprehend the long-term benefits of the Warner merger. Large quantities of Time shares were held by institutional investors. The board feared that even though there appeared to be wide support for the Warner transaction, Paramount's cash premium would be a tempting prospect to these investors. In mid-June, Time sought permission from the New York Stock Exchange to alter its rules and allow the Time–Warner merger to proceed without stockholder approval. Time did so at Warner's insistence. The New York Stock Exchange rejected Time's request on June 15; and on that day, the value of Time stock reached $182 per share.

The following day, June 16, Time's board met to take up Paramount's offer. The board's prevailing belief was that Paramount's bid posed a threat to Time's control of its own destiny and retention of the "Time Culture." Even after Time's financial advisors made another presentation of Paramount and its business attributes, Time's board maintained its position that a combination with Warner offered greater potential for Time. Warner provided Time a much desired production capability and an established international marketing chain. Time's advisors suggested various options, including defensive measures. The board considered and rejected the idea of purchasing Paramount in a "Pac Man" defense. The board considered other defenses, including a recapitalization, the acquisition of another company, and a material change in the present capitalization structure or dividend policy. The board determined to retain its same advisors even in light of the changed circumstances. The board rescinded its agreement to pay its advisors a bonus based on the consummation of the Time–Warner merger and agreed to pay a flat fee for any advice rendered. Finally, Time's board formally rejected Paramount's offer.

At the same meeting, Time's board decided to recast its consolidation with Warner into an outright cash and securities acquisition of Warner by Time; and Time so informed Warner. Time accordingly restructured its proposal to acquire Warner as follows: Time would make an immediate all-cash offer for 51% of Warner's outstanding stock at $70 per share. The remaining 49% would be purchased at some later date for a mixture of cash and securities worth $70 per share. To provide the funds required for its outright acquisition of Warner, Time would assume 7–10 billion dollars worth of debt, thus eliminating one of the principal transaction-related benefits of the original merger agreement. Nine billion dollars of the total purchase price would be allocated to the purchase of Warner's goodwill.

Warner agreed but insisted on certain terms. Warner sought a control premium and guarantees that the governance provisions found in the original merger agreement would remain intact. Warner further sought agreements that Time would not employ its poison pill against Warner and that, unless enjoined, Time would be legally bound to complete the transaction. Time's board agreed to these last measures only at the insistence of Warner. For its part, Time was assured of its ability to extend its efforts into production areas and international markets, all the while maintaining the Time identity and culture. The Chancellor found the initial Time–Warner transaction to have been negotiated at arms length and the restructured Time–Warner transaction to have resulted from Paramount's offer and its expected effect on a Time shareholder vote.

On June 23, 1989, Paramount raised its all-cash offer to buy Time's outstanding stock to $200 per share. Paramount still professed that all aspects of the offer were negotiable. Time's board met on June 26, 1989 and formally rejected Paramount's $200 per share second offer. The board reiterated its belief that, despite the $25 increase, the offer was still inadequate. The Time board maintained that the Warner transaction offered a greater long-term value for the stockholders and, unlike Paramount's offer, did not pose a threat to Time's survival and its "culture." . . .

II.

The Shareholder Plaintiffs first assert a *Revlon* claim. They contend that the March 4 Time–Warner agreement effectively put Time up for sale, triggering *Revlon* duties, requiring Time's board to enhance short-term shareholder value and to treat all other interested acquirors on an equal basis. The Shareholder Plaintiffs base this argument on two facts: (i) the ultimate Time–Warner exchange ratio of .465 favoring Warner, resulting in Warner shareholders' receipt of 62% of the combined company; and (ii) the subjective intent of Time's directors as evidenced in their statements that the market might perceive the Time–Warner merger as putting Time up "for sale" and their adoption of various defensive measures.

The Shareholder Plaintiffs further contend that Time's directors, in structuring the original merger transaction to be "takeover-proof," triggered *Revlon* duties by foreclosing their shareholders from any prospect of obtaining a control premium. In short, plaintiffs argue that Time's board's decision to merge with Warner imposed a fiduciary duty to maximize immediate share value and not erect unreasonable barriers to further bids. Therefore, they argue, the Chancellor erred in finding: that Paramount's bid for Time did not place Time "for sale"; that Time's transaction with Warner did not result in any transfer of control; and that the combined Time–Warner was not so large as to preclude the possibility of the stockholders of Time–Warner receiving a future control premium.

Paramount asserts only a *Unocal* claim in which the shareholder plaintiffs join. Paramount contends that the Chancellor, in applying the first part of the *Unocal* test, erred in finding that Time's board had reasonable grounds to believe that Paramount posed both a legally cognizable threat to Time shareholders and a danger to Time's corporate policy and effectiveness. Paramount also contests the court's finding that Time's board made a reasonable and objective investigation of Paramount's offer so as to be informed before rejecting it. Paramount further claims that the court erred in applying *Unocal*'s second part in finding Time's response to be "reasonable." Paramount points primarily to the preclusive effect of the revised agreement which denied Time shareholders the opportunity both to vote on the agreement and to respond to Paramount's tender offer. Paramount argues that the underlying motivation of Time's board in adopting these defensive measures was management's desire to perpetuate itself in office. . . .

A.

We first take up plaintiffs' principal *Revlon* argument, summarized above. In rejecting this argument, the Chancellor found the original Time–Warner merger agreement not to constitute a "change of control" and concluded that the transaction did not trigger *Revlon* duties. The Chancellor's conclusion is premised on a finding that "[b]efore the merger agreement was signed, control of the corporation existed in a fluid aggregation of unaffiliated shareholders representing a voting majority—in other words, in the market." The Chancellor's findings of fact are supported by the record and his conclusion is correct as a matter of law. However, we premise our rejection of plaintiffs' *Revlon* claim on different grounds, namely, the absence of any substantial evidence to conclude that Time's board, in negotiating with Warner, made the dissolution or break-up of the corporate entity inevitable, as was the case in *Revlon*.

Under Delaware law there are, generally speaking and without excluding other possibilities, two circumstances which may implicate *Revlon* duties. The first, and clearer

272

one, is when a corporation initiates an active bidding process seeking to sell itself or to effect a business reorganization involving a clear break-up of the company. However, Revlon duties may also be triggered where, in response to a bidder's offer, a target abandons its long-term strategy and seeks an alternative transaction involving the breakup of the company. Thus, in *Revlon*, when the board responded to Pantry Pride's offer by contemplating a "bust-up" sale of assets in a leveraged acquisition, we imposed upon the board a duty to maximize immediate shareholder value and an obligation to auction the company fairly. If, however, the board's reaction to a hostile tender offer is found to constitute only a defensive response and not an abandonment of the corporation's continued existence, *Revlon* duties are not triggered, though *Unocal* duties attach. . . .

B.

We turn now to plaintiffs' *Unocal* claim. We begin by noting, as did the Chancellor, that our decision does not require us to pass on the wisdom of the board's decision to enter into the original Time–Warner agreement. That is not a court's task. Our task is simply to review the record to determine whether there is sufficient evidence to support the Chancellor's conclusion that the initial Time–Warner agreement was the product of a proper exercise of business judgment. . . .

In *Unocal*, we held that before the business judgment rule is applied to a board's adoption of a defensive measure, the burden will lie with the board to prove (a) reasonable grounds for believing that a danger to corporate policy and effectiveness existed; and (b) that the defensive measure adopted was reasonable in relation to the threat posed. Directors satisfy the first part of the *Unocal* test by demonstrating good faith and reasonable investigation. We have repeatedly stated that the refusal to entertain an offer may comport with a valid exercise of a board's business judgment.

Unocal involved a two-tier, highly coercive tender offer. In such a case, the threat is obvious: shareholders may be compelled to tender to avoid being treated adversely in the second stage of the transaction. In subsequent cases, the Court of Chancery has suggested that an all-cash, all-shares offer, falling within a range of values that a shareholder might reasonably prefer, cannot constitute a legally recognized "threat" to shareholder interests sufficient to withstand a *Unocal* analysis. AC Acquisitions Corp. v. Anderson, Clayton & Co., Del.Ch., 519 A.2d 103 (1986); see Grand Metropolitan, PLC v. Pillsbury Co., Del.Ch., 558 A.2d 1049 (1988); City Capital Associates v. Interco, Inc., Del.Ch., 551 A.2d 787 (1988). In those cases, the Court of Chancery determined that whatever threat existed related only to the shareholders and only to price and not to the corporation.

From those decisions by our Court of Chancery, Paramount and the individual plaintiffs extrapolate a rule of law that an all-cash, all-shares offer with values reasonably in the range of acceptable price cannot pose any objective threat to a corporation or its shareholders. Thus, Paramount would have us hold that only if the value of Paramount's offer were determined to be clearly inferior to the value created by management's plan to merge with Warner could the offer be viewed—objectively—as a threat.

Implicit in the plaintiffs' argument is the view that a hostile tender offer can pose only two types of threats: the threat of coercion that results from a two-tier offer promising unequal treatment for nontendering shareholders; and the threat of inadequate value from an all-shares, all-cash offer at a price below what a target board in good faith deems to be the present value of its shares. See, e.g., Interco, 551 A.2d at 797; see also BNS, Inc. v. Koppers, D.Del., 683 F.Supp. 458 (1988). Since Paramount's offer was all-cash, the only conceivable "threat," plaintiffs argue, was inadequate value. We disapprove of such a narrow and rigid construction of *Unocal*, for the reasons which follow.

Plaintiffs' position represents a fundamental misconception of our standard of review under *Unocal* principally because it would involve the court in substituting its judgment as to what is a "better" deal for that of a corporation's board of directors. To the extent that the Court of Chancery has recently done so in certain of its opinions, we hereby reject such approach as not in keeping with a proper *Unocal* analysis. See, e.g., Interco, 551 A.2d 787, and its progeny; but see TW Services, Inc. v. SWT Acquisition Corp., Del.Ch., C.A. No. 1047, Allen, C. 1989 WL 20290 (March 2, 1989).

The usefulness of *Unocal* as an analytical tool is precisely its flexibility in the face of a variety of fact scenarios. *Unocal* is not intended as an abstract standard; neither is it a structured and mechanistic procedure of appraisal. Thus, we have said that directors may consider, when evaluating the threat posed by a takeover bid, the "inadequacy of the price offered, nature and timing of the offer, questions of illegality, the impact on 'constituencies' other than shareholders ... the risk of nonconsummation, and the quality of securities being offered in the exchange." 493 A.2d at 955. The open-ended analysis mandated by *Unocal* is not intended to lead to a simple mathematical exercise: that is, of comparing the discounted value of Time–Warner's expected trading price at some future date with Paramount's offer and determining which is the higher. Indeed, in our view, precepts underlying the business judgment rule militate against a court's engaging in the process of attempting to appraise and evaluate the relative merits of a long-term versus a short-term investment goal for shareholders. To engage in such an exercise is a distortion of the Unocal process and, in particular, the application of the second part of *Unocal*'s test, discussed below.

In this case, the Time board reasonably determined that inadequate value was not the only legally cognizable threat that Paramount's all-cash, all-shares offer could present. Time's board concluded that Paramount's eleventh hour offer posed other threats. One concern was that Time shareholders might elect to tender into Paramount's cash offer in ignorance or a mistaken belief of the strategic benefit which a business combination with Warner might produce. Moreover, Time viewed the conditions attached to Paramount's offer as introducing a degree of uncertainty that skewed a comparative analysis. Further, the timing of Paramount's offer to follow issuance of Time's proxy notice was viewed as arguably designed to upset, if not confuse, the Time stockholders' vote. Given this record evidence, we cannot conclude that the Time board's decision of June 6 that Paramount's offer posed a threat to corporate policy and effectiveness was lacking in good faith or dominated by motives of either entrenchment or self-interest....

We turn to the second part of the *Unocal* analysis. . . . As applied to the facts of this case, the question is whether the record evidence supports the Court of Chancery's conclusion that the restructuring of the Time–Warner transaction, including the adoption of several preclusive defensive measures, was a reasonable response in relation to a perceived threat.

Paramount argues that, assuming its tender offer posed a threat, Time's response was unreasonable in precluding Time's shareholders from accepting the tender offer or receiving a control premium in the immediately foreseeable future. Once again, the contention stems, we believe, from a fundamental misunderstanding of where the power of corporate governance lies. Delaware law confers the management of the corporate enterprise to the stockholders' duly elected board representatives. 8 Del.C. § 141(a). The fiduciary duty to manage a corporate enterprise includes the selection of a time frame for achievement of corporate goals. That duty may not be delegated to the stockholders. Directors are not obliged to abandon a deliberately conceived corporate plan for a short-term shareholder profit unless there is clearly no basis to sustain the corporate strategy. See, e.g., Revlon, 506 A.2d 173.

Although the Chancellor blurred somewhat the discrete analyses required under *Unocal*, he did conclude that Time's board reasonably perceived Paramount's offer to be a significant threat to the planned Time–Warner merger and that Time's response was not "overly broad." We have found that even in light of a valid threat, management actions that are coercive in nature or force upon shareholders a management-sponsored alternative to a hostile offer may be struck down as unreasonable and nonproportionate responses.

Here, on the record facts, the Chancellor found that Time's responsive action to Paramount's tender offer was not aimed at "cramming down" on its shareholders a management-sponsored alternative, but rather had as its goal the carrying forward of a pre-existing transaction in an altered form. Thus, the response was reasonably related to the threat. The Chancellor noted that the revised agreement and its accompanying safety devices did not preclude Paramount from making an offer for the combined Time–Warner company or from changing the conditions of its offer so as not to make the offer dependent upon the nullification of the Time–Warner agreement. Thus, the response was proportionate. We affirm the Chancellor's rulings as clearly supported by the record.

Discussion Questions:

1. In *Interco* and *TW Services*, cited above, the Delaware Chancery Court applied *Unocal* to require a target board to redeem (i.e., eliminate) its poison pill. This "hard look" at the reasonableness of a pill seemed to be invited by the language of *Moran* itself. (Recall the Court's language that "the Rights Plan [poison pill] is not absolute," and the board "will not be able to arbitrarily reject the offer.") But in *Time-Warner*, the Delaware Supreme Court criticizes this hard look, finding that such an approach "would involve the court in substituting its judgment as to what is a 'better' deal for that of a corporation's board of directors." But is it correct that a forced redemption of a poison pill substitutes the court's judgment for the board's? Who exactly gets to decide, when a poison pill is eliminated?

2. What is the standard that the Court establishes for reviewing a board's decision to engage in a stock-for-stock merger? How deferential do you think this standard is? (Why do you think commentators argued that *Time Warner* endorsed the "Just Say No" defense?)

Paramount Communications, Inc. v. QVC Network, Inc.
637 A.2d 34 (Del. 1994)

VEASEY, C.J.:

In this appeal we review an order of the Court of Chancery . . . , preliminarily enjoining certain defensive measures designed to facilitate a so-called strategic alliance between Viacom Inc. ("Viacom") and Paramount Communications Inc. ("Paramount") approved by the board of directors of Paramount . . . and to thwart an unsolicited, more valuable, tender offer by QVC Network Inc. ("QVC"). In affirming, we hold that the sale of control in this case, which is at the heart of the proposed strategic alliance, implicates enhanced judicial scrutiny of the conduct of the Paramount Board under [*Unocal* and *Revlon*]. . . .

. . . Paramount owns and operates a diverse group of entertainment businesses, including motion picture and television studios, book publishers, professional sports teams and amusement parks.

There are 15 persons serving on the Paramount Board. Four directors are officer-employees. . . . Paramount's 11 outside directors are distinguished and experienced business persons who are present or former senior executives of public corporations or financial institutions.

. . . Viacom is controlled by Sumner M. Redstone ("Redstone"), its Chairman and Chief Executive Officer, who owns indirectly approximately 85.2 percent of Viacom's voting Class A stock and approximately 69.2 percent of Viacom's nonvoting Class B stock. . . . Viacom has a wide range of entertainment operations, including a number of well-known cable television channels such as MTV, Nickelodeon, Showtime, and The Movie Channel. . . .

. . . Barry Diller ("Diller"), [is] the Chairman and Chief Executive Officer of QVC, [and] is also a substantial stockholder. QVC sells a variety of merchandise through a televised shopping channel. . . .

Beginning in the late 1980s, Paramount investigated the possibility of acquiring or merging with other companies in the entertainment, media, or communications industry. Paramount considered such transactions to be desirable, and perhaps necessary, in order to keep pace with competitors in the rapidly evolving field of entertainment and communications. Consistent with its goal of strategic expansion, Paramount made a tender offer for Time Inc. in 1989, but was ultimately unsuccessful. . . .

Although Paramount had considered a possible combination of Paramount and Viacom as early as 1990, recent efforts to explore such a transaction began at a dinner meeting between Redstone and Davis on April 20, 1993....

On September 12, 1993, the Paramount Board . . . unanimously approved the Original Merger Agreement whereby Paramount would merge with and into Viacom. The terms of the merger provided that each share of Paramount common stock would be converted into 0.10 shares of Viacom Class A voting stock, 0.90 shares of Viacom Class B nonvoting stock, and $9.10 in cash. In addition, the Paramount Board agreed to amend its "poison pill" Rights Agreement to exempt the proposed merger with Viacom. The Original Merger Agreement also contained several provisions designed to make it more difficult for a potential competing bid to succeed. We focus, as did the Court of Chancery, on three of these defensive provisions: a "no-shop" provision (the "No-Shop Provision"), the Termination Fee, and the Stock Option Agreement.

First, under the No-Shop Provision, the Paramount Board agreed that Paramount would not solicit, encourage, discuss, negotiate, or endorse any competing transaction unless: (a) a third party "makes an unsolicited written, bona fide proposal, which is not subject to any material contingencies relating to financing"; and (b) the Paramount Board determines that discussions or negotiations with the third party are necessary for the Paramount Board to comply with its fiduciary duties.

Second, under the Termination Fee provision, Viacom would receive a $100 million termination fee if: (a) Paramount terminated the Original Merger Agreement because of a competing transaction; (b) Paramount's stockholders did not approve the merger; or (c) the Paramount Board recommended a competing transaction.

The third and most significant deterrent device was the Stock Option Agreement, which granted to Viacom an option to purchase approximately 19.9 percent (23,699,000 shares) of Paramount's outstanding common stock at $69.14 per share if any of the triggering events for the Termination Fee occurred. In addition to the customary terms that are normally associated with a stock option, the Stock Option Agreement contained two provisions that were both unusual and highly beneficial to Viacom: (a) Viacom was permitted to pay for the shares with a senior subordinated note of questionable marketability instead of cash, thereby avoiding the need to raise the $1.6 billion purchase price (the "Note Feature"); and (b) Viacom could elect to require Paramount to pay Viacom in cash a sum equal to the difference between the purchase price and the market price of Paramount's stock (the "Put Feature"). Because the Stock Option Agreement was not "capped" to limit its maximum dollar value, it had the potential to reach (and in this case did reach) unreasonable levels.

After the execution of the Original Merger Agreement and the Stock Option Agreement on September 12, 1993, Paramount and Viacom announced their proposed merger. In a number of public statements, the parties indicated that the pending transaction was a virtual certainty. Redstone described it as a "marriage" that would "never be torn asunder" and stated that only a "nuclear attack" could break the deal....

Despite these attempts to discourage a competing bid, Diller sent a letter to Davis on September 20, 1993, proposing a merger in which QVC would acquire Paramount for approximately $80 per share, consisting of 0.893 shares of QVC common stock and $30 in cash. QVC also expressed its eagerness to meet with Paramount to negotiate the details of a transaction. When the Paramount Board met on September 27, it was advised by Davis that the Original Merger Agreement prohibited Paramount from having discussions with QVC (or anyone else) unless certain conditions were satisfied. In particular, QVC had to supply evidence that its proposal was not subject to financing contingencies....

[After] QVC provided Paramount with evidence of QVC's financing, [t]he Paramount Board . . . decided to authorize management to meet with QVC. Davis also informed the Paramount Board that Booz-Allen & Hamilton ("Booz-Allen"), a management consulting firm, had been retained to assess, inter alia, the incremental earnings potential from a Paramount-Viacom merger and a Paramount-QVC merger. Discussions proceeded slowly, however, due to a delay in Paramount signing a confidentiality agreement. In response to Paramount's request for information, QVC provided two binders of documents to Paramount on October 20.

On October 21, 1993, QVC filed this action and publicly announced an $80 cash tender offer for 51 percent of Paramount's outstanding shares (the "QVC tender offer"). Each remaining share of Paramount common stock would be converted into 1.42857 shares of QVC common stock in a second-step merger. The tender offer was conditioned on, among other things, the invalidation of the Stock Option Agreement....

Confronted by QVC's hostile bid, which on its face offered over $10 per share more than the consideration provided by the Original Merger Agreement, Viacom realized that it would need to raise its bid in order to remain competitive.... In effect, the opportunity for a "new deal" with Viacom was at hand for the Paramount Board. With the QVC hostile bid offering greater value to the Paramount stockholders, the Paramount Board had considerable leverage with Viacom.

At a special meeting on October 24, 1993, the Paramount Board approved the Amended Merger Agreement and an amendment to the Stock Option Agreement. The Amended Merger Agreement was, however, essentially the same as the Original Merger Agreement, except that it included a few new provisions. One provision related to an $80 per share cash tender offer by Viacom for 51 percent of Paramount's stock, and another changed the merger consideration so that each share of Paramount would be converted into 0.20408 shares of Viacom Class A voting stock, 1.08317 shares of Viacom Class B nonvoting stock, and 0.20408 shares of a new series of Viacom convertible preferred stock. The Amended Merger Agreement also added a provision giving Paramount the right not to amend its Rights Agreement to exempt Viacom if the Paramount Board determined that such an amendment would be inconsistent with its fiduciary duties because another offer constituted a "better alternative." Finally, the Paramount Board was given the power to terminate the Amended Merger Agreement if it withdrew its recommendation of the Viacom transaction or recommended a competing transaction.

Although the Amended Merger Agreement offered more consideration to the Paramount stockholders and somewhat more flexibility to the Paramount Board . . . , the defensive measures designed to make a competing bid more difficult were not removed or modified. . . .

On November 6, 1993, Viacom unilaterally raised its tender offer price to $85 per share in cash and offered a comparable increase in the value of the securities being proposed in the second-step merger. At a telephonic meeting held later that day, the Paramount Board agreed to recommend Viacom's higher bid to Paramount's stockholders.

QVC responded to Viacom's higher bid on November 12 by increasing its tender offer to $90 per share and by increasing the securities for its second-step merger by a similar amount. . . .

At its meeting on November 15, 1993, the Paramount Board determined that the new QVC offer was not in the best interests of the stockholders. The purported basis for this conclusion was that QVC's bid was excessively conditional. The Paramount Board did not communicate with QVC regarding the status of the conditions because it believed that the No-Shop Provision prevented such communication in the absence of firm financing. . . .

Under normal circumstances, neither the courts nor the stockholders should interfere with the managerial decisions of the directors. . . .

Nevertheless, there are rare situations which mandate that a court take a more direct and active role in overseeing the decisions made and actions taken by directors. In these situations, a court subjects the directors' conduct to enhanced scrutiny to ensure that it is reasonable. The decisions of this Court have clearly established the circumstances where such enhanced scrutiny will be applied. . . . The case at bar implicates two such circumstances: (1) the approval of a transaction resulting in a sale of control, and (2) the adoption of defensive measures in response to a threat to corporate control.

When a majority of a corporation's voting shares are acquired by a single person or entity, or by a cohesive group acting together, there is a significant diminution in the voting power of those who thereby become minority stockholders. Under the statutory framework of the General Corporation Law, many of the most fundamental corporate changes can be implemented only if they are approved by a majority vote of the stockholders. . . . Because of the overriding importance of voting rights, this Court and the Court of Chancery have consistently acted to protect stockholders from unwarranted interference with such rights.

In the absence of devices protecting the minority stockholders, stockholder votes are likely to become mere formalities where there is a majority stockholder. For example, minority stockholders can be deprived of a continuing equity interest in their corporation by means of a cash-out merger. *Weinberger,* 457 A.2d at 703. Absent effective protective provisions, minority stockholders must rely for protection solely on the fiduciary duties owed to them by the directors and the majority stockholder, since the minority stockholders have lost the power to influence corporate direction through the ballot. The acquisition of majority status and the consequent privilege of exerting the powers of majority ownership come at a price. That price is usually a control premium which recognizes not only the value of a control block of shares, but also compensates the minority stockholders for their resulting loss of voting power.

In the case before us, the public stockholders (in the aggregate) currently own a majority of Paramount's voting stock. Control of the corporation is not vested in a single person, entity, or group, but vested in the fluid aggregation of unaffiliated stockholders. In the event the Paramount-Viacom transaction is consummated, the public stockholders will receive cash and a minority equity voting position in the surviving corporation. Following such consummation, there will be a controlling stockholder who will have the voting power to: (a) elect directors; (b) cause a break-up of the corporation: (c) merge it with another company; (d) cash-out the public stockholders: (e) amend the certificate of incorporation; (f) sell all or substantially all of the corporate assets; or (g) otherwise alter materially the nature of the corporation and the public stockholders' interests. Irrespective of the present Paramount Board's vision of a long- term strategic alliance with Viacom, the proposed sale of control would provide the new controlling stockholder with the power to alter that vision.

Because of the intended sale of control, the Paramount-Viacom transaction has economic consequences of considerable significance to the Paramount stockholders. Once control has shifted, the current Paramount stockholders will have no leverage in the future to demand another control premium. As a result, the Paramount stockholders are entitled to receive, and should receive, a control premium and/or protective devices of significant value. There being no such protective provisions in the Viacom-Paramount transaction, the Paramount directors had an obligation to take the maximum advantage of the current opportunity to realize for the stockholders the best value reasonably available.

. . . In the sale of control context, the directors must focus on one primary objective—to secure the transaction offering the best value reasonably available for the stockholders— and they must exercise their fiduciary duties to further that end. . . .

. . . Moreover, the role of outside, independent directors becomes particularly important because of the magnitude of a sale of control transaction and the possibility, in certain cases, that management may not necessarily be impartial. . . .

[The] *Barkan* [decision] teaches some of the methods by which a board can fulfill its obligation to seek the best value reasonably available to the stockholders. 567 A.2d at 1286-87. . . . They include conducting an auction, canvassing the market, etc. Delaware law recognizes that there is "no single blueprint" that directors must follow. . . .

In determining which alternative provides the best value for the stockholders, a board of directors is not limited to considering only the amount of cash involved. . . . Where stock or other non-cash consideration is involved, the board should try to quantify its value, if feasible, to achieve an objective comparison of the alternatives. . . . While the assessment of these factors may be complex, the board's goal is straightforward: Having informed themselves of all material information reasonably available, the directors must decide which alternative is most likely to offer the best value reasonably available to the stockholders.

Board action in the circumstances presented here is subject to enhanced scrutiny. Such scrutiny is mandated by: (a) the threatened diminution of the current stockholders' voting power; (b) the fact that an asset belonging to public stockholders (a control premium) is being sold and may never be available again[;] and (c) the traditional concern of Delaware courts for actions which impair or impede stockholder voting rights. . . .

The key features of an enhanced scrutiny test are: (a) a judicial determination regarding the adequacy of the decisionmaking process employed by the directors, including the information on which the directors based their decision; and (b) a judicial examination of the reasonableness of the directors' action in light of the circumstances then existing. The directors have the burden of proving that they were adequately informed and acted reasonably.

Although an enhanced scrutiny test involves a review of the reasonableness of the substantive merits of a board's actions, a court should not ignore the complexity of the directors' task in a sale of control. There are many business and financial considerations implicated in investigating and selecting the best value reasonably available. The board of directors is the corporate decisionmaking body best equipped to make these judgments. Accordingly, a court applying enhanced judicial scrutiny should be deciding whether the directors made a reasonable decision, not a perfect decision. If a board selected one of several reasonable alternatives, a court should not second-guess that choice even though it might have decided otherwise or subsequent events may have cast doubt on the board's determination. Thus, courts will not substitute their business judgment for that of the directors, but will determine if the directors' decision was, on balance, within a range of reasonableness. . . .

The Paramount defendants and Viacom assert that the fiduciary obligations and the enhanced judicial scrutiny discussed above are not implicated in this case in the absence of a "break-up" of the corporation, and that the order granting the preliminary injunction should be reversed. This argument is based on their erroneous interpretation of our decisions in *Revlon* and *Time-Warner*. . . .

Although [the earlier] *Macmillan* and *Barkan* [decisions] are clear in holding that a change of control imposes on directors the obligation to obtain the best value reasonably available to the stockholders, the Paramount defendants have interpreted our decision in *Time-Warner* as requiring a corporate break-up in order for that obligation to apply. The facts in *Time-Warner*, however, were quite different from the facts of this case. . . . In *Time-Warner*, the Chancellor held that there was no change of control in the original stock-for-stock merger between Time and Warner because Time would be owned by a fluid aggregation of unaffiliated stockholders both before and after the merger. . . .

In our affirmance of the Court of Chancery's well-reasoned decision, this Court held that "The Chancellor's findings of fact are supported by the record and *his conclusion is correct as a matter of law.*" 571 A.2d at 1150 (emphasis added). Nevertheless, the Paramount defendants here have argued that a break-up is a requirement and have focused on the following language in our *Time-Warner* decision:

> However, we premise our rejection of plaintiffs' *Revlon* claim on different grounds, namely, the absence of any substantial evidence to conclude that Time's board, in negotiating with Warner, made the dissolution or break-up of the corporate entity inevitable, as was the case in *Revlon.*

> Under Delaware law there are, generally speaking and without excluding other possibilities, two circumstances which may implicate *Revlon* duties. The first, and clearer one, is when a corporation initiates an active bidding process seeking to sell itself or to effect a business reorganization involving a clear breakup of the company. However, *Revlon* duties may also be triggered where, in response to a bidder's offer, a target abandons its long-term strategy and seeks an alternative transaction involving the breakup of the company. *Id.* at 1150 (emphasis added) (citation and footnote omitted).

The Paramount defendants have misread the holding of *Time-Warner.* Contrary to their argument, our decision in *Time-Warner* expressly states that the two general scenarios discussed in the above-quoted paragraph are not the only instances where "*Revlon* duties" may be implicated. The Paramount defendants' argument totally ignores the phrase "without excluding other possibilities." Moreover, the instant case is clearly within the first general scenario set forth in *Time-Warner.* The Paramount Board, albeit unintentionally, had "initiated an active bidding process seeking to sell itself" by agreeing to sell control of the corporation to Viacom in circumstances where another potential acquirer (QVC) was equally interested in being a bidder.

The Paramount defendants' position that both a change of control and a break-up are required must be rejected. Such a holding would unduly restrict the application of *Revlon,* is inconsistent with this Court's decisions in *Barkan* and *Macmillan,* and has no basis in policy. There are few events that have a more significant impact on the stockholders than a sale of control or a corporate break-up. Each event represents a fundamental (and perhaps irrevocable) change in the nature of the corporate enterprise from a practical standpoint. It is the significance of each of these events that justifies: (a) focusing on the directors' obligation to seek the best value reasonably available to the stockholders; and (b) requiring a close scrutiny of board action which could be contrary to the stockholders' interests.

Accordingly, when a corporation undertakes a transaction which will cause: (a) a change in corporate control; or (b) a break-up of the corporate entity, the directors' obligation is to seek the best value reasonably available to the stockholders. This obligation arises because the effect of the Viacom- Paramount transaction, if consummated, is to shift control of Paramount from the public stockholders to a controlling stockholder, Viacom. Neither

282

Time-Warner nor any other decision of this Court holds that a "break-up" of the company is essential to give rise to this obligation where there is a sale of control. . . .

We now turn to duties of the Paramount Board under the facts of this case and our conclusions as to the breaches of those duties that warrant injunctive relief. . . .

Under the facts of this case, the Paramount directors had the obligation: (a) to be diligent and vigilant in examining critically the Paramount-Viacom transaction and the QVC tender offers; (b) to act in good faith; (c) to obtain, and act with due care on, all material information reasonably available, including information necessary to compare the two offers to determine which of these transactions, or an alternative course of action, would provide the best value reasonably available to the stockholders; and (d) to negotiate actively and in good faith with both Viacom and QVC to that end.

Having decided to sell control of the corporation, the Paramount directors were required to evaluate critically whether or not all material aspects of the Paramount-Viacom transaction (separately and in the aggregate) were reasonable and in the best interests of the Paramount stockholders in light of current circumstances, including: the change of control premium, the Stock Option Agreement, the Termination Fee, the coercive nature of both the Viacom and QVC tender offers, the No-Shop Provision, and the proposed disparate use of the Rights Agreement as to the Viacom and QVC tender offers, respectively.

These obligations necessarily implicated various issues, including the questions of whether or not those provisions . . . : (a) adversely affected the value provided to the Paramount stockholders; (b) inhibited or encouraged alternative bids; (c) were enforceable contractual obligations in light of the directors' fiduciary duties; and (d) in the end would advance or retard the Paramount directors' obligation to secure for the Paramount stockholders the best value reasonably available under the circumstances.

The Paramount defendants contend that they were precluded by certain contractual provisions including the No-Shop Provision, from negotiating with QVC or seeking alternatives. Such provisions, whether or not they are presumptively valid in the abstract, may not validly define or limit the directors' fiduciary duties under Delaware law or prevent the Paramount directors from carrying out their fiduciary duties under Delaware law. To the extent such provisions are inconsistent with those duties, they are invalid and unenforceable. . . .

Since the Paramount directors had already decided to sell control, they had an obligation to continue their search for the best value reasonably available to the stockholders. This continuing obligation included the responsibility, at the October 24 board meeting and thereafter, to evaluate critically both the QVC tender offers and the Paramount-Viacom transaction to determine if: (a) the QVC tender offer was, or would continue to be, conditional; (b) the QVC tender offer could be improved; (c) the Viacom tender offer or other aspects of the Paramount-Viacom transaction could be improved; (d) each of the respective offers would be reasonably likely to come to closure, and under what circumstances; (e) other material information was reasonably available for consideration by the Paramount directors; (f) there were viable and realistic alternative courses of action; and (g) the timing constraints could be managed so the directors could consider these matters carefully and deliberately....

When entering into the Original Merger Agreement, and thereafter, the Paramount Board clearly gave insufficient attention to the potential consequences of the defensive measures demanded by Viacom. The Stock Option Agreement had a number of unusual and potentially "draconian" provisions, including the Note Feature and the Put Feature. Furthermore, the Termination Fee, whether or not unreasonable by itself, clearly made Paramount less attractive to other bidders, when coupled with the Stock Option Agreement. Finally, the No-Shop Provision inhibited the Paramount Board's ability to negotiate with other potential bidders, particularly QVC which had already expressed an interest in Paramount.

Throughout the applicable time period, and especially from the first QVC merger proposal on September 20 through the Paramount Board meeting on November 15, QVC's interest in Paramount provided the opportunity for the Paramount Board to seek significantly higher value for the Paramount stockholders than that being offered by Viacom....

The Paramount directors had the opportunity in the October 23-24 time frame, when the Original Merger Agreement was renegotiated, to take appropriate action to modify the improper defensive measures as well as to improve the economic terms of the Paramount-Viacom transaction. Under the circumstances existing at that time, it should have been clear to the Paramount Board that the Stock Option Agreement, coupled with the Termination Fee and the No-Shop Clause, were impeding the realization of the best value reasonably available to the Paramount stockholders. Nevertheless, the Paramount Board made no effort to eliminate or modify these counterproductive devices, and instead continued to cling to its vision of a strategic alliance with Viacom. Moreover, based on advice from the Paramount management, the Paramount directors considered the QVC offer to be "conditional" and asserted that they were precluded by the No-Shop Provision from seeking more information from, or negotiating with, QVC.

By November 12, 1993, the value of the revised QVC offer on its face exceeded that of the Viacom offer by over $1 billion at then current values. This significant disparity of value cannot be justified on the basis of the directors' vision of future strategy, primarily because the change of control would supplant the authority of the current Paramount Board to continue to hold and implement their strategic vision in any meaningful way. Moreover, their uninformed process had deprived their strategic vision of much of its credibility....

When the Paramount directors met on November 15 to consider QVC's increased tender offer, they remained prisoners of their own misconceptions and missed opportunities to eliminate the restrictions they had imposed on themselves. Yet, it was not "too late" to reconsider negotiating with QVC. . . . Nevertheless, the Paramount directors remained paralyzed by their uninformed belief that the QVC offer was "illusory." This final opportunity to negotiate on the stockholders' behalf and to fulfill their obligation to seek the best value reasonably available was thereby squandered....

Viacom argues that it had certain "vested" contract rights with respect to the No-Shop Provision and the Stock Option Agreement. In effect, Viacom's argument is that the Paramount directors could enter into an agreement in violation of their fiduciary duties and then render Paramount, and ultimately its stockholders, liable for failing to carry out an agreement in violation of those duties. Viacom's protestations about vested rights are without merit. This Court has found that those defensive measures were improperly designed to deter potential bidders, and that such measures do not meet the reasonableness test to which they must be subjected. They are consequently invalid and unenforceable under the facts of this case.

The No-Shop Provision could not validly define or limit the fiduciary duties of the Paramount directors. To the extent that a contract, or a provision thereof, purports to require a board to act or not act in such a fashion as to limit the exercise of fiduciary duties, it is invalid and unenforceable. . . .

Viacom, a sophisticated party with experienced legal and financial advisors, knew of (and in fact demanded) the unreasonable features of the Stock Option Agreement. It cannot be now heard to argue that it obtained vested contract rights by negotiating and obtaining contractual provisions from a board acting in violation of its fiduciary duties. . . .

The realization of the best value reasonably available to the stockholders became the Paramount directors' primary obligation under these facts in light of the change of control. That obligation was not satisfied, and the Paramount Board's process was deficient. The directors' initial hope and expectation for a strategic alliance with Viacom was allowed to dominate their decisionmaking process to the point where the arsenal of defensive measures established at the outset was perpetuated (not modified or eliminated) when the situation was dramatically altered. QVC's unsolicited bid presented the opportunity for significantly greater value for the stockholders and enhanced negotiating leverage for the directors. Rather than seizing those opportunities, the Paramount directors chose to wall themselves off from material information which was reasonably available and to hide behind the defensive measures as a rationalization for refusing to negotiate with QVC or seeking other alternatives. Their view of the strategic alliance likewise became an empty rationalization as the opportunities for higher value for the stockholders continued to develop.

For the reasons set forth herein, the . . . Order of the Court of Chancery has been AFFIRMED, and this matter has been REMANDED for proceedings consistent herewith. . . .

Discussion Questions:

1. In the original deal structure, how did Sumner Redstone (HLS '47) maintain control of the combined company? Why (do you think) the Paramount board would allow him to control the combined company?

2. What are the policy reasons in favor of imposing *Revlon* duties on a target board when a merger shifts control to a controlling shareholder in the acquirer? What are the potential costs of this approach? (Recall our discussion of the pros and cons of *Revlon* itself.)

3. Rob Kindler, then an attorney at Cravath, Swaine & Moore (and now the Vice Chairman of Morgan Stanley) explained the Court's decision as follows:

   > The problem was that QVC came in with their bid, and then [Paramount] had to re-negotiate [its] deal with Viacom. And the court said, "Let me see if I get this straight—you signed up a new deal with Viacom, knowing that you had a competing bidder, and you signed up a new deal with Viacom over some weekend, and it never dawned on you to ask them to change any of the breakups? . . . Viacom needed your approval to sign up this new restructured deal, and you never even thought about asking Viacom to cap the option, or to reduce the option, or reduce the breakup fee? That shows us that you were willing to do a deal with Viacom at any cost."[23]

   From the other side of the table, recall that Redstone described the deal as a "marriage" that would "never be torn asunder" and stated that only a "nuclear attack" could break the deal." If Paramount and Viacom had a "redo" on the deal, how would you advise them to frame it in their public statements?

4. After the stock option lockup was struck down in this case, Delaware practitioners migrated to termination fees, and stock option lockups became non-existent. Is this an appropriate reading of the Court's decision? Or is it an over-reaction to poor facts and a poorly structured lockup in this case?

The Current U.S. Debate (2017)

So where are we now?

The *Airgas* excerpt below summarizes the current state of Delaware fiduciary law for takeover defenses. A board can maintain a poison pill for as long as it likes and for the mere reason that it believes the offer price to be inadequate. This means that the only way to overcome determined resistance by an incumbent board is to replace it in a proxy fight.

Until recently, most large corporations' charters did not permit replacing a majority of the board in a single annual meeting. Their boards were staggered, i.e., only a third of the directors were up for re-election each year (re-read DGCL 141(d), (k)(1)). Consequently, an acquirer had to win proxy fights at two successive annual meetings to replace the majority of an intransigent board. This takes at a minimum one year and a couple months, and the acquirer would have had to keep the tender offer open (and capital tied up, etc.) during

---

[23] Guhan Subramanian Interview with Rob Kindler, in New York, N.Y. (Aug. 10, 1999), transcript at 6.

that entire time. Hardly any challenger was willing to attempt this. *Airgas* is about one of the very few exceptions.

In recent years, however, the incidence of staggered boards has declined precipitously among the largest U.S. corporations. By 2012, only a fourth of the corporations in the S&P 500 index had staggered boards. Between 2012 and 2014, most of these hold-outs "destaggered" as well. The impetus came from a law school clinic, the Shareholder Rights Project (SRP) based at Harvard Law School. Acting on behalf of several institutional shareholders, the SRP submitted destaggering proposals for the corporations' annual meetings. Under Rule 14a-8, the targeted corporations had to include these proposals on their proxies. Other shareholders generally supported these proposals, and most recipient corporations soon agreed to destagger. At the same time, staggered boards remain the norm in IPO charters—the charters of corporations selling their stock to the public for the first time.

Air Products & Chemicals, Inc., v. AirGas, Inc.
16 A.3d 48 (2011)

CHANDLER, Chancellor.

This case poses the following fundamental question: Can a board of directors, acting in good faith and with a reasonable factual basis for its decision, when faced with a structurally non-coercive, all-cash, fully financed tender offer directed to the stockholders of the corporation, keep a poison pill in place so as to prevent the stockholders from making their own decision about whether they want to tender their shares—even after the incumbent board has lost one election contest, a full year has gone by since the offer was first made public, and the stockholders are fully informed as to the target board's views on the inadequacy of the offer? If so, does that effectively mean that a board can "just say never" to a hostile tender offer?

The answer to the latter question is "no." A board cannot *"just* say no" to a tender offer. Under Delaware law, it must first pass through two prongs of exacting judicial scrutiny by a judge who will evaluate the actions taken by, and the motives of, the board. Only a board of directors found to be acting in good faith, after reasonable investigation and reliance on the advice of outside advisors, which articulates and convinces the Court that a hostile tender offer poses a legitimate threat to the corporate enterprise, may address that perceived threat by blocking the tender offer and forcing the bidder to elect a board majority that supports its bid.

In essence, this case brings to the fore one of the most basic questions animating all of corporate law, which relates to the allocation of power between directors and stockholders. That is, "when, if ever, will a board's duty to 'the corporation and its shareholders' require [the board] to abandon concerns for 'long term' values (and other constituencies) and enter a current share value maximizing mode?" More to the point, in the context of a hostile tender offer, who gets to decide when and if the corporation is for sale?

Since the Shareholder Rights Plan (more commonly known as the "poison pill") was first conceived and throughout the development of Delaware corporate takeover jurisprudence during the twenty-five-plus years that followed, the debate over who ultimately decides whether a tender offer is adequate and should be accepted—the shareholders of the corporation or its board of directors—has raged on. Starting with *Moran v. Household International, Inc.* in 1985, when the Delaware Supreme Court first upheld the adoption of the poison pill as a valid takeover defense, through the hostile takeover years of the 1980s, and in several recent decisions of the Court of Chancery and the Delaware Supreme Court, this fundamental question has engaged practitioners, academics, and members of the judiciary, but it has yet to be confronted head on.

For the reasons much more fully described in the remainder of this Opinion, I conclude that, as Delaware law currently stands, the answer must be that the power to defeat an inadequate hostile tender offer ultimately lies with the board of directors. As such, I find that the Airgas board has met its burden under *Unocal* to articulate a legally cognizable threat (the allegedly inadequate price of Air Products' offer, coupled with the fact that a majority of Airgas's stockholders would likely tender into that inadequate offer) and has taken defensive measures that fall within a range of reasonable responses proportionate to that threat. I thus rule in favor of defendants. Air Products' and the Shareholder Plaintiffs' requests for relief are denied, and all claims asserted against defendants are dismissed with prejudice.

INTRODUCTION

This is the Court's decision after trial, extensive post-trial briefing, and a supplemental evidentiary hearing in this long-running takeover battle between Air Products & Chemicals, Inc. ("Air Products") and Airgas, Inc. ("Airgas"). The now very public saga began quietly in mid-October 2009 when John McGlade, President and CEO of Air Products, privately approached Peter McCausland, founder and CEO of Airgas, about a potential acquisition or combination. After McGlade's private advances were rebuffed, Air Products went hostile in February 2010, launching a public tender offer for all outstanding Airgas shares.

Now, over a year since Air Products first announced its all-shares, all-cash tender offer, the terms of that offer (other than price) remain essentially unchanged. After several price bumps and extensions, the offer currently stands at $70 per share and is set to expire today, February 15, 2011—Air Products' stated "best and final" offer. The Airgas board unanimously rejected that offer as being "clearly inadequate." The Airgas board has repeatedly expressed the view that Airgas is worth at least $78 per share in a sale transaction—and at any rate, far more than the $70 per share Air Products is offering.

So, we are at a crossroads. Air Products has made its "best and final" offer—apparently its offer to acquire Airgas has reached an end stage. Meanwhile, the Airgas board believes the offer is clearly inadequate and its value in a sale transaction is at least $78 per share. At this stage, it appears, neither side will budge. Airgas continues to maintain its defenses, blocking the bid and effectively denying shareholders the choice whether to tender their shares. Air Products and Shareholder Plaintiffs now ask this Court to order Airgas to redeem its poison pill and other defenses that are stopping Air Products from moving forward with its hostile offer, and to allow Airgas's stockholders to decide for themselves whether they want to tender into Air Products' (inadequate or not) $70 "best and final" offer.

A week-long trial in this case was held from October 4, 2010 through October 8, 2010. Hundreds of pages of post-trial memoranda were submitted by the parties. After trial, several legal, factual, and evidentiary questions remained to be answered. In ruling on certain outstanding evidentiary issues, I sent counsel a Letter Order on December 2, 2010 asking for answers to a number of questions to be addressed in supplemental post-trial briefing. On the eve of the parties' submissions to the Court in response to that Letter Order, Air Products raised its offer to the $70 "best and final" number. At that point, defendants vigorously opposed a ruling based on the October trial record, suggesting that the entire trial (indeed, the entire case) was moot because the October trial predominantly focused on the Airgas board's response to Air Products' then-$65.50 offer and the board's decision to keep its defenses in place with respect to that offer. Defendants further suggested that any ruling with respect to the $70 offer was not ripe because the board had not yet met to consider that offer.

I rejected both the mootness and ripeness arguments. As for mootness, Air Products had previously raised its bid several times throughout the litigation but the core question before me—whether Air Products' offer continues to pose a threat justifying Airgas's continued maintenance of its poison pill—remained, and remains, the same. And as for ripeness, by the time of the December 23 Letter Order the Airgas board had met and rejected Air Products' revised $70 offer. I did, however, allow the parties to take supplemental discovery relating to the $70 offer. A supplemental evidentiary hearing was held from January 25 through January 27, 2011, in order to complete the record on the $70 offer. Counsel presented closing arguments on February 8, 2011.

Now, having thoroughly read, reviewed, and reflected upon all of the evidence presented to me, and having carefully considered the arguments made by counsel, I conclude that the Airgas board, in proceeding as it has since October 2009, has not breached its fiduciary duties owed to the Airgas stockholders. I find that the board has acted in good faith and in the honest belief that the Air Products offer, at $70 per share, is inadequate.

Although I have a hard time believing that inadequate price alone (according to the target's board) in the context of a nondiscriminatory, all-cash, all-shares, fully financed offer poses any "threat"—particularly given the wealth of information available to Airgas's stockholders at this point in time—under existing Delaware law, it apparently does. Inadequate price has become a form of "substantive coercion" as that concept has been developed by the Delaware Supreme Court in its takeover jurisprudence. That is, the idea that Airgas's stockholders will disbelieve the board's views on value (or in the case of merger arbitrageurs who may have short-term profit goals in mind, they may simply ignore

289

the board's recommendations), and so they may mistakenly tender into an inadequately priced offer. Substantive coercion has been clearly recognized by our Supreme Court as a valid threat.

Trial judges are not free to ignore or rewrite appellate court decisions. Thus, for reasons explained in detail below, I am constrained by Delaware Supreme Court precedent to conclude that defendants have met their burden under *Unocal* to articulate a sufficient threat that justifies the continued maintenance of Airgas's poison pill. That is, assuming defendants have met their burden to articulate a legally cognizable threat (prong 1), Airgas's defenses have been recognized by Delaware law as reasonable responses to the threat posed by an inadequate offer—even an all-shares, all-cash offer (prong 2).

In my personal view, Airgas's poison pill has served its legitimate purpose. Although the "best and final" $70 offer has been on the table for just over two months (since December 9, 2010), Air Products' advances have been ongoing for over sixteen months, and Airgas's use of its poison pill—particularly in combination with its staggered board—has given the Airgas board over a full year to inform its stockholders about its view of Airgas's intrinsic value and Airgas's value in a sale transaction. It has also given the Airgas board a full year to express its views to its stockholders on the purported opportunistic timing of Air Products' repeated advances and to educate its stockholders on the inadequacy of Air Products' offer. It has given Airgas *more time than any litigated poison pill in Delaware history*—enough time to show stockholders four quarters of improving financial results, demonstrating that Airgas is on track to meet its projected goals. And it has helped the Airgas board push Air Products to raise its bid by $10 per share from when it was first publicly announced to what Air Products has now represented is its highest offer. The record at both the October trial and the January supplemental evidentiary hearing confirm that Airgas's stockholder base is sophisticated and well-informed, and that essentially all the information they would need to make an informed decision is available to them. In short, there seems to be no threat here—the stockholders know what they need to know (about both the offer and the Airgas board's opinion of the offer) to make an informed decision.

That being said, however, as I understand binding Delaware precedent, I may not substitute my business judgment for that of the Airgas board. The Delaware Supreme Court has recognized inadequate price as a valid threat to corporate policy and effectiveness. The Delaware Supreme Court has also made clear that the "selection of a time frame for achievement of corporate goals . . . may not be delegated to the stockholders." Furthermore, in powerful dictum, the Supreme Court has stated that "[d]irectors are not obliged to abandon a deliberately conceived corporate plan for a short-term shareholder profit unless there is clearly no basis to sustain the corporate strategy." Although I do not read that dictum as eliminating the applicability of heightened *Unocal* scrutiny to a board's decision to block a non-coercive bid as underpriced, I do read it, along with the actual holding in *Unitrin,* as indicating that a board that has a good faith, reasonable basis to believe a bid is inadequate may block that bid using a poison pill, irrespective of stockholders' desire to accept it.

Here, even using heightened scrutiny, the Airgas board has demonstrated that it has a reasonable basis for sustaining its long term corporate strategy—the Airgas board is independent, and has relied on the advice of three different outside independent financial advisors in concluding that Air Products' offer is inadequate. Air Products' *own three nominees* who were elected to the Airgas board in September 2010 have joined wholeheartedly in the Airgas board's determination, and when the Airgas board met to consider the $70 "best and final" offer in December 2010, it was one of those Air Products Nominees who said, "We have to protect the pill." Indeed, one of Air Products' *own directors* conceded at trial that the Airgas board members had acted within their fiduciary duties in their desire to "hold out for the proper price," and that "if an offer was made for Air Products that [he] considered to be unfair to the stockholders of Air Products . . . [he would likewise] use every legal mechanism available" to hold out for the proper price as well. Under Delaware law, the Airgas directors have complied with their fiduciary duties. Thus, as noted above, and for the reasons more fully described in the remainder of this Opinion, I am constrained to deny Air Products' and the Shareholder Plaintiffs' requests for relief.

[...]

Discussion Questions:

1. How would you characterize Chancellor Chandler's opinion validating Airgas's use of the poison pill? Do you side with Chancellor Chandler's "personal view" or the ruling of the court? (And does it influence your opinion that the Airgas stock price exceeded Air Products' $70 "best and final" offer just a few months later, in November 2011, and the company was sold to Air Liquide for $143 per share in May 2016?)

2. Opinions are sharply divided about the desirability of takeover defenses in general, and of staggered boards in particular. Managers and their advisors argue that defenses allow boards to focus on long-term value creation rather than on catering to short-term pressures from the stock market. Opponents claim that defenses shield slack and prevent efficient reallocations of productive assets. The accountability argument for takeovers is easy to understand. What about the short-termism counterargument? Why would stock markets exert short-termist pressures on boards?

Chapter 9 – Buyouts by Controlling Shareholders

Buyouts by controlling shareholders (a.k.a. "freeze-outs," "squeeze-outs," and "minority buyouts") stand at the intersection of two types of corporate transaction that corporate law treats with special case: first, they are fundamental transactions (like M&A), and so the economic consequences are often significant; and second, they are conflict transactions, because the controlling shareholder is buying out the minority shareholders of the company. This creates the possibility that the controlling shareholder will abuse its power, e.g., by timing the buyout opportunistically, or not paying fair value to the exiting shareholders.

Corporate law tries to mitigate these potential abuses by supplying procedural protections to minority shareholders as a matter of fiduciary duty. The following cases document the evolution of these procedural protections in Delaware.

Weinberger v. UOP., Inc.
457 A.2d 701 (Del. 1983)

MOORE, Justice:

This post-trial appeal was reheard en banc from a decision of the Court of Chancery. It was brought by the class action plaintiff below, a former shareholder of UOP, Inc., who challenged the elimination of UOP's minority shareholders by a cash-out merger between UOP and its majority owner, The Signal Companies, Inc. Originally, the defendants in this action were Signal, UOP, certain officers and directors of those companies, and UOP's investment banker, Lehman Brothers Kuhn Loeb, Inc. The present Chancellor held that the terms of the merger were fair to the plaintiff and the other minority shareholders of UOP. Accordingly, he entered judgment in favor of the defendants.

Numerous points were raised by the parties, but we address only the following questions presented by the trial court's opinion:

> 1) The plaintiff's duty to plead sufficient facts demonstrating the unfairness of the challenged merger;

> 2) The burden of proof upon the parties where the merger has been approved by the purportedly informed vote of a majority of the minority shareholders;

> 3) The fairness of the merger in terms of adequacy of the defendants' disclosures to the minority shareholders;

4) The fairness of the merger in terms of adequacy of the price paid for the minority shares and the remedy appropriate to that issue; and

5) The continued force and effect of *Singer v. Magnavox Co.,* Del.Supr., 380 A.2d 969, 980 (1977), and its progeny.

In ruling for the defendants, the Chancellor re-stated his earlier conclusion that the plaintiff in a suit challenging a cash-out merger must allege specific acts of fraud, misrepresentation, or other items of misconduct to demonstrate the unfairness of the merger terms to the minority. We approve this rule and affirm it.

The Chancellor also held that even though the ultimate burden of proof is on the majority shareholder to show by a preponderance of the evidence that the transaction is fair, it is first the burden of the plaintiff attacking the merger to demonstrate some basis for invoking the fairness obligation. We agree with that principle. However, where corporate action has been approved by an informed vote of a majority of the minority shareholders, we conclude that the burden entirely shifts to the plaintiff to show that the transaction was unfair to the minority. *See, e.g., Michelson v. Duncan,* Del.Supr., 407 A.2d 211, 224 (1979). But in all this, the burden clearly remains on those relying on the vote to show that they completely disclosed all material facts relevant to the transaction.

Here, the record does not support a conclusion that the minority stockholder vote was an informed one. Material information, necessary to acquaint those shareholders with the bargaining positions of Signal and UOP, was withheld under circumstances amounting to a breach of fiduciary duty. We therefore conclude that this merger does not meet the test of fairness, at least as we address that concept, and no burden thus shifted to the plaintiff by reason of the minority shareholder vote. Accordingly, we reverse and remand for further proceedings consistent herewith.

[...]

Our treatment of these matters has necessarily led us to a reconsideration of the business purpose rule announced in the trilogy of *Singer v. Magnavox Co., supra; Tanzer v. International General Industries, Inc.,* Del.Supr., 379 A.2d 1121 (1977); and *Roland International Corp. v. Najjar,* Del.Supr., 407 A.2d 1032 (1979). For the reasons hereafter set forth we consider that the business purpose requirement of these cases is no longer the law of Delaware.

I.

The facts found by the trial court, pertinent to the issues before us, are supported by the record, and we draw from them as set out in the Chancellor's opinion.

Signal is a diversified, technically based company operating through various subsidiaries. Its stock is publicly traded on the New York, Philadelphia and Pacific Stock Exchanges. UOP, formerly known as Universal Oil Products Company, was a diversified industrial company

293

engaged in various lines of business, including petroleum and petro-chemical services and related products, construction, fabricated metal products, transportation equipment products, chemicals and plastics, and other products and services including land development, lumber products and waste disposal. Its stock was publicly held and listed on the New York Stock Exchange.

In 1974 Signal sold one of its wholly-owned subsidiaries for $420,000,000 in cash. *See Gimbel v. Signal Companies, Inc.,* Del. Ch., 316 A.2d 599, *aff'd,* Del.Supr., 316 A.2d 619 (1974). While looking to invest this cash surplus, Signal became interested in UOP as a possible acquisition. Friendly negotiations ensued, and Signal proposed to acquire a controlling interest in UOP at a price of $19 per share. UOP's representatives sought $25 per share. In the arm's length bargaining that followed, an understanding was reached whereby Signal agreed to purchase from UOP 1,500,000 shares of UOP's authorized but unissued stock at $21 per share.

This purchase was contingent upon Signal making a successful cash tender offer for 4,300,000 publicly held shares of UOP, also at a price of $21 per share. This combined method of acquisition permitted Signal to acquire 5,800,000 shares of stock, representing 50.5% of UOP's outstanding shares. The UOP board of directors advised the company's shareholders that it had no objection to Signal's tender offer at that price. Immediately before the announcement of the tender offer, UOP's common stock had been trading on the New York Stock Exchange at a fraction under $14 per share.

The negotiations between Signal and UOP occurred during April 1975, and the resulting tender offer was greatly oversubscribed. However, Signal limited its total purchase of the tendered shares so that, when coupled with the stock bought from UOP, it had achieved its goal of becoming a 50.5% shareholder of UOP.

Although UOP's board consisted of thirteen directors, Signal nominated and elected only six. Of these, five were either directors or employees of Signal. The sixth, a partner in the banking firm of Lazard Freres & Co., had been one of Signal's representatives in the negotiations and bargaining with UOP concerning the tender offer and purchase price of the UOP shares.

However, the president and chief executive officer of UOP retired during 1975, and Signal caused him to be replaced by James V. Crawford, a long-time employee and senior executive vice president of one of Signal's wholly-owned subsidiaries. Crawford succeeded his predecessor on UOP's board of directors and also was made a director of Signal.

By the end of 1977 Signal basically was unsuccessful in finding other suitable investment candidates for its excess cash, and by February 1978 considered that it had no other realistic acquisitions available to it on a friendly basis. Once again its attention turned to UOP.

The trial court found that at the instigation of certain Signal management personnel, including William W. Walkup, its board chairman, and Forrest N. Shumway, its president, a feasibility study was made concerning the possible acquisition of the balance of UOP's outstanding shares. This study was performed by two Signal officers, Charles S. Arledge, vice president (director of planning), and Andrew J. Chitiea, senior vice president (chief financial officer). Messrs. Walkup, Shumway, Arledge and Chitiea were all directors of UOP in addition to their membership on the Signal board.

Arledge and Chitiea concluded that it would be a good investment for Signal to acquire the remaining 49.5% of UOP shares at any price up to $24 each. Their report was discussed between Walkup and Shumway who, along with Arledge, Chitiea and Brewster L. Arms, internal counsel for Signal, constituted Signal's senior management. In particular, they talked about the proper price to be paid if the acquisition was pursued, purportedly keeping in mind that as UOP's majority shareholder, Signal owed a fiduciary responsibility to both its own stockholders as well as to UOP's minority. It was ultimately agreed that a meeting of Signal's executive committee would be called to propose that Signal acquire the remaining outstanding stock of UOP through a cash-out merger in the range of $20 to $21 per share.

The executive committee meeting was set for February 28, 1978. As a courtesy, UOP's president, Crawford, was invited to attend, although he was not a member of Signal's executive committee. On his arrival, and prior to the meeting, Crawford was asked to meet privately with Walkup and Shumway. He was then told of Signal's plan to acquire full ownership of UOP and was asked for his reaction to the proposed price range of $20 to $21 per share. Crawford said he thought such a price would be "generous", and that it was certainly one which should be submitted to UOP's minority shareholders for their ultimate consideration. He stated, however, that Signal's 100% ownership could cause internal problems at UOP. He believed that employees would have to be given some assurance of their future place in a fully-owned Signal subsidiary. Otherwise, he feared the departure of essential personnel. Also, many of UOP's key employees had stock option incentive programs which would be wiped out by a merger. Crawford therefore urged that some adjustment would have to be made, such as providing a comparable incentive in Signal's shares, if after the merger he was to maintain his quality of personnel and efficiency at UOP.

Thus, Crawford voiced no objection to the $20 to $21 price range, nor did he suggest that Signal should consider paying more than $21 per share for the minority interests. Later, at the executive committee meeting the same factors were discussed, with Crawford repeating the position he earlier took with Walkup and Shumway. Also considered was the 1975 tender offer and the fact that it had been greatly oversubscribed at $21 per share. For many reasons, Signal's management concluded that the acquisition of UOP's minority shares provided the solution to a number of its business problems.

Thus, it was the consensus that a price of $20 to $21 per share would be fair to both Signal and the minority shareholders of UOP. Signal's executive committee authorized its management "to negotiate" with UOP "for a cash acquisition of the minority ownership in UOP, Inc., with the intention of presenting a proposal to [Signal's] board of directors ... on

March 6, 1978". Immediately after this February 28, 1978 meeting, Signal issued a press release stating:

> The Signal Companies, Inc. and UOP, Inc. are conducting negotiations for the acquisition for cash by Signal of the 49.5 per cent of UOP which it does not presently own, announced Forrest N. Shumway, president and chief executive officer of Signal, and James V. Crawford, UOP president.
>
> Price and other terms of the proposed transaction have not yet been finalized and would be subject to approval of the boards of directors of Signal and UOP, scheduled to meet early next week, the stockholders of UOP and certain federal agencies.

The announcement also referred to the fact that the closing price of UOP's common stock on that day was $14.50 per share.

Two days later, on March 2, 1978, Signal issued a second press release stating that its management would recommend a price in the range of $20 to $21 per share for UOP's 49.5% minority interest. This announcement referred to Signal's earlier statement that "negotiations" were being conducted for the acquisition of the minority shares.

Between Tuesday, February 28, 1978 and Monday, March 6, 1978, a total of four business days, Crawford spoke by telephone with all of UOP's non-Signal, i.e., outside, directors. Also during that period, Crawford retained Lehman Brothers to render a fairness opinion as to the price offered the minority for its stock. He gave two reasons for this choice. First, the time schedule between the announcement and the board meetings was short (by then only three business days) and since Lehman Brothers had been acting as UOP's investment banker for many years, Crawford felt that it would be in the best position to respond on such brief notice. Second, James W. Glanville, a long-time director of UOP and a partner in Lehman Brothers, had acted as a financial advisor to UOP for many years. Crawford believed that Glanville's familiarity with UOP, as a member of its board, would also be of assistance in enabling Lehman Brothers to render a fairness opinion within the existing time constraints.

Crawford telephoned Glanville, who gave his assurance that Lehman Brothers had no conflicts that would prevent it from accepting the task. Glanville's immediate personal reaction was that a price of $20 to $21 would certainly be fair, since it represented almost a 50% premium over UOP's market price. Glanville sought a $250,000 fee for Lehman Brothers' services, but Crawford thought this too much. After further discussions Glanville finally agreed that Lehman Brothers would render its fairness opinion for $150,000.

During this period Crawford also had several telephone contacts with Signal officials. In only one of them, however, was the price of the shares discussed. In a conversation with Walkup, Crawford advised that as a result of his communications with UOP's non-Signal directors, it was his feeling that the price would have to be the top of the proposed range, or $21 per share, if the approval of UOP's outside directors was to be obtained. But again, he did not seek any price higher than $21.

Glanville assembled a three-man Lehman Brothers team to do the work on the fairness opinion. These persons examined relevant documents and information concerning UOP, including its annual reports and its Securities and Exchange Commission filings from 1973 through 1976, as well as its audited financial statements for 1977, its interim reports to shareholders, and its recent and historical market prices and trading volumes. In addition, on Friday, March 3, 1978, two members of the Lehman Brothers team flew to UOP's headquarters in Des Plaines, Illinois, to perform a "due diligence" visit, during the course of which they interviewed Crawford as well as UOP's general counsel, its chief financial officer, and other key executives and personnel.

As a result, the Lehman Brothers team concluded that "the price of either $20 or $21 would be a fair price for the remaining shares of UOP". They telephoned this impression to Glanville, who was spending the weekend in Vermont.

On Monday morning, March 6, 1978, Glanville and the senior member of the Lehman Brothers team flew to Des Plaines to attend the scheduled UOP directors meeting. Glanville looked over the assembled information during the flight. The two had with them the draft of a "fairness opinion letter" in which the price had been left blank. Either during or immediately prior to the directors' meeting, the two-page "fairness opinion letter" was typed in final form and the price of $21 per share was inserted.

On March 6, 1978, both the Signal and UOP boards were convened to consider the proposed merger. Telephone communications were maintained between the two meetings. Walkup, Signal's board chairman, and also a UOP director, attended UOP's meeting with Crawford in order to present Signal's position and answer any questions that UOP's non-Signal directors might have. Arledge and Chitiea, along with Signal's other designees on UOP's board, participated by conference telephone. All of UOP's outside directors attended the meeting either in person or by conference telephone.

First, Signal's board unanimously adopted a resolution authorizing Signal to propose to UOP a cash merger of $21 per share as outlined in a certain merger agreement and other supporting documents. This proposal required that the merger be approved by a majority of UOP's outstanding minority shares voting at the stockholders meeting at which the merger would be considered, and that the minority shares voting in favor of the merger, when coupled with Signal's 50.5% interest would have to comprise at least two-thirds of all UOP shares. Otherwise the proposed merger would be deemed disapproved.

UOP's board then considered the proposal. Copies of the agreement were delivered to the directors in attendance, and other copies had been forwarded earlier to the directors participating by telephone. They also had before them UOP financial data for 1974-1977, UOP's most recent financial statements, market price information, and budget projections for 1978. In addition they had Lehman Brothers' hurriedly prepared fairness opinion letter finding the price of $21 to be fair. Glanville, the Lehman Brothers partner, and UOP director, commented on the information that had gone into preparation of the letter.

Signal also suggests that the Arledge-Chitiea feasibility study, indicating that a price of up to $24 per share would be a "good investment" for Signal, was discussed at the UOP directors' meeting. The Chancellor made no such finding, and our independent review of the record, detailed *infra,* satisfies us by a preponderance of the evidence that there was no discussion of this document at UOP's board meeting. Furthermore, it is clear beyond peradventure that nothing in that report was ever disclosed to UOP's minority shareholders prior to their approval of the merger.

After consideration of Signal's proposal, Walkup and Crawford left the meeting to permit a free and uninhibited exchange between UOP's non-Signal directors. Upon their return a resolution to accept Signal's offer was then proposed and adopted. While Signal's men on UOP's board participated in various aspects of the meeting, they abstained from voting. However, the minutes show that each of them "if voting would have voted yes".

On March 7, 1978, UOP sent a letter to its shareholders advising them of the action taken by UOP's board with respect to Signal's offer. This document pointed out, among other things, that on February 28, 1978 "both companies had announced negotiations were being conducted".

Despite the swift board action of the two companies, the merger was not submitted to UOP's shareholders until their annual meeting on May 26, 1978. In the notice of that meeting and proxy statement sent to shareholders in May, UOP's management and board urged that the merger be approved. The proxy statement also advised:

> The price was determined after *discussions* between James V. Crawford, a director of Signal and Chief Executive Officer of UOP, and officers of Signal which took place during meetings on February 28, 1978, and in the course of several subsequent telephone conversations. (Emphasis added.)

In the original draft of the proxy statement the word "negotiations" had been used rather than "discussions". However, when the Securities and Exchange Commission sought details of the "negotiations" as part of its review of these materials, the term was deleted and the word "discussions" was substituted. The proxy statement indicated that the vote of UOP's board in approving the merger had been unanimous. It also advised the shareholders that Lehman Brothers had given its opinion that the merger price of $21 per share was fair to UOP's minority. However, it did not disclose the hurried method by which this conclusion was reached.

As of the record date of UOP's annual meeting, there were 11,488,302 shares of UOP common stock outstanding, 5,688,302 of which were owned by the minority. At the meeting only 56%, or 3,208,652, of the minority shares were voted. Of these, 2,953,812, or 51.9% of the total minority, voted for the merger, and 254,840 voted against it. When

Signal's stock was added to the minority shares voting in favor, a total of 76.2% of UOP's outstanding shares approved the merger while only 2.2% opposed it.

By its terms the merger became effective on May 26, 1978, and each share of UOP's stock held by the minority was automatically converted into a right to receive $21 cash.

II.

A.

A primary issue mandating reversal is the preparation by two UOP directors, Arledge and Chitiea, of their feasibility study for the exclusive use and benefit of Signal. This document was of obvious significance to both Signal and UOP. Using UOP data, it described the advantages to Signal of ousting the minority at a price range of $21-$24 per share. Mr. Arledge, one of the authors, outlined the benefits to Signal:

Purpose Of The Merger

1) Provides an outstanding investment opportunity for Signal—(Better than any recent acquisition we have seen.)

2) Increases Signal's earnings.

3) Facilitates the flow of resources between Signal and its subsidiaries—(Big factor—works both ways.)

4) Provides cost savings potential for Signal and UOP.

5) Improves the percentage of Signal's 'operating earnings' as opposed to 'holding company earnings'.

6) Simplifies the understanding of Signal.

7) Facilitates technological exchange among Signal's subsidiaries.

8) Eliminates potential conflicts of interest.

Having written those words, solely for the use of Signal, it is clear from the record that neither Arledge nor Chitiea shared this report with their fellow directors of UOP. We are satisfied that no one else did either. This conduct hardly meets the fiduciary standards applicable to such a transaction. While Mr. Walkup, Signal's chairman of the board and a UOP director, attended the March 6, 1978 UOP board meeting and testified at trial that he had discussed the Arledge-Chitiea report with the UOP directors at this meeting, the record does not support this assertion. Perhaps it is the result of some confusion on Mr. Walkup's part. In any event Mr. Shumway, Signal's president, testified that he made sure the Signal outside directors had this report prior to the March 6, 1978 Signal board meeting, but he did not testify that the Arledge-Chitiea report was also sent to UOP's outside directors.

Mr. Crawford, UOP's president, could not recall that any documents, other than a draft of the merger agreement, were sent to UOP's directors before the March 6, 1978 UOP meeting. Mr. Chitiea, an author of the report, testified that it was made available to Signal's directors, but to his knowledge it was not circulated to the outside directors of UOP. He specifically testified that he "didn't share" that information with the outside directors of UOP with whom he served.

None of UOP's outside directors who testified stated that they had seen this document. The minutes of the UOP board meeting do not identify the Arledge-Chitiea report as having been delivered to UOP's outside directors. This is particularly significant since the minutes describe in considerable detail the materials that actually were distributed. While these minutes recite Mr. Walkup's presentation of the Signal offer, they do not mention the Arledge-Chitiea report or any disclosure that Signal considered a price of up to $24 to be a good investment. If Mr. Walkup had in fact provided such important information to UOP's outside directors, it is logical to assume that these carefully drafted minutes would disclose it. The post-trial briefs of Signal and UOP contain a thorough description of the documents purportedly available to their boards at the March 6, 1978, meetings. Although the Arledge-Chitiea report is specifically identified as being available to the Signal directors, there is no mention of it being among the documents submitted to the UOP board. Even when queried at a prior oral argument before this Court, counsel for Signal did not claim that the Arledge-Chitiea report had been disclosed to UOP's outside directors. Instead, he chose to belittle its contents. This was the same approach taken before us at the last oral argument.

Actually, it appears that a three-page summary of figures was given to all UOP directors. Its first page is identical to one page of the Arledge-Chitiea report, but this dealt with nothing more than a justification of the $21 price. Significantly, the contents of this three-page summary are what the minutes reflect Mr. Walkup told the UOP board. However, nothing contained in either the minutes or this three-page summary reflects Signal's study regarding the $24 price.

The Arledge-Chitiea report speaks for itself in supporting the Chancellor's finding that a price of up to $24 was a "good investment" for Signal. It shows that a return on the investment at $21 would be 15.7% versus 15.5% at $24 per share. This was a difference of only two-tenths of one percent, while it meant over $17,000,000 to the minority. Under such circumstances, paying UOP's minority shareholders $24 would have had relatively little long-term effect on Signal, and the Chancellor's findings concerning the benefit to Signal, even at a price of $24, were obviously correct. *Levitt v. Bouvier*, Del.Supr., 287 A.2d 671, 673 (1972).

Certainly, this was a matter of material significance to UOP and its shareholders. Since the study was prepared by two UOP directors, using UOP information for the exclusive benefit of Signal, and nothing whatever was done to disclose it to the outside UOP directors or the minority shareholders, a question of breach of fiduciary duty arises. This problem occurs because there were common Signal-UOP directors participating, at least to some extent, in the UOP board's decision-making processes without full disclosure of the conflicts they faced.[7]

B.

In assessing this situation, the Court of Chancery was required to:

> examine what information defendants had and to measure it against what they gave to the minority stockholders, in a context in which 'complete candor' is required. In other words, the limited function of the Court was to determine whether defendants had disclosed all information in their possession germane to the transaction in issue. And by 'germane' we mean, for present purposes, information such as a reasonable shareholder would consider important in deciding whether to sell or retain stock.

> * * * * * *

> . . . Completeness, not adequacy, is both the norm and the mandate under present circumstances.

Lynch v. Vickers Energy Corp., Del.Supr., 383 A.2d 278, 281 (1977) (*Lynch I*). This is merely stating in another way the long-existing principle of Delaware law that these Signal designated directors on UOP's board still owed UOP and its shareholders an uncompromising duty of loyalty. The classic language of *Guth v. Loft, Inc.,* Del.Supr., 5 A.2d 503, 510 (1939), requires no embellishment:

> A public policy, existing through the years, and derived from a profound knowledge of human characteristics and motives, has established a rule that demands of a corporate officer or director, peremptorily and inexorably, the most scrupulous observance of his duty, not only affirmatively to protect the interests of the corporation committed to his charge, but also to refrain from doing anything that would work injury to the corporation, or to deprive it of profit or advantage which his skill and ability might properly bring to it, or to enable it to make in the reasonable and lawful exercise of its powers. The

---

[7] Although perfection is not possible, or expected, the result here could have been entirely different if UOP had appointed an independent negotiating committee of its outside directors to deal with Signal at arm's length. *See, e.g., Harriman v. E.I. duPont de Nemours & Co.,* 411 F.Supp. 133 (D.Del.1975). Since fairness in this context can be equated to conduct by a theoretical, wholly independent, board of directors acting upon the matter before them, it is unfortunate that this course apparently was neither considered nor pursued. *Johnston v. Greene,* Del.Supr., 121 A.2d 919, 925 (1956). Particularly in a parent-subsidiary context, a showing that the action taken was as though each of the contending parties had in fact exerted its bargaining power against the other at arm's length is strong evidence that the transaction meets the test of fairness. *Getty Oil Co. v. Skelly Oil Co.,* Del.Supr., 267 A.2d 883, 886 (1970); *Puma v. Marriott,* Del.Ch., 283 A.2d 693, 696 (1971). [...]

rule that requires an undivided and unselfish loyalty to the corporation demands that there shall be no conflict between duty and self-interest.

Given the absence of any attempt to structure this transaction on an arm's length basis, Signal cannot escape the effects of the conflicts it faced, particularly when its designees on UOP's board did not totally abstain from participation in the matter. There is no "safe harbor" for such divided loyalties in Delaware. When directors of a Delaware corporation are on both sides of a transaction, they are required to demonstrate their utmost good faith and the most scrupulous inherent fairness of the bargain. *Gottlieb v. Heyden Chemical Corp.,* Del.Supr., 91 A.2d 57, 57-58 (1952). The requirement of fairness is unflinching in its demand that where one stands on both sides of a transaction, he has the burden of establishing its entire fairness, sufficient to pass the test of careful scrutiny by the courts. *Sterling v. Mayflower Hotel Corp.,* Del.Supr., 93 A.2d 107, 110 (1952); *Bastian v. Bourns, Inc.,* Del.Ch., 256 A.2d 680, 681 (1969), *aff'd,* Del.Supr., 278 A.2d 467 (1970); *David J. Greene & Co. v. Dunhill International Inc.,* Del.Ch., 249 A.2d 427, 431 (1968).

There is no dilution of this obligation where one holds dual or multiple directorships, as in a parent-subsidiary context. *Levien v. Sinclair Oil Corp.,* Del.Ch., 261 A.2d 911, 915 (1969). Thus, individuals who act in a dual capacity as directors of two corporations, one of whom is parent and the other subsidiary, owe the same duty of good management to both corporations, and in the absence of an independent negotiating structure (see note 7, *supra*), or the directors' total abstention from any participation in the matter, this duty is to be exercised in light of what is best for both companies. *Warshaw v. Calhoun,* Del. Supr., 221 A.2d 487, 492 (1966). The record demonstrates that Signal has not met this obligation.

C.

The concept of fairness has two basic aspects: fair dealing and fair price. The former embraces questions of when the transaction was timed, how it was initiated, structured, negotiated, disclosed to the directors, and how the approvals of the directors and the stockholders were obtained. The latter aspect of fairness relates to the economic and financial considerations of the proposed merger, including all relevant factors: assets, market value, earnings, future prospects, and any other elements that affect the intrinsic or inherent value of a company's stock. Moore, *The "Interested" Director or Officer Transaction,* 4 Del.J. Corp.L. 674, 676 (1979); Nathan & Shapiro, *Legal Standard of Fairness of Merger Terms Under Delaware Law,* 2 Del.J. Corp.L. 44, 46-47 (1977). *See Tri-Continental Corp. v. Battye,* Del.Supr., 74 A.2d 71, 72 (1950); 8 *Del.C.* § 262(h). However, the test for fairness is not a bifurcated one as between fair dealing and price. All aspects of the issue must be examined as a whole since the question is one of entire fairness. However, in a non-fraudulent transaction we recognize that price may be the preponderant consideration outweighing other features of the merger. Here, we address the two basic aspects of fairness separately because we find reversible error as to both.

D.

Part of fair dealing is the obvious duty of candor required by *Lynch I, supra.* Moreover, one possessing superior knowledge may not mislead any stockholder by use of corporate information to which the latter is not privy. *Lank v. Steiner,* Del. Supr., 224 A.2d 242, 244 (1966). Delaware has long imposed this duty even upon persons who are not corporate officers or directors, but who nonetheless are privy to matters of interest or significance to their company. *Brophy v. Cities Service Co.,* Del. Ch., 70 A.2d 5, 7 (1949). With the well-established Delaware law on the subject, and the Court of Chancery's findings of fact here, it is inevitable that the obvious conflicts posed by Arledge and Chitiea's preparation of their "feasibility study", derived from UOP information, for the sole use and benefit of Signal, cannot pass muster.

The Arledge-Chitiea report is but one aspect of the element of fair dealing. How did this merger evolve? It is clear that it was entirely initiated by Signal. The serious time constraints under which the principals acted were all set by Signal. It had not found a suitable outlet for its excess cash and considered UOP a desirable investment, particularly since it was now in a position to acquire the whole company for itself. For whatever reasons, and they were only Signal's, the entire transaction was presented to and approved by UOP's board within four business days. Standing alone, this is not necessarily indicative of any lack of fairness by a majority shareholder. It was what occurred, or more properly, what did not occur, during this brief period that makes the time constraints imposed by Signal relevant to the issue of fairness.

The structure of the transaction, again, was Signal's doing. So far as negotiations were concerned, it is clear that they were modest at best. Crawford, Signal's man at UOP, never really talked price with Signal, except to accede to its management's statements on the subject, and to convey to Signal the UOP outside directors' view that as between the $20-$21 range under consideration, it would have to be $21. The latter is not a surprising outcome, but hardly arm's length negotiations. Only the protection of benefits for UOP's key employees and the issue of Lehman Brothers' fee approached any concept of bargaining.

As we have noted, the matter of disclosure to the UOP directors was wholly flawed by the conflicts of interest raised by the Arledge-Chitiea report. All of those conflicts were resolved by Signal in its own favor without divulging any aspect of them to UOP.

This cannot but undermine a conclusion that this merger meets any reasonable test of fairness. The outside UOP directors lacked one material piece of information generated by two of their colleagues, but shared only with Signal. True, the UOP board had the Lehman Brothers' fairness opinion, but that firm has been blamed by the plaintiff for the hurried task it performed, when more properly the responsibility for this lies with Signal. There was no disclosure of the circumstances surrounding the rather cursory preparation of the Lehman Brothers' fairness opinion. Instead, the impression was given UOP's minority that a careful study had been made, when in fact speed was the hallmark, and Mr. Glanville, Lehman's partner in charge of the matter, and also a UOP director, having spent the weekend in Vermont, brought a draft of the "fairness opinion letter" to the UOP directors' meeting on March 6, 1978 with the price left blank. We can only conclude from the record that the rush imposed on Lehman Brothers by Signal's timetable contributed to the difficulties under which this investment banking firm attempted to perform its responsibilities. Yet, none of this was disclosed to UOP's minority.

Finally, the minority stockholders were denied the critical information that Signal considered a price of $24 to be a good investment. Since this would have meant over $17,000,000 more to the minority, we cannot conclude that the shareholder vote was an informed one. Under the circumstances, an approval by a majority of the minority was meaningless. *Lynch I,* 383 A.2d at 279, 281; *Cahall v. Lofland,* Del.Ch., 114 A. 224 (1921).

Given these particulars and the Delaware law on the subject, the record does not establish that this transaction satisfies any reasonable concept of fair dealing, and the Chancellor's findings in that regard must be reversed.

E.

Turning to the matter of price, plaintiff also challenges its fairness. His evidence was that on the date the merger was approved the stock was worth at least $26 per share. In support, he offered the testimony of a chartered investment analyst who used two basic approaches to valuation: a comparative analysis of the premium paid over market in ten other tender offer-merger combinations, and a discounted cash flow analysis.

In this breach of fiduciary duty case, the Chancellor perceived that the approach to valuation was the same as that in an appraisal proceeding. Consistent with precedent, he rejected plaintiff's method of proof and accepted defendants' evidence of value as being in accord with practice under prior case law. This means that the so-called "Delaware block" or weighted average method was employed wherein the elements of value, i.e., assets, market price, earnings, etc., were assigned a particular weight and the resulting amounts added to determine the value per share. This procedure has been in use for decades. *See In re General Realty & Utilities Corp.,* Del.Ch., 52 A.2d 6, 14-15 (1947). However, to the extent it excludes other generally accepted techniques used in the financial community and the courts, it is now clearly outmoded. It is time we recognize this in appraisal and other stock valuation proceedings and bring our law current on the subject.

While the Chancellor rejected plaintiff's discounted cash flow method of valuing UOP's stock, as not corresponding with "either logic or the existing law" (426 A.2d at 1360), it is significant that this was essentially the focus, i.e., earnings potential of UOP, of Messrs. Arledge and Chitiea in their evaluation of the merger. Accordingly, the standard "Delaware block" or weighted average method of valuation, formerly employed in appraisal and other stock valuation cases, shall no longer exclusively control such proceedings. We believe that a more liberal approach must include proof of value by any techniques or methods which are generally considered acceptable in the financial community and otherwise admissible in court [...]

Fair price obviously requires consideration of all relevant factors involving the value of a company. This has long been the law of Delaware as stated in *Tri-Continental Corp.*, 74 A.2d at 72:

> The basic concept of value under the appraisal statute is that the stockholder is entitled to be paid for that which has been taken from him, viz., his proportionate interest in a going concern. By value of the stockholder's proportionate interest in the corporate enterprise is meant the true or intrinsic value of his stock which has been taken by the merger. In determining what figure represents this true or intrinsic value, the appraiser and the courts must take into consideration all factors and elements which reasonably might enter into the fixing of value. Thus, market value, asset value, dividends, earning prospects, the nature of the enterprise and any other facts which were known or which could be ascertained as of the date of merger and which throw any light on *future prospects* of the merged corporation are not only pertinent to an inquiry as to the value of the dissenting stockholders' interest, but *must be considered* by the agency fixing the value. (Emphasis added.)

[...]

Although the Chancellor received the plaintiff's evidence, his opinion indicates that the use of it was precluded because of past Delaware practice. While we do not suggest a monetary result one way or the other, we do think the plaintiff's evidence should be part of the factual mix and weighed as such. Until the $21 price is measured on remand by the valuation standards mandated by Delaware law, there can be no finding at the present stage of these proceedings that the price is fair. Given the lack of any candid disclosure of the material facts surrounding establishment of the $21 price, the majority of the minority vote, approving the merger, is meaningless.

[...]

The judgment of the Court of Chancery, finding both the circumstances of the merger and the price paid the minority shareholders to be fair, is reversed. The matter is remanded for further proceedings consistent herewith. Upon remand the plaintiff's post-trial motion to enlarge the class should be granted.

* * * * * *

REVERSED AND REMANDED.

Discussion Questions:

1. What flaws did the Court find in the negotiation process? What should Signal and its representatives have done differently? To generalize, how "nicely" does a controlling

shareholder have to play with minority shareholders in a freeze-out merger negotiation?

2. As a result of the failures in the process, the Court imposes "entire fairness" review, with the burden on the defendant directors to show fairness. Was there a procedural mechanism that the Court suggests would have avoided this outcome? What benefit would such a procedural mechanism have given the parties, according to the Court?

3. Building on *Weinberger's* theme of procedural protections for minority shareholders in freeze-out transactions, subsequent Delaware case law clarified that Special Committee approval *or* majority-of-the-minority shareholder approval shifted the burden to the plaintiffs to entire fairness, but *both* protections provided no further benefit. What incentives do you think such a system creates for transactional planners? (The next case changes this calculus in important ways.)

In re MFW Shareholders Litigation
67 A.3d 496 (Del. Ch. 2013)

STRINE, Chancellor.

I. Introduction

This case presents a novel question of law. Here, MacAndrews & Forbes—a holding company whose equity is solely owned by defendant Ronald Perelman—owned 43% of M&F Worldwide ("MFW"). MacAndrews & Forbes offered to purchase the rest of the corporation's equity in a going private merger for $24 per share. But upfront, MacAndrews & Forbes said it would not proceed with any going private transaction that was not approved: (i) by an independent special committee; and (ii) by a vote of a majority of the stockholders unaffiliated with the controlling stockholder (who, for simplicity's sake, are termed the "minority"). A special committee was formed, which picked its own legal and financial advisors. The committee met eight times during the course of three months and negotiated with MacAndrews & Forbes, eventually getting it to raise its bid by $1 per share, to $25 per share. The merger was then approved by an affirmative vote of the majority of the minority MFW stockholders, with 65% of them approving the merger.

MacAndrews & Forbes, Perelman, and the other directors of MFW were, of course, sued by stockholders alleging that the merger was unfair. After initially seeking a preliminary injunction hearing in advance of the merger vote with agreement from the defendants and receiving a good deal of expedited discovery, the plaintiffs changed direction and dropped their injunction motion in favor of seeking a post-closing damages remedy for breach of fiduciary duty.

The defendants have moved for summary judgment as to that claim. The defendants argue that there is no material issue of fact that the MFW special committee was comprised of independent directors, had the right to and did engage qualified legal and financial advisors to inform itself whether a going private merger was in the best interests of MFW's minority stockholders, was fully empowered to negotiate with Perelman over the terms of his offer and to say no definitively if it did not believe the ultimate terms were fair to the MFW minority stockholders, and after an extensive period of deliberation and negotiations, approved a merger agreement with Perelman. The defendants further argue that there is no dispute of fact that a majority of the minority stockholders supported the merger upon full disclosure and without coercion. Because, the defendants say, the merger was conditioned up front on two key procedural protections that, together, replicate an arm's-length merger—the employment of an active, unconflicted negotiating agent free to turn down the transaction and a requirement that any transaction negotiated by that agent be approved by the disinterested stockholders—they contend that the judicial standard of review should be the business judgment rule. Under that rule, the court is precluded from inquiring into the substantive fairness of the merger, and must dismiss the challenge to the merger unless the merger's terms were so disparate that no rational person acting in good faith could have thought the merger was fair to the minority. On this record, the defendants say, it is clear that the merger, which occurred at a price that was a 47% premium to the stock price before Perelman's offer was made, cannot be deemed waste, a conclusion confirmed by the majority-of-the-minority vote itself.

[...]

The question [is] . . . what standard of review should apply to a going private merger conditioned upfront by the controlling stockholder on approval by both a properly empowered, independent committee and an informed, uncoerced majority-of-the-minority vote. [...]

. . . . Although rational minds may differ on the subject, the court concludes that when a controlling stockholder merger has, from the time of the controller's first overture, been subject to (i) negotiation and approval by a special committee of independent directors fully empowered to say no, and (ii) approval by an uncoerced, fully informed vote of a majority of the minority investors, the business judgment rule standard of review applies. This conclusion is consistent with the central tradition of Delaware law, which defers to the informed decisions of impartial directors, especially when those decisions have been approved by the disinterested stockholders on full information and without coercion. [...]

[Before addressing the question of what standard of review should apply, the Court satisfied itself that "the procedural devices used to protect the minority"—the MFW special committee and the majority-of-the-minority vote condition—"are entitled to cleansing effect under Delaware's traditional approach to the business judgment rule." Thus "both of the protections having sufficient integrity to invoke the business judgment standard." The court further concluded that "the [Delaware] Supreme Court has never had a chance to answer the question the defendants now pose and therefore it remains open for consideration." Reviewing prior decisions, the court acknowledged that "this court must and will give heavy consideration to the reasoning of our Supreme Court's prior decisions. In particular, the prior cases make emphatic the strong public policy interest our common law of corporations has in the fair treatment of minority stockholders and the need to ensure that controlling stockholders do not extract unfair rents using their influence.

Fidelity to not just *Lynch*, but cases like *Weinberger*, requires that the question before the court receive an answer that gives that public policy interest heavy weight.[139]" The court then turned to the main question.]

V. <u>The Business Judgment Rule Governs And Summary Judgment Is Granted</u>

This case thus presents, for the first time, the question of what should be the correct standard of review for mergers between a controlling stockholder and its subsidiary, when the merger is conditioned on the approval of both an independent, adequately empowered special committee that fulfills its duty of care, and the uncoerced, informed vote of a majority of the minority stockholders.

In prior cases, this court has outlined the development of the case law in this area,[140] as have distinguished scholars,[141] and there is no need to repeat that recitation. The core legal question is framed by the parties' contending positions. For their part, the defendants say that it would be beneficial systemically to minority stockholders to review transactions structured with both procedural protections under the business judgment rule. Absent an incentive to do so, the defendants argue that controlling stockholders will not agree upfront to both protections, thus denying minority stockholders access to the transaction structure most protective of their interests—one that gives them the benefit of an active and empowered bargaining agent to negotiate price and to say no, plus the ability to freely decide for themselves on full information whether to accept any deal approved by that agent. This structure is not common now because controlling stockholders have no incentive under the law to agree to it, and such an incentive is needed because it involves the controller ceding potent power to the independent directors and minority stockholders.[142] The defendants argue that the benefits of their preferred approach are considerable, and that the costs are negligible because there is little utility to having an expensive, judicially intensive standard of review when stockholders can protect themselves by voting no if they do not like the recommendation of a fully empowered independent committee that exercised due care. In support of that argument, the defendants can cite to empirical evidence showing that the absence of a legally recognized transaction structure that can invoke the business judgment rule standard of review has resulted not in litigation that generates tangible positive results for minority stockholders in the form of additional money in their pockets, but in litigation that is settled for fees because there is no practical way of getting the case dismissed at the pleading stage and the costs of discovery and entanglement in multiyear litigation exceed the costs of paying

---

[139] *Lynch* I, 638 A.2d 1110; *Weinberger*, 457 A.2d 701.

[140] *E.g., In re Pure Res., Inc., S'holders Litig.*, 808 A.2d 421 (Del. Ch. 2002); *In re Cysive, Inc. S'holders Litig.*, 836 A.2d 531 (Del. Ch. 2003); *In re Cox Commc'ns, Inc. S'holders Litig.*, 879 A.2d 604 (Del. Ch. 2005); *CNX*, 4 A.3d 397; *see also* Allen et al., *Function over Form*, at 1306-09; Leo E. Strine, Jr., *The Inescapably Empirical Foundation of the Common Law of Corporations*, 27 Del. J. Corp. L. 499, 506-13 (2002).

[141] *E.g.,* Gilson & Gordon, *Controlling Shareholders*, at 796-803, 805-27; Subramanian, *Fixing Freezeouts*, at 11-22.

[142] *See, e.g.,* Subramanian, *Fixing Freezeouts*, at 59.

attorneys' fees.[143] Finally, the defendants note that Delaware law on controlling stockholder going private transactions is now inconsistent, with the intrinsically more coercive route of using a tender offer to accomplish a going private transaction escaping the full force of equitable review, when a similarly structured merger where a less coercive chance to say no exists would not.[144]

In response, the plaintiffs argue that a requirement that every controlling stockholder transaction be subject to fairness review is good for minority stockholders. The plaintiffs, rather surprisingly, argue that giving stockholders the protection of a majority-of-the-minority vote in addition to a special committee adds little value because, in their view, stockholders will always vote for a good premium deal, and long-term stockholders will sell out to arbitrageurs in advance of the vote, leaving the minority vote in the hands of stockholders who will invariably vote for the deal. That said, the plaintiffs conceded in their briefing that minority stockholders would benefit if more controlling stockholders would use a structure that gave minority stockholders an independent bargaining and veto agent as well as a majority-of-the-minority vote. But they contend that the cost of not having an invariable judicial inquiry into fairness outweighs that benefit.

After considering these arguments, the court concludes that the rule of equitable common law that best protects minority investors is one that encourages controlling stockholders to accord the minority this potent combination of procedural protections.

There are several reasons for this conclusion. The court begins with a Delaware tradition. Under Delaware law, it has long been thought beneficial to investors for courts, which are not experts in business, to defer to the disinterested decisions of directors, who are expert, and stockholders, whose money is at stake. Thus, when no fiduciary has a personal self-interest adverse to that of the company and its other stockholders, the fiduciary is well-informed, and there is no statutory requirement for a vote, the business judgment rule standard of review applies and precludes judicial second-guessing so long as the board's decision "can be attributed to any rational business purpose."[148] Outside the controlling

---

[143] *See generally* Elliott J. Weiss & Lawrence J. White, *File Early, Then Free Ride: How Delaware Law (Mis)Shapes Shareholder Class Actions*, 57 Vand. L. Rev. 1797 (2004) [hereinafter Weiss & White, *File Early*]; *see also* Cox, 879 A. 2d at 613-14 (discussing Weiss & White, *File Early*); Aff. of Lawrence J. White, *Cox*, C.A. No. 613-N (Del. Ch. Jan. 13, 2005) (summarizing Weiss & White, *File Early*).

[144] *Compare In re Siliconix Inc. S'holders Litig.*, 2001 WL 716787 (Del. Ch. June 21, 2001), *with Lynch I*, 638 A.2d 1110. The implication of the Supreme Court's decision in *Solomon v. Pathe* and cases following it, such as *Siliconix*, is that a going private transaction proposed by a controller by the tender offer method is not subject to equitable review. *Solomon v. Pathe Commc'ns Corp.*, 672 A.2d 35 (1996). Although this implication has been affected by later cases such *Pure* and *Cox*, it remains the case that it is not certain that a controlling stockholder owes the same equitable obligations when it seeks to acquire the rest of a corporation's equity by a tender offer, rather than by a statutory merger. *See* Gilson & Gordon, *Controlling Shareholders*, at 796-832; Subramanian, *Fixing Freezeouts*, at 11-22.

[148] *Sinclair Oil Corp. v. Levien*, 280 A.2d 717, 720 (Del. 1971); *see Cede & Co. v. Technicolor, Inc.*, 634 A.2d 345, 361 (Del. 1993) ("To rebut the [business judgment] rule, a shareholder plaintiff assumes the burden of providing evidence that directors, in reaching their challenged decision, breached

stockholder merger context, it has long been the law that even when a transaction is an interested one but not requiring a stockholder vote, Delaware law has invoked the protections of the business judgment rule when the transaction was approved by disinterested directors acting with due care.

[...]

But tradition should admittedly not persist if it lacks current value. If providing an incentive for a disinterested bargaining agent and a disinterested approval vote are of no utility to minority investors, it would not make sense to shape a rule that encourages their use.

But even the plaintiffs here admit that this transactional structure is the optimal one for minority stockholders. They just claim that there is some magical way to have it spread that involves no cost. That is not so, however. Absent doing something that is in fact inconsistent with binding precedent—requiring controlling stockholders to use both protections in order to get any credit under the entire fairness standard—there is no way to create an incentive for the use of both protections other than to give controllers who grant both protections to the minority the benefit of business judgment rule review.

A choice about our common law of corporations must therefore be made, and the court is persuaded that what is optimal for the protection of stockholders and the creation of wealth through the corporate form is adopting a form of the rule the defendants advocate. By giving controlling stockholders the opportunity to have a going private transaction reviewed under the business judgment rule, a strong incentive is created to give minority stockholders much broader access to the transactional structure that is most likely to effectively protect their interests. In fact, this incentive may make this structure the common one, which would be highly beneficial to minority stockholders. That structure, it is important to note, is critically different than a structure that uses only one of the procedural protections. The "or" structure does not replicate the protections of a third-party merger under the DGCL approval process, because it only requires that one, and not both, of the statutory requirements of director and stockholder approval be accomplished by impartial decisionmakers. The "both" structure, by contrast, replicates the arm's-length merger steps of the DGCL by "requir[ing] two independent approvals, which it is fair to say serve independent integrity-enforcing functions."[156]

When these two protections are established up-front, a potent tool to extract good value for the minority is established. From inception, the controlling stockholder knows that it cannot bypass the special committee's ability to say no. And, the controlling stockholder knows it cannot dangle a majority-of-the-minority vote before the special committee late in the process as a deal-closer rather than having to make a price move. From inception, the controller has had to accept that any deal agreed to by the special committee will also have

---

[the duties of] loyalty or due care. If a shareholder plaintiff fails to meet this evidentiary burden, the business judgment rule attaches to protect corporate officers and directors and the decisions they make, and our courts will not second-guess these business judgments." (Citations omitted)).

[156] *In re Cox Commc'ns, Inc. S'holders Litig.*, 879 A.2d 604, 618 (Del. Ch. 2005).

to be supported by a majority of the minority stockholders. That understanding also affects the incentives of the special committee in an important way. The special committee will understand that those for whom it is bargaining will get a chance to express whether they think the special committee did a good or poor job. [...]

The premise that independent directors with the right incentives can play an effective role on behalf of minority investors is one shared by respected scholars sincerely concerned with protecting minority investors from unfair treatment by controlling stockholders. Their scholarship and empirical evidence indicates that special committees have played a valuable role in generating outcomes for minority investors in going private transactions that compare favorably with the premiums received in third-party merger transactions.[162]

[...]

When all these factors are considered, the court believes that the approach most consistent with Delaware's corporate law tradition is the one best for investors in Delaware corporations, which is the application of the business judgment rule. That approach will provide a strong incentive for the wide employment of a transactional structure highly beneficial to minority investors, a benefit that seems to far exceed any cost to investors, given the conditions a controller must meet in order to qualify for business judgment rule protection. Obviously, rational minds can disagree about this question, and our Supreme Court will be able to bring its own judgment to bear if the plaintiffs appeal. But, this court determines that on the conditions employed in connection with MacAndrews & Forbes's acquisition by merger of MFW, the business judgment rule applies and summary judgment is therefore entered for the defendants on all counts. IT IS SO ORDERED.

[...]

Discussion Questions:

1. If you were advising a controlling shareholder considering a freeze-out transaction, how would you advise them in view of *MFW*? What are the potential risks of your proposed approach? (Hint: consider the phenomena underlying the surge in appraisal rights, as discussed previously.)

2. Until *MFW*, there was a doctrinal tension between freeze-out tender offers (which were subject to business judgment review under the *Siliconix-Glassman* line of cases) and freeze-out mergers (which were subject to entire fairness review under the *Weinberger* line of cases). Vice Chancellor Laster noted this tension in *In re CNX Gas Corp. Shareholder Litigation*, 2010 WL 2291842 (Del. Ch. 2010):

---

[162] *See, e.g.,* Guhan Subramanian, *Post-Siliconix Freeze-Outs: Theory and Evidence*, 36 J. Legal Stud. 1, 13 tbl. 1 (2007) [hereinafter, Subramanian, *Post-Siliconix*] (reporting long-term cumulative abnormal returns of 39% in completed going private transactions between 2001 and 2005, almost all of which used a special committee).

The standard of review for a controller's unilateral two-step freeze-out . . . is an issue with real-world consequences. In his study of post-*Siliconix* freeze-outs, Professor Guhan Subramanian found that stockholders received greater consideration in single-step [merger] freeze-outs . . . than in unilateral two-step freeze-outs. . . . Professor Subramanian noted that "[i]nterviews as well as informal conversations with New York City and Delaware lawyers indicate that [the finding of lower returns for stockholders in *Siliconix* deals] is consistent with practitioner experience." *Id.*

Controllers and their advisors take the governing legal regime into account when determining whether and how to proceed with a transaction. Professor Subramanian found that controllers moved decidedly towards unilateral two-step transactions after the blazing of the *Siliconix-Glassman* trail. *Id.* at 10-11.

These data raise policy questions. All else equal, a legal regime that makes it easier for controllers to freeze out stockholders will increase the number of transactions but result in lower premiums. Conversely, a legal regime that imposes greater procedural requirements will enable target stockholders to receive higher premiums but reduce the overall level of transactional activity. Either approach is legitimate and defensible. Either approach could result in the greatest aggregate benefits for stockholders, depending on the typical premium and overall level of deal activity.

MFW therefore leveled the playing field between freeze-out mergers and freeze-out tender offers. But until then, if controlling shareholders were able to pay less in freeze-out tender offers, why (do you think) would *any* controlling shareholder execute its freeze-out as a merger rather than as a tender offer?

Chapter 10 – The Enforcement of Corporate Law

Like most litigation, shareholder litigation presents an obvious dilemma. On one hand, fiduciary duties are toothless without shareholder litigation to enforce them. That is why courts encourage it with generous fee awards, as in *Americas Mining, infra.* On the other hand, litigation is extremely expensive, especially the corporate sort. In particular, defendants can incur substantial costs in discovery even if the case never goes to trial, let alone results in a verdict for the plaintiff. In fiduciary duty suits, the main cost is the disruption caused by depositions of directors and managers and, more generally, their distraction from ordinary business. Opportunistic plaintiffs may threaten such litigation costs to extract a meritless settlement.

In recognition of this threat, Delaware courts screen derivative suits with special procedural hurdles. The main hurdle, and the main subject of *Aronson*, is that the complaint must provide some initial reason for why a shareholder should be allowed to prosecute the suit instead of the board. In essence, courts will allow discovery only if the derivative complaint alleges *particularized facts* that, if true, would create a reasonable doubt that a majority of the directors cannot impartially assess the expeditiousness of the suit, either because they themselves violated their fiduciary duties or because they are beholden to others who did or who are otherwise likely to be liable to the corporation. In particular, it is *not* sufficient simply to name all directors as defendants; the complaint must make it plausible that they are actually liable. Courts address this question on a motion to dismiss. Even if they do not grant that motion, courts may dismiss the suit at any later time during discovery if a "special litigation committee" so recommends (see *Zapata* as reported by *Aronson*).

Reading *Aronson* is complicated by arcane and even misleading terminology. Some signposts may be helpful. Formally, the case arises under Delaware Chancery Rule 23.1(a), which states:

> The [derivative] complaint shall also allege with particularity the efforts, if any, made by the plaintiff to obtain the action the plaintiff desires from the directors [i.e., the plaintiff's *demand* to the board to direct the corporation to sue] and the reasons for the plaintiff's failure to obtain the action or for not making the effort.

For this rule to make any sense, it must be read to require dismissal if the board rightfully rejected the plaintiff's demand, or, if no demand was made, the plaintiff's reasons for failing to make a demand were not legally compelling. In practice, derivative plaintiffs never make a formal demand—the directors will hardly ever agree to sue themselves, and the Delaware Supreme Court has ruled that making a demand waives certain claims plaintiffs might otherwise have. Hence the relevant question in *Aronson* and other cases is: when is demand "futile"? Both the demand requirement and the powers of the special litigation committee only apply to derivative suits; they do not apply to direct suits (which are usually filed as class actions). The test for distinguishing direct from derivative actions is "(1) who suffered the alleged harm (the corporation or the suing stock-holders, individually); and (2) who would receive the benefit of any recovery or other remedy (the corporation or the stock-holders, individually)?" *Tooley v. Donaldson, Lufkin & Jenrette*, 845 A. 2d 1031, at 1033 (Del. 2004). In practice, this means that shareholders can sue directly over mergers and other transactions that affect their status as shareholders, but not over transactions such as executive compensation that affect shareholders merely financially.

Aronson v. Lewis
473 A.2d 805 (Del. 1984)

MOORE, Justice:

In the wake of *Zapata Corp. v. Maldonado,* Del.Supr., 430 A.2d 779 (1981), this Court left a crucial issue unanswered: when is a stockholder's demand upon a board of directors, to redress an alleged wrong to the corporation, excused as futile prior to the filing of a derivative suit? We granted this interlocutory appeal to the defendants, Meyers Parking System, Inc. (Meyers), a Delaware corporation, and its directors, to review the Court of Chancery's denial of their motion to dismiss this action, pursuant to Chancery Rule 23.1, for the plaintiff's failure to make such a demand or otherwise demonstrate its futility. The Vice Chancellor ruled that plaintiff's allegations raised a "reasonable inference" that the directors' action was unprotected by the business judgment rule. Thus, the board could not have impartially considered and acted upon the demand. See *Lewis v. Aronson,* Del.Ch., 466 A.2d 375, 381 (1983).

We cannot agree with this formulation of the concept of demand futility. In our view demand can only be excused where facts are alleged with particularity which create a reasonable doubt that the directors' action was entitled to the protections of the business judgment rule. Because the plaintiff failed to make a demand, and to allege facts with particularity indicating that such demand would be futile, we reverse the Court of Chancery and remand with instructions that plaintiff be granted leave to amend the complaint.

I.

The issues of demand futility rest upon the allegations of the complaint. The plaintiff, Harry Lewis, is a stockholder of Meyers. The defendants are Meyers and its ten directors, some of whom are also company officers.

In 1979, Prudential Building Maintenance Corp. (Prudential) spun off its shares of Meyers to Prudential's stockholders. Prior thereto Meyers was a wholly owned subsidiary of Prudential. Meyers provides parking lot facilities and related services throughout the country. Its stock is actively traded over-the-counter.

This suit challenges certain transactions between Meyers and one of its directors, Leo Fink, who owns 47% of its outstanding stock. Plaintiff claims that these transactions were approved only because Fink personally selected each director and officer of Meyers.

Prior to January 1, 1981, Fink had an employment agreement with Prudential which provided that upon retirement he was to become a consultant to that company for ten years. This provision became operable when Fink retired in April 1980. Thereafter, Meyers agreed with Prudential to share Fink's consulting services and reimburse Prudential for 25% of the fees paid Fink. Under this arrangement Meyers paid Prudential $48,332 in 1980 and $45,832 in 1981.

On January 1, 1981, the defendants approved an employment agreement between Meyers and Fink for a five year term with provision for automatic renewal each year thereafter, indefinitely. Meyers agreed to pay Fink $150,000 per year, plus a bonus of 5% of its pre-tax profits over $2,400,000. Fink could terminate the contract at any time, but Meyers could do so only upon six months' notice. At termination, Fink was to become a consultant to Meyers and be paid $150,000 per year for the first three years, $125,000 for the next three years, and $100,000 thereafter for life. Death benefits were also included. Fink agreed to devote his best efforts and substantially his entire business time to advancing Meyers' interests. The agreement also provided that Fink's compensation was not to be affected by any inability to perform services on Meyers' behalf. Fink was 75 years old when his employment agreement with Meyers was approved by the directors. There is no claim that he was, or is, in poor health.

Additionally, the Meyers board approved and made interest-free loans to Fink totalling $225,000. These loans were unpaid and outstanding as of August 1982 when the complaint was filed. At oral argument defendants' counsel represented that these loans had been repaid in full.

The complaint charges that these transactions had "no valid business purpose", and were a "waste of corporate assets" because the amounts to be paid are "grossly excessive", that Fink performs "no or little services", and because of his "advanced age" cannot be "expected to perform any such services". The plaintiff also charges that the existence of the Prudential consulting agreement with Fink prevents him from providing his "best efforts" on Meyers' behalf. Finally, it is alleged that the loans to Fink were in reality "additional compensation" without any "consideration" or "benefit" to Meyers.

The complaint alleged that no demand had been made on the Meyers board because:

> 13. . . . such attempt would be futile for the following reasons:
>
> (a) All of the directors in office are named as defendants herein and they have participated in, expressly approved and/or acquiesced in, and are personally liable for, the wrongs complained of herein.

(b) Defendant Fink, having selected each director, controls and dominates every member of the Board and every officer of Meyers.

(c) Institution of this action by present directors would require the defendant-directors to sue themselves, thereby placing the conduct of this action in hostile hands and preventing its effective prosecution.

Complaint, at ¶ 13.

The relief sought included the cancellation of the Meyers-Fink employment contract and an accounting by the directors, including Fink, for all damage sustained by Meyers and for all profits derived by the directors and Fink.

II.

Defendants moved to dismiss for plaintiff's failure to make demand on the Meyers board prior to suit, or to allege with factual particularity why demand is excused. See Del.Ch.Ct.R. 23.1, supra.

[...] According to the Vice Chancellor, the test of futility is "whether the Board, at the time of the filing of the suit, could have impartially considered and acted upon the demand". *Id.* at 381.

[...] the Vice Chancellor maintained that a plaintiff "must only allege facts which, if true, show that there is a reasonable inference that the business judgment rule is not applicable for purposes of considering a pre-suit demand pursuant to Rule 23.1". *Id.* The court concluded that this transaction permitted such an inference. *Id.* at 384-86.

[...]

The trial court [...] stated that board approval of the Meyers-Fink agreement, allowing Fink's consultant compensation to remain unaffected by his ability to perform any services, may have been a transaction wasteful on its face. *Id.* [citing *Fidanque v. American Maracaibo Co.*, Del.Ch., 92 A.2d 311 (1952)]. Consequently, demand was excused as futile, because the Meyers' directors faced potential liability for waste and could not have impartially considered the demand. *Id.* at 384.

III.

The defendants make two arguments, one policy-oriented and the other, factual. First, they assert that the demand requirement embraces the policy that directors, rather than stockholders, manage the affairs of the corporation. They contend that this fundamental principle requires the strict construction and enforcement of Chancery Rule 23.1. Second, the defendants point to four of plaintiff's basic allegations and argue that they lack the factual particularity necessary to excuse demand. Concerning the allegation that Fink dominated and controlled the Meyers board, the defendants point to the absence of any facts explaining how he "selected each director". With respect to Fink's 47% stock interest, the defendants say that absent other facts this is insufficient to indicate domination and control. Regarding the claim of hostility to the plaintiff's suit, because defendants would have to sue themselves, the latter assert that this bootstrap argument ignores the possibility that the directors have other alternatives, such as cancelling the challenged agreement. As for the allegation that directorial approval of the agreement excused demand, the defendants reply that such a claim is insufficient, because it would obviate the demand requirement in almost every case. The effect would be to subvert the managerial power of a board of directors. Finally, as to the provision guaranteeing Fink's compensation, even if he is unable to perform any services, the defendants contend that the trial court read this out of context. Based upon the foregoing, the defendants conclude that the plaintiff's allegations fall far short of the factual particularity required by Rule 23.1.

IV.

A.

A cardinal precept of the General Corporation Law of the State of Delaware is that directors, rather than shareholders, manage the business and affairs of the corporation. 8 *Del.C.* § 141(a). Section 141(a) states in pertinent part:

> "The *business and affairs* of a corporation organized under this chapter *shall be managed by or under the direction* of a board of directors except as may be otherwise provided in this chapter or in its certificate of incorporation."

8 *Del.C.* § 141(a) (Emphasis added). The existence and exercise of this power carries with it certain fundamental fiduciary obligations to the corporation and its shareholders. *Loft, Inc. v. Guth,* Del.Ch., 2 A.2d 225 (1938), *aff'd,* Del.Supr., 5 A.2d 503 (1939). Moreover, a stockholder is not powerless to challenge director action which results in harm to the corporation. The machinery of corporate democracy and the derivative suit are potent tools to redress the conduct of a torpid or unfaithful management. The derivative action developed in equity to enable shareholders to sue in the corporation's name where those in control of the company refused to assert a claim belonging to it. The nature of the action is two-fold. First, it is the equivalent of a suit by the shareholders to compel the corporation to sue. Second, it is a suit by the corporation, asserted by the shareholders on its behalf, against those liable to it.

By its very nature the derivative action impinges on the managerial freedom of directors. Hence, the demand requirement of Chancery Rule 23.1 exists at the threshold, first to insure that a stockholder exhausts his intracorporate remedies, and then to provide a safeguard against strike suits. Thus, by promoting this form of alternate dispute resolution, rather than immediate recourse to litigation, the demand requirement is a recognition of the fundamental precept that directors manage the business and affairs of corporations.

In our view the entire question of demand futility is inextricably bound to issues of business judgment and the standards of that doctrine's applicability. The business judgment rule is an acknowledgment of the managerial prerogatives of Delaware directors under Section 141(a). See *Zapata Corp. v. Maldonado,* 430 A.2d at 782. It is a presumption that in making a business decision the directors of a corporation acted on an informed basis, in good faith and in the honest belief that the action taken was in the best interests of the company. *Kaplan v. Centex Corp.,* Del.Ch., 284 A.2d 119, 124 (1971); *Robinson v. Pittsburgh Oil Refinery Corp.,* Del.Ch., 126 A. 46 (1924). Absent an abuse of discretion, that judgment will be respected by the courts. The burden is on the party challenging the decision to establish facts rebutting the presumption. See *Puma v. Marriott,* Del.Ch., 283 A.2d 693, 695 (1971).

The function of the business judgment rule is of paramount significance in the context of a derivative action. It comes into play in several ways—in addressing a demand, in the determination of demand futility, in efforts by independent disinterested directors to dismiss the action as inimical to the corporation's best interests, and generally, as a defense to the merits of the suit. However, in each of these circumstances there are certain common principles governing the application and operation of the rule.

First, its protections can only be claimed by disinterested directors whose conduct otherwise meets the tests of business judgment. From the standpoint of interest, this means that directors can neither appear on both sides of a transaction nor expect to derive any personal financial benefit from it in the sense of self-dealing, as opposed to a benefit which devolves upon the corporation or all stockholders generally. *Sinclair Oil Corp. v. Levien,* Del.Supr., 280 A.2d 717, 720 (1971); *Cheff v. Mathes,* Del.Supr., 199 A.2d 548, 554 (1964); *David J. Greene & Co. v. Dunhill International, Inc.,* Del.Ch., 249 A.2d 427, 430 (1968). See also 8 *Del.C.* § 144. Thus, if such director interest is present, and the transaction is not approved by a majority consisting of the disinterested directors, then the business judgment rule has no application whatever in determining demand futility. See 8 *Del.C.* § 144(a)(1).

Second, to invoke the rule's protection directors have a duty to inform themselves, prior to making a business decision, of all material information reasonably available to them. Having become so informed, they must then act with requisite care in the discharge of their duties. While the Delaware cases use a variety of terms to describe the applicable standard of care, our analysis satisfies us that under the business judgment rule director liability is predicated upon concepts of gross negligence. See Veasey & Manning, *Codified Standard— Safe Harbor or Uncharted Reef?* 35 Bus.Law. 919, 928 (1980).

However, it should be noted that the business judgment rule operates only in the context of director action. Technically speaking, it has no role where directors have either abdicated their functions, or absent a conscious decision, failed to act. But it also follows that under applicable principles, a conscious decision to refrain from acting may nonetheless be a valid exercise of business judgment and enjoy the protections of the rule. . . .

Delaware courts have addressed the issue of demand futility on several earlier occasions. *See Sohland v. Baker,* Del. Supr., 141 A. 277, 281-82 (1927); *McKee v. Rogers,* Del.Ch., 156 A. 191, 193 (1931); *Miller v. Loft,* Del.Ch., 153 A. 861, 862 (1931); *Fleer v. Frank H. Fleer Corp.,*

Del.Ch., 125 A. 411, 414 (1924); *Harden v. Eastern States Public Service Co.*, Del.Ch., 122 A. 705, 707 (1923); *Ellis v. Penn Beef Co.*, Del.Ch., 80 A. 666, 668 (1911). *Cf. Mayer v. Adams*, Del.Supr., 141 A.2d 458, 461 (1958) (minority demand on majority shareholders). The rule emerging from these decisions is that where officers and directors are under an influence which sterilizes their discretion, they cannot be considered proper persons to conduct litigation on behalf of the corporation. Thus, demand would be futile. *See, e.g., McKee v. Rogers*, Del.Ch., 156 A. 191, 192 (1931) (holding that where a defendant controlled the board of directors, "[i]t is manifest then that there can be no expectation that the corporation would sue him, and if it did, it can hardly be said that the prosecution of the suit would be entrusted to proper hands"). *But see, e.g., Fleer v. Frank H. Fleer Corp.*, Del.Ch., 125 A. 411, 415 (1924) ("[w]here the demand if made would be directed to the particular individuals who themselves are the alleged wrongdoers and who therefore would be invited to sue themselves, the rule is settled that a demand and refusal is not requisite"); *Miller v. Loft, Inc.*, Del.Ch., 153 A. 861, 862 (1931) ("if by reason of hostile interest or guilty participation in the wrongs complained of, the directors cannot be expected to institute suit, . . . no demand upon them to institute suit is requisite").

However, those cases cannot be taken to mean that any board approval of a challenged transaction automatically connotes "hostile interest" and "guilty participation" by directors, or some other form of sterilizing influence upon them. Were that so, the demand requirements of our law would be meaningless, leaving the clear mandate of Chancery Rule 23.1 devoid of its purpose and substance.

The trial court correctly recognized that demand futility is inextricably bound to issues of business judgment, but stated the test to be based on allegations of fact, which, if true, "show that there is a reasonable inference" the business judgment rule is not applicable for purposes of a pre-suit demand. *Lewis*, 466 A.2d at 381.

The problem with this formulation is the concept of reasonable inferences to be drawn against a board of directors based on allegations in a complaint. As is clear from this case, and the conclusory allegations upon which the Vice Chancellor relied, demand futility becomes virtually automatic under such a test. Bearing in mind the presumptions with which director action is cloaked, we believe that the matter must be approached in a more balanced way.

Our view is that in determining demand futility the Court of Chancery in the proper exercise of its discretion must decide whether, under the particularized facts alleged, a reasonable doubt is created that: (1) the directors are disinterested and independent [or[24]] (2) the challenged transaction was otherwise the product of a valid exercise of business judgment. Hence, the Court of Chancery must make two inquiries, one into the independence and disinterestedness of the directors and the other into the substantive nature of the challenged transaction and the board's approval thereof. As to the latter inquiry the court does not assume that the transaction is a wrong to the corporation

---

[24] The paragraph that follows, as well as subsequent case law, make clear that the original articulation as an "and" should be read as an "or." – Eds.

requiring corrective steps by the board. Rather, the alleged wrong is substantively reviewed against the factual background alleged in the complaint. As to the former inquiry, directorial independence and disinterestedness, the court reviews the factual allegations to decide whether they raise a reasonable doubt, as a threshold matter, that the protections of the business judgment rule are available to the board. Certainly, if this is an "interested" director transaction, such that the business judgment rule is inapplicable to the board majority approving the transaction, then the inquiry ceases. In that event futility of demand has been established by any objective or subjective standard.[8] *See, e.g., Bergstein v. Texas Internat'l Co.,* Del.Ch., 453 A.2d 467, 471 (1982) (because five of nine directors approved stock appreciation rights plan likely to benefit them, board was interested for demand purposes and demand held futile). This includes situations involving self-dealing directors. *See Sinclair Oil Corp. v. Levien,* Del.Supr., 280 A.2d 717 (1971); *Sterling v. Mayflower,* Del.Supr., 93 A.2d 107 (1952); *Trans World Airlines, Inc. v. Summa Corp.,* Del.Ch., 374 A.2d 5 (1977); *David J. Greene & Co. v. Dunhill International, Inc.,* Del.Ch., 249 A.2d 427 (1968).

However, the mere threat of personal liability for approving a questioned transaction, standing alone, is insufficient to challenge either the independence or disinterestedness of directors, although in rare cases a transaction may be so egregious on its face that board approval cannot meet the test of business judgment, and a substantial likelihood of director liability therefore exists. *See Gimbel v. Signal Cos., Inc.,* Del.Ch., 316 A.2d 599, *aff'd,* Del.Supr., 316 A.2d 619 (1974); *Cottrell v. Pawcatuck Co.,* Del.Supr., 128 A.2d 225 (1956). In sum the entire review is factual in nature. The Court of Chancery in the exercise of its sound discretion must be satisfied that a plaintiff has alleged facts with particularity which, taken as true, support a reasonable doubt that the challenged transaction was the product of a valid exercise of business judgment. Only in that context is demand excused.

B.

Having outlined the legal framework within which these issues are to be determined, we consider plaintiff's claims of futility here: Fink's domination and control of the directors, board approval of the Fink-Meyers employment agreement, and board hostility to the plaintiff's derivative action due to the directors' status as defendants.

Plaintiff's claim that Fink dominates and controls the Meyers' board is based on: (1) Fink's 47% ownership of Meyers' outstanding stock, and (2) that he "personally selected" each Meyers director. Plaintiff also alleges that mere approval of the employment agreement illustrates Fink's domination and control of the board. In addition, plaintiff argued on

---

[8] We recognize that drawing the line at a majority of the board may be an arguably arbitrary dividing point. Critics will charge that we are ignoring the structural bias common to corporate boards throughout America, as well as the other unseen socialization processes cutting against independent discussion and decisionmaking in the boardroom. The difficulty with structural bias in a demand futile case is simply one of establishing it in the complaint for purposes of Rule 23.1. We are satisfied that discretionary review by the Court of Chancery of complaints alleging specific facts pointing to bias on a particular board will be sufficient for determining demand futility.

appeal that 47% stock ownership, though less than a majority, constituted control given the large number of shares outstanding, 1,245,745.

Such contentions do not support any claim under Delaware law that these directors lack independence. In *Kaplan v. Centex Corp.,* Del.Ch., 284 A.2d 119 (1971), the Court of Chancery stated that "[s]tock ownership alone, at least when it amounts to less than a majority, is not sufficient proof of domination or control". *Id.* at 123. Moreover, in the demand context even proof of majority ownership of a company does not strip the directors of the presumptions of independence, and that their acts have been taken in good faith and in the best interests of the corporation. There must be coupled with the allegation of control such facts as would demonstrate that through personal or other relationships the directors are beholden to the controlling person. *See Mayer v. Adams,* Del.Ch., 167 A.2d 729, 732, *aff'd,* Del.Supr., 174 A.2d 313 (1961). To date the principal decisions dealing with the issue of control or domination arose only after a full trial on the merits. Thus, they are distinguishable in the demand context unless similar particularized facts are alleged to meet the test of Chancery Rule 23.1. *See e.g., Kaplan,* 284 A.2d at 123; *Chasin v. Gluck,* Del.Ch., 282 A.2d 188 (1971); *Greene v. Allen,* Del.Ch., 114 A.2d 916 (1955); *Loft, Inc. v. Guth,* Del.Ch., 2 A.2d 225, 237 (1938), *aff'd,* Del.Supr., 5 A.2d 503 (1939).

The requirement of director independence inhers in the conception and rationale of the business judgment rule. The presumption of propriety that flows from an exercise of business judgment is based in part on this unyielding precept. Independence means that a director's decision is based on the corporate merits of the subject before the board rather than extraneous considerations or influences. While directors may confer, debate, and resolve their differences through compromise, or by reasonable reliance upon the expertise of their colleagues and other qualified persons, the end result, nonetheless, must be that each director has brought his or her own informed business judgment to bear with specificity upon the corporate merits of the issues without regard for or succumbing to influences which convert an otherwise valid business decision into a faithless act.

Thus, it is not enough to charge that a director was nominated by or elected at the behest of those controlling the outcome of a corporate election. That is the usual way a person becomes a corporate director. It is the care, attention and sense of individual responsibility to the performance of one's duties, not the method of election, that generally touches on independence.

We conclude that in the demand-futile context a plaintiff charging domination and control of one or more directors must allege particularized facts manifesting "a direction of corporate conduct in such a way as to comport with the wishes or interests of the corporation (or persons) doing the controlling". *Kaplan,* 284 A.2d at 123. The shorthand shibboleth of "dominated and controlled directors" is insufficient. In recognizing that *Kaplan* was decided after trial and full discovery, we stress that the plaintiff need only allege specific facts; he need not plead evidence. Otherwise, he would be forced to make allegations which may not comport with his duties under Chancery Rule 11.

Here, plaintiff has not alleged any facts sufficient to support a claim of control. The personal-selection-of-directors allegation stands alone, unsupported. At best it is a conclusion devoid of factual support. The causal link between Fink's control and approval of the employment agreement is alluded to, but nowhere specified. The director's approval, alone, does not establish control, even in the face of Fink's 47% stock ownership. *See Kaplan v. Centex Corp.,* 284 A.2d at 122, 123. The claim that Fink is unlikely to perform any services under the agreement, because of his age, and his conflicting consultant work with Prudential, adds nothing to the control claim. Therefore, we cannot conclude that the complaint factually particularizes any circumstances of control and domination to overcome the presumption of board independence, and thus render the demand futile.

C.

Turning to the board's approval of the Meyers-Fink employment agreement, plaintiff's argument is simple: all of the Meyers directors are named defendants, because they approved the wasteful agreement; if plaintiff prevails on the merits all the directors will be jointly and severally liable; therefore, the directors' interest in avoiding personal liability automatically and absolutely disqualifies them from passing on a shareholder's demand.

Such allegations are conclusory at best. In Delaware mere directorial approval of a transaction, absent particularized facts supporting a breach of fiduciary duty claim, or otherwise establishing the lack of independence or disinterestedness of a majority of the directors, is insufficient to excuse demand. Here, plaintiff's suit is premised on the notion that the Meyers-Fink employment agreement was a waste of corporate assets. So, the argument goes, by approving such waste the directors now face potential personal liability, thereby rendering futile any demand on them to bring suit. Unfortunately, plaintiff's claim falls in its initial premise. The complaint does not allege particularized facts indicating that the agreement is a waste of corporate assets. Indeed, the complaint as now drafted may not even state a cause of action, given the directors' broad corporate power to fix the compensation of officers.

In essence, the plaintiff alleged a lack of consideration flowing from Fink to Meyers, since the employment agreement provided that compensation was not contingent on Fink's ability to perform any services. The bare assertion that Fink performed "little or no services" was plaintiff's conclusion based solely on Fink's age and the *existence* of the Fink-Prudential employment agreement. As for Meyers' loans to Fink, beyond the bare allegation that they were made, the complaint does not allege facts indicating the wastefulness of such arrangements. Again, the mere existence of such loans, given the broad corporate powers conferred by Delaware law, does not even state a claim.

In sustaining plaintiff's claim of demand futility the trial court relied on *Fidanque v. American Maracaibo Co.,* Del. Ch., 92 A.2d 311, 321 (1952), which held that a contract providing for payment of consulting fees to a retired president/director was a waste of corporate assets. *Id.* In *Fidanque,* the court found after trial that the contract and payments were in reality compensation for past services. *Id.* at 320. This was based upon facts not present here: the former president/director was a 70 year old stroke victim, neither the agreement nor the record spelled out his consulting duties at all, the consulting salary equalled the individual's salary when he was president and general manager of the corporation, and the contract was silent as to continued employment in the event that the retired president/director again became incapacitated and unable to perform his duties. *Id.* at 320-21. Contrasting the facts of *Fidanque* with the complaint here, it is apparent that plaintiff has not alleged facts sufficient to render demand futile on a charge of corporate waste, and thus create a reasonable doubt that the board's action is protected by the business judgment rule. *Cf. Beard v. Elster,* Del.Supr., 160 A.2d 731 (1960); *Lieberman v. Koppers Company Line, Inc.,* Del.Ch., 149 A.2d 756, *aff'd, Lieberman v. Becker,* Del.Supr., 155 A.2d 596 (1959).

D.

Plaintiff's final argument is the incantation that demand is excused because the directors otherwise would have to sue themselves, thereby placing the conduct of the litigation in hostile hands and preventing its effective prosecution. This bootstrap argument has been made to and dismissed by other courts. *See, e.g., Lewis v. Graves,* 701 F.2d 245, 248-49 (2d Cir.1983); *Heit v. Baird,* 567 F.2d 1157, 1162 (1st Cir. 1977); *Lewis v. Anselmi,* 564 F.Supp., 768, 772 (S.D.N.Y.1983). Its acceptance would effectively abrogate Rule 23.1 and weaken the managerial power of directors. Unless facts are alleged with particularity to overcome the presumptions of independence and a proper exercise of business judgment, in which case the directors could not be expected to sue themselves, a bare claim of this sort raises no legally cognizable issue under Delaware corporate law.

V.

In sum, we conclude that the plaintiff has failed to allege facts with particularity indicating that the Meyers directors were tainted by interest, lacked independence, or took action contrary to Meyers' best interests in order to create a reasonable doubt as to the applicability of the business judgment rule. Only in the presence of such a reasonable doubt may a demand be deemed futile. Hence, we reverse the Court of Chancery's denial of the motion to dismiss, and remand with instructions that plaintiff be granted leave to amend his complaint to bring it into compliance with Rule 23.1 based on the principles we have announced today.

* * *

REVERSED AND REMANDED.

[...]

Discussion Questions:

1. The *Aronson* court ultimately rules that "demand was not futile" in this case, i.e., the shareholder-plaintiff was not entitled to prosecute this suit. What should the shareholder have done to achieve a different outcome, and would this have been

feasible? In light of this, do you think *Aronson*'s hurdle for derivative suits is appropriate, too high, or too low?

2. The *Aronson* court repeatedly cites *Zapata v. Maldonaldo*. In *Aronson*'s words (which we edited out), *Zapata* held that "even in a demand-excused case, a board has the power to appoint a committee of one or more independent disinterested directors to determine whether the derivative action should be pursued or dismissal sought. [T]he Court of Chancery, in passing on a committee's motion to dismiss a derivative action in a demand excused case, must apply a two-step test. First, the court must inquire into the independence and good faith of the committee and review the reasonableness and good faith of the committee's investigation. Second, the court must apply its own independent business judgment to decide whether the motion to dismiss should be granted" (internal references omitted). *Zapata* is still good law, and boards often try to get derivative suits dismissed this way, which may happen at any point until the final verdict. If you were a plaintiff attorney, would you rather get dismissed at the demand futility stage or later under *Zapata*?

Attorneys Fees: The Juice that Fuels the System of Corporate Law Enforcement

To generate a substantial amount of shareholder litigation, merely allowing shareholders suits, direct or derivative, is not sufficient. Somebody needs to have an incentive to bring the suit. If shareholder-plaintiffs only recovered their pro rata share of the recovery (indirectly in the case of a derivative suit), incentives to bring suit would be very low and, in light of substantial litigation costs, usually insufficient. Litigation would be hamstrung by the same collective action problem as proxy fights. Under the *common fund doctrine*, however, U.S. courts award a substantial part of the recovery to the plaintiff or, in the standard case, to the plaintiff lawyer. As *Americas Mining* shows, that award can be very substantial indeed.

The litigation incentives generated by such awards strike some as excessive. For a while, virtually every M&A deal attracted shareholder litigation, albeit mostly with much lower or no recovery. Corporations tried various tactics to limit the amount of litigation they face, prompting recent amendments of the DGCL Sections 102(f) and 115.

Americas Mining Corp. v. Theriault
51 A.3d 1213 (Del. 2012)

HOLLAND, J., for the majority:

This is an appeal from a post-trial decision and final judgment of the Court of Chancery awarding more than $2 billion in damages and more than $304 million in attorneys' fees. The Court of Chancery held that the defendants-appellants, Americas Mining Corporation ("AMC"), the subsidiary of Southern Copper Corporation's ("Southern Peru") controlling shareholder, and affiliate directors of Southern Peru (collectively, the "Defendants"), breached their fiduciary duty of loyalty to Southern Peru and its minority stockholders by causing Southern Peru to acquire the controller's 99.15% interest in a Mexican mining company, Minera México, S.A. de C.V. ("Minera"), for much more than it was worth, *i.e.,* at an unfair price. . . . [4]

The Plaintiff challenged the transaction derivatively on behalf of Southern Peru. The Court of Chancery found the trial evidence established that the controlling shareholder, Grupo México, S.A.B. de C.V. ("Grupo Mexico"), through AMC, "extracted a deal that was far better than market" from Southern Peru due to the ineffective operation of a special committee (the "Special Committee"). To remedy the Defendants' breaches of loyalty, the Court of Chancery awarded the difference between the value Southern Peru paid for Minera ($3.7 billion) and the amount the Court of Chancery determined Minera was worth ($2.4 billion). The Court of Chancery awarded damages in the amount of $1.347 billion plus pre- and post-judgment interest, for a total judgment of $2.0316 billion. The Court of Chancery also awarded the Plaintiff's counsel attorneys' fees and expenses in the amount of 15% of the total judgment, which amounts to more than $304 million.

[...]

ATTORNEYS' FEE AWARD

The Plaintiff petitioned for attorneys' fees and expenses representing 22.5% of the recovery plus post-judgment interest. The Court of Chancery awarded 15% of the $2.031 billion judgment, or $304,742,604.45, plus post-judgment interest until the attorneys' fee and expense award is satisfied ("Fee Award"). The Court of Chancery found that the Fee Award "fairly implements the most important factors our Supreme Court has highlighted under *Sugarland,* including the importance of benefits," and "creates a healthy incentive for plaintiff's lawyers to actually seek real achievement for the companies that they represent in derivative actions and the classes that they represent in class actions."

On appeal, the Defendants contend "the Court of Chancery abuse[d] its discretion by granting an unreasonable fee award of over $304 million that pays the Plaintiff's counsel over $35,000 per hour worked and 66 times the value of their time and expenses." [...]

Common Fund Doctrine

Under the common fund doctrine, "a litigant or a lawyer who recovers a common fund for the benefit of persons other than himself or his client is entitled to a reasonable attorney's fee from the fund as a whole." The common fund doctrine is a well-established basis for

---

[4] Grupo Mexico held—and still holds—its interest in Southern Peru through its wholly-owned subsidiary Americas Mining Corporation ("AMC"). Grupo Mexico also held its 99.15% stake in Minera through AMC. AMC, not Grupo Mexico, is a defendant to this action, but I refer to them collectively as Grupo Mexico in this opinion because that more accurately reflects the story as it happened.

awarding attorneys' fees in the Court of Chancery. It is founded on the equitable principle that those who have profited from litigation should share its costs.

"Typically, successful derivative or class action suits which result in the recovery of money or property wrongfully diverted from the corporation ... are viewed as fund creating actions." In this case, [...] the $2.031 billion judgment resulted in the creation of a common fund. Accordingly, Plaintiff's counsel, whose efforts resulted in the creation of that common fund, are entitled to receive a reasonable fee and reimbursement for expenses from that fund. [...]

Sugarland

Factors Applied

The determination of any attorney fee award is a matter within the sound judicial discretion of the Court of Chancery. In this case, the Court of Chancery considered and applied each of [...]

The aptly-named *Sugarland* factor[s], perhaps never more aptly-named than today, [...]

Benefit Achieved

With regard to the first and most important of the *Sugarland* factors, the benefit achieved, the Court of Chancery found that "[t]he plaintiffs here indisputably prosecuted this action through trial and secured an immense economic benefit for Southern Peru." The Court of Chancery stated that "this isn't small and this isn't monitoring. This isn't a case where it's rounding, where the plaintiffs share credit." The Court of Chancery concluded that "anything that was achieved ... by this litigation [was] by these plaintiffs." With pre-judgment interest, the benefit achieved through the litigation amounts to more than $2 billion. Post-judgment interest accrues at more than $212,000 per day. The extraordinary benefit that was achieved in this case merits a very substantial award of attorneys' fees.

The Defendants take issue with the fact that the Fee Award was based upon the total damage award, which included pre-judgment interest. They contend that including such interest in the damage award is reversible error because the Plaintiff took too long to litigate this matter. The record reflects that the Court of Chancery considered the slow pace of the litigation in making the Fee Award. In response to the Defendants' arguments, the trial judge stated: "I'm not going to ... exclude interest altogether. I get that argument.... The interest I awarded is fairly earned by the plaintiffs. It's a lower amount. And, again, I've taken that [pace of litigation] into account by the percentage that I'm awarding." The Court of Chancery's decision to include pre-judgment interest in its determination of the benefit achieved was not arbitrary or capricious, but rather was the product of a logical and deductive reasoning process.

Difficulty and Complexity

The Court of Chancery carefully considered the difficulty and complexity of the case. It noted that the Plaintiff's attorneys had succeeded in presenting complex valuation issues in a persuasive way before a skeptical court:

> They advanced a theory of the case that a judge of this court, me, was reluctant to embrace. I denied their motion for summary judgment. I think I gave [Plaintiff's counsel] a good amount of grief that day about the theory. I asked a lot of questions at trial because I was still skeptical of the theory. It faced some of the best lawyers I know and am privileged to have come before me, and they won. . . .
>
> I think when you talk about *Sugarland* and you talk about the difficulty of the litigation, was this difficult? Yes, it was. Were the defense counsel formidable and among the best that we have in our bar? They were. Did the plaintiffs have to do a lot of good work to get done and have to push back against a judge who was resistant to their approach? They did.

The Plaintiff's attorneys established at trial that Southern Peru had agreed to overpay its controlling shareholder by more than fifty percent ($3.7 billion compared to $2.4 billion). In doing so, the Court of Chancery found that the Plaintiff had to "deal with very complex financial and valuation issues" while being "up against major league, first-rate legal talent." This factor supports a substantial award of attorneys' fees.

Contingent Representation

The Plaintiff's attorneys pursued this case on a contingent fee basis. They invested a significant number of hours and incurred more than one million dollars in expenses. The Defendants litigated vigorously and forced the Plaintiff to go to trial to obtain any monetary recovery. Accordingly, in undertaking this representation, the Plaintiff's counsel incurred all of the classic contingent fee risks, including the ultimate risk—no recovery whatsoever. The Court of Chancery acknowledged that the fee award was "going to be a lot per hour to people who get paid by the hour," but that in this case, the Plaintiff's attorneys' compensation was never based on an hourly rate. Therefore, the Court of Chancery found that an award representing 15% of the common fund was reasonable in light of the absolute risk taken by Plaintiff's counsel in prosecuting the case through trial on a fully contingent fee basis.

Standing and Ability of Counsel

The Court of Chancery acknowledged that it was familiar with Plaintiff's counsel and had respect for their skills and record of success. The Defendants do not contest the skill, ability or reputation of the Plaintiff's counsel. They argue, however, that the Court of Chancery "should have weighed more heavily Plaintiff's counsel's undoubted ability against the causal manner in which this case was litigated." The record does not support that argument.

First, the Court of Chancery credited the Defendants' arguments that a rescission-based remedy was inappropriate because of the Plaintiff's delay in litigating the case. Second, the Court of Chancery noted that the record could justify a much larger award of attorneys' fees, but it ultimately applied a "conservative metric because of Plaintiff's delay." Accordingly, the record reflects that the Court of Chancery's Fee Award took into account the length of time involved in getting this case to trial.

Time and Effort of Counsel

The effort by the Plaintiff's attorneys was significant. The Plaintiff's attorneys reviewed approximately 282,046 pages in document production and traveled outside the United States to take multiple depositions. They also engaged in vigorously contested pretrial motion practice. They invested their firms' resources by incurring over a million dollars of out-of-pocket expenses. Most significantly, however, the Plaintiff's attorneys took this case to trial and prevailed. We repeat the Court of Chancery's statement: "anything that was achieved . . . by this litigation [was] by [the Plaintiff's attorneys]."

The primary focus of the Defendants' challenge to the Court of Chancery's Fee Award is on the hourly rate that it implies, given that Plaintiff's counsel spent 8,597 hours on this case. They argue that the Court of Chancery abused its discretion by failing to consider the hourly rate implied by the Fee Award as a "backstop check" on the reasonableness of the fee. The Court of Chancery recognized the implications of this argument: "I get it. It's approximately—on what I awarded, approximately $35,000 an hour, if you look at it that way." However, the Court of Chancery did not look at it that way.

Sugarland does not require, as the Defendants argue, courts to use the hourly rate implied by a percentage fee award, rather than the benefit conferred, as the benchmark for determining a reasonable fee award. To the contrary, in *Sugarland,* this Court refused to adopt the Third Circuit's lodestar approach, which primarily focuses on the time spent. [...]

Instead, we held that the *benefit achieved* by the litigation is the "common yardstick by which a plaintiff's counsel is compensated in a successful derivative action." [...]

The Defendants' alternative to their hourly argument is a challenge to the fairness of the percentage awarded by the Court of Chancery. The Defendants contend that the Court of Chancery erred by failing to apply a declining percentage analysis in its fee determination. According to the Defendants, this Court's decision in *Goodrich v. E.F. Hutton Group, Inc.* supports the *per se* use of a declining percentage. We disagree.

In *Goodrich,* we discussed the declining percentage of the fund concept, noting that the Court of Chancery rightly "acknowledged the merit of the emerging judicial consensus that the percentage of recovery awarded should 'decrease as the size of the [common] fund increases.'" We also emphasized, however, that the multiple factor *Sugarland* approach to determining attorneys' fee awards remained adequate for purposes of applying the equitable common fund doctrine. Therefore, the use of a declining percentage, in applying the *Sugarland* factors in common fund cases, is a matter of discretion and is not required *per se*.

[...]

Fee Award Percentage Discretionary

In determining the amount of a reasonable fee award, our holding in *Sugarland* assigns the greatest weight to the benefit achieved in the litigation. When the benefit is quantifiable, as in this case, by the creation of a common fund, *Sugarland* calls for an award of attorneys' fees based upon a percentage of the benefit. The *Sugarland* factor that is given the greatest emphasis is the size of the fund created, because a "common fund is itself the measure of success ... [and] represents the benchmark from which a reasonable fee will be awarded."

Delaware case law supports a wide range of reasonable percentages for attorneys' fees, but 33% is "the very top of the range of percentages." The Court of Chancery has a history of awarding lower percentages of the benefit where cases have settled before trial. When a case settles early, the Court of Chancery tends to award 10-15% of the monetary benefit conferred. When a case settles after the plaintiffs have engaged in meaningful litigation efforts, typically including multiple depositions and some level of motion practice, fee awards in the Court of Chancery range from 15-25% of the monetary benefits conferred. "A study of recent Delaware fee awards finds that the average amount of fees awarded when derivative and class actions settle for both monetary and therapeutic consideration is approximately 23% of the monetary benefit conferred; the median is 25%." Higher percentages are warranted when cases progress to a post-trial adjudication.

The reasonableness of the percentage awarded by the Court of Chancery is reviewed for an abuse of discretion. The question presented in this case is how to properly determine a reasonable percentage for a fee award in a megafund case. A recent study by the economic consulting firm National Economic Research Associates ("NERA") demonstrates that overall as the settlement values increase, the amount of fee percentages and expenses decrease. The study reports that median attorneys' fees awarded from settlements in securities class actions are generally in the range of 22% to 30% of the recovery until the recovery approaches approximately $500 million. Once in the vicinity of over $500 million, the median attorneys' fees falls to 11%.

Appellate courts that have examined a "megafund rule" requiring a fee percentage to be capped at a low figure when the recovery is quite high, have rejected it as a blanket rule. It is now accepted that "[a] mechanical, a *per se* application of the 'megafund rule' is not necessarily reasonable under the circumstances of a case." For example, although the Third Circuit recognized that its jurisprudence confirms the use of a sliding scale as "appropriate" for percentage fee awards in large recovery cases, it has held that trial judges are not required to use a declining percentage approach in every case involving a large settlement.
[...]

In *Goodrich*, [...] We reasoned that "[t]he adoption of a mandatory methodology or particular mathematical model for determining attorney's fees in common fund cases would be the antithesis of the equitable principles from which the concept of such awards originated." [...]

Fee Award Reasonable Percentage

The percentage awarded as attorneys' fees from a common fund is committed to the sound discretion of the Court of Chancery. [...]

We review an award of attorneys' fees for an abuse of discretion. [...]

In this case, the Court of Chancery carefully weighed and considered all of the *Sugarland* factors. The record supports its factual findings and its well-reasoned decision that a reasonable attorneys' fee is 15% of the benefit created. [...]

Conclusion

The judgment of the Court of Chancery, awarding more than $2 billion in damages and more than $304 million in attorneys' fees, is affirmed.

BERGER, J., concurring and dissenting:

I concur in the majority's decision on the merits, but I would find that the trial court did not properly apply the law when it awarded attorneys' fees, and respectfully dissent on that issue.

The majority finds no abuse of discretion in the trial court's decision to award more than $304 million in attorneys' fees. The majority says that the trial court applied the settled standards set forth in *Sugarland Industries, Inc. v. Thomas,* and that this Court may not substitute its notions of what is right for those of the trial court. But the trial court did not apply *Sugarland,* it applied its own world views on incentives, bankers' compensation, and envy.

To be sure, the trial court recited the *Sugarland* standards. Its analysis, however, focused on the perceived need to incentivize plaintiffs' lawyers to take cases to trial. The trial court hypothesized that a stockholder plaintiff would be happy with a lawyer who says, "If you get really rich because of me, I want to get rich, too." Then, the trial court talked about how others get big payouts without comment, but that lawyers are not viewed the same way:

> [T]here's an idea that when a lawyer or law firms are going to get a big payment, that there's something somehow wrong about that, just because it's a lawyer. I'm sorry, but investment banks have hit it big.... They've hit it big many times. And to me, envy is not an appropriate motivation to take into account when you set an attorney fee.

330

The trial court opined that a declining percentage for "mega" cases would not create a healthy incentive system, and that the trial court would not embrace such an approach. Rather, the trial court repeatedly pointed out that "plenty of market participants make big fees when their clients win," and that if this were a hedge fund manager or an investment bank, the fee would be okay. In sum, the trial court said that the fundamental test for reasonableness is whether the fee is setting a good incentive, and that the only basis for reducing the fee would be envy. That is not a decision based on *Sugarland.*

[...]

Discussion Questions:

1. How does the court determine the right amount of the fee award? What criteria does it use, and what purposes does it aim to achieve? Are the criteria well calibrated to the purposes?

2. Who is opposing the fee award, and why? (This is a hard question—to answer it you will need to diagram the various corporate entities and "follow the money.")

3. Are the damage and fee awards sufficient to deter fiduciary duty violations similar to those at issue in this case?

4. Take a step back: virtually all penalties against the corporation in derivative actions are paid by the company's insurance. In a competitive insurance market, the premiums paid for the insurance are approximately equal to the claims paid out. Directors, as we have already discussed, almost never pay anything out-of-pocket, so one must wonder what deterrent effect such penalties have. The only constituency that wins is the plaintiffs' attorneys. Does this make any sense as an enforcement regime? Notice that Delaware could shut down derivative litigation very quickly, by denying fee requests. But Delaware does not do this—why not? Does Delaware's position reflect "capture" by the plaintiffs' bar, or a reasonable middle-ground position on the benefits of derivative litigation?

Settlement

Settlements of class and derivative actions require court approval under Del. Ch. Rules 23(e) and 23.1(c), respectively. In *In re Riverbed Tech., Inc. S'holders Litig.,* 2015 WL 5458041 (Del. Ch. 2015), Vice-Chancellor Glasscock explained the rationale for this requirement in the context of a class action:

> Settlements in class actions present a well-known agency problem: A plaintiff's attorney may favor a quick settlement where the additional effort required to fully develop valuable claims on behalf of the class may not generate an additional fee as lucrative to the plaintiff's attorney as accepting a quick and moderate fee, then pursuing other interests. The interest of the

principal—the individual plaintiff/stockholder—is often so small that it serves as scant check on the perverse incentive described above, notwithstanding that the aggregate interest of the class in pursuing litigation may be great—the very problem that makes class litigation appropriate in the first instance.[25]

In particular, as class representatives, plaintiff attorneys have the power to forfeit claims on behalf of the entire class in a settlement. Plaintiff attorneys are thus in a position to "sell" shareholder claims—possibly below value but keeping the "price" (fees) for themselves:

> In combination, the incentives of the litigants may be inimical to the class: the individual plaintiff may have little actual stake in the outcome, her counsel may rationally believe a quick settlement and modest fee is in his best financial interest, and the defendants may be happy to "purchase," at the bargain price of disclosures of marginal benefit to the class and payment of the plaintiffs' attorney fees, a broad release from liability.[26]

In spite of these concerns, Delaware courts had developed a practice of approving settlements containing broad releases of shareholder claims in return for moderate corporate disclosures and six-figure attorney fees. Starting with *Riverbed* and culminating with Chancellor Bouchard's authoritative opinion in *Trulia*, the Chancery Court announced a change in its practice.

In re Trulia, Inc. Stockholder Litigation
129 A.3d 884 (Del. 2016)

BOUCHARD, C.

This opinion concerns the proposed settlement of a stockholder class action challenging Zillow, Inc.'s acquisition of Trulia, Inc. in a stock-for-stock merger that closed in February 2015. Shortly after the public announcement of the proposed transaction, four Trulia stockholders filed essentially identical complaints alleging that Trulia's directors had breached their fiduciary duties in approving the proposed merger at an unfair exchange ratio. Less than four months later, after taking limited discovery, the parties reached an agreement-in-principle to settle.

The proposed settlement is of the type often referred to as a "disclosure settlement." It has become the most common method for quickly resolving stockholder lawsuits that are filed routinely in response to the announcement of virtually every transaction involving the acquisition of a public corporation. In essence, Trulia agreed to supplement the proxy materials disseminated to its stockholders before they voted on the proposed transaction to include some additional information that theoretically would allow the stockholders to

---

[25] Riverbed Tech. at *7.
[26] *Id.*, at *9.

be better informed in exercising their franchise rights. In exchange, plaintiffs dropped their motion to preliminarily enjoin the transaction and agreed to provide a release of claims on behalf of a proposed class of Trulia's stockholders. If approved, the settlement will not provide Trulia stockholders with any economic benefits. The only money that would change hands is the payment of a fee to plaintiffs' counsel.

Because a class action impacts the legal rights of absent class members, it is the responsibility of the Court of Chancery to exercise independent judgment to determine whether a proposed class settlement is fair and reasonable to the affected class members. For the reasons explained in this opinion, I conclude that the terms of this proposed settlement are not fair or reasonable because none of the supplemental disclosures were material or even helpful to Trulia's stockholders, and thus the proposed settlement does not afford them any meaningful consideration to warrant providing a release of claims to the defendants. Accordingly, I decline to approve the proposed settlement.

On a broader level, this opinion discusses some of the dynamics that have led to the proliferation of disclosure settlements,[15] noting the concerns that scholars, practitioners and members of the judiciary have expressed that these settlements rarely yield genuine benefits for stockholders and threaten the loss of potentially valuable claims that have not been investigated with rigor. I also discuss some of the particular challenges the Court faces in evaluating disclosure settlements through a non-adversarial process.

Based on these considerations, this opinion offers the Court's perspective that disclosure claims arising in deal litigation optimally should be adjudicated outside of the context of a proposed settlement so that the Court's consideration of the merits of the disclosure claims can occur in an adversarial process without the defendants' desire to obtain an often overly broad release hanging in the balance. The opinion further explains that, to the extent that litigants continue to pursue disclosure settlements, they can expect that the Court will be increasingly vigilant in scrutinizing the "give" and the "get" of such settlements to ensure that they are genuinely fair and reasonable to the absent class members.

I. BACKGROUND

The facts recited in this opinion are based on the allegations of the Verified Amended Class Action Complaint in C.A. No. 10022-CB, which was designated as the operative complaint in the consolidation action; the brief plaintiffs submitted in support of their motion for a preliminary injunction; and the briefs and affidavits submitted in connection with the

---

[15] In this Opinion, I use the term "disclosure settlement" to refer to settlements in which the sole or predominant consideration provided to stockholders in exchange for releasing their claims is the dissemination of one or more disclosures to supplement the proxy materials distributed for the purpose of soliciting stockholder approval for a proposed transaction. An example of a disclosure settlement in which the supplemental disclosures would be the predominant but not sole consideration is one that, in addition to supplemental disclosures, includes an insubstantial component of other non-monetary consideration, such as a minor modification to a deal protection measure.

proposed settlement. Because of the posture of the litigation, the recited facts do not represent factual findings, but rather the record as it was presented for the Court to evaluate the proposed settlement.

A. The Parties

Defendant Trulia, Inc., a Delaware corporation, is an online provider of information on homes for purchase or for rent in the United States. Individual defendants Pete Flint, Robert Moles, Theresia Gouw, Gregory Waldorf, Sami Inkinen, Erik Bardman, and Steve Hafner were members of Trulia's board of directors when the merger was approved.

Defendant Zillow, Inc., a Washington corporation, is a real estate marketplace that helps home buyers, sellers, landlords and others find and share information about homes. Defendant Zebra Holdco, Inc. ("Holdco"), now known as Zillow Group, Inc., is a Washington corporation that was formed to facilitate the merger at issue and is now the parent company of Zillow and Trulia.

Plaintiffs Christopher Shue, Matthew Sciabacucci, Chaile Steinberg, and Robert Collier were Trulia stockholders at all times relevant to this action.

B. The Announcement of the Merger and the Litigation

On July 28, 2014, Trulia and Zillow announced that they had entered into a definitive merger agreement under which Zillow would acquire Trulia for approximately $3.5 billion in stock. The transaction was structured to include two successive stock-for-stock mergers whereby separate subsidiaries of Holdco would acquire both Trulia and Zillow. After these mergers, Trulia and Zillow would exist as wholly-owned subsidiaries of Holdco, and the former stockholders of Trulia and Zillow would receive, respectively, approximately 33% and 67% of the outstanding shares of Holdco.

After the merger was announced, the four plaintiffs filed class action complaints challenging the Trulia merger and seeking to enjoin it. Each of the complaints alleged essentially identical claims: that the individual defendants had breached their fiduciary duties, and that Zillow, Trulia, and Holdco aided and abetted those breaches.

On September 11, 2014, Holdco filed a registration statement containing Trulia and Zillow's preliminary joint proxy statement with the United States Securities and Exchange Commission. On September 24, 2014, one of the four plaintiffs filed a motion for expedited proceedings and for a preliminary injunction.

On October 13, 2014, the Court granted an unopposed motion to consolidate the four cases into one action and to appoint lead counsel. On October 14, at 10:37 a.m., plaintiffs filed a motion to expedite the proceedings in the newly consolidated case. The Court never heard the motion, however, because the parties promptly agreed on an expedited schedule, which they documented in a stipulated case schedule filed on October 14 at 12:12 p.m., less than two hours after the motion to expedite was filed.

Over the next few weeks, plaintiffs reviewed documents produced by defendants and deposed one director of Trulia (Chairman, CEO, and co-founder Pete Flint) and a banker from J.P. Morgan Securities LLC, Trulia's financial advisor in the transaction.

On November 14, 2014, plaintiffs filed a brief in support of their motion for a preliminary injunction. In that brief, plaintiffs asserted that the individual defendants had breached their fiduciary duties by "failing to obtain the highest exchange ratio available for the Company's stockholders in a single-bidder process, failing to properly value the Company, agreeing to preclusive provisions in the Merger Agreement that impede the Board's ability to consider and accept superior proposals, and disseminating materially false and misleading disclosures to the Company's stockholders. . . ." The discussion of the merits in that brief, however, focused only on disclosure issues. Plaintiffs provided no argument in support of any other aspect of their claims.

On November 17, Trulia and Zillow filed a definitive joint proxy statement regarding the transaction on Schedule 14A (the "Proxy").

C. The Parties Reach a Settlement

On November 19, 2014, the parties entered into a Memorandum of Understanding detailing an agreement-in-principle to settle the litigation for certain disclosures to supplement those contained in the Proxy, subject to confirmatory discovery. The same day, Trulia filed a Form 8-K with the Securities and Exchange Commission containing the disclosures (the "Supplemental Disclosures").

On December 18, 2014, Trulia and Zillow held special meetings of stockholders at which each company's stockholders voted on and approved the transaction. Trulia's stockholders overwhelmingly supported the transaction. Of the Trulia shares that voted, 99.15% voted in favor of the transaction. In absolute terms, 79.52% of Trulia's outstanding shares voted in favor the transaction.

On February 10, 2015, plaintiffs conducted a confirmatory deposition of a second Trulia director, Gregory Waldorf. On February 17, 2015, the transaction closed.

On June 10, 2015, the parties executed a Stipulation and Agreement of Compromise, Settlement, and Release (the "Stipulation") in support of a proposed settlement reiterating the terms of the Memorandum of Understanding. In the Stipulation, the parties agreed to seek certification of a class consisting of all Trulia stockholders from July 28, 2014 (when the transaction was announced) through February 17, 2015 (when the transaction closed). The Stipulation included an extremely broad release encompassing, among other things, "Unknown Claims" and claims "arising under federal, state, foreign, statutory, regulatory, common law or other law or rule" held by any member of the proposed class relating in any conceivable way to the transaction. The Stipulation further provided that plaintiffs' counsel intended to seek an award of attorneys' fees and expenses not to exceed $375,000, which defendants agreed not to oppose.

Beginning on July 17, 2015, Trulia disseminated notices to the proposed class members in accordance with a scheduling order the Court had entered.

D. Procedural Posture

On September 16, 2015, after receiving a brief and an affidavit from plaintiffs advocating for approval of the proposed settlement, I held a hearing to consider the fairness of the terms of the proposed settlement. Defendants made no submissions concerning the proposed settlement before the hearing, and no stockholder filed an objection to it. After the hearing, I took the request to approve the settlement under advisement and asked the parties for supplemental briefing on whether disclosures must meet the legal standard of materiality in order to constitute an adequate benefit to support a settlement, and on the rationale and justification for including "unknown claims" among the claims that would be released by the proposed settlement.

On September 22, 2015, Sean J. Griffith, a professor at Fordham University School of Law who has researched disclosure settlements and objected to them in the past, requested permission to appear as *amicus curiae* in order to submit a brief on the topics for which I requested supplemental briefing. I approved this request on September 23, and the parties submitted their supplemental briefing on October 16.

Along with their supplemental briefing, plaintiffs submitted an affidavit from Timothy J. Meinhart, a managing director of Willamette Management Associates, which provides business valuation and transaction financial advisory services. The affidavit addresses certain concerns about some (but not all) of the disclosures that I raised at the settlement hearing. Plaintiffs and defendants also informed the Court that, following the hearing, the parties had agreed to a revised stipulation with a narrower release.

Specifically, the parties removed "Unknown Claims" and "foreign" claims from the ambit of the release and added a carve-out so that the release would not cover "any claims that arise under the Hart-Scott-Rodino, Sherman, or Clayton Acts, or any other state or federal antitrust law." As revised, the release still encompasses "any claims arising under federal, state, statutory, regulatory, common law, or other law or rule" held by any member of the proposed class relating in any conceivable way to the transaction, with the exception of the carve-out for claims arising under state and federal antitrust law.

II. LEGAL ANALYSIS

A. Legal Standard

Under Court of Chancery Rule 23, the Court must approve the dismissal or settlement of a class action. Although Delaware has long favored the voluntary settlement of litigation, the fiduciary character of a class action requires the Court to independently examine the fairness of a class action settlement before approving it. "Approval of a class action settlement requires more than a cursory scrutiny by the court of the issues presented." The

Court must exercise its own judgment to determine whether the settlement is reasonable and intrinsically fair. In doing so, the Court evaluates not only the claim, possible defenses, and obstacles to its successful prosecution, but also "the reasonableness of the 'give' and the 'get,'" or what the class members receive in exchange for ending the litigation.

Before turning to that analysis here, I pause to discuss some of the dynamics that have led to the proliferation of disclosure settlements and the concerns that have been expressed about this phenomenon, and to offer the Court's perspective on how disclosure claims in deal litigation should be adjudicated in the future.

B. Considerations Involving Disclosure Claims in Deal Litigation

Over two decades ago, Chancellor Allen famously remarked in *Solomon v. Pathe Communications Corporation* that "[i]t is a fact evident to all of those who are familiar with shareholder litigation that surviving a motion to dismiss means, as a practical matter, that economical[ly] rational defendants . . . will settle such claims, often for a peppercorn and a fee." The Chancellor's remarks were not made in the context of a settlement, but they touch upon some of the same dynamics that have fueled disclosure settlements of deal litigation.

Today, the public announcement of virtually every transaction involving the acquisition of a public corporation provokes a flurry of class action lawsuits alleging that the target's directors breached their fiduciary duties by agreeing to sell the corporation for an unfair price. On occasion, although it is relatively infrequent, such litigation has generated meaningful economic benefits for stockholders when, for example, the integrity of a sales process has been corrupted by conflicts of interest on the part of corporate fiduciaries or their advisors. But far too often such litigation serves no useful purpose for stockholders. Instead, it serves only to generate fees for certain lawyers who are regular players in the enterprise of routinely filing hastily drafted complaints on behalf of stockholders on the heels of the public announcement of a deal and settling quickly on terms that yield no monetary compensation to the stockholders they represent.

In such lawsuits, plaintiffs' leverage is the threat of an injunction to prevent a transaction from closing. Faced with that threat, defendants are incentivized to settle quickly in order to mitigate the considerable expense of litigation and the distraction it entails, to achieve closing certainty, and to obtain broad releases as a form of "deal insurance." These incentives are so potent that many defendants self-expedite the litigation by volunteering to produce "core documents" to plaintiffs' counsel, obviating the need for plaintiffs to seek the Court's permission to expedite the proceedings in aid of a preliminary injunction application and thereby avoiding the only gating mechanism (albeit one friendly to plaintiffs) the Court has to screen out frivolous cases and to ensure that its limited resources are used wisely.

Once the litigation is on an expedited track and the prospect of an injunction hearing looms, the most common currency used to procure a settlement is the issuance of supplemental disclosures to the target's stockholders before they are asked to vote on the proposed transaction. The theory behind making these disclosures is that, by having the additional information, stockholders will be better informed when exercising their franchise rights. Given the Court's historical practice of approving disclosure settlements when the additional information is not material, and indeed may be of only minor value to the stockholders, providing supplemental disclosures is a particularly easy "give" for defendants to make in exchange for a release.

Once an agreement-in-principle is struck to settle for supplemental disclosures, the litigation takes on an entirely different, non-adversarial character. Both sides of the caption then share the same interest in obtaining the Court's approval of the settlement. The next step, after notice has been provided to the stockholders, is a hearing in which the Court must evaluate the fairness of the proposed settlement. Significantly, in advance of such hearings, the Court receives briefs and affidavits from plaintiffs extolling the value of the supplemental disclosures and advocating for approval of the proposed settlement, but rarely receives any submissions expressing an opposing viewpoint.

Although the Court commonly evaluates the proposed settlement of stockholder class and derivative actions without the benefit of hearing opposing viewpoints, disclosure settlements present some unique challenges. It is one thing for the Court to judge the fairness of a settlement, even in a non-adversarial context, when there has been significant discovery or meaningful motion practice to inform the Court's evaluation. It is quite another to do so when little or no motion practice has occurred and the discovery record is sparse, as is typically the case in an expedited deal litigation leading to an equally expedited resolution based on supplemental disclosures before the transaction closes. In this case, for example, no motions were decided (not even a motion to expedite), and discovery was limited to the production of less than 3,000 pages of documents and the taking of three depositions, two of which were taken before the parties agreed in principle to settle and one of which was a "confirmatory" deposition taken thereafter.

The lack of an adversarial process often requires that the Court become essentially a forensic examiner of proxy materials so that it can play devil's advocate in probing the value of the "get" for stockholders in a proposed disclosure settlement. Consider the following example. During discovery, plaintiffs will typically receive copies of board presentations made by financial advisors who ultimately opine on the fairness of the transaction from a financial point of view. It is all too common for a plaintiff to identify and obtain supplemental disclosure of a laundry list of minutiae in a financial advisor's board presentation that does not appear in the summary of the advisor's analysis in the proxy materials—summaries that commonly run ten or more single-spaced pages in the first instance. Given that the newly added pieces of information were, by definition, missing from the original proxy, it is not difficult for an advocate to make a superficially persuasive argument that it is better for stockholders to have more information rather than less. In an adversarial process, defendants, armed with the help of their financial advisors, would be quick to contextualize the omissions and point out why the missing details are immaterial (and may even be unhelpful) given the summary of the advisor's analysis already disclosed in the proxy. In the settlement context, however, it falls to law-trained judges to attempt to perform this function, however crudely, as best they can.

It is beyond doubt in my view that the dynamics described above, in particular the Court's willingness in the past to approve disclosure settlements of marginal value and to routinely grant broad releases to defendants and six-figure fees to plaintiffs' counsel in the process, have caused deal litigation to explode in the United States beyond the realm of reason. In just the past decade, the percentage of transactions of $100 million or more that have triggered stockholder litigation in this country has more than doubled, from 39.3% in 2005 to a peak of 94.9% in 2014. Only recently has the percentage decreased, falling to 87.7% in 2015 due to a decline near the end of the year. In Delaware, the percentage of such cases settled solely on the basis of supplemental disclosures grew significantly from 45.4% in 2005 to a high of 76.0% in 2012, and only recently has seen some decline. The increased prevalence of deal litigation and disclosure settlements has drawn the attention of academics, practitioners, and the judiciary.

Scholars have criticized disclosure settlements, arguing that non-material supplemental disclosures provide no benefit to stockholders and amount to little more than deal "rents" or "taxes," while the liability releases that accompany settlements threaten the loss of potentially valuable claims related to the transaction in question or other matters falling within the literal scope of overly broad releases. One recent study provides empirical data suggesting that supplemental disclosures make no difference in stockholder voting, and thus provide no benefit that could serve as consideration for a settlement. Another paper, written by a practitioner, provides examples of cases in which unexplored but valuable claims that almost were released through disclosure settlements later yielded significant recoveries for stockholders. A particularly vivid example is the recently concluded *Rural/Metro* case. In that case, the Court of Chancery initially considered it a "very close call" to reject a disclosure settlement that would have released claims which subsequently yielded stockholders over $100 million, mostly from a post-trial judgment, after new counsel took over the case.

Members of this Court also have voiced their concerns over the deal settlement process, expressing doubts about the value of relief obtained in disclosure settlements, and explaining their reservations over the breadth of the releases sought and the lack of any meaningful investigation of claims proposed to be released. Judges outside of Delaware have expressed similar concerns.

Given the rapid proliferation and current ubiquity of deal litigation, the mounting evidence that supplemental disclosures rarely yield genuine benefits for stockholders, the risk of stockholders losing potentially valuable claims that have not been investigated with rigor, and the challenges of assessing disclosure claims in a non-adversarial settlement process, the Court's historical predisposition toward approving disclosure settlements needs to be reexamined. In the Court's opinion, the optimal means by which disclosure claims in deal litigation should be adjudicated is outside the context of a proposed settlement so that the Court's consideration of the merits of the disclosure claims can occur in an adversarial process where the defendants' desire to obtain a release does not hang in the balance.

Outside the settlement context, disclosure claims may be subjected to judicial review in at least two ways. One is in the context of a preliminary injunction motion, in which case the adversarial process would remain intact and plaintiffs would have the burden to demonstrate on the merits a reasonable likelihood of proving that "the alleged omission or misrepresentation is material." In other words, plaintiffs would bear the burden of showing "a substantial likelihood that the disclosure of the omitted fact would have been viewed by the reasonable investor as having significantly altered the `total mix' of information made available."

A second way is when plaintiffs' counsel apply to the Court for an award of attorneys' fees after defendants voluntarily decide to supplement their proxy materials by making one or more of the disclosures sought by plaintiffs, thereby mooting some or all of their claims. In that scenario, where securing a release is not at issue, defendants are incentivized to oppose fee requests they view as excessive. Hence, the adversarial process would remain in place and assist the Court in its evaluation of the nature of the benefit conferred (*i.e.,* the value of the supplemental disclosures) for purposes of determining the reasonableness of the requested fee.

In either of these scenarios, to the extent fiduciary duty claims challenging the sales process remain in the case, they may be amenable to dismissal. Harkening back to Chancellor Allen's words in *Solomon,* the Court would be cognizant of the need to "apply the pleading test under Rule 12 with special care" in stockholder litigation because "the risk of strike suits means that too much turns on the mere survival of the complaint." [...]

The preferred scenario of a mootness dismissal appears to be catching on. In the wake of the Court's increasing scrutiny of disclosure settlements, the Court has observed an increase in the filing of stipulations in which, after disclosure claims have been mooted by defendants electing to supplement their proxy materials, plaintiffs dismiss their actions without prejudice to the other members of the putative class (which has not yet been certified) and the Court reserves jurisdiction solely to hear a mootness fee application. From the Court's perspective, this arrangement provides a logical and sensible framework for concluding the litigation. After being afforded some discovery to probe the merits of a fiduciary challenge to the substance of the board's decision to approve the transaction in question, plaintiffs can exit the litigation without needing to expend additional resources (or causing the Court and other parties to expend further resources) on dismissal motion practice after the transaction has closed. Although defendants will not have obtained a formal release, the filing of a stipulation of dismissal likely represents the end of fiduciary challenges over the transaction as a practical matter.

In the mootness fee scenario, the parties also have the option to resolve the fee application privately without obtaining Court approval. Twenty years ago, Chancellor Allen acknowledged the right of a corporation's directors to exercise business judgment to expend corporate funds (typically funds of the acquirer, who assumes the expense of defending the litigation after the transaction closes) to resolve an application for attorneys' fees when the litigation has become moot, with the caveat that notice must be provided to the stockholders to protect against "the risk of buy off" of plaintiffs' counsel. As the Court recently stated, "notice is appropriate because it provides the information necessary for an interested person to object to the use of corporate funds, such as by 'challeng[ing] the fee payment as waste in a separate litigation,' if the circumstances warrant." In other words, notice to stockholders is designed to guard against potential abuses in the private resolution of fee demands for mooted representative actions. With that protection in place, the Court has accommodated the use of the private resolution procedure on several recent occasions and reiterates here the propriety of proceeding in that fashion.

Returning to the historically trodden but suboptimal path of seeking to resolve disclosure claims in deal litigation through a Court-approved settlement, practitioners should expect that the Court will continue to be increasingly vigilant in applying its independent judgment to its case-by-case assessment of the reasonableness of the "give" and "get" of such settlements in light of the concerns discussed above. To be more specific, practitioners should expect that disclosure settlements are likely to be met with continued disfavor in the future unless the supplemental disclosures address a plainly material misrepresentation or omission, and the subject matter of the proposed release is narrowly circumscribed to encompass nothing more than disclosure claims and fiduciary duty claims concerning the sale process, if the record shows that such claims have been investigated sufficiently. In using the term "plainly material," I mean that it should not be a close call that the supplemental information is material as that term is defined under Delaware law. Where the supplemental information is not plainly material, it may be appropriate for the Court to appoint an *amicus curiae* to assist the Court in its evaluation of the alleged benefits of the supplemental disclosures, given the challenges posed by the non-adversarial nature of the typical disclosure settlement hearing.

Finally, some have expressed concern that enhanced judicial scrutiny of disclosure settlements could lead plaintiffs to sue fiduciaries of Delaware corporations in other jurisdictions in the hope of finding a forum more hospitable to signing off on settlements of no genuine value. It is within the power of a Delaware corporation to enact a forum selection bylaw to address this concern. In any event, it is the Court's opinion, based on its extensive experience in adjudicating cases of this nature, that the historical predisposition that has been shown towards approving disclosure settlements must evolve for the reasons explained above. We hope and trust that our sister courts will reach the same conclusion if confronted with the issue.

With the foregoing considerations in mind, I consider next the "give" and the "get" of the proposed settlement in this case.

C. The Supplemental Disclosures Are not Material and Provided no Meaningful Benefit to Stockholders

Under Delaware law, when directors solicit stockholder action, they must "disclose fully and fairly all material information within the board's control." Delaware has adopted the standard of materiality used under the federal securities laws. Information is material "if there is a substantial likelihood that a reasonable shareholder would consider it important in deciding how to vote." In other words, information is material if, from the perspective of a reasonable stockholder, there is a substantial likelihood that it "significantly alter[s] the 'total mix' of information made available."

Here, the joint Proxy that Trulia and Zillow stockholders received in advance of their respective stockholders' meetings to consider whether to approve the proposed transaction ran 224 pages in length, excluding annexes. It contained extensive discussion concerning, among other things, the background of the mergers, each board's reasons for recommending approval of the proposed transaction, prospective financial information concerning the companies that had been reviewed by their respective boards and financial advisors, and explanations of the opinions of each company's financial advisor. In the case of Trulia, the opinion of J.P. Morgan was summarized in ten single-spaced pages.

The Supplemental Disclosures plaintiffs obtained in this case solely concern the section of the Proxy summarizing J.P. Morgan's financial analysis, which the Trulia board cited as one of the factors it considered in deciding to recommend approval of the proposed merger. Specifically, these disclosures provided additional details concerning: (1) certain synergy numbers in J.P. Morgan's value creation analysis [...].

Relevant to considering the materiality of information disclosed in this section of the Proxy, then-Vice Chancellor Strine observed in *In re Pure Resources, Inc. Shareholders Litigation* that there were "conflicting impulses" in Delaware case law about whether, when seeking stockholder action, directors must disclose "investment banker analyses in circumstances in which the bankers' views about value have been cited as justifying the recommendation of the board." The Court held that, under Delaware law, when the board relies on the advice of a financial advisor in making a decision that requires stockholder action, those stockholders are entitled to receive in the proxy statement "a fair summary of the substantive work performed by the investment bankers upon whose advice the recommendations of their board as to how to vote on a merger or tender rely." This "fair summary" standard has been a guiding principle for this Court in considering proxy disclosures concerning the work of financial advisors for more than a decade.

A fair summary, however, is a *summary.* By definition, it need not contain all information underlying the financial advisor's opinion or contained in its report to the board. Indeed, this Court has held that the summary does not need to provide sufficient data to allow the stockholders to perform their own independent valuation. The essence of a fair summary is not a cornucopia of financial data, but rather an accurate description of the advisor's methodology and key assumptions. In my view, disclosures that provide extraneous details do not contribute to a fair summary and do not add value for stockholders.

With the foregoing principles in mind, I consider next whether any of the four specific Supplemental Disclosures that plaintiffs obtained here were material or whether they provided any benefit to Trulia's stockholders at all.

1. Synergy Numbers in the Value Creation Analysis

The Supplemental Disclosures provided some additional details in the sections of J.P. Morgan's analysis entitled "Value Creation Analysis-Intrinsic Value Approach" and "Value Creation Analysis-Market-Based Approach." In the "Intrinsic Value Approach" analysis, J.P.

342

Morgan compared the implied equity value derived from its discounted cash flow analysis of Trulia on a standalone basis to Trulia stockholders' pro forma ownership of the implied equity value of the combined company. In the "Market-Based Approach," J.P. Morgan compared the public market equity value of Trulia on a standalone basis to Trulia stockholders' pro forma ownership of the implied equity value of the combined company.

As supplemented, the disclosure concerning the Intrinsic Value Approach reads in relevant part as follows, with the information that was added to the original disclosure in the Proxy appearing in bolded text:

The pro forma combined company equity value was equal to: (1) the Trulia standalone discounted cash flow value of $2.9 billion, plus (2) the Zillow standalone discounted cash flow value of $6.2 billion, plus (3) $2.2 billion, representing the present value of (a) Trulia's management expected after-tax synergies of $2.4 billion, less (b) Trulia's management estimates of (i) the one-time costs to achieve such synergies of $65.0 million and (ii) transaction expenses of $85 million. **The present value of after-tax synergies was based on an estimate of $175.0 million in synergies to be fully realized starting in 2016, extrapolated through 2029 based on assumptions provided by Trulia's management.**

Plaintiffs argue that the disclosure of the $175 million synergies figure in the quote above was important because it is substantially different from the $100 million in synergies that J.P. Morgan used in the Market-Based Approach, which figure already was disclosed in the Proxy. According to plaintiffs, "[h]ad [stockholders] initially known that the market-based approach analysis was skewed downward by using lower synergies numbers, their view as to the resulting implied value and reliability of [J.P. Morgan's] analysis may have changed appreciably." There are three fundamental problems with this argument.

First, although plaintiffs question why J.P. Morgan used two different synergies figures in two different analyses, they provide no explanation as to why doing so would be inappropriate. To the contrary, it seems logical that an intrinsic value approach (which is based on a comparison derived from a discounted cash flow analysis) would use synergies based on long-term management projections, while a market-based approach (which is based on a comparison to the public market equity value of Trulia) would use synergies based on what would be publicly announced to investors. Regardless, the Proxy accurately disclosed which synergies assumptions the financial advisor deemed appropriate to use in each analysis.

Second, the $175 million synergies figure that plaintiffs consider so important was not new information. It already was disclosed in the Proxy, which contained the following table providing information about management's synergies expectations:

The following table presents summary estimated synergies that Trulia's management also prepared in respect of the combined company following the completion of the mergers for the calendar years ending 2014 through 2024 in connection with Trulia's evaluation of the mergers.

Trulia Management Estimated synergies (in millions, unaudited)

[Column 1: year, column 2: Total Operating Synergies[1]]

2014E	$-
2015E	$23
2016E	$175
2017E	$225
2018E	$285
2019E	$349
2020E	$416
2021E	$480
2022E	$535
2023E	$574
2024E	$594

Because the $175 million figure for 2016 synergies already appeared in this table, inserting it into a methodological paragraph a few pages later is of no benefit to stockholders. In my view, the supplemental disclosure may have added confusion more than anything else, because it lacks explanatory context and does not clearly describe the nature of management's estimate of synergies that was disclosed in the original Proxy.

Third, plaintiffs exaggerate the significance of juxtaposing the synergy figures used in the Intrinsic Value Approach with those used in the Market-Based Approach. In contrast to the Intrinsic Value Approach, the Market-Based Approach was placed in the end of the summary of the financial advisor's analysis in the "Other Information" section, was termed an "illustrative value creation analysis," and "was presented merely for informational purposes." As plaintiffs concede, a "fair reading" of the Proxy indicates that the Market-Based Approach analysis was less important than the Intrinsic Value Approach analysis. Thus, the notion that the disclosure of the $175 million synergies figure used in one analysis (which already was disclosed in the Proxy) was significant because it was higher than the $100 million figure used in a second, different analysis is based on a false equivalence of the relative importance of the two analyses.

---

[1] "Total Operating Synergies" means the expected EBIT effect of revenue synergies plus the EBIT effect of cost savings/cost avoidance less one-time costs to achieve and retain such synergies. "EBIT" means earnings before interest and taxes. An assumed tax rate of 40% was applied to Total Operating Synergies to determine estimated after-tax synergies. Projected synergies (including costs to achieve synergies) were prepared by Trulia's management through fiscal year 2016 after discussion with Zillow's management. The management of Trulia provided J.P. Morgan with assumptions relating to projected synergies for fiscal years 2017 through 2024 deemed appropriate by Trulia's management. The management of Trulia then directed J.P. Morgan to use these assumptions in extrapolating such estimated synergies for fiscal years extending beyond those for which the management of Trulia had provided projections. The management of Trulia then reviewed and approved such extrapolation of the synergies.

In sum, the disclosures in the original Proxy already provided a fair summary of J.P. Morgan's methodology and assumptions in its two "Value Creation" analyses. Inserting additional minutiae underlying some of the assumptions could not reasonably have been expected to significantly alter the total mix of information and thus was not material. Indeed, in my view, the supplemental information was not even helpful to stockholders.

[...]

For the reasons explained above, none of plaintiffs' Supplemental Disclosures were material or even helpful to Trulia's stockholders. The Proxy already provided a more-than-fair summary of J.P. Morgan's financial analysis in each of the four respects criticized by the plaintiffs. As such, from the perspective of Trulia's stockholders, the "get" in the form of the Supplemental Disclosures does not provide adequate consideration to warrant the "give" of providing a release of claims to defendants and their affiliates, in the form submitted or otherwise. Accordingly, I find that the proposed settlement is not fair or reasonable to Trulia's stockholders.

III. CONCLUSION

For the foregoing reasons, approval of the proposed settlement is DENIED.

IT IS SO ORDERED.

[...]

Discussion Questions:

1. Chancellor Bouchard's "opinion further explains that . . . the Court will be increasingly vigilant in scrutinizing . . . settlements." What precedential value does this language have, formally speaking? What precedential value do you think it has in practice?

2. Chancellor Bouchard disapproves of settlements for disclosures "of marginal value." Why are settlements for "plainly material" disclosures less suspicious? Do "plainly material" disclosures guarantee that the settlement is in the class' best interest?

3. Chancellor Bouchard also disapproves of "broad releases from liability." Can a broad release—including, e.g., antitrust claims—ever be justified? Chancellor Bouchard is also concerned that "defendants are incentivized to settle quickly in order to mitigate the considerable expense of litigation and the distraction it entails [and] to achieve closing certainty." Is this problem specific to class and derivative actions? Is it a problem for the class members? Is it a problem for stockholders? Does blocking settlements solve this problem? What settlements should be approved? What litigation should be encouraged, and, once encouraged, under which conditions should it be allowed to terminate?

Chapter 11 – Insider Trading

We now turn to our final substantive topic of the course, which is the murky terrain of insider trading. Insider trading is formally an area of securities law, but we cover it in our Corporations course for two reasons. <u>First</u>, by invoking questions of "duties" and "to whom the duty is owed," insider trading doctrine shares certain features of corporate law. <u>Second</u>, as a very practical matter, insider trading is highly relevant for most students of corporate law—in fact, perhaps the most personally relevant part of the entire course. Most corporate attorneys will have reason to possess material, non-public information. Careers and lives have been changed because of improper use of this information. While he was teaching at HLS, Professor Alan Dershowitz famously told his Criminal Law students that "a greater percentage of you will become criminal defendants than will be defense lawyers."[27] Our admittedly unscientific survey suggests that the most likely way that corporate attorneys end up as criminal defendants is through insider trading.

Geeta Anand, Jenny Markon, and Chris Adams, *ImClone's Ex-CEO Arrested, Charged with Insider Trading*
***Wall Street Journal* (June 13, 2002)**

Shortly after 6 a.m. EDT yesterday, four FBI agents gathered in front of a building here in the upscale Soho neighborhood where Samuel Waksal lives in a large duplex loft. . . .

Upstairs, still asleep in his pajamas, Dr. Waksal was awakened by a phone call from the agents, asking him to let them up.

Once inside the loft, the agents arrested Dr. Waksal, who recently resigned as chief executive officer of ImClone Systems Inc., on criminal charges of trying to sell ImClone stock and tipping off family members after learning that regulators would soon reject his company's promising cancer drug.

The 54-year-old Dr. Waksal, who had given up an illustrious career as an immunologist to become a biotechnology entrepreneur, asked the agents not to handcuff him in front of his 28-year-old daughter, Aliza. Dr. Waksal was wearing the handcuffs when he left the building, after being allowed to change into street clothes. . . .

Federal officials said they are still looking at "everyone" involved in ImClone trading that might be connected to Dr. Waksal. One investor under scrutiny: home-decor doyenne Martha Stewart, a close friend of Dr. Waksal who sold 3,928 shares of ImClone on the afternoon of Dec. 27, the day before ImClone announced the FDA's rejection of the drug. . . .

There are some bright line rules. Section 16(a) of the 1934 Securities & Exchange Act ("the '34 Act") requires directors, officers, and shareholders holding 10% or more of the corporation's stock to file public reports of any transactions in the corporation's securities,

---

[27] Dinitia Smith, *Trying to Save Leona*, New York Magazine (Mar. 12, 1990).

and Section 16(b) requires these designated persons to disgorge to the corporation any profits from any "matched pair" of purchases/sales in the corporation's stock within any six-month period. Regulation FD (for "Fair Disclosure") also tries to level the playing field between insiders and outsiders, by requiring a corporation (or any person acting on its behalf) to release material, non-public information "[s]imultaneously, in the case of an intentional disclosure," and "[p]romptly, in the case of a non-intentional disclosure."

There is also an important safe-harbor for pre-existing plans under Rule 10b5-1. For example, a CEO who is trying to liquidate some of her holdings in her company's stock to finance her child's college education could set up a 10b5-1 plan to sell stock over time. The plan must be on "auto-pilot" in order for it to qualify for 10b5-1's safe harbor.

The bulk of insider trading regulation is not done by these bright-line rules (which, like most bright-line rules, are both over- and under-encompassing), but rather by Section 10 of the 1934 Act. Section 10(b) provides that it shall be unlawful "to use or employ, in connection with the purchase or sale of any security . . . any manipulative or deceptive device or contrivance in contravention of such rules and regulations as the Commission may proscribe as necessary or appropriate in the public interest or for the protection of investors."

By far the most important Rule promulgated by the SEC under Section 10(b) is Rule 10b-5, which you should read in your Statutory Supplement. As you can see, it is an extremely broad rule. It was drafted by Milton Freeman, a young attorney at the SEC, who in 1942 was tasked with drafting a Rule to be able to bring an enforcement action against a Boston CEO who (according to the SEC) was buying shares of his own company while "talking down" the earnings, when in fact the corporate earnings were at blockbuster levels for the upcoming year. Forgoing the extensive hearings, op-eds, and comment periods that would be typical today for promulgation of such a momentous Rule, Freeman later recounted the meeting at which 10b-5 was adopted: "I do not remember if we got there that morning or after lunch. We passed a piece of paper around to all the commissioners. All the commissioners read the rule and they tossed it on the table, indicating approval. Nobody said anything except Sumner Pike. 'Well,' he said, 'we are against fraud, aren't we?' That is how it happened."

Tracking the elements of common law fraud, which it resembles in certain respects, there are several elements of a Rule 10b-5 action: (1) a false or misleading statement or omission; (2) which a reasonable shareholder would consider important (i.e., materiality); (3) with a specific intent to deceive, manipulate, or defraud (i.e., scienter); (4) involving a purchase or sale of securities (i.e., standing); (5) on which the injured party reasonably relied; and (6) which caused damages.

Of these elements, the first has historically been doctrinally the most intricate. Because insider trading cases invariably involve an omission (not an affirmative statement), there must be some duty to disclose that triggers liability under insider trading doctrine. Three theories of duty have developed over the years. The *Equal Access Theory* holds that *anyone* who trades while in possession of material non-public information violates Rule 10b-5.

(This is clearly the most expansive articulation of what Rule 10b-5 prohibits.) The *Fiduciary Duty Theory* holds that those who owe a fiduciary duty to the corporation's shareholders (in which the insider trading takes place) must not trade in possession of material non-public information. And the *Misappropriation Theory* holds that those who misappropriate material non-public information violate Rule 10b-5 if they trade on that information. The cases below document the U.S. Supreme Court's grappling with these alternative theories of liability under Rule 10b-5.

Chiarella v. U.S.
445 U.S. 222 (1980)

MR. JUSTICE POWELL delivered the opinion of the Court.

The question in this case is whether a person who learns from the confidential documents of one corporation that it is planning an attempt to secure control of a second corporation violates § 10 (b) of the Securities Exchange Act of 1934 if he fails to disclose the impending takeover before trading in the target company's securities.

I.

Petitioner is a printer by trade. In 1975 and 1976, he worked as a "markup man" in the New York composing room of Pandick Press, a financial printer. Among documents that petitioner handled were five announcements of corporate takeover bids. When these documents were delivered to the printer, the identities of the acquiring and target corporations were concealed by blank spaces or false names. The true names were sent to the printer on the night of the final printing.

The petitioner, however, was able to deduce the names of the target companies before the final printing from other information contained in the documents. Without disclosing his knowledge, petitioner purchased stock in the target companies and sold the shares immediately after the takeover attempts were made public. By this method, petitioner realized a gain of slightly more than $30,000 in the course of 14 months. Subsequently, the Securities and Exchange Commission (Commission or SEC) began an investigation of his trading activities. In May 1977, petitioner entered into a consent decree with the Commission in which he agreed to return his profits to the sellers of the shares. On the same day, he was discharged by Pandick Press.

In January 1978, petitioner was indicted on 17 counts of violating § 10 (b) of the Securities Exchange Act of 1934 (1934 Act) and SEC Rule 10b-5. After petitioner unsuccessfully moved to dismiss the indictment, he was brought to trial and convicted on all counts.

The Court of Appeals for the Second Circuit affirmed petitioner's conviction. 588 F. 2d 1358 (1978). We granted certiorari, 441 U. S. 942 (1979), and we now reverse.

II.

[...]

This case concerns the legal effect of the petitioner's silence. The District Court's charge permitted the jury to convict the petitioner if it found that he willfully failed to inform sellers of target company securities that he knew of a forthcoming takeover bid that would make their shares more valuable. [...]

§ 10 (b) does not state whether silence may constitute a manipulative or deceptive device. Section 10 (b) was designed as a catchall clause to prevent fraudulent practices. 425 U. S., at 202, 206. But neither the legislative history nor the statute itself affords specific guidance for the resolution of this case. When Rule 10b-5 was promulgated in 1942, the SEC did not discuss the possibility that failure to provide information might run afoul of § 10 (b). [...]

At common law, misrepresentation made for the purpose of inducing reliance upon the false statement is fraudulent. But one who fails to disclose material information prior to the consummation of a transaction commits fraud only when he is under a duty to do so. And the duty to disclose arises when one party has information "that the other [party] is entitled to know because of a fiduciary or other similar relation of trust and confidence between them." In its *Cady, Roberts* decision, the Commission recognized a relationship of trust and confidence between the shareholders of a corporation and those insiders who have obtained confidential information by reason of their position with that corporation. This relationship gives rise to a duty to disclose because of the "necessity of preventing a corporate insider from . . . tak[ing] unfair advantage of the uninformed minority stockholders." *Speed* v. *Transamerica Corp.,* 99 F. Supp. 808, 829 (Del. 1951).

The federal courts have found violations of § 10 (b) where corporate insiders used undisclosed information for their own benefit. *E. g., SEC* v. *Texas Gulf Sulphur Co.,* 401 F. 2d 833 (CA2 1968), cert. denied, 404 U. S. 1005 (1971). [...] Accordingly, a purchaser of stock who has no duty to a prospective seller because he is neither an insider nor a fiduciary has been held to have no obligation to reveal material facts. See *General Time Corp.* v. *Talley Industries, Inc.,* 403 F. 2d 159, 164 (CA2 1968), cert. denied, 393 U. S. 1026 (1969).

[...]

Thus, administrative and judicial interpretations have established that silence in connection with the purchase or sale of securities may operate as a fraud actionable under § 10 (b) despite the absence of statutory language or legislative history specifically addressing the legality of nondisclosure. But such liability is premised upon a duty to disclose arising from a relationship of trust and confidence between parties to a transaction. Application of a duty to disclose prior to trading guarantees that corporate insiders, who have an obligation to place the shareholder's welfare before their own, will not benefit personally through fraudulent use of material, nonpublic information.

III.

In this case, the petitioner was convicted of violating § 10 (b) although he was not a corporate insider and he received no confidential information from the target company. Moreover, the "market information" upon which he relied did not concern the earning power or operations of the target company, but only the plans of the acquiring company. Petitioner's use of that information was not a fraud under § 10 (b) unless he was subject to an affirmative duty to disclose it before trading. In this case, the jury instructions failed to specify any such duty. In effect, the trial court instructed the jury that petitioner owed a duty to everyone; to all sellers, indeed, to the market as a whole. The jury simply was told to decide whether petitioner used material, nonpublic information at a time when "he knew other people trading in the securities market did not have access to the same information." Record 677.

The Court of Appeals affirmed the conviction by holding that "[a]nyone—corporate insider or not—who regularly receives material nonpublic information may not use that information to trade in securities without incurring an affirmative duty to disclose." 588 F. 2d, at 1365 (emphasis in original). [...] The use by anyone of material information not generally available is fraudulent, this theory suggests, because such information gives certain buyers or sellers an unfair advantage over less informed buyers and sellers.

This reasoning suffers from two defects. First, not every instance of financial unfairness constitutes fraudulent activity under § 10 (b). See *Santa Fe Industries, Inc.* v. *Green,* 430 U. S. 462, 474-477 (1977). Second, the element required to make silence fraudulent—a duty to disclose—is absent in this case. No duty could arise from petitioner's relationship with the sellers of the target company's securities, for petitioner had no prior dealings with them. He was not their agent, he was not a fiduciary, he was not a person in whom the sellers had placed their trust and confidence. He was, in fact, a complete stranger who dealt with the sellers only through impersonal market transactions.

We cannot affirm petitioner's conviction without recognizing a general duty between all participants in market transactions to forgo actions based on material, nonpublic information. Formulation of such a broad duty, which departs radically from the established doctrine that duty arises from a specific relationship between two parties, see n. 9, *supra,* should not be undertaken absent some explicit evidence of congressional intent.

As we have seen, no such evidence emerges from the language or legislative history of § 10 (b). Moreover, neither the Congress nor the Commission ever has adopted a parity-of-information rule. [...]

IV.

In its brief to this Court, the United States offers an alternative theory to support petitioner's conviction. It argues that petitioner breached a duty to the acquiring corporation when he acted upon information that he obtained by virtue of his position as an employee of a printer employed by the corporation. The breach of this duty is said to support a conviction under § 10 (b) for fraud perpetrated upon both the acquiring corporation and the sellers.

We need not decide whether this theory has merit for it was not submitted to the jury. [...]

MR. CHIEF JUSTICE BURGER, dissenting.

I believe that the jury instructions in this case properly charged a violation of § 10 (b) and Rule 10b-5, and I would affirm the conviction.

I.

As a general rule, neither party to an arm's-length business transaction has an obligation to disclose information to the other unless the parties stand in some confidential or fiduciary relation. See W. Prosser, Law of Torts § 106 (2d ed. 1955). This rule permits a businessman to capitalize on his experience and skill in securing and evaluating relevant information; it provides incentive for hard work, careful analysis, and astute forecasting. But the policies that underlie the rule also should limit its scope. In particular, the rule should give way when an informational advantage is obtained, not by superior experience, foresight, or industry, but by some unlawful means. One commentator has written:

> "[T]he way in which the buyer acquires the information which he conceals from the vendor should be a material circumstance. The information might have been acquired as the result of his bringing to bear a superior knowledge, intelligence, skill or technical judgment; it might have been acquired by mere chance; or it might have been acquired by means of some tortious action on his part. . . . *Any time information is acquired by an illegal act it would seem that there should be a duty to disclose that information.*" Keeton, Fraud—Concealment and Non-Disclosure, 15 Texas L. Rev. 1, 25-26 (1936) (emphasis added).

I would read § 10 (b) and Rule 10b-5 to encompass and build on this principle: to mean that a person who has misappropriated nonpublic information has an absolute duty to disclose that information or to refrain from trading.

The language of § 10 (b) and of Rule 10b-5 plainly supports such a reading. By their terms, these provisions reach *any* person engaged in *any* fraudulent scheme. [...]

The history of the statute and of the Rule also supports this reading. The antifraud provisions were designed in large measure "to assure that dealing in securities is fair and without undue preferences or advantages among investors." H. R. Conf. Rep. No. 94-229, p. 91 (1975). These provisions prohibit "those manipulative and deceptive practices which have been demonstrated to fulfill no useful function." S. Rep. No. 792, 73d Cong., 2d Sess., 6 (1934). An investor who purchases securities on the basis of misappropriated nonpublic information possesses just such an "undue" trading advantage; his conduct quite clearly serves no useful function except his own enrichment at the expense of others.

This interpretation of § 10 (b) and Rule 10b-5 is in no sense novel. It follows naturally from legal principles enunciated by the Securities and Exchange Commission in its seminal *Cady, Roberts* decision. 40 S. E. C. 907 (1961). There, the Commission relied upon two factors to impose a duty to disclose on corporate insiders: (1) ". . . access . . . to information intended to be available only for a corporate purpose *and not for the personal benefit of anyone*" (emphasis added); and (2) the unfairness inherent in trading on such information when it is inaccessible to those with whom one is dealing. Both of these factors are present whenever a party gains an informational advantage by unlawful means. [...]

MR. JUSTICE BLACKMUN, with whom MR. JUSTICE MARSHALL joins, dissenting.

Although I agree with much of what is said in Part I of the dissenting opinion of THE CHIEF JUSTICE, *ante,* p. 239, I write separately because, in my view, it is unnecessary to rest petitioner's conviction on a "misappropriation" theory. The fact that petitioner Chiarella purloined, or, to use THE CHIEF JUSTICE's word, *ante,* at 245, "stole," information concerning pending tender offers certainly is the most dramatic evidence that petitioner was guilty of fraud. He has conceded that he knew it was wrong, and he and his co-workers in the printshop were specifically warned by their employer that actions of this kind were improper and forbidden. But I also would find petitioner's conduct fraudulent within the meaning of § 10 (b) of the Securities Exchange Act of 1934, 15 U. S. C. § 78j (b), and the Securities and Exchange Commission's Rule 10b-5, 17 CFR § 240.10b-5 (1979), even if he had obtained the blessing of his employer's principals before embarking on his profiteering scheme. Indeed, I think petitioner's brand of manipulative trading, with or without such approval, lies close to the heart of what the securities laws are intended to prohibit.

The Court continues to pursue a course, charted in certain recent decisions, designed to transform § 10 (b) from an intentionally elastic "catchall" provision to one that catches relatively little of the misbehavior that all too often makes investment in securities a needlessly risky business for the uninitiated investor. [...]

Discussion Questions:

1. According to the majority, why is the equal access theory inconsistent with rule 10b-5? In other words, what else is required for a 10b-5 violation, besides trading while in possession of material non-public information?

2. As Burger's dissent points out, *Chiarella* did not simply trade while in possession of material non-public information: Chiarella misappropriated that information from his employer. Why is such misappropriation not sufficient to subject his trades to 10b-5 liability? Or is it? Cf. Part IV of the majority opinion and *O'Hagan, infra.*

3. Do you think the equal access theory would be good policy? What interests would it protect, if any? What desirable activities might it hamper?

Dirks v. SEC
463 U.S. 646 (1983)

JUSTICE POWELL delivered the opinion of the Court.

I.

In 1973, Dirks was an officer of a New York broker-dealer firm who specialized in providing investment analysis of insurance company securities to institutional investors. On March 6, Dirks received information from Ronald Secrist, a former officer of Equity Funding of America. Secrist alleged that the assets of Equity Funding, a diversified corporation primarily engaged in selling life insurance and mutual funds, were vastly overstated as the result of fraudulent corporate practices. Secrist also stated that various regulatory agencies had failed to act on similar charges made by Equity Funding employees. He urged Dirks to verify the fraud and disclose it publicly.

Dirks decided to investigate the allegations. He visited Equity Funding's headquarters in Los Angeles and interviewed several officers and employees of the corporation. The senior management denied any wrongdoing, but certain corporation employees corroborated the charges of fraud. Neither Dirks nor his firm owned or traded any Equity Funding stock, but throughout his investigation he openly discussed the information he had obtained with a number of clients and investors. Some of these persons sold their holdings of Equity Funding securities, including five investment advisers who liquidated holdings of more than $16 million.

While Dirks was in Los Angeles, he was in touch regularly with William Blundell, the Wall Street Journal's Los Angeles bureau chief. Dirks urged Blundell to write a story on the fraud allegations. Blundell did not believe, however, that such a massive fraud could go undetected and declined to write the story. He feared that publishing such damaging hearsay might be libelous.

During the 2-week period in which Dirks pursued his investigation and spread word of Secrist's charges, the price of Equity Funding stock fell from $26 per share to less than $15 per share. This led the New York Stock Exchange to halt trading on March 27. Shortly thereafter California insurance authorities impounded Equity Funding's records and uncovered evidence of the fraud. Only then did the Securities and Exchange Commission (SEC) file a complaint against Equity Funding and only then, on April 2, did the Wall Street Journal publish a front-page story based largely on information assembled by Dirks. Equity Funding immediately went into receivership.

The SEC began an investigation into Dirks' role in the exposure of the fraud. After a hearing by an Administrative Law Judge, the SEC found that Dirks had aided and abetted violations of § 17(a) of the Securities Act of 1933, 48 Stat. 84, as amended, 15 U. S. C. § 77q(a), § 10(b) of the Securities Exchange Act of 1934, 48 Stat. 891, 15 U. S. C. § 78j(b), and SEC Rule 10b-5, 17 CFR § 240.10b-5 (1983), by repeating the allegations of fraud to members of the investment community who later sold their Equity Funding stock. The SEC concluded: "Where 'tippees'—regardless of their motivation or occupation—come into possession of material `corporate information that they know is confidential and know or should know came from a corporate insider,' they must either publicly disclose that information or refrain from trading." 21 S. E. C. Docket 1401, 1407 (1981) (footnote omitted) (quoting *Chiarella* v. *United States,* 445 U. S. 222, 230, n. 12 (1980)). Recognizing, however, that Dirks "played an important role in bringing [Equity Funding's] massive fraud to light," 21 S. E. C. Docket, at 1412, the SEC only censured him.

Dirks sought review in the Court of Appeals for the District of Columbia Circuit. The court entered judgment against Dirks "for the reasons stated by the Commission in its opinion." [...]

In view of the importance to the SEC and to the securities industry of the question presented by this case, we granted a writ of certiorari. 459 U. S. 1014 (1982). We now reverse.

II.

In the seminal case of *In re Cady, Roberts & Co.,* 40 S. E. C. 907 (1961), the SEC recognized that the common law in some jurisdictions imposes on "corporate 'insiders,' particularly officers, directors, or controlling stockholders" an "affirmative duty of disclosure . . . when dealing in securities." [...]

III.

We were explicit in *Chiarella* in saying that there can be no duty to disclose where the person who has traded on inside information "was not [the corporation's] agent, . . . was not a fiduciary, [or] was not a person in whom the sellers [of the securities] had placed their trust and confidence." [...] This requirement of a specific relationship between the shareholders and the individual trading on inside information has created analytical difficulties for the SEC and courts in policing tippees who trade on inside information. Unlike insiders who have independent fiduciary duties to both the corporation and its shareholders, the typical tippee has no such relationships.[14] In view of this absence, it has been unclear how a tippee acquires the *Cady, Roberts* duty to refrain from trading on inside information.

---

[14] Under certain circumstances, such as where corporate information is revealed legitimately to an underwriter, accountant, lawyer, or consultant working for the corporation, these outsiders may become fiduciaries of the shareholders. The basis for recognizing this fiduciary duty is not simply that such persons acquired nonpublic corporate information, but rather that they have entered into a special confidential relationship in the conduct of the business of the enterprise and are given access to information solely for corporate purposes. When such a person breaches his fiduciary relationship, he may be treated more properly as a tipper than a tippee. For such a duty to be imposed, however, the corporation must expect the outsider to keep the disclosed nonpublic information confidential, and the relationship at least must imply such a duty.

354

A.

The SEC's position, as stated in its opinion in this case, is that a tippee "inherits" the *Cady, Roberts* obligation to shareholders whenever he receives inside information from an insider: [...]

In effect, the SEC's theory of tippee liability in both cases appears rooted in the idea that the antifraud provisions require equal information among all traders. This conflicts with the principle set forth in *Chiarella* that only some persons, under some circumstances, will be barred from trading while in possession of material nonpublic information. [...]

Imposing a duty to disclose or abstain solely because a person knowingly receives material nonpublic information from an insider and trades on it could have an inhibiting influence on the role of market analysts, which the SEC itself recognizes is necessary to the preservation of a healthy market. It is commonplace for analysts to "ferret out and analyze information," 21 S. E. C. Docket, at 1406, and this often is done by meeting with and questioning corporate officers and others who are insiders. And information that the analysts obtain normally may be the basis for judgments as to the market worth of a corporation's securities. The analyst's judgment in this respect is made available in market letters or otherwise to clients of the firm. It is the nature of this type of information, and indeed of the markets themselves, that such information cannot be made simultaneously available to all of the corporation's stockholders or the public generally.

B.

The conclusion that recipients of inside information do not invariably acquire a duty to disclose or abstain does not mean that such tippees always are free to trade on the information. The need for a ban on some tippee trading is clear. Not only are insiders forbidden by their fiduciary relationship from personally using undisclosed corporate information to their advantage, but they also may not give such information to an outsider for the same improper purpose of exploiting the information for their personal gain. [...] Similarly, the transactions of those who knowingly participate with the fiduciary in such a breach are "as forbidden" as transactions "on behalf of the trustee himself." [...]

Thus, some tippees must assume an insider's duty to the shareholders not because they receive inside information, but rather because it has been made available to them *improperly*. And for Rule 10b-5 purposes, the insider's disclosure is improper only where it would violate his *Cady, Roberts* duty. Thus, a tippee assumes a fiduciary duty to the shareholders of a corporation not to trade on material nonpublic information only when the insider has breached his fiduciary duty to the shareholders by disclosing the information to the tippee and the tippee knows or should know that there has been a breach. [...] Tipping thus properly is viewed only as a means of indirectly violating the *Cady, Roberts* disclose-or-abstain rule.

C.

In determining whether a tippee is under an obligation to disclose or abstain, it thus is necessary to determine whether the insider's "tip" constituted a breach of the insider's fiduciary duty. All disclosures of confidential corporate information are not inconsistent with the duty insiders owe to shareholders. [...] Whether disclosure is a breach of duty therefore depends in large part on the purpose of the disclosure. [...] the test is whether the insider personally will benefit, directly or indirectly, from his disclosure. Absent some personal gain, there has been no breach of duty to stockholders. And absent a breach by the insider, there is no derivative breach. [...]

The SEC argues that, if inside-trading liability does not exist when the information is transmitted for a proper purpose but is used for trading, it would be a rare situation when the parties could not fabricate some ostensibly legitimate business justification for transmitting the information. We think the SEC is unduly concerned. In determining whether the insider's purpose in making a particular disclosure is fraudulent, the SEC and the courts are not required to read the parties' minds. Scienter in some cases is relevant in determining whether the tipper has violated his *Cady, Roberts* duty. But to determine whether the disclosure itself "deceive[s], manipulate[s], or defraud[s]" shareholders, *Aaron v. SEC*, 446 U. S. 680, 686 (1980), the initial inquiry is whether there has been a breach of duty by the insider. This requires courts to focus on objective criteria, *i. e.*, whether the insider receives a direct or indirect personal benefit from the disclosure, such as a pecuniary gain or a reputational benefit that will translate into future earnings. [...] There are objective facts and circumstances that often justify such an inference. For example, there may be a relationship between the insider and the recipient that suggests a *quid pro quo* from the latter, or an intention to benefit the particular recipient. The elements of fiduciary duty and exploitation of nonpublic information also exist when an insider makes a gift of confidential information to a trading relative or friend. The tip and trade resemble trading by the insider himself followed by a gift of the profits to the recipient.

Determining whether an insider personally benefits from a particular disclosure, a question of fact, will not always be easy for courts. But it is essential, we think, to have a guiding principle for those whose daily activities must be limited and instructed by the SEC's inside-trading rules, and we believe that there must be a breach of the insider's fiduciary duty before the tippee inherits the duty to disclose or abstain. In contrast, the rule adopted by the SEC in this case would have no limiting principle.

IV.

Under the inside-trading and tipping rules set forth above, we find that there was no actionable violation by Dirks. It is undisputed that Dirks himself was a stranger to Equity Funding, with no pre-existing fiduciary duty to its shareholders. He took no action, directly or indirectly, that induced the shareholders or officers of Equity Funding to repose trust or confidence in him. There was no expectation by Dirks' sources that he would keep their information in confidence. Nor did Dirks misappropriate or illegally obtain the information about Equity Funding. Unless the insiders breached their *Cady, Roberts* duty to shareholders in disclosing the nonpublic information to Dirks, he breached no duty when he passed it on to investors as well as to the Wall Street Journal.

It is clear that neither Secrist nor the other Equity Funding employees violated their *Cady, Roberts* duty to the corporation's shareholders by providing information to Dirks. The tippers received no monetary or personal benefit for revealing Equity Funding's secrets, nor was their purpose to make a gift of valuable information to Dirks. As the facts of this case clearly indicate, the tippers were motivated by a desire to expose the fraud. See *supra,* at 648-649. In the absence of a breach of duty to shareholders by the insiders, there was no derivative breach by Dirks. See n. 20, *supra.* Dirks therefore could not have been "a participant after the fact in [an] insider's breach of a fiduciary duty." [...]

JUSTICE BLACKMUN, with whom JUSTICE BRENNAN and JUSTICE MARSHALL join, dissenting.

The Court today takes still another step to limit the protections provided investors by § 10(b) of the Securities Exchange Act of 1934. See *Chiarella* v. *United States,* 445 U. S. 222, 246 (1980) (dissenting opinion). The device employed in this case engrafts a special motivational requirement on the fiduciary duty doctrine. This innovation excuses a knowing and intentional violation of an insider's duty to shareholders if the insider does not act from a motive of personal gain. Even on the extraordinary facts of this case, such an innovation is not justified.

I.

As the Court recognizes, *ante,* at 658, n. 18, the facts here are unusual. After a meeting with Ronald Secrist, a former Equity Funding employee, on March 7, 1973, App. 226, petitioner Raymond Dirks found himself in possession of material nonpublic information of massive fraud within the company. In the Court's words, "[h]e uncovered . . . startling information that required no analysis or exercise of judgment as to its market relevance." *Ibid.* In disclosing that information to Dirks, Secrist intended that Dirks would disseminate the information to his clients, those clients would unload their Equity Funding securities on the market, and the price would fall precipitously, thereby triggering a reaction from the authorities. App. 16, 25, 27.

Dirks complied with his informant's wishes. Instead of reporting that information to the Securities and Exchange Commission (SEC or Commission) or to other regulatory agencies, Dirks began to disseminate the information to his clients and undertook his own investigation. One of his first steps was to direct his associates at Delafield Childs to draw up a list of Delafield clients holding Equity Funding securities. On March 12, eight days before Dirks flew to Los Angeles to investigate Secrist's story, he reported the full allegations to Boston Company Institutional Investors, Inc., which on March 15 and 16 sold approximately $1.2 million of Equity securities. See *id.,* at 199. As he gathered more information, he selectively disclosed it to his clients. To those holding Equity Funding securities he gave the "hard" story—all the allegations; others received the "soft" story—a recitation of vague factors that might reflect adversely on Equity Funding's management. See *id.,* at 211, n. 24.

Dirks' attempts to disseminate the information to nonclients were feeble, at best. On March 12, he left a message for Herbert Lawson, the San Francisco bureau chief of The Wall Street Journal. Not until March 19 and 20 did he call Lawson again, and outline the situation. William Blundell, a Journal investigative reporter based in Los Angeles, got in touch with Dirks about his March 20 telephone call. On March 21, Dirks met with Blundell in Los Angeles. Blundell began his own investigation, relying in part on Dirks' contacts, and on March 23 telephoned Stanley Sporkin, the SEC's Deputy Director of Enforcement. On March 26, the next business day, Sporkin and his staff interviewed Blundell and asked to see Dirks the following morning. Trading was halted by the New York Stock Exchange at about the same time Dirks was talking to Los Angeles SEC personnel. The next day, March 28, the SEC suspended trading in Equity Funding securities. By that time, Dirks' clients had unloaded close to $15 million of Equity Funding stock and the price had plummeted from $26 to $15. The effect of Dirks' selective dissemination of Secrist's information was that Dirks' clients were able to shift the losses that were inevitable due to the Equity Funding fraud from themselves to uninformed market participants.

II.

A.

No one questions that Secrist himself could not trade on his inside information to the disadvantage of uninformed shareholders and purchasers of Equity Funding securities. See Brief for United States as *Amicus Curiae* 19, n. 12. Unlike the printer in *Chiarella,* Secrist stood in a fiduciary relationship with these shareholders. [...]

The Court also acknowledges that Secrist could not do by proxy what he was prohibited from doing personally. [...]

B.

The Court holds, however, that Dirks is not liable because Secrist did not violate his duty; according to the Court, this is so because Secrist did not have the improper purpose of personal gain. *Ante,* at 662-663, 666-667. In so doing, the Court imposes a new, subjective limitation on the scope of the duty owed by insiders to shareholders. The novelty of this limitation is reflected in the Court's lack of support for it.

[...]

C.

The fact that the insider himself does not benefit from the breach does not eradicate the shareholder's injury. Cf. Restatement (Second) of Trusts § 205, Comments *c* and *d* (1959) (trustee liable for acts causing diminution of value of trust); 3 A. Scott, Law of Trusts § 205, p. 1665 (3d ed. 1967) (trustee liable for any losses to trust caused by his breach). [...]

III.

The improper-purpose requirement not only has no basis in law, but it also rests implicitly on a policy that I cannot accept. The Court justifies Secrist's and Dirks' action because the general benefit derived from the violation of Secrist's duty to shareholders outweighed the harm caused to those shareholders, see Heller, *Chiarella*, SEC Rule 14e-3 and *Dirks:* "Fairness" versus Economic Theory, 37 Bus. Lawyer 517, 550 (1982); Easterbrook, Insider Trading, Secret Agents, Evidentiary Privileges, and the Production of Information, 1981 S. Ct. Rev. 309, 338—in other words, because the end justified the means. Under this view, the benefit conferred on society by Secrist's and Dirks' activities may be paid for with the losses caused to shareholders trading with Dirks' clients.

[...]

Dirks and Secrist were under a duty to disclose the information or to refrain from trading on it. I agree that disclosure in this case would have been difficult. *Ibid.* I also recognize that the SEC seemingly has been less than helpful in its view of the nature of disclosure necessary to satisfy the disclose-or-refrain duty. The Commission tells persons with inside information that they cannot trade on that information unless they disclose; it refuses, however, to tell them how to disclose. See *In re Faberge, Inc.,* 45 S. E. C. 249, 256 (1973) (disclosure requires public release through public media designed to reach investing public generally). This seems to be a less than sensible policy, which it is incumbent on the Commission to correct. The Court, however, has no authority to remedy the problem by opening a hole in the congressionally mandated prohibition on insider trading, thus rewarding such trading.

[...]

Discussion Question:

1. According to the majority, when are tippees liable under rule 10b-5? And why wasn't Dirks himself liable under this Rule?

2. Reg. FD (for "fair disclosure") was promulgated in 2000, seventeen years after *Dirks*. But if Reg FD had been in place at the time, would Secrist have violated it?

U.S. v. O'Hagan
521 U.S. 642 (1997)

Ginsburg, J., delivered the opinion of the Court, in which Stevens, O'Connor, Kennedy, Souter, and Breyer, JJ., joined, and in which Scalia, J., joined as to Parts I, III, and IV. Scalia, J., filed an opinion concurring in part and dissenting in part, *post*, p. 679. Thomas, J., filed an opinion concurring in the judgment in part and dissenting in part, in which Rehnquist, C. J., joined, *post, p. 680.*

[...]

I.

Respondent James Herman O'Hagan was a partner in the law firm of Dorsey & Whitney in Minneapolis, Minnesota. In July 1988, Grand Metropolitan PLC (Grand Met), a company based in London, England, retained Dorsey & Whitney as local counsel to represent Grand Met regarding a potential tender offer for the common stock of the Pillsbury Company, headquartered in Minneapolis. Both Grand Met and Dorsey & Whitney took precautions to protect the confidentiality of Grand Met's tender offer plans. O'Hagan did no work on the Grand Met representation. Dorsey & Whitney withdrew from representing Grand Met on September 9, 1988. Less than a month later, on October 4, 1988, Grand Met publicly announced its tender offer for Pillsbury stock.

On August 18, 1988, while Dorsey & Whitney was still representing Grand Met, O'Hagan began purchasing call options for Pillsbury stock. Each option gave him the right to purchase 100 shares of Pillsbury stock by a specified date in September 1988. Later in August and in September, O'Hagan made additional purchases of Pillsbury call options. By the end of September, he owned 2,500 unexpired Pillsbury options, apparently more than any other individual investor. See App. 85, 148. O'Hagan also purchased, in September 1988, some 5,000 shares of Pillsbury common stock, at a price just under $39 per share. When Grand Met announced its tender offer in October, the price of Pillsbury stock rose to nearly $60 per share. O'Hagan then sold his Pillsbury call options and common stock, making a profit of more than $4.3 million.

The Securities and Exchange Commission (SEC or Commission) initiated an investigation into O'Hagan's transactions, culminating in a 57-count indictment. The indictment alleged that O'Hagan defrauded his law firm and its client, Grand Met, by using for his own trading purposes material, nonpublic information regarding Grand Met's planned tender offer. *Id.,* at 8. According to the indictment, O'Hagan used the profits he gained through this trading to conceal his previous embezzlement and conversion of unrelated client trust funds. *Id.,* at 10. O'Hagan was charged with 20 counts of mail fraud, in violation of 18 U. S. C. § 1341; 17 counts of securities fraud, in violation of § 10(b) of the Securities Exchange Act of 1934 (Exchange Act), 48 Stat. 891, 15 U. S. C. § 78j(b), and SEC Rule 10b—5, 17 CFR § 240.10b—5 (1996); 17 counts of fraudulent trading in connection with a tender offer, in violation of § 14(e) of the Exchange Act, 15 U. S. C. § 78n(e), and SEC Rule 14e—3(a), 17 CFR § 240.14e—3(a) (1996); and 3 counts of violating federal money laundering statutes, 18 U. S. C. §§ 1956(a)(1)(B)(i), 1957. See App. 13-24. A jury convicted O'Hagan on all 57 counts, and he was sentenced to a 41-month term of imprisonment.

A divided panel of the Court of Appeals for the Eighth Circuit reversed all of O'Hagan's convictions. 92 F. 3d 612 (1996). Liability under § 10(b) and Rule 10b—5, the Eighth Circuit held, may not be grounded on the "misappropriation theory" of securities fraud on which the prosecution relied. *Id.,* at 622. The Court of Appeals also held that Rule 14e—3(a)—which prohibits trading while in possession of material, nonpublic information relating to a tender offer—exceeds the SEC's § 14(e) rulemaking authority because the Rule contains no breach of fiduciary duty requirement. *Id.,* at 627. The Eighth Circuit further concluded that O'Hagan's mail fraud and money laundering convictions rested on violations of the securities laws, and therefore could not stand once the securities fraud convictions were reversed. [...]

II.

We address first the Court of Appeals' reversal of O'Hagan's convictions under § 10(b) and Rule 10b—5. [...]

A.

[...]

Liability under Rule 10b—5, our precedent indicates, does not extend beyond conduct encompassed by § 10(b)'s prohibition. [...]

Under the "traditional" or "classical theory" of insider trading liability, § 10(b) and Rule 10b—5 are violated when a corporate insider trades in the securities of his corporation on the basis of material, nonpublic information. Trading on such information qualifies as a "deceptive device" under § 10(b), we have affirmed, because "a relationship of trust and confidence [exists] between the shareholders of a corporation and those insiders who have obtained confidential information by reason of their position with that corporation." *Chiarella* v. *United States,* 445 U. S. 222, 228 (1980). That relationship, we recognized, "gives rise to a duty to disclose [or to abstain from trading] because of the 'necessity of preventing a corporate insider from . . . tak[ing] unfair advantage of . . . uninformed . . . stockholders.' " *Id.,* at 228-229 (citation omitted). The classical theory applies not only to officers, directors, and other permanent insiders of a corporation, but also to attorneys, accountants, consultants, and others who temporarily become fiduciaries of a corporation. See *Dirks* v. *SEC,* 463 U. S. 646, 655, n. 14 (1983).

The "misappropriation theory" holds that a person commits fraud "in connection with" a securities transaction, and thereby violates § 10(b) and Rule 10b—5, when he misappropriates confidential information for securities trading purposes, in breach of a duty owed to the source of the information. See Brief for United States 14. Under this theory, a fiduciary's undisclosed, self-serving use of a principal's information to purchase or sell securities, in breach of a duty of loyalty and confidentiality, defrauds the principal of the exclusive use of that information. In lieu of premising liability on a fiduciary relationship between company insider and purchaser or seller of the company's stock, the misappropriation theory premises liability on a fiduciary-turned-trader's deception of those who entrusted him with access to confidential information.

The two theories are complementary, each addressing efforts to capitalize on nonpublic information through the purchase or sale of securities. The classical theory targets a corporate insider's breach of duty to shareholders with whom the insider transacts; the misappropriation theory outlaws trading on the basis of nonpublic information by a corporate "outsider" in breach of a duty owed not to a trading party, but to the source of the information. The misappropriation theory is thus designed to "protec[t] the integrity of the securities markets against abuses by 'outsiders' to a corporation who have access to confidential information that will affect th[e] corporation's security price when revealed, but who owe no fiduciary or other duty to that corporation's shareholders." *Ibid.*

In this case, the indictment alleged that O'Hagan, in breach of a duty of trust and confidence he owed to his law firm, Dorsey & Whitney, and to its client, Grand Met, traded on the basis of nonpublic information regarding Grand Met's planned tender offer for Pillsbury common stock. App. 16. This conduct, the Government charged, constituted a fraudulent device in connection with the purchase and sale of securities.

B.

We agree with the Government that misappropriation, as just defined, satisfies § 10(b)'s requirement that chargeable conduct involve a "deceptive device or contrivance" used "in connection with" the purchase or sale of securities. We observe, first, that misappropriators, as the Government describes them, deal in deception. A fiduciary who "[pretends] loyalty to the principal while secretly converting the principal's information for personal gain," Brief for United States 17, "dupes" or defrauds the principal. [...]

The misappropriation theory advanced by the Government is consistent with *Santa Fe Industries, Inc.* v. *Green,* 430 U. S. 462 (1977), a decision underscoring that § 10(b) is not an all-purpose breach of fiduciary duty ban; rather, it trains on conduct involving manipulation or deception. See *id.,* at 473-476. In contrast to the Government's allegations in this case, in *Santa Fe Industries,* all pertinent facts were disclosed by the persons charged with violating § 10(b) and Rule 10b—5, see *id.,* at 474; therefore, there was no deception through nondisclosure to which liability under those provisions could attach, see *id.,* at 476. Similarly, full disclosure forecloses liability under the misappropriation theory: Because the deception essential to the misappropriation theory involves feigning fidelity to the source of information, if the fiduciary discloses to the source that he plans to trade on the nonpublic information, there is no "deceptive device" and thus no § 10(b) violation— although the fiduciary-turned trader may remain liable under state law for breach of a duty of loyalty.[7]

We turn next to the § 10(b) requirement that the misappropriator's deceptive use of information be "in connection with the purchase or sale of [a] security." This element is satisfied because the fiduciary's fraud is consummated, not when the fiduciary gains the

---

[7] Where, however, a person trading on the basis of material, nonpublic information owes a duty of loyalty and confidentiality to two entities or persons—for example, a law firm and its client—but makes disclosure to only one, the trader may still be liable under the misappropriation theory.

confidential information, but when, without disclosure to his principal, he uses the information to purchase or sell securities. The securities transaction and the breach of duty thus coincide. This is so even though the person or entity defrauded is not the other party to the trade, but is, instead, the source of the nonpublic information. [...]

The misappropriation theory comports with § 10(b)'s language, which requires deception "in connection with the purchase or sale of any security," not deception of an identifiable purchaser or seller. The theory is also well tuned to an animating purpose of the Exchange Act: to insure honest securities markets and thereby promote investor confidence. See 45 Fed. Reg. 60412 (1980) (trading on misappropriated information "undermines the integrity of, and investor confidence in, the securities markets"). Although informational disparity is inevitable in the securities markets, investors likely would hesitate to venture their capital in a market where trading based on misappropriated nonpublic information is unchecked by law. [...]

III.

We consider next the ground on which the Court of Appeals reversed O'Hagan's convictions for fraudulent trading in connection with a tender offer, in violation of § 14(e) of the Exchange Act and SEC Rule 14e—3(a). A sole question is before us as to these convictions: Did the Commission, as the Court of Appeals held, exceed its rulemaking authority under § 14(e) when it adopted Rule 14e—3(a) without requiring a showing that the trading at issue entailed a breach of fiduciary duty? We hold that the Commission, in this regard and to the extent relevant to this case, did not exceed its authority.

The governing statutory provision, § 14(e) of the Exchange Act, reads in relevant part:

> "It shall be unlawful for any person . . . to engage in any fraudulent, deceptive, or manipulative acts or practices, in connection with any tender offer . . . . The [SEC] shall, for the purposes of this subsection, by rules and regulations define, and prescribe means reasonably designed to prevent, such acts and practices as are fraudulent, deceptive, or manipulative." [...]

Relying on § 14(e)'s rulemaking authorization, the Commission, in 1980, promulgated Rule 14e—3(a). That measure provides:

"(a) If any person has taken a substantial step or steps to commence, or has commenced, a tender offer (the 'offering person'), it shall constitute a fraudulent, deceptive or manipulative act or practice within the meaning of section 14(e) of the [Exchange] Act for any other person who is in possession of material information relating to such tender offer which information he knows or has reason to know is nonpublic and which he knows or has reason to know has been acquired directly or indirectly from:

> "(1) The offering person,

"(2) The issuer of the securities sought or to be sought by such tender offer, or

"(3) Any officer, director, partner or employee or any other person acting on behalf of the offering person or such issuer, to purchase or sell or cause to be purchased or sold any of such securities or any securities convertible into or exchangeable for any such securities or any option or right to obtain or to dispose of any of the foregoing securities, unless within a reasonable time prior to any purchase or sale such information and its source are publicly disclosed by press release or otherwise." 17 CFR § 240.14e—3(a) (1996).

As characterized by the Commission, Rule 14e—3(a) is a "disclose or abstain from trading" requirement. [...]

We need not resolve in this case whether the Commission's authority under § 14(e) to "define . . . such acts and practices as are fraudulent" is broader than the Commission's frauddefining authority under § 10(b), for we agree with the United States that Rule 14e—3(a), as applied to cases of this genre, qualifies under § 14(e) as a "means reasonably designed to prevent" fraudulent trading on material, nonpublic information in the tender offer context. A prophylactic measure, because its mission is to prevent, typically encompasses more than the core activity prohibited. [...]

Because Congress has authorized the Commission, in § 14(e), to prescribe legislative rules, we owe the Commission's judgment "more than mere deference or weight." *Batterton* v. *Francis,* 432 U. S. 416, 424-426 (1977). Therefore, in determining whether Rule 14e—3(a)'s "disclose or abstain from trading" requirement is reasonably designed to prevent fraudulent acts, we must accord the Commission's assessment "controlling weight unless [it is] arbitrary, capricious, or manifestly contrary to the statute." *Chevron U. S. A. Inc.* v. *Natural Resources Defense Council, Inc.* , 467 U. S. 837, 844 (1984). In this case, we conclude, the Commission's assessment is none of these.

In adopting the "disclose or abstain" rule, the SEC explained:

"The Commission has previously expressed and continues to have serious concerns about trading by persons in possession of material, nonpublic information relating to a tender offer. This practice results in unfair disparities in market information and market disruption. Security holders who purchase from or sell to such persons are effectively denied the benefits of disclosure and the substantive protections of the Williams Act. If furnished with the information, these security holders would be able to make an informed investment decision, which could involve deferring the purchase or sale of the securities until the material information had been disseminated or until the tender offer had been commenced or terminated." 45 Fed. Reg. 60412 (1980) (footnotes omitted).

The Commission thus justified Rule 14e—3(a) as a means necessary and proper to assure the efficacy of Williams Act protections.

The United States emphasizes that Rule 14e—3(a) reaches trading in which "a breach of duty is likely but difficult to prove." Reply Brief 16. "Particularly in the context of a tender offer," as the Tenth Circuit recognized, "there is a fairly wide circle of people with confidential information," *Peters,* 978 F. 2d, at 1167, notably, the attorneys, investment bankers, and accountants involved in structuring the transaction. The availability of that information may lead to abuse, for "even a hint of an upcoming tender offer may send the price of the target company's stock soaring." *SEC* v. *Materia,* 745 F. 2d 197, 199 (CA2 1984). Individuals entrusted with nonpublic information, particularly if they have no long-term loyalty to the issuer, may find the temptation to trade on that information hard to resist in view of "the very large short-term profits potentially available [to them]." *Peters,* 978 F. 2d, at 1167.

"[I]t may be possible to prove circumstantially that a person [traded on the basis of material, nonpublic information], but almost impossible to prove that the trader obtained such information in breach of a fiduciary duty owed either by the trader or by the ultimate insider source of the information." *Ibid.* The example of a "tippee" who trades on information received from an insider illustrates the problem. Under Rule 10b—5, "a tippee assumes a fiduciary duty to the shareholders of a corporation not to trade on material nonpublic information only when the insider has breached his fiduciary duty to the shareholders by disclosing the information to the tippee and the tippee knows or should know that there has been a breach." *Dirks* , 463 U. S., at 660. To show that a tippee who traded on nonpublic information about a tender offer had breached a fiduciary duty would require proof not only that the insider source breached a fiduciary duty, but that the tippee knew or should have known of that breach. "Yet, in most cases, the only parties to the [information transfer] will be the insider and the alleged tippee." *Peters,* 978 F. 2d, at 1167.

In sum, it is a fair assumption that trading on the basis of material, nonpublic information will often involve a breach of a duty of confidentiality to the bidder or target company or their representatives. The SEC, cognizant of the proof problem that could enable sophisticated traders to escape responsibility, placed in Rule 14e—3(a) a "disclose or abstain from trading" command that does not require specific proof of a breach of fiduciary duty. That prescription, we are satisfied, applied to this case, is a "means reasonably designed to prevent" fraudulent trading on material, nonpublic information in the tender offer context. See *Chestman,* 947 F. 2d, at 560 ("While dispensing with the subtle problems of proof associated with demonstrating fiduciary breach in the problematic area of tender offer insider trading, [Rule 14e— 3(a)] retains a close nexus between the prohibited conduct and the statutory aims."); accord, *Maio,* 51 F. 3d, at 635, and n. 14; *Peters,* 978 F. 2d, at 1167. Therefore, insofar as it serves to prevent the type of misappropriation charged against O'Hagan, Rule 14e—3(a) is a proper exercise of the Commission's prophylactic power under § 14(e). [...]

Justice Scalia, concurring in part and dissenting in part.

[...]

While the Court's explanation of the scope of § 10(b) and Rule 10b—5 would be entirely reasonable in some other context, it does not seem to accord with the principle of lenity we apply to criminal statutes (which cannot be mitigated here by the Rule, which is no less ambiguous than the statute). [...] In light of that principle, it seems to me that the unelaborated statutory language: "[t]o use or employ, in connection with the purchase or sale of any security . . . any manipulative or deceptive device or contrivance," § 10(b), must be construed to require the manipulation or deception of a party to a securities transaction.

Discussion Questions:

1. The misappropriation theory rests 10b-5 liability on deceiving the source of the information. What exactly is the deception, and does it occur "in connection with the purchase or sale of any security" (see SEA §10(b) and Rule 10b-5)?

2. Does Rule 14e-3 expand liability beyond Rule 10b-5? If so, what is the statutory basis for the expansion?

3. Did *O'Hagan* overrule *Chiarella* and *Dirks*?

4. Could the defendant in *Chiarella* have been convicted under *O'Hagan*'s theory of Rule 10b-5? If so, why wasn't he? Hint: re-read part IV of *Chiarella*.

5. Could the defendant in *Chiarella* have been convicted under Rule 14e-3? If so, why wasn't he?

6. Does *O'Hagan's* misappropriation theory of 10b-5 insider trading liability replace the "classical theory" as endorsed and applied by *Chiarella* and *Dirks*—liability premised on a duty to the shareholders of the corporation whose shares are being traded? Or are the two theories complementary? What behavior would violate Rule 10b-5 under the classical theory but not under the misappropriation theory?

From the pages of

FORTUNE

Roger Parloff, *The Gray Art of Not Quite Insider Trading*: Scores of arrests and the indictment of SAC Capital have Wall Street spooked. But what's the crime exactly? The SEC and the Supreme Court disagree. So nobody's sure—and that's how regulators like it.
Fortune **(Aug. 15, 2013)**

"We used to be able to talk to investigators on drug trials," says Source A, a hedge fund portfolio manager. Like all the analysts, research directors, and portfolio managers who cooperated for this article, Source A requested anonymity. People don't want their names in a story about gray areas of equities research that border on insider trading. Four or five years ago, Source A continues, he and other health care analysts still used to get in touch with doctors who were serving as investigators on Phase II or Phase III trials, studies required by the U.S. Food and Drug Administration before a pharmaceutical can be approved as safe and effective. He might have been able to reach as many as eight out of 10 investigators running a study, and sometimes he could reach the principal investigator, the overseer of the whole thing.

"Say each investigator has 11 patients," Source A continues. "'You could almost go patient by patient," asking how they were doing.

The outcome of these drug trials would have an enormous impact on the stock price of the pharmaceutical firm developing the drug. For a small company, the stock might go down 90% or up 100%, depending on the result, and even the stock of a big company, like Pfizer, might move 5%.

The doctors on these studies were providing the analysts with nonpublic information. They may well have been violating confidentiality agreements they had signed with the pharmaceutical companies that commissioned the studies. Source A was paying the doctors for their information, in that he'd reach them through expert-network firms that his hedge fund had on retainer, and the networks paid the doctors for their time.

Isn't that insider trading? In fact, doesn't it sound a lot like the top charge currently being leveled in the marquee insider-trading case of our time: the indictment, filed in July, against Steven A. Cohen's hedge fund, SAC Capital Advisors, which the government alleges made $276 million in July 2008 by obtaining nonpublic information from a doctor overseeing a study of an Alzheimer's drug?

Yet Source A doesn't think his conversations with drug-study doctors in the past ever crossed the line from good, aggressive research into criminality. As we'll see, he's probably right.

This story is about the layers of gray that wash over the world in which hedge fund portfolio managers and stock analysts operate, a world of which the general public knows little. It's about what insider trading is, why it's so hard to define, why prosecutors and regulators like it that way, and why analysts don't.

To be sure, neither Source A nor most of his peers contact drug-study doctors anymore. But that's not necessarily because it was illegal then or now. Rather, it's because general counsels and compliance officers across the industry have gotten a lot antsier about keeping their colleagues from getting anywhere close to the line. The primary stimulus for the new scrupulousness is no mystery. In the summer of 2006 Manhattan U.S. Attorney Preet Bharara commenced a massive insider-trading investigation that burst into public view in October 2009 with the arrest of Raj Rajaratnam, founder and head of the $7 billion Galleon Group hedge fund. So far, Bharara has arrested 83 individuals, of whom 74 have already been convicted.

His top target is Cohen, who has not been criminally charged but who does face civil suit by the U.S. Securities and Exchange Commission that seeks to ban him from the industry for life. (Cohen has denied wrong-doing.) [On November 4, 2013 federal prosecutors announced that SAC Capital would plead guilty to insider trading violations, pay a $1.8 billion fine, and end its investment advisory business.] Cohen's family of funds may be the most prosperous ever, employing about 1,000 people and managing, at its peak, $15 billion in assets. The fund has rewarded investors with annual returns as high as 70% in some years, even when netted of Cohen's staggering fees: 3% of assets, plus 50% of profits. . . .

Let's go back to Source A. Why wasn't he guilty of insider trading if he was paying doctors for nonpublic information about drug trials they were involved in? And if he wasn't guilty, why does the government think SAC Capital is?

Insider trading involves, among other things, trading on "material nonpublic information." Source A did not consider the information obtained from each drug-study doctor he spoke with to be material. Information is "material," the Supreme Court has said, if "there is a substantial likelihood that a reasonable investor would consider it important in deciding" whether to trade a security.

The drug studies that Source A was hearing about were "double blind," meaning that neither the doctors nor the patients knew who were getting the placebos and who were getting the test drug. In addition, each doctor he contacted had access to only tiny samples of patients, and the studies were ongoing, not completed. No rational person would run out and place a trade based solely on impressions gained in a conversation with one of these very imperfectly informed doctors. So the information gained from each conversation wasn't material.

Still, Source A says, he could learn pertinent tidbits. A conversation might have gone like this, he continues:

Analyst: Do you think your patients are getting the placebo or the test drug?

Doctor: I'm seeing rashes in nine of 12 patients, so they probably got the drug.

Analyst: Are the patients with rashes doing better?

Doctor: Yes, they seem to be.

Such a conversation, in aggregate with lots of other conversations and a wide range of other research, might add up to something compelling.

This is the so-called mosaic theory, which is the research analyst's North Star and presumed safe harbor. The SEC has generally endorsed the mosaic theory in commentary accompanying certain rules releases. If a stock analyst collects numerous nonmaterial nuggets of information from different sources, and then adds them together, he should be okay, even if the agglomeration of his information becomes material. The image that emerges from the mosaic can be material, so long as no individual tile is.

Now let's compare that with what Cohen's indicted portfolio manager Mathew Martoma is accused of doing. Through an expert network Martoma met Sidney Gilman, a renowned neurologist who was also the chairman of the safety monitoring committee on a Phase II trial of an Alzheimer's drug being studied by Wyeth and Elan. Gilman, now 80, came to regard Martoma as a friend and pupil, according to the SEC. In July 2008, Gilman emailed Martoma a PowerPoint presentation of the study's final results 12 days before Gilman was to present them for the first time at a professional conference, Gilman has told the government. Martoma began dumping his position in Wyeth and Elan shortly after Gilman sent him the PowerPoint. "We want people kicking tires and uncovering frauds, so public pension funds aren't invested in Enron."

"That's the worst thing I've ever seen," says Source A. "That's different from, 'The patients look like they're doing well now: It doesn't matter what doctors are telling you before the card is flipped. That's not inside information. Martoma played blackjack with the cards exposed." (Martoma has pleaded not guilty and is scheduled to go to trial in November. Gilman is cooperating with the government in exchange for not being charged.)

Still, while everyone seems to agree that what Martoma is charged with is illegal insider trading, not everyone's sure that what Source A used to do was fine and dandy. Source B, the executive at a different hedge fund, is uneasy when told of those facts.

"Talking to scientists on a clinical trial about what's going on before it's been made public?" he asks skeptically. "And paying them for the information? That's very, very gray. I'd be uncomfortable with that, but I can't tell you it's definitively wrong."

Insider trading is a serious crime. Rajaratnam got 11 years for it in September 2011. How, then, can there be so much confusion about what it is? Isn't it defined in the insider-trading statute? That's where all the problems begin. There is no insider-trading statute.

Most modern-day, insider-trading prosecutions are brought under the general federal statute forbidding securities fraud. Fraud involves lying, deception, or trickery. But most stock sales occur over exchanges, where the buyer and seller never meet, let alone mislead each other. Ordinarily, silence can't be fraud. So the mere fact that the buyer of a stock knows something important that the seller doesn't is not enough to make him guilty of insider trading.

Our contemporary notion of insider trading began taking shape in 1961. That year the U.S. Securities and Exchange Commission concluded that since corporate officers and directors owe a special duty of trust and confidence—a "fiduciary" duty—to their shareholders, they do commit fraud if they buy company stock from one of their shareholders, or sell company stock to someone (who thereby becomes one of their shareholders), based on material nonpublic information. Such trades are now known as "classic" insider trading. Furthermore, if the corporate insider tips someone outside the corporation to inside information so that he can trade on it, the tippee may be guilty too.

Gradually, the SEC and federal judges extended the concept of insider trading to reach some situations in which not only was the trader not a corporate insider, but his information hadn't ever come from any corporate insider. The case of the former *Wall*

Street Journal columnist R. Foster Winans is a famous illustration. For several months in 1983, Winans would regularly leak his "Heard on the Street" columns to a couple of Kidder Peabody brokers just before they were published. The brokers traded on the stocks mentioned in the columns and then shared the profits with Winans. Winans was not himself a corporate insider and none of the information he published was illegally leaked to him by corporate insiders. Nevertheless, he was charged with insider trading on the theory that he'd breached his fiduciary duty to his employer, the *Journal*, which forbade its journalists from trading the companies they were writing about. (This became known as the misappropriation theory of insider trading, because Winans misappropriated information that belonged to his employer.) Though Winans was, in the end, convicted on a different theory of wrongdoing, the U.S. Supreme Court explicitly accepted the misappropriation theory in a different prosecution in 1997.

The anomaly of Winans' situation was that, while he was forbidden from trading on the information contained in the columns he wrote, the *Journal* itself was theoretically free to do so, since it couldn't violate a duty to itself. In fact, many journalism organizations effectively do trade on the market-moving information they gather or, more precisely, they sell it to traders so that they can do so.

That's what brought Thomson Reuters unwanted publicity this past June. As the *Journal* and CNBC then reported, Thomson Reuters has for years paid the University of Michigan more than $1 million annually to distribute the results of a market-moving consumer sentiment survey the university conducts. The university releases its findings to the public at 10 a.m. every other Friday. But Thomson Reuters, with the university's blessing, releases those figures to its paying subscribers five minutes earlier, at 9:55 a.m., so that they can get a trading jump on the nonpaying public. In addition, until July of this year, Thomson Reuters also released the study findings two seconds earlier still, at 9:54:58 a.m., in machine-readable form, to certain super-premium subscribers-hedge funds that specialize in high-speed trading. The funds paid $5,000 per month for this extra headstart, plus $1,025 per month for the hookup fee, according to the *Journal.* In the two-second window they could easily trade hundreds of thousands of shares, racking up sure thing profits worth hundreds of thousands of dollars.

In July, Thomson Reuters suspended the advantage it sold to high-speed traders at the behest of the New York attorney general, who is investigating whether it violated state law. But no one alleges that Thomson Reuters' practices amount to insider trading. (Thomson Reuters denies wrongdoing and says its distribution policies were fully disclosed.)

All this focus on arcane "fiduciary duties" leads to weird loopholes, anomalies, and ambiguities—another source of gray pervading the insider-trading field. This scholasticism may have reached a comic apogee in the case of a Ukrainian national named Oleksandr Dorozhko, who in 2007 allegedly hacked into the servers of Thomson Reuters Financial over the Internet, stole quarterly earnings figures for a health care company hours before its announcement, shorted the stock, and made $286,000 overnight. That's got to be insider trading, right?

Not necessarily, explains Donna Nagy, a law professor at the University of Indiana. The hacker owed no fiduciary duty to either Thomson or the health care company, she points out, so he wasn't defrauding either in the usual sense. In light of that fact, the U.S. Court of Appeals for the Second Circuit decided in 2009 that the trial-level judge would have to explore the precise nature of the hack Dorozhko allegedly used to break into the servers. If he misrepresented his identity, for instance, then he defrauded companies. But if he merely "exploited a weakness" in the "electronic code," it wasn't fraud, and the case would have to be dismissed. (After that ruling, Dorozhko stopped cooperating with his lawyer and effectively defaulted.)

Isn't it a major problem having such fuzzy parameters for such a serious crime?

"Yes," says Stephen Bainbridge, a professor at the UCLA School of Law and author of a treatise on insider trading. "But it's a problem the SEC and Congress have deliberately created and preserved." At least twice, he notes, in 1984 and 1988, Congress and the SEC mulled over whether they should write a statute sharply defining the crime but opted not to. "They decided that creating a definition would be a blueprint for fraud," Bainbridge explains. "It would allow clever Wall Street types to figure out loopholes—conduct that wasn't covered through oversight." By keeping the law fuzzy, Congress could "preserve wiggle room for the SEC to respond to new types of fraud."

But can't we at least discard all these vexing, ethereal fiduciary duties? Why not just outlaw any trading on material nonpublic information by anyone, period?

In 1968 the U.S. Court of Appeals for the Second Circuit—the appeals court that hears more insider-trading cases than any other because of its jurisdiction over New York and Connecticut—seemed to do just that. In a landmark case involving the mining company Texas Gulf Sulphur, whose insiders bought stock before their company announced that it had discovered a rich new ore deposit, the court said flatly: "Anyone in possession of material inside information must either disclose it to the investing public or . . . Abstain from trading."

This became known as the parity-of-information view, because it focused on whether the parties to the trade had equal access to information.

But in a pair of cases decided in the early 1980s, the Supreme Court squarely rejected the Second Circuit's broad approach. It did so in part out of fealty to the language of the relevant statute, which was about "fraud." But policy concerns also motivated the court, as became quite explicit in the second ruling of the pair, *Dirks* v. *Securities and Exchange Commission.* That case, decided in 1983, proved something of a Magna Carta for stock analysts.

The facts of the case were odd. Ronald Secrist, a former officer of a public life insurance company, discovered that his former company was committing a massive accounting fraud. Secrist asked Raymond Dirks, a broker-dealer, to expose the fraud. Dirks contacted the *Wall Street Journal* but couldn't persuade it to go with a story. Simultaneously, Dirks counseled his clients to dump their stock in the insurer or to short it (i.e., bet on it to go

371

down in value). The stock plummeted, authorities launched probes, and the insurer was, in fact, charged with fraud. But so was Dirks, for his alleged insider trading.

In a 6-3 decision, Justice Lewis Powell Jr., writing for the majority, concluded that since Secrist obtained no personal benefit from tipping Dirks to the fraud—he did it for the public good—Secrist hadn't breached any duty to his company. And if the tipper hadn't breached any duty, the court found, neither had his tippee, Dirks.

Punishing a person "solely because [he] knowingly receives material nonpublic information from an insider and trades on it could have an inhibiting influence on the role of market analysts," wrote Justice Powell for the majority. "Market efficiency in pricing is significantly enhanced by [analysts'] initiatives to ferret out and analyze information," he continued, "and thus the analyst's work redounds to the benefit of all investors."

The message was that if we want to ensure that stocks are valued accurately—promoting "market efficiency"—we must give stock analysts an incentive to do extensive, critical research of companies. The fact that these analysts gain informational advantages over others in the market is not, then, necessarily illegal. Sometimes, in fact, it benefits society.

The *Dirks* ruling seemed to drive a stake through the heart of the parity-of-information view of insider trading. Yet the latter refused to die.

"The SEC was never happy with the way the Supreme Court defined insider trading," says professor Bainbridge of UCLA. It continued to fight for its favored view—"If you have material information, you can't trade," as he puts it—by bringing suits that aggressively interpreted the law and issuing rules that tried to expand the definition.

As a result, says Yale Law School professor Jonathan Macey, today "there are two laws of insider trading." There's the law the Supreme Court has laid down and the law the SEC embraces. "If you're advising clients, you have to know both," he explains, because most clients don't want to incur the attorney fees and bad press of having to defend an SEC action, even if they might win it in the courts five years down the road.

In the wake of *Dirks* there followed a period in which certain powerful stock analysts enjoyed a privileged position in the investing firmament. By the late 1990s, a CEO could, with impunity, meet with one of these analysts and openly ladle out material nonpublic information, knowing the analyst would turn around and give it to his clients so that they could get rich with it. The practice was known as selective disclosure, and it was widely assumed to be lawful because of the *Dirks* ruling, in which, remember, the court said that both the corporate insider and his tippee were protected if the insider received no "personal gain" from leaking inside information.

The theory here, explains Harvey Goldschmid, a former SEC commissioner who is now a professor at Columbia Law School, was that "the CEO was giving the information not for his personal benefit, but for corporate goodwill." He was seeking to ensure better stock valuations, mitigate volatility, and so on.

Yet the conduct still walked, talked, and quacked like insider trading. In addition, there was concern that the C-suite personnel were, in effect, "buying off analysts and perverting their willingness to criticize and dig," as Goldschmid says. Basically, the analysts wouldn't want to risk losing access to inside information by issuing dour reports and buzzkilling "sell" recommendations.

Though some within the SEC wanted to bring insider-trading charges against selective disclosers, according to Goldschmid, who was the commission's general counsel at the time, the commission in the end opted for a less combative approach. In Regulation FD (for "fair disclosure"), which took effect in October 2000, it banned selective disclosure, decreeing that if C-suite officers were going to disclose material nonpublic information they had to do so in a public forum.

Reg FD leveled the playing field for research analysts and turbocharged demand for their services. It also gave researchers some guidance about how to lawfully ply their trade, because the commentary accompanying it officially endorsed the "mosaic theory."

A company "is not prohibited from disclosing a non-material piece of information to an analyst," the SEC wrote at the time, "even if, unbeknownst to the [company], that information helps the analyst complete a 'mosaic' of information that, taken together, is material." It went on: "Analysts can provide a valuable service in sifting through and extracting information that would not be significant to the ordinary investor to reach material conclusions. We do not intend... to discourage this sort of activity."

The devil being in the details, however, researchers and regulators soon developed differing notions about precisely what the mosaic theory was meant to protect.

Suppose someone wants to get a sense of a company's upcoming quarterly earnings. Let's approach the question in steps, beginning with the most clearly innocuous information-gathering techniques and gradually moving up the ladder to dicier approaches.

There's nothing conceivably wrong, for instance, with an analyst camping out at the port of Newark, for instance, and counting how many Toyotas are offloaded from ships. There are "channel-checking" firms that engage in research like this for analysts.

Similarly, it's unimpeachably clean to send "mall walkers" to key shopping centers on Black Friday, the day after Thanksgiving, to monitor traffic at a number of Abercrombie & Fitch or Gap stores.

It's also often possible for analysts to chat with individual store managers about how sales are doing. "Say I'm trying to estimate McDonald's sales," says Source B. "I could go find 20 representative stores," he says. He could send a researcher to talk to store managers at each. "You could interpolate sales with some reasonable degree of accuracy," he continues. "I'm seeing this trend; it's confirming my thesis; I think that's a go." For a national chain with 32,000 stores, such information can't possibly be material, and if the analyst doesn't pay the store managers—i.e., the manager is getting no "personal benefit"—the analyst has an additional layer of protection under *Dirks.*

Now let's pose a hypothetical. Suppose it were possible to talk to all 2,000 store managers in a chain, giving the portfolio manager granular data about 100% of the companies' retail sales. Would that still be protected under the mosaic theory? As long as all the information came from independent sources, Says source B it should be okay. "That's mosaic theory," he says.

But Donald Langevoort, a law professor at Georgetown University Law Center and a former SEC staffer, is dubious. "1 thousand interviews with 2,000 store managers? Those insiders have given you collectively the biggest tip in the world. I'd be happy to take that case before a jury [as an SEC enforcement lawyer], especially if each manager had been given something of value, like theater tickets."

Of course it's unrealistic to interview 2,000 store managers, so let's ratchet up the stakes a notch. What if the analyst speaks to a district manager, whose region accounts for 10% of a company's total sales? Or two district managers? Or six?

Five years ago some analysts were certainly speaking to such insiders. Today, on the other hand—and certainly since Rajaratnma's arrest—many hedge funds and expert-network firms forbid analysts from speaking to midlevel corporate insiders because the practice goes too close to the line. In addition, by paying insiders to violate their fiduciary duties to their corporations, analysts subject their funds to the risk of civil suit by the corporation being researched for "tortious interference" with the district managers' contracts with the company. (In November 2010 the Tampa-based research firm Retail Intelligence Group was sued by discounter Big Lots Inc. on this theory. The case was settled.)

Still, there are other ways to get information of nearly equal quality. Public companies often have big customers, suppliers, distributers, or franchisees that are private companies and whose CEOs are willing to speak to analysts. Technology companies, with their hundreds of components and lengthy supply chains, are especially vulnerable to informational seepage. Analysts sometimes make contacts within the Asian factories to which Western companies outsource their manufacturing functions.

Suppose, then, that an analyst speaks to a franchisee who runs 200 Wendy's restaurants? Is that still protected by the mosaic theory, or is this "tile" of information too big and revealing? No one knows. Some compliance officers use 5% of revenues as a rule-of-thumb cutoff. Under that rule, the hypothetical Wendy's franchisee would probably be fair game, since Wendy's now has more than 6,600 locations. But how many additional franchisees can the analyst approach? A few dozen, say, with aggregate insight into 60% of sales? No one knows.

To the reader, playing it safe may seem like the obvious default answer to all these questions. Yet hedge fund managers don't see things that way. If a fund forgoes a lawful research technique, its investment advice won't be as good as it could have been, nor as good as its competitors'.

"You're acting as a fiduciary for your investors," stresses Source B. "If you think there's value there, and it's legal, aren't you obligated to use it? You want to go into a fistfight with one arm tied behind your back?"

CPSIA information can be obtained
at www.ICGtesting.com
Printed in the USA
LVHW03s2354160818
587263LV00007B/145/P